Costing

Fourth Edition

T. Lucey MSocSc, FCMA, FCCA, JDipMA

Terry Lucey has been an accountant and consultant in industry and
has had over twenty years examining and teaching experience at all
levels of professional studies and for diploma and degree courses in
business studies. He was previously Head of Department of Business
Studies at the University of Wolverhampton and is now a consultant
and Visiting Fellow at Aston Business School, Aston University.

Amongst his other published works are:
'*Investment Appraisal: Evaluating Risk and Uncertainty*', '*Accounting
and Computer Systems*' (co-author), '*Quantitative Techniques*',
'*Management Information Systems*', '*Management Accounting*', '*First
Course in Cost and Management Accounting*' and several ACCA and
CIMA Study and Revision manuals.

DP Publications Ltd
Aldine House, Aldine Place
142/144 Uxbridge Road,
London W12 8AW
1993

Acknowledgements

The author would like to express thanks to the following for giving permission to reproduce past examination questions:

Institute of Chartered Accountants in England and Wales (ICA)
Chartered Association of Certified Accountants (ACCA)
Chartered Institute of Management Accountants (CIMA)
Chartered Institute of Public Finance and Accountancy (CIPFA)
Association of Accounting Technicians (AAT)

Each question used is cross referenced to the appropriate Institute or Association and the title of the paper.

Terminology

A major objective of the study of any technical subject, like accounting or costing, is to gain familiarity with the precise definitions of the technical terminology used. The terminology adopted in this book is based on the official terminology of Managing Accounting published by CIMA. Appropriate definitions have been reproduced from the Terminology, by kind permission of the Chartered Institute of Management Accountants.

A CIP catalogue record for this book is available from the British Library

First Published 1981
Reprinted 1982
Second edition 1984
Reprinted 1985, 1986, 1987, 1988 (twice)
Third edition 1989
Reprinted 1990, 1991, 1992
Fourth Edition 1993
Reprinted 1994

Copyright T. Lucey © 1993

ISBN 1 85805 015 4

Printed by The Guernsey Press Co. Ltd.,
Braye Road, Vale,
Guernsey, Channel Islands

Contents

Preface   iii

Chapter 1   What is costing   1
2   The Framework of Cost Accounting   7
3   Classification and Coding   14
4   Materials – Purchasing, Reception and Storage   24
5   Materials – Stock Recording and Inventory Control   33
6   Materials – Pricing Issues and Stocks   43
7   Labour – Remuneration methods   54
8   Labour – Recording, Costing and Allied Procedures   64
9   Overheads   72
10   Cost Accounts   110
11   Costing methods – Introduction   145
12   Costing methods – Job and Batch costing   148
13   Costing methods – Contract costing   164
14   Costing methods – Operation and Service costing   180
15   Costing methods – Process costing   189
16   Costing methods –Joint product and by-product costing   210
17   Planning, Control and Decision Making   223
18   Cost behaviour   230
19   Marginal Costing and Absorption Costing   251
20   Marginal Costing and Decision Making   266
21   Break Even Analysis   294
22   Capital Investment Appraisal   314
23   Budgets   329
24   Standard Costing – Introduction   365
25   Standard Costing – variance analysis (Material, labour and overheads)   374
26   Standard Costing – variance analysis (Sales and Standard Marginal costs)   403
27   Uniform costing   436
28   Costing and Computers   439

Case Exercises   450

Progress Tests   464

Table A   Present Value Factors   479
Table B   Present Value Annuity Factors   480

Examination Technique   481
Solutions to Exercises and Examination Questions set at end of chapters   483
Index   485

Preface

1. Aims

This book is designed to provide a thorough understanding of the theory and practice of cost accountancy.

It is particularly relevant for:

a. Students preparing themselves for the examinations of the following bodies; Institute of Chartered Accountants, Chartered Association of Certified Accountants, Chartered Institute of Management Accountants, Chartered Institute of Public Finance and Accountancy and the Association of Accounting Technicians.

b. Students on Foundation Courses in Accounting, Degree and Diploma courses in Accounting and Business Studies and Students on Business/ Technician Education Council (B/TEC) courses.

c. Managers and others in industry, commerce, local authorities and similar organisations who wish to gain a working knowledge of the principles and processes of cost accountancy.

2. Scope of the book

The book covers in comprehensive fashion the principles, techniques and methods involved in cost accountancy.

In the first part of the book there is a detailed coverage of the objectives, principles, techniques and methods of cost accountancy relating to the analysis and gathering of costs and cost ascertainment. The second part of the book concentrates upon the use of cost information for planning, control and decision making. At each stage, concepts are illustrated by practical examples and placed into context so that the reader is aware of the importance and relationships of the various aspects of costing.

This book does not cover all the more advanced topics contained in some Management Accounting syllabuses. These are covered in the author's book 'Management Accounting', also published by DP Publications.

However, because there are many overlaps between Cost and Management Accounting, topics common to both are included in this book. Examples include; budgetary control, standard costing and marginal costing. Whatever the intended final level of study, thorough knowledge of the basics of cost accounting is an essential requirement. This point is stressed again and again in Examiner's Reports.

3. Teaching approach

The book has been written in a standardised format with numbered paragraphs, end of chapter summaries, with a review question and examination questions at the end of each chapter. This approach has been tested and found effective by thousands of students and the book can be used for independent study or in conjunction with tuition at a collage.

4. How to use the book effectively

For each case of study the book is divided into self contained chapters with numbered paragraphs. Each chapter is followed by *self review* questions, cross referenced to appropriate paragraph(s). You should attempt to answer the self review questions *unaided* then check your answer with the text.

In addition each chapter contains a number of test exercises and examination questions *with* suggested solutions. The test exercises are usually shorter and simpler than the examination questions and will be found useful for practice and consolidation. The examination questions have mostly been drawn from past professional examinations and have been selected not merely to repeat the material in the chapters but to extend knowledge and understanding. They should be considered an integral part of the book. *Always* make some attempt at the question before reading the solution. It will be noted that some chapters have more examination questions than others. This reflect the weighting given to the particular topic by the various professional bodies in the examinations.

Also at the end of each chapter there is a further selection of test exercises and examination questions, *without* answers. These can be used by lecturers for classwork and assignments when the book is being used as a course text or as extra practice when the book is used for independent study.

Four Progress Tests containing Multiple Choice Questions have been included to provide additional practice and as a means of self-assessment. Each test covers approximately a quarter of the topics in the book and you should attempt the tests progressively as you work through the book.

5. Sequence of study

The book should be studied in the sequence of the chapters. The sequence has been arranged so that there is a progressive accumulation of knowledge and any given chapter either includes all the principles necessary or draws upon a previous chapter(s).

Notes to the fourth edition

The response to this book continues to be extremely encouraging and I would like to express my appreciation for the positive feedback and constructive suggestions received from both lecturers and students worldwide.

There have been extensive revisions and additions and it is hoped that this new edition will be found to be of continuing value to students and lecturers.

Particular features of the Fourth Edition:

a. New material has been included on the latest developments in cost accounting including; Activity Based Costing and Activity Based Budgeting, the impact of Just-in-Time Purchasing and Production Systems, Throughput and Back-flush Accounting and so on

b. The Terminology throughout has been updated in accordance with the latest 'Terminology of Management Accounting'.

c. There are numerous detail revisions and extensions of coverage throughout the text including; more material on Service and Public Sector Costing, Zero-Based Budgeting, Contract Costing, the effect of inflation and so on.

d. More case exercises have been included covering Public Sector Costing and Activity Based Costing.

e. There is a wide selection of past Examination questions drawn from the most recent Professional Examinations.

f. Four Progress Tests containing Multiple Choice Questions have been included, These can be used for practice and self-assessment.

Special assistance to lecturers

A separate Lecturers Supplement is available free to lecturers who adopt the book as a course text and is available from the publishers. Application should be made on departmental headed notepaper.

The supplement contains:
- Guidance notes on the Case exercises
- Solutions to all the exercises and examination questions in the book.
- OHP masters of key diagrams from the book.

T Lucey
1993

1: What is costing?

1. Topics covered in this chapter

> 1. Definition and scope of cost accounting.
>
> 2. Relationships of cost accounting to management accounting and financial accounting.
>
> 3. Introduction to the contents of the book.

2. Cost accounting – definition

This may be defined as; 'The establishment of budgets, standard costs and actual costs of operations, processes, activities or products; and the analysis of variances, profitability, or the social use of funds.' *Terminology*.

Detailed explanations of the principles, methods and application of cost accounting form the basis of the subsequent chapters in this book.

3. Development of cost accounting

Ever since the use of money replaced barter, people have been concerned with costs. However, it was the concentration of manufacturing facilities into factories which gave impetus to the development of recognisable costing systems. Whilst the early developments were almost entirely related to manufacturing concerns, nowadays costing is used very widely indeed; in hospitals, transport undertakings, local authorities, offices, banks as well as in every manufacturing concern.

4. The scope of cost accounting

The cost accounting system of any organisation is the foundation of the internal financial information system. Management need a variety of information to plan, to control and to make decisions. Information regarding the financial aspects of performance is provided by the costing system. Examples of the information provided by a typical costing system and how it is used are given in the following table and in the following paragraphs.

Information provided by Costing System	Possible uses by Management
Cost per unit of production or service or for a process	As a factor in Pricing Decisions, Production Planning and Cost Control.
Cost of running a section, department, or factory	Organisational planning, cost control.
Wage costs for a unit of production or per period of production	Production planning, decisions on alternative methods, wages cost control.
Scrap/Rectification costs	Material cost control, production planning.
Cost behaviour with varying levels of activity	Profit planning, make or buy decisions, cost control.

Examples of costing information and uses.
Table 1.1

Note:

1. The examples given of uses are not mutually exclusive and it is common to find cost information being used for purposes other than those shown above.

2. The table provides a few examples only. In practice much more information is produced and used.

3. In most cases the usefulness of costing information is enhanced when the actual results and costs are compared to some target or standard figure.

5. Cost accounting and control

An important part of the managerial task is to ensure that operations, departments, processes and costs are under control and that the organisation and its constituent parts are working efficiently towards agreed objectives. Although there are numerous other control systems within a typical organisation, for example, Product Control, Quality Control, and Inventory Control, the Cost Accounting system is the key financial control system and monitors the results of all activities and all other control systems. The detailed analysis and location of all expenditure, the calculation of job and product costs, the analysis of losses and scrap, the monitoring of labour and departmental efficiency and the other outputs of the Costing system provide a sound basis of information for financial control.

6. Cost accounting and decision making

Decision making is concerned with making a choice between alternatives and frequently an important factor in making that choice is the financial implications of the various alternatives.

Correctly presented cost information can be of great value to management in decision making and accordingly material on short and long term decision making is included later in the book.

Note: Students should be aware that much of decision making (and planning) is considered to be within the field of Management Accounting rather than Cost Accounting and accordingly, for greater depth and coverage of these topics, students are advised to refer to the author's book *'Management Accounting'* DP *Publications.*

7. Cost accounting and planning

The analysis and recording of past costs and activities is but one element of cost accounting. Management are also concerned to know what costs will be in the future so that appropriate plans and decisions can be made in good time. Also, having some standard or target against which to compare actual costs greatly assists the control function. The future oriented aspects of cost accounting, namely *budgeting* and *standard costing*, are dealt with in Chapters 23 to 26.

8. Cost accounting, estimating and pricing

Pricing decisions are complex and many interacting factors need to be considered including; the type of market in which the firm operates, the degree of competition, demand and the elasticity of demand, the cost structure of the product and firm, the state of the economy and numerous other factors. Pricing is NOT simply a cost based decision although past costs and expected future costs are factors to be considered in pricing decisions.

9. Costing must be useful

It cannot be emphasised too strongly that if the information produced by the costing system is not useful for managerial decision making, for control or for planning, then it has no value and should not be prepared. To ensure its usefulness the following factors should be considered:

a. Is the costing system appropriate to the organisation the way services are provided or goods manufactured?

b. Do the reports, statements and analyses produced by the costing system contain the relevant information for the intended purpose?

c. Are the reports and statements produced at appropriate intervals and early enough to be effective?

d. Are they addressed to the person responsible for planning/decision making/control?

e. Is the information produced in a relevant form and to a sufficient degree of accuracy for the intended purpose?

It follows from these factors that every costing system will, in certain respects, be unique, because it must be designed to suit the particular organisation, products and processes and personalities involved.

10. Costing and management accounting

The definition of management accounting is: 'An integral part of management concerned with identifying, presenting and interpreting information used for:

a. formulating strategy;

b. planning and controlling activities;

c.   decision taking;

d.   optimising the use of resources;

e.   disclosure to shareholders and others external to the entity;

f.   disclosure to employees;

g.   safeguarding assets.

The above involves participation in management to ensure that there is effective:

a.   formulation of plans to meet objectives (strategic planning);

b.   formulation of short term operation plans (budgeting/profit planning);

c.   acquisition and use of finance (financial management) and recording of transactions (financial accounting and cost accounting);

d.   communication of financial and operating information;

e.   corrective action to bring plans and results into line (financial control);

f.   reviewing and reporting on systems and operations (internal audit, management audit).' *Terminology*

It will be seen that there are similarities between the objectives of both management and cost accounting and indeed in practice there is no true dividing line. In general, management accounting is wider in scope and uses more advanced techniques. However, a fundamental requirement for management accounting is the existence of a sound costing system to provide basic data. Without this, sophisticated techniques will be useless.

Both management accounting and cost accounting are in the main concerned with the provision of information (often in great detail) for internal planning, control and decision making purposes with considerable emphasis on the costs of functions, activities, processes, and products.

11. Costing and financial accounting

Financial accounting can be defined as: 'The classification and recording of monetary transactions of an entity in accordance with established concepts, principles, accounting standards and legal requirements and presentation of a view of those transactions during and at the end of an accounting period' *Terminology*.

Financial accounting originated to fulfil the stewardship function of businesses and this is still an important feature. Most of the external financial aspects of the organisation, eg, dealing with Accounts Payable and Receivable, preparation of Final Accounts etc, are dealt with by the financial accounting system. Of course internal information is also prepared, but in general it can be said that financial accounting presents a broader, more overall view of the organisation with primary emphasis upon classification according to type of transaction (eg, salaries, materials) rather than the cost and management accounting emphasis on functions, activities, products and processes and on internal planning and control information.

12. Summary of relationships between cost and management and financial accounting

The objectives of the various facets of accounting have been given above and the differences discussed. However, it must be realised that they all form part of the financial information system of an organisation and in many organisations the various facets are totally integrated with no artificial divisions between them.

13. Overview of costing

Having defined cost, management and financial accounting and discussed the relationships between them, it is now possible to show more detail of cost accounting. Figure 1.1 summarises the major parts of the cost accounting process and shows in diagrammatic from how data are transformed into information. The rest of the book provides detailed explanations for each of the elements in the diagram.

14. Costing and management accounting – the future

Enormous changes are taking place in the way companies are organised and how goods are manufactured or services supplied. Computers are used extensively not just for administrative purposes but to plan production, design products and to control machines. Production is highly automated, product life cycles are becoming shorter and markets more competitive. In general there is an increasing rate of change which will continue into the foreseeable future.

To deal with this, cost and management accounting (CMA) systems must be flexible and adaptable. Full use must be made of modern information processing and communications systems and, in addition, the principles and methods of CMA must be continually challenged and updated where necessary to meet current and expected conditions.

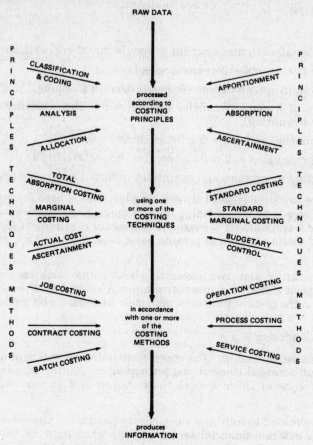

Figure 1.1 Overview of costing

Much of cost and management accounting developed in the early part of this century to meet the requirements of the factories which then existed and the way that products were made.

Typically there was a low level of mechanisation, wages were a high proportion of total costs and there was a relatively slow rate of change of methods and products. Contrast this with a modern factory using Just-in-Time (JIT) systems. A JIT system is where production only takes place to meet demand, there are low or zero inventories, and there is an emphasis on perfect quality. Manufacture is highly automated and typically wages may only be 5–10% of total costs. Production is continually changing, there is constant drive for improvement and batch quantities are low because goods are made to meet demand not to move into stock. It is a *demand-pull* system rather than *production-push*.

In order to provide relevant information the CMA system must take full account of the production system and the nature of the organisation. Above all, the greatest care must be taken not to use inappropriate and outmoded principles and techniques which were developed to suit earlier, and now superseded, conditions. As W. Raffish has said, 'It's not that traditional cost accounting doesn't work – it's that the world it was designed for is rapidly disappearing!'

15. Summary

a. Cost accounting is concerned with the ascertainment and control of costs.

b. The purpose of cost accounting is to provide detailed information for control, planning and decision making.

c. To be of use, costing information must be appropriate, relevant, timely, well presented and sufficiently accurate for the purpose intended.

d. Cost accounting and management accounting are closely related.

e. The emphasis of financial accounting is upon classification by type of transaction and type of expenditure rather than the functional analysis of cost accounting.

f. Cost, financial and management accounting all contribute to the financial information system of an organisation and increasingly in practice are totally integrated.

16. Points to note

a. Cost and financial information is not the only information required for management decision making, but it is usually an important if not a crucial factor.

b. Decision making is concerned with the future and with future costs and revenues. Cost accounting, which is based on historical data, can nevertheless provide some guide to future costs and is frequently a critical part of the information upon which a decision is made.

c. Because there is no real dividing line between cost and management accounting, many of the topics introduced in this book, particularly in the latter part, are equally relevant to students studying costing or management accountancy.

d. Cost and management accountancy is essentially for internal purposes. Financial accountancy is for stewardship purposes and is the basis of external reporting.

e. Not all of the costing principles, techniques and methods described in this book will be applicable to a given firm. Some of the principles, techniques and methods are the basis of regularly produced information, whilst other may only be used in providing information for 'one off' decisions.

f. The increasing emphasis on cost effectiveness, 'value for money' and the growth of competition means that costing is being applied ever more widely. Local authorities use costing principles for many of their services as well as for their own internal administration. Transport undertakings, in both the public and private sectors monitor costs and services in a detailed fashion, hospitals, banks, water authorities, colleges and universities and numerous other non-manufacturing organisations rely heavily on their costing systems to monitor costs, control activities and to provide information for decision making. Accordingly, throughout the book examples are given of costing applications and problems drawn from a wide range of service organisation as well as from the manufacturing sector, which has been the traditional home of cost accounting.

Author's Note

Before tackling the Self-Testing Questions for the first time the reader is advised to read para. 4 of the Preface which explains the purpose behind each type of question. *Where answers are provided to exercises and examination questions at end of chapters, they will be found on pages 483 et seq.*

Student self-testing

Self Review Questions

1. Define cost accounting. (2)

2. Give 6 examples of costing information and its uses. (4 to 8)

3. What is the relationship between costing, management accounting and financial accountancy? (10 to 11)

Exercises and examination questions with answers

Exercises

A1.1 Most of the applications of cost accounting appear to relate to manufacturing companies. Can cost accounting be applied in other organisations? If so, give 6 examples of organisations where cost accounting could usefully be employed.

A1.2 For each of the six examples of organisations given in question 1 give an example of assistance that a cost accounting system could provide.

Examination questions

A1.3 A manufacturing company produces three products in two departments. It has 60 employees, 20 of whom work in the machining department, 30 in the assembly department and 10 are management and staff.

The managing director owns the business which he founded three years ago with only five employees. He is an engineer by training and has relied on the auditors to prepare half yearly trading and profit statements and balance sheets. These he has received ten weeks after the end of each half year.

The managing director is considering installing a cost accounting system. He has asked you to prepare a report to:

a. describe briefly the main aims of the cost accounting system;

b. list six specific types of information which could be obtained from the system, that cannot be obtained from the half yearly accounts now prepared by the auditors, which would be of significant help to him in running the business. You are required to write the report.

(CIMA, Cost Accounting 1)

A1.4 A domestic appliance manufacturer has recently installed several very expensive semi-automatic machines to take over some of the manufacturing operations currently performed by skilled workers.

Required: Outline the ways in which a cost accountant could contribute to the efficient and economic operation of the new equipment.

(ACCA, Costing)

A1.5 One year ago you were appointed to the newly created position of Cost Accountant with a small manufacturing company. You have now installed a costing system and the Managing Director has asked you to write informing him of the kind of information the system should provide.

Required: A report to the Managing Director setting out six principal items of information obtainable from a Costing System.

(AAT, Cost Accounting & Budgeting)

Exercises and examination questions without answers

Exercises

B1.1 On occasions information is produced by the cost accounting system which is of little value for management purposes because it is produced too late or is inaccurate or inappropriate. Give six reasons why this may occur and suggest possible ways to overcome the problems mentioned.

B1.2 Why will some features of every cost accounting system be unique to the particular organisation involved? Give examples from your own experience, if possible, of unique features found in various cost accounting systems.

Examination questions

B1.3 A small business with fifty employees and three main sections, cutting, machining and finishing, manufactures four products. The management has relied on a financial accounting system created and developed to meet statutory obligations but it is now considering the installation of a costing system.

You are required to prepare a report for management listing nine benefits you would expect to follow from the introduction of a cost accounting system.

(CIMA Cost Accounting 1)

B1.4 a. The managing director of your organisation, a manufacturer of garden furniture, disagrees with you over the need for a costing system within your organisation. He says that the only requirement for the classification of costs is by the financial accountant into cost of sales, distribution cost and administration expense for the published accounts and anything beyond is unnecessary.

Required:

Write a report to the Managing Director stating your case as to why you believe he is wrong and specifying the following:

i. The manner in which he has classified cost in his statement.

ii. Four alternative classifications of cost and the ways in which they can assist management decision making, planning and control.

(AAT Cost Accounting & Budgeting part question)

2: The framework of cost accounting

1. Topics covered in this chapter

1. Basic costing definitions
2. The build-up of Overheads
3. Conventional cost build-up
4. Introduction to Activity Based Costing and Activity Based Accounting

2. A cost

This may be defined as:

'The amount of expenditure (actual or notional) incurred on, or attributable to, a specified thing or activity.' *Terminology.*

It will be clear from a study of this definition that it relates to *past costs* which are the basis of cost ascertainment. At the simplest level, costs include two components, quantity used and price, ie,

$$\text{cost} = \text{quantity used} \times \text{price}$$

3. Cost units

Costs are always related to some object or function or service. For example, the cost of a car, a haircut, a ton of coal etc. Such units are known as *cost units* and can be formally defined as 'A quantitative unit of product or service in relation to which costs are ascertained.' *Terminology*

The cost unit to be used in any given situation is that which is most relevant to the purpose of the cost ascertainment exercise. This means that in any one organisation numerous cost units may be used for particular parts of the organisation or for differing purposes.

For example, in a factory manufacturing typewriters the following cost units might be used in the cost accounting system.

Cost Unit	Used for
a typewriter	production cost ascertainment
kilowatt-hours	electricity cost ascertainment
computer minutes of operation	computer running cost ascertainment
tonne-miles	transport cost ascertainment
canteen meals	catering cost ascertainment

Cost units may be *units of production,* eg tonnes of cement, typewriters, gallons of beer, or *units of service,* eg consulting hours, number of invoices processed, patient nights, kilowatt-hours, etc. They may be *identical* units as in the above examples, or they may be dissimilar as in a jobbing engineering factory where the cost unit will be the JOB or BATCH, each of which will be costed individually.

4. Direct costs

Costs may be classified in numerous ways, but a fundamental and important method of classification is into *direct* and *indirect costs.* Direct costs (comprising direct material costs, direct wages cost and direct expenses) are those costs which can be directly identified with a job, batch, product or service. Typical examples are

❏ *Direct materials*

The raw materials used in a product, bought in parts and assemblies incorporated into the finished product.

❏ *Direct wages or Direct labour cost*

The remuneration paid to production workers for work directly related to production, the salaries directly attributable to a saleable service (audit clerk's salaries for example).

❑ *Direct expenses*

Expenses incurred specifically for a particular product, job, batch or service; royalties paid per unit for a copyright design, plant or tool hire charges for a particular job or batch.

It follows therefore that direct costs do not have to be spread between various categories because the whole cost can be attributed directly to a production unit or saleable service.

The total of direct costs is known as PRIME COST,

ie DIRECT MATERIAL + DIRECT LABOUR + DIRECT EXPENSES = PRIME COST

Invariably when direct costs are mentioned, the costing of production cost units is involved. Technically this need not be so, but unless the context of the question clearly points to some other conclusion, any reference to direct costs should be taken to refer to production costs units.

5. Indirect costs

All material, labour and expense costs which cannot be identified as direct costs are termed indirect costs. The three elements of indirect costs; indirect materials, indirect labour and indirect expenses are collectively known as OVERHEADS. Typical examples of indirect costs in the production area are the following:

INDIRECT MATERIALS	Lubricating oil, stationery, consumable materials, maintenance materials, spare parts for machinery, etc.
INDIRECT LABOUR	Factory supervision, maintenance wages, storemen's wages, etc.
INDIRECT EXPENSES	Rent and rates for the factory, plant insurance, etc.

INDIRECT MATERIALS + INDIRECT LABOUR + INDIRECT EXPENSES = OVERHEADS

Note: In practice overheads are usually separated in categories such as Production Overheads, Administration Overheads, Selling Overheads. The above are examples of Production Overheads.

6. Cost build-up

Having defined direct and indirect costs, the framework of cost build-up can be shown thus:

DIRECT MATERIAL		INDIRECT MATERIAL	
+		+	
DIRECT LABOUR	= **PRIME COST**	INDIRECT LABOUR	= **OVERHEADS**
+		+	
DIRECT EXPENSE		INDIRECT EXPENSE	

PRIME COST + OVERHEADS = TOTAL COST

Note: The above shows cost ascertainment at its most basic. Additional refinements are dealt with later in the book.

7. Conversion cost

This is the term used to describe the costs of converting purchased materials into finished or semi-finished products.

It is thus total production cost minus initial material input costs ie, the sum of additional direct materials, direct wages, direct expenses and absorbed production overhead. The above is the definition given in *Terminology*, but students should be aware that alternative interpretations exist. For example, economists define conversion cost as total cost less material costs, ie, all overheads are included, not just production overheads.

Alternatively, the term conversion cost is used to describe the cost of converting materials from one stage of manufacture to the next stage which need not be the finished state.

8. Added value

This is the increase in market value of a product excluding the costs of bought out materials and services. It is thus equivalent to the economist's conversion cost plus profit. Added value is an important concept and considerable research has been undertaken into methods of incorporating added value concepts into internal and external accounting statements. Added value helps to highlight the relative efficiency of the firm without the analysis being obscured by external input costs which are largely uncontrollable.

9. The build-up of overheads

Overheads invariably include a large number of types of indirect costs so that the build-up of overheads is a more complicated process than the calculation of prime cost which merely consists of direct costs clearly related to the cost unit being produced. To understand this process, three further basic costing definitions are required, ie, *cost centre*, *cost allocation*, and *cost apportionment*.

10. Cost centre

This can be defined as 'A production or service location, function, activity or item of equipment whose costs may be attributed to cost units'. *Terminology*.

Typical examples of cost centres are: The Plating shop, The Works Office, The 1,000 ton Power Press, The Milling Machines (consisting of 20 similar machines), Sales Representatives, Invoicing Section, Inspection, etc.

In practice a cost centre is simply a method by which costs are gathered together, according to their incidence, usually by means of cost centre codes. Thus a purchase of carbon paper for use in the Invoicing Section would have a code representing say Office sundries – 457, and a code representing the Invoicing section as a cost centre, say 303, and would be coded:

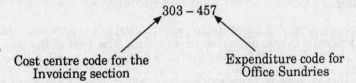

303 – 457

Cost centre code for the   Expenditure code for
Invoicing section   Office Sundries

Similarly another purchase of carbon paper but for use in the Works Office (cost centre code 106) would be coded:

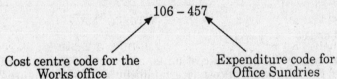

106 – 457

Cost centre code for the   Expenditure code for
Works office   Office Sundries

11. Cost allocation

This can be defined as 'That part of cost attribution which charges a specific cost to a cost centre or cost unit' *Terminology*.

The key part of this definition is 'specific cost'. Where a cost, without division or splitting, can be clearly identified with a cost centre or cost unit, then it can be allocated (via the cost accounting coding system) to that cost centre or cost unit. It follows that direct costs can be allocated to particular cost units or groups of particular cost units, but cost allocation can, of course, apply equally to indirect costs. The examples shown in Para. 10 are examples of cost allocation of an indirect material cost.

12. Cost apportionment

Frequently it is not possible to identify a discrete item of cost with a cost centre and it is necessary to split a cost over several cost centres on some agreed basis. A classic example is that of Rates which are levied upon the premises as a whole, but which, for internal cost ascertainment purposes, need to be shared or apportioned between the cost centres. The basis normally used for Rates being the floor area occupied by the various cost centres. The formal definition of cost apportionment is

'That part of cost attribution which shares costs among two of more cost centres or cost units in proportion to the estimated benefit received, using a proxy eg, square metres.' *Terminology*

The basis upon which the apportionment is made varies from cost to cost. The basis chosen should produce, as far as possible, a fair and equitable share of the common cost for each of the receiving cost centres. The choice of an appropriate basis is a matter of judgement to suit the particular circumstances of the organisation and wherever possible there should be a cost/cause relationship.

Typical bases used are as follows:

Basis	Costs which may be apportioned on this basis
Floor Area	Rates, Rent, Heating, Cleaning, Lighting, Building Depreciation
Volume or Space Occupied	Heating, Lighting, Building Depreciation
Number of Employees in each Cost Centre	Canteen, Welfare, Personnel, General Administration, Industrial Relations, Safety
Book (or Replacement) Value of Plant, Equipment, Premises, etc.	Insurance, Depreciation
Stores Requisitions	Store-Keeping
Weight of Materials	Store-Keeping, Materials Handling

The process of apportionment is an essential part of the build-up of overheads, because many indirect costs apply to numerous cost centres rather than just to one.

Note: Although cost apportionment is a normal part of the cost ascertainment process, it must be realised that it is a convention only and costs so apportioned are not verifiable.

13. Overhead absorption

Direct costs, by definition, are readily identifiable to cost units, but overheads, which are often considerable, cannot be related directly to cost units, but nevertheless form part of the total cost of a product. Accordingly overheads must be shared out in some equitable fashion among all of the cost units produced.

The process by which this is done is know as *overhead absorption* or *overhead recovery*. Typically an overhead absorption rate, based on factors such as direct machine or labour hours is calculated and the overheads 'shared out' over the cost units or jobs according to the number of machine or labour hours involved.

14. The build-up of total cost

Having now defined the basic terminology of cost units, cost centres, cost allocation, cost apportionment and overhead absorption, the framework of cost ascertainment is shown in Figure 2.1.

15. Activity based costing (ABC)

The approach to product costing outlined above is what may be termed the traditional approach. This is widely used and must be thoroughly understood by students.

ABC is a recent approach to product costing, pioneered by Professors Kaplan and Cooper of Harvard University. ABC is an attempt to reflect more accurately in product costs those activities which influence the level of support overheads. Support overheads include such items as Inspection, Despatch, Production Planning, Set-up, Tooling and similar costs.

Traditionally all overheads were absorbed on production volume, as measured by labour or machine hours. This means that high volume standardised products would be charged with most overheads and short run production with lower overheads in spite of the fact that short run production causes more set-ups, retooling, production planning and thereby generates more support overhead costs. Thus, traditional volume related overhead absorption tends to *overcost* products made in *long runs* and *undercost* products made in *short runs*.

ABC seeks to overcome this problem by relating support overheads to products, not by production volume, but by a number of specific factors known as *cost drivers*. A cost driver is an activity which causes cost. Table 2.1. shows some typical cost driver and the costs which the activity influences (or drives).

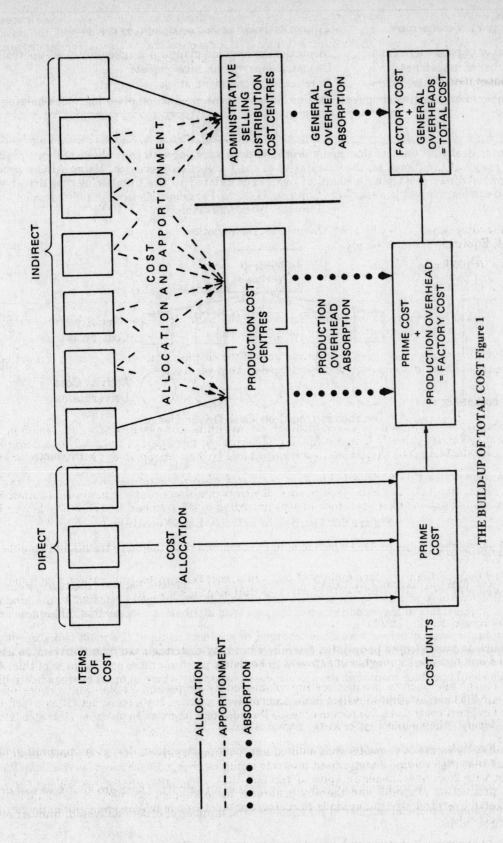

Figure 2.1 The conventional build-up of total costs

Examples of cost drivers	Typical costs influenced or 'driven' by cost driver
Number of production runs	Inspection, production planning & scheduling, set-up, tooling
Number of despatches	Despatch department, invoicing etc
Number of purchase orders	Purchasing department, stock-holding etc
Number of engineering changes	Technical department, production planning, stock-holding etc

Table 2.1

ABC seeks to deal with the fact that many overhead costs vary not with the *volume* of items produced but with the *range* of the items, ie, the complexity of the production processes. Using ABC a product cost consists of its direct costs plus a share of overheads related to the number of cost driver units the production causes.

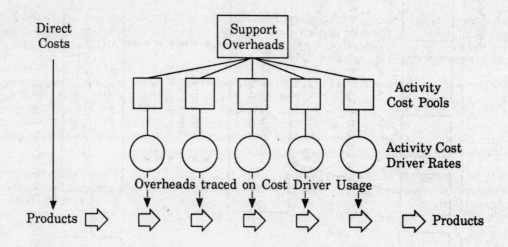

Figure 2.2 Outline of activity-based costing

Figure 2.2 shows the outline of ABC which should be compared with the more traditional approach shown in Figure 2.1.

It will be seen from the diagrams that there are considerable similarities between the two systems. In both systems, direct costs go straight to the product and overheads are charged or 'traced' to the product using a two stage process. It is in the second stage of the overhead attribution process that differences arise.

In a traditional system overheads would be charged to products using at the most two absorption bases (labour hours and/or machine hours). On the other hand, ABC systems use many drivers as absorption bases (eg number of set-ups, number of orders, number of despatches and so on). Because of this, ABC cost driver rates should produce more realistic product costs, especially where support overheads are high.

In outline an ABC system is developed and used as follows.

Step 1   Identify the main activities in the organisation.

Examples include: materials handling, purchasing, reception, despatch, machining, assembly and so on.

Step 2   Identify the factors which determine the costs of an activity. These are known as *cost drivers*.

Examples include: number of purchase orders, number of orders delivered, number of set-ups and so on.

Step 3   Collect the costs of each activity. These are known as *cost pools* and are similar to conventional cost centres.

Step 4 Charge support overheads to products on the basis of their usage of the activity, expressed in terms of the chosen cost driver(s). For example, if the total costs of Purchasing were £200,000 and there were 1,000 Purchase orders (the chosen cost driver), products would be charged £200 for each purchase order. Thus a batch generating 3 purchase orders would be charged 3 × £200 = £600 for Purchasing overheads.

The use of ABC also requires a change in the way overheads are classified. This is described later in the book when overheads are covered in detail.

16. Activity based accounting (ABA)

Activity Based Costing, described above, is but one part of what is a new approach to internal accounting. This approach focuses on analysing, recording, controlling and reporting on the costs and wider performance of *activities* rather than the traditional narrow emphasis on merely the costs of departments and cost centres.

Activity based accounting includes; Activity Based Costing (for product costing), Activity Based Budgeting or Activity Cost Management (for cost planning and control) and Activity Performance Measurement (for performance monitoring using both financial and non-financial indicators). All of these approaches are covered in detail later in the book.

ABA is not merely a new technical system. It has strong behavioural influences and is being widely used to promote cost reduction and increase efficiency. For example, Tektronik designed its ABC system to encourage designers to use existing standard parts in new products rather than designing new components or using unique bought in parts. Rexel Engineering's activity based system focuses attention on value added and non-value added activities with the objective of being able to make specific, guided cost reductions rather than blanket overhead cuts which could damage operations.

In general, activity based systems encourage continuous improvement rather than just report on the cost of past operations. It is because of this that their use is becoming more widespread and many leading organisations already use some form of activity based accounting. Examples include; IBM, British Telecom, ICI, Hewlett-Packard, Kodak, Lever Brothers, Johnson Paints, British Airways, Coca Cola, Lucas and so on.

17. Summary
a. Costs must be considered in relation to cost units which may be units of production, a job or batch, or units of saleable service.

b. Direct costs are those which are readily identifiable to a cost unit. Direct labour, Direct Materials and Direct Expenses form Prime Cost.

c. Conversion cost is the cost of converting materials into products. Added value is the increase in market value of a product less bought out materials and services, ie, it includes profit unlike conversion cost.

d. All costs not identifiable as direct are termed Indirect Costs. Indirect Labour, Indirect Material and Indirect Expenses are collectively known as Overheads.

e. Cost centres may be physical locations, items of equipment, groups of personnel etc. They are a method of gathering indirect costs via the coding system of the firm.

f. Cost allocation is the allotment of whole items of cost. Cost apportionment is the sharing of a common cost amongst cost centres.

g. Overhead absorption (or recovery) is the process by which overheads are included in the cost of cost units, ie, Prime Cost plus overheads absorbed = Total Cost.

h. Activity Based Costing (ABC) attributes support overhead costs (eg set-up, planning, despatch, purchasing) to products or product lines using cost drivers ie, the activities which cause the cost.

i. Traditional product costing and ABC treat Direct costs and some Production Overheads (eg power costs) in the same way. The treatment of support overheads differs. Traditionally, all were absorbed on production volume whereas ABC uses a range of cost drivers to attribute various support overheads to the product or the product line.

j. ABC is one facet of Activity Based Accounting (ABA). ABA also includes Activity Based Budgeting or Activity Cost Management and Activity Performance Measurement using both financial and non-financial indicators.

18. Points to note:

a. The word cost is rarely used on its own. It is invariably qualified in some way, eg Prime Cost, Factory Cost, Indirect Cost etc.

b. The process of apportionment is sometimes known as *pro-rating costs*. Although many of the bases used, eg Rates apportioned on floor area, appear sensible, it must be realised that the whole process of apportionment is merely a convention. There is no way of proving that apportioned costs are correct.

c. Alternative names for overheads include *burden* and *on-cost*, but students are recommended always to use the term overheads.

d. Costing is a tool for practical purposes and a common-sense view should be taken over each factor. For example, some costs, although direct, may be of such small value that they may be classified as indirect and included in production overheads. An example of this might be paint used to stencil a number on a machine tool. The effort required to establish how much paint is used on each machine would not be worthwhile.

e. On occasions it may be possible to classify a cost normally regarded as indirect as a direct cost and this should be done whenever possible. An example of this is commission paid to an agent or salesman to gain a particular job where the job is classed as the cost unit.

f. The ascertainment of product cost relies on clear identification of the product or service. in manufacturing companies this is usually self-evident but in many service organisations the problem is more complex. For example, a major clearing bank defined well over 150 products/services which it supplied. Many of these were interrelated and many shared common facilities. In such circumstances product cost ascertainment becomes a difficult operation.

Student self-testing

Self Review Questions

1. What is a cost? (2)

2. Define a cost unit and give examples. (3)

3. What is a direct cost? (4)

4. What is the make-up of prime cost? (4)

5. What are indirect costs? (5)

6. What is the difference between conversion cost and added value? (7 & 8)

7. Define a cost centre and give examples (10)

8. What is the difference between cost allocation and cost apportionment? (11 & 12)

9. Give examples of typical apportionment bases for: Heating, Insurance and Wage Administration costs. (12)

10. What is Activity Based Costing? (15)

11. What does Activity Based Accounting include? (16)

Exercises and examination questions with answers

Exercises

A2.1 Give five examples (other than those in the chapter) of each of the following:

    a.   Cost units in manufacturing firms

    b.   Cost units in service firms

A2.2 Your Managing Director has asked you to consider changing all the firm's cost accounting reports to include the added value of the products. How would you deal with this request and what advantages (if any) might accrue from this practice?

A2.3 From a costing viewpoint what are the effects of the increasing automation of manufacturing facilities?

Examination questions

A2.4 a. Identify and explain the essential elements of an effective cost control system.

　 b. Outline possible problems which may be encountered as a result of the introduction of a system of cost control into an organisation.

(ACCA, Costing)

A2.5 a. You are required to:

　　 i. explain the terms 'cost centre' and 'cost unit',

　　 ii. suggest suitable cost units which may be used to aid control within the following organisations:

　　　　 1. a hospital;

　　　　 2. a road haulage business;

　　　　 3. a hotel with 40 double rooms and 5 single rooms;

　　　　 4. public transport authority.

(CIMA Cost Accounting)

A2.6 'It is now fairly widely accepted that conventional cost accounting distorts management's view of business through unrepresentative overhead allocation and inappropriate product costing.

This is because the traditional approach usually absorbs overhead costs accross products and orders solely on the basis of the direct labour involved in their manufacture. And as direct labour as a proportion of total manufacturing cost continues to fall, this leads to more and ,more distortion and misrepresentation of the impact of particular products on total overhead costs.'

(From an article in Financial Times, 2 March 1990)

You are required to discuss the above and to suggest what approaches are being adopted by management accountants to overcome such critisism.

(CIMA Cost Accounting)

A2.7 The traditional methods of cost allocation, cost apportionment and absorption into products are being challenged by some writers who claim that much information given to management is misleading when these methods of dealing with fixed overheads are used to determine product costs.

You are required to explain what is meant by *cost allocation*, *cost apportionment* and *absorption* and to describe briefly the alternative approach of *activity based costing* in order to ascertain total product costs.

(CIMA Cost Accounting)

Exercises and examination questions without answers

Exercises

B2.1 'It is good accounting practice to classify costs as direct wherever this is possible'. Discuss.

B2.2 What bases of apportionment would you consider most appropriate for the following items.

　 a. Canteen deficit
　 b. Balance of maintenance department costs after charging out large jobs
　 c. Charge for Security Services
　 d. Depreciation
　 e. Personnel department costs
　 f. Air conditioning costs
　 g. Costing department costs.

B2.3 Cost accounting is only useful in manufacturing companies. Discuss.

Examination questions

B2.4 You have recently been appointed accountant to a general engineering firm engaged in the production of special purpose machines. Orders are obtained by the firm's technical representatives who, having ascertained customers' needs provide the necessary information to the Estimator who prepares and submits the required quotation.

Recent trading results have been unsatisfactory, and the management feel that a costing system would provide greater opportunity for control and would help to improve the firm's profitability.

You have been requested to install a suitable costing system. How would you proceed?

(ACCA, Costing)

B2.5 a. i.   Explain what you understand by the term 'cost unit'.

        ii. What might be an appropriate cost unit for each of the following:

            Steelworks

            Hospital

            Professional accounting office

            Salesmen's expenses within a specific organisation

            Restaurant

(AAT Cost Accounting & Budgeting, part question)

B2.6 'It is probably impossible to obtain an absolutely accurate true cost of a product or service' said a speaker at a students' society meeting.

You are required to comment on the above statement, referring in your answer to

a.   the definition of 'cost' as a noun and as a verb;

b.   whether or not you are in agreement with the statement, supporting your conclusion with an explanation;

c.   the purposes for which costs are needed by business.

(CIMA Cost Accounting)

3: Classification and coding

1. Topics covered in this chapter

1. Subjective and objective classifications
2. Coding principles
3. Features of coding systems
4. Types of coding systems.

2. Classification

Before any attempts can be made to collect, analyse and control costs, it is essential that all items (labour, material, overheads, etc) can be precisely classified and also that their destination in the costing system (direct to cost units or indirectly to cost centres) can be identified. Classification is the process of arranging items into groups according to their degree of similarity and is formally defined as:

'The arrangement of items in logical groups having regard to their nature (subjective classification) or purpose (objective classification).' *Terminology*.

The first part of this definition relates to the nature of expenditure, eg expenditure on raw materials and the latter part indicates where the expenditure is to be charged, eg in the case of raw materials, direct to the cost unit.

3. Classification and objectives

The way items are classified must be related to the objectives of the systems using the classification. For examples, the classification of materials must aid all the systems involved with materials and these would typically include: purchasing, storage, stock control, production control, inspection, as well as the costing and accounting systems. Examples of the material classifications which would be found in a typical manufacturing company are the following:

a. Raw materials, ie, bought in material which is used in the manufacture of the product. According to the organisation, raw materials could be further classified into steel, timber, etc, etc.

b. Components and sub-assemblies, ie, bought in components and subassemblies which are incorporated in the product.

c. Work-in-progress, ie, partly completed assemblies and products incorporating raw materials and/or sub-assemblies.

d. Consumable materials, ie, materials used in the operation of the factory and during production which do not appear in the product, eg cleaning rags, detergents, etc.

e. Maintenance materials, ie, materials of all types used in maintaining machinery, buildings and vehicles, eg spare parts, lubricating oils and greases, cement, etc.

f. Office materials, ie, materials used in the operation of offices, eg stationery, carbons, etc.

g. Tools, ie, jigs, tools, fixtures, clamps, etc.

Note:

a. The above classifications are not exhaustive and others are frequently found.

b. Invariably there are sub-divisions within the above broad classifications. The extent of sub-division depends on the requirements of material control in all its facets.

4. Coding

A code is defined as, 'A system of symbols designed to be applied to a classified set of items, to give a brief accurate reference facilitating entry, collation and analysis.' *Terminology*.

It will be seen from the above definition that coding is the way that the classification system is applied, ie, items are classified, then coded. The importance of well designed coding systems cannot be over-emphasised. Coding is important with normal accounting systems, but becomes vital with mechanised and computerised systems. Accordingly an understanding of coding systems is vital to accountants. Coding is necessary:

a. To identify uniquely items, materials and parts which cannot be done from descriptions.

b. To avoid ambiguity which would arise from using descriptions.

c. To aid processing, particularly important with computer based systems.

d. To reduce data storage. In the majority of cases a code is much shorter than a description.

5. Features of good coding systems

a. Unique – each item should have one, and only one, code.

b. Clear symbolisation – codes should consist of either all numeric or all alphabetic characters. In general, particularly with computer based systems, numeric codes would be preferred. Also, the use of numerous strokes, dashes, colons or brackets should be avoided. The following would be an example of bad notation,

56-503/291:8

c. Distinctiveness – codes which represent different items should, so far as practicable, look distinctive. Errors may occur if virtually identical codes describe different items. For example, if a code for raw materials was 9-3816 and a code for a bought in component was 7-3816, confusion may occur even though the codes are unique.

d. Brevity – codes should be as brief as possible consistent with meeting the requirements of the classification system. In general it has been found that seven digits is the maximum number of digits which can be reliably remembered.

e. Uniformity – codes should be equal length and of the same structure. This makes it easy to see whether any characters are missing. Having fixed length codes also considerably facilitates processing.

f. Exhaustive – the coding structure should be exhaustive which means that it should encompass the full range of the classification as it exists and, of equal importance, be able to cope with new items as they arise. This latter point is a major practical problem when designing coding systems.

g. Ambiguity – the notation used for the coding system should avoid ambiguity. If there is a mixed alpha/numeric system, the letters I and O should not be used because of possible confusion with the numerals 1 and 0 (zero). In addition, when an all alphabetic system is used, the letters I, Q, S and G are most similar to other letters and numerals and should be avoided where possible.

h. Significant – Where possible the coding should be significant. This means that the actual code should signify something about the item being coded. For example, part of the code for vehicle tyres could indicate the actual size of the tyre. Thus a code for a 165 × 13 tyre would include 165.

i. Mnemonic – On occasions when an alphabetic system is used the actual code is derived from the item's description or name. Most people are probably familiar with the letter code used by airlines to denote various airports, for example

LHR stands for London Heathrow
LGW stands for London Gatwick

6. Practical aspects of coding systems

The previous paragraph has explained various features of coding systems. To implement coding systems which are useful, various practical matters need to be considered.

a. For most data processing purposes a 'closed notation' is preferable, ie, all codes should be of the same length. This effectively means sacrificing some of expansibility which is possible using an expansible notation such as the Universal Decimal Classification used for book classification in libraries. This system is capable of indefinite expansion, but each sub-division requires extra digit(s) and is less suitable for accounts purposes.

b. Because of the need to introduce new items from time to time, most coding systems used for costing purposes are forms of block coding. An example of this is the following:

Item	*Block assigned*
Raw material	1000 – 2999
Work in progress	3000 – 3999
Indirect materials	4000 – 4999

This system allows, within limits, new items to be introduced into the correct block without destroying the coding structure.

c. Indexing – Ideally a code should be self indexing, as for example names in alphabetical order, but this is rarely possible. Accordingly a clear index or coding list should be readily available.

d. Centralised control – Depending on the particular circumstances new codes should only be issued centrally. It should not be possible for branches, junior staff, etc, to introduce a new code into the system.

e. Check digit verification – Because of the supreme importance of correct identification through the code number, particularly using computers, many important code numbers; account numbers, part numbers etc, have an extra digit suffixed which makes them self checking and guards against many of the common coding errors, eg transposition, incorrect character(s), character(s) missing etc. The most common method used is termed Modulus 11 check digit verification.

f. Code layouts – Although there is the general need to keep codes as brief as possible, the requirements of particular systems often mean that codes are unavoidably lengthy. Experience would indicate that lengthy codes are better remembered and transcribed if they are grouped or subdivided into three's.

For example, 658 – 291 – 204 is better than 658291204.

g. Pre-printing – Wherever possible, codes should be pre-printed on forms so that errors are reduced.

7. Types of coding systems

The best coding systems, whether for manual or computer use, are those which are simple to understand flexible and capable of expansion. At the design stage it is important to look ahead and to try to allow for growth, both in volume and diversity. Some of the main types of coding systems are:

Group classification codes

These are codes where a specified digit, usually the first, indicates item classification. For example;

$$7XXX \quad \text{represents Hexagon bars}$$
$$8XXX \quad \text{represents Round bars}$$
$$9XXX \quad \text{represents Square bars}$$

where XXX represents other digits.

Hierarchical codes

These are developments of group classification codes where each digit represents a classification. Each digit to the right represents a smaller and smaller sub-classification.

Probably the best known example of a hierarchical code is the Universal Decimal code used in libraries. This is extremely flexible and can incorporate numerous sub-classifications within the primary one at the expense of having variable length codes.

However for business and accounting purposes, codes of a standard length are preferable. Hierarchical coding can still be used in these circumstances albeit with some potential loss of detail. For example;

6	represents Screws
62	represents Countersunk screws
63	represents Round-headed screws
621	represents Countersunk slotted screws
622	represents Countersunk star screws
.....	etc

up to the agreed length of code.

Significant digit codes

These are codes where some of the digits are part of the description of the item being coded. For example:

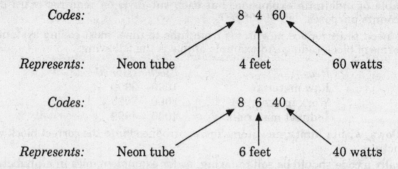

Codes: 8   4   60

Represents: Neon tube   4 feet   60 watts

Codes: 8   6   40

Represents: Neon tube   6 feet   40 watts

The use of significant codes enables the description of an item to be largely derived from its code.

In practice the various systems may be mixed to provide one that suits the organisations requirements. For accounting purposes the most common system is some form of hierarchical coding. This is developed into a published 'Chart of Accounts' which specifies the various expenditure headings.

In addition, for cost accounting purposes, there must be a set of cost centre codes which specify the location or use of the expenditure. Sometimes the type of expenditure and its location or use are combined into one code, sometimes there are two separate codes.

8. Summary

a. Accurate classification of all items is a vital pre-requisite to any form of analysis and control.

b. Classification is the process of grouping together items which are similar.

c. The classification system must meet the objectives of all the systems which may use the classifications.

d. Coding is the way that the classification system is applied.

e. The features of good coding systems include; uniqueness, distinctiveness, exhaustiveness, unambiguousness, brevity and uniformity.

f. To ensure that coding systems actually work in practice, care should be taken over the need to allow space for expansion, indexing, central control, self-checking codes, code layouts and pre-printing.

g. Coding systems may be of various types including; Group Classification Codes, Hierarchical Codes, Significant Digit Codes or some combination.

9. Points to note

a. Most coding systems used in accounting are composite systems. Typically they might contain two sections, the first section indicating the nature of the expenditure (termed subjective classification) and the second section indicating the cost centre or cost unit to be charged (termed objective classification).

    For example;

283 – 691

Expense code for, say, salaries   Location of expenditure, in this case cost centre 691

b. The Financial Accounting System would be concerned with the subjective classification of an item and not the location of the expenditure, the objective classification.

Student self-testing

Self Review Questions

1. What is classification and why is the process of prime importance? (2)

2. What is coding and why is it necessary? (4)

3. What are the features of good coding systems? (5)

4. What is 'closed notation, 'block coding' and 'check digit verification'? (6)

5. Distinguish between Group Classification, Hierarchical and Significant Digit coding systems. (7)

6. What is subjective and objective classification and what is their importance in costing systems? (9)

Exercises and examination questions with answers

Exercises

A3.1 The following are items of cost and expenditure in a manufacturing company:

    a. Wages paid to fork-lift truck drivers
    b. Finance Director's salary
    c. Depreciation of production machinery
    d. Heating of factory
    e. Small tools used in the Production Dept.
    f. Repairs to machinery
    g. Steel used in the product
    h. Wages of personnel department staff
    i. Chargehand's wages
    j. Sales advertising
    k. Wages of production workers
    l. Overtime payments made to production workers.

You are required to give the subjective classification and the likely objective classification for each item.

A3.2 Devise a simple block coding system and code each of the items in question A3.1 in respect of the nature of the item and where it will be charged.

A3.3 Give five likely effects of incorrectly coding a payment of *direct* wages as *indirect*.

Examination questions

A3.4 a. List the main groups of items you would expect to find in a functional classification of marketing costs.

    b. How would you expect marketing costs to be analysed for management control purposes? What purposes are served by such analyses?

(ACCA, Costing)

A3.5 Y Limited has recently appointed a new stores controller, who has decided to introduce a new stores control system. He has asked you as Cost Accountant, to design for him a new Materials Code.

    a. You are required to prepare a report to the Stores Controller, in which you should briefly:

       i. explain the principles to be observed in designing a Materials Classification Code;

       ii. state the advantages of such a coding system in a system of stores control.

    b. Assume that the design of your coding system has been completed. Included in the range of Y Limited's products is a series of flat sections of varying dimensions and in four different raw materials, aluminium, brass, copper and stainless steel. Examples of coding of two of these are:

Material	Length	Dimensions Thickness	Width	Code Number
Stainless steel	4'	$\frac{7}{8}''$	$3\frac{3}{4}''$	04081415
Brass	$8\frac{1}{2}'$	$1\frac{3}{8}''$	2''	02172208

       i. Determine the code for the following:

       Aluminium $- 6'6'' \times \frac{1}{4}'' \times 3\frac{1}{2}''$

       Copper $- 1' \times \frac{3}{8}'' \times 4\frac{1}{4}''$

       ii. Describe the type of bar as defined by these codes: 03112903   01071 721

(CIMA, Costing)

A3.6 Cost must be classified to facilitate its arrangement in as flexible a manner as possible.

    Required:

    a. Explain the meaning of the 'classification of cost' and give some practical examples of the ways cost is classified.

b. Design a code number series for use in a costing system integrated with a financial accounting system. Detail some practical examples of the code numbers.

c. Detail four advantages of using code numbers for stock materials.

(AAT, Cost Accounting & Budgeting)

A3.7 The overhead expenses of an international company are coded within a seven digit system as follows: First and second digits – location.   Third and fourth digits – function.   Final three digits – type of expense

Extracts from within the costing system are as follows:

Location	Code Number	Type of Expense	Code Number
London	10	Factory rent	201
Dublin	11	Plant depreciation	202
Lagos	12	Stationery	203
Nairobi	13	Telephone	204
Kuala Lumpur	17	Travel	207
Hong Kong	18	Entertainment	209
Function			
Production	20		
Marketing	21		
Administration	24		

The code number for factory rent in Nairobi factory is 1320201. Stationery purchased by the cost office in Kingston is 1523203. Required:

i. State the seven digit code which represents the following:

a. Depreciation of plant in the Dublin factory.

b. Administration telephone costs incurred in Lagos.

c. Salesman in Singapore entertaining overseas visitors.

d. Salary expenses of Research and Development Department at Port of Spain.

ii. Give two advantages of using a coding system for the classification of costs and revenues.

(AAT Cost Accounting & Budgeting, part question)

Exercises and examination questions without answers

Exercises

B3.1 A firm supplies plastic sheets made of either PVC or Acetate. A coding system is used and the following are examples:

A PVC sheet 2 metres long 10 centimetres wide and 2 millimetres thick is coded, 1.04.010.020.
An Acetate sheet 1.5 metres long 8 centimetres wide and 3 millimetres thick is coded, 2.03.008.030.

Code the following items:

PVC sheet 0.5 metres long, 12 centimetres wide and 4 millimetres thick.
Acetate sheet 5.5 metres long, I metre wide and 2.5 millimetres thick.

B3.2 Problems are being experienced in your organisation with incorrect or missing code numbers on a number of internal documents. List five ways in which this problem can be alleviated.

Examination questions

B3.3 a. In connection with control of materials, you are required to:

i. explain the meaning and principles of classification;

ii. explain the principles of coding;

iii. state four advantages of using a coding system.

b. A company manufactures shoes and slippers in half-sizes in the following ranges:

	Sizes
Mens	6 to $9\frac{1}{2}$
Ladies	3 to 9
Boys	1 to $5\frac{1}{2}$
Girls	1 to 5

The company uses a seven-digit code to identify its finished products, which, reading from left to right, is built up as follows: Digit one indicates whether the products are mens, ladies, boys or girls. The numbers used are:

1 – mens
2 – ladies
3 – boys
4 – girls

Digit two denotes type of footwear (shoes or slippers). Digit three denotes colour (5 is green; 6 is burgundy). Digit four denotes the material of the upper part of the product. Digit five denotes the material of the sole. Digits six and seven denote size.

Examples:

Code 1613275 represents a pair of mens slippers, brown suede, rubber sole, size $7\frac{1}{2}$.

Code 1324195 represents a pair of mens shoes, black leather, leather sole, size $9\frac{1}{2}$.

You are required to set suitable code numbers to the following, stating any assumptions you make:

i. boys shoes, brown leather uppers, rubber soles, size 4;

ii. ladies slippers, green felt uppers, rubber soles, size $4\frac{1}{2}$;

iii. girls shoes, burgundy leather uppers, leather soles, size $3\frac{1}{2}$.

(CIMA Cost Accounting 1)

B3.4 Within the costing system of a manufacturing company the following types of expense are incurred:

Reference number	
1	Cost of oils used to lubricate production machinery
2	Motor vehicle licences for lorries
3	Depreciation factory plant and equipment
4	Cost of chemicals used in the laboratory
5	Commission paid to sales representatives
6	Salary of the secretary to the Finance Director
7	Trade discount given to customers
8	Holiday pay of machine operatives
9	Salary of security guard in raw material warehouse
10	Fees to advertising agency
11	Rent of finished goods warehouse
12	Salary of scientist in laboratory
13	Insurance of the company's premises
14	Salary of supervisor working in the factory
15	Cost of typewriter ribbons in the general office
16	Protective clothing for machine operatives

Required:

Place each expense within the following classifications: Production Overhead, Selling and Distribution Overhead, Administration Overhead, Research and Development Overhead. Each type of expense should appear only once in your answer. You may use the reference numbers in your answers.

(AAT Cost Accounting & Budgeting, part question)

B3.5 a. Your company is considering installing a costing system and is examining ways in which different classifications of cost can assist management.

Required:

Prepare a report for the Finance Director outlining:

i. How costs can be classified.

ii How the different classifications of cost can assist management.

(AAT Cost Accounting & Budgeting, part Question)

4: Materials – purchasing, reception and storage

1. Topics covered in this chapter

> 1. Essentials of material control
> 2. Purchasing procedure
> 3. Reception, inspection, storage
> 4. Just-in-Time purchasing and production
> 5. Materials requirements planning.

2. The essentials of materials control

From the costing viewpoint the essentials of materials control prior to actual use in production can be summarised as follows:

a. Materials of the appropriate quality and specification should be purchased only when required and appropriately authorised.

b. The suppliers chosen should represent an appropriate balance between quality, price and delivery.

c. Materials should be properly received and inspected.

d. Appropriate storage facilities should be provided and stock levels physically checked on a regular basis.

e. Direct materials used in production should be charged to production on an appropriate and consistent pricing basis.

f. Indirect materials used in production and non production departments should be appropriately charged to the correct cost centre and included in the overheads of the cost centre.

g. The documentation, accounting systems and controls at each stage should be well designed and effective.

h. Stock taking must be well organised to ensure that stock quantities on hand are available when required.

3. The material control process

Figure 4.1 shows the elements of the material control process (prior to actual production material control).

The important features of purchasing, receipt, storage and issue are dealt with below whilst inventory control and materials costing are dealt with in subsequent chapters.

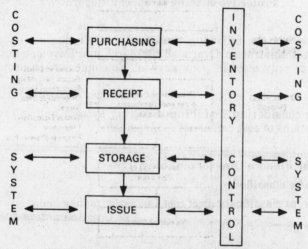

Figure 4.1 The material control process

4. Purchasing

Because such a large proportion of a firm's costs are represented by bought in materials and services, the purchasing function is of great importance and has become highly specialised. The responsibility of the purchasing function includes price, quality and delivery all of which are crucial factors. Late or non-delivery, poor and substandard materials, incorrect specifications etc. are all likely to have at least as great an impact on profitability as paying an unnecessarily high price. The avoidance of production delays, excessive scrap caused by incorrect materials and the avoidance of excessive stocks are among the aims of an efficient purchasing function. Frequently the purchasing function of a group or of a firm with numerous branches is centralised.

This has many advantages including: larger quantity discounts, uniform standards, possibility of more continuous supplies in difficult times etc, but there may be disadvantages such as longer response times; some lack of flexibility in catering for specialised needs and general remoteness from the scene of operations.

5. Purchasing procedures

Although the exact system obviously varies from firm to firm, Figure 4.2 is typical.

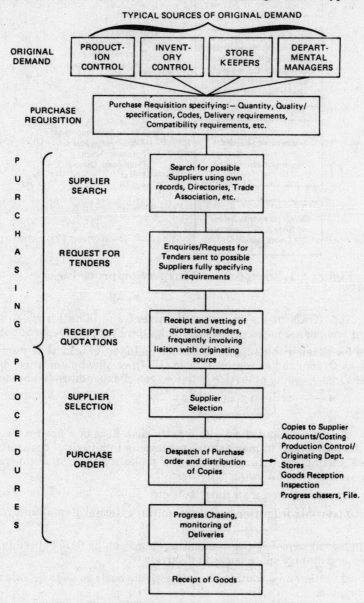

Figure 4.2 Outline of purchasing procedures

Notes to Figure 4.2:

a. Although the diagram shows each of the originating sources producing a Purchase Requisition, frequently Production and Inventory Control may produce a schedule of requirements (often computer based) specifying delivery dates and call off rates.

b. The Purchase Order is the basis of the legal contract between the firm and the supplier and should unambiguously define the required goods or services. Virtually all organisations refuse to recognise an invoice from a supplier which is not covered by a purchase order. The issue of Purchase Orders must be closely controlled and signing restricted to a few senior people.

c. Progress chasing is shown as a purchasing procedure which it frequently is. However, it is sometimes the responsibility of Production Control and Works Administration.

6. Reception and inspection procedures

Again, whilst details vary, Figure 4.3 shows a typical situation.

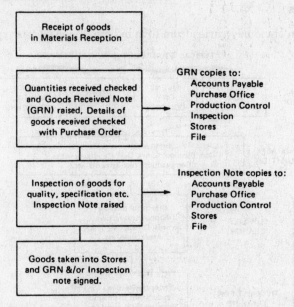

Figure 4.3 Reception and inspection procedures.

Notes:

a. The Goods Received Note (GRN) is an important document and is necessary so that the Supplier's invoice can be verified and passed for payment usually by the Purchase Department.

b. The usual procedure for passing the supplier's invoice includes: checks that items invoiced were as ordered (from Purchase Order) and as received (from GRN), verification of price, discounts and credit terms (from Purchase Order), coding of invoice both for type of expenditure and place to be charged.

7. Storekeeping

It is salutary to compare the controls and checks on a petty cash float of a few hundred pounds with the frequently haphazard procedures used in many stores containing hundreds of thousands of pounds worth of stock. Storekeeping is an important function and can make a substantial contribution to efficient operations. Storekeeping includes the following activities:

a. Efficient and speedy issue of required materials, tools etc.

b. Receipt of parts and materials from Goods Reception (ie, external items) and from Production (ie, internal items)

c. Organising storage in logical sequences, thus ensuring items can be found speedily, that all items can be precisely identified and storage space is used effectively.

d. Organising Stock Checks either on a continuous or a periodic basis so as to be able to provide accurate stock figures when required.

e. Protecting items in store from damage and deterioration.

f. Securing the stores from pilfering, theft and fire.

Notes:

a. It will be noted that the clerical tasks associated with *stores recording* are not mentioned above as, except in the very smallest stores, these tasks are carried out separately from actual storekeeping. Stores recording procedures are dealt with subsequently.

8. Storage – issues and returns

The issue of materials must be appropriately authorised and amount issued recorded so that the appropriate charge can be made to production or to the receiving cost centre. The usual way this is done is by a *materials requisition* (MR).

An MR would contain:

Quantity – Part No – Description – Job or Centre to be charged – Authorisation

On presenting an MR to the storeman, it would be checked for correctness and authorisation and if satisfactory, the issue would be made. The MR would be retained by stores who would insert date of issue and forward the MR to Stores Records (for updating the Stock Records) and thence to the Cost Department (for pricing and charging). The storeman must ensure that the MR is amended when the issue cannot be made exactly as the original request, eg where only a part issue is made or an alternative material is acceptable when that originally requested is unavailable.

The procedure for goods returned to store is similar to that outlined above except that the document involved is termed a *material return note* and, of course, the goods are taken into stores rather than issued.

9. Storage – stocktaking

There are two approaches to the task of stocktaking – Periodic (usually annual) and Continuous.

❏ *Periodic Stocktaking*

The objective of periodic stocktaking is to find out the physical quantities of materials of all types (raw materials, finished goods, W-I-P etc) at a given date. This is a substantial task even in a modest organisation and becomes a difficult if not impossible task in a large firm. The following factors need to be considered:

a. Adequate numbers of staff should be available who should receive clear and precise instructions on the procedures.

b. Ideally the stocktake should be done at a weekend or overnight so as not to interfere with production.

c. The stocktake should be organised into clearly defined physical areas and the checkers should count or estimate all materials in the area.

d. Adequate technical assistance should be available to identify materials, part no's etc. Far greater errors are possible because of wrong classification than wrong counting.

e. Great care should be taken to ensure that only valid stock items are included and that all valid items are checked.

f. The completed stock sheets should have random, independent checks to verify their correctness.

g. The quantities of each type of material should be checked against the stock record to expose any gross errors which may be due to stocktaking errors or faults or errors in the recording system. Small discrepancies are inevitable.

h. The pricing and extension of the Stock Sheets, where done manually, should be closely controlled. Frequently the pricing and value calculations are done by computer, the only action necessary being to input quantities and stock and part numbers.

❏ *Continuous stocktaking*

To avoid some of the disruptions caused by periodic stocktaking and to be able to use better trained staff, many organisations operate a system whereby a proportion of stock is checked daily so that over the year all stock is checked at least once and many items, particularly the major value or fast moving items, would be checked several times. Where continuous stocktaking is adopted, it is invariably carried out by staff independent from the storekeepers.

Note: Continuous stocktaking is absolutely essential when an organisation uses what is known as the *Perpetual Inventory System*. This is a stock recording system whereby the stock balance is shown on the record *after every stock movement*, either issue or receipt. With this system the balances on the stock record represent the stock on hand and balances would be used in monthly and annual accounts as the closing stock. Continuous stocktaking is necessary to ensure that the perpetual inventory system is functioning correctly and that minor stock discrepancies are corrected.

10. Storage – centralisation vs. decentralisation

There is no conclusive answer as to whether there should be a centralised stores or several stores situated in branches or departments. Each system has its advantages and disadvantages which are given below.

Advantages of Centralisation

a. Lower stock on average.

b. Less risk of duplication.

c. Higher quality staff may be usefully employed to specialise in various aspects of storekeeping.

d. Closer control is possible on a central site.

e. Possibly more security from pilferage.

f. Some aspects of paperwork may be reduced, eg, purchase requisitions. g. Stocktaking is facilitated.

h. Likelihood that more advanced equipment will be viable, eg, materials handling, visual displays.

Disadvantages of Centralisation

a. Less convenient for outlying branches/departments.

b. Possible loss of local knowledge.

c. Longer delays possible in obtaining materials.

d. Greater internal/external transport costs in fetching and carrying materials.

11. Changes in production and purchasing systems

There are a number of changes taking place in industry which are altering dramatically the way that products are made and production is organised. These changes naturally influence supporting activities such as purchasing and storage. Several of the more important developments are outlined below. These include; Just-in-Time Purchasing, Just-in-Time Production and Materials Requirements Planning.

12. Just-in-time (JIT) systems

JIT systems were developed in Japan, notably at Toyota, and are considered as one of the main contributions to Japanese manufacturing success.

The aim of JIT systems is to produce the required items, of high quality, exactly at the time they are required. JIT systems are characterised by the pursuit of excellence at all stages with a climate of continuous improvement.

A JIT environment is characterised by:

❏ a move towards zero inventory

❏ elimination of non-value added activities

❏ an emphasis on perfect quality ie, zero defects

❏ short set-ups

❏ a move towards a batch size of one

❏ 100% on time deliveries

❏ a constant drive for improvement

❏ Demand-pull manufacture

It is this latter characteristic which gives rise to the name of Just-in-Time. Production only takes place when there is actual customer demand for the product so JIT works on a *pull-through* basis which means that products are not made to go into stock.

Contrast this with the traditional manufacturing approach of *production-push* where products are made in large batches and move into stock.

There are two aspects to JIT systems, JIT Purchasing and JIT Production.

13. JIT purchasing

This seeks to match the usage of materials with the delivery of materials from external suppliers. This means that material stocks can be kept at near-zero levels. For JIT purchasing to work requires the following:

a. Confidence that suppliers will deliver exactly on time.

b. That suppliers will deliver materials of 100% quality so that there will be no rejects, returns and consequent production delays.

The reliability of suppliers is all-important and JIT purchasing means that the company must build up close working relationships with their suppliers. This is usually achieved by doing more business with fewer suppliers and placing long term purchasing orders in order that the supplier has assured sales and can plan to meet the demand.

14. JIT production

JIT production works on a demand-pull basis and seeks to eliminate all waste and activities which does not add value to the product. As an example, consider the lead times associated with making and selling a product. These include:

- ❏ Inspection time
- ❏ Transport time
- ❏ Queuing time
- ❏ Storage time
- ❏ Processing time

Of these, only processing time adds value to the product whereas all the others add cost, but not value.

The ideal for JIT systems is to convert materials to finished products with a lead time equal to processing time so eliminating all activities which do not add value. A way of emphasising the importance of reducing throughput time is to express the above lead times as follows:

> Throughput time = Value-added time + Non-value added time

The JIT pull system means that components are not made until requested by the next process. The usual way this is done is by monitoring parts consumption at each stage and using a system of markers (known as kanbans) which authorise production and movement to the process which requires the parts. A consequence of this is that there may be idle time at certain work stations but this is considered preferable to adding to work-in-progress inventory.

Poor and uncertain quality is a prime source of delays hence the drive in JIT systems for zero defects and Total Quality Control (TQC). When quality is poor, higher WIP is needed to protect production from delays caused by defective parts. Higher inventory is also required when there are long set-up and changeover times. Accordingly there is continual pressure in JIT systems to reduce set-up times and eventually eliminate them so that the optimal batch size can become one. With a batch size of one, the work can flow smoothly to the next stage without the need to store it and schedule the next machine to accept the item.

15. JIT production implications

To operate JIT manufacturing successfully and achieved the targets of low inventories and on-time deliveries means that:

a. The production processes must be shortened and simplified. Each product family is made in a work-cell based on flowline principles. The JIT system increases the variety and complexity within work cells. These contain groups of dissimilar machines which thus requires workers to be more flexible and adaptable.

b. Using JIT the emphasis is on 'doing the job right the first time' thus avoiding defects and reworking. JIT systems require quality awareness programmes, statistical checks on output quality and continual worker training.

c. Factory layouts must be changed to reduce movement. Traditionally machines were grouped by function; all the drilling machines together, the grinding machines and so on. This meant a part had to travel long distances moving from one area of the factory to another often stopping along the way in a storage area. All these are non-value added activities which have to be reduced or eliminated.

d. There must be full employee involvement. As an example it has been reported that the 60,000 employees of Toyota produced a total of 2.6 million improvement suggestions per annum. In most cases, after line management approval, the working groups simply get on with implementing their ideas. Arguably one of the most important behavioural implications of JIT is that the status quo is continually challenged and there is a never ending search for improvements.

16. Benefits from JIT

Successful users of JIT systems are making substantial savings. These arise from numerous areas:

a. Lower investment required in all forms of inventory

b. Space savings from the reduction in inventory and improved layouts

c. Greater customer satisfaction resulting from higher quality better deliveries and greater product variety

d. The buffers provided by traditional inventories masked other areas of waste and inefficiency. Examples include; co-ordination and work flow problems, bottle necks, supplier unreliability and so on. Elimination of these problems improves performance dramatically

e. The flexibility of JIT and the ability to supply small batches enables companies to respond more quickly to market changes and to be able to satisfy market niches.

17. Materials requirement planning (MRP)

MRP is a computerised information, planning and control system which has the objective of maintaining a smooth production flow.

It is concerned with:

❑ maximising the efficiency in the timing of orders for raw materials or parts that are placed with external suppliers

❑ efficient scheduling of the manufacture and assembly of the final product

The operation of an MRP System requires the following:

a. A master production schedule showing the quantities and timings required for the finished product(s)

b. A Bill of Materials (BOM) which shows the breakdown of each finished product into sub-assemblies components and raw materials

c. An Inventory file containing the balance on hand, scheduled receipts and numbers already allocated for each sub-assembly, component and type of raw material

d. A parts manufacturing and purchasing file containing lead times of all purchased items and lead times and production sequences of all sub-assemblies and components produced internally.

MRP has evolved into MRPII which attempts to integrate material resource planning, factory capacity planning and labour scheduling into a single manufacturing control system.

18. Summary

a. The material control process includes:

   Purchasing, Receipt, Storage and Issue, Inventory Control, and associated costing procedures.

b. The purchasing function is very important and aims for an appropriate balance of price, quality and delivery.

c. The Purchase Requisition giving precise details of quantity required, specification, delivery etc. initiates the main purchasing procedures.

d. The main purchasing procedures are: supplier search, supplier selection, ordering and processing deliveries.

e.   Goods must be properly received, inspected and a Goods Received Note (GRN) raised.

f.   The GRN is an important document which is used in the supplier invoice approval procedure.

g.   Storekeeping involves issue and receipt of materials, storage space organisation, protection of materials from deterioration, stocktaking etc.

h.   Items should not be issued from stores unless covered by a Materials Requisition (MR).

i.   The MR is used for amending the stock records and for charging the issue direct to production or to a particular cost centre.

j.   Stocktaking is carried out on a Periodic (usually annual) or Continuous basis. Continuous stocktaking is essential for Perpetual Inventory systems.

k.   Centralised stores have the advantage of lower stocks, better facilities and staff and some administrative savings, but may cause inconvenience and delays.

l.   The newer production systems such as Just-in-time and Materials Requirements Planning are radically altering traditional approaches to manufacturing, purchasing and storage. Manufacture and purchasing take place only when required, stocks are reduced or eliminated, there is a continual drive for improvement and zero defects.

19. Points to note

a.   Many variations exist on the basic systems outlined in this chapter. In particular where there is continuous or assembly line operation, purchasing procedures are often integrated with production control and deliveries are received continuously, frequently directly to the production floor. Whatever the system, adequate, well designed controls are essential.

b.   Because there is no clear advantage one way or the other, many organisations have a large central store supported by a number of smaller outlying stores.

c.   The process of Continuous Stocktaking is sometimes known as Stock Audit.

d.   Where a substantial quantity of items are required from stores say, for a particular job, the issue may be authorised by a Bill of Materials or Requirements Schedule, detailing all the items required rather than individual material Requisitions. Frequently the Requirements Schedules are computer produced and the items required would be listed in the most economical sequence for the storemen, ie, in location sequence or 'Picking order.'

Student self-testing

Self Review Questions

1.   What are the essentials of material control? (2)

2.   Outline the main steps in the Purchasing Procedure. (5)

3.   Where does the Goods Received Note (GRN) originate and what is its purpose? (6)

4.   What are the major activities involved in storekeeping? (7)

5.   What is Periodic and Continuous Stock taking? (9)

6.   In what circumstances is it essential to use continuous stocktaking? (9)

7.   What are the advantages and disadvantages of centralised storage? (10)

8.   What are the features which make a JIT environment? (12)

9.   What benefits are claimed for JIT? (16)

10.   What is Materials Requirement Planning? (17)

Exercises and examination questions with answers

Exercises

A4.1 Invariably goods, services and the supply of materials are obtained by the use of a Purchase Order. Design the layout of a Purchase Order, showing what essential information the order should contain.

A4.2 Give six advantages of continuous stocktaking.

A4.3 Give five reasons why stock-taking errors occur.

A4.4 Give five differences of JIT Purchasing from conventional purchasing.

Examination questions

A4.5 A manufacturing company has a high growth record and is unable to satisfy the demand for its products. It is unable to expand its production facilities on its present site, so is planning to move to a development area where it can build a factory which will be much larger than its existing factory.

As cost accountant you have been asked to help in the planning stage and your particular responsibility is for the planning of a new store for raw materials and components.

You are required to state the factors to be considered in respect of the following:

a. centralised or de-centralised stores;

b. the use of a continuous stock-taking system;

c. the layout of stores.

(CIMA Cost Accounting 1)

A4.6 The manufacturing company by which you are employed has just taken a six monthly physical check of all its stocks. The valuations of this physical stock-taking differs considerably from balances at the stocktaking date shown in the stock accounts in the ledger.

You are required to state the steps you would take to investigate how the differences had arisen so that an accurate stock value may be obtained.

(CIMA Financial Accounting 2)

A4.7 Outline the accountant's contribution to the process of material cost control in a manufacturing organisation where material is a significant element of total cost.

(ACCA, Costing)

Exercises and examination questions without answers

Exercises

B4.1 Even where the firm utilises a number of separate stores rather than a single, central store, buying is usually dealt with centrally.

Why do you think this is so? Give four advantages of centralised purchasing.

B4.2 Flowchart the processes involved in passing an invoice from a supplier taking care to identify the procedures involved at each stage and the links with other systems and procedures in the organisation.

B4.3 What are the main controls that should be present in a purchasing system?

B4.4 List eight features which characterise J.I.T manufacturing.

Examination question

B4.5 You are required to:

a. i. explain the term 'materials control' indicating the scope of its coverage within a manufacturing business;

    ii. differentiate between 'stock control' and 'store-keeping';

    iii. explain the term 'pareto (80/20) distribution'.

b. demonstrate your understanding of a. iii. above by:

    i. classifying, for stock control purposes, the items shown below;

    ii. drawing a graph that will enable management to understand the significance of your classification in b. i.

Stock item reference number	Annual usage (units)	Cost per unit £
7212	1,200	62.5
7213	800	150.0
7214	1,400	15.0
7215	2,000	11.4
7216	2,600	12.0
7217	5,000	3.2
7218	5,000	1.6
7219	2,000	3.0

(CIMA Cost Accounting 1)

5: Materials stock recording and inventory control

1. Topics covered in this chapter

1.   Stock recording
2.   Perpetual inventory
3.   Inventory control
4.   Control level calculations
5.   Economic Ordering Quantity (EOQ).

2. Stock recording

However sophisticated the Inventory or Stock Control system is in the firm, a basic prerequisite is that stock movements (issue and receipt) are accurately recorded. In addition the stock record typically shows various control levels which relate to the Inventory Control system and which are explained later in this chapter. In some firms several stock records may be kept regarding a particular materials, but this practice can introduce errors and discrepancies and has little to commend it.

The most frequently encountered records of stocks are *Bin Cards* and *Stock Record Cards*.

3. Bin cards

Where found, these are attached to or adjacent to the actual materials and the entries made at the time of issue either by the storeman or a stores clerk. They show only basic information relating to physical movements. A typical layout of a Bin Card is shown in Figure 5.1.

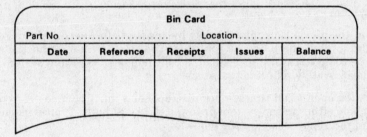

Bin Card				
Part No		Location		
Date	**Reference**	**Receipts**	**Issues**	**Balance**

Figure 5.1 Bin card

Notes:

a.   The reference column would be used for inserting the GRN or Material Requisition number.

b.   The use of Bin cards is declining partly because of the difficulty of keeping them up to date and partly because of the increasing integration of stock recording and inventory control procedures, frequently using computers.

4. Stock record cards

To obtain a full picture of the stock position of an item it is necessary to know not only the physical stock balance, but also the Free Stock Balance. This is defined as

Free stock balance = Physical stock
+ outstanding replenishment orders
– unfulfilled requirements or allocations

The free stock balance is a notional, not physical stock and is the key figure in Inventory Control. It is necessary to know *physical stock* for issue purposes, for stocktaking, and for controlling maximum and minimum stock levels and it is necessary to know the *free stock* position for replenishment ordering (these points are expanded below under Inventory Control). A typical Stock Record Card is shown in Figure 5.2.

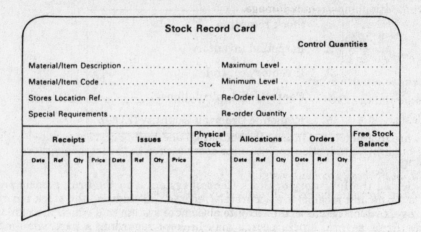

Figure 5.2 Stock record card

Notes:

a.   The entries in the Ref (Reference) columns would be Receipts (GRN No), Issues (Material Requisition No), Allocations (Job No or Customer's order No) and Orders (Purchase Order No).

b.   The above illustration shows a card for a manual or mechanised system, but even when the Stock Record is computerised, the same type of information is normally included in the computer file.

5. Perpetual inventory system

This system, mentioned in the previous chapter, simply means that after each issue or receipt the physical balance is calculated. The total of the balances represent the stock on hand and the system avoids the necessity for wholesale, periodic stocktaking. Instead, a continuous stocktaking system must be operated to ensure that the records accurately reflect actual stocks.

If the records are to be relied upon at all times, stock discrepancies must be investigated immediately and appropriate corrections made either to the system or to the record or both. Typical causes of discrepancies between actual stocks and recorded stocks are the following:

a.   Errors caused by incorrect recording and calculation.

b.   Incorrect coding causing the wrong part to be issued and/or wrong card to be altered.

c.   Under or over issues not noted.

d.   Parts and materials returned to stores and not documented.

e.   Shrinkage, pilferage, evaporation, losses due to breaking bulk etc.

f.   Loss or non-use of GRN's, material requisitions and other appropriate documentation.

6. Inventory control

(This subject is covered in greater depth in 'Quantitative Techniques', T. Lucey, DP PUBLICATIONS).

This can be defined as the system used in a firm to control the firm's investment in stock. This includes; the recording and monitoring of stock levels, forecasting future demands and deciding when and how many to order. The overall objective of inventory control is to minimise, in total, the costs associated with stock. These costs can be categorised into three groups:

Carrying costs:

a.   Interest on capital invested in stocks.

b.   Storage charges (rent, lighting, heating, refrigeration and air conditioning).

c.   Stores staffing, equipment, maintenance and running costs.

d. Material handling costs.

e. Audit, stocktaking, stock recording costs.

f. Insurance and security.

g. Deterioration and obsolescence.

h. Pilferage, evaporation and vermin damage.

Costs of obtaining Stock:

(Frequently known as ordering costs)

a. Clerical and administrative costs of Purchasing, Accounting and Goods Reception.

b. Transport Costs.

c. Where goods are manufactured internally, the set up and tooling costs associated with each production run plus the planning, production control costs associated with the internal order.

Costs of being without Stock (Stockout costs):

a. Lost contribution through the lost sale caused by the Stockout.

b. Loss of future sales because customers may go elsewhere.

c. Cost of production stoppages caused by stockouts of W-I-P and raw materials.

d. Extra costs associated with urgent, often small quantity, replenishment orders.

Some of the above items may be difficult to quantify, particularly stockout costs, but nevertheless may be of considerable importance. The avoidance of stockout costs is the basic reason why stocks are held in the first place.

7. Inventory control terminology

Some common inventory control items are now defined and illustrated in Figure 5.3.

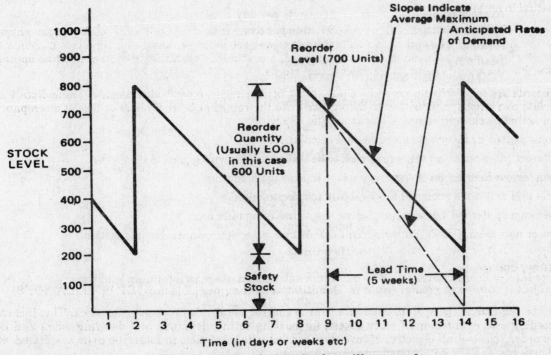

Figure 5.3 Stock terminology illustrated

a. *Lead or procurement time.* The period of time between ordering (externally or internally) and replenishment, ie, when the goods are available for use.

b. *Economic Ordering Quantity (EOQ) or Economic Batch Quantity (EBQ).* This is a calculated reorder quantity which minimises the balance of cost between carrying costs and ordering costs.

   c. *Buffer Stock or Minimum Stock or Safety Stock.* A stock allowance to cover errors in forecasting the lead time or the demand during the lead time.

   d. *Maximum Level.* A stock level calculated as the maximum desirable which is used as an indicator to management to show when stocks have risen too high.

   e. *Reorder Level.* The level of stock (usually free stock) at which a further replenishment order should be placed. The recorder level is dependent on the lead time and the rate of demand during the lead time.

   f. *Reorder Quantity.* The quantity of the replenishment order, frequently, but not always, the EOQ.

The diagram shows a simple stock position with the following assumptions and values:

> Regular rate of demand of 100 units per week
> Fixed lead time of 5 weeks
> Re-order quantity 600 units
> Maximum rate of demand 140 units per week
> Safety stock 200 units
> Reorder level 700 units

Notes:

   a. It will be seen that the 200 safety stock is necessary to cope with periods of maximum demand during the lead time.

   b. With constant rates of demand, as shown, the average stock is the safety stock plus $\frac{1}{2}$ reorder quantity

$$\text{ie, in example above average stock} = 200 + \frac{1}{2}(600)$$

$$= \textbf{500 units}$$

8. Calculating control levels

Typical methods of calculating the major control levels: Reorder Level, Minimum Level, and Maximum Level, are illustrated below using the following data:

Average usage	100 units per day
Minimum usage	60 units per day
Maximum usage	130 units per day
Lead time	20–26 days
EOQ (previously calculated)	4000 units

Reorder level = Maximum usage × maximum lead time

$$= 130 \times 26$$

$$= \underline{\textbf{3380 units}}$$

Minimum level = Reorder level – average usage in average lead time

$$= 3380 - (100 \times 23)$$

$$= 3380 - 2300$$

$$= \underline{\textbf{1080 units}}$$

Maximum level = Reorder level + EOQ – minimum anticipated usage in minimum lead time

$$= 3380 + 4000 - (60 \times 20)$$

$$= \underline{\textbf{6180 units}}$$

Notes:

   a. These are the normal control levels encountered in basic inventory control systems. Each time an entry is made, a comparison would be made between actual stock and the control level.

   b. Reorder level is a definite action level; maximum and minimum levels are levels at which management would be warned that a potential danger may occur.

c. The minimum level is set so that management are warned when usage is above average and buffer stock is being used. There may be no danger, but the situation needs watching.

d. The maximum level is set so that management will be warned when demand is the minimum anticipated and consequently stock may rise above maximum intended.

e. The calculation of control levels is done relatively infrequently in manual systems, but in a computer based system calculations would take place automatically to reflect current and forecast future conditions.

9. Economic ordering quantity (EOQ)

It will be recalled from paragraph 7 that the EOQ is a calculated order quantity which minimises the balance of cost between ordering and carrying costs. To be able to calculate a basic EOQ certain assumptions are necessary.

a. That there is a known, constant stockholding cost.

b. That there is a known, constant ordering cost.

c. That rates of demand are known.

d. That there is a known, constant price per unit.

e. That replenishment is made instantaneously ie, the whole batch is delivered at once.

The above assumptions are wide ranging and it is unlikely that all could be made in practice. Nevertheless the EOQ calculation is a useful starting point in establishing an appropriate reorder quantity.

The EOQ formula is given below and its derivation given in 'Quantitative Techniques', DP Publications.

$$EOQ = \sqrt{\frac{2.Co.D}{Cc}}$$

where: Co = Ordering cost per order

D = Demand per annum

Cc = Carrying cost per item per annum

Example

Find the EOQ where the forecasted demand is 1000 units per month, the ordering cost is £350 per order, the units cost £8 each and it is estimated that carrying costs are 15% per annum.

Here: Co = £350

D = 1000 × 12

= 12,000 units per annum

Cc = £8 × 15%

= £1.2 per item per annum

Thus: EOQ = $\sqrt{\dfrac{2 \times 350 \times 1200}{1.2}}$

= 2646 units

Notes:

a. It will be seen that it is necessary to bring the factors involved to the correct time scale.

b. The EOQ formula given above is for replenishment in one batch. Where replenishment takes place gradually, for example where the items are manufactured internally and placed into stock as they are made, the formula changes slightly as follows

$$\textbf{EOQ (with gradual replenishment)} = \sqrt{\frac{2.Co.D}{Cc\left(1-\dfrac{D}{R}\right)}}$$

where: R = Replenishment rate per annum

10. Summary

a. The two most common stock records are the Bin Card, or Stock Record Card (or its computer equivalent).

b. The bin card, where used, shows the basic Issues, Receipts and Physical Balance.

c. As well as physical information the Stock Record Card shows the Free Stock balance and the major control levels; Reorder level, Maximum level, and Minimum level.

d. The perpetual inventory system means that after each stock movement the balance on hand is calculated. To ensure that the records keep in line with actual stocks, continuous stocktaking is carried out.

e. Inventory control is the system used in a firm to control the investment in stocks and has the overall objective of minimising in total the three costs associated with stocks: carrying costs, ordering costs and stockout costs.

f. Reorder level is an action point, maximum and minimum levels are management indicators.

g. The EOQ is a calculated order quantity to minimise the balance of ordering and carrying costs and the basic formula is

$$EOQ = \sqrt{\frac{2.Co.D}{Cc}}$$

11. Points to note

a. Keeping stock records aligned with actual stocks is a major practical problem which is rarely solved completely successfully.

b. The inventory control system described in this chapter is the Reorder Level System, sometimes known as the TWO BIN System.

c. An alternative control system is known as the Periodic Review System where all stock levels are reviewed at fixed intervals and replenishment orders issued. These orders would be based on estimated usage, lead time etc. and would not be the EOQ used in the Reorder Level System.

d. The newer approaches to production, such as Just-in-Time, challenge the philosophy behind the traditional EOQ approach. Just-in-Time systems seek to eliminate stocks entirely and where possible, move towards a batch size of one. This applies especially to Work-in-Progress stocks.

Student self-testing

Self Review Questions

1. What is a Bin Card? (3)
2. What is the Free Stock Balance? Why is this figure of importance? (4)
3. What is the Perpetual Inventory System? (5)
4. What are the key elements in inventory control? (6)
5. What are the three categories of costs associated with stocks? (6)
6. Define: Lead time, EOQ, Buffer Stock, Reorder level. (7)
7. How is the Minimum Stock level calculated? (8)
8. What are the assumptions necessary to use the basic EOQ formula? (9)
9. What is the EOQ formula? (9)
10. What is the EOQ formula with gradual replenishment? (9)

Exercises and examination questions with answers

Exercises

A5.1 An investigation into stores procedures and record keeping showed that for Part No. Y292 the physical stock differed from the Bin Card and also from the Record Card kept in the works office which did not agree with the Bin Card. Give reasons for the differences.

A5.2 What is the relationship between Perpetual Inventory Systems and Continual Stocktaking?

A5.3 What is the Economic Order Quantity when demand is 25 per working day, ordering costs are £150 per order, the items cost £3 each and carrying costs are 12% per year. There are 250 working days in a year.

Examination questions

A5.4 The Managing Director of a company manufacturing and selling a range of goods has been looking through the previous period's accounts and has noted that the cost of direct materials purchased, expressed as a percentage of sales, is higher than the budgeted material cost of sales, expressed as a percentage of sales. He concludes from this comparison that the company has been wasting or losing significant amounts of material.

Required:

a. Provide *four* reasons why the Managing Director's conclusions regarding material waste/losses could be incorrect.

b. Assuming that the Managing Director is correct, identify THREE points where material waste/losses could have occurred, and for each point you have identified, outline a control procedure which could assist in reducing the material waste or losses.

(ACCA, Costing).

A5.5 a. Explain what is meant by the term 'economic order quantity'. Your explanation should be supported by a sketch or graph, which need not be on graph paper.

b. Using the information stated below, you are required to prepare a schedule showing the associated costs if 1, 2, 3, 4, 5 or 6 orders were placed during a year for a single product.

From your schedule, state the number of orders to be placed each year and the economic order quantity.

Annual usage of product	600 units
Unit cost of product	£2.4
Cost of placing an order	£6.0
Stock holding cost as a percentage of average stock value	20%

c. Comment briefly on three problems met in determining the economic order quantity.

(CIMA, Cost Accounting 1)

A5.6 The following information is provided concerning a particular raw material:

Average usage	1,000 kilos per day
Minimum usage	800 kilos per day
Maximum usage	1,350 kilos per day
Order quantity	9,000 kilos

The stock level is reviewed at the end of each day and an order is placed the following day if the normal re-order level has been reached. Delivery is reliably expected at the beginning of the fourth day following order.

Required:

a From the above information calculate three normal control levels used for stock control purposes.

b. Draw a graph demonstrating the changing level of stock of the material based on the following actual usage over a 14 day period:

First five days	1,020 kilos per day
Next four days	1,200 kilos per day
Final five days	900 kilos per day

The stock at the beginning of day 1 was 6,000 kilos. Show clearly on the graph three control levels calculated in (a).

c. Contrast the actual minimum stock level over the period with the normal control level established, and comment on the difference and any action required.

(ACCA, Cost and Management Accounting 1)

A5.7 The following data relates to an item of raw material:

Cost of raw material	£10 per unit
Usage per day	100 units
Minimum lead time	20 days
Maximum lead time	30 days
Cost of ordering material	£400 per order
Carrying costs	10% p.a.

N.B. Assume that each year consists of 48 working weeks of 5 days per week.

Required

Calculate:

a. the re-order level;

b. the re-order quantity;

c. the maximum level;

d. the minimum level.

(AAT, Cost Accounting & Budgeting, part question)

A5.8 a. Explain what you understand by the following terms, and briefly state the principal features of each:

stock control

store keeping

b. Receipts and issues of Material X for the month of August are as follows:

	Receipts units	Total value	Issues units
1st August	2,000	£4,000	
2nd August	3,000	6,600	
3rd August	2,000	6,000	
4th August			3,000
5th August	3,000	7,500	
6th August			6,000

There were no opening stocks of Material X.

Required: Using a FIFO method of valuation, show the price charged to each issue, and the closing stock valuation at 6th August. Assume that records are maintained using a perpetual inventory system.

c. Assume that you discover that the actual number of units of an item in stock represents 1.5 times the maximum level set for that item. Briefly explain what you might do.

(AAT, Cost Accounting & Budgeting, part question)

Exercises and examination questions without answers

Exercises

B5.1 Calculate three control levels for a Stock Control System having the following characteristics:

Average usage	3,000 units per week
Minimum usage	2,200 units per week
Maximum usage	4,200 units per week
Lead time	10-14 weeks
EOQ	35,000 units

B5.2 a. Draw a graph of the following information relating to a period of 24 days.

Opening Stock 100 Kg

Usage		
	First 8 days	15 Kg per day
	Second 8 days	12 Kg per day
	Third 8 days	20 Kg per day

The reorder level is 70 Kg and the reorder quantity is 120 Kg. Goods are delivered at the end of the third day after reaching reorder level.

b. From the graph determine the maximum stock in the period, the minimum stock in the period and the closing stock.

B5.3 Calculate the Economic Order quantity when the demand is 200 per week, the ordering cost is £150 per order, the items cost £6 each and the carrying costs are 18% per annum.

Examination questions

B5.4 The Managing Director of your company has been looking at the company's last Balance Sheet and is concerned at the high level of stocks contained in the working capital. In particular he considers the control of raw material stocks is relatively inefficient and has asked you to report on the fixing of economic levels of stock holding.

The company is an engineering company manufacturing components for which there is a regular demand and raw material stocks comprise a large range of items of varying types and values.

Prepare a short report to the Managing Director and in doing so you should state:

a. The stock levels you would fix and the factors that would influence the fixing of these levels.

b. How these levels would operate.

c. The major advantages to be derived from such a system.

(CIPFA, Management Accounting)

B5.5 A large local government authority places orders for various stationery items at quarterly intervals. In respect of an item of stock coded A32, data are:

❏ annual usage 5,000 boxes

❏ minimum order quantity 500 boxes

❏ cost per box £2

Usage of material is on a regular basis and on average, half of the amount purchased is held in inventory. The cost of storage is considered to be 25% of the inventory value. The average cost of placing an order is estimated at £12.5.

The chief executive of the authority has asked you to review the present situation and to consider possible ways of effecting cost savings.

You are required to:

a. tabulate the costs of storage and ordering item A32 for each level of orders from four to twelve placed per year;

b. ascertain from the tabulation the number of orders which should be placed in a year to minimise these costs;

c. produce a formula to calculate the order level which would minimise these costs – your formula should explain each constituent part of the formula and their relationships;

d. give an example of the use of the formula to confirm the calculation in b. above.

e. calculate the percentage saving on the annual cost which could be made by using the economic order quantity system;

f. suggest two other approaches which could be introduced in order to reduce the present cost of storage and ordering of stationery.

(CIMA, Cost Accounting 2)

B5.6   In the context of a company's stock control, the following information relates to item number 7829:

	Units
Stock levels: maximum	6,000
minimum	1,000
Re-order level – when free balance reaches	1,600
Re-order quantity	2,000
Opening balances at 1st August included:	
Stock in the stores	1,600
Ordered from suppliers awaiting delivery	2,200
Allocated	1,200

Transactions for the three months ended 31st October included:

	August	September	October
Received	1,200	2,400	3,600
Issued	1,400	3,600	2,200
Allocated	1,800	4,600	1,400
Returns to supplier (not replaced)	200	800	400
Transfers (by transfer notes) from Department X to Department Y	600	–	800
Returns to stores	600	400	200

You are required to:

a. design a stores record card to provide for the above information;

b. enter on the card, for item number 7829, the appropriate transactions for the three months. The balances at the end of each month should be shown for:

    i.   allocated stock;

    ii. stock on order;

    iii. stock in stores;

    iv. free balance.

(CIMA, Cost Accounting 1)

B5.7 a. During the night of 30th April a fire at the premises of P Limited destroyed all the work-in-progress stock but not the raw materials nor the finished goods stocks. A physical stocktaking on 1st May valued the stocks on hand as follows:

	£'000
Raw materials	60
Finished goods	80

At 31st March the stocks on hand were:

	£'000
Raw materials	30
Work-in-progress	20
Finished goods	50

During April, sales were £60,000, raw materials purchases £50,000, carriage on purchases of raw materials £8,000, and direct labour costs incurred £40,000. Production overhead absorption rate is 50% of the direct labour cost.

The sales and gross profits for the four months of December to March are shown below and it has been agreed with the insurers that the average gross profit over this period be used for the basis of a claim.

	Sales £	Gross profit £
December	53,000	12,340
January	42,000	11,920
February	47,000	10,860
March	54,000	13,880

You are required to determine the value of work-in-progress stock lost in the fire which will be the basis of a claim on P Limited's insurers. Present your answer in the form of a statement, showing your supporting calculations.

b. A basic rule in stock valuation is that stock should be valued at the lower of cost and net realisable value, taking each item or group of similar items separately.

You are required, in the context of stock valuation for a manufacturer, to explain the terms 'cost' and 'net realisable value' as used in the above statement.

(CIMA, Cost Accounting 1)

6: Materials – pricing issues and stocks

1. Topics covered in this chapter

1. Objectives of materials pricing

2. Pricing systems (LIFO, FIFO, Average Price etc)

3. Accounting for stocks.

2. Accurate recording

There is little point in detailed analysis of pricing systems for charging purposes unless the basic records are accurate and up to date. The system of issues, job recording, scrap records, material returns, material transfers, defective material returns, inspection records etc, etc. must be continually monitored to ensure its relevance and accuracy.

3. Objectives of material pricing

There are two main objectives of material pricing:

a. To charge to production on a consistent and realistic basis the cost of materials used.

b. To provide a satisfactory basis of valuation for inventory on hand.

These objectives should be achieved by a materials pricing system which is the simplest effective one and which is administratively realistic.

4. Problems of materials pricing

In practice the problem of pricing material issues, which thus determine product costs, is complicated by several factors:

a. Rapidly changing prices for bought in materials and components.

b. The stock of any given material is usually made up of several deliveries which may have been made at different prices.

c. The frequent impossibility (and undesirability from a costing viewpoint) of identifying items with their delivery consignment.

d. The sensitivity of profit calculations to the pricing method adopted particularly where materials form a large part of total cost.

No one pricing method has all the advantages and it is necessary to use the most appropriate system to fulfil the requirements of a particular situation. The features of the various pricing systems are described below.

5. General features of pricing systems

When an issue is made from Stores, the Materials Requisition would be passed to the Cost Department to be priced and extended for appropriate ledger entries to be made. At the simplest these entries would be:

Debit

Work-in-Progress Control A/C
(for direct material issues)

or

Overhead Control A/C
(for indirect material issues)

Credit

Stores Ledger Control A/C

To be able to use some of the pricing systems described below (eg, the FIFO and LIFO methods) the stock recording system has to be comprehensive enough not only to record overall quantities and prices, but also the number or quantity received in any one batch. This is so that issues can be nominally identified against batches which is necessary to establish the appropriate price to be charged.

6. First in first out (FIFO)

Using this method issues are priced at the price of the oldest batch in stock until all units of the batch have been issued when the price of the next oldest is used and so on.

Characteristics

a. It is an actual cost system

b. It is a good representation of sound storekeeping practice whereby oldest items are issued first.

c. Because it is actual cost system unrealised profits or losses do not arise.

d. The stock valuation is based on the more recently acquired materials and thus more nearly approaches current market values.

e. The FIFO system is acceptable to the Inland Revenue and is acceptable according to SSAP 9 (Stocks and Work-in-Progress).

f. Product costs, being based on the oldest material prices, lag behind current conditions.

   In periods of rising prices (inflation) products costs are understated and profits overstated; in periods of falling prices (deflation) product costs are overstated and profits understated.

g. Because of the necessity to keep track of each batch, the system is administratively clumsy.

h. Renders cost comparison between jobs difficult because the material issue price may vary from batch to batch even with issues made on the same day.

7. Last in first out (LIFO)

Using this method, issues are charged out at the price of the most recent batch received and continue to be charged thus until a new batch is received.

Characteristics

a. It is an actual cost system.

b. LIFO will frequently result in many batches being only partly charged to production where a subsequent batch is received.

c. Product costs will tend to be based fairly closely on current prices and will therefore be more realistic.

d. Stocks are valued at the oldest prices.

e. The LIFO system is generally not acceptable to the Inland Revenue and is not recommended by SSAP 9.

f. Administratively clumsy.

g. Renders cost comparison between jobs difficult.

h. In periods of rising prices LIFO, by keeping down disclosed profits, provides a hedge against inflation.

8. Average price method

The average price method is a perpetual weighted average system where the issue price is recalculated after each receipt taking into account both quantities and money value.

Characteristics

a. Although realistic, it is not an actual buying in price, except by coincidence.

b. The average price method is acceptable to the Inland Revenue and is one of the methods recommended by SSAP 9.

c. It is less complicated to administer than LIFO and FIFO.

d. It has an effect on product costs and stock valuation somewhere between the LIFO and FIFO systems.

e. The average price method makes cost comparison between jobs using similar materials somewhat easier.

f. With constantly fluctuating purchase prices, the average price method is likely to give more satisfactory results than LIFO or FIFO as it will tend to even out the price fluctuations.

g. Because it is based on actual costs, no unrealised stock profits and losses occur.

9. Specific or unit price

Where the item issued can be identified with the relevant invoice, the actual cost can be charged. This is usually only possible with special purpose items bought for a particular job.

10. Standard price

This is defined as:

'A predetermined price fixed on the basis of a specification of a product or service and of all factors affecting that price'.

In effect a standard or planned price is an average price predicted for a future period and all issues and returns would be made at the standard price for the period concerned.

Characteristics

a. Not an actual cost, therefore stock profits and losses may arise.

b. Administratively simple. Only quantities issued and received need be recorded, not the money values as they are predetermined.

c. Very real practical difficulty in establishing an acceptable and realistic standard price; particularly in volatile conditions.

d. If a realistic standard price can be established, some guidance to purchasing efficiency may be obtained.

e. Because material price variations are eliminated, manufacturing cost comparisons can be made more easily.

Note: A standard issue price for materials may be used even where the firm does not use a full standard costing system – described in Chapter 23 onwards.

11. Replacement price

A typical example of this method, sometimes known as the market price method, charges out issues at the buying in price on the day of issue. There are many variants to this system. For example, buying in prices may be established by means of a price index or actual prices updated on a monthly basis.

Characteristics

a. Not an actual cost price, therefore stock profits and losses may occur.

b. Issues would be priced at up to date values.

c. Major administrative problem in keeping replacement prices up to date.

d. Replacement pricing is more frequently used with estimating rather than normal stock issues.

e. Not acceptable to Inland Revenue.

f. Makes cost comparison between jobs difficult.

12. Base stock method

Although not strictly a method of valuing issues it is included in this section for completeness. The method assumes that initial purchases were to provide a buffer or base stock and that this base stock should appear in all subsequent stock valuations at its original value. Issues would be valued by one of the methods described earlier in this chapter. The base stock method would result in stock values which were totally unrealistic and its use is not recommended.

13. Comparison of pricing methods

Because of the effect on product costs and stock valuations, there is a need for an organisation to be consistent in its issue pricing methods. Apart from specific or unit prices all the methods are merely conventions, each with advantages and disadvantages. Provided that the system is used consistently and suits the operating conditions of the firm, any of the system could be used. However, because of SSAP recommendations and the Inland Revenue, the use of the FIFO or the Average price systems appear to be most common.

Based on the stores data below, issue prices using the FIFO, LIFO, Average Price and Standard Price systems are shown in the following accounts.

Stores data for part no 10x for October where the standard price is 4.50 per unit.

Date	Receipts	Purchase Price	Issues
1/10	150 units	4.00	
5/10	100 units	4.50	
6/10			80 units
12/10			100 units
20/10	90 units	4.80	
24/10			80 units

Stores Ledger Account using the Average Price Method

Receipt date	GRN No	Qty	Price £	Total £	Issue date	Mat'l req	Issue details	£	Balance (memorandum only)	£
1/10	5832	150	4.00	600					150 @ 4.00	600
5/10	6291	100	4.50	450					250 @ 4.20*	1050
					6/10	257	80 @ 4.20	336	170 @ 4.20	714
					12/10	492	100 @ 4.20	420	70 @ 4.20	294
20/10	7057	90	4.80	432					160 @ 4.5375†	726
					24/10	794	80 @ 4.5375	363	80 @ 4.5375	363
						Bal c/f	80	363		
		340		1482			340	1482		

Average Price calculations

$$*\quad \begin{array}{rlll} & 150 & \text{units @} & \pounds 4 & = & \pounds 600 \\ \text{plus} & 100 & \text{units @} & \pounds 4.5 & = & 450 \\ = & 250 & \text{units} & & = & \pounds 1050 \end{array}$$

$\therefore$ average price = $\pounds \dfrac{1050}{250} = \pounds 4.20$

$$\dagger\quad \begin{array}{rlll} & 70 & \text{units @} & \pounds 4.2 & = & \pounds 294 \\ \text{plus} & 90 & \text{units @} & \pounds 4.80 & = & 432 \\ = & 160 & \text{units} & & = & \pounds 726 \end{array}$$

$\therefore$ average price = $\pounds \dfrac{726}{160} = \pounds 4.5375$

Stores Ledger Account using the Standard Price Method

Receipt date	GRN No	Qty	Price £	Total £	Issue date	Mat'l req	Issue details	£	Balance (memorandum only)	£
1/10	5832	150	4.50	675					150 @ 4.50	675
5/10	6291	100	4.50	450					250 @ 4.50	1125
					6/10	257	80 @ 4.50	360	170 @ 4.50	765
					12/10	492	100 @ 4.50	450	70 @ 4.50	315
20/10	7057	90	4.50	405					160 @ 4.50	720
					24/10	794	80 @ 4.50	360	80 @ 4.50	360
						Bal c/f	80	360		
		340		1530			340	1530		

Stores Ledger Account using the FIFO Method

Receipt date	GRN No	Qty	Price £	Total £	Issue date	Mat'l req	Issue details	£	Balance (memorandum only)	£
1/10	5832	150	4.00	600					150 @ 4.00	600
5/10	6291	100	4.50	450					150 @ 4.00 ⎱ 100 @ 4.50 ⎰	1050
					6/10	257	80 @ 4.00	320	70 @ 4.00 ⎱ 100 @ 4.50 ⎰	730
					12/10	492	70 @ 4.00 ⎱ 30 @ 4.50 ⎰	415	70 @ 4.50	315
20/10	7057	90	4.80	432					70 @ 4.50 ⎱ 90 @ 4.80 ⎰	747
					24/10	794	70 @ 4.50 ⎱ 10 @ 4.80 ⎰	363	80 @ 4.80	384
					Bal c/f		80 @ 4.80	384		
		340		1482			340	1482		

Stores Ledger Account using the LIFO Method

Receipt date	GRN No	Qty	Price £	Total £	Issue date	Mat'l req	Issue details	£	Balance (memorandum only)	£
1/10	5832	150	4.00	600					150 @ 4.00	600
5/10	6291	100	4.50	450					150 @ 4.00 ⎱ 100 @ 4.50 ⎰	1050
					6/10	257	80 @ 4.50	360	150 @ 4.00 ⎱ 20 @ 4.50 ⎰	690
					12/10	492	20 @ 4.50 ⎱ 80 @ 4.00 ⎰	410	70 @ 4.00	280
20/10	7057	90	4.80	432					70 @ 4.00 ⎱ 90 @ 4.80 ⎰	712
					24/10	794	80 @ 4.80	384	70 @ 4.00 ⎱ 10 @ 4.80 ⎰	328
					Bal c/f		80	328		
		340		1482			340	1482		

Notes:

a. The account using standard prices is shown fully completed for illustration purposes only. If the standard price method was to be used then quantities only need to be recorded thus saving clerical work.

b. It will be noted that receipts, issues and balances are all at standard price. The gain/loss on purchasing would be written off elsewhere in the accounts, the stores ledger being entirely at standard price.

It will be seen that the various pricing systems produce issue prices ranging from £4 to £4.8 and closing stock valuations ranging from £328 to £384.

14. Stock valuation

The application of any of the issue pricing methods automatically results in a closing stock valuation of the particular item in the stores ledger. The summation of the individual items ie, the balance on the Stores Ledger Control Account, represents a valuation of closing stock. Invariably this valuation is used for operating statements and internal management accounts. In addition this valuation is frequently the basis of stock valuation for use in the financial accounts, but on occasion some adjustment to the figure is made. The general rule of stock valuation for financial accounting purposes is cost, net realisable value or replacement cost, whichever is the lowest.

15. What purchase price to use?

So far the last three chapters have conveniently assumed that there is a clear cut purchase price which is entered in the cost accounts and which forms the basis of pricing issues and stocks. In practice this is not always the case and various charges, taxes and discounts may create some ambiguity. A number of the more commonly encountered complications are dealt with below.

a. *Value Added Tax (VAT)*

Most of the goods and services supplied to a typical organisation have an additional charge (currently at $17\frac{1}{2}$%) levied on the value of the goods or services and this appears on invoices. This tax charge is part of an organisation's input tax which can be reclaimed so that the VAT charge should not be included in the cost accounts.

b. *Transport, storage and delivery charges*

Where the purchaser has to bear these charges they form part of the cost of the goods and so should be included in the cost accounts. Where these charges are invoiced per unit or by weight (or can be easily prorated) then they would be included in the direct material cost. Often this is not practicable, or the amounts involved are small, in which case the additional charges would be allotted to production overheads.

c. *Quantity or Trade Discounts*

These are discounts given against a list price for ordering in large quantities. For example, on a list price of £5 per unit a discount of 5% may be given for purchases over 50 units and a 10% discount for purchases of over 100. Where such discounts are available it is clearly good purchasing practice to take maximum advantage of the price reductions possible. From the cost accounting viewpoint the net price of the items is the one which should be used so that, based on the example above, the price would be £4.50 per unit if ordering in lots of over 100.

d. *Cash discount*

This is a small percentage allowance which can be obtained by settling invoices promptly. For example, a supplier's terms may be $1\frac{1}{2}$% discount for settlement within 7 days otherwise Net Monthly.' The cash discount is generally considered to be a financial accounting item which would not normally be included in the cost accounts.

e. *Packing and container charges*

Where packing or containers are charged separately the cost accounting treatment varies according to whether the containers are returnable or not.

i. Non-returnable packing and container charges. The cost of the packing or containers is part of the purchase price of the materials and would normally be included in the direct or indirect costs as appropriate.

ii. Returnable packing and containers where full credit is given. The normal assumption would be that containers are returned and full credit received so that the container cost would not be included in the cost accounts. In certain circumstances however, experience may show that, because of damage or losses, the organisation does not receive credit for all packing and containers charged. In such cases a suitable addition could be made to the direct material cost or, if the amount is small, a charge could be made to production overheads.

iii. Returnable packing and containers where only a partial credit is given. The net cost of the containers (amount charged less credit received) is an addition to the material cost and would be included in the cost accounts.

16. Summary

a. There must be a consistent, reasonably simple method of pricing issues so that production is charged a realistic figure for materials consumed.

b. The problems involved in pricing issues arise from changing purchase prices, the frequent impossibility of identifying materials with particular purchases and administrative problems.

c. The major pricing methods are First in First out (FIFO), Last in First out (LIFO), Average price and Standard price.

d. SSAP 9, Stocks and Work in Progress, recommend the use of either unit (or specific) price, FIFO, or Average price.

e. Many of the pricing systems are administratively clumsy, requiring either the monitoring of batches or frequent price calculations.

f. Some of the administrative problems can be overcome by the use of a Standard price system, but there is the very real practical problem of establishing a standard price. If conditions are such that frequent revisions of the standard price are necessary, many of the advantages of the system are lost.

17. Points to note

a. It will be apparent that there is no such thing as 'true' issue price. It is a question of judgement which system is best suited to a particular organisation.

b. The stores ledger accounts shown in this chapter are examples of the perpetual inventory system described in Chapter 4, ie, where a balance is shown after each receipt and issue.

c. Regardless of SSAP recommendations and Inland Revenue acceptability, any pricing or stock valuation system could be used for internal purposes. However, to avoid duplication of effort there is merit in using a system for internal purposes which will be acceptable as a basis of stock valuation for financial accounting purposes.

d. The issue pricing systems described in this Chapter are the most common. Other systems exist, an example of which is 'Next in First Out' (NIFO). In this system, issued are priced at the 'next' price ie, the price of items which have been ordered but not received. This price would be close to current market prices. This system is complicated and rarely used.

Student self-testing

Self Review Questions

1. What are the objectives of issue pricing systems? (3)

2. What are the basic ledger entries for material issues: to production? indirect materials? (5)

3. What is the FIFO System ? (6)

4. What is the effect of the FIFO system in times of inflation? (6)

5. What are the characteristics of the LIFO system? (7)

6. Describe the average price method. (8)

7. What is a specific or unit price? (9)

8. Define a standard issue price. (10)

9. What is replacement price? (11)

10. Using any of the issue pricing systems, how is the closing stock valuation established? (14)

Exercises and examination questions with answers

Exercises

A6.1 The following information is available about a component.

Opening Stock	1st Jan	500 at £2 each
Deliveries	6th Jan	160 at £2.20 each
	20th Jan	180 at £2.25 each
Issues	2 Jan	300
	16 Jan	210

Complete three separate stores ledger accounts assuming that issues are priced using:

a. LIFO

b. FIFO

c. Average Price

A6.2 Which of the following items would be considered as part of the cost of materials taken in stores?

   a. Cash discount

   b. Trade discount

   c. VAT

   d. Freight and carriage charges

   e. Cost of non-returnable containers

   f. Cost of returnable containers

A6.3 At what price per unit would Part No. 52Y be entered in the Stores Ledger if the following invoice was received from a supplier?

Invoice	£
150 units Part No. 52Y @ £5 ea =	750
less 20% discount	150
	600
plus VAT @ $17\frac{1}{2}$%	105
	705
plus Packing Charges 5 non-returnable pallets	25
	730

Note: A $2\frac{1}{2}$% discount will be given for payment in 30 days.

Examination questions

A6.4 The Managing Director of a company manufacturing one product, a standard sized office desk, asks you as the recently appointed works accountant to investigate the material control procedures operating in the factory. You have arranged for a physical stock count of raw materials, work-in progress and finished goods to take place at the beginning and end of April. The results of this stocktaking and other data relevant to the consumption of material during April are shown below.

Physical Stocktaking	*Opening Stock at Beginning of April*	*Closing Stock at End of April*
Finished Goods	650 desks	925 desks
Work-in-Progress	300 desks	160 desks
degree of completion:		
Timber	66.67% complete*	75.0% complete
Varnish	25.0% complete	37.5% complete

(ie, the 300 desks had been issued with 66.67% of the timber necessary to complete the desk.)

Raw Materials:

Timber	40,000 square feet	55,000 square feet
Varnish	1,600 litres	700 litres

Other Data:

Sales	4,600 desks

	Timber	Varnish
Works Manager's estimate of material consumption per desk, including an allowance for normal waste	30 square feet	0.47 litres
Purchase price of opening stock	£1.40 per square foot	£1.20 per litre

Purchases of materials:

5 April	125,000 square feet at £1.50 per square foot	400 litres at £1.10 per litre
19 April	70,000 square feet at £1.70 per square foot	1,800 litres at £1.30 per litre

Value of material issued to production:

12 April	£120,000	£1,200
26 April	£164,000	£1,550

The value of material issued to production has been obtained by using the following methods of pricing material issues:

> Timber – last in, first out
>
> Varnish – first in, first out

Required:

a. Calculate the quantity of timber and varnish issued on each of the dates shown in the question and the consequent book-stocks of each material at the end of April. Compare the closing book-stocks of each material with the results of the physical stock count.

b. Calculate the total quantity of each material which, according to the works manager's estimates, should have been consumed and compared with the quantities of materials actually consumed.

c. Discuss the possible reasons for any differences revealed by your comparisons in a. and b. above.

(ACCA, Costing)

A6.5 For the six months ended 31st October, an importer and distributor of one type of washing machine has the following transactions in his records. There was an opening balance of 100 units which had a value of £3,900.

Date	Bought Quantity in units	Cost per unit £
May	100	41
June	200	50
August	400	51.875

The price of £51.875 each for the August receipt was £6.125 per unit less than the normal price because of the large quantity ordered.

Date	Sold Quantity in units	Price each £
July	250	64
September	350	70
October	100	74

From the information given above and using weighted average, FIFO and LIFO methods for pricing issues, you are required for each method to:

a. show the stores ledger records including the closing stock balance and stock valuation;

b. prepare in columnar format, trading accounts for the period to show the gross profit using each of the three methods of pricing issues;

c. comment on which method, in the situation depicted, is regarded as the best measure of profit, and why.

(CIMA, Cost Accounting 1)

A6.6 You have been appointed as Inventory Accountant to a company where material is a major element of cost. The Chief Accountant wants to install an efficient material control and pricing system within the company and seeks your advice upon a number of issues:

a. Material XY has fluctuated in price over period 11,November 1990 and the Chief Accountant is unsure what price to cost the issues to Job 124.

You are given the following information:

Material XY		Kilos	Cost
November 1	Opening Balance	20,000	£60,000
November 3	Receipts	5,000	£4 per kilo
November 10	Receipts	12,000	£5 per kilo
November 17	Issues	24,000	
November 20	Receipts	17,000	£4.50 per kilo
November 27	Issues	20,000	

Required:

    i.   Cost the issues on 17 November and 27 November to Job 124 using two different methods of pricing.

    ii.   On the assumption that the Direct Labour for Job 124 is £50,000 and Overhead is recovered on the basis of 110% of Direct Material, calculate the selling price for Job 124 if profit is 10% of selling price on the basis of the two methods that you selected in i.

    iii.   Comment critically upon the results that you have arrived at on the two methods used in i. and ii.

b.   At the moment there are a number of stores spread throughout the factory, each duplicating the holding of stock. Stock- taking is carried out once a year which require the suspension of production for one week with overtime rates being paid to the stock checkers. The Chief Accountant maintains that the cost levels associated with the present system are too high and with the planned growth of the Company taken into consideration a more efficient cost-effective system is required.

Required:

Evaluate

    i.   Continuous stock-taking

    ii.   Centralised store-keeping, as methods whereby the Chief Accountant's objectives can be met

c.   The ordering of Material KL has caused concern in the past according to the Chief Accountant. There have been occasions when an excessive amount of stock has been carried beyond any possible demand and when the problem has been addressed and the stock level cut , orders have been unfulfilled and sales lost because the Company has run out of Material KL. The Chief Accountant has now said he wants a policy that achieves:

    i.   Adequate stock of material KL, thus minimising the risk of shortage and production dislocation balanced with,

    ii.   Avoidance of excessive stock levels of material KL and the consequent tying up of scarce funds.

You are given the following information:

    i.   Budgeted average demand for material KL is 400 kilos per week and production is maintained for 50 weeks in the year.

    ii.   The ordering cost is £150 per order.

    iii.   The standard material cost of KL is £6 per kilo and carrying costs are $33\frac{1}{3}\%$ of that figure per annum for each kilo.

    iv.   The maximum usage in any one week is 600 kilos and the minimum 400.

On average the orders take anything from one to three weeks to be delivered after they have been placed.

Required:

In order to meet the Chief Accountant's objectives what is:

    i.   The optimum order quantity that should be placed?

    ii.   The reorder level for stock of KL?

    iii.   The minimum level of stock that should be held?

    iv.   The minimum level of stock that should be held?

(AAT Cost Accounting & Budgeting)

Exercises and examination questions without answers

Exercises

B6.1 a. Calculate the closing stock value using:

    i.   LIFO

    ii. FIFO and

    iii. Average prices.

Receipts	(1st March)	60 units at £15
	(7th March)	60 units at £18
	(3rd March)	25 units
	(10th March)	55 units

    b. Which, if any, of these values would be acceptable for both cost accounting and financial accounting purposes?

B6.2 The Works Director, on examining the costs of a job just completed, finds that material has been charged to the job at £15 per Kg using the FIFO pricing system in operation whereas he knows that the current price is £19 per Kg. He asks you to explain this, exclaiming that 'If this example is typical, all the job costs are wrong and they are not worth preparing.'

Examination questions

B6.3 For the purpose of measuring business income it has been suggested that 'the use of LIFO and replacement cost depreciation will almost completely adjust for the misleading result obtained by applying the historical cost convention.'

You are required to:

a. explain what it meant by 'misleading result obtained by applying the historical cost convention';

b. provide definitions of

    i.   LIFO

    ii. replacement cost depreciation;

c. explain how the use of the principles referred to will 'almost completely adjust for the misleading result obtained by applying the historical cost convention'.

(ACCA, Costing)

B6.4 On 1 January Mr G started a small business buying and selling a special yarn. He invested his savings of £40,000 in the business and, during the next six months, the following transactions occurred:

	Yarn Purchases			Yarn Sales		
Date of Receipt	Quantity Boxes	Total Cost	Date of Despatch	Quantity Boxes	Total value	
		£			£	
13 January	200	7,200	10 February	500	25,000	
8 February	400	15,200				
11 March	600	24,000	20 April	600	27,000	
12 April	400	14,000				
15 June	500	14,000	25 June	400	15,200	

The yarn is stored in premises Mr G has rented and the closing stock of yarn, counted on 30 June, was 500 boxes. Other expenses incurred, and paid in cash, during the six month period amounted to £2,300. Required:

a. Calculate the value of the material issues during the six month period, and the value of the closing stock at the end of June, using the following methods of pricing:

    i.   first in, first out,

    ii. last in, first out, and

    iii. weighted average (calculations to two decimal places only).

b. Calculate and discuss the effect each of the three methods of material pricing will have on the reported profit of the business. and examine the performance of the business during the first six month period.

(ACCA Costing)

7: Labour – remuneration methods

1. Topics covered in this chapter

1.	Principles of remuneration
2.	Time based remuneration
3.	Incentive schemes
4.	Trends in labour costing.

2. Trends in remuneration

At present approximately one third of manual workers are paid by some form of incentive scheme. This overall percentage masks extremely wide variations from industry to industry. For example, in general engineering around 80% of workers are paid wholly or partly by some form of incentive scheme, whereas in process industries the figure is as low as 15%.

There is a general tendency (with, of course, exceptions) for larger firms to move away from direct incentive schemes to schemes such as measured day work. There is also a tendency for workers to become salaried employees which has clear costing implications as direct labour costs become more fixed in nature rather than varying with output.

3. Remuneration methods

The two main categories of remuneration are

a. Time based

b. Related in some way or another to output or performance.

Within these two categories there are innumerable variations some of which have general applicability whilst others are of a local and specialised nature. Remuneration systems are frequently complex and administratively cumbersome, but because the system is the result of negotiations, disputes and agreements over the years, attempts to rationalise and simplify are frequently met with hostility and suspicion. The two major categories of remuneration together with typical variations are dealt with below.

The newer forms of production organisation, such as Just-in-Time systems mean more and more workers will be paid time rates and will not have their pay dependent on individual output levels. There are two main reasons for this. Firstly, parts are now only produced as and when required. This means that the repetitive production of components that move into stock is avoided as one of the key objectives of Just-in-Time is to eliminate all forms of stock. Secondly, what counts in JIT is the output of the group (known as a *production cell*) as a whole. As a consequence workers have to be flexible and adaptable and move from task to task according to demand. In such circumstances individual incentive schemes are of little or no value.

In addition more and more wages and salaries, traditionally classed as overheads, are now being traced to product lines and classed as direct. For example, IBM are now grouping many support functions around specific product lines so that identification of costs is more direct. This is, of course, part of the trend towards Activity Cost Management whereby there is much closer identification of people and expenditure to specific value adding activities.

4. Time based systems

a. *Basic System.*

At the simplest level workers would be paid for the number of hours worked at a basic rate per hour up to, say, 40 hours per week. Time worked in addition to 40 hours would be classed as overtime and is usually paid at a higher rate, for example 'time and a quarter' (ie, $1\frac{1}{4} \times$ basic rate per hour) depending on the number of extra hours worked and when the overtime was worked.

Although workers' pay is not related to output, this does not mean that output and performance is unimportant. On the contrary, it is normal practice to monitor output and performance closely by shop floor supervision and managerial control systems so that workers are paid for actually working and not merely attending.

Advantages:

i.   Simple to understand and administer

ii. Simplifies wage negotiations in that only one rate needs to be determined unlike the continuous complex negotiations over individual rates usual in some incentive schemes.

Disadvantages:

i.   No real incentive to increase output.

ii. All employees in the grade paid the same rate regardless of performance.

iii. Constant supervision may be necessary.

Most appropriate for:

i.   Work where quality is all important eg, jig and tool making.

ii. Work where incentive schemes would be difficult or impossible to install eg, indirect labour, stores assistants, clerical work etc.

iii. Work where the output level is not under the employees' control eg, power station workers.

b.   *High day rate system*

This is a time based system which is designed to provide a strong incentive by paying rates well above normal basic time rates in exchange for above average output and performance. For its successful application it is necessary to ensure that the output levels are the result of detailed work studies and that there is agreement from the labour force and the unions involved on the required production level. A typical application of this system is on assembly line production in the car industry and in domestic appliance manufacture.

Advantages

i.   It is claimed to attract higher grade workers.

ii. Provides a direct incentive without the complications of individual piecework rates.

iii. Simple to understand and administer.

Disadvantages

i.   May cause other local employers to raise their rates to attract the better workers thus nullifying the original effect.

ii. Problems occur when the original target production figures are not met.

Most appropriate for: Easily measurable output to which groups of workers contribute, eg, car assembly.

Note: The system is also called Measured Day Work and in practice such schemes may well have quite complex structures and rules.

c.   *Common bonuses found in time based systems*

In addition to the time rates explained above, bonuses or extra payments are frequently made. Some common examples are:

i.   Shift bonus. Where a worker agrees to work shifts, particularly where rotating shifts are used, he receives an extra amount.

ii. Timekeeping bonus. Where a person's timekeeping has been good over the week a bonus may be paid.

iii. Continuous working bonus. Where the plant has achieved continuous production without strikes, go slows or stoppages a weekly bonus is paid. This system appears to have had some success in one of the large car manufacturers.

Note: Many variants exist, for example, many firms which operate a time based system pay, in addition, some form of output bonus and conversely some of the above bonuses are found in firms where the main method of remuneration is by an incentive scheme.

5. General features of incentive schemes

All incentive schemes relate payment to output in some way or another. There are innumerable variations; some schemes apply to individuals whilst other apply to groups of workers, some have a direct and immediate relationship to output whilst other are more indirect.

From a properly organised and well planned system both the firm and the employees can benefit. The employee from the extra income arising from increased production, and the firm from the reduced overheads per unit of the increased production. Unfortunately not all schemes achieve this ideal, but careful attention to the following factors will help to achieve this objective.

a. Remuneration should reflect workers' effort and performance and payment should be made without delay, preferably soon after completion of the task.

b. The scheme should be reasonably simple to assist administration and to enable employees to calculate their own bonus.

c. Performance levels should be demonstrably fair ie, they should be in reach of the average worker working reasonably hard.

d. There should be no artificial limit on earnings and earnings should be safeguarded when problems arise outside the employee's control.

e. The scheme should not be introduced until there has been full consultation and agreement with employees and unions.

f. The full implications of the scheme, performance levels, rates etc. must be considered, so that it will have a reasonable length of life. Rapid changes, particularly artificial ones to curtail earnings, destroy trust and cause problems.

6. Advantages and disadvantages of incentive schemes

Advantages

a. Increases production thereby increasing wages but also reducing overheads per unit, particularly where there are substantial fixed overheads.

b. May enable firm to remain competitive in inflationary conditions.

c. May improve morale by ensuring that extra effort is rewarded.

d. More efficient workers may be attracted by the opportunity to earn higher wages.

Disadvantages

a. Frequently there are problems in establishing performance levels and rates with frequent and continuing disputes.

b. Some incentive schemes are complex and expensive to administer.

c. Some groups of workers, although relatively unskilled, may earn high wages through incentive schemes whilst others engaged on skilled work may become resentful when differentials are eroded.

7. Individual incentive schemes

In general incentive schemes which relate to an individual worker seem to be the more usual and successful, probably because of the immediacy and direct relationship between effort and reward. The following are typical examples.

8. Straight piecework

At its most basic the worker would be paid an agreed rate per unit for the number of units produced. On occasions the number of operations would be the basis of payment or, where various types of articles are produced, a piecework time allowance per article would be sent and the worker paid for the piecework hours produced. For example, assume the following data:

Week No. 37

Employee No. 58107

Clock hours 40

Output

300 units of A,	Piecework time allowance	1.8 mins/unit
150 units of B,	Piecework time allowance	1.5 mins/unit
100 units of C,	Piecework time allowance	2.2 mins/unit

/ continued over

> *Piecework rate*
>   10p per minute produced.
>
> *Total production*
> $= (300 \times 1.8) + (150 \times 1.5) + (100 \times 2.2)$ piecework minutes
> $= 985$ piecework minutes
>
> *Gross wages*
> $= 985 \times 10p$
> $= \textbf{£98.50}$

Note:

It will be seen that the piecework time produced is not equivalent to actual clock hours. Piecework time allowances are merely a device for measuring the work content of dissimilar items.

Rarely, if ever, is piecework found on its own. Usually it is accompanied by certain safeguards, typical of which are: Guaranteed day rates and in lieu bonuses.

a. Piecework with guaranteed day rates. If earnings from piecework fall below normal day rates then there is a guarantee that day rates would be paid. This is to safeguard earnings when there are delays, shortages, tool breakage's etc. which make it impossible for the employee to earn bonus pay.

b. In lieu bonuses. Where a worker is normally covered by an incentive scheme and is transferred to ordinary day work, frequently an in lieu bonus is paid on top of normal day rates. Such a bonus is often paid to support workers (fork lift truck drivers, labourers etc.) whose work is not amenable to the incentive scheme used for the rest of the factory.

9. Differential piecework

One objection to straight piecework systems is that, because a flat rate per unit is paid, the incentive effect at higher production levels declines. Differential piecework seeks to overcome this by increasing the rate progressively at various production levels, eg,

up to	100	units per day 10p/unit
	101-150	units per day 12p/unit
	151-200	units per day 15p/unit

Differential piecework would, of course, normally be accompanied by the usual safeguards of guaranteed day rates or in lieu bonuses.

Note:
On occasions in differential schemes the whole of the output is paid at the higher rate when the next production threshold is reached.

10. Group incentive schemes

Although individually based incentive schemes are common and frequently successful, on occasions they are inappropriate and some form of group scheme is used. These schemes are likely to be more appropriate.

a. Where production is based on a group or gang basis, eg, road surfacing, coal mining.

b. Where production is integrated and all efforts are directed toward the same end, eg, all forms of production line manufacture, cars, domestic appliances etc.

c. Where the production methods or product makes it infeasible to measure individual performance.

Any of the incentive methods (piecework, differential piecework, premium bonus systems etc.) can be used, with appropriate adaption, for group scheme. In addition because of the wider scope of a group scheme, incentives based on cost savings, delivery dates, quality norms are also used.

Apart from the choice of the incentive scheme there is the problem of how to share the bonus amongst the group. Whatever method is used, it must have the full agreement of the group and unions involved.

11. Advantages and disadvantages of group schemes

Advantages

a. may engender closer cooperation in the group and a team spirit.

b. Administratively simpler with far less recording of labour times, production rates etc.

c. Support workers not directly associated with production can easily be included in the scheme.

d. Greatly reduces the number of rates to be negotiated.

e. May encourage more flexible working arrangements within the group.

Disadvantages

a. Less direct than individual schemes so may not provide the same incentive.

b. Less hardworking members of a group receive the same bonus and this may cause friction.

c. Not always easy to obtain agreement on proportions of the bonus which group members will receive.

12. Incentive schemes in practice

A significant proportion of production workers are paid under some form of incentive or bonus scheme and there is no doubt that some schemes are extremely effective. Many others are not and recognition of some of the following problems will help to ensure a workable and efficient scheme.

a. An incentive scheme will not solve the problems of badly managed, poorly organised, ill-equipped factories.

b. To ensure only good production is paid for, sound quality control and inspection procedures are vital.

c. All incentive schemes should be based on efficient working methods following comprehensive work studies. Notwithstanding this, it should be recognised that rate fixing is a subjective process which will only be finalised after employer/employee/union negotiations.

d. Care should be taken not to enter into sham productivity deals ie, where pay increases have been granted involving increased productivity which does not materialise.

13. Profit sharing

Although this would not normally be classed as an incentive scheme, profit sharing is part of the package of benefits that an employee could receive. It can be defined as the payment to employees of a proportion of company profits. The amount received by individuals is usually related to their salary or wage level and the profit share may be given in cash or in shares of the company. In the latter case the system becomes a form of co-ownership. Profit sharing appears to be regarded as a welcome but minor bonus too remote from the workplace to have any real incentive effect.

14. Trends in labour costing

In the past labour costs were a major proportion of total cost. This meant that it was worthwhile carrying out a thorough analysis of labour costs and making the necessary detailed accounting entries.

The position today is very different. Factories are highly automated and labour is a small (and reducing) proportion of total cost. Table 7.1 shows an analysis of Product Costs carried out by Walley and Piper in 1989.

Industry	Direct material	Direct labour	Overhead
Aerospace	51.7	19.3	29.0
Computers	69.9	7.5	22.5
Electronics	48.6	15.1	36.3
Industrial equipment	46.0	12.8	41.2
Metal products	52.0	15.7	32.3
Motor vehicles and parts	63.8	7.8	28.4
Scientific and photographic	52.3	11.3	36.5
Average	54.4	12.9	32.6

Table 7.1 Product cost by industry (% of total cost)

In these circumstances simpler costing systems are being used for labour with some companies eliminating direct labour accounting completely. For example, Hewlett-Packard in both their US and UK factories now treat labour as part of overheads and not as a separate item of cost. This means that there are now only two elements in product costs; materials and overheads.

15. Summary

a. There is a trend away from direct incentive schemes to measured day work, particularly for the larger companies.

b. In addition to a basic time based system there are high day rate or measured day work systems which aim to attract good workers by paying above average rates for above average performance.

c. Incentive schemes seek to increase production and should be, as far as possible; simple, directly related to performance, paid promptly, installed after full consultation, reasonably permanent.

d. Straight piecework pays a fixed rate per unit, whereas differential piecework pays extra amounts per unit above certain quantities; the aim being to provide greater incentive to higher output.

e. Group incentive schemes may use any of the incentive methods (piecework, premium bonus etc.) and are most suitable where a cooperative team effort is required.

f. Any form of incentive scheme must be based on proper work organisation, sound quality control and proper consultation.

g. Profit sharing may be by cash payout or share distribution. Frequently it is considered too remote to have any direct incentive effect.

h. In today's highly automated factories labour is a small and reducing element of cost. As a consequence labour costing is becoming less important and in some cases labour is not costed separately but is treated as part of overheads.

16. Points to note

a. Incentive schemes may increase the labour cost per unit but as long as the reduction in overhead cost per unit is sufficient, the scheme should be worthwhile.

b. Incentive schemes are not only applicable to manufacturing. The Government is attempting to introduce 'Performance Related Pay' across the Public Sector. Civil servants, local government officials, teachers and others are being targeted.

c. It is common costing practice to charge overtime wages above basic rate to overheads rather than direct wages. For example, if the basic rate is £4 per hour and overtime is paid at 'time and a quarter' then £4 per hour would be charged to direct wages and £1 per hour charged to overheads. The reasons for this is that it is generally fortuitous which particular job is done during overtime hours and which is done during normal hours and so it would be unjust to penalise the job which happened to be done during overtime.

There are circumstances where this practice is not adopted and where all wages, including the overtime premium, would be charged to direct wages. Examples include: process industries where there is continuous production of identical units and situations where overtime is worked at the request of a customer to bring forward a delivery date and the total wages can be charged to the job.

d. As production becomes more planned and organised and stocks are reduced or eliminated, as in JIT systems, direct incentive schemes become less appropriate. The main requirements for incentive schemes; repetitive production for stock, output individually determined and so on, run directly counter to the newer manufacturing philosophies.

Student self-testing

Self Review Questions

1. What are the two major categories of remuneration methods? (3)
2. What is 'time and a half'? (4)
3. In what circumstances is the use of the High Day Rate System appropriate? (4)
4. What bonuses are commonly encountered in conjunction with time based remuneration schemes? (4)
5. What factors should be considered when designing incentive schemes? (5)
6. What are the advantages and disadvantages of incentive schemes? (6)
7. What is straight piecework? (8)
8. What is an 'in lieu' bonus? (8)

9. What are the objectives of differential piecework systems? (9)

10. In what circumstances are group incentive schemes most appropriate? (10)

11. What is profit sharing? (13)

Exercises and examination questions with answers

Exercises

A7.1 Draw a graph showing the earnings per hour, for an output range of 0 – 400 units per hour if the worker is paid under the following wage systems:

a. Daywork at £4 per hour

b. Straight piecework at 2p per unit

c. Differential piecework at 2p per unit from 0 – 200 units, 2.5p per unit for 201 to 250 units, 2.75p per unit for 251 to 300 units and 3p per unit for all units above 301.

A7.2 A new incentive scheme has recently been introduced and the first period's results have been analysed. After studying the results the Managing Director has said that although he was pleased to see the increase in production he was disturbed to see that the average labour cost per unit had risen. In view of this it was his opinion that the scheme should be discontinued. You are required to reply to the Managing Director's comments.

A7.3 A worker is paid by differential piecework. The scheme is as follows:

up to 50	units per day	50p per unit
51– 70	units per day	60p per unit
71– 80	units per day	65p per unit
81– 100	units per day	70p per unit

His daily outputs for a five day week were 68 units, 83 units, 59 units, 94 units and 47 units. What will be his gross pay for the week?

Examination questions

A7.4 A manufacturing company seeking to control its labour costs produces a labour cost report each month. The report for October is reproduced below.

Labour Cost Report

	October £	September £
Direct labour	28,100	24,400
Supervision	3,000	3,000
Material handlers	3,100	2,800
Inspectors	3,400	3,640
Repairs and maintenance labour	3,200	3,200
Administrative labour	2,400	2,400
Total labour costs	£43,200	£39,440
Sales value of production	160,000	136,000
Total labour costs as a percentage of sales value of Production	27%	29%

You are required to comment on:

a. labour efficiency in October compared with that in September and state four possible factors which may have caused the percentage in October to be lower than in September;

b. the effectiveness of labour cost control by means of this report and suggest two better ways of controlling labour costs.

(CIMA, Cost Accounting 1)

A7.5 Cost accounting theory suggests that direct wages are variable with output. However, it is recognised that there is a fixed element present in wages. Therefore, direct wages are, in fact, semi-variable. Required:

a. Discuss the factors which have contributed towards this semi-variable element in wages.

b. How would a Cost Accountant account for the following in ascertaining total costs?

    i. overtime premium;

    ii. incentive payment;

    iii. sick pay and holiday pay to operatives;

    iv. idle time.

c. An organisation operates an individual premium bonus scheme in which an operatives performance is calculated and paid for as follows: Each task is given a target expressed in standard minutes. The amount of weekly output achieved is stated as a total of standard minutes. The weeks total of standard minutes is expressed as a percentage of attendance time (to the nearest whole number). The operator is paid:

Percentage Performance	Rate Paid Per hour
0 – 75	£2. 20
76 – 90	£2. 40
91 – 110	£2. 80
111 and over	£3. 40

Three products are assembled and have the following standard times:

    Product A – 42 standard minutes

    Product B – 60 standard minutes

    Product C – 75 standard minutes

Required:

Calculate the gross pay for each operator from the following information:

Operator	Hours Attended	Performance Products Assembled		
		A	B	C
A	38	15	13	11
B	39	15	10	8
C	42	15	18	16

(AAT, Cost Accounting & Budgeting)

A7.6 a. 'The same cost may be classified in a variety of different ways for different purposes.'

Identify three different ways of classifying the wages of an employee and give an example of the purpose of each method of classification.

b. Discuss the possible effects, on a company's costs, of changing the method of remunerating its direct workers from a time-rate to a piece-rate based scheme.

(ACCA, Costing)

A7.7 a. The following information is available:

Normal working day:	8 hours
Guaranteed rate of pay (on time basis)	£5.5 per hour
Standard time allowed to produce 1 unit:	3 minutes
Piecework price	£0.1 per standard minute
Premium Bonus:	75% of time saved, in addition to hourly pay.

Required:

For the following levels of output produced in one day:

    80 units

    120 units

    210 units

Calculate earnings based on:

    i. piecework, where earnings are guaranteed at 80% of time-based pay.

    ii. premium bonus system.

(AAT Cost Accounting & Budgeting, part question)

A7.8 a. Overtime premiums and shift allowances can be traced to specific batches, jobs or products and should be considered to be direct labour rather than indirect labour.

You are required to discuss the above statement.

b. Your managing director, after hearing a talk at a branch meeting on just-in-time (JIT) manufacturing would like the management to consider introducing JIT at your unit which manufactures typewriters and also keyboards for computing systems.

You are required, as the assistant management accountant, to prepare a discussion paper for circulation to the directors and senior management, describing just-in-time manufacturing, the likely benefits which would follow its introduction and the effect its introduction would probably have on the cost accounting system.

(CIMA Cost Accounting)

Exercises and examination questions without answers

Exercises

B7.1 A foundry is investigating what wages will be paid using various payment methods; daywork, piecework, and a bonus system which pays workers day wages plus half the surplus of standard hours produced times the piecework rate.

Data available.

8 hour day

Day rate £7 per hour

Standard time = 2 standard minutes per casting

Piecework price = £5 per standard hour

Output levels per day; 300, 350 and 400 castings.

B7.2 A factory has a system of incentives for direct workers based on piecework. This works well and no complaints have been heard from the direct operatives.

However, the indirect workers who are not included in the scheme complain that as they service and support production operations and are essential to factory efficiency they, too, should have an incentive scheme of their own or be included in the scheme for the direct workers.

What factors should be considered in resolving this problem?

B7.3 The production workers at a factory, previously on a piecework scheme, are now to be paid a fixed salary. From a costing viewpoint give 5 likely consequences of this.

Examination question

B7.4 A company selling chemicals direct to farmers remunerates its field sales force on a commission and year end bonus basis. The commission is 20% of standard gross margin (planned selling price less the standard cost of goods sold on a full absorption cost basis), contingent only on the collection of the account. A customer's credit is approved by the company's credit department. Price concessions are granted on occasions by the top sales management, but sales commission is not reduced by the granting of such discounts. A year end bonus of 15% of commissions earned is paid to salesmen who equal or exceed their annual sales target or quota. The annual sales target is usually established by applying approximately a 5% increase to the previous year's sales.

You are required to state with reasons:

a. what features of their remuneration plan are likely to be effective in motivating the salesmen to help meet the company's goals of higher profits and return on investment, and

b. what features are likely to be counter effective.

(ICA, Management Accounting)

B7.5 The chairman of Zed Manufacturing plc. has recently attended a conference on incentive schemes, and has become enthusiastic about the possible introduction of a value added incentive scheme. He has asked you, as assistant management accountant, to prepare a report to the board of directors, in which you should explain:

a. the concept of value added:

b. the operation of a value added incentive scheme;

c. three advantages of operating such a scheme.

(CIMA, Cost Accounting 2)

B7.6 A small company classifies all its production overhead of £2,400 per week as fixed. The company currently produces 150 components per week on a sub-contracting basis and has been asked by its major customer to increase its output. Management is reluctant to operate for more than the normal 40 hours each week but in an attempt to meet its customer's wishes decides to offer an incentive scheme to its four direct operators whose current rates of pay are as follows:

	Hourly rate £
C Ahmed	3. 00
A Brown	3.00
D Choudery	4. 00
G Spencer (working Foreman)	5.00

With the agreement of the employees, who are not members of a trade union, their basic hourly rates are to be reduced for a trial period of four weeks to those shown below but with *each* of them being given a bonus of £0.60 for every unit produced.

	Revised hourly rate £
C Ahmed	1.50
A Brown	1.50
D Choudery	2.50
G Spencer	3.50

After the first week of the trial period, production was 180 units. The production manager studied the results and believed the introduction of the bonus was too costly because the increase of 20% in production had increased labour costs by 32%. He is considering recommending changes to the newly – introduced scheme.

You are required to:

a.   i. calculate how the increase in labour cost of 32% was derived;

    ii. comment on whether the production manager was correct in assuming that the bonus scheme was too costly, showing your supporting calculations.

b. list *eight* of the general principles which should be borne in mind when an incentive scheme for direct labour personnel is being considered.

(CIMA, Cost Accounting 1)

B7.7 a. Give *three* reasons why direct production labour cost might be regarded as a fixed cost rather than as a variable cost.

b. A company currently remunerates its factory workers on a time basis and is now considering the introduction of alternative methods of remuneration. The following information relates to two employees for one week:

	Y	Z
Hours worked	44	40
Rate of pay per hour	£3.50	£4.50
Units of output achieved	480	390

The time allowed for each unit of output is 7 standard minutes. For purposes of piecework calculations each minute is valued at £0.05. Required:

    i. Calculate the earnings of each employee where earnings are based on:

a. piecework rates with earnings guaranteed at 80% of pay calculated on an hourly basis.

b. premium bonus scheme in which bonus (based on 75% of time saved) is added to pay calculated on an hourly basis.

    ii. Describe *two* situations in which the time basis of remuneration is likely to be more appropriate than piecework schemes.

(AAT Cost Accounting & Budgeting, part question)

8: Labour – recording, costing and allied procedures

1. Topics covered in this chapter

> 1. Attendance and output records
>
> 2. Wages procedure
>
> 3. Job evaluation and merit rating
>
> 4. The Personnel Function.

2. The necessary records

Whatever the system of remuneration, records of attendance time for each worker are required. In addition, depending on the incentive scheme involved, records will be required for operations, processes, parts and products including both times taken and quantities produced.

These records form the basis of wage calculations and for such costing data as: direct and indirect labour costs, overhead build-up, labour cost control. In many cases nowadays the recording is done electronically and not by using traditional forms and paperwork. The recording may be done by entries on terminals, automatic counting or weighing or by various forms of scanning using bar codes. Whatever the recording methods used the principles and objectives remain the same.

The two types of records; those for attendance and those for output are described below.

3. Attendance records

In all but the very smallest concerns this is done by the use of clock cards, one for each worker, and a time recording clock usually based at the entrance to the factory. The clock card is the basis of time recording and whatever additional time records are kept, they must be reconciled with the total attendance time recorded on the clock card by the time recording clock.

4. Output records

The records necessary must be tailored to the requirement of incentive and labour cost control systems in operation. Unnecessary recording incurs extra clerical costs and may slow down production and should be avoided. The following are typical records: daily and weekly time sheets, job cards, operation cards.

5. Daily and weekly time sheets

These are records, filled in by the worker and countersigned, which show how he spent his time during the day or week. The general objective is to reconcile all the time in attendance (recorded on the clock card) with time bookings either to jobs or operations ie, direct wages, or to non-productive attendance such as a machine breakdown which would be analysed by the cost department as indirect wages.

Weekly times sheets tend to be more inaccurate but require less clerical effort. It really depends on whether the worker deals with numbers of small jobs, when daily time sheets would be preferred, or is employed on jobs which last a considerable time when weekly sheets may be adequate.

A typical time sheet is shown in Figure 8.1.

6. Job cards

Unlike time sheets which relate to individual employees and may contain bookings relating to numerous jobs, a job card relates to a single job or batch and is likely to contain entries relating to numerous employees.

On completion of the job it will contain a full record of the times and quantities involved in the job or batch. The use of job cards, particularly for jobs which stretch over several weeks, makes reconciliation of work time and attendance time a difficult task. These cards are difficult to incorporate directly into the wages calculation procedures.

7. Operation cards

These cards, sometimes known as *piecework tickets*, are provided for each operation or stage of manufacture so that each operation will have at least one card. In this way a job will have a number of operation cards and although this increases the paper work, it does enable the operation cards to be used directly in the wage calculation procedures. A typical operation card is shown in Figure 8.2.

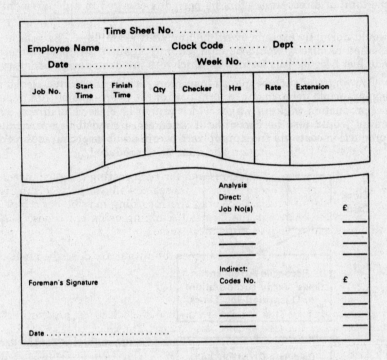

Figure 8.1 Time sheet

Operation Card				
Operators Name		Total Batch Quantity...........		
Clock No.		Start Time		
Pay Week No................ Date .... Stop Time				
Part No.		Works Order No.		
Operation		Special Instructions		
Quantity Produced	No. Rejected	Good Production	Rate	£
Inspector		Operative		
Foreman		Date		
PRODUCTION CANNOT BE CLAIMED WITHOUT A PROPERLY SIGNED CARD				

Figure 8.2 Operation card (or piecework ticket)

8. Wages procedures

The flowchart (figure 8.3) shows in outline a typical wages procedure from the original clock card to basic cost accounting entries.

9. Labour costing

Using job cards and/or times sheets and/or output records and the payroll, the cost department carries out a detailed analysis of all wages paid to enable the labour costs for products, operations, jobs, cost centres and departments to be established. This is done for cost ascertainment and cost control purposes. Features of various aspects of labour costing are dealt with below.

a. *Direct Wages.* That proportion of the wages of production employees directly attributable to production (ie, as ascertained from job cards and/or time sheets) is charged to the job or operation in which engaged and the total of direct wages for the period is charged to a departmental Work-in-Progress control A/c.

   Direct wages would normally exclude overtime and shift premiums. The reason for this is that such premiums, if classed as direct, would be charged only against the job(s) done during the overtime period which is unjust because it is fortuitous which jobs are done during ordinary or overtime.

b. *Indirect wages.* The wages of such people as inspectors, stores assistants, clerks and labourers would be coded to the appropriate department to form part of the overheads of that department. In addition, the proportion of production workers' wages which cannot be classed as direct, eg, idle time, overtime and shift premium would also be classified as indirect, included in overheads and subsequently absorbed into production costs via the appropriate overhead absorption rates as described in Chapter 9.

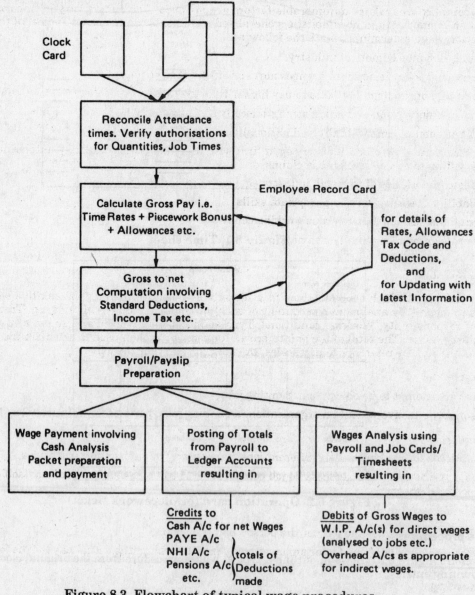

Figure 8.3 Flowchart of typical wage procedures

c. *Labour cost control.* The cost department activities described above provide the raw data for cost ascertainment and also for cost control purposes. Cost control at its simplest will show various comparisons, for example, direct and indirect wages, suitably analysed, compared with the same classifications for the last period for each cost centre and department and will also show various ratios. The simplest of these would be the ratio of direct to indirect wages, compared period by period for each cost centre and department. In this way trends of labour costs will be shown and may give some guidance to management on cost control.

The above points are only a brief introduction to cost control and substantially more detail is given in Chapters 23–25 on standard costing and budgetary control.

10. Related factors

In addition to the recording and costing procedures described above, there are numerous other matters which have an impact on labour and labour costs. Some of the more important of these are dealt with below, namely – wage determination, job evaluation, merit rating, personnel policies and labour turnover.

11. Wages determination

This is a complex area where innumerable factors are involved. The factors vary in importance from one organisation to another and no simplistic, generalised statements can be made. Typical of the factors to be considered in wage determination are the following.

a. General economic climate of industry.

b. Government policy ie, is there a wages norm or official income policy?

c. Profitability of the firm. Is it able to pay higher than average wages?

d. Extent of unionisation and union strength locally and nationally.

e. Extent of unemployment locally and nationally.

f. Cost structure of firm and industry eg, a firm with high fixed costs of largely automatic plant may be more willing to accede to high pay claims.

g. Strategic importance of firm and industry eg, electricity industry.

h. Availability of workers with appropriate skills.

i. Extent of hazardous or dangerous working conditions.

j. Wage rates prevailing locally and nationally.

12. Job evaluation

This is a technique which seeks to show in a reasonably objective manner the relative worth of jobs. It attempts to do this by analysing the content of each job under various categories, eg, Training required, Degree of responsibility, Working conditions, Types of decisions involved and so on, and giving a points score for each factor. The total of the points' scores for each job is then used to establish the ranking of one job to another and, by reference to pay scales, the normal salary for the job.

Advantages

a. Makes an attempt to be objective in ranking jobs.

b. Reasonably effective within an organisation at ranking jobs, particularly relatively low level ones.

Disadvantages

a. Not suitable for ranking widely different jobs, particularly in different organisations.

b. Gives a spurious air of objectivity to job comparison. The Job Evaluation process itself contains many subjective elements.

Notes:

a. Job Evaluation studies the job not the person doing the job.

b. Job Evaluation is only one factor amongst many in determining the actual pay for the job.

13. Merit rating

Unlike job evaluation, merit rating is concerned with the individual employee. It seeks to rate an employee's performance to assist in determining whether a person should receive a merit award, promotion, demotion etc. It does this by considering the performance and attributes of an employee under various categories, for example, initiative, attendance, accuracy, willingness etc, etc, and giving a number of points for each factor. Merit rating under various guises is frequently encountered in staff appraisal schemes, particularly in larger firms, and is considered to be of value in providing a reasonably standardised basis to the difficult task of individual appraisal.

14. The personnel function

Most firms of any size have a Personnel department who have responsibility for numerous tasks involving labour. Typically these include:

a. Advertising, recruiting and engaging labour.

b. Discharge, transfer, administration of appraisal schemes.

c. Industrial relations and union negotiations.

d. Maintenance of personnel records and provision of statistical information to Government Departments, Trade Associations etc.

e. Provisions of information to management on such matters as absenteeism, lateness, labour turnover, normal and overtime worked etc.

f. Staff development, training and educational schemes, including day release, apprenticeships and courses.

g. Welfare, sports and social facilities.

h. Safety and medical facilities.

i. Manpower planning and forecasting.

In general terms the Personnel function has the responsibility of providing an efficient labour force which is cost effective and keeping labour turnover to a minimum.

15. Labour turnover

This is usually expressed as a ratio, ie,

$$\frac{\text{Number of employees replaced per period}}{\text{Average total number of employees in the period}}$$

Although some labour movement is of value, high labour turnover rates destroy morale, increase costs and reduce productivity. People leave jobs for a variety of reasons, some of which are avoidable, and it is normal to analyse the reasons for leaving so as to take corrective action where possible. Typical of the reasons for labour turnover are the following:

a. Redundancy.

b. Dissatisfaction over prospects, pay, hours, conditions.

c. Lack of career structure.

d. Lack of training or day release.

e. Personal advancement.

f. Marriage, pregnancy.

g. Retirement.

h. Discharge.

i. Move from locality.

j. Changes in domestic circumstances.

16. Cost of labour turnover

These costs can be substantial, yet to some extent are avoidable through enlightened personnel policies and good management. The costs arise in the following areas:

a. Leaving costs, ie, interviews, preparation of documentation, disruption of output.

b. Replacement costs, ie, advertising, selection, personnel department procedures.

c. Training costs, ie, costs of required internal and external courses.

d. Learning cost, ie, slower initial production, increased scrap, tool breakages, increased accident rate.

17. Summary

a. Attendance records, usually in the form of clock cards, are always required.

b. Where incentive schemes are in operation, output records either by time sheets, job cards or piecework tickets are required.

c. Whether the recording of times, output etc, is made electronically or by using traditional paperwork the principles remain the same.

d. The main elements in the wages procedure are: time reconciliation, gross pay calculation, gross to net calculation, payroll and payslip preparation, wage payment.

e. The total of gross wages is charged to Work-in-Progress A/cs for direct wages and Overhead A/cs for indirect.

f. Overtime and shift premiums are generally classed as indirect and form part of production overheads.

g. Numerous factors determine the level of wages paid including: national and local rates, cost of living, prosperity of industry, union strength and militancy, working conditions etc.

h. Job evaluation seeks to analyse the content of each job under various factors so as to establish the relative worth of one job to another.

i. Merit rating seeks to assess the efficiency of an individual for the purpose of bonuses, promotion etc.

j. The personnel function is wide ranging and important and includes: engaging and discharging labour, union negotiations, staff development and training, welfare and safety.

k. Labour turnover should be monitored closely and the reasons for each employee leaving ascertained.

l. The costs of labour turnover can be high and include: engaging new labour, learning costs, training costs, lower initial productivity.

18. Points to note

Every aspect of labour relations can be critical and affect costs. The old 'scientific management' approach to labour as merely an adjunct to machinery is outmoded in modern conditions.

Student self-testing

Self Review Questions

1. What is a clock card ? (3)
2. Why are job cards difficult to incorporate into wages procedures? (6)
3. What is an operation card? (7)
4. Describe the steps in a typical wage procedure. (8)
5. Are overtime and shift premiums normally included in direct wages? (9a)
6. Give some examples of reports which might assist labour cost control. (9c)
7. What are some of the factors in wage determination? (11)
8. What is the object of Job Evaluation? (12)
9. What is Merit Rating? (13)
10. Give six functions normally carried out by a Personnel department. (14)
11. What is the labour turnover ratio? (15)

Exercises and examination questions with answers

Exercises

A8.1 A firm's basic rate is £3 per hour and overtime rates are time and a half for evenings and double time for weekends. The following details have been recorded on three jobs.

	Job X321	Job X786	Job Xl14
	Clock Hours	*Clock Hours*	*Clock Hours*
Normal time	480	220	150
Evening time	102	60	80
Weekend	10	30	16

You are required to calculate the labour cost chargeable to each of the jobs in the following circumstances:

a. Where overtime is worked occasionally to meet production requirements.

b. Where the overtime is worked at the customer's request to bring forward the delivery time.

A8.2 In practice it is unlikely that labour time and output records (eg, time sheets, piecework tickets, job cards) are perfectly accurate. Discuss the reasons for this lack of reliability and the implications for the cost accountant.

A8.3 In order to avoid criticism for spending too long on a job some production workers have been incorrectly classifying part of the time spent actually working on jobs as waiting time. What are the implications of this practice?

Examination questions

A8.4 Based on the data shown below, you are required to calculate the remuneration of each employee, as determined by each of the following methods:

   i. hourly rate;

   ii. basic piece rate;

   iii. individual bonus scheme, where the employee receives a bonus in proportion of the time saved to the time allowed:

Data			
Name of employee	Salmon	Roach	Pike
Units produced	270	200	220
Time allowed in minutes per unit	10	15	12
Time taken in hours	40	38	36
	£	£	£
Rate per hour	1.25	1.05	1.20
Rate per unit	0.20	0.25	0.24

b. Comment briefly on the effectiveness of method iii.

(CIMA, Cost Accounting 1)

A8.5 a. The following statement is an extract from an article about an electronics and telecommunications company. 'Turnover for the entire labour force is now stabilised at 23% per annum, consisting of 4% for management, and 30% for hourly paid workers, one third of whom are women.'

Explain what is meant by 'labour turnover' and list five cost implications.

b. The labour turnover of B Limited has risen disturbingly and for the last six 4-weekly periods the figures are given below. State the further information desirable for the tabulation to be more useful as a basis for managerial action.

Period	Average number employed	Number of leavers
1	1,000	60
2	1,200	120
3	1,100	100
4	1,000	100
5	1,000	110
6	1,000	130

c. State five possible reasons for a company having a high labour turnover rate.

(CIMA, Cost Accounting 1)

A8.6 X Ltd has an average of 42 workers employed in one of its factories in a period during which seven workers left were replaced.

The company pays a basic rate of £4.60 per hour to all its direct personnel. This is used as the standard rate. In addition, a factory wide bonus scheme is in operation. A bonus of half of the efficiency ratio in excess of 100% is added as a percentage to the basic hourly rate eg, if the efficiency ratio is 110% then the hourly rate is £4.83 (ie, £4.60 + (£4.60 × 5%)).

During the period 114,268 units of the company's single product were manufactured in 4,900 hours. The standard hour is 22 units.

Required:

a. calculate the labour turnover percentage for the period.

b. Identify the reasons for, and costs of, labour turnover, and discuss how it may be reduced.

c. Calculate the hourly wage rate paid for the period.

(ACCA Cost and Management Accounting, part question)

A8.7 The following information gives details of the gross pay calculated for a production worker:

	£
Basic pay for normal hours worked:	
40 hours at £5 per hour	200.00
Overtime:	
5 hours at time and a half	37.50
Group bonus payment	4.00
Gross wages for the week	241.50

Although paid for 40 hours in normal time, the worker was in fact unable to work for 6 hours because of machine breakdowns. Required: Analyse the total of £241.50 into direct and indirect costs. Give reasons for your answers. *(AAT Cost Accounting & Budgeting, part question)*

Exercises and examination questions without answers

Exercises

B8.1 Design a suitable form for use as a monthly Labour Turnover Report for management.

B8.2 The newly appointed Managing Director of a large organisation states that he wishes all salaries to be determined by systematic Job Evaluation and Merit rating procedures. He asserts that this will cure anomalies and eliminate subjective judgements.

Discuss the above statement.

Examination Questions

B8.3 a. Recent regulations affecting pay policies are causing many businesses to re-examine the use of incentive schemes as a method of remunerating employees. Discuss the general principles which should be applied to incentive schemes.

b. Certain organisations, for example car manufacturers, have abandoned premium bonus schemes and piece work schemes and substituted a 'high day rate' system. List the advantages and disadvantages expected from following such a policy. *(CIMA, Cost Accounting 1)*

B8.4 a. In the context of the output from a factory or group of workers, define and distinguish 'production' and 'productivity'.

b. X Y and Z are the members of a team making metal brackets. The expected output of the team is 6,000 brackets per week, each member working a 40 hours week and being paid a basic rate of £1.75 for each hour worked. A bonus of 50% of the team's productivity index in excess of 100 is added as a percentage to the basic hourly rate.

During week No. 50, X worked 40 hours, Y 39 hours and Z 38 hours and the output for the week was 6,786 brackets.

You are required to calculate for week No. 50:

i. the team's productivity index

ii. the effective hourly rate paid to the operatives

iii. the wages rate and efficiency variances of the team

c. Name the type of bonus scheme under which the member of the team are remunerated and demonstrate your understanding of the characteristics of that scheme by reference to your answers to (b). *(ACCA, Costing)*

B8.5 You are required to:

a. explain what is meant by 'idle time' and state the accounting entries which ought to be made in respect of idle time relating to direct production personnel;

b. draft, for the production manager, an idle time report form incorporating six possible reasons for the idle time occurring. *(CIMA, Cost Accounting 1)*

9: Overheads

1. Topics covered in this chapter

> 1. Bases of overhead absorption
> 2. Under/over absorption
> 3. Problem of service cost centres
> 4. Overhead analysis
> 5. Depreciation and obsolescence
> 6. Overheads and Activity Based Costing
> 7. Cost pools and cost drivers

2. Overhead absorption

This process was introduced in Chapter 2 from which it will be recalled that overhead absorption is the process by which overheads are included in the total cost of a product. The formal definition is:

'A means of attributing overheads to a product or service based for example, on direct labour hours, direct labour cost or machine hours'. *Terminology.*

Note that the Terminology definition given above relates to the traditional production volume based approach to overhead absorption not to an Activity Based approach. The traditional approach is described first in this chapter then the changes necessary to deal with Activity Based Costing.

Overhead absorption becomes of greater importance when dissimilar products are made which require different production processes or for jobs which, although using identical facilities, occupy the facilities for varying length of time. It is of importance in these circumstances because the overheads absorbed into the product or job should, as far as possible, reflect the load that the product or job places upon the production facilities.

To be able to compute the overhead to be absorbed by a cost unit it is necessary to establish an overhead absorption rate (OAR) which is calculated by using two factors; the overheads attributable to a given cost centre and the number of units of the absorption base (labour hours, machine hours, etc) that is deemed most suitable; thus

$$\text{OAR for cost centre} = \frac{\text{Total overheads of cost centre}}{\text{Total number of units of absorption base applicable to cost centre}}$$

The total overheads of a cost centre are established by the processes of cost allocation and cost apportionment described in Chapter 2. The various possible absorption bases are described below.

3. Bases of absorption

The objective of the overhead absorption process is to include in the total cost of a product an appropriate share of the firm's total overheads. An appropriate share is generally taken to mean an amount which reflects the effort and/or time taken to produce a unit or complete a job. In the unlikely event of identical products being produced by identical processes for the whole of a period, the total overheads could be shared equally amongst the products. Life is rarely so simple and to cope with practical situations various absorption bases have been developed. These bases are illustrated by the following example relating to Production Cost Centre 52.

Data relating to Cost Centre 52 for period 9:

Total Overhead for period	£6,000
Total Direct Labour hours for period	800
Total Direct Wages	£1,600
Total Direct Material used	£3,000
Total Machine Hours	1,200

Using these data the following absorption rates could be calculated using the formula given in Para. 2 above.

$$\text{Direct Labour hour OAR} = \frac{£6,000}{800 \text{ hrs}}$$

= £7. 5 overheads per labour hour

$$\text{Direct Wages OAR} = \frac{£6,000}{£1,600}$$

= £3. 75 overheads per £ of wages or 375% of wages

$$\text{Direct Material OAR} = \frac{£6,000}{£3,000}$$

= £2 overheads per £ of materials or 200% of materials

$$\text{Prime Cost OAR} = \frac{£6,000}{£4,600}$$

= £1.30 overheads per £ of Prime cost

$$\text{Machine Hour OAR} = \frac{£6,000}{1,200 \text{ hrs}}$$

= £5 overheads per machine hour

$$\text{Cost Unit OAR} = \frac{£6,000}{45 \text{ units}}$$

= £133 overhead per unit produced

4. Using the calculated OAR

When it has been decided what is the most appropriate rate to use for a given cost centre, the OAR is used to calculate the cost of a cost unit as in the following example.

A cost unit X has been produced in Cost Centre 52 and the following details recorded:

Cost Unit X

Direct Materials used	£23
Direct Wages	£27.50
Direct Labour Hours	12
Machine Hours	17

Assuming that it has been decided that the Direct Labour rate is the most appropriate method to use, calculate the cost of the cost unit using the data given above.

Cost Unit X

Direct Labour	27.50
Direct Materials	23.00
= Prime Cost	50.50
+ Overheads (12 hrs @ Labour Hour OAR of £7.5/hr)	90.00
	£140.50

In practice, as in the above example, the most appropriate OAR for a given cost centre is decided upon and used for all the cost calculations of units passing through that cost centre. Different cost centres may well have different absorption bases and the factors influencing the choice of base are given later in this chapter.

For comparative purposes the overheads which would be absorbed by cost unit X using each of the absorption bases is shown in the following table.

Cost Unit X Production Data

Direct Material	£23
Direct Wages	£27.50
Direct Labour hrs	12
Machine Hours	17

Absorption base	Direct labour hour	Direct wages	Direct material	Prime cost	Machine hour	Cost unit
OAR (from para 3)	£7.50 per hour	375% of wages	200% of materials	130% of prime cost	£5 per hour	£133 per unit
Cost Unit X data	12 labour hours	£27.50 wages	£23 materials	£50.50 prime cost	17 machine hours	1 unit
Calculation	12 × £7.5	3.75 × £27.50	2 × £23	1.3 × £50.50	17 × £5	1 × £133
Overhead absorbed by Cost Unit X	£90	£103.125	£46	£65.65	£85	£133

Table 9.1 Costs using different absorption bases

Notes:

1. Although each of the bases have been used in the table, this is for illustration only. In practice one base only, that deemed most appropriate, would be used for cost calculations.

2. It will be noted that the various absorption bases produce substantially different amounts of overheads to be absorbed into the cost unit, ranging from £46 to £133.

3. The wide range of overheads possible, as shown above, emphasises the point that there is no such thing as a single, accurate cost. *All* costs are based on conventions and judgement.

5. Choosing the appropriate absorption base

The factors to be considered in the choice of an appropriate base are given below, but it must be emphasised that the final choice is a matter of judgement and common-sense. There are no absolute rules or formulae. What is required is an absorption basis which realistically reflects the characteristics of a given cost centre and which avoids undue anomalies.

There is general acceptance that the time based methods (Labour Hours, Machine Hours and to a lesser extent Direct Wages) are more likely to reflect the load on a cost centre and hence the incidence of overheads and so students are recommended to choose one of these methods unless there are special factors involved.

❐ *Direct labour hour basis*

Most appropriate in a labour intensive cost centre and, providing the time booking system is good, easy to use. However, most production nowadays involves substantial use of machinery so the Labour Hour method may become increasingly inappropriate.

❐ *Machine hour basis*

Most appropriate in a mechanised cost centre. In such a cost centre many of the overheads are related to the machinery (power, repairs, depreciation etc), so a machine hour rate should reflect fairly accurately the incidence of overheads.

❐ *Direct wages*

This is a frequently used rate in practice and is easy to apply. Direct wages paid are related to time, but because of varying rates paid to different personnel, piecework and bonus systems, there is not an exact correlation between wages paid and time elapsed. If there was only one rate per hour paid throughout a cost centre and no form of incentive scheme, then the Direct Wages system would give identical results to the Labour Hour basis, but this is rarely the case.

❑ *Direct material*

This method has little to commend and if used could lead to absurd anomalies. For example, if an identical blanking process utilised either mild steel or stainless steel sheet and the stainless was five times the price of the ordinary steel, the Direct Material Absorption method would load the stainless product with five times the overhead, even though it was produced by an identical process taking identical time.

❑ *Prime cost*

Although part of Prime Cost is time related (direct wages), the inclusion of the direct material element would lead to possible anomalies as outlined above and accordingly its use is not recommended.

❑ *Cost unit*

Providing all the units produced in a period were identical with identical production processes and times, then this absorption method would give accurate results. However, such circumstances are unlikely, so the times when this method can be used are very rare.

6. Predetermined absorption rates

It will be recalled from the formal definition of overhead absorption given in Para. 2 that in most cases the rates are *pre-determined*. This simply means that the overhead absorption rate (OAR) is calculated prior to the accounting period, using estimated or budgeted figures for overheads and units of the absorption base chosen. Thus the general formula given in Para. 2 becomes

$$\text{Predetermined OAR for cost centre} = \frac{\text{Budgeted total overheads for cost centre}}{\text{Budgeted total number of units of absorption base}}$$

The major reason for this procedure is that the actual overheads and actual number of base units are not known in total until the end of the period and the actual OAR could not be calculated until then. This would mean that product costs could not be calculated until the end of a period and clearly this would introduce unacceptable delays into such procedures as invoicing and estimating. This is such a major disadvantage that virtually all absorption rates used are predetermined.

7. Under or over absorption

Using predetermined rates, overheads are absorbed into actual production throughout the accounting period. Because the predetermined rates are based on estimated production and estimated overheads, invariably, the overheads absorbed by this process do not agree with the actual overheads incurred for the period.

If the overheads absorbed are greater than actual overheads, this is known as OVER ABSORPTION. Conversely, if absorbed overheads are less than actual overheads, this is known as UNDER ABSORPTION. The following example shows a typical situation.

Assume that the data given on Para. 3 were budgeted figures and that the actual production, overheads and other data were as follows:

Cost Centre 52 Data for Period 9		
	Budgeted	*Actual*
Overheads	£6,000	£6,312
Direct Labour Hours	800	792
Direct Wages	£1,600	£1,705
Direct Materials	£3,000	£2,947
Machine Hours	1,200	1,172
Units produced	45	46

The predetermined overhead absorption rate for direct labour hours (which, it will be recalled, was judged the most appropriate for cost centre 52) was £7. 5 per hour

Total overheads absorbed by actual activity of 792 labour hours

$$= 792 \times 7.5$$
$$= £5,940 \text{ overheads absorbed into production, but actual overheads were } £6,312.$$

$$\therefore \text{ Under absorbed overheads } = £6,312 - 5,940 = £372$$

Note: It will be observed that under (or over) absorption can arise from either actual overheads differing from budget or a difference between the actual and budgeted amount of the absorption base or a combination of these two factors.

8. Dealing with under and over absorption

The budgeted figures used for calculating the predetermined OAR's are based on expected levels of production and overhead. There are many factors which cause actual results to differ from those expected and it must be realised that it is *actual* costs and overheads which determine the final profit. This means that the total of actual costs must appear in the final profit and loss account and not merely those calculated product costs which include actual prime cost plus overheads based on a predetermined OAR.

Accordingly, the amount of under absorbed overheads should be *added* to total costs before the profit is calculated and conversely the amount of over absorbed overheads should be *subtracted* from total cost.

This is now illustrated using the data from the previous paragraph relating to cost centre 52.

Actual direct material		*Actual direct labour*		*Actual prime cost*		*Absorbed overheads*		*Calculated production cost*		*Under absorption*		*Total production cost*
£2,947	+	£1,705	=	£4,652	+	£5,940	=	£10,592	+	£372	=	£10,964

P&L A/c

Notes:

a. The actual direct costs for each cost unit would of course be immediately available from the labour and material booking system for the job card.

b. The under (or over) absorption of overheads can only be established at the end of the period when actual activity or production and actual overheads are known.

c. Although eventually appearing in a Profit and Loss account or Operating Statement, the under or over absorption is sometimes put to a monthly suspense account as an intermediate stage and the net balance taken to P & L at the year end.

9. Absorbing non production overheads

The examples of absorption bases given in the preceding paragraphs relate to production overheads. However, a significant proportion of the overheads of a typical company are non-production overheads, eg Selling and Marketing Overheads, Research and Development Overheads, Distribution Overheads, Administrative Overheads etc. These overheads also form part of the total cost of a cost unit and have to be absorbed or charged to Profit and Loss account in some fashion.

Although the absorption bases for production overheads appear to have some rationale, the methods in common use for non-production overheads unfortunately are somewhat arbitrary. The different methods used are given below, but it must be emphasised that provided a given method is used consistently by an organisation, the choice between the methods is probably not important except where costs are used as the basis of pricing. In such cases the choice of method may be very important.

Type of overhead	*Absorption base(s) used*
SELLING and MARKETING	SALES VALUE or PRODUCTION COST
RESEARCH and DEVELOPMENT	PRODUCTION COST or CONVERSION COST or ADDED VALUE
DISTRIBUTION	PRODUCTION COST or SALES VALUE
ADMINISTRATION	PRODUCTION COST or CONVERSION COST or ADDED VALUE

Table 9.2 Typical absorption bases for non production overheads

Notes:

1. Conversion cost is Production cost less the cost of direct materials ie, the cost of converting materials into products.

2. Added value is the sales value of a product less the cost of bought out materials and services. Unlike conversion cost added value includes profit.

3. Many variations exist in practice in dealing with non-production overheads and frequently firms charge particular categories of overheads directly to the P & L A/C and do not attempt the somewhat arbitrary process of absorption. A typical example is that of Research and Development overheads.

In each case, if an absorption rate is required, the calculation would follow the pattern for predetermined OAR's given in Para. 6. As an example assume that it is required to calculate an OAR for Selling and Marketing overheads and it is company policy to use Sales Value as an absorption base. The following estimated figures have been established for the period:

$$\text{Estimated Selling and Marketing overheads} \quad £25,000$$

$$\text{Estimated total Sales Value} \quad £280,000$$

$$\text{Selling and Marketing predetermined OAR} = \frac{\text{Estimated overheads}}{\text{Estimated Sales Value}} = \frac{£25,000}{£280,000} = \textbf{9\% of Sales Value}.$$

10. Absorption costing

The process described in this chapter by which total overheads are absorbed into production naturally enough is known as *absorption costing*. The absorption of total overheads into product costs has implications for performance measurement, cost control and stock valuation and students should be aware that the process described is subject to criticism by some managers and accountants.

The criticism arises from the fact that overheads contain items, known as *fixed costs* – which do not change when the activity level changes and which would still have to be paid if there was no activity, eg rates – and items, known as *variable costs*, which vary more or less directly with activity, eg power consumption. To overcome some of the difficulties, an alternative method of costing has been developed, known as *marginal costing*, which, although using the process of absorption, excludes fixed costs from the absorption process. The explanation of fixed and variable costs and marginal costing is developed further in Chapter 19.

Figure 9.1 summarises the conventional method of establishing overheads and how these overheads are absorbed into production. The diagram should be studied together with the following notes.

Notes on Figure 9.1

Stage 1.   Cost elements

The raw data relating to Labour, Materials, Expenses are gathered from Invoices, Payroll, Goods Issued Notes and Requisitions.

Stage 2.   Coding

All the raw cost data needs to be classified and then coded in respect of the type of expense and location. This process is fundamental to all the costing and management accounting procedures.

Stage 3.   Cost analysis

Where discrete items of cost can be allotted to cost centres this is termed *allocation*. Where the cost has to be spread or shared over several cost centres this is known as *apportionment*. The bases of apportionment were discussed in Chapter 2.

Stage 4.   Service cost centres

These are cost centres which provide a service to production cost centres. Examples are Maintenance, Stores and Boiler House. Their costs are built up by the usual process of allocation and primary apportionment and then their total costs are apportioned (secondary apportionment) over the production cost centres, thus forming part of production overheads which are absorbed into the cost units produced. The problems of service cost centres are dealt with in more detail below.

Stage 5.   Production cost centres

These are the cost centres involved directly in the production process. Typical examples are, the Assembly shop, Drilling machines, Centre lathes, Spray shop.

Stage 6.   Overhead absorption.
The overheads of each production cost centre are absorbed into the costs of the units produced, usually in proportion to the time involved ie, by the Labour Hour or Machine Hour rate.

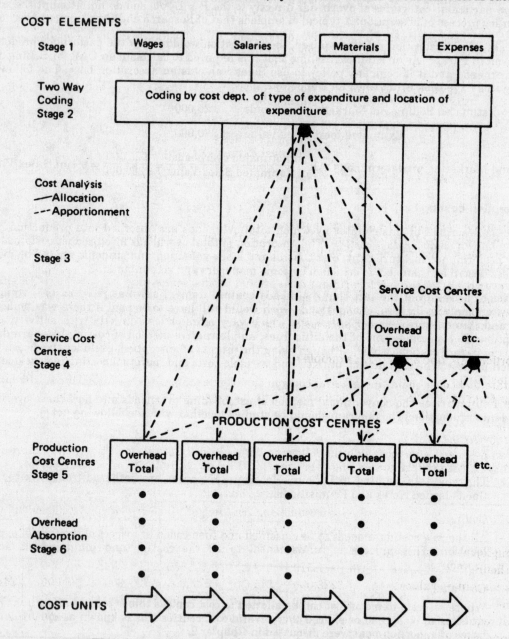

The conventional build-up of overheads. Figure 9.1

11. Service cost centres

Because no production cost units pass through the service cost centres, it is necessary to apportion the service department costs to the production cost centres so that all production costs (including those for the servicing departments) are absorbed into production. Typical bases for secondary apportionment, ie, the apportionment of service costs to production departments are given below:

Service Dept.	Possible bases of Apportionment to Production Cost Centres
Maintenance	Maintenance Labour Hours Maintenance Wages Plant values
Stores	No. of Requisitions Weight of Materials issued
Inspection	No. of Production Employees per cost centre No. of Inspection Tickets No. of Jobs
Production Control	No. of Production Employees per cost centre No. of Jobs
Power Generation	Metered Usage Notional Capacity Technical Estimate
Personnel Dept.	No. of Employees per Department

Notes:

a. The basis chosen should be one that is judged to be the most equitable way of sharing the service department's costs over the departments which use the service. This may mean that a particular and unique basis of apportionment may have to be derived. It must reflect the use made of the services provided.

b. Wherever possible, service department costs should be charged directly, ie, allocated. An example of this would be maintenance wages and materials. When a maintenance job is done for a department, the wages and materials used would be charged directly to the department concerned. In this way only unallocated service department costs need to be apportioned.

12. Apportionment and absorption example

To illustrate and consolidate the material covered so far an example follows which shows the build up of overheads from basic data and the calculation of suitable overhead absorption rates.

Example 1

Prepare an overhead analysis using the following data and calculate suitable overhead absorption rates for the Milling, Assembly and Spraying departments. The data relate to one accounting period.

	Basic Data					
	Production Cost Centres			Service Cost Centres		
	Milling	Assembly	Spraying	Stores	Maintenance	Totals
No of employees	30	75	25	6	14	150
Labour hours	1,510	3,320	950	252	595	6,627
Plant & machinery values	£225,000	£75,000	£45,000	£17,000	£85,000	£447,000
Area (m²)	7,500	10,000	3,500	500	1,000	22,500
Material requisitions	1,400	300	250		550	2,500
Maintenance hours (minor work)	75	30	45			150
KWH ('000)	300	70	50	10	170	600
Machine hours	8,400	1,100	300			9,800

During the period the following data were recorded:

	Milling	Assembly	Spraying	Stores	Maintenance	Totals
Indirect materials	£2,500	£1,000	£1,500	£300	£1,700	£7,000
Indirect labour	£5,250	£2,500	£2,250	£4,250	£11,750	£26,000
Major maintenance work	£18,500	£7,500	£4,500			£30,500

The following details were obtained from the accounts relating to the period.

	£
Fire Insurance	1,250
Power	4,500
Heating and Lighting	2,000
Rates	1,800
Machine depreciation	8,400
Machine insurance	850
Canteen deficit	4,250
Balance of maintenance costs (excl. major works)	17,500

Solution

Notes (to following table)

1. All apportionment's follow a similar principle. For example, the total Fire and Machine Insurance of £2,100 is divided by the total plant value of £447,000 which is then multiplied, in turn, by the value of the plant in each cost centre.

2. The secondary apportionment is carried out using a net plant value of £345,000 ie, less the values in stores and maintenance.

3. The additional complications which can arise with Service Depts. are dealt with below.

4. Maintenance is apportioned on Plant Values because maintenance hours are not available for the service C.C.s which naturally must have some maintenance.

Overhead Analysis

Overhead item	Apportionment basis	Total	Production Cost Centres			Service Cost Centres	
			Milling	Assembly	Spraying	Stores	Maintenance
		£	£	£	£	£	£
Allocated items							
Indirect material		7000	2500	1000	1500	300	1700
Indirect labour		26000	5250	2500	2250	4250	11750
Major maintenance		30500	18500	7500	4500		
Apportioned items							
Fire and machine insurance	Plant values (1.)	2100	1056	353	212	79	400
Power	Kwh	4500	2250	525	375	75	1275
Heating & lighting	Floor area	2000	667	889	311	44	89
Rates	Floor area	1800	600	800	280	40	80
Machine depreciation	Plant values	8400	4227	1411	847	316	1599
Canteen deficit	No. of employees	4250	850	2125	708	170	397
Maintenance	Plant values	17500	8806	2940	1764	658	3332
	Totals	104050	44706	20043	12747	5932	20622
Secondary apportionment							
Stores	Material requisitions		3322	712	593	– 5932	1305
Maintenance	Plant values (2.)		14300	4767	2860		– 21927
Total production dept overheads		£104050	62328	25522	16200		
Overhead absorption basis			Machine hrs	Labour hrs	Labour hrs		
Overhead absorption rates			£62,328	£25,522	£16,200		
			8,400	3,320	950		
			= £7.42	= £7.69	= £17.05		
			per machine hr	per lab. hr	per lab. hr		

13. Establishing service departmental costs

The necessity to apportion service costs has been described above. However, before this apportionment takes place, it is necessary to establish the total service department costs. This is discussed below in three differing circumstances: where service departments only do work for other departments and not each other; where some service departments do work for other service departments; and where service departments provide reciprocal services to each other as well as providing a service to production.

14. Services to non-service departments only

This is the simplest situation and is somewhat unlikely. It is the situation depicted in Figure 9.1 and total service department costs are easily arrived at by the usual process of allocation and primary apportionment from the raw data, ie, Stages 1, 2 and 3 from Figure 9.1.

15. Service departments working for other service departments

Where a service department provides a service to another service department, for example maintenance to stores, it is necessary to apportion the *servicing* departments costs before that of the *serviced* department. In the example given, maintenance costs would be apportioned to stores (and appropriate production cost centres), then the stores' costs would be apportioned between the various production cost centres. The reason for this is, of course, that the total cost of the stores must include an appropriate charge for maintenance work done.

16. Reciprocal services

A particular problem arises where two or more service departments work for each other as well as for production. For example, assume that Maintenance (M) do work for Stores (S) and Stores supply items to Maintenance. The total cost of M cannot be ascertained until the charge for S's service is known, and similarly the total cost of S cannot be found until the charge for M's work is known.

Some way has to be found to break into this circular problem so as to be able to ascertain service department costs. This can be done by three methods; continuous allotment, elimination, and using simultaneous equations. These methods will be illustrated by using the following example:

Example

A small factory has two service departments, Maintenance (M) and Stores (S) and three Production departments (P1, P2, and P3).

The service departments provide services for each other as well as for the Production departments and it has been agreed that the most appropriate bases of apportionment for service department costs are: Capital equipment values for Maintenance and number of requisitions for Stores.

The overheads applicable to each department following allocation and primary apportionment are:

Department	Overheads
M	6,800
S	2,700
P1	12,000
P2	19,500
P3	26,000
Total	£67,000

Data for apportionment of Service Department overheads

	M	S	P1	P2	P3
Capital values	£15,000	£10,000	£50,000	£76,000	£64,000
Proportion	–	5%	25%	38%	32%
No of requisitions	900	–	2400	1620	1080
Proportion	15%	–	40%	27%	18%

The above data are used for each of the solution methods described below.

17. The continuous allotment method

The principle involved in this method is that the appropriate proportion of the costs of the first service department are allotted to the second (ie, 5% of M to S), then the appropriate proportion of the second department is allotted back to the first department (ie, 15% of S to M) and so on until the amounts allotted to and fro become insignificant. This is now shown.

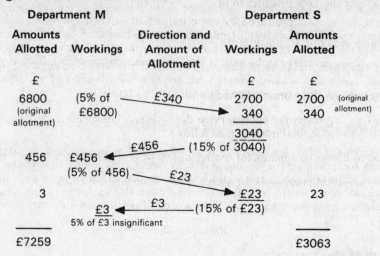

The notional service department overheads, ie, £7,259 and £3,063 are then used in the secondary apportionment thus:

	Departments				
	M	S	P1	P2	P3
	£	£	£	£	£
Original Allotment	6,800	2,700	12,000	19,500	26,000
Notional Overheads for M apportioned over serviced Depts.	−7,259	363	1,815	2,758	2,323
Notional Overheads for S apportioned over serviced Depts.	459	−3,063	1,225	827	552
	NIL	NIL	£15,040	£23,085	£28,875

Note: Amounts rounded to nearest £.

The final apportioned overheads equal the original total allotments,

ie, £15,040 + 23,085 + 28,875 = **£67,000**

18. The elimination method

This is a simpler method which apportions in turn service department costs to users. Once a service department's costs have been apportioned the department is eliminated from further apportionment's. This means that return charges from other service departments do not arise ie, the cost effects of reciprocal servicing is ignored. The sequence in which departments are eliminated can be related to either the amounts involved or the number of departments serviced. The method is illustrated below using the data from Example 1.

	Departments				
	M	S	P1	P2	P3
	£	£	£	£	£
Original Allotment	6,800	2,700	12,000	19,500	26,000
Apportion Total of M (ie, £6,800) and eliminate M	−6,800	340	1,700	2,584	2,176
Apportion Total of S (ie, £2,700 + 340)		−3,040	1,430	966	644
	NIL	NIL	£15,130	£23,050	£28,820

Notes:

1. In this case M was eliminated first as the largest amount was involved.

2. The apportionment's of M are in the original proportions ie, 5% –25% –38% –32%.

3. The apportionment's of S, because M is eliminated, are in the proportions of 40:27:18, ie, the original percentages omitting the 15% relating to M.

4. It is claimed that the results produced by the elimination method are less 'accurate' than the results obtained by other methods. However, it must be emphasised that the procedures of absorption and apportionment are merely conventions so that the concepts of accuracy and inaccuracy in this context have doubtful validity. All that can be said is that the methods produce different results.

19. Simultaneous equations (algebraic method)

This method utilises an equation for each service department, (in example 1, two equations) and solves these equations by the conventional methods, as follows:

Let m = total overheads for maintenance when the stores charges have been allotted

s = total overheads for stores when maintenance charges have been allotted.

$$m = 6,800 + 0.15s$$

$$\text{and } s = 2,700 + 0.05m$$

Rearranging these equations we obtain

$$m - 0.15s = 6,800 \text{ .... Equation I}$$

$$\text{and } s - 0.05m = 2,700 \text{ .... Equation II}$$

To solve Equations I and II it is necessary to eliminate one of the unknowns. This can be done in this example by multiplying Equation II by 20 and adding the result to Equation I thus

$$m - 0.15s = 6,800 \text{ .... Equation I}$$

$$\underline{20s - m = 54,000} \text{ .... } 20 \times \text{Equation II}$$

$$19.85s = 60,800$$

$$s = \underline{\underline{£3,063}}$$

Substituting the value for s in one of the equations, the value for m can be obtained.

Substituting in Equation I

$$m - 0.15 (3,063) = 6,800$$

$$m = \underline{\underline{£7,259}}$$

Having thus obtained the values for m and s, the secondary apportionment can take place as shown in the last part of Para. 17 above.

Notes:

a. In this case the values obtained for m and s correspond exactly to the values obtained by the continuous allotment method. Sometimes there is a slight discrepancy.

b. Simultaneous equations can also be solved using matrix algebra. This method is dealt with in detail in 'Quantitative Techniques', T. Lucey, DP Publications.

20. Depreciation

Most of the items which are classified as overheads, eg rent, rates, indirect labour and materials, office expenses, electricity and heating charges, have their values externally determined; eg the landlord fixes the rent, the local authority the rates and so on. However, a major item of overhead costs, that of depreciation, has its value determined internally and so consideration of the various depreciation methods is essential for accountants. Depreciation can be formally defined as,

'The measure of the wearing out, consumption or other loss of value of a fixed asset whether arising from use, effluxion of time or obsolescence through technology and market changes (SSAP 12)'. *Terminology*.

Effectively the conventions of accounting for depreciation spread the cost of a fixed asset over its life and consequently over the production involved.

A further difference between depreciation and other overheads such as rates and salaries, is that it is a notional item of expense. For items such as rates, electricity and salaries an actual cash flow takes place. However, for notional items such as depreciation no cash flows occurs, the charge being merely a book-keeping entry. This does not mean that depreciation is unimportant. It would be unrealistic not to include the cost of expensive plant and buildings in the cost of a product and depreciation is the most practical way this can be done.

21. Depreciation methods

There are numerous systems available each with particular characteristics, but they fall into two categories;

a. Those that are time based.

b. Those that are based on the volume produced or the level of activity.

Whatever method is used, it is necessary to establish the total amount that needs to be charged through depreciation. This amount, termed the 'net asset cost', is calculated as follows:

Net asset cost = Purchase price + Installation + delivery costs − Net scrap value.

Notes:

a. For registered organisations the purchase price is the Invoice value less VAT; for unregistered organisations it is the gross Invoice value.

b. Net scrap value is the amount realised on disposal less disposal costs.

The three most common methods of depreciation are, the Straight Line, Reducing Balance and the Production Unit (or Hour) methods.

22. Straight line depreciation

This method, sometimes known as the *equal instalment* method, writes down the value of the asset by an equal amount each year. The charge per year is found by the formula:

$$\text{Depreciation charge per year} = \frac{\text{Net Asset cost}}{\text{Estimated life in years}}$$

Example

The net asset cost of a power press is £38,000 and it is estimated to have a life of 10 years. What is the depreciation charge per year?

Solution

$$\text{Straight line depreciation p.a.} = \frac{£38,000}{10}$$

$$= \underline{£3,800}$$

Characteristics:

a. Simple to understand and calculate.

b. Charges an equal amount for depreciation over each year of the asset's life.

c. Takes no account of the volume of activity during the year.

d. Although an equal financial amount is charged each year, inflation causes this amount to have a declining impact on real values. In the example above, £3,800 charged in year 10 has only approximately 25% of the real value of the £3,800 charged in the first year, assuming a 15% inflation rate.

e. A time based method.

23. Reducing balance method (alternatively the diminishing balance method)

Under this method a fixed percentage of the written value of the asset is charged as depreciation each year. The effect of this is that decreasing amounts are charged each year in contrast with the straight line method which produces an equal charge each year. The fixed percentage to be used is the percentage which should be deducted from the written down value each year so that, over the life of the asset, the initial total installed cost is reduced to the net scrap value.

The percentage can be calculated by the following formula

$$\text{Percentage} = \left(1 - \sqrt[n]{\frac{s}{a}}\right) \times 100$$

where: n = estimated life in years
s = net scrap value
a = total installed cost

Example

If an asset has a total installed cost of £22,500 and an estimated net scrap value of £2,500 and is expected to last 10 years, what is the appropriate percentage to use for depreciation under the reducing balance method?

Solution

$n = 10;\ s = 2,500;\ a = 22,500$

$$\text{Percentage} = \left(1 - \sqrt[10]{\frac{2,500}{22,500}}\right) \times 100$$

and solving by logs:

$$\begin{array}{l} 3.3979 \\ \underline{4.3522} \\ \overline{1}.0457 \end{array} \quad \left(\text{ie } \frac{2,500}{22,500}\right)$$

$$10)\ \overline{1}.0457 \text{ (ie finding 10th root)}$$

$$= 10)\ \overline{10} + 9.0457$$

$$= \overline{1}.9046$$

$$\text{antilog} = \underline{0.8029}$$

$$\therefore \text{Percentage} = (1 - 0.8029) \times 100 \approx \underline{\mathbf{20\%}}$$

This percentage would be deducted from the written down value thus

		£	Depreciation charge £
Total installed cost	=	22,500	
Depreciation = £22,500 × 20%	=	−4,500	4,500 Year 1
		18,000	
Depreciation = £18,000 × 20%	=	−3,600	3,600 Year 2
		14,400	
Depreciation = £14,400 × 20%	=	−2,880	2,880 Year 3
		11,520	
Depreciation = £11,520 × 20%	=	−2,304	2,304 Year 4

and so on.

Notes:

a. In practice rates are not calculated for each asset in the manner shown above. Invariably assets are classified into various categories eg Motor Vehicles, Plant and Machinery etc, and a given percentage, usually determined by custom and practice, used for each category, eg Motor vehicles 30%, Plant 25% and so on.

b. An approximation of the percentage rate can be found by the following simple formula:

$$\frac{200}{n}\% \text{ where } n \text{ is the life of the asset.}$$

Characteristics of reducing balance method

a. The depreciation charges are heavier in the earlier years and progressively decline. An argument for this is that as maintenance charges are likely to increase as the years go by, the combined depreciation/maintenance charge will even out. Unfortunately this degree of regularity is unlikely in practice.

b. The method takes no account of the level of activity.

c. Simple to understand and calculate. Within a category of assets with the same percentage, the calculation of the total depreciation charge is simply the given percentage of the total written down value regardless of the varying ages of the assets.

d. A time based method.

24. Production unit method

Under this method the depreciation charge is based upon the estimated number of units to be produced by the machine over its life.

$$\text{Depreciation charge p.a.} = \frac{\text{Net asset cost}}{\text{Estimated life of machine*}} \times \text{Units produced in the year}$$

* expressed in units of production

Example

A machine with a net asset cost of £30,000 is expected to produce 240,000 units over its working life. In a given year actual production was 27,000 units. What is the depreciation charge for the year?

Solution

$$\text{Depreciation/unit} = \frac{£30,000}{240,000}$$

$$= £0.125$$

$$\therefore \text{Charge for year} = £0.125 \times 27,000$$

$$= \underline{\underline{£3,375}}$$

Note:

An alternative form of this method uses production hours instead of production units.

Characteristics:

a. Depreciation is directly related to activity thus becoming a variable cost.

b. Only appropriate for a relatively narrow range of assets ie, those directly producing identifiable units.

c. Administratively cumbersome.

d. Ignores the depreciation effects of time.

25. Other depreciation methods

Alternative depreciation methods which are less frequently encountered are briefly described below.

a. *Revaluation method*

The depreciation charge is the difference between the value of the asset(s) at the beginning of the year and the assessed value at the year end. Used for items where normal depreciation methods are inappropriate, eg Livestock, Tools, Site Plant.

b. *Sum of the digits*

Somewhat similar in application to the reducing balance method in that decreasing amounts are charged each year.

$$\text{Depreciation charge per year} = \frac{x}{\sum n} \text{ (Net asset cost)}$$

where n = estimated life of asset in years

$\sum n$ = the sum of the progression $1 + 2 + 3$ and so on up to n.

x = n for year 1; $n - 1$ for year 2; $n - 2$ for year 3 and so on.

Example

An asset has a net asset cost of £9,000 and a life of 5 years. What is the first year's depreciation using the sum of the digits method?

Solution

$n = 5$ $\therefore \sum n = 5 + 4 + 3 + 2 + 1$

                                    $= 15$

For Year 1 $x = n$

$\therefore$ Year 1   depreciation $= \frac{5}{15} (9,000)$

                                 $= \underline{\underline{£3,000}}$

c. *Repair reserve method*

In this method the annual charge comprises a normal straight line depreciation charge plus an estimated maintenance cost, ie,

$$\text{charge per annum} = \frac{\text{Net asset cost} + \text{Estimated maintenance charge over life of asset}}{\text{Estimated life}}$$

d. *Sinking fund*

This method differs fundamentally from all other methods described. The sinking fund method makes periodic investments external to the firm so that at the end of the life of the asset the realisation of the investment will produce cash equal to the cost of the asset. It will be remembered that other depreciation methods involve book-keeping entries only and no cash flow is involved. The formula is as follows:

$$\text{charge per annum} = \text{Net asset cost} \times S_{\overline{n}|r}$$

where n = estimated life in years
                r = interest rate of sinking fund and
       $S_{\overline{n}|r}$ = a value obtained from Sinking Fund Tables.

For example, an asset has a net asset cost of £18,000, is expected to last 5 years and investment opportunities exist at 8%. What is the charge per annum?

Charge per annum $= £18,000 \times S_{\overline{5}|8\%}$

                          $= £18,000 \times .17046$ (value from Sinking Fund Tables)

                          $= \underline{\underline{£3,068}}$

26. Plant register

To be able to allocate and apportion depreciation charges (however calculated) an up to date record of all assets must be kept. This is termed a *plant register*. This may be on a card index system or, more frequently nowadays, on a computer file. Typically such a record would contain the following details:

a. Plant description, serial number, supplier details including original cost.

b. Technical data relating to speeds, capacities, fuel usage etc.

c. Location.

d. Depreciation method, estimated life and residual value, amounts written off, written down value.

e. Details of capital allowances, balancing charges or allowances.

f. Disposal details.

g. Maintenance expenditure (usually reserved for major overhauls).

h. Details of additions and enhancements.

27. Obsolescence

This may be defined as:

'The loss of value of a fixed asset due to advances in technology and changes in market conditions for the product.' *Terminology*.

There are some relationships between normal depreciation and the concept of obsolescence, but the main distinction is that obsolescence may be rapid and is usually difficult to forecast. Consequently it is not normal practice to make regular charges relating to obsolescence. Instead, when an asset is retired prematurely due to obsolescence, it is normal practice to charge the resulting loss directly to the general profit and loss account rather than to a particular product or department.

28. Asset in use after being fully depreciated

When the useful life of an asset is underestimated, it may arise that an asset is fully depreciated, yet still in use. In such circumstances it is usual to continue to charge depreciation so as to maintain cost comparability with previous periods and so that current costs reflect all the costs of using the asset. The excess of depreciation so charged can either be used to create a reserve against obsolescence or credited to the general profit and loss account.

It is frequently possible to judge that the original life estimate is incorrect before the asset is fully written off. In such cases a new life estimate is made with a consequent change in the depreciation charge, so obviating the problem of having an asset in use which is fully written off.

29. Replacement value and historic cost

All the preceding paragraphs have assumed that depreciation is based on the original cost of the asset. Students should be aware that there are strong arguments for basing depreciation on current replacement values, not historical cost. The reason for this is that depreciation based on replacement values more nearly approximates to real economic values which are of greater importance to decision making management. However, the arguments for and against the use of replacement costs raise fundamental issues of accounting theory outside the scope of this book.

30. Special overhead problems

There are some items to which special consideration should be given as to whether they form part of overheads or not.

a. *Taxation*

Taxation is regarded as an appropriation of profit and is invariably omitted from routine costing systems. However, for many decision and planning purposes the effects of taxation can be crucial so it should be included in special studies and reports where appropriate.

b. *Value Added Tax*

Because input VAT can be claimed back it does not represent a cost, so it is never included in the cost accounts.

c. *Interest*

Although there are some strong theoretical arguments for the inclusion of interest in the cost accounts, there are severe problems in devising a practical scheme. In general therefore interest payments or imputed interest is not included in the routine costing system. However, in a similar fashion to taxation, interest should be included in cost statements and investigation reports where it may have an effect on the decision to be taken. Typical examples include: the costs of alternative actions involving different capital investment, lease or buy decisions, financing decisions etc.

d. *Notional costs*

This is a hypothetical cost which is entered in the cost accounts so as to represent a benefit enjoyed by the organisation even though no actual cost is incurred. For example, the owner occupier of premises does not pay rent, yet some accountants would consider it correct to make a notional charge to overheads equivalent to the current rents for similar properties.

In this way cost comparability with other organisations would be possible and the firm's costs would reflect a situation closer to current economic values. This could be vital if the firm was involved in any form of cost plus pricing. Obviously any notional charge into overheads and thence product costs would have to be counterbalanced by a credit to the general profit and loss account.

31. Overheads and activity based costing (ABC)

ABC has developed to deal with what were seen as defects in the way that conventional absorption costing absorbs support overheads into product costs. Conventionally, all overheads were absorbed on production volume (measured as labour or machine hours) even though many support overheads vary, not with production volume, but with the range and complexity of production.

When support overheads were only a small proportion of total costs the methods of absorption used probably did not matter too much. Today however the position is dramatically different. Direct costs are a declining proportion of total cost and support overheads relating to such things as technical engineering and design services, planning, tooling, data processing etc. are a major proportion of costs in many modern factories. It is therefore of considerable importance that support overheads are traced to product costs in a more realistic manner.

As already explained in Chapter 2 this is done by collecting overheads into *cost pools* and using *cost drivers* to charge the product with a suitable amount of overheads to reflect its usage of the particular support overhead. To do this means classifying overheads in a different manner.

32. Overhead classification using ABC

Using traditional classification systems, variable costs are those that vary with production volume. Examples include; direct materials, power costs and so on. On the other hand Fixed costs are those that do not vary with production volume. This embraces the majority of costs, including most overheads.

Using ABC, Kaplan and Cooper advocate classifying overhead costs in a different way. They propose: *short-term variable costs, long-term variable costs* and *fixed costs*.

❏ *Short-term variable costs*

These are cost that do vary with production volume and would be those also classified as variable under traditional methods. A typical example would be power costs. These vary in direct relationship to production volume, expressed as machine hours.

It is suggested that short-term variable overhead costs are traced to products using production volume-related cost drivers as appropriate. Examples include: direct labour hours, machine hours, direct material cost or weight. Unlike traditional systems where only one or two absorption bases are used, ABC recognises that there could be several cost drivers whenever labour hours, machine hours and material costs are used in different proportions by products. In most organisations, there will only be a small proportion of overheads that can be classed as short-term variable costs.

❏ *Long-term variable costs*

These are overhead costs which do not vary with production volume but do vary with other measures of activity, but not immediately. For example, costs for support activities such as stock handling, production scheduling, set-ups etc, are fixed in the shorter term but vary in the longer term according to the range and complexity of the products manufactured. ABC requires these costs be traced to products by *transaction based cost drivers*.

Most support overheads can be classified as long-term variable costs and thus traced to products using appropriate cost drivers. In traditional systems most of these would be classified as fixed.

❏ *Fixed costs*

Using ABC these are classified as costs which do not vary, for a given time period with any activity indicator. An example would be the salary of the Managing Director. Research by Kaplan and Cooper suggests that these are a relatively small proportion of the total costs.

33. Cost pools and cost drivers

A key idea behind ABC is to focus attention on what factors cause or drive costs, known as *cost drivers*.

Cost drivers can be defined as:

> *Activities or transactions which are significant determinants of cost.*

There are difficulties in choosing realistic cost drivers and Cooper warns:

'There are no simple rules that pertain to the selection of cost drivers. The best approach is to identify the resources that constitute a significant proportion of the products and determine their cost behaviour. If several are long-term variable costs, a transaction-based system should be considered.' If it is decided that an activity based system is required then appropriate cost drivers are chosen and the costs associated with each activity are gathered together in *cost pools*.

Cost pools are similar in principle to cost centres in traditional systems. Costs are pooled, or collected, on the basis of the activity that drives the costs regardless of conventional departmental boundaries. For example if the cost driver is 'number of set-ups' then all costs relating to the activity of setting-up will be pooled together.

Cost pools are therefore not necessarily related to departmental boundaries nor do they encompass all the activities of a single department as the cost drivers may differ for the various activities carried out within the same department. Most conventional departments do not perform a single function so that, in general, the number of activities (and consequently cost pools) is greater than the number of departments. Figure 9.2 shows typical departmental groupings and the larger number of activities carried out.

Typical departments	Typical major activities
Manufacturing	Drilling, Forming, Assembly etc
Engineering services	Maintenance
Quality control	Product and tool design
	Internal transport
	Material acquisition/storing
	Inspection
	Order processing
	Factory loading/planning/control
	Shipping
	Invoicing
	Supplier liaison
	Material scheduling/ordering
	Production control
	All aspects of management and financial accounting
	Personnel administration including hiring/training etc
	... ...

Figure 9.2 Departments and activities

The development of ABC and the designation of cost pools and appropriate cost drivers is not merely a cost recording and cost attribution process. It is more fundamental than that and forces the organisation to ask the following important questions:

❑ What does this department achieve?

Does, for example, the department add value or does it simply add cost? Why is it needed? Can we do without it?

❑ What causes the activity for which the department is responsible?

This question can force a re-appraisal of the underlying causes of costs. As Johnson has said 'people cannot manage costs, they can only manage the activities which cause costs'.

Focusing on the drivers which cause overheads and tracing overheads to products on the usage of cost drivers enables a higher proportion of overheads to be product related. Using traditional systems most support overheads cannot be related to products except in the most general, arbitrary way. It is this feature of ABC which, it is claimed, produces greater accuracy.

34. Selecting cost drivers

Ideally there should be a direct cause/effect relationship between the consumption of overheads and the chosen cost driver. There should be a causal relationship between the amount of resource use, and therefore level of cost, and the volume of the selected cost driver. The relationship is not necessarily a short-term one. This is because salaries and related personnel costs make up a significant proportion of most support overheads and these costs are not easily adjusted in the short-run, hence, Professor Kaplan's definition of 'long-run variable costs'.

The number of cost pools and cost drivers used in practice varies widely, from hundreds in some organisations to dozens in others. As always, a balance must be struck between a complicated and expensive scheme with many cost pools and cost drivers and the loss in accuracy from having a simpler, less costly system.

The number and type of cost drivers chosen will depend on numerous factors including

a. The required accuracy of product costing. In general the greater accuracy required, the more cost drivers.

b. The extent that a given cost driver captures the actual consumption of an activity by a product. The more closely a cost driver correlates with activity use the fewer distortions in product cost and the fewer cost drivers.

c. The extent to which a cost driver can be related to many activities or cost pools. The cost pool should be homogeneous in the sense that it can fairly be represented by one cost driver. Where this is not possible the pool may need to be sub-divided and numerous cost drivers used which will, of course make the system more complex and costly to administer.

d. The extent that one cost can be fairly applied to diverse products. For example if the cost driver, 'number of inspections' was used to trace Inspection Costs to products, distortions will be introduced if inspections take varying amounts of time for different products. If this was the case, inspection hours may be a better cost driver or there may be a need for several cost drivers to trace costs fairly.

35. Cost drivers used in practice

Naturally, the cost pools and cost drivers chosen must suit the organisation, the products or services and the objectives of the ABC system. As a consequence they will vary from organisation to organisation and there are no universally applicable examples.

Some that have been used in practice are shown in Figure 9.3 on the following page.

It should be emphasised that not all the cost drivers shown in figure 9.3 against the various cost pools would be used within one organisation. The most appropriate one or two for each cost pool would be selected and used to trace the costs to the product.

36. Example of cost driver calculation and use

An organisation has introduced ABC and has separated its main activities into reasonably homogeneous cost pools. Cost drivers have been selected for each cost pool, the usage of which correlates approximately to the amount of overheads in the cost poll. These are shown below:

Cost Pool	Cost Driver
Material Procurement	No of orders
Material Handling	No of material movements
Set-ups	No of set-ups
Maintenance	No of maintenance hours
Quality control	No of inspections
Machinery (power, depreciation etc)	No of machine hours

(Note that in a traditional costing system *all* these production overheads would be absorbed on production volume measured as direct labour or machine hours. In this example, only machinery costs are deemed to be primarily driven by production volume and machine hours are considered a reasonable measure of this.)

Customer order processing	No of orders No of customers No of orders by size No of customer visits
Production control	No of engineering changes No of machine/layout changes No of parts operational No of personnel No of schedule changes Delivery performance No of production batches No of set-ups No of works orders
Material planning / Inventory control	No of parts No of deliveries No of material movements No of stock discrepancies No of shortages No of on-time movements No of schedule movements No of receipts Material weight/volume
Engineering support	No of set-ups No of engineering changes No of product changes No of production hours No of defects No of tool changes No of change notices No of breakdowns
Inspection and quality control	No of inspections No of rejects Checking frequency No of parts No of suppliers No of receipts No of product changes Batch sizes No of customers
General accounting	No of suppliers/customers Frequency of despatches Frequency of deliveries No of invoices No of accounting reports No of purchase/sales orders No on payroll No of accounting changes

Figure 9.3 Examples of cost drivers

Example

Budgeted overheads and cost driver volumes

Cost pool	Budgeted overhead	Cost driver	Budgeted volume	Cost driver rate
	£000			
Mat. Procurement	1100	No of orders	4,500	$\frac{£1100}{4500}$ =£244 per order
Mat. handling	1850	No of movements	2,750	$\frac{£1850}{2750}$ =£637 per move
Set-up	900	No of set-ups	525	$\frac{£900}{525}$ = £1714 per set-up
Maintenance	2650	Maintenance hours	21,000	$\frac{£2650}{21000}$ =£126 per hour
Quality control	2300	No of inspections	8,500	$\frac{£2300}{8500}$ =£271 per inspection
Machinery	3600	No of machine hours	125,000	$\frac{£3600}{125000}$ =£28.8per hour

The calculated cost driver rates are used to trace the appropriate amount of overheads to the product.

For example a batch of 4200 Part No X528 had a direct cost (material and labour) of £363,500 and usage of activities as follows:

84	material orders
49	material movements
22	set-ups
610	maintenance hours
90	inspections
1060	machine hours

What was the cost of the batch?

Solution

Cost of batch of 4,200 Part No X5288		
		£
Direct Costs		363,500
Overheads	£	
84 material orders @ £244	20496	
49 material movements @ £673	32977	
22 set-ups @ £1714	37708	
610 maintenance hours @ £126	76860	
90 inspections @ £271	24390	
1060 machine hours @ £28.8	30528	222,959
Batch cost		£586,459

37. Merits of ABC

The following are the main claims made regarding ABC:

a. More realistic product costs are provided especially in Advanced Manufacturing Technology (AMT) factories where support overheads are a significant proportion of total costs.

b. More overheads can be traced to the product. In modern factories there are a growing number of non-factory floor activities. ABC is concerned with all activities so takes product costing beyond the traditional factory floor basis.

c. ABC recognises it is activities which cause cost, not products and it is products which consume activities.

d. ABC focuses attention on the real nature of cost behaviour and helps in reducing costs and identifying activities which do not add value to the product.

e. ABC recognises the complexity and diversity of modern production by the use of multiple cost drivers, many of which are transaction based rather than based solely on production volume.

f. ABC provides a reliable indication of long-run variable product cost which is relevant to strategic decision making.

g. ABC is flexible enough to trace costs to processes, customers, areas of managerial responsibility, as well as products costs.

h. ABC provides useful financial measures (eg cost driver rates) and non-financial measures (eg transactions volumes).

38. Problems with ABC

Undoubtedly ABC removes some of the major deficiencies of traditional absorption costing but, not surprisingly, it has its own problems. These include:

❑ the choice of cost drivers. It is a simplistic assumption that a chosen cost driver is an adequate summary measure of complex activities.

❑ the assumption of a direct, linear relationship between the usage of a cost driver and the amount of overheads. Very few costs indeed are truly variable in this sense whether in the short or long term.

❑ the problem of common costs. It is often difficult to attribute costs to single activities; some costs support several activities.

❑ tracing difficulties. It is not always apparent which product should carry the traced overhead. For example, if a set-up takes place from which a range of products benefit, which one should bear the set-up cost? Should it be the first one after the set up or all the products which benefit?

❑ complexity. A full ABC system having numerous cost pools and cost drivers is more complex and consequently more expensive to operate. This need not be a problem provided that the benefits outweigh the costs.

39. Summary

a. Overheads are built up by a process of allocation and apportionment. They are 'shared out' over production by means of overhead absorption.

b. Overhead absorption rates (OAR) are usually predetermined and are calculated by the general formula.

$$OAR = \frac{\text{Budgeted overheads for cost centre}}{\text{Budgeted units of absorption base}}$$

c. The appropriate absorption basis to use is the one which most accurately reflects the incidence of overheads in a given cost centre.

d. Possible absorption bases include: Direct Labour hours, Direct Wages, Machine hours, Prime Cost etc.

e. In general the most appropriate absorption bases are those based on time, particularly Direct Labour Hours and Machine Hours.

f. Because predetermined OAR's are based on estimates of overheads and activity, the amount of overhead absorbed into production is unlikely to agree with the actual overheads incurred so that under or over absorption is likely to occur.

g. When absorbed overheads are greater than actual overheads, there is OVER ABSORPTION; when they are less there is UNDER ABSORPTION.

h. The amount of under or over absorption is eventually charged to the Profit and Loss account or Operating Statement.

i. Non-production overheads form part of total cost and sometimes are absorbed into product costs (usually by a percentage of Production Cost) or charged directly to Profit and Loss account.

j. Where all costs, including both fixed and variable, are included in production costs the process is termed Absorption Costing. Where only variable costs are included in production costs and fixed costs are charged to Profit and Loss account each period the system is known as Marginal Costing.

k. The overheads of service departments are built up by allocation and primary apportionment and are then spread over the production departments by secondary apportionment in proportion to usage.

l. The three methods of establishing service department overheads when reciprocal servicing occurs are: continuous allotment, elimination and the use of simultaneous equations.

m. Depreciation occurs through wear and tear and the passage of time. The accounting charge known as depreciation is a way of spreading the cost of an asset over its working life.

n. The most common methods of depreciation are: straight line, reducing balance, and production unit.

o. Other depreciation methods include: revaluation, sum of the digits, sinking fund and repair reserve.

p. Obsolescence is the loss in value due to supercession. It is not normal practice to make regular charges relating to obsolescence, but to write the loss off to the general profit and loss account when it occurs.

q. Taxation and interest are not included in routine costing. They may, however, be included as part of the special information regarding a particular decision.

r. ABC collects overheads into cost pools and traces these to products using cost drivers.

s. Kaplan considers that most support overheads are long-term variable costs that vary more with product complexity and diversity than production volume.

t. Ideally cost pools should be homogenous and should have a single cost driver that relates directly with the amount of resource use but, in practice, the choice of cost drivers is difficult.

u. ABC recognises that it is activities which cause costs helps in reducing costs and identifying non-value added activities.

40. Points to note

a. Typically a product passes through several production cost centres, absorbing overheads from each one, often using a different absorption base in each cost centre, eg labour hours, machine hours as appropriate.

b. Any overheads under or over absorbed in a period must be dealt with in that period and should not be carried forward to a future period.

c. In some simple costing systems a single, factory wide OAR is calculated. This means that there is no need to accumulate overheads for various cost centres and overheads would be absorbed by the application of the one OAR for all types of work. Obviously this is easy to do but there is a loss of accuracy because the overheads absorbed do not necessarily reflect the loading or costs of the different cost centres.

d. Non production overheads (administration, selling, research etc) are an increasing proportion of the total costs of firms.

e. Because there are so many assumptions and conventions involved in establishing overheads, there is little point in pursuing minute accuracy over such matters as the bases of apportionment, depreciation and reciprocal service costs.

Student self-testing

Self Review Questions

1. What is the objective of overhead absorption? (2)
2. How are overhead absorption rates calculated? (2)
3. Give six examples of absorption bases. (3)
4. What factors govern the choice of the absorption base? (5)
5. When is the Direct Labour Hour Basis – The Machine Hour Basis – most appropriate? (5)
6. Why are predetermined absorption rates invariably used? (6)
7. How does over/under absorption arise? (7)
8. How is under/over absorption dealt with? (8)
9. How are non-production overheads absorbed? (9)
10. What is the distinction between absorption costing and marginal costing? (10)
11. How are production overheads built up and eventually absorbed into production? (10)
12. What is a service cost centre? (11)
13. Give six examples of bases of apportionment of service department costs to production cost centres. (11)

14. What are the three methods of establishing service department costs when reciprocal servicing takes place? (16)
15. Describe the continuous allotment method. (17)
16. What is the simultaneous equation method? (19)
17. Define depreciation. (20)
18. Why is depreciation a notional charge? (20)
19. What is the 'net asset cost'? (21)
20. Describe straight line depreciation. (22)
21. Are equal amounts charged each year using the reducing balance method? (23)
22. What is the formula for the reducing balance method? (23)
23. What is the production unit method of depreciation? (24)
24. Give three other methods of depreciation. (25)
25. What is the major difference between the sinking fund method and all other methods? (25)
26. What are typical details kept in a Plant Register? (26)
27. Distinguish between depreciation and obsolescence. (27)
28. What is the costing treatment of an asset which is still in use after being fully depreciated? (28)
29. Is taxation a part of cost? (30)
30. Should imputed interest be included in routine costing statements and records? (30)
31. How are overheads classified in ABC systems? (32)
32. How do cost pools differ from traditional cost centres? (33)
33. What factors need to be considered when selecting cost drivers? (34)
34. What merits are claimed for ABC systems? (37)
35. What problems may arise in ABC systems? (38)

Exercises and examination questions with answers

Exercises

A9.1   a.   Calculate five different overhead absorption rates for cost centre 17 based on the following budgeted data.

Labour hours for period	1,400
Total direct wages for period	£3,600
Total direct materials for period	£7,500
Total machine hours for period	2,850
Total units produced for period	535
Total overheads for period	£12,900

         b.   A cost unit has been produced in Cost Centre 17 and the following details recorded:

Direct materials used	£16.50
Direct wages	£17.50
Direct labour hours	$5\frac{1}{2}$
Machine hours	$8\frac{1}{2}$

Calculate the costs of the above unit using each of the absorption bases calculated in (a).

         c.   What basis of overhead absorption would you recommend if you are informed that Cost Centre 17 comprises a number of numerically controlled machine tools with semi-skilled operators and that over half of the cost centre's overheads relate to machine depreciation? Give reasons.

A9.2   a.   Give three reasons why over or under absorption of overheads may arise.

         b.   Calculate the amount of over/under absorption of overheads (if any) given the following data:

Cost Centre 258 for Period 2

	Budgeted	Actual
Direct labour hours	5,600	5,925
Direct wages	£19,040	£20,450
Machine hours	3,300	3,418
Direct materials	£26,200	£28,213
Units produced	81,000	85,296
Overheads	£57,500	£61,257

It is considered that overhead absorption based on labour hours is the most appropriate basis for Cost Centre 258.

A9.3 Discuss the advantages and disadvantages of basing product costs on a single blanket overhead rate for the whole factory instead of separate overhead rates for the various production cost centres.

A9.4 A blanking machine cost £20,000 and required alterations to the premises of £8,500 to install it. Its life is expected to be 12 years when it could be sold as scrap for £1,500.

Calculate the depreciation charge per annum using the Straight Line method and the charge for the first year if the Reducing Balance method was used.

A9.5 Two products X and Y are made using similar equipment and methods. The data for last period are

	X	Y
Units produced	6000	8000
Labour hours per unit	1	2
Machine hours per unit	4	2
Set-ups in period	15	45
Orders handled in the period	12	60

Overheads for period	£
Relating to production set-ups	179,000
Relating to order handling	30,000
Relating to machine activity	55,000
	264,000

Calculate the overheads to be absorbed per unit of each product based on:

a. Conventional absorption costing using a labour hour absorption rate

b. An ABC approach using suitable cost drivers.

Examination questions

A9.6 The following data relates to a manufacturing department for a period:

	Budget Data £	Actual Data £
Direct material cost	100,000	150,000
Direct Labour cost	250,000	275,000
Production overhead	250,000	350,000
Direct labour hours	50,000 hours	55,000 hours

Job ZX was one of the jobs worked on during the period. Direct material costing £7,000 and direct Labour (800 hours) costing £4,000 were incurred. Required:

i. Calculate the production overhead absorption rate predetermined for the period based on:

a. percentage of direct material cost;

b. direct labour hours.

ii. Calculate the production overhead cost to be charged to Job ZX based on the rates calculated in answer to (i) above.

iii. Assume that the direct labour hour rate of absorption is used. Calculate the under or over absorption of production overheads for the period and state an appropriate treatment in the accounts.

iv. Comment briefly on the relative merits of the two methods of overhead absorption used in (i) above.

(AAT, Cost Accounting & Budgeting, part question)

A9.7 A light engineering company calculates its production overhead absorption rate at the end of each month by dividing the total actual overheads incurred by the total number of units produced in that month. This blanket absorption rate is then applied retrospectively to the month's production.

A variety of products are manufactured by the company and total demand is such that there are some unavoidable seasonal fluctuations in production activity. Production departments vary from light assembly work to semi-automatic machine shops and within each department the processing time for different products varies considerably, in some cases products do not pass through every department.

Required:

Critically examine the effect of the above system of overhead absorption on the company's product costs, pricing policy and consequent profitability.

(ACCA, Costing)

A9.8 Superdoop plc,* is a manufacturing company operating three production departments. Shown below are next year's budgeted manufacturing costs, per unit, for each of the three products manufactured by the company.

	Product X		Product Y		Product Z	
	£ per unit	£ per unit	£ per unit	£ per unit	£ per unit	£ per unit
Direct materials		24.0		36.0		48.0
Direct wages:						
Department A	10.0		8.0		14.0	
Department B	12.0		15.0		21.0	
Department C	6.0		3.0		2.0	
		28.0		26.0		37.0
Production overheads:						
Department A	11.2		8.0		4.8	
Department B	6.0		7.5		10.5	
Department C	2.5	19.7	2.5	18.0	2.5	17.8
Total budgeted manufacturing cost per unit		71.7		80.0		102.8

Prime costs are variable, production overhead contains both fixed and variable elements.

The company operates a full absorption costing system and next year's budgeted overhead absorption rates, based upon next year's budgeted overheads and activity are:

Department A	Department B	Department C
£1.60 per machine hour	50% of direct wages	£2.50 per unit

Next year's budgeted total direct wages for Department B, analysed by product are:

Product X	Product Y	Product Z
£158,400	£412,500	£147,000

Stocks of work-in-progress are not carried.

Required:

a. Describe the circumstances in which it would be appropriate to use each of the absorption methods indicated in the question.

b. Calculate next year's total budgeted overheads for each of the three departments in Superdoop p.l.c.

c. Assume that, next year, the actual results are exactly as those predicted in the budget except that production of Product Z is 200 units higher than that budgeted and, as a consequence, the overheads over-absorbed in the three departments are as follows:

Department A	£840
Department B	£1,680
Department C	£200

Analyse the overheads incurred in Departments A and B between fixed and variable.

(ACCA, Costing)

A9.9 From the data given you are required to:

a. prepare an 'overhead analysis sheet' showing the basis for apportionments made (calculated to the nearest £1);

b. calculate (to two decimal places of £1) an overhead absorption rate based on direct labour hours for:
   i. the assembly department;
   ii. the finishing department;

c. state briefly, for each overhead item or group of items, why the basis of apportionment was chosen;

d. for purposes of apportioning costs, state what other information you would have preferred to have used for any of the items instead of the information given.

Data: The information given relates to a four-week accounting period. In addition to the cost centres listed there is an 'occupancy' cost centre which is charged with all the costs concerned with occupation of the building. The total of this cost centre should be apportioned before the stores costs are apportioned.

Department:	Machining	Assembly	Finishing	Stores
Area occupied, in sq. feet	24,000	36,000	16,000	4,000
Plant and equipment at cost, in £'000	1,400	200	60	10
Number of employees	400	800	200	20
Direct labour hours	16,000	32,000	4,000	
Direct wages	£32,600	£67,200	£7,200	
Number of requisitions on stores	400	1,212	200	

Allocated costs:

	Total £	Machining £	Assembly £	Finishing £	Stores £
Indirect wages	34,000	9,000	15,000	4,000	6,000
Indirect materials	2,400	400	1,400	600	
Maintenance	2,100	1,400	600	100	
Power	2,200	1,600	400	200	
Total	40,700	12,400	17,400	4,900	6,000

Other costs:

Rent	£2,000
Rates	600
Insurance on building	200
Lighting and heating	400
Depreciation on plant and equipment	16,700
Wage related costs (holiday pay, graduated national insurance and company pension scheme)	28,200
Factory administration and personnel	7,100
Insurance on plant and equipment	1,670
Cleaning of factory premises by outside contract cleaners	800
	£57,670

(CIMA, Cost Accounting 1)

A9.10 The overhead allocated to the three production cost centres and two service cost centres of the manufacturing division of a company were:

Production cost centre:	1	£20,000
	2	£24,000
	3	£36,000
Service cost centre:	S	£13,500
	T	£9,500

After a study it is decided that the costs of service centres should be apportioned as follows:

		Production cost centres			Service cost centres	
		1	2	3	S	T
		%	%	%	%	%
Service cost centre:	S	Nil	55	35	–	10
	T	45	35	15	5	–

You are required to calculate the total overhead chargeable to each production cost centre by each of the following methods:

a. Ignoring the service that each of the two service cost centres gives to the other;

b. Using a 'two-step' method of apportionment whereby costs of the service that serves most cost centres is apportioned first, and the other service cost centre is then apportioned to the production cost centres;

c. Using the 'repeated distribution' or 'continuous allotment' method of apportioning the costs of service cost centres among the production and the two service cost centres.

(CIMA, Cost Accounting)

A9.11 AC Limited is a small company which undertakes a variety of jobs for its customers.

Budgeted Profit and Loss Statement
for the year ending 31st December

	£	£
Sales		750,000
Costs:		
Direct materials	100,000	
Direct wages	50,000	
Prime cost	150,000	
Fixed production overhead	300,000	
Production cost	450,000	
Selling, distribution and administration cost	160,000	
Profit		610,000
		£140,000

Budgeted data:

Labour hours for the year	25,000
Machine hours for the year	15,000
Number of jobs for the year	300

An enquiry has been received and the production department has produced estimates of the prime cost involved and of the hours required to complete job A57.

	£
Direct materials	250
Direct wages	200
Prime cost	£450
Labour hours required	80
Machine hours required	50

You are required to:

a. calculate by different methods six overhead absorption rates;
b. comment briefly on the suitability of each method calculated in (a);
c. calculate cost estimates for job A57 using in turn each of the six calculated in (a).

(CIMA, Cost Accounting 1)

A9.12 A large hotel has recently reorganised its costing system and split activities into four cost centres

1. Accommodation
2. Catering
3. Leisure
4. Outings

The hotel is moving towards standardising its services and selling a hotel package to its customers which will include accommodation, meals, use of leisure facilities and a number of outings. There is to be a predetermined price per day for the use of each cost centre by the customer.

Labour and material can be identified and allocated to the cost centres in the budget but other overheads listed below cannot be so readily identifiable.

	Accomm-odation	Catering	Leisure	Outings	Total
	£	£	£	£	£
Labour	110,000	100,500	35,000	38,500	284,000
Materials	19,000	36,000	16,000	13,000	84,000
Power					84,000
Rent and Rates					72,000
Depreciation					60,000
Advertising					76,000
Office expenses					240,000

You are given the following information about the cost centres from the budget for the coming year.

	Accomm-odation	Catering	Leisure	Outings
Floor area (sq metres)	1,200	400	600	200
No of employees	32	16	24	8
Machinery value	£10,000	£20,000	£60,000	£30,000
Kilowatt hours	5,000	2,500	12,500	1,000
Expected customer usage in days	15,000	12,000	8,000	3,000

You are told that advertising is to be apportioned to the cost centres on the basis of customer usage and office expenses apportioned on the basis of total cost per cost centre before the apportionment of the office expenses.

The budget for the coming year has been based upon the strategy that customers will have the standard accommodation and catering package with the leisure facilities and outings package as optional. Hotel policy for the coming year is to operate a profit margin of 30% on price.

Required

a) Prepare a cost statement for the four cost centres showing the budgeted total cost and the budgeted cost per customer day per cost centre.

b) Calculate the price to be charged to a married couple who want to stay at the hotel for one week. They require accommodation and catering for seven days, use of the leisure facilities for three days and want to go on outings on three days.

c) The actual results for the hotel for the year under review were as follows:

Cost centre	Total cost £	Customer days Usage
Accommodation	320,000	15,250
Catering	275,000	13,000
Leisure	200,000	6,800
Outings	125,000	3,200

Calculate the under/over absorption of costs per cost centre.

(AAT, Cost Accounting and Budgeting)

A9.13 Having attended a CIMA course on activity based costing (ABC) you decide to experiment by applying the principles of ABC to the four products currently made and sold by your company. Details of the four products and relevant information are given below for one period

Product	A	B	C	D
Output in units	120	100	80	120
Costs per unit	£	£	£	£
Direct material	40	50	30	60
Direct labour	28	21	14	21
Machine hours per unit	4	3	2	3

The four products are similar and are usually produced in production runs of 20 units and sold in batches of 10 units.

The production overhead is currently absorbed by using a machine hour rate, and the total of the production overhead for the period has been analysed as follows:

	£
Machine department costs (rent, business rates, depreciation and supervision)	10,430
Set up costs	5,250
Stores receiving	3,600
Inspection/Quality control	2,100
Materials handling and dispatch	4,620

You have ascertained that the 'cost drivers' to be used are as listed below for the overhead costs shown:

Cost	Cost driver
Set up costs	Number of production runs
Stores receiving	Requisitions raised
Inspection/Quality control	Number of production runs
Materials handling and dispatch	Orders executed

The number of requisitions raised on the stores was 20 for each period and the number of orders executed was 42, each order being for a batch of 10 of a product.

You are required:

a) to calculate the total costs for each product if all overhead costs are absorbed on a machine hour basis;

b) to calculate the total costs for each product, using activity based costing;

c) to calculate and list the unit product costs from your figures in (a) and (b) above, to show the differences and to comment briefly on any conclusions which may be drawn which could have profit and pricing implications.

(CIMA, Cost Accounting)

A9.14 A manufacturing company has prepared the following budgeted information for 1992:

	£
Direct material	800,000
Direct labour	200,000
Direct expenses	40,000
Production overhead	600,000
Administrative overhead	328,000
Budgeted activity levels include	units
Budgeted production	600,000
Machine hours	50,000
Labour hours	40,000

It has recently spent heavily upon advanced technological machinery and reduced its workforce. As a consequence it is thinking about changing its basis for overhead absorption from a percentage of direct labour costs to either a machine hour or labour hour basis. The administrative overhead is to be absorbed as a percentage of factory cost.

Required:

a) Prepare pre-determined overhead absorption rates for production overhead based upon the three different bases for absorption mentioned above.

b) Outline the reasons for calculating a pre-determined overhead absorption rate.

c) Select the overhead absorption rate that you think the organisation should use giving reasons for your decision.

d) The company has been asked to price job AX, this job requires the following:

Direct material	£3,788
Direct labour	£1,100
Direct expenses	£422
Machine hours	120
Labour hours	220

Compute the price for this job using the absorption rate selected in c) above, given that the company profit margin is equal to 10% of the price.

e) The company previously paid its direct labour workers upon a time basis but is now contemplating moving over to an incentive scheme.

Required.

Draft a memo to the Chief Accountant outlining the general characteristics and advantages of employing a successful incentive scheme.

(AAT Cost Accounting & Budgeting)

Exercises and examination questions without answers

Exercises

B9.1 Prepare an overhead analysis from the following data using the processes of allocation and apportionment. Where apportionment is used the basis should be stated.

Basic data								
	Production cost centres				Service cost centres			Total
	Machining	Fabricat'n	Assembly	Plating	Stores	Maint'nce	Qual. ctrl	
No. of employees	85	35	40	40	8	22	10	240
Plant & mach. values	£185,000	£45,000	£65,000	£110,000	£25,000	£55,000	£15,000	£500,000
Area (M²)	8,500	10,000	7,500	2,500	500	750	250	30,000
kW H ('000)	480	220	250	650		80		1,680
Material requisitions	1,200	200	750	750		600		3,500
Maintenance hours booked on minor work	125	50	60	65				300
During period 23 the following data were recorded								
Indirect labour	£5,200	£2,600	£12,500	£4,400	£2,300	£3,800	£1,800	£32,600
Indirect materials	£3,500	£750	£3,100	£1,750	£650	£3,400	£1,100	£14,250
Major maintenance work	£12,500	£8,200	£4,200	£7,600			£6,500	£39,000

In addition for Period 23 the following details were extracted from the Cost Accounts and other records.

	£
Rates	2,600
Machine depreciation	7,800
Fire insurance	650
Factory admin, costs	11,000
Power	3,250
Heating & Lighting	1,400
Machine insurance	350
Balance of Maintenance dept. costs (excl. major works)	29,300

B9.2 Projections for the next accounting year show that the Production Overhead is expected to increase from 250% of Direct Wages to 400% of Direct Wages.

Explain what factors may have contributed to the expected increase and in what circumstances such an increase could be acceptable.

B9.3 What overheads in total will be allotted to Production Departments M and N given the following:

Overheads (resulting from allocation and primary apportionment)

	£
Production Dept. M	18,000
Production Dept. N	14,000
Service Dept. X	8,000
Service Dept. Y	6,000

It is expected that: Department X will do 50% of its work for M; 30% for N and 20% for Y. Department Y will do 60% for M; 30% for N and 10% for X.

B9.4 An asset has an installed cost for £35,000, an estimated life of 10 years and an estimated scrap value of £2,000

Calculate the first year charge for depreciation using the following methods.

a. Straight line
b. Reducing balance
c. Sum of digits
d. Repair reserve where maintenance is expected to cost £18,000 over the life of the asset.
e. Production unit where the lifetime output is estimated to be 200,000 and output in the first year estimated to be 15,000.

In addition calculate the sinking fund charge for the asset where investment opportunities exist at 12% and the asset is expected to cost £55,000 to replace in 10 years.

(The value of S $\overline{10}|12$% can be calculated using the formula

$$\frac{r}{(1 + r)^n - 1}$$

where n is the number of years and r is the rate of interest, or alternatively tables can be used from which the value will be found to be 0.0570).

B9.5 Overheads are a major part of product costs yet the procedures for establishing overheads and absorbing them into products are arbitrary and based on conventions. As a consequence there is no such thing as an accurate cost. Discuss.

Examination Questions

B9.6 Meklect Limited produce two types of lawnmower, a mechanical model, and an electric model. The company's trading summary for the year recently ended is as follows:

	£	£
Sales		550,000
Direct material and labour	389,000	
Factory overhead	40,000	
Administration overhead	30,000	
Marketing overhead	16,500	
		475,500
Profit		£74,500

The directors consider the profit/sales ratio (13.54%) to be inadequate and have asked you to analyse the trading summary in order to determine the profitability of each of the two models.

Your investigation reveals:

a.
Sales for the year were	£
5,000 mechanical models	325,000
3,000 electric models	225,000

b. Opening stock of raw material were £45,000 and closing stocks £54,000. Purchases during the year were £324,000.

c. £150,000 of material was used in the production of mechanical models and the remainder on the electric models.

d. The piecework labour rate is £10 for a mechanical model and £8 for an electric model.

e. Included in Factory Overhead are the following costs with indications of the directors' views of their apportionment:

	£	*Mechanical*	*Electric*
Indirect labour	15,000	one-third	two-thirds
Power	6,500	three-fifths	two-fifths
Depreciation	12,600	three-sevenths	four-sevenths

The remaining Factory Overhead is to be apportioned equally.

f. Administration Overhead includes a computer bureau's charge of £11,000 for producing sales invoices; this charge is to be apportioned according to invoiced sales value; the remaining Administration Overhead is to be apportioned equally to the two models.

g. Marketing Overhead is to be borne by the two models in proportion to invoiced sales values.

h. Finished Stocks and Work in Progress were the same at the end of the year as they were at the beginning. You are required to produce a statement to show:

i. the trading results for each model

ii. the unit cost and profit of each model, analysing cost as follows:

Direct material   Direct labour
Factory overhead   Administration overhead
Marketing overhead

and to add brief comments which you think may be helpful to the directors.   *(ACCA, Costing)*

B9.7 Due to recession in its industry, which has caused a reduction in its sales, a manufacturing company is proposing to reduce by one-fifth its productive capacity, as measured in terms of the number of direct labour hours of its operators. It is considering doing this by either:

a. putting some of its operators on short time; or

b. making a number of its operators redundant through dismissal. You are required to compare and contrast in tabular form the effects that each course of action is likely to have on the composition and level of the company's total annual:

    i.   direct materials cost;

    ii. direct wages;

    iii. production overhead;

    iv. other (non-production) overhead.   *(CIMA, Cost Accounting 2)*

B9.8   A Manufacturing concern absorbs overheads by means of budgeted departmental rates which are as follows:

Production departments	Absorption
Machine Shop	£1.20 per machine hour worked
Finishing Shop	80% on direct wages
Assembly	£0.25 per unit of finished product
Non-productive departments	125% on direct material costs, issued to Production

For the previous period the following was incurred:

	Direct materials issued	Direct wages earned	Machine hours worked	Actual overhead
	£	£		£
Machine Shop	4,160	6,650	9,600	11,570
Finishing Shop	23,520	12,700		– 9,470
Assembly	11,020	3,700		15,110
Non-productive depts.				49,135
	£38,700	£23,050		£85,285

During the period 58,500 units were manufactured. Required:

a. Calculate for each department and in total:

    i.   the amount of overhead absorbed into total costs;

    ii. the amount of under or over absorbed overhead.

b. Calculate the amount of profit or loss made by Job Number 872 which was completed during the period from the following information.

Selling Price £3 unit.   Quantity 1,152 units

	Material	Wages	Machine hours
	£	£	
Machine Shop	150	101	315
Finishing Shop	470	200	
Assembly	160	74	

c. State an alternative method of recovering overheads which the company could use, indicating whether this would be an improvement on the existing method.

                                                  (AAT, Cost Accounting and Budgeting,)

B9.9   An industrial concern manufactures three products known as P, Q and R. Each product is started in the Machining area and completed in the Finishing Shop.

The direct costs associated with each product forecast for the next trading period are:

	P	Q	R
	£	£	£
	18.50	15.00	22.50
Materials			
Wages:			
Machining area at £5 per hour	10.00	5.00	10.00
Finishing Shop at £4 per hour	6.00	4.00	8.00
	£34.50	£24.00	£40.50

There are machines in both departments and machine hours required to complete one of each products are:

Machine area	4	$1\frac{1}{2}$	3
Finishing Shop	$\frac{1}{2}$	$\frac{1}{2}$	1
Budget output in units	6,000	8,000	2,000

Fixed overheads are:

Machining area	£100,800
Finishing Shop	£94,500

Required:

a. an overhead absorption rate for Fixed Overheads using:
   i. a Labour Hour rate for each department,
   ii. a Machine Hour rate for each department;

b. the total cost of each product using:
   i. the Labour Hour rate,
   ii. the Machine Hour rate, as calculated in (a) above;

c. your comments to the Factory manager who has suggested that one overhead rate for both departments would simplify matters;

d. the fixed cost and the variable rate of overhead cost for the Machining area.

This has been constant over the previous five periods, and extracted from the following:

Period	Total overhead £	Labour hours
1	92,600	21,300
2	86,200	18,100
3	95,250	22,625
4	105,500	27,750
5	93,200	21,600

(AAT, Cost Accounting and Budgeting)

B9.10 PQ Limited absorbs its production overhead by using predetermined rates – a percentage on direct labour cost for department P and a machine hour rate (calculated to three decimal places) for Q.

The estimates made at the beginning of the financial year which ended on 31st October were:

	Dept. P £	Dept. Q £
Direct labour cost	450,000	150,000
Production overhead	517,500	922,500
	Hours	Hours
Direct labour	172,500	40,000
Machines	20,000	180,000

For the month of October, the cost sheet for Job No. 186 shows the following information:

	Dept. P	Dept Q
Materials used	£200	£800
Direct labour	£360	£190
Direct labour hours	120	47.5
Machine hours	20	260

Following the end of the financial year it was ascertained that actual production overhead incurred by department P was £555,000 and that incurred by department Q was £900,000.

You are required to:

a. calculate the overhead absorption rates for each of the departments P and Q;

b. determine the total production overhead cost to be charged to Job No 186 for October;

c. show the over/under absorbed overhead for each department and for the company as a whole for the year ended 31st October assuming that actual direct labour cost and machine hours worked were as originally estimated;

d. comment on the choice of an overhead absorption rate based on direct labour cost for department P.

(CIMA, Cost Accounting 1)

B9.11 SM Limited makes two products. Exe and Wye. For product costing purposes a single cost centre overhead rate of £3.40 per hour is used based on budgeted production overhead of £680,000 and 200,000 budgeted hours as shown below.

	Budgeted overhead	Budgeted hours
Department 1	480,000	100,000
Department 2	200,000	100,000
	£680,000	200,000

The number of hours required to manufacture each of the products is:

	Exe	Wye
Department 1	8	4
Department 2	2	6
	10	10

There were no work-in-progress or finished goods stocks at the beginning of the period of operations but at the end of the period 10,000 finished units of Exe and 5,000 finished units of Wye were in stock. There was no closing work-in-progress.

The prime cost per unit of Exe is £30. The pricing policy is to add 50% to the production cost to cover administration, selling and distribution costs and to provide what is thought to be a reasonable profit.

You are required to:

a. calculate what the effect is on the company's profit for the period, by using a single cost centre overhead rate compared with using departmental overhead rates;

b. show by means of a comparative statement what the price of Exe would be using (i) single cost centre overhead rate and (ii) departmental overhead rates;

c. discuss briefly whether the company should change its present policy on overhead absorption, stating reasons to support your conclusion.

(CIMA, Cost Accounting 1)

B9.12 A company re-apportions the costs incurred by two service cost centres, materials handling and inspection, to the three production cost centres of machining, finishing and assembly.

The following are the overhead costs which have been allocated and apportioned to the five cost centres:

	£000
Machining	400
Finishing	200
Assembly	100
materials handling	100
Inspection	50

Estimates of the benefits received by each cost centre are as follows:

	Machining	Finishing	Assembly	Materials handling	Inspection
	%	%	%	%	%
Materials handling	30	25	35	–	10
Inspection	20	30	45	5	–

You are required to

a. calculate the charge for overhead to each of the three production cost centres, including the amounts re-apportioned from the two service centres, using

   i. the continuous allotment (or repeated distribution) method, and

   ii. an algebraic method;

b. comment on whether re-apportioning service cost centre costs is generally worthwhile and suggest an alternative treatment for such costs;

c. discuss the following statement:

'Some writers advocate that an under- or over-absorption of overhead should be apportioned between the cost of goods sold in the period to which it relates and to closing stocks. However, the United Kingdom practice is to treat under- or over-absorption of overhead as a period cost.'

(CIMA Cost Accounting)

B9.13 You are the Cost Accountant of an industrial concern and have been given the following budgeted information regarding the four cost centres within your organisation.

	Department 1	Department 2	Maintenance Department	Canteen	Total
	£	£	£	£	£
Indirect Labour	60,000	70,500	25,000	15,000	170,000
Consumables	12,000	16,000	3,000	10,000	41,000
Heating and Lighting					12,000
Rent and Rates					18,000
Depreciation					30,000
Supervision					24,000
Power					20,000
					315,000

You are also given the following information:

	Department 1	Department 2	Maintenance Department	Canteen	Total
Floor area (in sq. metres)	10,000	12,000	5,000	3,000	30,000
Book value of machinery in £	150,000	120,000	20,000	10,000	300,000
No. of employees	40	30	10		80
Kilowatt hours	4,500	4,000	1,000	500	10,000

You are also told:

i. The canteen staff are outside contractors.

ii. Departments 1 and 2 are production centres and the maintenance department and canteen are service cost centres.

iii. The maintenance department provides 4,000 service hours to Department 1 and 3,000 service hours to Department 2.

iv. That Department 1 is machine intensive and department 2 is labour intensive.

v. That 6,320 machine hours and 7,850 labour hours are budgeted for Departments 1 and 2 respectively for 1991.

Required:

a. An overhead cost statement showing the allocation and apportionment of overhead to the four cost centres for 1991, clearly showing the basis of apportionment.

b. calculate the overhead absorption rates for Department 1 on the basis of the machine hours and Department 2 on the basis of labour hours.

c. On the basis that for 1991 actual overheads for Department 1 turn out to be £155,000 and machine hours worked 6,000, whilst actual overheads for Department 2 turn out to be £156,000 and labour hours worked 7,900, calculate the under or over recovery of overheads for each department.

d. The Managing Director of your organisation suggests to you that one blanket rate rather than separate overhead absorption rates for Department 1 and 2 based on machine hours and labour hours respectively would be more beneficial for future years.

Draft a reply to this assertion.

(AAT Cost Accounting & Budgeting)

B9.14 A company produces several products which pass through the two production departments in its factory. These two departments are concerned with filling and sealing operations. There are two service departments, maintenance and canteen, in the factory.

Predetermined overhead absorption rates, based on direct labour hours, are established for the two production departments. The budgeted expenditure for these departments for the period just ended, including the apportionment of service department overheads, was £110,040 for filling, and £53,300 for sealing. Budgeted direct labour hours were 13,100 for filling and 10,250 for sealing.

Service department overheads are apportioned as follows:

Maintenance	– Filling	70%
	– Sealing	27%
	– Canteen	3%
Canteen	– Filling	60%
	– Sealing	32%
	– Maintenance	8%

During the period just ended, actual overhead costs and activity were as follows:

	£	Direct Labour hours
Filling	74,260	12,820
Sealing	38,115	10,075
Maintenance	25,050	
Canteen	24,375	

Required:

a. Calculate the overheads absorbed in the period and the extent of the under/over absorption in each of the two production departments.

b. State, and critically assess, the objectives of overhead apportionment and absorption.

(ACCA Cost & Management Accounting)

B9.15 One of the Directors of Company X has been looking at the budgets that have been recently prepared and shows concern at the production costs budget. The overhead absorption rate, based on a percentage on direct wages has increased from 200% to 300%.

Required:

a. An explanation of how overhead absorption rates are calculated and used.

b. An explanation of what factors may have caused the above increase.

c. An explanation of the circumstances that could make this increase acceptable.

d. Suggest possible apportionment methods for the following overhead cost items.

    i. Rent and rates

    ii. Supervisors salaries

    iii. Canteen costs

    iv. Machine depreciation.

e. Calculate under or over absorption of overhead from the following information.

	Machine Dept	Finishing Dept
Budgeted labour hrs	2,200	4,000
Budgeted overhead costs	£11,000	£16,000
Actual labour hrs	2,350	3,900
Actual overhead costs	£11,250	£16,720

(AAT Cost Accounting & Budgeting)

10: Cost Accounts

1. Topics covered in this chapter

> 1. Integrated and interlocking cost accounts
> 2. Reconciliation of financial and cost accounts
> 3. Developments in cost accounting
> 4. Back-flush accounting.

2. Accounting systems for costs

Because there are no statutory requirements to maintain detailed cost records some small firms keep only traditional financial accounts and prepare cost information in an ad-hoc fashion. In all but the very smallest firm this approach is likely to be unsatisfactory and the majority of firms maintain cost accounts in some form or other.

There is a vast range of systems in operation ranging from simple analysis systems to computer based accounting systems incorporating standards, variance analysis and the automatic production of control and operating statements. Invariably the systems are tailored to suit the particular firm and so will have unique features. Nevertheless there will be recognisably common aspects to most systems and the records will be maintained using proper double entry principles.

Whatever system is adopted for recording costs, it will depend on accurate coding of source data, ie, items such as invoices, job tickets, time sheets and requisitions. (The principles of coding have been dealt with in Chapter 3). Despite the variety of cost accounting systems, two particular categories are frequently encountered. These are known as *integrated cost accounts* and *interlocking cost accounts*. Descriptions of these terms follow.

Integrated cost accounts

This is a single, comprehensive accounting system with no division between financial and cost accounts. It follows therefore that the same bases for matters such as stock valuation and depreciation will be used and that there is no need for reconciliation between cost profit and financial profit. Financial profit will be the cost profit adjusted by any non-cost items, eg, income from investments, charitable donations etc.

Interlocking cost accounts

This system (of which there are many variants) uses separate cost accounts which periodically are reconciled with the financial accounts. Naturally the cost accounts use the same basic data (purchases, wages etc) as the financial accounts, but frequently adopt different bases for matters such as depreciation and stock valuation. The interlocking of the two systems is carried out by the use of control accounts in each set of account, ie,

> a cost ledger control account in the financial ledger and
>
> a financial ledger control account in the cost ledger.

3. Integrated cost accounts

Figure 10.1 shows the main flow of accounting entries in a typical integrated system. It has been kept free from the many complications and variations that occur in practice to show clearly the underlying principles. It should be studied in conjunction with the notes which follow.

Notes on integrated accounts

a. No distinction is made between 'cost accounts' and 'financial accounts'.

b. The emphasis is on functional analysis, eg selling overheads, rather than analysis by nature, eg salaries, telephone etc.

c. If analysis by nature is required, as in a traditional nominal ledger, then the prime data needs to be coded accordingly and natural accounts kept in addition to functional accounts.

d. The traditional form of Profit and Loss account disappears to be replaced by a Costing Profit and Loss account, or, as it is frequently known, an Operating Statement.

4. Example of integrated accounts

Example

Acme Manufacturing Ltd. operate an integrated accounting system and it is required to record the following balances and transactions in the ledger accounts and prepare Final Accounts at the month's end.

Opening balance at 1st June 19XX

		£	£
Issued share capital			250,000
Reserves			65,000
Depreciation provision (plant)			38,000
Creditors control			42,750
Buildings		80,000	
Plant & Machinery (at cost)		146,500	
Bank		23,291	
Debtors		49,856	
Stocks:	Raw materials	41,200	
	W-I-P	24,260	
	Finished Goods	30,643	
		395,750	395,750

The following information is supplied regarding the month's transactions.

	£
Purchases of raw materials	122,600
Gross wages and salaries	
Production direct wages (including £6,800 accrued)	24,910
Production indirect wages	6,253
Production salaries	2,985
Administration salaries	11,058
Selling and distr. salaries	6,219
Expenses	
Production control	4,286
Administration	7,017
Selling and distribution	4,935
Cash payments	
Creditors	155,296
Salaries and wages	41,025
Cash receipts – Debtors	185,473
Discounts allowed	2,100
Discounts received	3,926
Overheads recovered	
Production	28,750
Administration	18,500
Selling and distribution	10,800
Provisions	
Depreciation on plant	9,520
Bad debts	4,100
Factory cost of completed production	155,000
Factory cost of goods sold	173,000
Sales	220,800
Material issues	
Production	83,621
Works maintenance	6,509

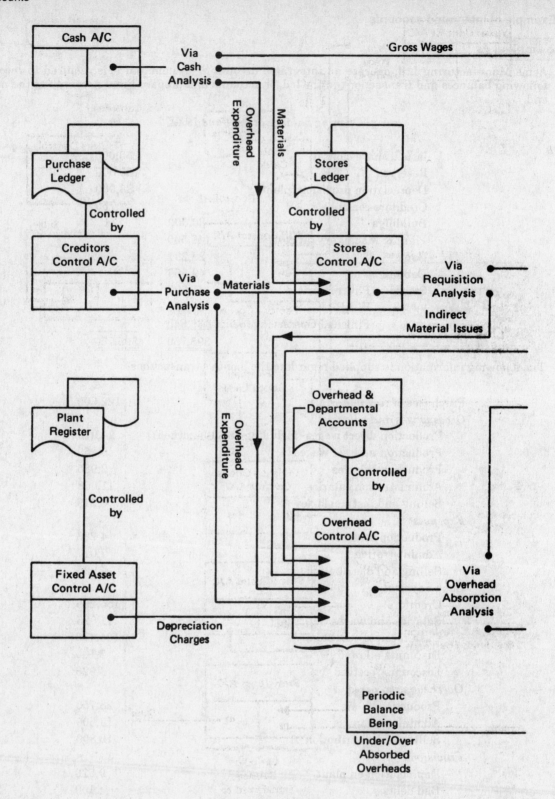

Figure 10.1 Typical accounting entries in an integrated cost accounting system

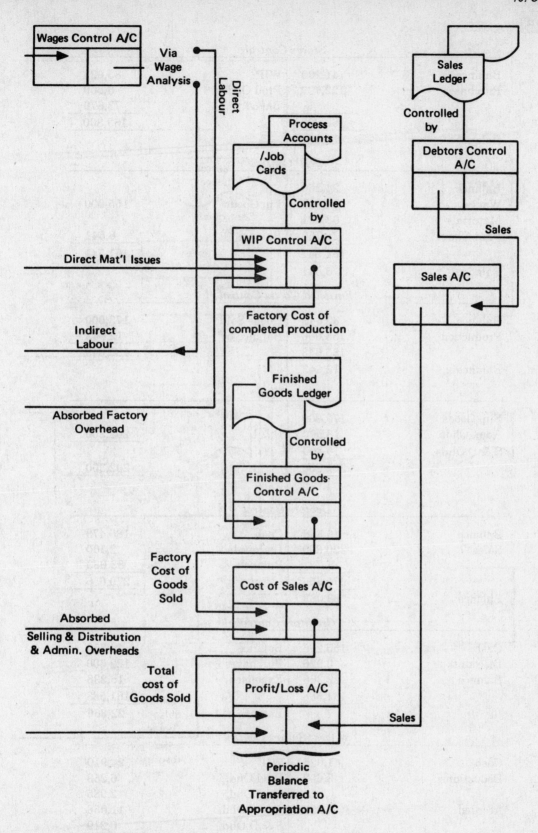

Figure 10.1 (cont.) Typical accounting entries in an integrated cost accounting system

Solution

Stores Control

Balance	41,200	WIP	83,621
Purchases	122,600	Prod Ohds	6,509
		Bal c/f	73,670
	163,800		163,800
Balance	73,670		

WIP Control

Balance	24,260		
Wages	24,910	Fin Goods	155,000
Materials	83,621		
Prod Ohds	28,750	Balance	6,541
	161,541		161,541
Balance	6,541		

Finished Goods Control

Balance	30,643	Goods Sold	173,000
Production	155,000	Balance c/f	12,643
	185,643		185,643
Balance	12,643		

Cost of Sales

Fin. Goods	173,000		
Adm. Ohds.	18,500	P & L	202,300
S & D Ohds.	10,800		
	202,300		202,300

Debtors Control

Balance	49,856	Cash	185,473
Sales	220,800	Discounts	2,100
		Balance	83,083
	270,656		270,656
Balance	83,083		

Creditors Control

Cash	155,296	Balance	42,750
Discounts	3,926	Purchases	122,600
Balance	22,366	Expenses	16,238
	181,588		181,588
		Balance	22,366

Wages/Salary Control

Cash	41,025	WIP	24,910
Deductions	3,600	Prod.Ohd.	6,253
		Prod.Ohd.	2,985
Accrued	6,800	Amm. Ohd.	11,058
		S & D Ohd.	6,219
	51,425		51,425
		Balance	6,800

Prodn Ohd Control

Wages	6,253		
Salaries	2,985		
Expenses	4,286	WIP	28,750
Depreciation	9,520	Under Recov.	803
Materials	6,509		
	29,553		29,553

Admin Ohd Control

Salaries	11,058		
Expenses	7,017	Cost of Sales	18,500
Over Recovery	475		
	18,500		18,500

S&D Ohd Control

Salaries	6,219		
Expenses	4,935	Cost of Sales	10,800
		Under Recovery	354
	11,154		11,154

Bad Debts Provision

		P & L	4,100

Wages / Salaries Deductions

		Wages	3,600

Share Capital

		Balance	250,000

Reserves

		Balance	65,000
		Profit	15,494
			80,494

Discount Allowed

Debtors	2,100	P & L	2,100

Discount Received

P & L	3,926	Creditors	3,926

Bank

Balance	23,291	Creditors	155,296
Debits	185,473	Wages	41,025
		Balance c/f	12,443
	208,764		208,764
Balance	12,443		

Buildings

Balance	80,000		

Plant & Machinery

Balance	146,500		

Depreciation Prov Plant

Balance c/f	47,250	Balance	38,000
		Prod. Ohd	9,520
	47,520		47,520
		Balance	47,520

Ohd Adjustment A/c

Prod. Ohds.	803	Admin. Ohds	425
S & D Ohds.	354	P & L	732
	1,157		1,157

Sales

P & L	220,800	Debtors	220,800

Profit and Loss

Cost of Sales	202,300	Sales	220,800
Overhead adjustment	732	Discount Received	3,296
Discounts allowed	2,100		
Bad Debts Prov.	4,100		
Transfer to Reserve	15,494		
	224,726		224,726

Balance Sheet

Share Capital		250,000	Buildings		80,000
Reserves		80,494	Plant	148,500	
			less Depreciation	47,520	98,980
					178,980
Current Liabilities			Current Assets		
Creditors	22,366		Cash	12,443	
Accrued Wages	6,800		Debtors	83,083	
Deductions	3,600	32,766	less B.D.P.	4,100	78,893
			Stocks		
			Raw Matls	73,670	
			WIP	6,541	
			Fin Goods	12,643	184,280
		£363,260			£363,260

5. Interlocking cost accounts

This system, with its many variants, is commonly encountered in practice. There are separate cost accounting and financial accounting systems in which the basic accounting data are used in the normal manner in the financial accounts and then the data and documents passed to the cost department. There the source data on costs will be re-classified into the functional analysis necessary for costing purposes, using such supplementary information as labour and machine times, production statistics, material requisitions and scrap reports.

The financial accounting system has the normal debit and credit entries within itself and in addition has a memorandum account frequently termed the Cost Ledger Control A/C. This account will have posted to it all items which are to be transferred to the cost accounting system.

In the cost ledger there will be the necessary accounts for costing purposes, eg Stores Control A/C, W-l-P Control A/C etc. and, in addition, an account which is equal and opposite to the memorandum financial account. The cost ledger account is sometimes termed the Cost Ledger Contra Account, but to avoid confusion with the memorandum cost ledger control account in the financial accounts, it is frequently called the Financial (or General) Ledger Control A/C.

The Financial Ledger Control account is an essential element of the cost ledger because it forms part of the double entry system within the ledger. It also enables the financial and cost ledgers to be interlocked because it must agree with the memorandum Cost Ledger Control account in the financial ledger. A summary of the two ledgers is shown below.

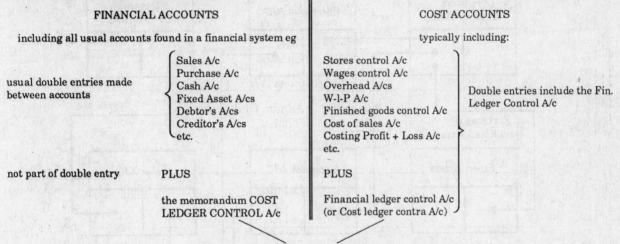

	FINANCIAL ACCOUNTS	COST ACCOUNTS
	including all usual accounts found in a financial system eg	typically including:
usual double entries made between accounts	Sales A/c Purchase A/c Cash A/c Fixed Asset A/cs Debtor's A/cs Creditor's A/cs etc.	Stores control A/c Wages control A/c Overhead A/cs W-l-P A/c Finished goods control A/c Cost of sales A/c Costing Profit + Loss A/c etc. Double entries include the Fin. Ledger Control A/c
not part of double entry	PLUS the memorandum COST LEDGER CONTROL A/c	PLUS Financial ledger control A/c (or Cost ledger contra A/c)

These two accounts should be in agreement.

Note: There is no double entry connection between the Financial accounts and the Cost accounts although the use of the memorandum control account in the financial ledger and the financial ledger control A/c in the cost ledger enables the two sets of accounts to be kept in agreement.

Figure 10.2 shows the main flow in an interlocking system and should be studied in conjunction with the following notes.

Notes on Figure 10.2 relating to the Financial Ledger

a. Typical entries relating to items which will be transferred to the cost accounts ie, wages, purchases etc. are shown as M1, M2 etc. The normal double entries are given together with the entry in the memorandum Cost Ledger Control A/c.

b. Examples of two entries are given which do not affect the cost ledger, the Purchase of a fixed asset and payment of dividends. It will be seen that for these items there is no memorandum entry.

c. Other items which appear in the financial accounts, but not in the cost accounts, include:

   i. Financial charges such as stamp duty, interest on loans, issue expenses, loss on sale of capital assets and similar financial items.

   ii. Financial income such as dividends received, interest received on loans and deposits and profits from the sales of fixed assets.

   iii. Appropriations of profit such as dividends paid, transfers to reserve and taxation.

d. Although there are no double entries spanning the cost and financial ledgers, control must be maintained over the information and documents transferred. The cost ledger control account assists this process together with batch control totals, pre-lists and documents counts.

Notes on Figure 10.2 relating to Cost Ledger

a. Comparison with Figure 10.1 will show a similar pattern of accounts in both integral and interlocking systems.

b. It will be seen that the Financial Ledger Control A/c is a necessary part of the double entry system within the cost ledger (alternative names for this account are General Ledger Control A/c or the Cost Ledger Contra A/c).

c. The balance on the Financial Ledger Control account represents the total of all the balances of the impersonal accounts in the cost ledger.

d. If work of a capital nature is carried out in the factory, this needs to be transferred to the financial accounts via the Financial Ledger Control account.

e. Periodic reconciliation of the cost and financial ledgers is necessary. This is dealt with in detail later in this chapter.

FINANCIAL LEDGER

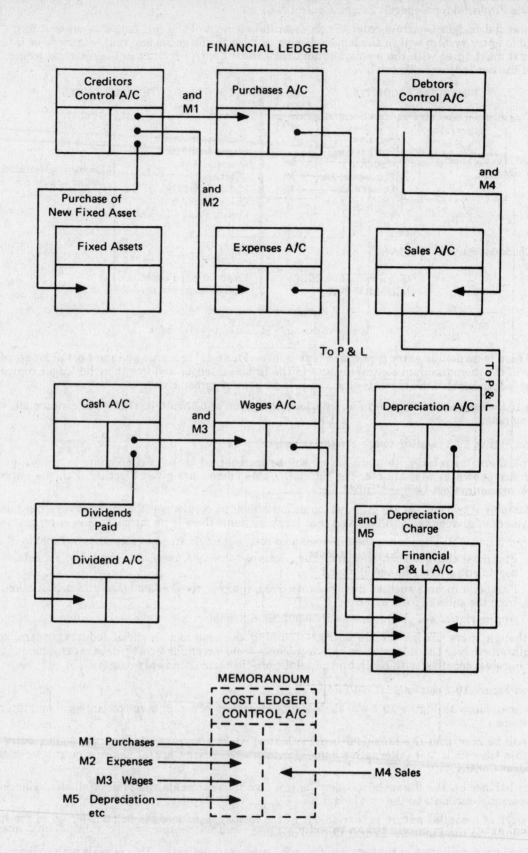

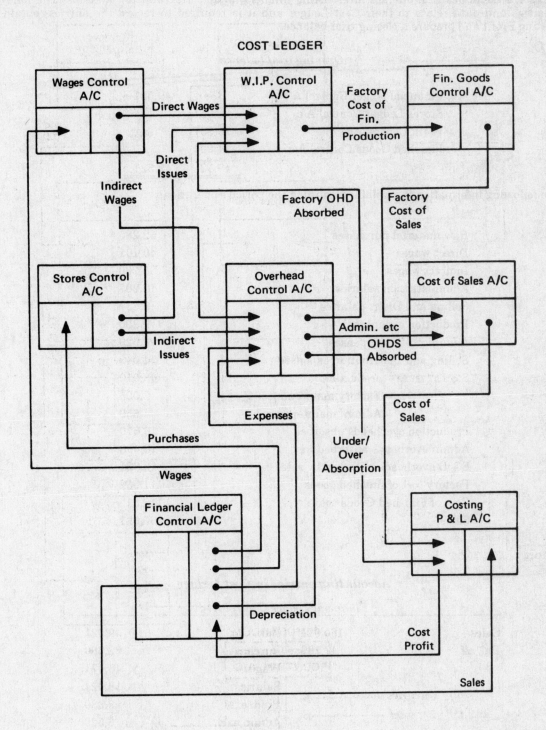

Figure 10.2

Typical accounting entries in an interlocking system with separate financial & cost accounts.

6. Example of accounts using a separate cost ledger

Example

Jackson Assemblies Ltd. operate interlocking financial and cost accounting systems. The following balances and data relate to their Cost Ledger and it is required to record the entries, obtain the Costing Profit and prepare a closing trial balance.

Cost Ledger
Opening trial balance

	£	£
Financial ledger Control A/c		49,521
Stores Ledger Control A/c	8,951	
W-l-P Control A/c	26,367	
Finished Goods Control A/c	14,203	
	49,521	49,521

The following information is available regarding the period's operations.

	£
Raw material purchases	62,280
Direct wages	40,191
Indirect wages	6,280
Administration salaries	11,207
Selling and Distr. Salaries	6,817
Production expenses	9,380
Administration expenses	6,529
Selling and Distribution expenses	4,043
Stores issues – production	43,010
– Factory maintenance	2,005
– Admin. maintenance	659
Production overheads absorbed	16,670
Admin overheads absorbed	18,493
S + D overheads absorbed by sales	10,621
Factory cost of finished goods	111,032
Cost of Finished Goods sold	118,815
Sales	160,921

Solution

Accounting entries in Cost Ledger

Financial Ledger Control A/c

Sales	160,921	Bal.	49,521
Bal. c/f	47,183	Purchases	62,280
		Wages	46,471
		Salaries	18,024
		Prod. exs.	9,380
		Admin exc.	6,529
		S & D exs.	4,043
		Profit	11,856
	208,104		208,104
		Bal.	47,183

Stores Ledger Control A/c

Bal.	8,951	W-I-P	43,010
F.L. control	62,280	Prod. Ohd.	2,005
		Admin Ohd.	659
		Bal c/f	25,557
	71,231		71,231
Bal.	25,557		

Finished Goods Control A/c

Bal.	14,203	Cost of Sales	118,815
W-I-P	111,032	Bal. c/f	6,420
	125,235		125,235
Bal. c/f	6,420		

Admin. overhead Control A/c

Salaries	11,207		
Expenses	6,529	Cost of Sales	18,493
Material	659		
Ohd. adj A/c	98		
	18,493		18,493

Wages Control A/c

F.L			
Control A/c	46,471	W-I-P	40,191
		Prod. Ohds	6,280
	46,471		46,471

W-I-P Control A/c

Bal.	26,367		
Issues	43,010	Fin. goods	111,032
Wages	40,191	Bal c/f	15,206
Prodn Ohds	16,670		
	126,238		126,238
Bal. c/f	15,206		

Production Overheads Control A/c

Wages	6,280	W-I-P	16,670
Exps.	9,380		
Stores	2,005	Ohd adjstmt (under recovery)	995
	17,665		17,665

Selling + Distr. overhead Control A/c

Salaries	6,817	Cost of Sales	10,621
Expenses	4,043	Ohd Adj A/c	239
	10,860		10,860

Salaries Control A/c

F.L.			
Control A/c	18,024	Adm. Ohds.	11,207
		S + D Ohds.	6,817
	18,024		18,024

Overhead Adjustment A/c

Prod. Ohds	995	Admin Ohds	98
S + D Ohds.	239	P + L	1,136
	1,234		1,234

Cost of Sales A/c

Admin. Ohds.	18,493		
Fin. Goods	118,815	P + L	147,929
S + D Ohds.	10,621		
	147,929		147,929

Costing P&L A/c

Cost of Sales	147,929	Sales	160,921
Ohd. Adj.	1,136		
Profit	11,856		
	160,921		160,921

Closing Trial Balance

Financial ledger Control A/c		47,183
Stores ledger Control A/c	25,557	
W-I-P Control A/c	15,206	
Finished Goods Control A/c	6,420	
	47,183	47,183

7. Reconciliation of cost and financial accounts

Differences can arise between the profits shown by the cost accounts and the financial accounts. Periodically these differences must be reconciled to ensure that there are no errors in either set of accounts.

Differences arise due to several factors:

a. Items appearing in financial accounts and not in cost accounts. Typical examples are; dividends received, profits and losses on sales of assets, interest paid or received, share issue and preliminary expenses, and fines paid by the company.

b. Items appearing only in the cost accounts. These are infrequent and usually relate to imputed charges for such matters as rent and interest.

c. Differences in the treatment of depreciation and different stock valuations.

The reconciliation is carried out using a memorandum reconciliation account as shown in the following example.

Example

The profit shown in the financial accounts is £18,592 and for the same period the cost accounts showed a profit of £20,496.

Comparison of the two sets of accounts revealed the following:

Stock Valuations	Cost Accounts	Financial Accounts
Raw Materials	£	£
Opening Stock	6,821	7,259
Closing Stock	5,483	5,128
Finished Goods		
Opening Stock	13,291	12,905
Closing Stock	11,430	11,131

Dividends and interest received of £552 and a loss of £1,750 on the sale of a milling machine were not entered in the cost accounts.

Reconcile the profit figures.

Solution

Memorandum Reconciliation A/c

	£		£
Profit as per Financial A/cs	18,592	Profit as per cost A/cs	20,496
Stock differences			
	£	Item not credited	
Raw material – opening	438	Dividends + interest recd.	
– closing	355	Stock difference	552
Finished Goods closing	299 1,092	Finished Goods-Opening	386
Items not charged in cost accounts			
Loss on sale of machine	1,750		
	£21,434		£21,434

8. Illustration of integrated accounts

To consolidate the material covered in this chapter a comprehensive example follows of a full set of accounts for one month for Acme Manufacturing Ltd who maintain a fully integrated system.

Example

Opening Balance Sheet

	£		£
Share Capital	1,000,000	Buildings (cost £600,000)	450,000
General Reserve	85,000	Plant & Machinery (cost £840,000)	585,000
P & L Appropriation	17,500	Vehicles (cost £360,000)	144,800
Debentures	400,000	Stocks – Raw Materials	102,550
Bought Ledger Control	43,250	– W-I-P	32,200
		– Finished Goods	69,250
		Sales Ledger Control	84,050
		Cash at Bank	77,900
	1,545,750		1,545,750

The transactions for the period were:

	£
Credit sales	384,500
Raw material purchases	147,000
Expense and overhead purchases	49,250
Cash from debtors	173,280
Cash to creditors	139,100
Cash drawn for wages and salaries	84,220
PAYE deductions	15,300
Works costs of goods sold	292,255
Production to Finished Goods Stock	306,405

The following allocations were made:

	Wages and Salaries £	Materials £	Expenses £
Direct costs	48,200	134,200	14,100
Production Dept's.			
Fabrication	8,300	8,520	9,800
Finishing	8,670	4,810	7,050
Service Dept's:			
Stores	3,550	13,270	3,000
Maintenance	11,600	18,450	4,350
Selling and Admin.	19,260		10,950

The following data are available from production and other records within the organisation.

	Percentage of value of			No of Stores Requisitions	Maintenance Hours
	Buildings	Plant	Vehicles		
Production					
Fabrication Dept.	20	35	5	250	600
Finishing Dept.	30	15	15	450	300
Stores Dept.	5	15	5	–	–
Maintenance Dept.	20	25	10	250	–
Selling and Admin.	25	10	65	50	100

The depreciation rates are:

Buildings	5% p.a. on cost
Plant	10% p.a. on cost
Vehicles	20% p.a. on cost

Overheads absorbed during the period:

	£
Fabrication Dept	63,200
Finishing Dept.	43,905

Based on the above information it is required to make the appropriate ledger entries, prepare Trading and Profit and Loss accounts for the period and a closing Balance Sheet.

Solution

Ledger Accounts

Share Capital

		Bal	1,000,000

P & L Appropriation

		Bal.	17,500
		P & L	52,270
			69,770

Plant and Machinery

Bal.	585,000	Depreciation	7,000
		Bal.	578,000
	585,000		585,000
Bal.	578,000		

Raw Materials Control

Bal.	102,550	W-I-P	134,200
Bought Ledger	147,000	Fabrication	8,520
		Finishing	4,810
		Stores	13,270
		Maintenance	18,450
		Bal.	70,300
	249,550		249,550
Bal.	70,300		

Finished Goods Control

Bal.	69,250	Trading A/c	292,255
W-I-P	306,405	Bal.	83,400
	375,655		375,655
Bal.	83,400		

General Reserve

		Bal.	85,000

Debentures

		Bal.	400,000

Buildings

Bal.	450,000	Depreciation	2,500
		Bal.	447,500
	450,000		450,000
Bal.	447,500		

Vehicles

Bal.	144,800	Depreciation	6,000
		Bal.	138,800
	144,800		144,800
Bal.	138,800		

WIP Control

Bal.	32,200		
Wages	48,200	Finished Goods	306,405
Materials	134,200	Bal.	29,400
Expenses	14,100		
Fabrication Ohds.	63,200		
Finishing Ohds.	43,905		
	335,805		335,805
		Bal.	29,400

Sales Ledger Control

Bal.	84,050	Bank	173,280
Sales	384,500	Bal.	295,270
	468,550		468,550
Bal.	295,270		

Bank

Bal.	77,900	Bought Ledger	139,100
Sales Ledger	173,280	Wage & Salaries	84,220
		Bal.	27,860
	251,180		251,180
Bal.	27,860		

Wage & Salary Control

Bank	84,220	WIP Control	48,200
PAYE	15,360	Fabrication Ohds.	8,300
		Finishing Ohds.	8,670
		Stores	3,550
		Maintenance	11,600
		Selling & Admin.	19,260
	99,580		99,580

Fabrication Overhead

Wage & Salaries	8,300		
Materials	8,520		
Building Deprec.	500	Absorbed Overhead	63,200
Plant Deprec.	2,450		
Vehicle Deprec.	300		
Expenses	9,800		
Stores Ohds.	5,324		
Maintenance	25,544		
Overhead Adj.	2,462		
	63,200		63,200

Stores Overhead

Wage & Salaries	3,550	Fabrication	5,324
Materials	13,270	Finishing	9,583
Building Deprec.	125	Maintenance	5,324
Plant Deprec.	1,050	S & D	1,064
Vehicle Deprec.	300		
Expenses	3,000		
	21,295		21,295

PAYE

		Wage & Salaries	15,360

Expense Control

Bought Ledger	49,250	WIP	14,100
		Fabrication	9,800
		Finishing	7,050
		Stores	3,000
		Maintenance	4,350
		S & D	10,950
	49,250		49,250

Finishing Overhead

Wage & Salaries	8,670		
Materials	4,810	Absorbed Overhead	43,905
Building Deprec.	750	Overhead Adjustment	1,680
Plant Deprec.	1,050		
Vehicle Deprec.	900		
Expenses	7,050		
Stores Ohds.	9,583		
Maintenance	12,772		
	45,585		45,585

Maintenance Overhead

Wage & Salaries	11,600	Fabrication	25,544
Materials	18,450	Finishing	12,772
Building Deprec.	500	S & D	4,258
Plant Deprec.	1,750		
Vehicle Deprec.	600		
Expenses	4,350		
Stores Ohds.	5,324		
	42,574		42,574

Selling & Admin. Overheads

Wage & Salaries	19,260		
Building Deprec.	625		
Plant Deprec.	700	P & L	40,757
Vehicle Deprec.	3,900		
Expenses	10,950		
Stores Ohds.	1,064		
Maintenance	4,258		
	40,757		40,757

Overhead Adjust ment A/c

Finishing Dept.	1,680	Fabrication Dept	2,462
P & L A/c	782		
	2,462		2,462

Bought Ledger Control

Bank	139,100	Bal.	43,250
		Materials	147,000
Bal.	100,400	Expenses	49,250
	239,500		239,500
		Bal.	100,400

Sales

Trading A/c	384,500	Sales Ledger	384,500

Trading A/c

Cost of Sales	292,255	Sales	384,500
Gross Profit	92,245		
	384,500		384,500

P & L A/c

S. & D. Ohds.	40,757	Gross Profit	92,245
P & L Approp.	52,270	Overhead Adj.	782
	93,027		93,027

Closing Balance Sheet

Share Capital	1,000,000	Buildings	447,500
General Reserve	85,000	Plant & Machinery	578,000
P & L Appropriation	69,770	Vehicles	138,800
Debentures	400,000	Stocks – Raw Materials	70,300
Bought Ledger Control	100,400	–WIP	29,400
PAYE	15,360	– Finished Goods	83,400
		Sales Ledger Control	295,270
		Cash at Bank	27,860
	£1,671,530		£1,671,530

Workings

				£
Depreciation	– Buildings	$\dfrac{5\% \times 600,000}{12}$	=	2,500
	– Plant	$\dfrac{10\% \times 840,000}{12}$	=	7,000
	– Vehicles	$\dfrac{20\% \times 360,000}{12}$	=	6,000

Apportionments

	Buildings £	Plant £	Vehicles £
Fabrication	500	2,450	300
Finishing	750	1,050	900
Stores	125	1,050	300
Maintenance	500	1,750	600
S & D	625	700	3,900
	2,500	7,000	6,000

Stores overhead apportionment (based on requisitions)

Fabrication	25%
Finishing	45%
Maintenance	25%
S & D	5%

Maintenance overhead apportionment (based on hours)

Fabrication	60%
Finishing	30%
S & D	10%

9. Developments in cost accounting

Conventional cost accounting systems as described so far track the detailed movement of costs stage by stage. Typically this begins with the introduction of raw materials into a Stores account or Raw materials account, the subsequent issue of materials to production and the consequent entries into a Work-in-Progress account (together with labour and overhead entries). When the goods are completed, entries are made from the WIP account into the Finished Goods account.

The entries outlined above are triggered by a vast number of works tickets, documents and notes relating to material issues, parts completed, goods finished and so on. Cost accounting methods developed in this way because this was the way that production was traditionally organised and still is in many factories.

However, enormous changes have taken place in the way goods are made, materials are purchased and production is organised and, as is to be expected, changes are also occurring in cost accounting methods. The production changes are most apparent in firms using Just-in-Time Purchasing and manufacturing methods; the key features of which are:

JIT Purchasing characterised by:

❑ Goods delivered immediately before demand or use.

❑ Increase in number of deliveries, each containing a smaller number of units.

❑ Goods/materials delivered in 'shop/factory ready' containers reducing materials handling.

❑ Long-term agreements with fewer suppliers specifying price, delivery and acceptable quality levels.

❑ Minimal checking by purchaser of quality and quantity of deliveries.

Frequently when JIT purchasing is adopted deliveries are made directly to the factory floor in exact accordance with production and delivery schedules.

JIT manufacturing characterised by:

- ☐ Elimination of non-value adding activities such as storage, transport etc.
- ☐ Commitment to high quality. The target is zero defects.
- ☐ Production on demand; not for stock.
- ☐ Nil or very small raw material and WIP stocks.
- ☐ A commitment to continuous improvement.
- ☐ Simplification, space saving and reduction in lead times.

The above are fundamental developments and it is important that there are corresponding changes in the cost accounting system. This is a critical point because accounting methods must be tailored to suit the underlying operations, and not vice versa.

One important change being adopted by many firms is called *backflush accounting*.

10. Backflush accounting

This is a simpler cost accounting system designed to reduce or eliminate detailed accounting entries. Instead of the detailed tracking of material movements through stores and production a backflush system focuses on the output of the firm (ie, the finished goods) and then works backwards to attribute costs between cost of goods sold and finished goods inventory and/or raw materials inventory with no separate accounting for WIP. The formal definition of back flush accounting is:

> A cost accounting system which focuses on the output of an organisation and then works backwards to attribute costs to stock and cost of sales.

There are several variants of back flush accounting depending on the inventory accounts maintained and the number and type of *trigger points* (these determine when entries are made in the accounts). Conversion costs (labour and overheads) are recorded as in traditional systems and then applied to products at various trigger points. Normally any conversion costs not applied to products are written off immediately as expenses incurred in the period.

Figure 10.3 shows key features of three variants of backflush accounting.

	Variant A	Variant B	Variant C
Trigger points for initiating accounting entries	1. Purchase of raw materials, components 2. Manufacture of finished goods	1. Purchase of raw materials, components 2. Sale of finished goods	Manufacture of finished goods
Inventory a/cs kept	1. Combined raw material & WIP a/c ie Raw & in Progress (RIP) a/c 2. Finished goods a/c	RIP a/c	Finished goods a/c
Main features of variants	Two trigger points Use of combined RIP a/c	Two trigger points Use of combined RIP a/c No finished goods a/c because the trigger is sales not manufacture	Simplest of all Finished goods a/c only Single trigger point Less feasible if there are significant stocks of materials and WIP

Figure 10.3 Variants of backflush accounting

11. Examples of backflush accounting

Example

The following data will be used to illustrate the three variants:

	£'000
Material/ component purchases for period	2300
Conversion costs for period	1250
Units of finished goods made	50,000
Units of finished goods sold	49,000

The standard cost of a unit of output is £70 (£45 materials, £25 conversion cost)

There are no opening stocks and for simplicity it is assumed that there are no variations from standard cost.

Required: The backflush accounting entries using:

    i.   Variant A

    ii.   Variant B

    iii   Variant C

Note: In each of the following solution the transactions and transfers have been numbered 1 2 3 etc and are explained following the accounts

Solution - Variant A

Triggers   – Purchase of materials

                – Manufacturing of finished units-

RIP a/c

		£000			£000
1.	Creditors	2,300	3.	Finished goods	2,250
				Balance	50
		2,300			2,300
	Balance	50			

Conversion Costs a/c

		£000			£000
2.	Creditors	1,250	4.	Finished goods	1,250

Finished Goods a/c

		£000			£000
3.	RIP a/c	2,250	5.	Cost of goods sold	3,430
4.	Conversion cost	1,250		Balance	70
		3,500			3,500
	Balance	70			

Cost of Goods Sold a/c

		£000			£000
5.	Finished goods	3,430		Profit & loss a/c	3,430

Notes:

1. Purchase of materials/components for period of £2,300,000
2. Conversion costs for period of £1,250,000
3. Transfer to Finished Goods A/C, materials used for production (50,000 × £45) = £2,250,000
4. Transfer to Finished Goods A/C the conversion costs of production (50,000 × £25) = £1,250,000
5. Transfer from Finished Goods to Cost of Goods Sold the cost of the units sold:
   (49,000 × £70) = £3,430,000

Closing stocks

It will be seen that the closing stocks are:

Raw Materials	£50,000	
Finished Goods	£70,000	(ie, 1000 × £70)
Total	£120,000	

The effect of this method is that £25000 of this periods' conversion cost (1000 × £25) is carried forward to next period in the Finished Goods balance.

Solution - Variant B

Triggers − Purchase of materials
  − Sale of finished units

RIP a/c

		£000				£000
1.	Creditors	2300	3.	Cost of goods sold		2205
				Balance		95
		2300				2300
	Balance	95				

Conversion costs

		£000				£000
2.	Creditors	1250	4.	Cost of goods sold		1225
			5.	Period exs		25
		1250				1250

Cost of Goods Sold

		£000		£000
3.	RIP	2205		
4.	Conv. Cost	1225	P&L	3430
		3430		3430

Period Expenses

		£000		£000
5.	Conv. Cost	25	P&L	25

Notes:

1. as in Variant A
2. as above
3. Transfer to C.O.G.S. of material costs in the units sold (49,000 × £45) £2,205,000
4. Transfer to C.O.G.S. of conversion costs in units sold (49,000 × £25) £1,225,000
5. Transfer to Period Expenses of the conversion costs incurred but not attributed to units sold:

   (£1250 − 1225) = £25,000. These are charged against this periods P&L A/C.

Closing stocks

The closing stocks are:

  RIP A/C £95,000

This balance comprises the £50,000 raw materials over purchased plus the materials contained in the units made but not sold ie 1000 × £45 = £45000.

It will be seen that in this method there will is no finished goods stock account and no conversion costs are carried forward in inventory valuations.

The rationales claimed for this variant are that it removes the incentive to produce for stock and it focuses attention on the overall organisational objective of producing saleable goods rather than on individual sub-unit goals such as increasing labour efficiency at a single production cost centre.

Solution - Variant C

Trigger – Manufacture of Finished units

Conversion Costs

	£000			£000
Creditors	1,250	2.	Finished goods	1,250

Finished Goods A/C

		£000			£000
1.	Creditors	2250	4.	Cost of goods sold	3430
3.	Con. Cost	1250		Balance	70
		3500			3500
Bal		70			

Cost of Goods Sold A/C

		£000			£000
4.	Finished goods	3,430	P & L		3,430

Notes:

1. Entry of material purchases for the number of units completed (50,000 × £45) £2,250,000
2. Conversion costs for period £1,250,000
3. Transfer of conversion costs for units completed to Finished Goods (50,000 × £25) £1,250,000
4. Transfer to C.O.G.S. of the cost of the units sold (49,000 × £70) = £3,430,000

Closing stocks

Finished Goods A/C £70,000 (ie 1000 × £70)

In this variant the £50,000 of Raw materials purchased but not yet manufactured into finished units is not entered into the internal product costing system. For this reason this variant is only suitable where the JIT system operates with minimum raw material and WIP inventories.

Where there are low inventories or there is little change in levels from period to period then the inventory valuations derived from backflush costing will not be greatly different than those from conventional systems and thus are likely to be accepted for external financial reporting.

12. Summary

a. Integrated cost accounts are a single system of accounting with no divisions between financial and cost accounts.

b. Interlocking cost accounts are systems in which separate financial and cost accounts are kept.

c. Separate accounts are frequently encountered and are controlled ('interlocked') by a memorandum Cost Ledger Control A/c in the financial ledger and a Financial Ledger Control A/c in the cost ledger. The Financial Ledger Control A/c in the cost ledger forms part of the double system within the cost ledger.

d. Where separate cost and financial ledgers are maintained, periodic reconciliation is necessary.

e. Cost accounting methods must suit the underlying operations especially where JIT purchasing and production are used.

f. Backflush accounting aims to streamline and simplify cost accounting and focuses on the output and then attributes costs to inventories and cost of sales.

13. Points to note

a. Whatever system is adopted, proper double entry standards should be maintained in the accounting system.

b. Even when the accounting system is computerised the principles shown regarding the accounting entries still apply.

c. By adopting backflush accounting and other simplifications Hewlett-Packard reduced the number of cost accounting entries from over 100,000 per period to under 10,000.

Student self-testing

Self Review Questions

1. What are integrated cost accounts? (2)

2. What are interlocking cost accounts? (2)

3. Using integrated cost accounts is the emphasis on functional analysis or analysis by nature of expense? (3)

4. Using interlocking cost accounts what is the 'Cost Ledger Control A/C' in the Financial ledger? (5)

5. Why do differences arise between the cost and financial accounts? (7)

6. What is backflush accounting. (10)

7. Describe three of the variants that might be found. (10)

Exercises and examination questions with answers

Exercises

A10.1 A company operates interlocking financial and cost accounting book-keeping systems. The following balances and data relate to the Cost Ledger.

Cost Ledger

	£	£
Opening Balances		24,283
Financial ledger control A/c	10,652	
W-I-P Control A/c	9,318	
Raw Material Control A/c	4,313	
Finished Goods Control A/c	24,283	24,283

The following data concerns the period's operations.

	£
Raw material purchases	41,286
Direct wages	20,444
Indirect wages	6,135
Selling & Distribution Salaries	5,157
Admin. salaries	9,106
Admin. expenses	7,213
	£
Production expenses	8,680
S & D expenses	5,217
Stores Issues	
– Production	36,291
– Factory maintenance	2,958
– Office maintenance	1,307
Production overhead absorbed	19,800
Admin. overhead absorbed by finished goods	17,200
S & D overheads absorbed by Sales	10,100
Factory cost of finished goods	78,280
Cost of finished goods sold	92,500
Sales	143,650

You are required to write up all the necessary accounts, prepare the Costing Profit & Loss Account and give the closing trial balance.

A10.2 The profit shown in the financial accounts was £11,287 and for the same period the cost account showed a profit of £2,704.

Examination of the accounts showed the following differences:

	Cost Accounts £	Financial Accounts £
Depreciation	9,826	10,520
Stock Valuations Opening Stocks	27,510	25,500
Closing Stocks	18,218	18,750
Profit on sale of asset	–	850
Dividends received	–	2,635
Imputed rent charge	3,250	–

Reconcile the profit figures.

A10.3   A firm maintains separate Cost and Financial Ledgers. The opening trial balance in the Cost Ledger was as follows:

Cost Ledger – Opening Trial Balance

	£	£
Financial Ledger Control A/c		24,952
Stores Ledger Control A/c	3,916	
W-I-P Control A/c	12,521	
Finished Goods Control A/c	8,515	
	24,952	24,952

During the period sales were £37,529 and purchases, wages and overheads totalled £29,286.

At the end of the period, by coincidence, the stores ledger and W-I-P Control accounts were the same values as in the opening trial balance and the balance on the Financial Ledger Control A/C was £21,242.

What was the profit for the period and the balance on the Finished Goods Control A/C?

Examination questions

A10.4   a.   A company maintained separate cost and financial accounts, and the costing profit for the last year differed to that revealed in the financial accounts, which was shown as £50,000.

The following information is available:

i.

	Cost accounts £	Financial Accounts £
Opening Stock of Raw Material	5,000	5,500
Closing Stock of Raw Material	4,000	5,300
Opening Stock of Finished Goods	12,000	15,000
Closing Stock of Finished Goods	14,000	16,000

ii.   Dividends of £1,000 were received by the company.

iii.   A machine with net book value of £10,000 was sold during the year for £8,000.

iv.   The company charged 10% interest on its opening capital employed of £80,000 to its process costs.

Required:

i.   Determine the profit figure which was shown in the cost accounts.

ii.   Explain what advantages a business might obtain from the integration of cost and financial accounting data.

(AAT Cost Accounting & Budgeting, part question)

A10.5   Shown below is one week's basic payroll data for the assembly department of Wooden Ltd, a manufacturer of a range of domestic furniture.

	Direct Workers	Indirect workers
Total attendance time	800 hours	350 hours
Basic hourly rate of pay	£1.50	£1.00
Overtime hours worked	100 hours	40 hours
Shift Premium	£150	£50
Group Bonus	£160	£70
Employees' deductions:		
Income Tax	£250	£100
National Insurance	£75	£35
Employer's Contributions:		
National Insurance	£125	£55

Overtime, which is paid at basic time rate plus one-half, is used as a means of generally increasing the factory output. However, 20% of the overtime shown above, for both direct and indirect workers, was incurred at the specific request of a special customer who requires, and is paying for, a particular batch of coffee tables to be completed quickly.

Analysis of the direct workers' time from returned work tickets shows:

Productive Time		590 hours
Non Productive Time:	Machine Breakdown	50 hours
	Waiting for Materials	40 hours
	Waiting for Instructions	45 hours
	Idle Time	75 hours

Required:

a. Assuming the company operates an historical batch costing system, fully integrated with the financial accounts, write up the assembly department's wages, work in progress and production overhead control accounts, and other relevant accounts.

b. Explain the reasons for, and effect on product costs of, your treatment of the following items:

   i. Employer's National Insurance Contributions
   ii. Group Bonus
   iii. Overtime Earnings.

(ACCA, Costing)

A10.6 In the absence of the accountant you have been asked to prepare a month's cost accounts for a company which operates a batch costing system fully integrated with the financial accounts. The cost clerk has provided you with the following information, which he thinks is relevant.

Balances at beginning of month:	£
Stores Ledger Control Account	24,175
Work in Progress Control Account	19,210
Finished Goods Control Account	34,164
Prepayments of production overheads brought forward from previous month	2,100

Transactions during the month:	£
Materials purchased	76,150
Materials issued: to production	26,350
for factory maintenance	3,280
Materials transferred between batches	1,450

	Direct Workers £	Indirect Workers £
Total wages paid – Net	17,646	3,342
– Employees deductions	4,364	890

	£
Direct wages charged to batches from work tickets	15,236
Recorded non-productive time of direct workers	5,230
Direct wages incurred on production of capital equipment, for use in the factory	2,670
Selling and distribution overheads incurred	5,240
Other production overheads incurred	12,200
Sales	75,400
Cost of finished goods sold	59,830
Cost of goods completed and transferred into finished goods store during the month	62,130
Physical stock value of work in progress at end of month	24,360

The production overhead absorption rate is 150% of direct wages and it is the policy of the company to include a share of production overheads in the cost of capital equipment constructed in the factory.

Required:

a. Prepare the following accounts for the month:
    Stores Ledger Control Account
    Work in Progress Control Account
    Finished Goods Control Account
    Production Overhead Control Account
    Profit/Loss Account

b. Identify any aspects of the accounts which you consider should be investigated.

c. Explain why it is necessary to value a company's stocks at the end of each period and also why, in a manufacturing company, expense items such as factory rent, wages of direct operatives, power costs etc. are included in the value of work in progress and finished goods stocks.
               (ACCA, Costing)

A10.7 K Limited operates separate cost accounting and financial accounting systems. The following manufacturing and trading statement has been prepared from the financial accounts for the quarter ended 31st March:

	£	£
Raw materials:		
Opening stock	48,000	
Purchases	108,800	
	156,800	
Closing stock	52,000	
Raw Materials consumed		104,800
Direct wages		40,200
Production overhead		60,900
Production cost incurred		205,900
Work-in-progress:		

	£	£
Opening stock	64,000	
Closing stock	58,000	
		6,000
Cost of goods produced carried down		211,900
Sales		440,000
Finished goods:		
Opening stock	120,000	
Cost of goods produced brought down	211,900	
	331,900	
Closing stock	121,900	
Cost of goods sold		210,000
Gross profit		230,000

From the cost accounts, the following information has been extracted:

Control account balances at 1st January:	£
Raw material stores	49,500
Work-in-progress	60,100
Finished goods	115,400
Transactions for the quarter:	£
Raw materials issued	104,800
Cost of goods produced	222,500
Cost of goods sold	212,100
Loss of materials damaged by flood (insurance claim pending)	2,400

A notional rent of £4,000 per month has been charged in the cost accounts. Production overhead was absorbed at the rate of 185% of direct wages.

You are required to:

a. prepare the following control accounts in the cost ledger: raw materials stores; work-in-progress; finished goods; production overhead;

b. prepare a statement reconciling the gross profit as per the cost accounts and the financial accounts;

c. comment on the possible accounting treatment(s) of the under- or over-absorption of production overhead, assuming that the financial year of the company is 1st January to 31st December.

(CIMA, Cost Accounting 1)

A10.8 a. Describe briefly the purpose of the;'wages control account'.

b. A manufacturing company has approximately 600 weekly paid direct and indirect production workers. It incurred the following costs and deductions relating to the payroll for the week ended 2 May:

	£	£
Gross wages		180,460
Deductions:		
Employees' national insurance	14,120	
Employees' pension fund contributions	7,200	
Income Tax (PAYE)	27,800	
Court order retention's	1,840	
Trade union subscriptions	1,200	
Private health care contributions	6,000	
Total deductions		58,160
Net wages paid		122,300

The employer's national insurance contribution for the week was £18,770.

From the wages analysis the following information was extracted:

	Direct workers £	Indirect workers £
Paid for ordinary time	77,460	38,400
Overtime wages at normal hourly rates	16,800	10,200
Overtime premium (treat as overhead)	5,600	3,400
Shift premiums/allowances	8,500	4,500
Capital work-in-progress expenditure*	–	2,300*
Statutory sick pay	5,700	3,300
Paid for idle time	4,300	–
	118,360	62,100

* Work done by building maintenance workers concerning floor area for a warehouse extension.

You are required to show journal entries to indicate clearly how each item should be posted into the accounts

    i.   from the payroll, and

    ii.   from the wages Control account to other accounts, based on the wages analysis.

Note: Narrations for the journal entries are not required.

(CIMA Cost Accounting)

A10.9   V Ltd operates interlocking financial and cost accounts. The following balances were in the cost ledger at the beginning of a month, the month (Month 12) of the financial year:

	Dr.	Cr.
Raw material stock control A/c	£28,944	
Finished goods stock control A/c	£77,168	
Financial ledger control A/c		£106,112

There is no work in progress at the end of each month.

21,600 kilos of the single raw material were in stock at the beginning of Month 12. Purchases and issues during the month were as follows:

Purchases:

7th,   17,400 kilos at £1.35 per kilo
20th,   19,800 kilos at £1.35 per kilo

Issues:
1st,   7,270 kilos
8th,   8,120 kilos
15th,   8,080 kilos
22nd, 9,115 kilos

A weighted average price per kilo (to four decimal places of a £) is used to value issues of raw material to production. A new average price is determined after each material purchase, and issues are charged out in total to the nearest £.

Costs of labour and overhead incurred during Month 12 were £35,407. Production of the company's single product was 17,150 units.

Stocks of finished goods were:

Beginning of Month 12, 16,960 units.

End of Month 12, 17,080 units.

Transfers from finished goods stock on sale of the product are made on a FIFO basis.

Required:

a.   Prepare the raw material stock control account, and the finished goods stock control account, for Month 12. (Show detailed workings to justify the summary entries made in the accounts.)

b.   Explain the purpose of the financial ledger control account.

(ACCA Cost & Management Accounting, part question)

A10.10 Your organisation operates separate financial and cost accounts. The Cost Accountant tells you that the financial profit has been determined as £75,000.

You are also told the following:

    i.   Debenture interest of £13,000 was paid during the year.

    ii.   Rent of £25,000 was received during the year.

    iii. There was a write off of goodwill amounting to £20,000.

    iv. Machinery that had a net book value of £15,000 was sold for £21,000.

    v.   A notional rent charge of £14,000 was charged in respect of the Company's premises.

    vi. Discounts allowed amounted to £7,000 and discounts received amounted to £5,000.

vii. The cost accounts included overheads recovered on the basis of £25 per machine hour. 8,000 machine hours were worked and the actual overhead incurred was £220,000.

viii. The financial accounts use first in first out to value material, whilst the cost accounts charge materials out on a last in first out basis. This has given the following stock values:

	Financial Accounts £	Cost Accounts £
Opening stock of raw materials	16,000	21,000
Opening stock of finished goods	47,000	42,000
Closing stock of raw materials	27,000	34,000
Closing stock of finished goods	39,000	40,000

Required:

b. Using the above data determine the costing profit for the Cost Accountant.

(AAT Cost Accounting & Budgeting, part question)

Exercises and examination questions without answers

Exercises

B10.1 The following balances were calculated for December 31st and January 31st.

	Balance at December 31st	Balance at January 31st
Stores Control A/c	54,192	51,282
W-l-P Control A/c	17,803	22,607
Finished Goods Control A/c	34,522	29,602

The following data relates to transactions in January.

	£
Material purchases	65,800
Direct labour	29,920
Indirect labour	11,860
Indirect material to production cost centres	2,790
Indirect production expenses	22,440

Production overhead is absorbed at 120% of direct wages. Prepare the three control accounts (Stores, W-l-P and Finished Goods) for January showing the production cost of goods sold and over/under absorption of production overhead.

B10.2 The profit in the financial accounts was £23,280. Examination of the cost and financial accounts showed the following differences .

	Cost Accounts	Financial Accounts
Stock Valuations:		
Opening	43,286	37,520
Closing	39,580	34,280
Profit on sale of asset	–	2,530
Dividends received		4,110
Depreciation	13,530	11,200
Imputed interest	2,100	–

What is the profit of the Cost Accounts?

B10.3 For a period a profit of £18,286 was shown in the financial accounts.

Examination of the Cost Accounts and the Financial Accounts showed the following differences:

	Cost Accounts £	Financial Accounts £
Depreciation	10,168	8,521
Profit on sale of asset	–	2,580
Stock valuations: opening	23,257	21,446
closing	19,275	20,510

What profit was shown in the Cost Accounts?

Examination Questions

B10.4 M limited operates an integral accounting system and, based on the data given below, you are required to prepare the relevant ledger accounts for the month ended 31st October and a trial balance at that date.

Trial Balance at 1st October

	£	£ £
Capital and reserves		1,210,000
Debtors	60,000	
Creditors		75,000
Plant and machinery	240,000	
Provision for depreciation, plant and machinery		60,000
Freehold buildings	400,000	
Stocks:		
Raw materials	350,000	
Work in process:		
direct materials	35,300	
direct wages	24,200	
production overhead	60,500	120,000
Work in process 2:		
direct materials	63,500	
direct wages	34,600	
production overhead	51,900	
	150,000	
Finished goods	30,000	
Bank	31,000	
Sales		500,000
Cost of sales	370,000	
Abnormal loss	4,500	
Administration overhead	60,000	
Selling and distribution overhead	40,000	
Production overhead over/under absorbed		10,500
	1,855,500	1,855,500

Transactions for the month ended 31st October, included:

	£
Direct wages incurred:	
process 1	42,400
process 2	64,600
Direct wages paid	100,000
Production salaries paid	85,000
Production expenses paid	125,000

	£
Paid to creditors	165,000
Received from debtors	570,000
Administration overhead paid	54,000
Selling and distribution overhead paid	42,000
Materials purchased on credit	105,000
Materials returned to suppliers	5,000
Materials issued to:	
process 1	68,000
process 2	22,000
Goods sold on credit:	
at sales price	550,000
at cost	422,400

	Direct Materials	Direct Wages
	£	£
Abnormal loss in:		
process 1	800	600
process 2	1,400	800
Transfer from process 1 to process 2	76,300	47,400
Transfer from process 2	273,900	69,800

Provision for depreciation of plant and machinery is on a straight line method at 20% per annum on cost.

(CIMA, Cost Accounting 2)

B10.5 Using the information given below for the month of October, in respect of A Limited, you are required to:

a. write up the integrated accounts;

b. prepare a trading and profit and loss account for October;

c. compile a trial balance as at 31st October;

d. comment on the difference in the level of stocks and state which administration cost will be increased following the changed levels of stocks.

1. List of balances at 1st October:

	£000
Fixed assets - production	1,000
Provision for depreciation of fixed assets	400
Material stores control	100
Work-in-progress stock	50
Finished goods stock	20
Debtors	600
Creditors	290
Creditors for P.A.Y.E. and national insurance	85
Wages control – credit balance (accrued direct wages)	20
Cash	5
Bank - overdrawn	300
Share capital	600
Profit and loss appropriation: credit balance	80

2. Transactions for the month of October:

	£000
Received from debtors	380
Paid to creditors	170
Expenses paid by cheque: production	60
administration	40
selling	30
Bank interest on overdraft	10
Paid to creditor for P.A.Y.E. and national insurance	60
Depreciation of fixed assets (for production)	25
Materials received and invoiced	110
Materials price variance, favourable, extracted as materials are received	10
Materials issued to production, at standard prices	80
Materials issued to production maintenance	20
Transfers from work-in-progress to finished goods	230
Sales on credit	310
Sales for cash	10
Production cost of goods sold	200

	Gross	PAYE/ Nat. Ins.	
	£000	£000	£000
Direct wages paid	86	20	66
Direct wages accrued	22	–	22
Indirect wages paid (production)	24	4	20
Administrative staff salaries paid	12	4	8
Selling staff salaries paid	20	4	16
Employer's contribution, national insurance: production			9
administration			3
selling			2
Cash paid into bank			13

Production overhead is absorbed on the basis of 150% on direct wages; any under or over absorption is transferred to profit and loss account. Administration and selling costs are not absorbed into product costs.

(CIMA, Cost Accounting 1)

B10.6 You are required to:

a. compare and contrast the operation of integrated accounts with a system where the financial and cost accounts are kept separately, stating two advantages and two disadvantages of a system of integrated accounts;

b. draw a diagram or flowchart to show the flow of accounting entries within an integrated system, where standard costing is not used, for the following transactions;

    i. purchase of raw materials, on credit terms;

    ii. issue to production of part of the consignment received in (i) above;

    iii. cash payment of wages to direct workers and to indirect workers associated with production;

    iv. electricity for production purposes, obtained on credit;

    v. depreciation of machinery used for production;

    vi. absorption of production overhead, using a predetermined rate.

CIMA (Cost Accounting 1)

B10.7 A company manufactures a single product from one basic raw material. The standard purchase price of the raw material is £3.50 per kilo, and standard usage is five kilos per unit of finished product. Material price variance is identified on purchase of raw material. Actual direct labour costs and production overhead absorbed are charged to units of finished product based upon weighted average costs. The production overhead absorption rate is 200% of direct labour cost.

Balances in the company's integrated accounts at the beginning of a period included:

Raw materials:
    Direct materials, 5,240 kilos
    Indirect materials, £1,484

Production overhead:
    Accrued at the end of the previous period, £3,840

Work in Progress:
    Direct material, £4,550
    Direct labour and production overhead, £1,950
    260 units, complete as to direct material, 50% complete as to direct labour and production overhead.

Finished goods:
    1,470 units, £47,775.

Costs incurred during the period were:

Raw materials purchased:
    Direct material, 7,600 kilos, £26,904
    Indirect materials, £2,107.

Raw materials issued:
    Direct material, 7,460 kilos.
    Indirect materials, £1,963.

Production wage paid:

	Direct workers £	Indirect workers £
Gross	8,670	2,235
Employees' deductions	2,688	693
Net	5,982	1,542

The cost of the productive time of direct workers was £7,950. The balance of the wages paid to direct workers is charged to production overhead.

Other production overhead incurred: £9,252

Period sales: 1,520 units.

Production output of the single product during the period was:

Completed and transferred to finished goods stock, 1,450 units.

Closing work in progress 310 units, completed as to direct material, 60% complete as to direct labour and production overhead

A physical stock check of the basic raw material at the end of the period revealed that 5,310 kilos remained in stock. Production overhead to be accrued totalled £4,170.

Required:

Prepare accounting entries for the period in the following accounts:
    i.   raw material stock,
    ii.   production wages,
    iii. production overhead,
    iv.   work in progress,
    v.   finished goods stock.

(ACCA Cost & management Accounting)

B10.8 XY Limited commenced trading on 1 February with fully paid issued share capital of £500,000, Fixed Assets of £275,000 and Cash at Bank of £225,000. By the end of April, the fopllowing transactions had taken place:

1. Purchases on credit from suppliers amounted to £572,500 of which £525,000 was raw materials and £47,500 was for items classified as production overhead.

2. Wages incurred for all staff were £675,000, represented by cash paid £500,000 and wage deductions of £175,000 in respect of income tax etc.

3. Payments were made by cheque for the following overhead costs:

	£
Production	20,000
Selling	40,000
Administration	25,000

4. Issues of raw materials were £180,000 to Department A, £192,500 to Department B and £65,000 for production overhead items.

5. Wages incurred were analysed to functions as follows:

	£
Work-in-progress - Department A	300,000
Work-in-progress - Department B	260,000
Production overhead	42,500
Selling overhead	47,500
Administration overhead	25,000
	675,000

6. Production overhead absorbed in the period by Department A was £110,000 and by Department B £120,000.

7. The production facilities, when not in use, were patrolled by guards from a security firm and £26,000 was owing for this service. £39,000 was also owed to a firm of management consultants which advises on production procedures; invoices for these two services are to be entered into the accounts.

8. The cost of finished goods completed was

	Department A £	Department B £
Direct labour	290,000	155,000
Direct materials	175,000	185,000
Production overhead	105,000	115,000
	570,000	555,000

9. Sales on credit were £870,000 and the cost of those sales was £700,000.

10. Depreciation of productive plant and equipment was £15,000.

11. cash received from debtors totalled £520,000.

12. Payments to creditors were £150,000.

You are required

a. to open the ledger accounts at the commencement of the trading period;

b. using intergrated accounting, to record the transactions for the three months ended 30 April;

c. to prepare, in vertical format, for presentation to management,

    i. a profit statement for the period;

    ii the balance sheet at 30 April.

(CIMA Cost Accounting)

11: Costing methods – introduction

1. Topics covered in this chapter:

> 1. Introduction to Costing Methods
> 2. Specific order costing
> 3. Operation or Unit Costing

2. What is a costing method?

A costing method is a method of costing which is designed to suit the way goods are processed or manufactured or the way that services are provided. It follows therefore that each firm will have a costing method which has unique features. Nevertheless there will be recognisably common features of the costing systems of firms who are broadly in the same line of business.

Conversely firms employing substantially different manufacturing methods, for example a food processors and a jobbing engineering factory, will have distinctly different costing methods. It must be clearly understood that whatever costing method is employed, the basic costing principles relating to analysis, allocation and apportionment will be used.

3. Categories of costing methods

There are two broad categories of product costing methods, namely specific order costing and continuous operation/process costing.

a. Specific order costing

This can be defined as;

'The basic costing method applicable where the work consists of separate contracts, jobs or batches.' *Terminology*.

In most cases the job or contract is the cost unit and frequently, but not always, the jobs or contracts are different from each other. The main sub-divisions of specific order costing are

i. Job costing

ii. Contract costing

iii. Batch costing

b. Continuous operation/process costing (sometimes called unit costing)

This can be defined as;

'The basic costing method applicable where goods or services result from a sequence of conditions or repetitive operations or processes to which costs are charged before being averaged over the units produced during the period.' *Terminology*.

The key feature of this definition is that operation (or unit) costing seeks to establish the average cost per unit during a period for a number of identical cost units. The main sub-divisions of operation costing are:

i. Process costing including Joint Product and By-product

ii. Service/function costing. This type of costing although not relating to production cost units uses similar principles whereby an average cost is established per unit of service. For example, an average cost per meal supplied could be calculated for the canteen which is a service cost centre.

These categories and sub-divisions are shown in figure 11.1.

Note to Figure 11.1

The dotted line indicates an area of overlap between the two major categories. Although each batch is separate and identifiable and may be different from any other batch, within a given batch there will be a number of identical cost units over which the total batch costs will be averaged. Thus batch costing may have some of the characteristics of both specific order and process costing.

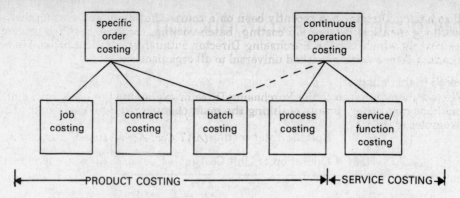

Figure 11.1 Costing Methods – Categories and sub-divisions

4. Costing methods and costing principles

An important difference between the principles of costing in relation to Specific Order Costing and Operation Costing is that, with Operation Costing, all costs ie, Labour, Materials and Overheads are allocated or apportioned to a *cost centre* from which these costs are shared out over the cost units produced. This differs from Specific Order Costing where labour and materials may be able to be *directly* charged to a *cost unit* with only overheads having to be allocated or apportioned to a cost centre before sharing the costs over cost units.

5. Costing methods and costing techniques

It must be emphasised that whatever costing method is used, it can be combined with any of the costing techniques if deemed appropriate. Thus, for example, a Process Costing system could utilise the technique of either, Total Absorption costing or Marginal costing or Standard Costing or Activity Based Costing.

6. Summary

a. Costing methods are designed to suit the method of manufacture or processing used by the firm.

b. Whatever method if used, it will employ basic costing principles relating to classification, analysis, allocation and apportionment.

c. The two main categories of costing methods are: specific order costing and continuous operation (or unit) costing.

d. Specific order costing can be sub-divided into: Job Costing, Contract Costing, and Batch Costing.

e. Continuous Operation or Unit Costing can be sub-divided into: Service Costing, and Process Costing which includes Joint-Product and By-Product costing.

f. Whatever is deemed the most appropriate costing technique, eg, Marginal Costing, Standard Costing etc, can be used with any of the costing methods.

7. Point to note

Different parts of the same firm may require different costing methods. It is essential to relate the costing method to the particular activity being costed.

Student self-testing

Self Review Questions

1. What is a costing method ? (2)

2. What are the five main types of costing methods? (3)

3 . What is the relationship of a costing technique to a costing method ? (4)

Examination question with answer

A11.1 You have been promoted to the position of Assistant Cost Accountant within your organisation. On the first day of your new appointment you receive two tasks; one from the Purchasing Director and one from the Cost Accountant.

The Purchasing Director has recently been on a course that discussed costing methods. Amongst the methods mentioned were job costing, batch costing, contract costing, process costing and service costing which left the Purchasing Director enthusiastic but confused. He has asked why there cannot be one costing method universal to all organisations,

Required:

a. Write a memorandum to the Purchasing Director explaining the need for the different costing methods mentioned, briefly outlining the main characteristics of each method and giving two examples of its use.

(AAT Cost Accounting & Budgeting, part question)

12: Costing methods – job and batch costing

1. Topics covered in this chapter:

> 1. Job costing defined
> 2. Procedure for job costing
> 3. Accounting for job costing
> 4. Batch costing
> 5. ABC and job/batch costing

2. Job costing – definition

This is defined as follows.

Job costing

'A form of specific order costing: the attribution of costs to jobs'. *Terminology*

3. Prerequisites for job costing

The main purposes of job costing are to establish the profit or loss on each job and to provide a valuation of W-I-P. To do this a considerable amount of clerical work is needed and to ensure an effective and workable system. the following factors are necessary:

a. A sound system of production control.

b. Comprehensive works documentation. Typically this includes: works order and/or operation tickets, bill of materials and/or materials requisitions, jig and tool requisitions, etc.

c. An appropriate time booking system using either time sheets or piecework tickets.

d. A well organised basis to the costing system with clearly defined cost centres, good labour analysis, appropriate overhead absorption rates and a relevant materials issue pricing system.

4. Typical procedures in a jobbing concern

Prior to examining the costing system it is necessary first to consider the typical flow of administrative procedures which ensure a job is manufactured correctly, delivered on time and charged for. An outline is shown in Figure 12.1.

5. Job costing procedures

The main objective is to charge all costs incurred to the particular job. The usual means by which this is done by creating a Job Cost Card (frequently just called the Job Card). The Job Cost Cards in total comprise the firm's work-in-progress and the detailed entries to the job cards would be debited in total to the work-in-progress account. The following diagram shows the major steps in a typical Job Costing process.

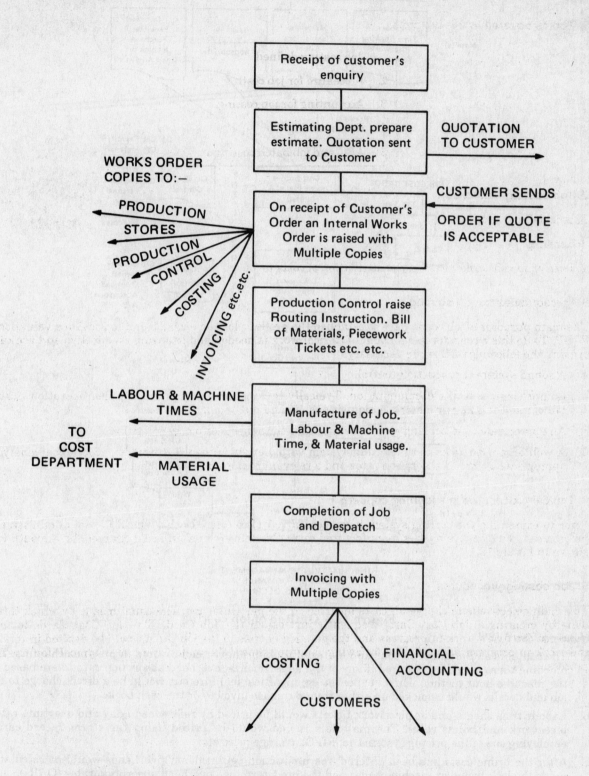

Figure 12.1 Typical non-costing procedures in a jobbing concern

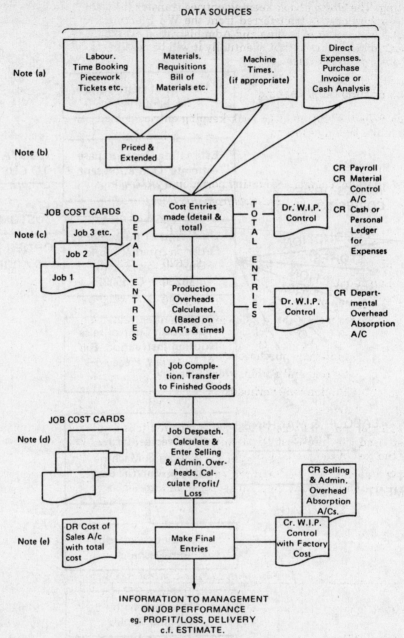

Figure 12.2 Outline of job costing

Notes on figure 12.2.

a. The contents and origin of Labour and Material bookings have been covered in previous chapters. The machine times would be required if any of the departmental overhead absorption rates were based on the machine hour method. Direct expenses eg, royalties, tool hire etc, would be a direct charge to the job and details would be picked up either from purchase invoices or the cash book.

b. Labour time sheets and/or piecework tickets would be priced by reference to day and overtime rates, piecework and bonus rates. The materials issued would be priced using the stores record cards, employing one of the pricing systems, ie, FIFO, average price etc.

c. After the prime costs had been entered, the production departments' overheads would be calculated using the labour and/or machine times and the predetermined overhead absorption rates (OARs).

d. Until a job is despatched, it would normally be valued in the Work-in-Progress account at factory or works cost only. On despatch (or, in some systems, transfer to finished goods), the works cost would be loaded with an appropriate amount of selling and administration overheads. Any delivery costs can be charged to the job, the total cost established and the profit or loss calculated.

e. The individual Job Cost Cards will be retained and used as a basis for management information and future estimating. The closing book-keeping entries transfer the total cost of jobs despatched to cost of sales and the Factory cost is transferred from the W-I-P account (or in some systems the Finished Goods account). The amount of Selling and Administration overheads charged to jobs is credited to the overhead absorption account, so that eventually it will be possible to establish whether there has been under or over absorption of overheads.

6. Illustration of job costing book-keeping

The example which follows illustrates the book-keeping entries depicted in Figure 12.2 and shows typical flows of information in a jobbing concern.

Example 1

The data below relate to a single accounting period in a jobbing engineering works.

Extracts from Job Cost Cards

	Opening W-I-P	Charged during period	Closing W-I-P
Materials	£10620	£32840	£12630
Labour	15250	53260	16170
Production overheads	10830	33520	9260

The financial accountant supplied the following information relating to the same period:

	£
Materials purchased	39150
Selling and admin. overheads	12780
Production overheads	30620
Sales	146330

The opening stock of material was £9200. All completed jobs are invoiced immediately to customers and you are advised that the Cost Department recover selling and administrative overheads at the rate of 10% of the cost of completed jobs.

Using the above information it is required to write up the Cost Ledger and prepare a Costing P & L A/C for the period assuming that the firm operates an interlocking system with separate financial and cost accounts.

Solution

Cost Ledger

Financial Ledger Control A/C

		Balance B/F	45900	
Sales	146330	Purchases	39150	
		S&D	12780	
Balance C/F	53570	Prod. ohds	30620	
		Wages	53260	
		Profit	18190	
	£199900		£199900	
		Balance	53570	

W-I-P Control

Balance B/F	36700		
Material	32840	Cost of Sales	118260
Wages	53260	Balance	38060
Prod. ohds.	33520		
	156320		156320
Balance B/F	38060		

Stores Control

Balance	9200	W-I-P	32840
F.L control	39150	Balance	15510
	48350		48350
Balance	15510		

Production Overhead Control

F. L. control	30620	W-I-P	33520
Ohd. Adj.	2900		
	33520		33520

Wages Control

F. L. control	53260	W-I-P	53260

S&D Overhead Control

F. L. control	12780	Cost of Sales	11826
		Ohd. Adj.	954
	12780		12780

Cost of Sales

W-I-P	118260		
S&D	11826	P&L	130086
	130086		130086

Overhead Adjustment

S&D ohd	954	Prod. ohd	2900
P&L	1946		
	2900		2900

Costing P&L

Cost of Sales	130086	Sales	146330
Profit	18190	Ohd. Adj	1946
	148276		148276

7. Job cost card

A typical job card is shown (Fig. 12.3). It is suitable for relatively small jobs or as the summary card for larger jobs which might have supporting schedules relating to Material, Labour and Overheads.

8. Batch costing

This is a form of costing which applies where a quantity of identical articles are manufactured as a batch. The most common forms of batch are:

a. where a customer orders a quantity of identical items, or

b. where an internal manufacturing order is raised for a batch of identical parts, sub-assemblies or products to replenish stocks.

In general the procedures for costing batches are similar to costing jobs. The batch would be treated as a job during manufacture and the costs collected as described previously in this chapter. On completion of the batch the cost per unit can be calculated by dividing the total batch cost by the number of good units produced. Batch costing is common in the engineering component industry, footwear and clothing manufacture and similar industries.

9. Illustration of job/batch costing

The following example shows a typical cost build-up for a batch of similar parts and illustrates typical job costing procedures and the subsequent calculation of the unit cost and profit.

JOB COST CARD																Job No.			
Customer						Customers Order No.							Start Date						
Job Description													Delivery Date						
Estimate Ref.						Invoice No.							Despatch Note No.						
Quoted Price						Invoice Price													

(Table continues with sections: Material, Labour, Overheads, Expenses, Job Cost Summary)

Material

| Date | Req. No. | Qty. | Price | Cost £ | Cost p |

Labour

| Date | Lab Anal Ref. | Cost Ctre | Hrs. | Rate | Bonus | Cost £ | Cost p | M/c Hrs. | OAR | Cost £ | Cost p |

Overheads

Total C/F (Material), Total C/F (Labour), Total C/F (Overheads)

Expenses

| Date | Ref. | Description | Cost £ | Cost p |

Job Cost Summary

	Actual £	Actual p	Estimate £	Estimate p
Direct Materials B/F				
Direct Expenses B/F				
Direct Labour B/F				
= Prime Cost				
Factory Overheads B/F				
= Factory Cost				
Selling & Admin. Overheads % on Factory Cost				
= Total Cost				
Invoice Price				
Job Profit/Loss				

Total C/F (Expenses)

Comments

Job Cost Card Completed by ....

Figure 12.3 Typical job cost card

Example 2

A company manufacturers small assemblies to order and has the following budgeted overheads for the year, based on normal activity levels.

Department	Budgeted Overheads £	Overhead Absorption Base
Blanking	18000	1500 labour hours
Machining	43000	2500 machine hours
Welding	20000	1800 labour hours
Assembly	15000	1000 labour hours

Selling and Administrative overheads are 20% of Factory cost.

An order for 250 assemblies type X 128 , made as Batch 5931, incurred the following costs:

Materials: £3107

Labour: 128 hours Blanking Shop at £5.25/hour
452 hours Machining Shop at £5.50/hour
90 hours Welding Shop at £5.25/hour
175 hours Assembly Shop at £4.80/hour

£525 was paid for the hire of special X-ray equipment for testing the welds. The time booking in the machine shop was 643 machine hours.

Calculate the total cost of the batch, the unit cost and the profit per assembly if the selling price was £150/assembly.

Solution

The first step is to calculate the overhead absorption rates for the production departments.

$$\text{Blanking} = \frac{£18000}{1500} = £12 \text{ OAR per labour hour}$$

$$\text{Machining} = \frac{£43000}{2500} = £17.2 \text{ OAR per machine hour}$$

$$\text{Welding} = \frac{£20000}{1800} = £11.1 \text{ OAR per labour hour}$$

$$\text{Assembly} = \frac{£15000}{1000} = £15 \text{ OAR per labour hour}$$

Total Cost – Batch No. 5931		£
Direct Material		3107
Direct Expense		525
	£	
Direct Labour	128 × 5.25	
	452 × 5.50	
	90 × 5.25	
	175 × 4.80	4470.5
= Prime Cost		£8102.5
Production Overheads Absorption		
	£	
Blanking	128 × 12	
Machining	643 × 17.2	
Welding	90 × 11.1	
Assembly	175 × 15	16219.6
= Factory Cost		£24322.1
+ Selling and Administrative overheads (20% of Factory Cost)	=	4864.42
= Total Cost		£29186.52

$$\text{Total Cost/unit} = \frac{£29186.52}{250} = £116.75$$

$$\text{Profit/unit} = \underline{\underline{£33.25}}$$

10. Using ABC for job/batch costing

Overheads can be charged to jobs or using either traditional labour or machine hour absorption rates or by using various cost drivers in ABC systems. If all jobs or batches were much the same and placed similar loads on support activities there would be little difference in the costs calculated by either method. Such uniformity is unlikely and jobs and batches do vary in the loads they place on production facilities and on support activities.

As a consequence, costs calculated by traditional methods and ABC system are likely to be different. The general effect is that more complex/diverse/small quantity production will tend to be costed higher using ABC as compared to traditionally calculated costs.

The following example illustrates the general principles:

Example 3

The following details have been recorded for 4 batches made in a period

Batch	A	B	C	D
Output in units	250	60	200	120
Cost per batch	£	£	£	£
Direct Material	1650	750	2100	900
Direct Labour	9200	1520	6880	2400
Labour hours per batch	1150	190	860	300

The total production overhead for the period has been analysed as follows:

	£
Machine related costs	14600
Materials handling & despatch	6800
Stores	8250
Inspection/Quality control	5850
Set-up	6200
Engineering support	8300
	50000

Cost drivers have been identified for the cost pools as follows:

Cost pool	Cost driver
Machine costs	Machine hours
Materials handling	Materials movements
Stores	Requisitions raised
Inspection	No. of inspections
Set-up	No. of set-ups
Engineering support	Engineering hours

The following cost driver volumes were recorded for the batches

Batch	A	B	C	D	Total
Machine hours per batch	520	255	610	325	1710
Material movements	180	70	205	40	495
Requisitions	40	21	43	26	130
Inspections	18	8	16	8	43
Set-ups	12	7	16	8	43
Engineering hours	65	38	52	35	190

Required:

a. The batch and unit costs using traditional costing based on a labour hour overhead absorption rate

b. the batch and unit costs using ABC

c. Compare the costs in (a) and (b)

d. Comment on the likely position if the firm uses cost-plus pricing.

Solution

a. Batch and unit costs using traditional overhead absorption based on labour hours.

$$\text{Labour hour OAR} = \frac{£50,000}{1150 + 190 + 860 + 300} = \textbf{£20 per hour}$$

Batch	A	B	C	D
Output (Units)	250	60	200	120
	£	£	£	£
Direct Material	1650	750	2100	900
Direct Labour	9200	1520	6880	2400
= Prime Cost	10850	2270	8980	3300
+ Overhead (Lab. hrs × OAR)	23000	3800	17200	6000
Total Batch Cost	33850	6070	26180	9300
Unit Cost	**135.40**	**101.17**	**130.9**	**77.50**

b. Batch and unit costs using ABC with various cost drivers.

Calculation of Cost Driver Rates

Cost Driver	*Cost Pool* Total number of cost driver	*Cost Driver Rate*
Machine hours	$\dfrac{£14600}{1710}$	£8.54 per mac. hour
Material movements	$\dfrac{£6800}{495}$	£13.74 per movement
Stores	$\dfrac{£8250}{130}$	£63.46 per requisition
Inspection	$\dfrac{£5850}{47}$	£124.47 per inspection
Set-ups	$\dfrac{£6200}{43}$	£144.19 per set-up
Engineering	$\dfrac{£8300}{190}$	£43.68 per hour

Batch unit costs using ABC

Batch		A		B		C		D
Quantity		250		60		200		120
		£		£		£		£
Prime cost		10850		2270		8980		3300
(+ overheads)								
Machine hrs @ £8.54	(520)	4441	(255)	2178	(610)	5209	(325)	2775
Movements @ £13.74	(180)	2473	(70)	962	(205)	2817	(40)	550
Requisitions @ £63.46	(40)	2538	(21)	1333	(43)	2729	(26)	1650
Inspections @ £124.47	(18)	2240	(8)	996	(16)	1992	(8)	996
Set-ups @ £144.19	(12)	1730	(7)	1009	(16)	2307	(8)	1153
Eng. hrs @ £43.68	(65)	2839	(38)	1660	(52)	2271	(35)	1529
= Total overheads		16261		8138		17325		8653
Total Batch cost		27111		10408		26305		11953
Unit Cost		**108.44**		**173.47**		**131.52**		**99.61**

c.　The unit costs compared

Batch A		Batch B		Batch C		Batch D	
Tradit-ional	ABC	Tradit-ional	ABC	Tradit-ional	ABC	Tradit-ional	ABC
£	£	£	£	£	£	£	£
135.40	108.44	101.17	173.47	130.9	131.52	77.50	99.61

It will be seen that in this example there are significant differences between the costs using the two systems. Batch C's costs are broadly the same but the costs of Batch B and D are much higher using ABC, whereas Batch A is lower.

Study of the usage of support overheads by the batches shows that Batches B and D have a higher relative usage of resources so incur greater overhead costs using ABC. Because the traditional method absorbs overheads on labour hours these differences in usage are effectively ignored. It is this feature which, it is claimed, makes product costs more accurate when ABC is used.

d.　Cost-plus pricing is a pricing method where a margin (say 40%) is added to costs to produce the selling price. Cost-plus pricing is widely used in many jobbing and batch production firms.

If the firm in the example uses cost-plus pricing then the quoted selling prices will differ considerably depending on whether the traditional or ABC method was used to calculate costs. If it is accepted that the ABC costs are the more accurate then serious errors in pricing may occur if the traditional costs were used as the basis. This would mean that, based on traditional costs, Batch A would be over-priced and Batches B and D under-priced.

In effect if pricing decisions were based on the less accurate costs then Batch A products would be subsidising Batch B and Batch D products and, in the long run, the firm would tend to receive more orders for the under-priced B and D products. This would be likely to lead to declining profits as these products place relatively higher demands on resources which should be reflected in higher prices.

11. Summary

a.　Job costing is employed where work is done to customer's requirements, eg in a factory or workshop.

b.　For job costing to be effective there must be a good system of production control, works documentation, material and labour booking.

c.　All costs incurred must be charged to the job, usually on to a job cost card.

d .　The job cost cards in total form the firm' s work-in progress .

e.　The detail entries to the job cards would be debited in total to the Work-in-Progress account.

f.　Prime costs are gathered from labour and material bookings on the shop floor and, in the case of expenses, from invoice or cash book analysis. Overheads can be charged to jobs *either* by the traditional methods using labour or machine hour absorption rates *or* by various cost driver rates using ABC. At present, overhead attribution by labour or machine hour rates is more common but this may change in the future if the use of ABC becomes more widespread.

g.　Batch costing is very similar to job costing and is used where a batch of identical units are manufactured. Costs are gathered as for job costing and when the batch is completed, the total cost is divided by the number of good units made to establish the unit cost.

12. Points to note

a.　Although job costing could be combined with any cost technique, for example standard costing or marginal costing, it is normally used with the total absorption technique. All the illustrations and narrative in this chapter have been based on the use of total absorption costing.

b.　A realistic attitude must be taken to job costing. If there are numerous, small value jobs it is unlikely that the full process described in this chapter would be followed. Instead a General Jobbing account might be used which would be charged with the costs of small jobs and credited with the selling prices. Some loss of control and information are, however, inevitable consequences of this procedure.

Student self-testing

Self Review Questions

1. Define job costing. (2)

2 . What factors need to be present before a job costing system can operate efficiently? (3)

3. What is a job cost card? (5) & (7)

4. How is it completed? (5)

5. How does batch costing differ from job costing? (8)

Exercises and examination questions with answers

Exercises

A12.1 Batch No.X37 incurred the following costs:

Dept   A   420 labour hours at £3.50

             B   686 labour hours at £3.00

Direct Materials £3,280

Factory Overheads are absorbed on labour hours and the rates are £8 per hour for Dept A and £5 per hour for Dept B.

The firm uses a cost plus system for setting selling prices and expects a 25% gross profit (Sales Value minus Factory Cost).

Administration overheads are absorbed as 10% of selling price.

Assuming that 1,000 units were produced in Batch No. X37:

a. Calculate the selling price per unit.

b. The total amount of administrative overheads recovered by Batch No. 37.

c. The notional net profit per unit.

A12.2 A firm deals with a variety of jobs which are separately costed. An investigation has shown that for a number of the smaller jobs the cost of calculating the job costs represents up to $\frac{1}{3}$ of the total cost of the job.

You are required to discuss this problem.

A12.3 What would be the likely effects of absorbing all overheads in a firm on labour hours when some jobs contain mostly labour and little machining whilst others use many machine hours but little labour? The firm uses a cost-plus system for pricing jobs.

Examination questions

A12.4 Suggest how the following items should be treated, in order to determine appropriate product costs, in a company employing a marginal historic batch costing system and outline the reasons for each of your recommended treatments:

a. Cost of products scrapped at final inspection.

b. The salary of a foreman in a production department.

c. Carriage inwards.

d. Cost of setting up time.

e. The cost of the power generating plant providing heat light and power throughout the factory.

f. Salesmens' salaries and travelling expenses.

(ACCA, Costing)

A12.5 The management of a company manufacturing electrical components is considering introducing an historic batch costing system into their factory.

Required:

a. Outline the information and procedures required in order to obtain the actual direct material cost of each batch of components manufactured.

b. Identify the elements which could make up a direct operative's gross wage and for each element explain, with supporting reasons, whether it should be regarded as part of the prime cost of the components manufactured.

(ACCA, Costing)

A12.6 A factory with three departments uses a single production overhead absorption rate expressed as a percentage of direct wages cost. It has been suggested that departmental overhead absorption rates would result in more accurate job costs. Set out below are the budgeted and actual data for the previous period, together with information relating to job No. 657.

Hours in thousands

	Direct wages £000's	Direct labour	Machine	Production overhead £000's
Budget:				
Department: A	25	10	40	120
B	100	50	10	30
C	25	25	–	75
Total:	150	85	50	225
Actual:				
Department: A	30	12	45	130
B	80	45	14	28
C	30	30	–	80
Total:	140	87	59	238

During this period job No. 657 incurred the actual costs and actual times in the departments as shown below:

	Direct material £	Direct wages £	Direct labour hour	Machine hours
Department: A	120	100	20	40
B	60	60	40	10
C	10	10	10	–

After adding production overhead to prime cost, one third is added to production cost for gross profit. This assumes that a reasonable profit is earned after deducting administration, selling and distribution costs.

You are required to:

a. calculate the current overhead absorption rate;

b. using the rate obtained in (a) above, calculate the production overhead charged to job No. 657 and state the production cost and expected gross profit on this job;

c. i. comment on the suggestion that departmental overhead absorption rates would result in more accurate job costs; and

  ii. compute such rates, briefly explaining your reason for each rate;

d. using the rates calculated in (c) (ii) above, show the overhead, by department and in total, that would apply to job No. 657;

e. show the over/under absorption, by department and in total, for the period using:

  i. the current rate in your answer to (a) above, and

  ii. your suggested rates in your answer to (c) (ii) above.

(CIMA, Cost Accounting 1)

A12.7 You have just taken up the position as the first full-time accountant for a jobbing engineering company. Previously the accounting work had been undertaken by the company's auditors who had produced the following summarised profit and loss statement for the financial year which ended on 31 March of this year:

	£	£	£
Sales			2,400,000
Direct material		1,000,000	
Direct labour - Grinding Dept	200,000		
Direct labour - Finishing Dept	260,000		
		460,000	
Production overhead - Grinding	175,000		
Production overhead - Finishing	208,000		
		383,000	
Administration costs		118,500	
Selling costs		192,000	
			2,153,500
Net profit			£246,500

The sales manager is currently negotiating a price for an enquiry for a job which has been allocated number 878 and he has been given the following information by his staff:

Preferred price to obtain a return of $16\frac{2}{3}$ % on selling price   £22,656

Lowest acceptable price   £18,880

These prices have been based on the following estimated costs for proposed job 878:

			£
Direct material			9,000
Direct labour - Grinding dept:	400 hours @ £5	2,000	
Direct labour - Finishing dept:	300 hours @ £6	1,800	
			3,800
			12,800
Add 47.5% to cover all other costs			6,080
Total cost			£18,880

The sales manager seeks your advice about the validity of the method he is using to quote for Job 878.

The company is currently busy with a fairly full order book but the Confederation of British Industry has forecast that a recession is imminent for the engineering industry.

You are required, as the accountant,

a. to criticise the method adopted for estimating the cost which are used as the basis for quoting prices for jobs;

b. to suggest a better method of estimating job costs and to calculate a revised job cost and price, based on the information available, to give to the sales manager;

c. to suggest how you would propose to improve the accounting information to assist with controlling costs and providing information for pricing purposes.

(CIMA Cost Accounting)

A12.8 A company provides a building repairs and maintenance service. A job costing system is in operation in order to identify the cost, and profit, of each job carried out. Several jobs are in progress at any one time. One such job is Job 126, which was started and completed in the month just ended.

Quantities of Material P were issued from stores to the job, as well as other materials as required. Raw material issues are priced at the end of each month on a weighted average basis. Overtime is worked as necessary to meet the general requirements of the business, and is paid at a premium of 30% over the basic rate for direct personnel. The basic rate is £6.00 per hour. Overheads are absorbed into job costs at the end of each month at an actual rate per direct labour hour. Idle time, material wastage, and rectification work after jobs are completed, are a normal feature of the business. Idle time is not expected to exceed 2% of direct hours charged to jobs. Wastage is not expected to exceed 1% of the cost of materials issued to jobs. Rectification costs are not expected to exceed 1.5% of direct costs. All such costs are not charged as direct costs of individual jobs.

Information concerning Job 126 is as follows:

Issues of Material P were 960 kilos. Issues of other materials were costed at £2,030. Of the total materials issued to the job, wastage cost £42 and materials used for rectification cost £33. The hours of direct personnel working on the job were 496. These included 37 overtime hours, 10 hours of idle time, and 12 hours spent on rectification work.

Information for all work carried out on jobs during the month is as follows:

Opening stock of Material p was 3,100 kilos, valued at £5,594. Purchases during the month were 3,500 kilos at £1.81 per kilo, and 3,800 kilos at £1.82 per kilo. 7,060 kilos of Material P were issued from stores to jobs, including 60 kilos which were subsequently wasted and 340 kilos which were used for rectification work.

Other materials issued to jobs were costed at £19,427 (including £236 wastage and £197 rectification).

Hours of direct personnel paid at basic rate were 3,640, with a further 290 hours paid at overtime rate. These total hours include 82 hours of idle time and 37 hours spent on rectification work.

Other costs incurred in the month were:

Supervisory labour	£3,760
Depreciation	£585
Cleaning materials	£63
Stationery and telephone	£275
Rent and rates	£940
Vehicle running costs	£327
Other administration	£688

Required:

a. prepare a statement of the costs associated with Job 126.

b. Provide, and comment upon, any additional information that may be useful in controlling the business.

(ACCA Cost & Management Accounting 1)

Exercises and examination questions without answers

Exercises

B12.1 Prepare the factory cost of Job No. 589 using the data below, where appropriate. Justify the figures you calculate.

Job No. 589.

Direct Material issues £235.

Note: The issues have been priced using the Average Price System as is normal in the firm but it has been brought to your notice that the replacement cost is £265.

Labour Costs	
Machining	30 hours at £4 per hour basic and
	4 hours at time and a half
Assembly	14 hours at £2 per hour
Finishing	8 hours at £2.5 per hour

Extract from the Overhead Analysis

	Department		
	Machining	Assembly	Finishing
	£	£	£
Actual overheads last year	125,296	83,781	37,530
Budgeted overheads this year	135,000	85,000	42,500
Actual labour hours last year	4,216	4,481	1,853
Budgeted labour hour this year	4,100	4,500	1,950
Machine hours last year	6,560	202	185
Budgeted machine hours this year	6,600	180	210

B12.2 During a period work was started on three jobs details of which were as follows:

	Job 1001	Job 1002	Job 1003
	£	£	£
Material Issues	850	625	350
Direct Wages	2,830	1,975	1,280
Direct Expenses	125	350	50

£75 of materials issued to Job 1002 were returned to stores and £25 of materials were transferred from Job 1001 to Job 1003 . Total production overheads for the period were £11,550 and overheads are absorbed at 200% of direct wages. Job 1001 was completed during the period and invoiced to the customer at £17,500.

Prepare

a. Job cost account for each job.

b. Overhead control account.

c. W-l-P control account.

d. Costing P & L account for the period.

B12.3 A firm has a Job Costing System using overhead recovery based on labour hours and a predetermined overhead absorption rates. In a period there is a substantial under recovery of overheads. Give possible reasons for this.

Examination questions

B12.4 The management of a company manufacturing special purpose industrial equipment are considering introducing a full absorption historic job costing system.

Required:

a. Explain how the information produced by the proposed costing system could be used and examine any weaknesses or inadequacies in the data provided by such a system.

b. Consider how the effective utilisation and the efficiency of the direct operatives may be measured in the above company.

(ACCA, Costing)

B12.5 a. A firm's computer department charges for the services which it provides to user departments.

The computer department has three main divisions of work:

i. development of systems and programs to be run on the computer

ii. data preparation

iii. computer operations

The budget for the department for the following year and the apportionments amongst its divisions of work is as follows.

		Divisions		
	Budget	Development	Data Preparation	Computer Operations
	£	%	%	%
Salaries	200,000	30	25	45
Compilation and Testing	60,000	100		
Maintenance	20,000		10	90
Materials	10,000	10	20	70
Power	10,000		25	75
Office costs	10,000	20	20	60

Other information:

i. The estimated number of staff hours of work which will be chargeable by the development division is 12,000 hours.

ii. The estimated number of key depressions on terminals for data preparation is 24,300,000.

iii. The estimated number of hours of computer operation available is 7,000 hours. Because of downtime, it is practice to recover costs over 'usable' hours which are estimated to be 60% of total available hours.

A user department has two jobs which require the services of the computer department, details of which are as follows:

	Job 1234	*Job 5678*
Development work	400 hours	20 hours
Data preparation		80,000 key depressions
Computer operations		5 hours

Required:

    i.   Prepare a table which shows total cost for each division of the computer department.

    ii. Calculate the costs which would be charged to Job 1234 and Job 5678.

b.   i.   Explain what you understand by the following terms:

           Cost unit

           Cost centre

    ii. Use the information in the question above to give *two* examples of each term, and give *two* *other* examples of each term.

AAT (Cost Accounting and Budgeting)

13: Costing methods – contract costing

1. Topics covered in this chapter:

> 1. Characteristics of contract costing
> 2. SSAP 9 requirements
> 3. Calculation of interim profits for incomplete contracts
> 4. Calculation of contract balances for Balance Sheet purposes
> 5. Contract accounts

2. What is contract costing?

Contract costing has many similarities to job costing and is usually applied to work which is

a. Undertaken to customer's special requirements
b. Relatively long duration
c. Site based, sometimes overseas
d. Frequently of a constructional nature

Because of the long time scale and size of many contracts, the necessity arises for intermediate valuations to be made of work done and for progress payments to be received from the client.

3. Characteristics of contract costing

Although details vary, certain characteristics are common to most contract costing systems:

a. Higher proportion of direct costs. Because of the self-contained nature of most site operations, many items normally classified as indirect can be identified specifically with a contract and/or site and thus can be charged directly, eg, telephones installed on site, site power usage, site vehicles, transportation, design and planning salaries.

b. Low indirect costs. For most contracts, the only item of indirect cost would be a charge for Head Office expenses. This is usually only a small proportion of the contract cost and is absorbed normally on some overall basis, such as a percentage of total contract cost.

c. Difficulties of cost control. Because of the scale of some contracts and the size of the site there are frequently major problems of cost control concerning: material usage and losses, pilferage, labour supervision and utilisation, damage to and loss of plant and tools, vandalism, etc.

d. Surplus materials. All materials bought for a contract would be charged directly to the contract. At the end of the contract, the contract account would be credited with the cost of the materials not used and, if they were transferred directly to another contract, the new contract account debited. If they were not required immediately, the materials would be stored and the cost debited to a stock account.

4. Contract plant

A feature of most contract work is the amount of plant used. This includes cranes, trucks, excavators, mixers and lorries. The usual ways in which plant costs are dealt with are as follows:

a. *When plant is leased*. The leasing charges are charged directly to the contract.

b. *When plant is purchased*. There are two methods in common use,

   i. charge new plant at cost to the contract for which it was purchased. When the plant is no longer required and is transferred to another contract or to base, the original contract would be credited with the second hand value of the plant. In this way the contract bears the charge for the depreciation incurred. It will be appreciated that this is an example of the revaluation method of depreciation.

   ii. where plant is moved frequently from contract to contract or where contracts are relatively short, a 'Plant Service Department' is created. This department organises the transfer of plant from contract to contract as required and each contract is charged a daily or weekly rental.

Note

Whatever method is used for charging the capital costs of plant, the ordinary running costs; fuel, repairs and insurance would be charged direct to the contract.

5. Progress payments

The contract normally provides for the client to make progress payments either at specific stages of the work, eg, when foundations are completed, first floor completion, or at particular agreed intervals. The basis for these interim payments is an architect's certificate of work satisfactorily completed. The architect's certificate shows the value of the work done at selling prices and this certificate accompanies the invoice sent to the customer. The amount paid is normally the certified value less a percentage retention which is released when the contract is fully completed and accepted by the customer.

Example 1

An architect assesses the value of work done to be £265,000. The client has already paid £110,000 and the agreed retention percentage is 15%. What is the amount of the current progress payment?

Solution

$$
\begin{aligned}
\text{Current payment} \quad &= \text{Value certified} - \text{Retention} - \text{Payments already made} \\
&= £265,000 - 15\% \,(265,000) - 110,000 \\
&= 265,000 - 39,750 - 110,000 \\
&= \textbf{£115,250}
\end{aligned}
$$

The accounting entries for this payment when received are

DR Bank A/C

CR Client A/C (or cash received on account)

6. Profit calculation and balance sheet entries for uncompleted contracts

The objective of contract costing is to show the profit and loss on each completed contract. However, when a contract is still in progress at the end of the financial year it is necessary to estimate the profit earned in the financial year (that is, part of the total contract profit) so as to avoid excessive fluctuations in company results from year to year. In addition, it is necessary to provide a realistic figure of the value of work-in-progress for balance sheet purposes.

Whilst anticipated losses should be allowed for, in full, as early as possible, the attributable profit in any period is conservatively estimated to allow for unforeseen difficulties and costs. The recommended approach for estimating attributable profit for the year, and the resulting Balance Sheet entries, is given in SSAP 9, Stocks and Long-term Contracts,. Key parts of the Standard are given below, followed by worked examples.

7. Key provisions of SSAP 9 *Relating to profit*

Students are recommended to read the whole of the Standard which gives valuable guidance on all aspects of stock valuation and dealing with long-term contracts. However, key parts of the Standard dealing with long-term contracts are reproduced below, referenced by the paragraph numbers from the Standard:

What is a long-term contract? Para 22 (extract)

'A contract that is required to be accounted for as long-term by this accounting standard will usually extend for a period exceeding one year. However, a duration exceeding one year is not an essential feature of a long-term contract. Some contracts with a shorter duration than one year should be accounted for as long-term contracts if they are sufficiently material to the activity of the period'

What is turnover? Para 8

'Companies should ascertain turnover in a manner appropriate to the stage of completion of the contracts, the businesses and the industries in which they operate.'

Turnover is further explained in Appendix 1, para 23.

> 'Turnover (ascertained in a manner appropriate to the industry, the nature of the contracts concerned and the contractual relationship with the customer) and related costs should be recorded in the profit and loss account as contract activity progresses. Turnover may sometimes be ascertained by reference to valuation of the work carried out to date. In other cases, there may be specific points during a contract at which individual elements of work done with separately ascertainable sales values and costs can be identified and appropriately recorded as turnover (eg. because delivery or customer acceptance has taken place). This accounting standard does not provide a definition of turnover in view of the different methods of ascertaining it as outlined above. However, it does require disclosure of the means by which turnover is ascertained.'

What are the general principles for deciding upon attributable profits or losses? Paras 9, 10 & 11

> 'Where the business carries out long-term contracts and it is considered that their outcome can be assessed with reasonable certainty before their conclusion, the attributable profit should be calculated on a prudent basis and included in the accounts for the period under review. The profit taken up needs to reflect the proportion of the work carried out at the accounting date and to take into account any known inequalities of profitability in the various stages of a contract. The procedure to recognise profit is to include an appropriate proportion of total contract value as turnover in the profit and loss account as the contract activity progresses. The costs incurred in reaching that stage of completion are matched with this turnover, resulting in the reporting of results that can be attributed to the proportion of work completed.

> Where the outcome of long-term contracts cannot be assessed with reasonable certainty before the conclusion of the contract, no profit should be reflected in the profit and loss account in respect of those contracts, although, in such circumstances, if no loss is expected it may be appropriate to show as turnover a proportion of the total contract value using a zero estimate of profit.

> If it is expected that there will be a loss on a contract as a whole, all of the loss should be recognised as soon as it is foreseen (in accordance with the prudence concept). Initially, the foreseeable loss will be deducted from the work in progress figure of the particular contract, thus reducing it to net realisable value. Any loss in excess of the work in progress figure should be classified as an accrual within 'Creditors' or under 'Provisions for liabilities and charges' depending upon the circumstances. Where unprofitable contracts are of such magnitude that they can be expected to utilise a considerable part of the company's capacity for a substantial period, related administration overheads to be incurred during the period to the completion of those contracts should also be included in the calculation of the provision for losses.'

These principles are explained further in Appendix I and Para 25 and part of Para 28 are given below.

Para 25

> 'In calculating the total estimated profit on the contract, it is necessary to take into account not only the total costs to date and the total estimated further costs to completion (calculated by reference to the same principles as were applied to cost to date) but also the estimated future costs of rectification and guarantee work, and any other future work to be undertaken under the terms of the contract. These are then compared with the total sales value of the contract. In considering future costs, it is necessary to have regard to likely increases in wages and salaries, to likely increases in the price of raw materials and to rises in general overheads, so far as these items are not recoverable from the customer under the terms of the contract.'

Para 28 (part)

> 'The amounts to be included in the year's profit and loss account will be both the appropriate amount of turnover and the associated costs of achieving that turnover, to the extent that these amounts exceed corresponding amounts recognised in previous years.'

Thus, in memorandum form, the overall contract outcome calculation is as follows:

	£	£
Total Contract value		XX
less Costs incurred to date	XX	
Estimated costs to completion	XX	
Rectification and guarantee work	XX	
Total estimated contract costs		XX
Estimated contract profit or loss		XX

If a loss is disclosed from the above calculation then this should be provided in full in the period's accounts. If an overall profit is expected and no additional problems are foreseen then it is correct to take credit in the current period for a reasonable proportion of the overall profit. This means that some appropriate amount of turnover and related costs will appear in the firm's P&L account for the year. As will be seen from the extracts given above, the Standard does not specify how this should be done.

8. Guidelines on calculating interim profits

Various possibilities exist for estimating the profit on incomplete contracts and several options are shown below. However a prudent view must always be taken and the profit should reflect the degree of completion. If the contract is at an early stage (say, less than 30% complete) no profit should be taken. Interim profits, however calculated, should only be taken when the final contract outcome can be assessed with reasonable confidence.

Options for estimating interim profit:

a. When substantial costs have been incurred (say the contract is 30 – 80% complete) a formula which has traditionally been used in the constructional industry is :

$$\text{Profit taken} = \tfrac{2}{3} \text{ or } \tfrac{3}{4} \text{ of the Notional profit} \times \frac{\text{cash received from progress payments}}{\text{value of work certified}}$$

where the Notional Profit is Value of Work Certified – Cost of Work Certified.

b. When the contract is nearing completion (say, over 80% complete) and the eventual profit can be assessed with reasonable certainty there is no need for excessive prudence and one of the following methods may be used:

i. $\text{Profit taken} = \dfrac{\text{Progress payments to date}}{\text{contract price}} \times \text{estimated total profit on completion}$

(Note: The above formula allows for the retention percentage in the unlikely event of their being no retention by the client the formula would be $\text{Profit taken} = \dfrac{\text{Value of work certified}}{\text{Contract price}} \times \text{estimated total profit}$)

The above method is probably the most usual but there are other possibilities:

ii. Profit taken = Value of work certified – Cost of work certified

or

iii. $\text{Profit taken} = \dfrac{\text{cost of work done}}{\text{Estimated total cost of contract}} \times \text{Estimated total profit.}$

Example 2

At their year end Apex Developments has three contracts in progress and their details are as follows:

Contract	AP10	AP11	AP12
	£	£	£
Contract price	150,000	275,000	185,000
Costs to date	35,000	144,000	154,000
Estimated costs to completion	88,000	96,000	7,000
Value of work certified	40,000	165,000	172,000
Progress payments received	34,000	140,250	146,200
Cost of work certified	28,000	138,000	150,000

What interim profits if any, should be taken on the three contracts? (no profits have been taken so far).

Solution

First check the degree of completion and whether the contracts are expected to make a profit on completion. Only if an overall profit is expected can taking an interim profit be considered. If any contract showed an expected overall loss, this must be taken, in full, in the current accounting year in accordance with the prudence concept.

	AP10	AP11	AP12
	£	£	£
Contract price	150,000	275,000	185,000
less estimated total costs	123,000	240,000	161,000
Estimated contract profit	27,000	35,000	24,000

Approximate degree of completion

$$\frac{\text{Costs to date}}{\text{Total costs}} = \quad \frac{35,000}{123,000} \quad \frac{144,000}{240,000} \quad \frac{154,000}{161,000}$$

$$= \quad 28\% \qquad 60\% \qquad 96\%$$

Thus all contracts are expected to make an overall profit on completion so taking an interim profit can be considered provided that the degree of completion justifies doing so.

Contract AP10

only 28% complete so it would be prudent not to take any profit until more of the contract is completed.

Contract AP11

60% complete so a prudent amount of profit can be taken. As there is a retention of 15% a reasonable method of calculation would be:

$$\text{Profit taken} = \frac{2}{3} \times \text{Notional Profit} \times \frac{\text{Progress payments}}{\text{Value of work certified}}$$

$$= \frac{2}{3} \times (165,000 - 138,000) \times \frac{140,250}{165,000}$$

$$= \pounds15,300$$

Note that the above figure is considerably below the difference between the value and cost of work certified, which is £27,000. This means that the amounts taken to the P&L account for turnover and cost of sales should be less than £165,000 and £138,000 respectively (this is dealt with below in Example 3).

Contract AP12

96% complete so a somewhat less prudent view can be taken of the interim profit. A reasonable calculation would be

$$\text{Profit taken} = \frac{\text{Progress payments}}{\text{Contract price}} \times \text{Estimated total profit} = \frac{146,200}{185,000} \times 24,000$$

$$= \pounds18,966$$

It will be seen from the initial data that, in each case, there was work done but not yet certified ie costs to date less cost of work certified. This must be carried at cost, not at sales value.

9. Profit and loss account entries for interim profits

Having calculated an appropriate interim profit, as shown above, the necessary Turnover and Cost of Sales figures must be derived, for insertion in the published P&L account of the firm. The turnover and cost of sales figures are based on the formulae used for the interim profit calculations and must obviously produce the agreed profit. The methods used are demonstrated below.

Example 3

Show the amounts of turnover and cost of sales relating to the three contracts in Example 2 which will be taken to the firms P&L account, according to the provisions of SSAP 9.

Solution

The amounts of Turnover and Cost of Sales which will be taken to the firms P&L A/C will be those which produce the profits as already calculated above ie;

Contract	
AP10	No Profit
AP11	£15,300 Profit
AP12	£18,966 Profit

Contract AP 10

As no profit is to be taken on this contract there are no allocations to Turnover and Cost of Sales in the firms P&L account.

Contract AP11

The turnover and Cost of Sales are obtained by weighting the Value and the Cost of Work certified respectively by the $\frac{2}{3}$ proportion and the proportion of payments made to value certified. This is merely the breakdown of the formula used to calculate the Interim profit above.

$$\text{Turnover} = \frac{2}{3} \times \text{Value of work certified} \times \frac{\text{Progress payment}}{\text{Value of work certified}}$$

$$= \frac{2}{3} \times 165{,}000 \times \frac{140{,}250}{165{,}000}$$

$$= \pounds93{,}500$$

$$\text{Cost of Sales} = \frac{2}{3} \times \text{Cost of work certified} \times \frac{\text{Progress payments}}{\text{Value certified}}$$

$$= \frac{2}{3} \times 138{,}000 \times \frac{140{,}250}{165{,}000}$$

$$= 78{,}200$$

$\therefore$ Entries in P&L relating to Contract AP11

	£
Turnover	93,500
Cost of Sales	78,200
= Profit	**15,300** as calculated.

Contract AP12

As a different formula from AP11 was used to calculate profit the calculation of Turnover and Cost of Sales is also different but is similarly based on the Interim Profit Formula used for AP12 in Example 2.

$$\text{Turnover} = \frac{\text{Progress Payments}}{\text{Contract price}} \times \text{Contract price}$$

$$= \frac{146{,}200}{185{,}000} \times 185{,}000$$

$$= \pounds146{,}200$$

$$\text{Cost of Sales} = \frac{\text{Progress Payments}}{\text{Contract price}} \times \text{Total Contract Price}$$

$$= \frac{146{,}200}{185{,}000} \times 161{,}000$$

$$= \pounds127{,}234$$

$\therefore$ Entries in P&L relating to contract AP12

	£
Turnover	146,200
Cost of Sales	127,234
= Profit	**18,966** as calculated

Summary for the 3 contracts

	AP10	AP11	AP12	Firms P&L A/C
		£	£	£
Turnover	–	93,500	146,200	239,700
Cost of Sales	–	78,200	127,234	205,434
Profit	–	15,300	18,966	34,266

Having dealt with the profit calculations and subsequent P&L account entries, we must now consider what balance sheet entries arise from incomplete contracts.

10. Key provisions of SSAP 9 relating to balance sheet entries

Part of the Standards recommendations regarding balance sheet entries have been shown above (in Standard Para 11) and other important extracts are shown below.

Para 13

'In the case of long-term contracts:

(a) long-term contract balances classified under the balance sheet heading of 'Stocks' are stated at total costs incurred, net of amounts transferred to the profit and loss account in respect of work carried out to date, less foreseeable losses and applicable payments on account. A suitable description in the financial statements would be 'at net cost, less foreseeable losses and payments on account'.

(b) cumulative turnover (ie, the total turnover recorded in respect of the contract in the profit and loss accounts of all accounting periods since inception of the contract) is compared with total payments on account. If turnover exceeds payments on account an 'amount recoverable on contracts' is established and separately disclosed within debtors. If payments on account are greater than turnover to date, the excess is classified as a deduction from any balance on that contract in stocks, with any residual balance in excess of cost being classified with creditors.'

In essence part (a) gives the value of net work-in-progress and part (b) shows the position when progress payments are greater or less than the value of turnover. All these terms are illustrated in the examples which follow.

11. Deriving the balance sheet entries

Some items which are entered into Contract accounts are conventionally treated and produce straightforward balance sheet entries. The two main items in this category are; Unused materials on site and Plant on site.

There are more difficulties however with work-in-progress and the differences between the amounts recognised as turnover and the progress payments received. SSAP 9 requires that the balances relating to long term contracts are split into two categories.

a. The costs of work done which is not yet recognised in the P&L account is shown under 'stocks' as 'Long term-contract balances'.

b. The difference between

	£
i. amounts taken as Turnover	XX
ii. *less* Progress payments received	XX
= Net difference	XX

will be grouped with 'Debtors' as 'Amounts recoverable on long-term contracts' if (i) is greater than (ii). Alternatively the net difference will be offset against the balances in (a) above if (ii) is greater than (i).

Thus it will be seen that various separate contract balances are calculated and then netted off to produce the final balances which appear, suitably aggregated, in the firms published Balance Sheet,

The main stages in this process are illustrated below.

Example 4

What are the balance sheet entries for the three contracts in example 2?

(The data on the contracts and the calculations of turnover cost of sales and profit are reproduced below for convenience)

Contract	AP10	AP11	AP12
	£	£	£
Contract price	150,000	275,000	185,000
Costs to date	35,000	144,000	154,000
Estimated costs to completion	88,000	96,000	7,000
Value of work certified	40,000	165,000	172,000
Progress payments received	34,000	140,250	146,200
Cost of work certified	28,000	138,000	150,000
Calculated turnover	–	93,500	146,200
Calculated cost of sales	–	78,200	127,234
Calculated Profit	–	15,300	18,966

Solution

There are two balances to be found, as specified in Para 10 (a) and 10 (b) which may have to be netted together. These are all shown in the table below:

Contract	AP10 £	AP11 £	AP12 £	Total £
Costs incurred but not allocated to cost of sales (a) (Note 1)	35,000	65,800	26,766	127,566
Amount taken as Turnover (from Ex. 3)	–	93,500	146,200	239,700
less Progress payments	34,000	140,250	146,200	320,450
Balance (b)	(34,000)	(46,750)	–	(80,750)
Netted balance (a–b) (Note 2)	1000	19,050	26,766	46,816

Note 1.

Workings for costs incurred but not allocated to Sales.

Contract	AP10 £	AP11 £	AP12 £	Total £
Costs to date	35,000	144,000	154,000	333,000
less Cost of Sales (Ex 3)	–	78,200	127,234	205,434
= Costs incurred but not allocated to sales	35,000	65,800	26,766	127,566

Note 2.

It will be seen that for these three contracts the Progress Payments are always at least equal to the Amount taken as Turnover. According to the rules given in Para 10 this means that the two main balances ((a) and (b)) can be netted against one another.

The Balance Sheet disclosures are thus:

	AP10 £	AP11 £	AP12 £	Total £
Stocks				
Long-term contract balances	1,000	19,050	26,766	46,816

Note: It will be seen that in this example Debtors did not arise. Debtors only arise when the Amount taken as Turnover *exceeds* the Progress Payments.

12. Comprehensive example.

To provide further practice and to illustrate other aspects of SSAP 9 a comprehensive example follows. You are recommended to attempt the problem yourself before working through the solution.

Example 5

Nationwide Contractors Plc. at 31st December 19_8 had three contracts in progress as follows:

Contract No.	NC852 £'000	NC794 £'000	NC881 £'000
Contract value	350	1460	850
Costs incurred to date	165	1100	182
Estimated future costs to complete	110	275	633
Estimated guarantee costs	–	–	95
Payments received on account	190	1200	145
Value of work certified	212	1125	110
Cost of work certified	165	1070	130
Start dates	30th Sep 19-7	4th Mar 19-7	1st Jan 19-8

(No profits have been taken so far)

It is required to assess whether any interim profits should be taken, to calculate the appropriate Turnover and Cost of Sales values and the Balance Sheet entries for the three contracts.

Solution

Estimated degree of completion and overall contract result

Contract No.	NC852	NC794	NC881
	£'000	£'000	£'000
Contract value	350	1460	850
Total expected costs	275	1375	910
Expected profit (loss)	75	85	(60)
Degree of completion	$\frac{165}{275} = 60\%$	$\frac{1100}{1375} = 80\%$	N.A. as all loss must be taken

Thus it will be seen that NC 852 and NC794 are expected to make a profit on completion and are well advanced so it is reasonable to take an interim profit. The whole of the loss on NC881, £60,000, must be brought into account in this accounting year.

Interim Profit calculations:

Contract NC852

$$\text{Profit} = \frac{2}{3} \times \text{Notional Profit} \times \frac{\text{Payments}}{\text{Value certified}} = \frac{2}{3} \times (212 - 165) \times \frac{190}{212} \text{ ('000s)}$$
$$= £28,100$$

Contract NC794

$$\text{Profit} = \frac{2}{3} \times (1125 - 1070) \text{ ('000s)} = £36,700$$

(Because, unusually, payments received for NC794 are above the value of work certified the usual retention effect has been ignored for this contract).

Turnover and Cost of Sales calculations:

	NC852	*NC794*	*NC881*
Turnover	$\frac{2}{3} \times \text{Value Cert} \times \frac{\text{Payments}}{\text{Value Cert}}$	$\frac{2}{3} \times \text{Value Cert}$	Value Certified
	$= \frac{2}{3} \times 212 \times \frac{190}{212}$	$= \frac{2}{3} \times 1125$	
	$= £126,700$	$= £750,000$	$= £110,000$
Cost of sales	$\frac{2}{3} \times \text{Cost Cert} \times \frac{\text{Payments}}{\text{Value Cert}}$	$\frac{2}{3} \times \text{Cost Cert}$	
	$= \frac{2}{3} \times 165 \times \frac{190}{212}$	$= \frac{2}{3} \times 1070$	Cost of sales to produce £60,000 loss
	$= £98,600$	$= £713,300$	$= £170,000$

Derivation of balances for Balance Sheet.

	NC852	NC794	NC881	Total
	£'000	£'000	£'000	£'000
Costs to Date	165	1100	182	1447
less Cost of Sales	98.6	713.3	170	981.9
= Costs incurred not allocated to Sales (a)	66.4	386.7	12	465.1
Turnover	126.7	750	110	986.7
less Progress payments	190	1200	145	1535
Balance (b)	(63.3)	(450)	(35)	(548.3)
Netted balance (a – b)	3.1	(63.3)	(23)	(83.2)

The results can now be summarised:

Values for P&L account of Nationwide Contractors for the three incomplete contracts

	NC852 £	NC794 £	NC881 £	Total £
Turnover	126,700	750,000	110,000	986,700
less Cost of Sales	98,600	713,300	170,000	981,900
Profit (loss)	28,100	36,700	(60,000)	4,800

Contract balances for Balance Sheet

	NC852 £	NC794 £	NC881 £	Total £
Stocks				
Long-term Contract balances	3,100			3,1000
With Creditors		63,300	23,000	86,600

Notes:

1. The figures have been chosen to illustrate the effect of having excess payments on account (as NC794) and a contract loss (as NC881)

2. It will be seen that there are no debtors. These can only arise when the progress payments received are less than the value taken as Turnover.

13. The accounting entries

A separate account will be kept for each contract with the general objective of establishing the overall contract profit or loss. To do this the following entries are required:

Contract Account

Typical Debit Entries	*Typical Credit Entries*
Debit Direct costs(Material, Labour)	Credit Plant, Materials transferred from Contract
Debit Direct expenses (Plant hire, Sub-contractors. Architects' fees, etc.)	Credit sales value of stages/final contract value
Debit Cost of Plant bought	
Debit any materials, plant etc, transferred to contract	
Debit Head Office Charges	
Debit Interim and Final Profit	

In addition there are, of course, contra entries within the contract account relating to carry forward/brought forward items, accruals and prepayments.

All of the above entries are shown in the following example.

14. Example of accounting for contracts

Example

The following information relates to Contract 87 on the Thornley site as at the 31st December 19-1.

Contract 87 – Thornley Site

Customer – Middlethorpe Corporation

	£
Wages	42,156
Materials delivered direct to site	54,203
Materials from Main Stores	657
Materials transferred to Riverview Site	1,590
Plant purchased (at cost)	12,500
Plant transferred to Thornley	5,250
Sub-contractors charges	19,580
Site expenses (power etc.)	5,086
Materials on Site 31st December	18,300
Plant on Site 31st December	14,750
Prepayments at 31st December	507
Accrued wages at 31st December	921
Sales value of stages completed	117,500
Cost of stages completed	102,300
Head Office charges are 10% of wages	
Progress payments received from client	115,000

The contract value is £550,000 and it is anticipated that there will be further costs of £375,000 (including guarantee and rectification claims). As this is the first year of the contract no profit has been taken previously.

From the above prepare the Contract Account for the year, the Balance sheet entries as at 31st December 19-1 and the opening entries for 1st January 19-2. It is company policy to take as interim profit the difference between the Sales Value and Cost of Stages completed.

Solution

CONTRACT No. 87   CUSTOMER: Middlethorpe Corporation

SITE: Thornley

Contract A/C

	£	£		£
Site Wages	42,156		Materials transferred out	1,590
+ accrued C/F	921	43,077	Prepayments C/D	507
Materials purchased	54,203			
Materials from Stores	657	54,860		
Plant purchased	12,500		Materials at site C/D	18,300
Plant transferred in	5,250	17,750	Plant at site C/D	14,750
Sub contractors		19,580	W-I-P C/D	7,214
Site expenses		5,086	(see note a)	
Head office Charges		4,308	Cost of stages completed	102,300
		£144,661		£144,661
Cost of stages completed		102,300		
			Sales value of stages	117,500
Profit for year		15,200		
(see note b)				
		117,500		117,500

Contract A/C (continued)

	£		£
1st Jan. 19-2 (see note c)			
Prepayments B/D	507		
Materials B/D	18,300	Accrued wages	921
Plant B/D	14,750		
W-I-P B/D	7,214		

Notes

a. The total costs to date are £109,514 ie. £144,661 less items C/D and transferred out. As the cost of stages completed is £102,300 the contract balance (W-I-P) is:

	£
	109,514
less Cost of sales	102,300
= Long term contract balance	£7,214

b. Before any profit can be taken for the year it is necessary to estimate the overall project outcome to see whether a profit or loss is expected, thus:

Expected contract outcome:

		£
Contract value		550,000
less Costs to date	109,514	
Future costs	375,000	484,514
Expected Overall Contract Profit		65,486

As an overall profit is expected it is reasonable to take a proportion into this year's accounts. The profit is the difference between the cost and sales value of the stages completed, as shown.

c. All the entries shown appear in the balance sheet as at 31st December 19-1 and would be aggregated with the other prepayments, accruals, stocks and work-in-progress of the firm.

In addition a balance sheet entry arises from the personal account of the client, Middlethorpe Corporation, thus:

Middlethorpe Corporation

		Cash (progress payments)	115,000	
Sales value of completed stages	117,500	Bal C/F (ie. Debtors)	2,500	
	117,500		117,500	
1st Jan 19-2 Bal B/F	2,500			

The £2500 balance on the Middlethorpe account would be grouped with debtors and termed 'Amounts recoverable on long-term contracts'.

Note that in this example a Debtor does arise because the amount taken for Turnover (£117,500) exceeds the Progress Payments (£115,000).

15. Summary

a. Contract costing is akin to job costing and is used on relatively large scale, long term contracts which are frequently site based.

b. Because of the separate nature of most site work, more costs can be identified as direct, including many which are normally considered indirect.

c. If plant is purchased for use on a site, the contract account would be charged with the purchase price and credited with the second hand value of the plan on the contract completion or when the plant was transferred. In this way the plant depreciation would be charged to the appropriate contract.

d. Progress payments are made based on an architect's certificate of work done less an agreed retention percentage.

e. If a contract is uncompleted at the year end, a conservative estimate is taken of the profit for the period. SSAP 9 provides recommendations for the method of profit calculation.

f. If a loss is expected for the contract as a whole this should be allowed for, in full, as early as possible.

g. Balance sheet entries may arise in connection with uncompleted contracts for; contract balances (W-I-P), debtors, excess payments on account and provision for losses.

Student self-testing

Self Review Questions

1. What are typical characteristics of work for which contract costing is used ? (2)
2. How are plant capital costs dealt with in contract accounts? (4)
3. What is a progress payment and how is it calculated ? (5)
4. When can profit on uncompleted contracts be taken? (6)
5. What are the general principles recommended by SSAP 9 for calculating attributable profit? (7)
6. What balance sheet entries may arise in connection with uncompleted contracts? (10)
7. Give five typical debit entries and two typical credit entries in a contract account. (13)

Exercises and examination questions with answers

Exercises

A13.1 Prepare columnar contract accounts for Bayes Construction Ltd who at present have two contracts in progress.

The following details were extracted at the 31st December.

Contract No. Commencement date	Y282 1st January	Z650 1st July
	£	£
Contract price	275,000	350,000
Expenditure:		
Materials	12,680	19,280
Wages	48,643	37,218
Site expenses	6,500	8,620
Plant purchases	150,000	65,000
Materials on site 31st December	2,100	6,400
Accrued wages	4,217	2,242
Value of work certified	110,000	85,000
Cash received on work certified	93,500	63,750
Work completed but not certified	3,500	2,200

Head office charges of £22,500 are charged to contracts in proportion to their prime costs. The plant was installed at the commencement of the contracts and depreciation is calculated at 20% per annum. Both contracts have been estimated to give an overall profit on completion.

A13.2 Site and contract work pose particular difficulties for cost control and accurate cost accounting.

You are required to describe the problems which might arise and how these can be overcome or mitigated.

A13.3 What are the arguments for and against charging individual contracts with Head Office costs?

Examination questions

A13.4 a. A long term contract is one that will usually extend for longer than one year.

Required:

i. Give two examples of long term contract work.

ii. List three characteristics of a long term contract other than its length.

b. In order to overcome the problem of profit recognition with a contract that extends over a number of years, attributable profit is allowed to be recognised before the contract is completed.

Required:

i. Explain the problem of profit recognition that is associated with long term contracts.

ii. Outline what you understand by attributable profit and in what circumstances it should and should not be taken.

iii. If it is thought that a loss might arise as a whole on a contract how should this be treated?

c. A long-term contract to build a factory in Radley was started up in November 1989 is expected to be completed in February 1991. The value of the contract is £1,400,000 and is at the stage that profit can be attributed to it. When work has been certified, the Company that issued the contract for the factory is sent an invoice for progress payments. You are given the following information relating to the year ended 3st October, 1990:

	£
Material issued to Site from Store	600,000
Materials returned to Store	50,000
Materials remaining on Site 31 October 1990	20,000
Wages paid	250,000
Wages accrued	30,000
Sub-contracters' charges	25,000
Plant purchased at cost	100,000
Value of plant on site at 31 October 1990	60,000
Overheads allocated to contract	25,000
Value of work certified at 31 October 1990	1,200,000
Progress payments received at 31 October 1990	1,000,000
Costs to completion	150,000

All costs to date form cost of work certified.

Required

Prepare the following for the year ended 31 October 1990:

i. The Radley contract account.

ii. The Contractee's account

iii. Contract profit and loss account

d. The rules have been changed recently as regard long-term contract work in progress.

Required

How is W.I.P. on long-term contracts determined under:

i. The old rules?

ii. The new rules?

(AAT, Cost Accounting and Budgeting)

A13.5 One of the building contracts currently engaged in by a construction company commenced 15 months ago and remains unfinished. The following information relating to work on the contract has been prepared for the year just ended.

	£000
Contract price	2,100
Value of work certified at end of year	1,840
Cost of work not yet certified	35
Costs incurred:	
Opening balances	
Cost of work completed	250
Materials on site (physical stock)	10
During the year	
Materials delivered to site	512
Wages	487
Hire of plant	96
Other expenses	74
Closing balance	
Materials on site (physical stock)	18

As soon as materials are delivered to the site, they are charged to the contract account. A record is also kept of materials as they are actually used on the contract. Periodically a stock check is made and any discrepancy between book stock and physical stock is transferred to a general contract materials discrepancy account. This is absorbed back into each contract, currently at a rate of 0.4% of materials booked. The stock check at the end of the year revealed a stock shortage of £4,000.

In addition to the direct charges listed above, general overheads of the company are charged to contracts at 5% of the value of work certified. General overheads of £13,000 had been absorbed into the cost of work completed at the beginning of the year.

It has been estimated that further costs to complete the contract will be £215,000. This estimate includes the cost of materials on site at the end of the year just finished, and also a provision for rectification.

Required:

a. Explain briefly the distinguishing features of contract costing.

b. Determine the profitability of the above contract, and recommend how much profit (to the nearest £000) should be taken for the year just ended. (Provide a detailed schedule of costs.)

c. State how your recommendation in

b. would be affected if the contract price was £3,500,000 (rather than £2,100,000) and if no estimate has been made of costs to completion.

(ACCA Costing)

Exercises and examination questions without answers

Exercises

B13.1 The following details have been extracted from the records for a building contract which Dunbar & Company are carrying out for the Hamcaster Local Authority.

As at 31st December 19-1

Cost of all work for year	£86,292
Cost of work not certified	£4,200
Value of work certified	£120,000

The client keeps a 10% retention. You are required to calculate the profit for the year using the traditional method.

B13.2 Having calculated the traditional profit you are required to calculate the profit using SSAP 9 recommendations.

The following information is available in addition to that already supplied.

	£
Contract value	600,000
Estimated costs to completion	415,000
Rectification costs expected after completion	105,000

Examination questions

B13.3 a. The following data relates to expenditure on the estate management (building services, grounds and gardens) of two colleges.

	College Alpha	College Beta
Number of students	4,000	10,000
Total area in cubic metres	877,000	2,800,000

	College Alpha		College Beta	
	Own workforce	Contractors	Own workforce	Contractors
Cost Element	£	£	£	£
Category A (work of a periodic nature)				
1. Painting	20,000	–	–	12,000
2. Maintenance	2,000	–	4,000	14,000
Category B (irregular work)				
1. Painting	1,500	–	10,800	–
2. Maintenance	7,000	47,000	14,500	13,000
Category C (grounds and gardens)				
3. General	18,000	3,000	35,000	–
Category D (unallocated)				
3. General	10,600	–	70,000	–

Required:

i. Tabulate the above information showing the expenditure per 1,000 cubic metres.

   Calculations should be in £'s to two decimal places.

ii. Comment briefly on your findings.

b. Contractors PLC has been engaged since 1st January 19x5 on the construction of an office for an electronics firm. The total contract price is £15m and the office block is expected to take 10 years to complete.

   At 31st December 19x5 site on plant was valued at £125,000 and unused materials on site were valued at £258,000. Site wages of £17,000 and direct expenses of £23,000 had been accrued. The long term contract work in progress value of the project was £653,000.

   The following details apply to the contract for 19x6:

	Costs Incurred	Cash Paid
	£	£
Site wages	150,000	153,000
Salaries	85,000	85,000
Sub-contracted work	63,000	63,000
Direct expenses	44,000	40,000

   Contractors PLC absorbs production overheads into contracts on a predetermined percentage based on wages incurred. The relevant budgeted figures for 19x6 were as follows:

	£
Production overheads	990,000
Wages	2,750,000

   At 31st December 19x6 site plant was valued at £97,000 and unused materials amounted to £39,000.

   Contractors PLC do not consider it appropriate to account for any attributable profit until a contract is at least half-way through its total life.

   Required: Prepare a contract account for the office block project for 19x6.

   (AAT Cost Accounting & Budgeting)

14: Operation and service costing

1. Topics covered in this chapter

1. Scope of operation costing
2. Service costing
3. Unit costs in the Public Sector
4. Performance measurement in the Public Sector

2. Operation costing – definition

This category of costing can be applied across a wide range of manufacturing and service organisations. The formal definition is

'The costing method applicable where goods or services result from a sequence of continuous or repetitive operations or processes. Costs are averaged over the units produced during the period'. *Terminology*

The key features of this defination are:

continuous operations or processes – virtually identical units of output – total costs divided by number of units to give average cost per unit.

3. Scope of operation costing

It will be seen that operation costing is a generic term embracing a group of costing methods of varying complexity. These are shown in the following diagram.

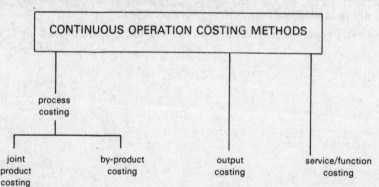

Output costing and service costing are relatively simple forms of costing and are described in this chapter. Process costing and its sub-divisions are dealt with in the next chapter.

4. Output costing

This is a costing method used where the organisation produces one product only. In consequence the whole production process is geared to the one product and is frequently highly mechanised. Typical examples of where output costing might be applied are: cement manufacture, certain dairies, mines, quarries etc. In such circumstances cost ascertainment is a simple process, ie,

$$\text{Cost per unit (or tonne)} = \frac{\text{Total costs for period}}{\text{Number of units (or tonnage) produced in the period}}$$

Note:

Where output costing is used, partly completed units at the end of a period would normally be ignored. This is because of their relative insignificance and the fact that they would tend to even out from period to period.

5. Service/function costing

This is defined as: 'Cost accounting for specific services or functions, eg, canteens, maintenance, personnel. These may be referred to as service centres, departments or functions.' *Terminology.*

Thus the services provided may be for sale, eg, public transport, hotel accommodation restaurants, power generation etc, or they may be provided within the organisation eg, maintenance, library, stores.

A particular difficulty is to define a realistic cost unit that represents a suitable measure of the service provided. Frequently a composite cost unit is deemed the more relevant, for example, the hotel industry may use the 'occupied bed-night' as an appropriate unit for cost ascertainment and cost control. Typical cost units used in service costing are shown below.

Service	Possible Cost Units
Transport	Tonne-Mile, Passenger-Mile, Miles travelled
Hospitals	Patient-days, no. of operations
Electricity	Kilowatt-hours
Hotels	Occupied bed-nights
Restaurants	Meals served
Colleges	Full time equivalent student

Each organisation will have to determine what cost is most appropriate for its own purposes. Frequently if a common cost unit is agreed, valuable cost comparisons can be made between similar establishments. This is common, for example, over a wide range of local authority services, between various hospitals, between power stations and other similar organisations.

Whatever cost unit is decided upon, the calculation of the cost per unit is done in a similar fashion to output costing, ie,

$$\text{Cost per service unit} = \frac{\text{Total costs per period}}{\text{No. of service units supplied in the period}}$$

It will be realised that the calculation shown above is similar to the calculation of cost driver rates using ABC. Service costing with homogeneous service centres or functions and cost units that are a good measure of the service provided is a form of activity based costing.

Example of service costing

Information has been collected about two hospitals over the last year.

	Loamshire General	Brownton Central
Number of beds	780	500
Number of in-patients	23,472	8165
Average stay	$7\frac{1}{2}$ days	Not recorded but bed-occupation percentage was 85%
Number of outpatient visits	216,500	63,920

Cost Breakdown

| | Loamshire General | | Browntown Central | |
	In-patients £	Out-patients £	In-patients £	Out-patients £
Direct patient care				
Supplies, drugs etc	1,821,520	693,600	1,551,350	285,450
Medical staff	8,729,100	3,308,950	6,832,700	1,975,050
Support services	2,210,500	2,563,700	1,845,380	1,591,620
Indirect costs				
General services	3,524,470	1,721,800	1,937,410	635,600
Totals	£16,285,590	£8,288,050	£12,166,840	£4,487,720

Calculate

a. Average length of stay in Brownton Central
b. Bed occupation percentage in Loamshire General
c. Cost per in-patient day for both hospitals
d. Cost per out-patient attendance for both hospitals
   and comment on the results.

Solution

a. Average stay in Browntown Central

$$\text{Potential in-patient days in a year} = 500 \text{ beds} \times 365 \text{ days}$$
$$= 182,500$$

$$\therefore 85\% \text{ occupancy} = 182,500 \times 0.85$$
$$= 155125 \text{ in-patient days.}$$

$$\therefore \text{Average stay} = \frac{155125}{8165}$$
$$= \textbf{19 days}$$

b. Bed occupation percentage in Loamshire General $= \dfrac{\text{Actual in-patient days}}{\text{Potential in-patient days}}$

$$= \frac{23472 \times 7.5}{780 \times 365} \%$$

$$= \frac{176040}{284700} \%$$

$$= \textbf{62\%}$$

c. Costs per in-patient day $= \dfrac{\text{Costs for in-patients}}{\text{No of in-patients days}}$

Loamshire General	Browntown Central
$\dfrac{£16,285,590}{23,472 \times 7.5}$	$\dfrac{£12,166,840}{8165 \times 19}$
= **£92.51**	**£78.43**

d. Cost per out-patient attendance $= \dfrac{\text{Costs for out-patients}}{\text{No of out-patients attendances}}$

Loamshire General	Browntown Central
$\dfrac{£8,288,050}{216,500}$	$\dfrac{£4,487,720}{63,920}$
= **£38.28**	**£70.21**

It will be seen that a composite cost unit (in-patient days) is used to calculate the costs. Although the calculated figures vary greatly between the hospitals it is difficult to draw any particular conclusions from this unless the hospitals catered for broadly the same type of patients, the same illnesses, were similarly equipped and so on. Browntown's in-patients had on average, stay of 19 days whilst Loamshires stayed only $7\frac{1}{2}$ days so it is likely that there are substantial differences between the hospitals. Cost comparisons between different units or organisations are only valid if like is compared with like.

The costs and occupancy percentages calculated are likely to be useful in comparing the performance within each hospital period to period. For example, Loamshire may be concerned to see a Bed- Occupancy percentage of only 62% and may monitor this period by period, in order to improve the percentage. It is likely that the lower occupancy percentage is a major factor in causing the relatively high cost of £92.51 per in-patient day. This is because the fixed costs of the hospital are spread over relatively few in-patient days. If the beds were occupied more intensively then it is likely that the cost per in-patient day would fall.

6. The use of unit costs in the public sector

Public Sector organisations cover an enormous range. Examples include; primary and secondary state education, Local Authorities, the National Health Service, Police and so on. Within these organisations there is rarely a profit figure to provide a measure of performance. Accordingly , most financial measures of performance tend to be cost-based. Costs are collected, related to some measure of throughput or output and a unit cost calculated as described above.

These unit costs have three main uses:

☐ *As Indicators of relative efficiency*

The Audit Commission make extensive use of unit costs to make comparisons between different establishments, local authorities and districts. Examples include comparisons of: cost per pupil in different Education Authorities, cost per patient-day at various hospitals, cost per night in police cells and so on.

☐ *As measures of Efficiency over time*

Unit costs allow the cost/output performance of the same organisation to be compared from year to year. They can help to indicate whether efficiency is increasing or decreasing over time so it is normal to remove the effects of inflation from the cost figures so that the underlying real performance may be seen. Various price indices may be used for removing the inflation effects but the Treasury recommended that the GDP (Gross Domestic Product) deflator should be used for all central government services in the UK including the National Health Service.

☐ *As an aid to cost control*

The regular production of Unit Costs and comparison with the costs of other establishments in the same field helps to control costs and engenders a more cost-conscious attitude.

For internal use, more detailed unit costs are often calculated which provide a sharper focus on particular costs. For example an overall unit cost per patient-day will be calculated in a hospital but this is often analysed into its component parts such as; clinicians cost per patient day, nursing costs per patient-day, administrative costs per patient-day and so on. In this way more detailed attention can be given to each element of cost.

Used as described above unit costs have certain advantages but they have a number of limitations which, in particular cases may make them less useful.

7. Limitations of unit costs

There are four main limitations:

1. Quality of performance is ignored.

    This is possibly the most serious problem. A unit cost is a summary figure which gives no guidance on the quality of performance. For example comparative unit costs per yard of street cleaned say nothing about the standard of cleanliness achieved. Cost per patient day for a hospital tells us nothing about the quality of care provided, whether the patients are cured and so on.

2. The throughput mix is likely to differ.

    Unless the throughput mix is more or less the same, cost comparisons between different establishments will be largely meaningless. The cost of a Local Authority Children's Home catering for disturbed and delinquent children will differ greatly to those Home's catering for normal children. Like must be compared with like.

3. Throughputs are used rather than outcomes.

Throughputs are numeric indicators of the level of activity. For example the number of heart by-pass operations, the number of children receiving education at a school etc. *Outcomes* are the impact which the activity has on the recipient of the service and are the underlying real objectives of providing the service. For example the objective of a Surgical Department is not to carry out 4000 by-pass operations but is to improve the quality of life of people with heart problems. In many cases in the Public Sector outcomes are not measurable so, in general, relatively easily measurable indicators of throughputs and costs are used as a proxy for real outcomes but they are not the same things.

4. There are significant inter-regional and inter-authority differences.

Crude national cost comparisons ignore the fact that there are genuine in-built differences between regions. For example, some local authorities on the south coast have high proportions of retired people.

Rural areas will have much higher collection costs per tonne of refuse because of the distance to be covered. Social deprivation and unemployment vary from area to area affecting health, social service and education costs so unthinking comparisons based on average unit costs have little value.

These and other problems mean that unit costs need to be used with caution and with regard to their possible limitations.

Performance measurements in the Public Sector is, of course, more comprehensive than the calculation of overall UnitCosts. This is explored below.

8. Performance measurement in the public sector

Over the last few years there has been a much greater emphasis on obtaining Value For Money (VFM) in public sector organisations such as Local Authorities the National Health Service, British Rail and so on. The drive for VFM has led to many structural changes in the organisations in an attempt to improve efficiency and control costs.

Examples include; outside tendering for Local Authority Services such as refuse collection and street cleaning, the establishment of Trust Hospitals and the creation of an Internal Market for health care, the Local Management of Schools and so on. This emphasis has also led to a considerable increase in the range of cost and financial information required for control, decision making and comparison.

As an example of the breadth of information that is now required in just one part of the Public Sector consider the following statistics suggested by the Local Authorities Code of Practice. See Figure 14.1

For the authority's total expenditure and for each function	Net cost per 1000 population Manpower per 1000 population
Primary education	Pupil/teacher ratio
Secondary education	Cost per pupil
School meals	Revenue/cost ratio Pupils receiving free meals as a proportion of school roll
Children in care	As a proportion of total under 18 population Cost per child in care
Care of elderly	Residents of council homes as a proportion of total over-75s Cost per resident each week
Home helps	Contact hours per 1000 population over 65
Police	Population per police officer Serious offences per 1000 population
Fire	Proportion of area at high risk
Public transport	Passenger journeys per week per 1000 population
Highways	Maintenance cost per kilometre
Housing	Rents as a proportion of total cost Management cost per dwelling Rent arrears as a percentage of year's rent income Construction cost per dwelling completed
Trading services	Revenue/gross cost ratio

Figure 14.1 Comparative statistics suggested in the Code of Practice

Calculation of these statistics requires a detailed cost accounting and recording system covering not merely costs but performance statistics of many types.

9. Other costing problems

Merely because the calculation of unit costs is a simple process in output costing and service costing, students should not be misled into thinking that no other costing problems exist in these industries. Many of the organisations involved are very substantial enterprises by any standard. Examples include power stations, large area hospitals, and city passenger transport undertakings. Such organisations have all the normal problems of large scale cost collection and analysis. They need to monitor and control their costs very closely and frequently employ sophisticated budgetary control systems. A particular problem in service organisations is caused by the high fixed cost of maintaining the total capacity which may be considerably under utilised at particular times. Examples include: electricity generation – where there is a substantial difference between peak and off peak demand, railways and bus services – where mid-day demand is substantially below rush hour periods, hotels – where there may be substantial differences between summer and winter or week day and weekend demand. The costing system should be comprehensive enough to show the effects of this type of demand on the costs of operation. Frequently this involves the analysis of costs into fixed and variable and the use of marginal costing techniques. These techniques are dealt with in detail later in the book.

10. Summary

a. Operation costing is applied where continuous operations or processes produce identical units of output. Total costs are averaged over all units produced

b. Operation costing is a general term covering the particular methods of Output Costing, Service Costing and Process Costing.

c. Output costing is used where one product only is produced. Examples include, quarries and cement works.

d. Service costing is applied to organisations supplying a service or to cost centres providing internal services.

e. The cost unit to be used needs to be defined carefully. It is frequently a composite figure such as Tonne-mile or Patient-night.

f. Organisations employing output costing and service costing have all the normal problems of cost collection and analysis and frequently employ sophisticated costing techniques as part of the information service to management.

g. Unit costs can be used as measures of efficiency, for comparison and for cost control.

h. Unit costs have several limitations-quality is ignored, mix is assumed constant, throughputs are used instead of outcomes etc, so need to be used with care.

11. Point to note

Some service organisations do not supply identical or near identical service units to customers. Examples include: Architectural/Design/Accountancy services. In such cases a form of Job costing is used.

Student self-testing

Self Review Questions

1. What are the key features of operation costing? (2)
2. What are the three major sub-divisions of operation costing? (3)
3. How is the cost per unit calculated using output costing? (4)
4. Define service costing. (5)
5. Give five examples of cost units found in service costing. (5)
6. For what purpose are unit costs used in the Public Sector? (6)
7. What are the limitation of unit costs? (7)
8. Give examples of Performance Measurement Statistics recommended for Local Authorities. (8)

Exercises and examination questions with answers

Exercises

A14.1 What managerial control problems arise when the facilities of a large scale service organisation are subject to substantial fluctuations in demand ? How can the cost accounting system provide assistance to management in such organisations?

A14.2 A firm operates a fleet of twenty lorries which are used for delivering goods to customers. The lorries bring back from the customers the returnable containers.

Describe a simple system of cost control covering the cost of running maintenance and depreciation. What cost unit would you recommend ?

Examination questions

A14.3 A small private company in a town with 190,000 inhabitants has decided to take advantage of the de-regulation of passenger transport services. It is proposing to operate a bus service on six particular routes where, after carrying out market research, it has been identified that there are opportunities to compete with existing services. Currently, the company has five 3-ton trucks which are engaged in light road haulage for regular established customers and has two mini-vans which are used as a courier service for fast delivery of letters and lightweight parcels.

The company has its own garage facilities for the repair and maintenance of its vehicles. The offices are located on the first floor above the garage and an upper floor, currently used for the storage of old records, is being cleared for conversion into office accommodation. At the rear of the garage and offices is a fenced compound where the vehicles are kept overnight. The compound is locked and floodlit during the hours of darkness and a security firm patrols regularly.

A suitably qualified person has been recruited to manage the bus operation and you have been engaged as the accountant for the expanding business. The owner of the company, a former transport manager, looks after selling and control of routing and utilisation of the five trucks and two mini-vans. His wife and a full-time bookkeeper undertake all the administrative work. Seven drivers and two garage mechanics are employed.

Cost accounting records kept have been of a rudimentary nature but the financial accounts, prepared at the end of every quarter by the company's auditors, show the business to be very profitable. The owner is conscious that with the expansion, better records will have to be maintained. From the accounts and in conjunction with the auditors, you ascertain that costs for the following expense headings are available:

> Depreciation
> Drivers' wages
> Employers' National Insurance contributions
> Fuel
> Holiday pay
> Insurance
> Management and staff salaries
> Mechanics' wages
> Oil
> Rent and rates for garage, office and compound
> Replacement parts and spares
> Road fund licences
> Security costs
> Tyre replacements

The newly-engaged passenger transport manager informs you that six minibuses at a total cost of £210,000 are on order. Each bus can seat twenty people and nine people are allowed to stand. The buses will each be operated by one person and the manager is currently interviewing drivers who hold PSV (public service vehicle) driving licences. He indicates that he will need information from you to ascertain the profitability of each route operated.

You are required, bearing in mind the objectives of cost accounting, to:

a. draft a form for the ascertainment of operating costs for the vehicles currently owned;

b. draft a form suitable for the proposed passenger service to show income and expenditure;

c. comment on the allocation and apportionment of overheads now that they have been increased substantially following the recruitment of yourself and the passenger transport manager.

(CIMA, Cost Accounting)

A14.4 You are represented with the following information for the coming year about a coach company that operates in your area.

	30 seat Coaches	50 seat Coaches
No. of coaches	5	10
No. of drivers	5	10
Weekly wage costs per driver	£220	£250
Cost of each coach	£20,000	£32,000
Fuel consumption – miles per gallon	12.5	8.0
Licence fee per coach	£350	£500
Insurance per coach	£340	£400

Repairs and maintenance for the year are budgeted at £65,000 and are to be apportioned between the coaches in the ratio of their total mileage. Administration expenses are budgeted at £93,600 and are to be apportioned to each coach in the ratio of drivers' wages costs.

You are told that each 30 seater is kept for 6 years, at which time it will have a resale value of £2,000 and that every 50 seater coach will be replaced after 7 years and have a resale value of £4,000. It is the policy of the company to depreciate the coaches on a straight line basis.

It is envisaged that each 30 seater coach will travel 500 miles per week and each 50 seater coach will travel 400 miles per week. The cost of fuel is budgeted at £2.20 per gallon. It is budgeted that each coach will be in operation 50 weeks per year and the drivers will be paid for 52 weeks.

Required:

a. Prepare costings to determine the operating cost per passenger mile on an absorption basis for;

  i. Each 30 seat coach

  ii. Each 50 seat coach

b. The company has been asked to tender for a contract to provide transport for an education authority for 40 weeks in the coming year. The contract would involve three of the coaches carrying 25 students 10 miles a day, 5 days a week and two coaches carrying 40 students 15 miles a day, 5 days a week.

Required:

Provide a total tender price on the basis of the costings you have prepared in a) above, given that the company requires a profit of 40% on contract price.

c. The company is worried that over the last year more coach drivers have left the company than in previous years.

Required:

Explain the possible reasons for the high rate of labour turnover and illustrate the costs involved as opposed to the benefits of stable workforce.

(AAT Cost Accounting & Budgeting)

Exercises and examination questions without answers

Exercises

B14.1 'Composite cost units such as tonne – mile, occupied bed-nights and patient-days, although commonly used in service costing, give a spurious air of simplicity and objectivity to cost accounting in service organisations.' Discuss.

B14.2 The records of a road haulage company show that costs, in total and per cost-unit are increasing disproportionately to the tonnage carried. Give possible reasons to explain these facts.

B14.3 A college with annual running costs of £8.5 millions has the following students:

Attendance

Type of Student	No.	Weeks p.a.	Hour per week
Full time	3200	36	30
Sandwich	1850	26	30
Part-time day	2400	28	9
Evening	4700	30	6
Short course	1000	2 (average)	20

      a. Determine a realistic cost unit for the college.

      b. Calculate the number of the units you have chosen in a. above for the college.

      c. Calculate the cost per unit.

Examination questions

B14.4 A change in government policy in the United kingdom has meant that, for the first time in their history, schools are to be individually responsible for their own budgets and the use of financial resources.

Knowing that you are studying for CIMA, a family friend who is a Headmaster of a secondary school which has 1,200 boys and girls aged from eleven to sixteen years has sought your advice about the financial information he ought to have to help him manage his school.

You are required, in the format of a report, to advise the Headteacher, bearing in mind the following points:

❏ The principles of cost accounting and financial control.

❏ Eighty to eighty five per cent of all costs are likely to be the salaries and wages of teachers, support staff and cleaners.

❏ Comparisons of cost of activities, it is hoped, will be made in the future against other similar schools.

❏ Personal computing facilities will be available.

Note: This question does not require special knowledge of UK schools but relates to any separately managed school which has budget responsibility.

(CIMA Cost Accounting)

15: Costing methods – process costing

1. Topics covered in this chapter

1.	Basis of process costing
2.	Normal and abnormal process losses
3.	Equivalent units
4.	FIFO and Average Cost valuations for Work-in-Progress

2. Process costing defined

Process costing is a form of operation costing used where production follows a series of sequential processes. It is used in a variety of industries including: oil refining, food processing, paper making, chemical and drug manufacture, paint and varnish manufacture. Although details vary from one concern to another, there are common features in most process costing systems. These include:

a. Clearly defined process cost centres and the accumulation of all costs (material, labour and overheads) by the cost centres.

b. The maintenance of accurate records of units and part units produced and the cost incurred by each process.

c. The averaging of the total costs of each process over the total production of that process, including partly completed units.

d. The charging of the cost of the output of one process as the raw materials input cost of the following process.

e. Clearly defined procedures for separating costs where the process produces two or more products (ie, Joint Products) or where By-products arise during production. (Joint product and By product costing are dealt with in the next chapter).

3. Choice of cost units

As previously explained, the cost unit chosen should be relevant to the organisation and its product. In most cases the appropriate unit arises naturally having regard to the process and the way the product is sold and priced. Examples include:

Industry	Possible Cost Units
Brewing	Litre, gallon, barrel
Paint, Varnish	Litre, Gallon
Food processing	Can, Case, Kilogram, Tonne, Gallon, etc.
Oil refining	Gallon or multiples, Barrel

4. Basis of process costing

The basis of all process costing systems is shown in Figure 15.1.

It will be seen that material passes through the various processes gathering costs as it progresses. The diagram shows the simplest possible situation. Typical complications which occur are the costing problems associated with process losses at various stages and the valuation of partly completed units at the end of an accounting period. These are dealt with later in the chapter.

5. Process losses

With many forms of production the quantity, weight or volume of the process *output* will be less than the quantity, weight or volume of the materials *input*. This may be due to various reasons:

a. evaporation, residuals, ash, swarf.

b. unavoidable handling, breakage and spoilage losses.

c. withdrawal for testing and inspection.

Because of increasing material costs, careful records must be maintained of losses occurring and the resulting cost implications. If losses are in accordance with normal practice, ie, standard levels, they are termed *normal process losses*. If they are above expectation, they are known as *abnormal process losses*.

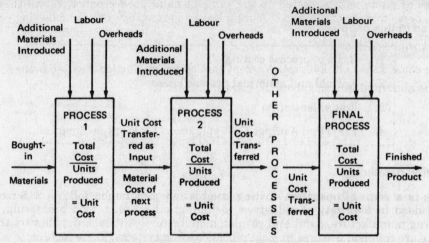

Figure 15.1 Process costing outline

6. Normal process losses

These are unavoidable losses arising from the nature of the production process and it is therefore logical and equitable that the cost of such losses is included as part of the cost of good production. If any value can be recouped from the sale of imperfect articles or materials then this would be credited to the process account thus reducing overall cost.

Example 1

A food manufacturing process has a normal wastage of 5% which can be sold as animal feedstuff at £5 tonne. In a given period the following data were recorded:

Input materials 160 tonnes at £23 per tonne. Labour and overheads £2896. Losses were at the normal level. Compute the cost per tonne.

Solution

INPUT	Tonnes	£
Materials	160	3680
Labour and overheads		2896
	160	6576
less Normal loss 5%	8	40 cr
Good production	152	6536

$$\text{Cost per tonne of good production} = \frac{6536}{152} = \textbf{£43}$$

Note:

The £40 credit to the Process account will be debited to a Scrap Sales account which will eventually be credited with the actual sale. Any balance on the Scrap Sales account will be taken to P&L account.

7. Abnormal process losses

Abnormal losses are those losses above the level deemed to be the normal loss rate for the process.

Abnormal losses cannot be foreseen and are due to such factors as; plant breakdown, industrial accidents, inefficient working or unexpected defects in materials. Conversely, unexpectedly favourable conditions might apply in a given period and actual losses may be lower than the calculated 'normal' loss. In such conditions *abnormal gains* would be made. The amount of abnormal loss or gain is calculated thus:

Abnormal loss (or gain) = Actual loss – Normal loss

It is an important costing principle, previously stated, that abnormal conditions should be excluded from routine reporting and only normal costs (which include normal process losses) charged to production. Accordingly the cost effects of abnormal losses or gains must be excluded from the Process Account. Abnormal losses or gains will be costed on the same basis as good production and therefore, like good production, will carry a share of the cost of normal losses. This is shown in the following example.

Example 2 - Abnormal loss

Assume the same data as in Example 1 except that actual production was 148 tonnes.

Compute the abnormal loss and show the relevant accounts.

Solution

$$\text{Abnormal loss} = \text{Actual loss} - \text{Normal loss}$$
$$= 12-8$$
$$= \textbf{4 tonnes}$$

As the abnormal losses are valued at the same cost as good production (ie, £43 tonne) the Process Account would be as follows.

Process A/C

	Tonnes	£		Tonnes	£
Material	160	3680	Good production	148	6364
Labour and Overheads		2896	Normal losses	8	40
			Abnormal losses	4	172
	160	6576		160	6576

The other relevant accounts would be:

Abnormal losses A/C

	£		£
Process A/C	172	Scrap sales	20
		P&L	152
	£172		£172

Scrap sales A/C

	£	
Process A/C	40	
Abnormal losses	20	

Note:

The sale of the 4 tonnes of abnormal losses at £5 tonne is credited to the Abnormal Losses A/c. This means that the net cost of £152 (£172-£20) is charged to the P&L A/c.

Example 3 - Abnormal gain

Again assume the same data as Example 1 except that actual production was 155 tonnes.

Calculate the abnormal gain and show the relevant accounts.

Solution

$$\text{Abnormal gain} = \text{Actual loss} - \text{Normal loss}$$
$$= 5 - 8$$
$$= \textbf{3 tonnes}$$

These gains are valued at the same rate as good production.

The relevant accounts are as follows:

Process A/C

	Tonnes	£		Tonnes	£
Material	160	3680	Good production	155	6665
Labour + Overheads		2896	Normal losses	8	40
Abnormal gains	3	129			
	163	£6705		163	£6705

Abnormal gains A/C

	£		£
Scrap sales A/C	15	Process A/C	129
P&L	114		
	129		129

Scrap sales A/C

	£		£
Process A/C	40	Abnormal gains	15

Note on Example 3:

a. Although an improvement in performance has been made, the Good Production is still valued at £43 per tonne.

b. The credit to the Scrap Sales A/c of £15 is necessary so that the account only shows the effect of the 5 tonnes actually lost.

8. The concept of equivalent units

At the end of any given period there are likely to be partly completed units. It is clear that some of the costs of the period are attributable to these units as well as those that are fully complete. To be able to spread costs equitably over part finished and fully complete units the concept of *equivalent units* is required. The number of equivalent units, for cost calculation purposes, is the number of equivalent fully complete units which the partly complete units (ie, the W-I-P) represent.

For example, assume that in a given period production was 2200 complete units and 600 partly complete. The partly complete units were deemed to be 75% complete.

$$\text{Total equivalent production} = \text{Completed units} + \text{Equivalent units in W-I-P}$$

$$= 2200 + \frac{3}{4}(600) = 2200 + 450$$

$$= \textbf{2650}$$

The total costs for the period would be spread over the total equivalent production.

ie $$\text{Cost per unit} = \frac{\text{Total Costs}}{\text{Total equivalent production (units)}}$$

9. Equivalent units and cost elements

The above illustration of equivalent units is the simplest possible. Frequently some overall estimate of completion is not possible or desirable and it becomes necessary to consider the percentage completion of each of the cost elements; material, labour and overheads. The same principles are used to calculate equivalent units, but each cost element must be treated separately and then the cost per unit of each element is added to give the cost of a complete unit. This is shown below.

Example 4

In a given period production and cost data were as follows:

Total Costs	Materials	£5,115
	Labour	3,952
	Overheads	3,000
		£12,067

Production was 1400 fully complete units and 200 partly complete. The degree of completion of the 200 units W-I-P was as follows

Material	75% complete
Labour	60% complete
Overheads	50% complete

Calculate the total equivalent production, the cost per complete unit and the value of the W-I-P.

Solution

Cost Element	Equivalent Units in W-I-P	+	Fully Complete Units	=	Total Effective production	Total costs Period £	Cost per Unit £
Material	$200 \times 75\% = 150$	+	1400	=	1550	5115	3.3
Labour	$200 \times 60\% = 120$	+	1400	=	1520	3952	2.6
Overheads	$200 \times 50\% = 100$	+	1400	=	1500	3000	2.00
						£12067	£7.90

From the table it will be seen that the cost of a complete unit = £7.90

$\therefore$ Value of completed production $\quad = 1400 \times £7.90$

$$= £11.060$$

$\therefore$ Value of W-I-P $\quad =$ Total Costs – Value of completed production

$$= £12067 - 11060$$

$$\mathbf{= £1007}$$

This can be verified by multiplying each element cost per unit by the number of equivalent units in the W-I-P of each cost element, thus:

Cost Element	No. of Equivalent Units in W-I-P	Cost per Unit	Value of WIP
Material	150	3.3	495
Labour	120	2.6	312
Overheads	100	2.00	200

£1007

Note on Example 4:

The way that the value of W-I-P can be cross checked by using the cost elements or the total values should be carefully studied. Remember-

Total cost for period = Value of completed units + Value of W-I-P

10. Input material and material introduced

It will be recalled from figure 15.1 that the output of one process forms the input material to the next process. The full cost of the completed units transferred forms the input material cost of the process and by its nature input material must be 100% complete.

Material introduced is extra material needed in the process and should always be shown separately from input material. Whenever there are partly completed units at the end of the period, they may contain two classifications of material, ie,

INPUT MATERIAL (ie, Previous process costs) always 100% complete.

MATERIAL INTRODUCED which may or may not be complete.

Note:

Input material may also be described as: Units transferred, Cost of goods or units transferred or Previous process costs.

11. Opening work in progress

It follows that where there are partly completed units at the end of one period (the closing W-I-P) there will be opening work in progress at the beginning of the next period. This opening work in progress will be partially complete and will have a value brought forward from the previous period, sometimes subdivided into the various elements of material, labour and overheads, each with a given degree of completion and value. Naturally in most practical situations there is both opening and closing work in progress and in such cases the problem arises of how to value the closing work in progress and the completed units transferred out.

There are two approaches to this problem; the *FIFO method* and the *Average cost* method.

12. FIFO method of valuation

Using this method it is assumed that units are dealt with on a first in – first out basis so that it is assumed that the first work done in a period is the completion of the opening W-I-P. The effect of this is that the closing W-I-P is valued at current period costs and part of the previous period's costs brought forward in the opening W-I-P valuation is attached to the cost of completed units.

13. Average cost method of valuation

Using this method an average unit cost is calculated using the total of the opening W-I-P valuation *plus* the current period costs. The effect of this is that both closing W-I-P and completed units are valued using the same average unit cost. This means that the previous period's costs (contained in the opening W-I-P valuation) influence the closing W-I-P valuation which is carried forward to the next period.

It is for this reason that it is sometimes argued that the Average Cost method makes the comparison of performance between periods more difficult than when the FIFO method is used. An alternative view is that the Average cost method is a useful device when costs fluctuate from period to period.

Neither of the valuation methods can be said to be 'incorrect' or 'correct', they are simply two different conventions which produce different answers. When costs are stable from one period to another and/or where the work-in-progress is a small proportion of throughput then the two systems produce similar results.

Examples follow which contrast the results obtained using both methods of valuation.

Example 5

Process 2 receives units from Process I and after carrying out work on the units transfers them to Process 3. For one accounting period the relevant data were as follows:

> Opening W-I-P 200 units (25% complete) valued at £2500
>
> 800 units received from Process I valued at £4300
>
> 840 units were transferred to Process 3
>
> Closing W-I-P 160 units (50% complete)
>
> The costs for the period were £16580 and no units were scrapped.

It is required to prepare the Process accounts for Process 2 using:

i.   the FIFO method of valuation,

ii.   the Average Cost method of valuation.

Solution - using FIFO method

Calculation of effective units of production

	Units
Completed units transferred out	840
+ Work contained in closing W-I-P (160 × 50%)	80
	920
− Work contained in opening W-I-P (200 × 25%)	50
∴ Effective units for period	870

$$\therefore \text{ Period cost per unit } = \frac{\text{Total cost for period (ie, Process costs + transfers in)}}{\text{Effective units for period}}$$

$$= \frac{£16580 + 4300}{870}$$

$$= £24$$

This figure is used to give the closing W-I-P valuation ie, $160 \times 50\% \times £24 = £1920$.

The valuation of the number of complete units transferred to Process 3 is found from the balance on the process account as follows:

Process 2 Account

	Units	£		Units	£
Opening W-I-P B/F	200	2500			
Receipts from Process 1	800	4300	Transfers to Process 3	840	21460
Process costs		16580	Closing WIP C/F	160	1920
	1000	23380		1000	23380

Note on Example 5 (FIFO METHOD):

The transfer value of £21460 is the balance on the account and is £1300 greater than the period cost per unit already calculated ie, $£21460 - (840 \times £24) = £1300$.

This is the amount by which the opening W-I-P valuation (based on the *previous* period's costs) is greater than the current period costs ie,

$$£2500 - (200 \times 25\% \times £24) = £1300.$$

Thus, it would be seen that only the current period cost levels, ie, the £24 per unit, are carried forward to the next period in the closing W-I-P valuation.

Solution - using Average Cost method

Using this system the effective units are the transfers to the next process (840 units) plus the work contained in the closing W-I-P (80 units ie, 50% of 160 units) that is a total of 920 units.

The costs involved are the total of the opening W-I-P valuation + the valuation of units transferred in + the process 2 costs ie,

$$£2500 + 4300 + 16580 = £23,380$$

$$\therefore \text{ average cost per unit } = \frac{23380}{920}$$

$$= £25.413$$

This is used to value both the closing stock and transfers out.

Thus Closing stock valuation $= 160 \times 50\% \times £25.413$

$$= £2033$$

Transfers to Process 3 $= 840 \times £25.413$

$$= £21347$$

The process account is as follows:

	Units	£		Units	£
Opening W-I-P B/F	200	2500			
Receipts from Process 1	800	4300	Transfers to Process 3	840	21347
Process Costs		16580	Closing WIP C/F	160	2033
	1000	23380		1000	23380

Notes on Example 5 (Average Cost method):

1. It will be seen that the effect of the average cost method is, in this example, to increase the value of closing stock and reduce the value of transfers to Process 3. This is because the previous period cost levels (as contained in the opening W-I-P valuation) were *higher* than the current cost levels. If the previous period cost levels were *lower* than current levels the average cost method would cause the closing W-I-P valuations to be lower than when using the FIFO system.

2. The above example has deliberately been kept simple to show clearly the principles involved. Examples follow which show the added complications of abnormal and normal scrap and where the elements (material, labour and overheads) of the opening and closing W-I-P are involved.

   It must be stressed however, that these added complications merely increase the amount of arithmetic involved, they do not alter the basic principles explained above so it is important that these are thoroughly understood before proceeding further.

Example 6

This example illustrates the treatment of opening and closing W-I-P where the W-I-P is broken down into its various elements.

The following data relate to Process Y for accounting period 2.

At the beginning of period 2 there were 800 units partly completed which had the following values:

	Value	
	£	% age complete
Input Material (from Process X)	8200	100
Material Introduced	5600	55
Labour	3200	60
Overheads	2400	45

During the period 4300 units were transferred from Process X at a value of £46,500 and other costs were:

	£
Material Introduced	24,000
Labour	19,500
Overheads	18,200

At the end of the period, the closing W-I-P was 600 units which were at the following stage of completion:

Input Material	100% complete
Material Introduced	50% complete
Labour	45% complete
Overheads	405 complete

The balance of 4500 units was transferred to Finished Goods.

Calculate the value of units transferred to Finished Goods and the value of W-I-P and prepare the Process account using

    i. the FIFO method and

    ii. the Average Cost method.

Solution – Using FIFO method

As previously the first step is to calculate the effective units of production for the period. This follows identical principles to Example 5 except that in this example it is necessary to consider the four elements of the units (Input material, material introduced, labour and overheads) instead of simply the units as a whole. When the effective production is ascertained the cost per unit, for each element, can be calculated.

Calculation of effective units and cost per unit

Cost element	Completed units	+	Equivalent units in closing W-I-P	–	Equivalent units in opening W-I-P	=	Total effective production	Costs	Cost per unit
								£	£
Input material	4500	+	600	–	800	=	4300	46500	10.814
Material Introduced	4500	+	300	–	440	=	4360	24000	5.505
Labour	4500	+	270	–	480	=	4290	19500	4.545
Overheads	4500	+	240	–	360	=	4380	18200	4.155
									25.019

∴ Closing stock valuation for 600 units

			£
Input material	= 100% complete	= 600 × £10.814 =	6488
Material introduced	= 50% complete	= 300 × £5.505 =	1651
Labour	= 45% complete	= 270 × £4.545 =	1227
Overheads	= 40% complete	= 240 × £4.155 =	997
			£10363

This value is used in the Process Account in the normal way with the value of the Transfers to Finished Goods being the balance on the account.

Process Account – Process Y (FIFO)

	Units	£		Units	£
Opening W-I-P B/F	800	19400			
Transfers in from Process X	4300	46500	Transfers to Fin. Goods	4500	117237
Material introduced		24000	Closing WIP C/F	600	10363
Labour		19500			
Overheads		18200			
	5100	127600		5100	127600

Solution - Using Average Cost method

Calculation of effective units and cost per unit

Cost Elements	Equivalent units in Closing WIP	+	Fully Complete Units	=	(a) Total Effective Production	Opening WIP Values	+	Period Costs	=	(b) Total Cost	Cost per Unit $\left(\frac{b}{a}\right)$
Input Material	600 × 100% = 600	+	4500	=	5100	£8200	+	£46500	=	£54700	£10.725
Material Intro	600 × 50% = 300	+	4500	=	4800	5600	+	24000	=	29600	6.167
Labour	600 × 45% = 270	+	4500	=	4770	3200	+	19500	=	22700	4.759
Overheads	600 × 40% = 240	+	4500	=	4740	2400	+	18200	=	20600	4.346
						£19400	+	£108200	=	£127600	£25.997

∴ Value of completed production = 4500 × £25.997

= **£116,987**

The value of the closing WIP can be found either by deducting the value of completed production from total costs or, more tediously, by calculating the various element values, as follows:

Value of closing WIP = Total cost – value of completed production

= £127,600 – 116,987 = **£10,613**

or this can be calculated by using the various element values ie,

600 × £10.725 =	6,435
300 × £6.167 =	1,850.10
270 × £4.759 =	1,284.93
240 × £4.346 =	1,043.04
	£10,613.07

(slight rounding error)

The process account can now be completed

Process Account – Process Y (Average Cost)

	Units	£		Units	£
Opening WIP B/F	800	19400			
			Transfers to Fin. Goods	4500	116987
Transfers from Process X	4300	46500	Closing WIP C/F	600	10613
Material Introduced		24000			
Labour		19500			
Overheads		18200			
	5100	£127600		5100	£127600

Example 7

This is a more complicated example which brings together the various facets of process costing covered in the chapter. It includes opening and closing W-I-P and normal and abnormal losses where the scrapped units are not fully complete.

The following data relate to Process 2 for one accounting period. Process 2 receives units from Process 1 and, after processing, transfers them to Process 3.

Opening W-I-P 600 units

	Value	Percentage complete
	£	
Input material	720	100
Material introduced	500	60
Labour	340	50
Overheads	270	40

Transfers from Process 1:4100 units valued at £5,200.

Transfers to Process 3:3500 units

	£
Materials introduced	2956
Labour	2200
Overheads	1900

Closing stock 800 units at the following stage of completion

Input material	100% complete
Material introduced	60% complete
Labour	50% complete
Overheads	40% complete

400 units were scrapped at the following stage of completion

Input material	100% complete
Material introduced	100% complete
Labour	40% complete
Overheads	30% complete

The normal loss is 10% of production and the scrapped units realised 40p each.

It is required to prepare the Process Account for Process 2 using

    i.   the FIFO method,

    ii.   the Average Cost method.

Solution - Using FIFO method

The first stage is to calculate the amount of normal loss to see whether there is any abnormal loss or gain involved.

The production for the period is calculated as follows:

Opening W-I-P	600	units
+ Transfers in	4100	
	4700	
– Closing W-I-P	800	
∴ Production	3900	units

∴ Normal loss is 10% of 3900 = 390, and as the actual number scrapped were 400, there were 10 units of abnormal loss.

The calculation of effective units for cost calculation purposes follows the same principles as in Examples 5 and 6 except that the number of units abnormal loss must be included in the total effective production because, as explained in Para 7, abnormal losses are costed on the same basis as good production.

Calculation of effective units and cost per unit

Cost Element	Completed Units	+	Equiv. Units in Closing WIP	+	Equiv. Units in Abnormal loss	–	Equiv. Units in Opening WIP	=	Total Effective Production	Costs £	Cost per Unit £
Input Material	3500	+	800	+	10	–	600	=	3710	5100	1.402
Material Intro.	3500	+	480	+	10	–	360	=	3630	2800*	0.771
Labour	3500	+	400	+	4	–	300	=	3604	2200	0.610
Overheads	3500	+	320	+	3	–	240	=	3583	1900	0.530

(* This is the cost of the material introduced, £2956, less the resale value of the normal loss, £156 ie, 390 @ 40p each. The resale value of the 10 units of abnormal loss is credited to the Abnormal loss account *not* the process account.)

The costs per unit calculated are then used to evaluate the value of the closing W-I-P and the abnormal loss

Closing W-I-P valuation

		£
Input material	800 equivalent units @ £1.402	1121.29
Material introduced	480 equivalent units @ 0.771	370.25
Labour	400 equivalent units @ 0.612	244.17
Overheads	320 equivalent units @ 0.530	169.69
		£1905.40
		say, £1905

Abnormal loss valuation

		£
Input material	10 equivalent units @ £1.402	14.02
Material introduced	10 equivalent units @ 0.771	7.71
Labour	4 equivalent units @ 0.610	2.44
Overheads	3 equivalent units @ 0.530	1.59
		£25.75
		say, £26

The process account can now be prepared.

Process 2 Account(FIFO)

	Units	£		Units	£
Opening WIP	600	1830			
Transfers from Process 1	4100	5200	Normal loss	390	156
Material		2956	Abnormal loss	10	26
Labour		2200	Transfers to Process 3	3500	11999
Overheads		1900	Closing WIP	800	1905
	4700	£14086		4700	£14086

Solution - Using Average Cost method

Calculation of effective units and cost per unit

Cost Element	Equiv. Units in Closing WIP	+	Equiv. Units in Abnormal loss	+	Complete units	=	Effective Production	Opening WIP value £	+	Period cost £	=	Total Costs (£)	Cost per Unit (£)
Input Material	800	+	10	+	3500	=	4310	720	+	5200	=	5920	1.35
Material Intro.	480	+	10	+	3500	=	3990	500	+	2800	=	3300	0.827
Labour	400	+	4	+	3500	=	3904	340	+	2200	=	2540	0.651
Overheads	320	+	3	+	3500	=	3823	270	+	1900	=	2170	0.568

The various costs per unit are used to evaluate the closing W-I-P, abnormal loss and the completed production:

Closing W-I-P

Equivalent units		Cost per unit		Value
800	×	1.35	=	1098.83
480	×	0.827	=	396.99
400	×	0.651	=	260.24
320	×	0.568	=	181.64
				1937.70
				say £1938

Abnormal loss

10	×	1.35	=	13.73
10	×	0.827	=	8.27
4	×	0.651	=	2.60
3	×	0.568	=	26.30
				£26.30
				say, £26

Completed production

3500	×	1.35	=	4807.42
3500	×	0.827	=	2894.74
3500	×	0.651	=	2277.15
3500	×	0.568	=	1986.66
				£11965.97
				say, £11966

These values are used in the Process account.

Process 2 Account (Average Cost)

	Units	£		Units	£
Opening WIP	600	1830			
			Normal loss	390	156
Transfers from Process 1	4100	5200	Abnormal loss	10	26
Material		2956	Transfers to Process 3	3500	11966
Labour		2200			
Overheads		1900	Closing WIP	800	1938
	4700	£14086		4700	£14086

Note:

If, instead of the abnormal loss, there had been an abnormal gain the treatment would be as follows for both Average cost and the FIFO methods. The total effective production would be found as in Example 6 *less* the number of abnormal gain units. These units would be evaluated at the cost per unit calculated and the Process account *debited* with the abnormal gain units and their value. It follows that abnormal gain units will always be fully complete whereas abnormal loss units may be partially or fully complete.

14. Summary

a. Process costing is used where production follows a number of sequential processes frequently of an automatic nature.

b. The cost unit chosen should be relevant to the organisation and the product. Examples include; gallons, barrels, tonnes, kilograms.

c. Material passes through the various processes gathering costs as it progresses. The output of one process forming the input material into the next process.

d. Losses due to breakage, evaporation, machining, testing and other causes must be carefully recorded.

e. Normal process losses are unavoidable losses in production and form part of the cost of good production.

f. Abnormal losses are losses above the normal anticipated level and should be costed on the same basis as good production.

g. When partly complete units occur at the end of a period the number of equivalent units of complete production must be calculated.

h. The concept of equivalent units can also be applied to the cost elements in production; material, labour and overheads.

i. There are two methods of calculating W-I-P values; the FIFO and average cost methods.

15. Points to note

a. Although the calculation of the cost of W-I-P is a common examination question, in practice where the W-I-P is a small fraction of throughput, period to period, it is likely to be ignored.

b. The technique of standard costing is particularly appropriate for use in process industries. Such applications are described in Chapter 26.

Student self-testing

Self Review Questions

1. What are the characteristics of process costing systems? (2)
2. Give 6 examples of cost units found in process costing? (3)
3. What are the reasons for process losses? (5)
4. What are the normal process losses and how are they dealt with in the costing system? (6)
5. What are abnormal process losses and how are they dealt with in the costing system? (7)
6. What is an equivalent unit? (8)
7. How is the value of W-I-P established in a process costing system? (9)
8. What is the distinction between 'Input Material' and 'Material Introduced' ? (10)

9. How is opening balance of W-I-P dealt with? (11)

10. Distinguish between the FIFO and average cost valuation methods. (12 & 13)

Exercises and examination questions with answers

Exercises

A15.1 A firm has two processes 1 and 2.

Material for 12,000 items was put into Process 1. There were no opening stocks and no process losses and there were transfers of 9,000 items to Process 2. The unfinished items were complete as to material and 50% complete as to labour and overhead. The costs of Process 1 were Direct Material £36,000, Direct Labour £32,000 and Overheads £8,000.

Process 2 completed 7,600 items and there were 600 scrapped which was considered normal. The balance was unfinished and deemed to be 25% complete in labour and overheads. The costs for Process 2 were; Labour £28,500 and Overheads £14,000. You are required to prepare process accounts for each process.

A15.2 Orion Ltd produce a single product which undergoes three processes. The following details relate to one period:

	Process		
	I	II	III
	£	£	£
Raw Materials (60,000 units)	80,000		
Materials Introduced	23,500	18,750	22,100
Direct Wages	15,600	12,000	13,400
Overheads allotted to Processes	3,800	4,600	3,200
Other overheads total £27,000			
	Units	Units	Units
Output in units	55,200	53,800	49,600

A normal loss of 5% of the input to each process is anticipated.

Units lost have the following scrap values:

After Process I	Nil
After Process II	£1
After Process III	£1.80

There was no opening or closing W-I-P.

Prepare ledger accounts for the period.

A15.3 A plastic manufacturing process has a normal wastage of 8% which can be sold as scrap at £2 per Kg.

In a given period, the following data were recorded:

Input 250 Kgs at	£7 Kg.
Labour and overheads	£3,500
Actual output	225 Kgs.

Show all relevant accounts.

A15.4 In a given period the production data and costs for a process were:

Production 2100 units fully complete

700 units partly complete

The degree of completion of the partly complete units was:

Material	80%	complete
Labour	60%	complete
Overheads	50%	complete

The costs for the period were

Material	£24800
Labour	£16750
Overheads	£36200

Calculate the total equivalent production, the cost per complete unit and the value of the W-I-P.

Examination questions

A15.5 A company manufactures a product that goes through two processes. You are given the following cost information about the processes for the month of November.

	Process 1	Process 2
Unit input	15,000	–
Finished unit input from Process 1	–	10,000
Finished unit output to Process 2	10,000	–
Finished unit output from Process 2	–	9,500
Opening WIP – Units	–	2,000
– Value	–	£26,200
Input – Materials	£26,740	
– Labour	£36,150	£40,000
– Overhead	£40,635	£59,700
Closing WIP – Units	4,400	1,800

You are told:

1. The closing WIP in Process 1 was 80% complete for material, 50% complete for labour and 40% complete for overhead.

2. The opening WIP in Process 2 was 40% complete for labour and 50% complete for overhead. It had value of labour £3,200, overheads £6,000 for work done in Process 2.

3. The closing WIP in Process 2 was two thirds complete for labour and 75% complete for overhead.

4. No further material needed to be added to the units transferred from Process 1.

5. Normal loss is budgeted at 5% of total input in process 1 and process 2. Total input is to be inclusive of any opening WIP.

6. Normal loss has no scrap value in Process 1 and can be sold for the input value from Process 1, in Process 2.

7. Abnormal losses have no sales value.

8. It is company policy to value opening WIP in a process by the weighted average method.

Required:

a. Prepare accounts for:
   i.   Process 1.
   ii. Process 2.
   iii. Normal loss.
   iv. Any abnormal loss/gain.

(AAT Cost Accounting & Budgeting, part question)

A15.6 A chemical compound is made by raw material being processed through two processes. The output of Process A is passed to Process B where further material is added to the mix. The details of the process costs for the financial period number 10 were as shown below:

Process A

Direct material	2,000 kilograms at £5 per kg
Direct labour	£7,200
Process plant time	140 hours at £60 per hour

Process B

Direct material	1,400 kilograms at £5 per kg
Direct labour	£4,200
Process plant time	80 hours at £72.50 per hour

The departmental overhead for Period 10 was £6,840 and is absorbed into the costs of each process on direct labour cost.

	Process A	Process B
Expected output was	80% of input	90% of input
Actual output was	1,400kgs	2,620 kgs

Assume no finished stock at the beginning of the period and no work-in-progress at either the beginning or end of the period.

Normal loss is contaminated material which is sold as scrap for £0.50 per kg from Process A and £1.825 per kg from Process B, for both of which immediate payment is received.

You are required to prepare the accounts for Period 10, for

    i.   Process A,

   ii.   Process B,

  iii.   Normal loss/gain,

  iv.   Abnormal loss/gain,

   v.   Finished goods,

  vi.   Profit and loss (extract).

(CIMA Cost Accounting)

A15.7 A company produces a single product from one of its manufacturing processes. The following information of process inputs, outputs and work in process relates to the most recently completed period:

	kg
Opening work in process	21,700
Materials input	105,600
Output completed	92,400
Closing work in process	28,200

The opening and closing work in process are respectively 60% and 50% complete as to conversion costs. Losses occur at the beginning of the process and have a scrap value of £0.45 per kg.

The opening work in process included raw material costs of £56,420 and conversion costs of £30,597. Costs incurred during the period were:

Materials input	£276,672
Conversion costs	£226,195

Required:

a. Calculate the unit costs of production (£ per kg to four decimal places) using:

    i.   the weighted average method of valuation and assuming that all losses are treated as normal;

   ii.   the FIFO method of valuation and assuming that normal losses are 5% of materials input.

(ACCA Cost and Management Accounting 1, part question)

A15.8 Armor p.l.c. operates a process which produces an industrial cleansing chemical and shown below are the costs incurred by the process during month 7 together with other relevant operating data.

Direct Materials transferred into process:

10,000 kilos at £0.15 per kilo	£1,500
Conversion Costs	£1,330

Output:

Finished Production	8,400 kilos
By-product	500 kilos
Toxic Waste	800 kilos

The toxic waste is the same chemical as the finished produced except that it has been polluted at the final operation. The cost of disposing of the toxic waste is £0.80 per kilo. The by-product is transferred to a subsidiary operation where it is packed at a cost of £0.25 per kilo. These costs are not included in the direct materials and conversion costs tabulated above.

The selling price of the by-product is £0.75 per kilo and the process is credited with the net realisable value of the by-product produced. During month 7, 30 kilos of the by-product were sold.

The normal output from the process, per 1,000 kilos of direct material is:

Finished Production	850 kilos
By-product	50 kilos
Toxic Waste	60 kilos
Loss as a result of evaporation	40 kilos

Required:

a. Prepare the following accounts recording month 7 transactions for the above process.

> Process Account.
>
> By-Product Account.
> Normal Toxic Waste Account.
> Any Relevant Abnormal Loss/Gain Accounts.

b. Explain the reasons for your treatment of the toxic waste including an explanation of how the total cost of abnormal toxic waste has been calculated.

(ACCA, Costing).

A15.9 Wye Chemicals p.l.c. manufactures a range of products in a variety of processes and the data given below relate to Process 3 for the month of April.

You are required to prepare:

a. a statement showing the cost per unit and the value of the output;

b. an account for Process 3;

c. an Abnormal Gain or Loss account.

	units	£
Transfer from Process 2	10,800	7,980
Transfer to Process 4	9,650	
Direct materials added during process		2,019
Direct wages incurred in process		2,889
Production overhead apportioned to process		6,482

There is a normal loss in process of 10% of throughput.

All units scrapped can be sold at £0.20 each.

Opening work-in-progress:	1,200 units	
Degree of completion:	materials added in process	40%
	direct wages	60%
	production overhead	70%
Closing work-in-progress:	1,000 units	
Degree of completion:	materials added in process	80%
	direct wages	60%
	production overhead	40%
Units scrapped:	1,350	
Degree of completion:	materials added in process	50%
	direct wages	40%
	production overhead	20%

(CIMA, Cost Accounting 2)

Exercises and examination questions without answers

Exercises

B15.1 In a period the following data were obtained relating to a process:

Materials	£23,200
Labour	18,250
Overheads	16,100

Production was 21,500 fully complete units and 1,200 partly complete units as follows:

Material	80% complete
Labour	50% complete
Overheads	40% complete

Calculate the total equivalent production, cost per complete unit and the value of the W-l-P.

B15.2 A process has a normal wastage of 5% which can be sold for £20 per tonne.

The following data were recorded during a period:

Input	320 tonnes at £55 per tonne
Labour	£7, 000
Actual output	308 tonnes

Show all relevant accounts.

B15.3 Process B receives the output from Process A and transfers its output to Process C.

During a period the following data were recorded regarding Process B.

Opening W-l-P:	500 Kgs (40% complete) valued at £11,500
Units received from A:	1,700 Kgs valued at £42,000
Units transferred to C:	1,750 Kgs.
Closing W-I-P	450 Kgs. (50% complete)

Labour and other costs for the period were £32,500 and no units were scrapped. Prepare the process accounts for Process B using:

a. the FIFO method of valuation

b. the Average cost method of valuation.

B15.4 There were 600 units of opening W-l-P for a process the details of which were as follows:

	£	% age complete
Input material (from previous process)	7,500	100
Material introduced	6,500	60
Labour	4,200	40

During the period 3,500 units were received from the previous process at a value of £41,500, labour costs were £22,500 and material costs £18,000.

Closing W-l-P was 800 units which were at the following stages of completion:

	% age completion
Input material	100
Material introduced	50
Labour	30

The balance of units were transferred to Finished Goods.

Calculate the value of units transferred to Finished Goods and the value of W-l-P and prepare the Process account using the FIFO method.

B15.5 As B15.4 but using the Average Cost method.

Examination questions

B15.6 a. The standard processing loss in refining certain basic materials into an industrial cleaning compound is 15%, this scrap being sold for 50p per kg.

At the beginning of Period 6, 8,000 kg of basic material was put into a process, the output of which was 7,000 kg of cleaning compound. The basic material cost 80p per kg, wages of process operators amounted to £1,200 and overhead applied to the process was £480.

Prepare the necessary accounts to show the results of the process.

b. The production of a product known as a Tojo requires the treatment of input units through three distinct processes at each of which refining material is added and labour and overhead costs are incurred.

Work in progress at the beginning of Period 9 consists of 8,000 input units which has passed through the first process, the cost to that point being £96,000. During Period 9, refining material which cost £31,594 was put into the process and labour costs amounted to £23,940. Process Overhead is applied at the rate of 40% of process labour.

7,200 units were completed during the Period and transferred to Process 3. Of the remainder, the firm's Chief Chemist estimated that in respect of refining material, labour and overhead, half were 75% complete at the end of Period 9, and the other half 40% complete.

You are required to write up Process 2 Account Period 9 showing clearly the cost to be transferred to process 3, and the value of the work in progress at the end of the period.

(ACCA, Costing)

B15.7 A concentrated liquid fertiliser is manufactured by passing chemicals through two consecutive processes. Stores record cards for the chemical ingredients used exclusively by the first process show the following data for May:

Opening stock	4,000 litres	£10,800
Closing stock	8,000 litres	£24,200
Receipts into store	20,000 litres	£61,000

Other process data for May is tabulated below.

	Process 1	Process 2
Direct Labour	£4,880	£6,000
Direct Expenses	£4,270	–
Overhead Absorption Rates	250% of Direct labour	100% of Direct labour
Output	8,000 litres	7,500 litres
Opening stock of Work in Process	Nil	Nil
Closing stock of Work in Process	5,600 litres	Nil
Normal Yield	85% of input	90% of input
Scrap Value of loss	Nil	Nil

In Process 1 the closing stock of work in process has just passed through inspection, which is at the stage where materials and conversion costs are 100% and 75% complete respectively.

In Process 2 inspection is the final operation.

Required:

a. Prepare the relevant accounts to show the results of the processes for May and present a detailed working paper showing your calculations and any assumptions in arriving at the data shown in those accounts.

b. If supplies of the required chemicals are severely restricted and all production can be sold immediately, briefly explain how you would calculate the total loss to the company if, at the beginning of June, 100 litres of the correct mix of chemicals were spilt on issue to Process 1.

(ACCA, Costing,)

B15.8 A company producing a single product from one process has an opening work in process of 3,200 units which were complete as to material but only 75% complete as to labour and overhead. These units at the end of September had been valued as follows:

	£
Direct materials	14,000
Direct wages	6,500
Production overhead (200% on direct wages)	13,000

During the month of October a further 24,800 units were put into process and the following costs charged to the process:

	£
Direct materials	96,000
Direct wages	59,125
Production overhead	118,250

Normal loss by evaporation was 500 units and 25,000 completed units were transferred to finished stock.

Work in process at the end of October was 2,500 units which were complete as to material and half complete as to labour and overhead.

The Average method of pricing is used.

You are required to prepare, for the month of October, a cost of production report or other suitable statement)s) for the operating management to show:

a. production cost per unit in total and by element of cost;

b. the total cost of production transferred to finished stock;

c. the valuation of closing work in process in total and by element of cost.

(CIMA, Cost Accounting 1)

B15.9 AB Chemicals Limited produces a compound by mixing certain ingredients within two separate processes. For a particular week the recorded costs were:

Process 1 – Material: 2,000 kilograms at £2 per kilogram Labour: £360
Process plant time: 24 hours at £200 per hour

Process 2 – Material: 3,100 kilograms at £6 per kilogram Labour: £240
Process plant time: 40 hours at £76.30 per hour.

Indirect production overhead for the week amounted to £2,400 and is absorbed on the basis of labour cost.

Normal outputs are: Process 1   80% of input
Process 2   90% of input

Discarded materials have scrap values of £0.30 per kilogram from Process 1 and £1.50 per kilogram from Process 2. Assume that sales of scrap are made for cash during the week. There was no work- in – progress at either the beginning or end of the week. Output during the week was 1,400 kilograms from Process 1 and 4,200 kilograms from Process 2.

You are required to:

a. show the accounts for:

i.   Process 1;

ii. Process 2;

iii. abnormal gain/loss;

iv. profit and loss – relating to transactions in any of the above accounts;

v.   finished goods.

b. explain, in relation to process costing, the concept of 'equivalent units' and give a simple example using your own figures.

(CIMA, Cost Accounting 1)

B15.10 a. Outline the characteristics of industries in which a process costing system is used and give two examples of such industries.

b. ATM Chemicals produces product XY by putting it through a single process. You are given the following details for November.

Input costs	
Material costs	25,000 kilos at £2.48 per kilo
Labour costs	8,000 hours at £5.50 per hour
Overhead costs	£63,000

You are also told the following:

i.   Normal loss is 4% of input.
ii. Scrap value of normal loss is £2.00 per kilo.
iii. Finished output amounted to 15,000 units.
iv. Closing work-in-progress amounted to 6,000 units and was fully complete for material, $\frac{2}{3}$ complete for labour and $\frac{1}{2}$ for overheads.
v.   There was no opening work-in-progress.

Required:

i.   Prepare the Process account for the month of November detailing the value of the finished units and the work-in-progress.

ii. prepare an Abnormal Loss account.

c. Distinguish between normal and abnormal losses, their costing treatment and how each loss may be controlled.

(AAT Cost & Budgeting)

B15.11 a. Explain the features that distinguish each of the following forms of accounting.

i.   Integrated accounts

ii. Inter-locking accounts.

b. The following information relates to the PM Company that uses a continuous process to produce its product.

Process 1

April – input of material 10,000 kilos at £2.80 per kilo

conversion costs £31,200

normal loss 10% of input

closing work in progress 3,000 kilos 60% complete for conversion costs.

Scrap value £1 per kilo

Output 6,000 kilos

The output from Process 1 is transferred to Process 2 where there was no opening work in progress at the beginning of April. The following information relates to Process 2.

Conversion costs £27,000

Normal loss 5% of input

Closing work in progress 1,000 kilos 70% complete for conversion costs.

Scrap value £2.25 per kilo

Output 4,900 kilos

Required:

Prepare accounts for Process 1 and Process 2 and for any losses or gains.

(AAT Cost Accounting & Budgeting, part question)

B15.12 C Limited manufactures a range of products and the data below refer to one product which goes through one process only. The company operates a thirteen four-weekly reporting system for process and product costs and the data given below relate to Period 10.

There was no opening work-in-progress stock.

5,000 units of material input at £2.94 per unit entered the process.

Further direct materials added	£13,830
Direct wages incurred	£6,555
Production overhead	£7,470

Normal loss is 3% of input.

Closing work-in-progress was 800 units but these were incomplete, having reached the following percentages of completion for each of the elements of cost listed:

Direct materials added	75%
Direct wages	50%
Production overhead	25%

270 units were scrapped after a quality control check when the units were at the following degrees of completion:

Direct materials added	$66\frac{2}{3}\%$
Direct wages	$33\frac{1}{3}\%$
Production overhead	$16\frac{2}{3}\%$

Units scrapped, regardless of the degree of completion, are sold for £1 each and it is company policy to credit the process account with the scrap value of normal loss units.

You are required

a. to prepare the Period 10 accounts for the

i. process account; and

ii. abnormal gain or loss;

b. to suggest two possible reasons to explain the gain or loss shown in a) (ii) above.

(CIMA Cost Accounting)

16: Costing methods – joint product and by product costing

1. Topics covered in this chapter

> 1. By-Products and joint product defined
> 2. Apportionment of joint costs
> 3. Physical unit basis
> 4. Sales value and notional sales value bases.

2. Definitions

A joint product is the term used when two or more products arise simultaneously in the course of processing, each of which has a significant sales value in relation to each other. Examples of industries where joint products arise are as follows:

Oil Refining

❏ The joint products include; diesel fuel, petrol, paraffin, lubricants.

Meat processing

❏ The joint products include; the various grades of meat and hides.

Mining

❏ The joint products frequently include the recovery of several metals from the same crushing.

On the other hand a By-Product is a product which arises incidentally in the production of the main product(s) and which has a relatively small sales value compared with the main product(s). Examples of by-products are;

Iron and steel manufacture

❏ furnace slag is sold for use in cement and brick manufacture and for road construction.

Meat trade

❏ bones, grease and certain offal are regarded as by-products.

Timber trade

❏ sawdust, small offcuts, bark are usually regarded as by-products.

After the point of separation both joint products and by-products may need further processing before they are saleable.

Note: It will be apparent from the foregoing that clear distinctions between by-products and joint products are not possible. The exact classification of a particular item is a matter of judgement depending on the particular circumstances. What is a by-product in one factory may be termed a joint product in another.

3. By-product costing

Because by-products, by definition, have a relatively small sales value, elaborate and expensive costing systems should be avoided. The most common methods of dealing with by-products are as follows:

a. By-product net realisable value is deducted from the total cost of production.

b. Total costs (main product and by-product, if any) are deducted from Total Sales value of main and by-products.

c. By-product receipts are treated as incidental other income and transferred to general P+L account. This method is generally considered unsatisfactory except where the value is very small.

d. By-products treated as joint products. This method is most appropriate where the value of the by-product is relatively large. Details of joint product costing are dealt with in Para. 4 below.

None of the by-product costing methods is wholly satisfactory, but method (a) above probably has least disadvantages. This method is illustrated in the following example.

Example 1

During a period 2400 units of Large were produced and sold at £10 per unit. Total production costs were £17,500. Arising from the main production process 60 kgs. of Little were produced which were sold at £8 per kg.

Special packing and distribution costs of £2.20 per kg were incurred for Little. What were the net production costs and gross profit for the period?

Solution

		£	£
	Production Costs		17,500
Less	Net Realisable Value of Little	480	
		-132	348
=	Net Production Cost		17,152
	Gross Profit		£6,848
	Sales Value of Large		£24,000

4. Joint-product costing

Because joint products arise due to the inherent nature of the production process, it follows that none of the products can be produced separately. The various products become identifiable at a point known as the 'split-off point'. Up to that stage all costs are joint costs, subsequent to the split-off point any costs incurred can be identified with specific products and they are known as 'subsequent' or 'additional processing costs'. This is shown diagrammatically in figure 16.1.

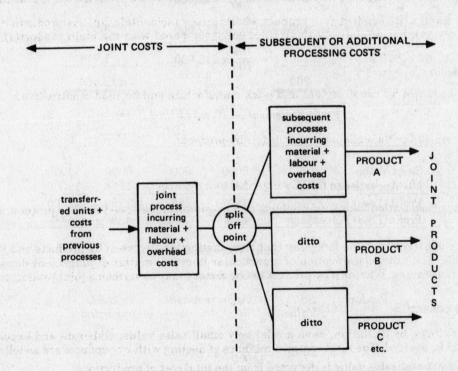

Figure 16.1 Joint product costing

It follows therefore that subsequent costs arising after the split-off point do not pose any particular costing problem because they are readily identifiable with a specific product and can be coded and charged accordingly. For product costing purposes the major problem in joint-product costing is to apportion the joint costs, ie, those prior to the split-off point, on an acceptable basis.

5. Apportioning joint costs

The commonest methods of apportioning joint costs are:

a. The physical unit basis. The joint costs are apportioned over the joint products in proportion to the physical weight or volume of the products.

b. The sales value basis. Here the joint costs are apportioned in proportion to the relative sales value of the products.

The two methods are illustrated in Example 2.

Example 2

A process produces three products, X, Y and Z. Total joint costs were £12,000 and outputs, selling prices and sales values were:

> X. 200 litres sold at £25 litre giving a sale value of £5000.
> Y. 400 litres sold at £15 litre giving a sale value of £6000.
> Z. 100 litres sold at £30 litre giving a sale value of £3000.

Apportion the joint costs and calculate the profit percentage on

> i.   the physical unit basis and
> ii. the sales value basis.

Solution

Physical unit basis

Cost Statement

Product	Output	Apportionment	Cost apportioned £
X	200	$\frac{200}{700} \times £12,000$	3,429
Y	400	$\frac{400}{700} \times £12,000$	6,857
Z	100	$\frac{100}{700} \times £12,000$	1,714
	700		£12,000

Profit Statement on Physical Unit Basis

	X	Y	Z	Total
	£	£	£	£
Sales Value	5000	6000	3000	14000
less Apportioned Costs	3429	6857	1714	12000
Profit/(Loss)	£1571	(£857)	£1286	£2000
Profit/(Loss) Percentage	31%	(14%)	43%	14%

Sales Value Basis

Cost Statement

Product	Sales Value	Apportionment	Costs apportioned £
X	£5000	$\frac{5000}{14000} \times £12,000$	4286
Y	£6000	$\frac{6000}{14000} \times £12,000$	5143
Z	£3000	$\frac{3000}{14000} \times £12,000$	2571
	£14000		£12000

Profit statement on Sales Value basis

	X	Y	Z	Total
	£	£	£	£
Sales Value	5000	6000	3000	14000
less Apportioned Costs	4286	5143	2571	12000
Profit	£714	£857	£429	£2000
Profit Percentage	14%	14%	14%	14%

Notes:

a. It will be seen that the sales value basis produces the same profit percentage for each product. The method is widely used for this reason and for the assumption that the price obtained for an item is directly related to its cost.

b. The cost apportionment is made on the sales value of the products (ie, Qty × price) and not the selling price per unit.

c. It must be emphasised that whatever method is used for apportioning joint costs, it is a convention only and its accuracy cannot be tested.

6. The notional sales value method

On occasions the products which emerge from the split-off point are not saleable without further processing. It follows therefore that, at the split-off point, sales values are not known so that joint costs cannot be apportioned until some estimate is made of a notional sales value at the split-off point.

This is done by deducting subsequent processing costs from the final sales value to arrive at a notional sales value at split-off point. This is illustrated below.

Example 3

A process with joint costs of £5000 produces 2 products W and V, both of which need further processing before sale. The relevant data are as follows:

Product	Output	Subsequent Processing Costs	Final Selling Price	Final Value Sales
				£
W	2000 Kgs	£1500	£2 Kg	4000
V	4500 Kgs	£1250	£1.50 Kg	6750

Calculate the notional Sales Value at split-off point, the apportionment of joint costs, the profit on each product and the profit percentage.

Solution

Cost Statement

Product	Final Sales Value	Subsequent Processing Costs	Notional Sales Value at Slit-off	Apportionment	Apportioned Costs
	£	£	£		£
W	4,000	1,500	2,500	$\frac{2500}{8000} \times £5000$	1,563
V	6,750	1,250	5,500	$\frac{5500}{8000} \times 5000$	3,437
	£10,750	£2,750	£8,000		£5,000

Profit Statement

	W £	W £	V £	V £	Total £	Total £
Final Sales Value		4000		6750		10750
less						
Apportioned Costs	1563		3437		5000	
Subsequent Costs	1500	3063	1250	4687	2750	7750
Profit		£937		£2063		£3000
Profit Percentage		23%		31%		28%

7. Joint products in service organisations

The illustrations so far in this chapter have been drawn from manufacturing industry but joint products or joint services also arise in service organisations. Wherever facilities – buildings, staff and equipment – are used in common to provide a variety of products or services then joint products may arise as in manufacturing.

Take for example, banking. Banks provide a range of financial services using, largely, a common pool of facilities. The services include: current and deposit accounts, foreign transactions, investments. insurance, trustee and taxation consultancy and so on. Although there are some identifiable costs specific to particular services, most of the costs are incurred in common for all the services so that the cost accounting system in a bank has to deal with precisely the same problems faced in, say, an oil refinery.

8. Cost apportionment and decision making

The procedures outlined so far are acceptable for stock valuation and conventional profit calculation purposes, but may produce misleading information for particular types of decisions. A common type of decision is whether to sell a joint product at the split-off point or whether to incur further processing costs and sell at an enhanced price. In such circumstances, the amount of the joint costs and the method by which the joint costs are apportioned are *irrelevant*.

All that matters is a comparison of the *increase* in *revenue* with the *increase* in *costs* necessary to achieve that revenue. This is an example of the use of incremental costing which is important in decision making. To illustrate this approach assume the same data as in Example 2 except that the firm has the opportunity to process further Product Y at an additional cost of £3/litre in which case the produce could be sold at £20/litre instead of £15/litre. Is this worthwhile?

	£
Incremental revenue possible = £5 litre × 400 litres =	2000
Incremental costs necessary = £3 litres × 400 litres =	1200
Extra Profit =	£800

The conclusion from this is that it is worthwhile incurring additional costs on a product as long as the additional sales value gained exceeds the additional costs.

9. Summary

a. When two or more products arise from a process and where each has a significant sales value, they are termed joint products. When a product of relatively small value arises incidentally it is termed a by-product.

b. The most common method of by-product costing is where the net realisable value of the by-product is deducted from the total production cost.

c. The point where joint-products are separately identifiable is the split-off point. Up to that point all costs are joint costs which, for product costing purposes, have to be spread over the products on a reasonable basis.

d. The main two methods of apportioning joint costs are the physical unit and the sales value bases.

e. The notional sales value basis is used where additional processing is necessary for the product to be saleable so that an actual sales value is not available at the split-off point.

f. To decide whether additional processing is worthwhile to gain extra revenue, all that is necessary is to compare the incremental costs and incremental revenue. Joint costs and methods of apportionment are irrelevant.

10. Point to note

Processing may produce Waste-Scrap-By-Products-Joint-Products in ascending order of value. The exact classification of any given item is a matter of judgement.

Student self-testing

Self Review Questions

1. What is a joint product? A by-product? (2)
2. What are three common methods of dealing with by-product costs? (3)
3. What is the 'split-off point' ? (4)
4. What are the two most common methods of apportioning joint costs? (5)
5. Why are notional sales values at split-off point sometimes calculated ? (6)
6. How is the decision made whether to sell at the split-off point or perform further processing? (7)

Exercises and examination questions with answers

Exercises

A16.1   The following data relate to three joint products:

	A	B	C
Sales Value	£24,000	£18,000	£15,000
Selling Costs	£3,500	£4,500	£1,000
Weight (Kgs)	180	240	150

Joint costs £35,000. Calculate the profit made by each product apportioning joint costs on:

a.   the sales value basis

b.   the physical basis.

A16.2   Two products, X and Y, are produced from the same material. The material costs 95p per Kg and the products appear after Process 1.

X can be sold directly but Y needs further processing in Process 2.

The following data relate to one period.

Process	Materials £	Labour £	Overhead £	Total £
1	144,000	21,000	15,000	180,000
2		10,000	18,000	28,000
	£144,000	£31,000	£33,000	£208,000

Product	Kgs. Sold	Closing Stock (Kgs.)	Sales
X	30,000	15,000	£52,500
Y	45,000		£150,750

There were no materials on hand at the end of the period.

You are required to calculate:

a.   the unit price of X and its market value at split off.

b.   The total joint cost to be apportioned between the two products.

c.   Calculate the total cost of X and Y using the sales value method of apportionment.

A16.3   Four joint products are produced from a refining process. In the past, no attempt has been made to apportion the joint costs and the Sales Manager obtained the best price he could for each product. The new accountant for the firm apportioned the joint costs over the products on a weight basis and found that this resulted in widely differing profit percentages. As a consequence the accountant asserted that the selling prices must be changed to take account of the cost of the products.

Discuss.

Examination questions

A16.4   Three products A, B and C are produced from a single process. Each product can be sold at the end of the process, or can be further processed independently to produce superior products, which are marketed under different names – respectively Alpha, Beta and Gamma.

Details for a period are:

	Initial Output	Sales Value	Further Process Costs	Rejection Rate
Product A	10,000 litres	£12 per litre	£7 per litre	
Product B	16,000 litres	£5 per litre	£3 per litre	
Product C	20,000 tonnes	£15 per tonne	£8 per tonne	
Product Alpha		£22 per litre		5%
Product Beta		£9 per litre		10%
Product Gamma		£24 per tonne		8%

The further processing costs are incurred at the commencement of the second stage of operation. During this stage rigorous quality control causes a percentage of input to be rejected, with zero scrap value.

Required:

i.   Calculate the apportionment of costs to products A, B and C, using the sales value of production as the basis for apportionment.

ii. Explain whether the initial process should be undertaken and which, if any, of the enhanced products should be produced.

(AAT Cost Accounting & Budgeting, part question)

A16.5   Three joint products are produced by passing chemicals through two consecutive processes. Output from the first process is transferred into the second process, from which the three joint products are produced and immediately sold.

The previous month's operating data for the processes is tabulated below:

	Process 1	Process 2
Direct Material (25,000 kilos at £4 per kilo)	£100,000	–
Direct Labour	£62,500	£69,000
Overheads	£45,000	£69,000
Normal Loss	10% of input	Nil
Scrap Value of Loss	£2 per kilo	–
Output	23,000 kilos	Joint Product A 9,000 kilos
		Joint Product B 8,000 kilos
		Joint Product C 6,000 kilos

There were no opening or closing stocks in either process and the selling prices of the output from Process 2 were:

Joint Product A	£24 per kilo
Joint Product B	£18 per kilo
Joint Product C	£12 per kilo

Required:

a.   Prepare an account for Process 1, together with any loss or gain accounts you consider necessary to record the month's activities.

b.   Calculate the profit attributable to each of the joint products by apportioning the total costs from Process 2:

i.   according to weight of output

ii.   by the market value of production.

c.   Critically examine the purpose of apportioning process costs to joint products.

(ACCA, Costing).

A16.6   XY Chemical Company Limited has three processing departments: 1, 2 and 3.

In department 1 batches of ingredients P, Q and R are mixed which, after processing, produce three products: QA, PA and PB.

QA requires no further processing and can be sold;

PA can either be sold or subjected to further processing in department 3;

PB requires further processing in department 2, having no saleable value in its present form.

In department 2, PB is mixed with ingredient S to produce PX, which is saleable.

In department 3, PA is mixed with ingredient S and, after processing produces PAS, which can be sold. It also produces a by-product AZ, which can be sold, but needs packing beforehand at a cost of £0.05 per lb.

Standard yields in each department are as follows:

Department 1– a batch of 50 lbs P, 70 lbs Q, and 30 lbs R will yield 30lbs PA, 20 lbs PB, and 50 lbs QA;

Department 2 –. a batch of 20 lbs PB and 50 lbs S will yield 50lbs PX;

Department 3 – a batch of 30 lbs PA and 20 lbs S will yield 10 lbs PAS and 40 lbs AZ.

Price and cost data are as follows:

Cost of ingredients:

Ingredient	Costs per lb.
P	£0.8
Q	0.6
R	0.2
S	0.3

Conversion cost per batch	£
Department: 1	32.00
2	10.00
3	24.00

Selling prices (per lb):	
PA	2.00
QA	3.00
PX	1.10
PAS	15.00
AZ	0.40

During period 5, a total of 80 batches was produced in all three departments. At the end of the period, the following proportions of the period's production remained unsold:

QA 10%: PX 15%: AZ 20%

With the above exception, opening and closing stocks were equal.

Fixed overhead of £6,000 per period is incurred; the company's practice is to treat it as a period cost and not to apportion it to departments, or to absorb it into product cost.

You are required:

1. on the assumption that the company apportions costs on the basis of weight at the split-off point, to calculate:

   a. the costs per batch of PA, PB, QA qnd PX:

   b. the costs per lb of PAS on the basis that the net revenue from the sale of AZ is treated as:

      i. income of the company as a whole;

      ii. a reduction in the cost of the main product in the department in which it is produced;

   c. the total profit that the company made during period 5.

   (Assume for this purpose that closing stocks of by-product AZ have no value).

2. If the company wished to apportion department 1 costs on the basis of the net sales value at the split-off point, to calculate:

   a. the net sales value per lb of PB;

   b. the costs per batch of PA, PB and QA, using the answer to '(a) above.

   (CIMA,Cost Accounting 2)

A16.7   PPI Limited is in the food processing industry and in one of its processes, three joint products are manufactured. Traditionally, the company has apportioned work incurred up to the joint products pre-separation point on the basis of weight of output of the product. You have recently been appointed cost accountant, and have been investigating process costs and accounting procedures. You are required to prepare statements for management to show:

a.   the profit and loss of each product as ascertained using the weight basis of apportioning pre-separation point costs;

b.   the optimal contribution which could be obtained from the manufacture of these products. The following process data for October are given:

Costs incurred up to separation point		£96,000	
	Product A	Product B	Product C
	£	£	£
Costs incurred after separation point	20,000	12,000	8,000
Selling price per tonne			
Completed product	500	800	600
Estimated, if sold at separation point	250	700	450
	tonnes	tonnes	tonnes
Output	100	60	80

The cost of any unused capacity after the separation point should be ignored.

(CIMA, Cost Accounting 2)

A16.8   BK Chemicals produces three joint products in one common process but each product is capable of being further processed separately after the split-off point. The estimated data given below relate to June:

	Product B	Product K	Product C
Selling price at split-off point (per litre)	£6	£8	£9
Selling price after further processing (per litre)	£10	£20	£30
Post-separation point costs	£20,000	£10,000	£22,500
Output in litres	3,500	2,500	2,000

Pre-separation point joint costs are estimated to be £40,000 and it is current practice to apportion these to the three products according to litres produced.

a.   You are required

    i.   to prepare a statement of estimated profit or loss for each product and in total for June if all three products are processed further, and

    ii.   to advise how profits could be maximised if one or more products are sold at the split-off point. Your advice should be supported by a profit statement.

b)   Discuss the problems associated with joint cost apportionments in relation to

    i.   planning

    ii.   control, and

    iii.   decision making.

(CIMA Cost Accounting, part question)

A16.9   C Ltd operates a process which produces three joint products. In the period just ended, costs of production totalled £509,640. Output from the process during the period was:

      Product W   276,000 kilos
      Product X   334,000 kilos
      Product Y   134,000 kilos

There were no opening stocks of the three products. Products W and X are sold in this state. Product Y is subjected to further processing. Sales of product W and X were:

      Product W   255,000 kilos at £0.945 per kilo
      Product X   312,000 kilos at £0.890 per kilo

128,000 kilos of product Y were further processed during the period. The balance of the period production of the three products W, X and Y remained in stock at the end of the period. The value of closing stock of individual products is calculated by apportioning costs according to weight of output.

The additional costs in the period of further processing product Y, which is converted into product Z, were:

Direct labour	£10,850
Production overhead	£7,070

96,000 kilos of product Z were produced from the 128,000 kilos of product Y. A by-product BP is also produced which can be sold for £0.12 per kilo. 8,000 kilos of BP were produced and sold in the period.

Sales of product Z during the period were 94,000 kilos, with a total revenue of £100,110. Opening stock of product Z was 8,000 kilos, valued at £8,640. The FIFO method is used for pricing transfers of product Z to cost of sales.

Selling and administration costs are charged to all main products when sold, at 10% of revenue.

Required

a. Prepare a profit and loss account for the period, identifying separately the profitability of each of the three main products.

b. C Ltd has now received an offer from another company to purchase the total output of product Y. (ie before further processing), for £0.62 per kilo. Calculate the viability of this alternative.

c. Discuss briefly the methods of, and rationale for, joint cost apportionment.

(ACCA, Cost and Management Accounting 1)

Exercises and examination questions without answers

Exercises

B16.1   A plastics company produces two joint products Uniplast and Duoplast.

Raw materials, costing £1 per Kg, enter the Mixing Department then pass to Heat Treatment where they become separated into Uniplast and Duoplast. 50% of the material becomes Uniplast and goes to the Edging Department where it is prepared for sale. The remaining 50% becomes Duoplast and is sent to the Finishing Department for completion.

The following costs are incurred in the manufacture of 100 Kgs of the product:

Departments

Costs per 100Kgs	Mixing	Heat Treatment	Edging	Finishing
Labour	£50	£30	£40	£50
Overheads	£30	£50	£35	£60

There are no process losses.

The selling prices per 100 kg are Uniplast £800 and Duoplast £1,000. Selling overheads are absorbed at the rate of 25% of the sales volume of each product.

You are required to calculate the net profit per 100 Kg of Uniplast and Duoplast.

B16.2   The joint costs of two products D and F have been apportioned on the physical weight basis as £2.80 per Kg for D and £1.60 per Kg for F.

The best price obtainable for D is £1. 95 per Kg but with further processing at a cost of 25p per Kg a selling price of £2.30 can be obtained. The Managing Director states that as the new selling price is still below cost there is no point in further processing.

Prepare a reply to the Managing Director.

Examination questions

B16.3   a. Explain briefly the distinction between joint products and by-products.

b. Discuss briefly the problems involved in calculating the cost of manufacture of joint products with particular reference to the apportionment of pre-separation point costs. A common method of apportioning these pre-separation point costs is by physical measurement; outline two other methods.

c. In a process line of the JP Manufacturing Company Limited, three joint products are produced. For the month of October the following data were available:

Product	X	Y	Z
Sales price per kilogram	£5	£10	£20
Post-separation point costs	£10,000	£5,000	£15,000
Output in kilograms	2,500	1,000	1,500

Pre-separation point costs amounted to £20,000.

The joint products are manufactured in one common process, after which they are separated and may undergo further individual processing. The pre-separation point costs are apportioned to joint products, according to weight.

You are required:

a. to prepare a statement showing the estimated profit or loss for each product and in total;

b. as an alternative to the costing system used in (a) above, to present a statement which will determine the maximum profit from the production of these joint products. The sales value of each product at separation point is as follows: X = £3 Y = £4 Z = £6

(CIMA, Cost Accounting 2)

B16.4 a. A chemical Exalete, passes through processes A and B before completion. In process B, a by-product Exaltent is produced which, after further processing in process C, is sold at a profit of 16 2/3% of selling price.

You are required, from the data given for the month of April, to prepare accounts for:

i.   processes A, B and C;

ii. abnormal loss;

iii. abnormal gain.

	Process		
	A	B	C
Output in units	4,200	3,800	100
Normal loss in process:			
% of input	20	5	–
	£	£	£
Scrap value of any loss in process, per unit	1.5	5	–
Costs			
Direct materials introduced (5,000 units)	30,000	–	–
Direct materials added	10,000	3,100	100
Direct wages incurred at £3 per hour	12,000	14,700	300
Direct expenses	7,500	1,170	–

Production overhead for the month, £72,000, is absorbed by a labour hour rate.

b. Define and explain briefly the accounting treatment of:

i.   by-products;

ii. joint products.

(CIMA, Cost Accounting 2)

B16.5 A distillation plant, which works continuously, processes 1,000 tonnes of raw material each day. The raw material costs £4 per tonne and the plant operating costs per day are £2,600. From the input of raw material the following output is produced:

	%
Distillate X	40
Distillate Y	30
Distillate Z	20
By-product B	10

From the initial distillation process, Distillate X passes through a heat process which costs £1,500 per day and becomes Product X which requires blending before sale.

Distillate Y goes through a second distillation process costing £3,300 per day and produces 75% of Product Y and 25% of Product X1.

Distillate Z has a second distillation process costing £2,400 per day and produces 60% of Product Z and 40% of Product X2.

The three streams of Products X, X1 and X2 are blended, at a cost of £1,155 per day to become the saleable final product XXX.

There is no loss of material from any of the processes.

By-product B is sold for £3 per tonne and such proceeds are credited to the process from which the by-product is derived.

Joint costs are apportioned on a physical unit basis.

You are required to:

a. draw a flow chart, flowing from left to right, to show for one day of production the flow of material and the build up of the operating costs for each product;

b. present a statement for management showing for each of the products XXX, Y and Z, the output for one day, the total cost and the unit cost per tonne;

c. suggest an alternative method for the treatment of the income receivable for by-product B than that followed in this question (figures are not required).

(CIMA, Cost Accounting)

B16.6 a. Three products are produced from a single process. During one period in which the process costs are expected to be £200,000, the following outputs are expected:

	Output	Selling Price
Product A	8,000 tonnes	£5 per tonne
Product B	20,000 tonnes	£5 per tonne
Product C	25,000 litres	£10 per litre

Each product can be modified after the initial process by using inputs of skilled labour, costing £8 per hour, to create superior products: Max A, Max B and Max C respectively. Labour requirements and selling prices are as follows:

	Skilled labour	Selling price
Max A	1 hour per tonne	£20 per tonne
Max B	1.5 hours per tonne	£23 per tonne
Max C	2 hours per litre	£22 per litre

Any modification work leads to a rejection rate of 10% of the input.

Required:

i. Calculate the apportionment to each product of the joint process costs in the period if the sales value of production basis of apportionment is used.

ii. Show which, if any, of the products should be modified into superior products.

iii. Assuming that the total available skilled labour hours for the period amounted to 6,000 hours show, giving reasons, which if any of the products should be modified.

(AAT Cost Accounting & Budgeting)

B16.7 QR Limited operates a chemical process which produces for different products Q, R, S and T from the input of one raw material plus water. Budget information for the forthcoming financial year is as follows:

	£000
Raw materials cost	268
Initial processing cost	464

Product	Output in litres	Sales £000	Additional processing cost £000
Q	400,000	768	160
R	90,000	232	128
S	5,000	32	–
T	9,000	240	8

The company policy is to apportion the costs prior to the split-off point on a method based on net sales value.

Currently, the intention is to sell product S without further processing but to process the other three products after the split-off point. However, it has been proposed that an alternative strategy would be able to sell four products at the split off point without further processing. If this were done the selling prices obtainable would be as follows:

	Per litre
	£
Q	1.28
R	1.60
S	6.40
T	20.00

You are required

a. to prepare a budgeted profit statement showing the profit or loss for each product, and in total, if the current intention is proceeded with;

b. to show the profit or loss by product, and in total, if the alternative strategy were to be adopted;

c. to recommend what should be done and why, assuming that there is no more profitable alternative use for the plant.

(CIMA Cost Accounting)

17: Planning, control and decision making

1. Topics covered in this chapter

1.	Long-term or corporate planning
2.	Introduction to short-term planning
3.	Introduction to feedback and control
4.	Decision making.

2. Wider view of costing

The student who has conscientiously studied the book so far will have a good knowledge of the language and procedures of basic costing. The material covered shows how data are gathered, classified, analysed and used for cost ascertainment. The rest of the book is concerned with the wider use of costing information for planning, control and decision making purposes.

It must be emphasised, however, that the existence of a sound, well organised basic costing system is fundamental to whatever use is made of the information, whether for routine cost ascertainment purposes or for a one-off decision. Before considering the various ways in which costing information can be of value to management, it is useful to examine some general considerations relating to planning, control and decision making.

3. Planning

Planning is a primary task of management. It is concerned with the future and relies upon information from many sources, both external and internal to the organisation, for it to be successful. Information for planning includes cost and financial data and also information relating to personnel, markets, competitors, production capacities and constraints, material supplies and so on.

Planning can be defined as; 'The establishment of objectives, and the formulation, evaluation and selection of the policies, strategies, tactics and action required to achieve these objectives. Planning comprises long term/strategic planning and short term operational planning. The latter usually refers to a period of one year.' *Terminology*. Thus it will be seen that the overall planning process covers both the long and short term and these two aspects are developed below.

4. Long term strategic planning

This can be defined as:

'The formulation, evaluation and selection of strategies for the purpose of preparing a long-term plan of action to attain objectives. Also known as *corporate planning* and *long range planning*.' *Terminology*.

The time span covered by a long term plan depends on the organisation, the industry in which it operates and the particular environment involved. Typically the periods involved are 3, 5, 7 or 10 years although longer periods are commonly encountered. An example is the long term plan relating to the Water Supply Industry which covers a 20 year period.

The process of long term or corporate planning is a detailed, lengthy process which in many organisations is considered an indispensable part of the management process. Figure 17.1 provides an overview of the process and shows the link with short term tactical planning.

5. Corporate planning

Figure 17.1 shows a considerable amount of detail about CP which, in essence, is concerned with several key questions;

What is the environment in which the organisation will have to operate in the future?
What is the existing state of the organisation and the environment in which it operates?
Where does the organisation want to go?
What is the best way to get there?

223

The strategic or corporate plan which is developed provides the framework within which short-term planning or budgeting takes place.

(Note: The stages and processes in CP are developed in greater detail in 'Management Accounting' T. Lucey, DP Publications).

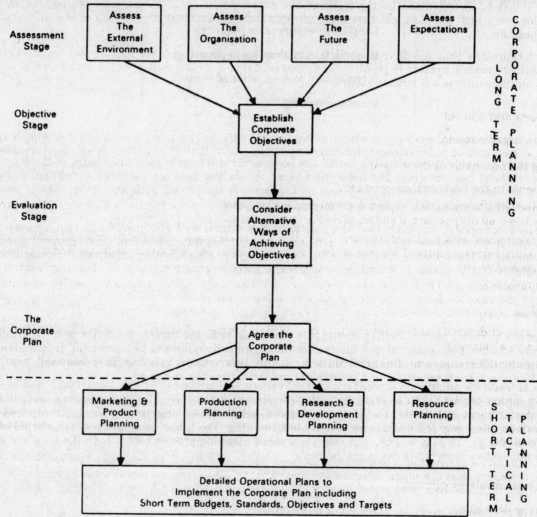

Figure 17.1 Corporate planning

6. Short term tactical planning/budgeting

The long term Corporate Plan serves as the longer term framework for the organisation as a whole but for operational purposes it is necessary to convert the Corporate Plan into a series of short term (usually 1 year) plans relating to sections, functions and departments. Short term tactical planning can be defined as; 'Planning the utilisation of resources to achieve specific objectives in the most effective and efficient way.' *Terminology*.

Those parts of a short-term plan to which monetary values can be attached become *budgets*.

A budget can be defined as; 'A plan expressed in money. It is prepared and approved prior to the budget period and may show income, expenditure and capital to be employed. May be drawn up showing incremental effects on former budgeted or actual figures or be compiled by zero-base budgeting'. *Terminology*.

The annual processes of short term planning and budgeting should be seen as stages in the progressive fulfilment of the Corporate Plan. The short term planning and budgeting processes steer the organisation towards the long term objectives defined in the Corporate Plan. It should be apparent that to gain the maximum advantage from short term planning and budgeting it is essential that some form of long term plan exists. Short term planning and budgeting are covered in detail in Chapter 22.

7. Control

The purpose of control is to help to ensure that operations and performance conform to the plans. There are two broad elements of the control process. Firstly, the comparison of actual and planned performance on a regular and continuing basis and secondly, the longer term process of reviewing the plan itself to see whether it needs modification in the light of the comparisons made or because of changes in the assumptions on which the plan was based, for example, new government regulations, material shortages new competition.

It follows therefore that effective control is not possible without planning and planning without a complementary control system is pointless. In organisational systems, control is exercised by the use of information frequently of a financial nature.

8. Feedback and control

Control in organisational systems is exercised by *information feedback loops* which gather information from the *output* side of a department, function or process which is used to govern *future performance* by adjusting the *input* side of the system.

The elements in the basic control cycle are;

a. A standard specifying the expected performance. This can be in the form of a budget, a procedure, a stock level, an output rate, a standard cost or some other target.

b. A measurement of actual performance. This should be made in an accurate, speedy, unbiased manner and using relevant units of measures. For example, time taken, £'s spent, units produced, efficiency ratings and so on.

c. Comparison of a. and b. Frequently the comparison is accompanied by an analysis which attempts to isolate the reasons for any variations. A well known example of this is the accounting process of variance analysis, described in Chapters 24 to 26.

d. Feedback of deviations or variations to a control unit. In an organisational context the 'control unit' would be a manager.

e. Actions by the manager to alter performance in accordance with the plan, target or standard.

The type of feedback mentioned is feedback of relatively small variations between actual and plan so that corrective action can be taken to bring operations in line with the plan. The implications of this is that existing performance standards and plans are essentially correct and appropriate. This type of feedback, also known as *single loop feedback*, is the normal feedback associated with budgetary control and standard costing systems.

Students should be aware that a higher order of feedback exists, known as *double loop feedback*, which is designed to ensure that the plans, budgets and standards – and indeed the organisational structures and control systems themselves, are revised to meet changes in conditions.

Figure 17.2 provides an overview of feedback and control cycles.

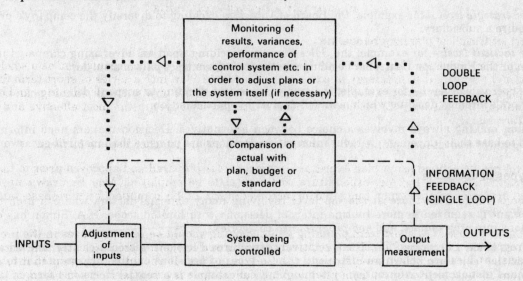

Figure 17.2 Control and feedback cycles

9. The decision process

Decision making is an all pervasive managerial task and because many decisions depend on financial factors it is important that the Cost Accountant is totally familiar with the processes involved and the sort of information that should be supplied to decision makers. The stages in the overall decision process are as follows:

a. *Definition of objectives*

The decision maker must be aware of the organisation's objectives which should, wherever possible, be quantified. If the organisation's objectives are clearly specified and are communicated widely there is less likelihood of *sub-optimal* decision making taking place. This is where local or departmental objectives are pursued to the detriment of overall organisational objectives.

b. *Consideration of alternatives*

There are always various ways of achieving objectives and ideally an exhaustive list should be prepared covering all possible alternatives. However, this is a theoretical ideal which is difficult to achieve in practice.

c. *Evaluation of alternatives*

This is the process of making quantitative and financial comparisons between the various alternatives so that the ultimate decision maker is provided with a relevant and correctly specified financial basis for the final decision. Clearly this is the stage in the decision process where the expertise of the Cost Accountant is most required so that relevant information can be supplied. What is relevant information for long and short run decision making is dealt with later in the book.

d. *Selection of the course of action*

This is the stage where the actual choice is made by the decision maker. Decision making involves personal, social, psychological and political factors as well as the more objective financial and quantitative considerations. An important factor in virtually all practical decisions is the risk and uncertainty involved. This means that it is important that the information supplied by the accountant shows the effects of risk and uncertainty and the range of likely outcomes.

Where uncertainty exists – which it does in virtually every situation – it can be positively misleading to provide information which shows only a single value of profit or contribution with no indication of the variability's which may occur.

Because this book is about cost accounting it naturally concentrates on financial matters. However it must be emphasised that many other factors may be of critical importance in a decision. Examples include; markets, the environment, legal factors, personal and psychological characteristics, production or service quality, reliability and so on. Decision making is not just a consideration of financial factors.

10. Levels of decision making

Management is involved with decision making at all levels;

at the strategic level – for example, the Board of Directors deciding to diversify the company's products or to acquire a subsidiary.

at the tactical level – for example, the Sales Manager deciding upon an advertising campaign in a given region or the Production Controller deciding whether to sub-contract part of an order.

at the operational level – for example, the credit Supervisor deciding to suspend deliveries to a bad payer or a work's foreman deciding which men will deal with a particular job.

Decision making always involves a choice between alternatives. Decision makers need information on which to base their judgement; without information decisions are no more than inspired guesswork.

11. Types of decisions

Decisions range from those at the top level involving many external factors where a high degree of judgement is required to more routine internal decisions with limited scope. H.A. Simon has classified decisions into *programmed* and *non-programmed* categories.

a. Programmed decisions. These are relatively structured decisions within a clearly defined area. The decision rules are known and frequently these types of decisions can be incorporated into computer based management information systems. A typical example is a reorder decision based on usage and reorder levels in an inventory control system.

b. **Non-programmed decisions.** These are decisions for which decision rules and procedures cannot be devised. Generally they are non-repetitive decisions, involving many external and internal factors, frequently with high levels of risk, and requiring information from a variety of sources.

12. Information for decision making

It is important to understand that all decision making relates to the future. It follows therefore that the decision maker requires information regarding such things as future costs and revenues, future material supplies and prices, the likely state of the market in the future and so on. Information for decision making must therefore be orientated towards the future and involves forecasting, estimating and extrapolation. Whilst it is self evident that we cannot foretell the future, it is found that past experience and records of performances, costs etc, frequently provide a sound basis for forecasting particular aspects of future operations.

However, this is only correct if future conditions are expected to be broadly similar to those in the past. If not, then an organisation's experience and records are likely to be of substantially diminished value. Information has no value in itself; its value derives from improvements in the decisions which are taken based upon the information. To enhance the value of information it must be capable of being used effectively and surveys have shown that information which has the following characteristics is more likely to be used.

Relevance – ie, appropriate to the manager's sphere of activity and to the decision in hand.

Timeliness – ie, produced and available to the manager in time for him to use. Frequently an approximate answer speedily prepared will be the most valuable.

Accuracy – ie, sufficiently accurate for it to be relied upon by the manager and sufficiently accurate for the intended purpose.

Understandable – ie, in a form readily usable by the manager. The avoidance of unexplained technical terms, the use of summaries, the use of graphical and other display methods are all ways to make information more understandable.

The types of decisions, and their information requirements, vary from level to level in the organisation.

Figure 17.3 shows a summary of the main characteristics of decisions and information for the three management levels.

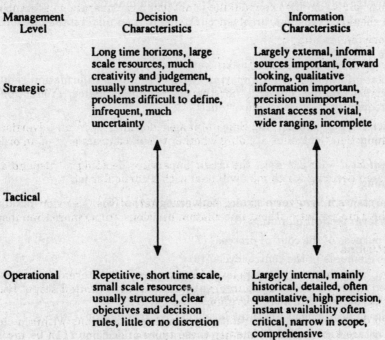

Management Level	Decision Characteristics	Information Characteristics
Strategic	Long time horizons, large scale resources, much creativity and judgement, usually unstructured, problems difficult to define, infrequent, much uncertainty	Largely external, informal sources important, forward looking, qualitative information important, precision unimportant, instant access not vital, wide ranging, incomplete
Tactical		
Operational	Repetitive, short time scale, small scale resources, usually structured, clear objectives and decision rules, little or no discretion	Largely internal, mainly historical, detailed, often quantitative, high precision, instant availability often critical, narrow in scope, comprehensive

Figure 17.3 Levels of decision making

Figure 17.4 gives examples of decision making at the three levels with typical information requirements.

Management Level	Decision Examples	Information Requirements
Strategic	Mergers and acquisitions, new product planning, capital investments, financial structuring	Market and economic forecasts, political and social trends, legislative, environmental and technological constraints and opportunities
Tactical	Pricing, capacity planning, budget preparation, purchasing contracts	Cost and sales analyses, performance measures, summaries of operations/production, budget/actual comparisons etc
Operational	Production scheduling, maintenance, re-ordering, credit approval	Sales orders, production requirements, performance measures, customer credit status, deliveries, despatches etc

Figure 17.4 Decision and information examples

13. Summary

a. Planning is concerned with the future and consists of five stages: Setting objectives, Assessing the environment, Reviewing resources, Establishing feasible goals, and Implementation.

b. Effective control must be preceded by planning, and planning without complementary control is pointless.

c. Control is exercised by feedback control loops whereby information regarding the output or performance is compared to the plan or standard and adjustments made (if necessary) to the inputs.

d. The decision process includes, the definition of objectives, consideration of alternatives, evaluation of alternatives and the selection of the course of action.

e. Management are involved with decision making at all levels, strategic, tactical and operational.

f. Decisions can be classified into programmed and non-programmed.

g. Future orientated information is necessary for decision making.

h. Information should be relevant, timely, accurate, and in an understandable form.

14. Point to note

Cost and financial information is an important part of the total information requirements for planning, control and decision making, but it is not the only element. Sales, production, personnel and other information is frequently of supreme importance.

Student self-testing

Self Review Questions

1. Define planning. (3)
2. What are the stages in long term strategic planning? (4) & (5)
3. Define short term tactical planning. (6)
4. What is the purpose of the control process? (7)
5. What are the elements in the control cycle? (8)
6. Distinguish between single and double loop feedback. (8)
7. What are the stages in the decision process? (9)
8. Give examples of decisions at the three levels in the organisation. (10)
9. Distinguish between programmed and non-programmed decisions. (11)
10. What are the characteristics of information which is more likely to be used in decision making? (12)

Exercises and examination questions with answers

Exercises

A17.1   The cost accounting system of the firms records the costs incurred in the past for products, departments, operations and processes. Accordingly the information contained within the cost accounting system is of no value for decision making purposes.

Discuss this statement.

A17.2   Why should the problems of control be considered at the planning stage?

A17.3   Give 3 examples of decision making at each of the main management levels ie, strategic, tactical, and operational.

Examination questions

A17.4   Coodsall plc. a multiple retailer, owns a hundred large department stores located throughout the country selling a wide range of household products. The company also operates four regional depots at which the goods, purchased from outside manufacturers, are stored, repacked and finally distributed by the company's own fleet of lorries to the particular stores in that region. In addition there is one head office at which the necessary central management and admistrative activities are performed.

Required:

a.   A discussion of the type of information the cost accountant could produce to assist the management of Coodsall plc., with particular reference to the provision of information in respect of:

i.   planning and decision-making activities

ii.   controlling and evaluating activities.

b.   Indicate the cost classifications required to support the provision of information in a.

(ACCA, Costing)

Exercises and examination questions without answers

Exercises

B17.1   'Many organisations operate budgetary systems without having a formal long term or corporate planning system. In such circumstances the budgetary systems are a waste of time.'

Discuss this statement.

B17.2   'Control looks backwards, planning and decision making look forwards.'

Discuss this statement and its influence on the type of information to be supplied by the cost accountant.

B17.3   Give 3 major differences between information for decision making at the strategic and operational levels.

18: Cost behaviour

1. Topics covered in this chapter

1. Importance of studying cost behaviour
2. Variable, semi-variable and fixed costs
3. Linear and non-linear costs
4. Calculating the characteristics of cost
5. Inflation and cost behaviour
6. Problems of cost prediction.

2. Reasons for the study of cost behaviour

If costs always remained unchanged and completely under control and if an organisation's activities and operations remained the same from period to period, then there would be little point in studying cost behaviour. Life is not as simple as that and an understanding of cost behaviour is vital for management and for accountants who advise them.

A knowledge of cost behaviour is necessary across the whole range of cost and management accounting activities, particularly in the areas of cost control, planning and decision making. Typical problems which need detailed analysis of cost behaviour before they can be solved are the following:

'What are the appropriate overhead costs if the throughput of the Assembly Department is increased by 15%'?

'Is it worthwhile to introduce second shift working to cope with a special export order'?

Should we accept a large contract at less than normal selling prices if it enables us to work at full capacity?'

'What would be the cost effects of treating more patients as day attenders rather than as conventional in-patients?'

'Will it be cheaper for a Local Authority to deal with Housing Maintenance by its own Direct Service Organisation or by private sub-contractors?'

3. Cost behaviour and the volume of activity

Whilst other factors influence costs, a major influence is the level or volume of activity, and many of the reasons for studying cost behaviour relate to changes or proposed changes in the level of activity. The level of activity is expressed in many varied ways, eg, tons produced, hours worked, standard hours produced, passenger/miles, invoices typed, sales, stores issues etc, etc.

Students should also be aware that many alternative terms are used for the concept of 'level of activity', typical ones being capacity, output, volume throughput. Activity level changes and the resulting cost changes form the basis of many practical decisions and many examination questions. The behaviour of cost in relation to changes in the level of activity is so important that it forms the basis of the accounting classifications of cost into fixed and variable costs.

4. Cost behaviour and time

Normally the situations where cost behaviour is analysed for planning and decision making are 'short run' in nature. This means that the relationship between cost and activity and the classifications of the costs themselves are most appropriate over a relatively short time span only. What is a 'relatively short time span' depends on the particular circumstances, it may be three months, six months, one year; it is unlikely to be as long as five years.

Over longer time periods unpredictable factors are bound to occur, methods will alter, technology will improve, so that predictions of cost behaviour are likely to be increasingly unreliable. In examination questions the time factor (in relation to cost behaviour!) is unlikely to be very significant, but in practice it can be a major problem.

5. Predicting cost behaviour

Except in completely new circumstances where no previous experience exists, predictions about cost levels and cost behaviour in the future are likely to be based on records of past costs and their associated levels of activity. Because of this, many of the statistical techniques of forecasting and extrapolation may be of value when studying cost behaviour. Care however must be taken when using any form of forecasting technique that past conditions are indeed a guide to the *future*.

It is the cost behaviour in the future that is being considered and if conditions in the future are likely to be significantly different from the past, then statistical forecasting techniques will be unable to produce valid predictions. Judgement will always play a part in cost prediction, but in many cases relatively simple statistical techniques can be of great assistance. Care must also be taken to base cost predictions on the facts of particular situations and not on arbitrary, general classifications.

An example of this is the almost invariable rule, particularly in examination questions, of assuming that direct labour is a fully variable cost, whereas because of wage agreements, guaranteed daily and weekly rates, the growth of salaried works personnel, the impact of technology etc, direct labour in many situations increasingly assumes many of the characteristics of a fixed cost, ie, it may, within limits, be relatively unchanged with varying levels of activity.

6. Variable cost definition

A variable cost can be defined as: 'A cost which tends to vary with the level of activity'. *Terminology*.

To this definition should be added the proviso 'in the short term' because over the longer term changing prices, methods and technology make any form of cost classification subject to change. A common assumption in accounting is that variable costs behave linearly in respect to volume changes. Naturally this is not always the case and such a simplifying assumption should only be made if it accords with the facts of the situation. This is explained in more detail below.

7. Variable cost behaviour

The patterns of variable cost behaviour are many and varied, but two main divisions of continuous variable cost patterns can be made, ie, *linear* and *non-linear* or *curvilinear*.

8. Linear variable costs

This is the simplest pattern and is where the relationship between variable cost and output can be shown as a straight line on a graph as in Figure 18.1:

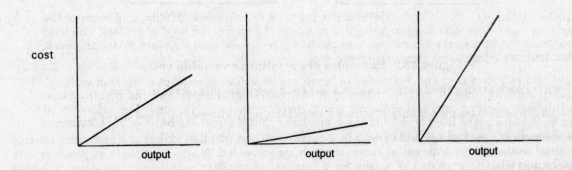

Figure 18.1 Examples of linear variable cost

For calculations and analysis it is usually more convenient to express the linear relationship algebraically thus

$$COST = bx$$

where: x = volume of output in units

        b = a constant representing the variable cost per unit.

Example 1

The materials contained in each assembly Z110 are

3 Brackets @ £1.25 each

30 Screws @ £0.02 each

6 Pulleys @ £0.67 each

What is the expected variable cost of materials for producing 40 Assemblies?

Solution

Material	*Cost/Assembly*
£	£
£3 × 1.25	= 3.75
30 × 0.02	= 0.60
6 × 0.67	= 4.02
	£8.37

$$\text{Cost} = bx$$
$$= £8.37 \times 40$$
$$= £334.8$$

9. Non-linear or curvilinear variable costs

In general where the relationship between variable cost and output can be shown as a curved line on a graph, it would be said to be *curvilinear*. Many types of curves exist and two typical ones are shown below in Figure 18.2.

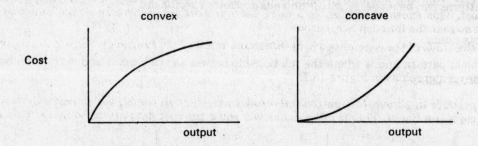

Figure 18.2 Examples of curvilinear variable costs

Convex – where each extra unit of output causes a *less than proportionate* increase in cost

Concave – where each extra unit of output causes a *more than proportionate* increase in cost.

A simple example of a cost which could result in a curvilinear cost function is that of a piecework scheme for individual workers with differential rates. If the rates increased by small amounts at progressively higher output levels the graphing of wages for a number of workers would result in a concave cost function.

Whether the curves are convex or concave, if they have particular characteristics, they may be categorised as known statistical functions. One of the more common types is described below, which is known as *parabola*, but many other types exist. The method by which a curve is identified is by the statistical technique of curve fitting.

Note:

Other statistical functions which may represent a cost function are: simple exponential or compound interest curve, logarithmic, Gompertz etc.

10. Curvilinear variable costs – the parabola

Where the slope of the cost function changes uniformly with changes in output (as the curves in fig. 18.2) the curve is known as a Parabola and can be expressed algebraically thus:

$$\text{Cost} = bx + cx^2 + dx^3 + \dots px^n$$

where: x = volume of output in units

$b, c, d, \dots p$ = constants representing the variable cost per unit.

Example 2

Analysis of cost and activity records for a project show that the variable cost can be accurately represented by the function:

$$\text{Cost} = £(bx + cx^2 + dx^3)$$

where $b = 8$ $c = 0.5$ and $d = 0.03$.

Calculate:

i.   Variable cost when production is 10 units

ii.   Variable cost when production is 15 units

Is the function convex or concave?

Solution

i.   Cost $= £8 \times 10 + 0.5 \times 10^2 + 0.03 \times 10^3$

        $= £160$

ii.   Cost $= £8 \times 15 + 0.5 \times 15^2 + 0.03 \times 15^3$

        $= £333.75$

It will be seen that the increase in activity from 10 to 15 units results in more than a doubling of variable cost. This shows that there is a more than proportionate increase in the unit cost of extra production so that the function is *concave*.

Note: It is the value of the constants which determine whether the function is convex or concave.

11. Linear approximation

It is common practice in accounting, particularly under examination conditions, to make the assumption that variable costs are linear. This is often done even when the cost data are curvilinear. This is shown thus:

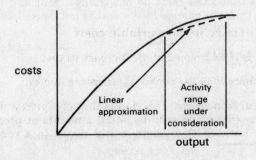 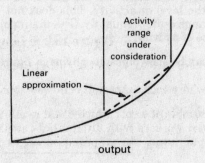

Features of linear approximation:

a.   Convenient and greatly simplifies calculations.

b.   May be reasonably accurate representation in the short run over a limited range of activity variations.

c.   May encourage too ready acceptance of the view that all variable costs are linear. All variable costs do not behave linearly and accurate cost prediction in practice must rely on analysis of cost and activity data, not upon overall blanket assumptions.

For examination purposes it can generally be assumed that, if a cost is identified as variable, it will be linear unless the context of the question clearly points to some other pattern.

12. Relationship of variable cost to other costs

Variable cost c.f. accounting concept of marginal cost.

Because of the assumption of linearity, variable cost equals accounting marginal cost ie, the cost of an extra unit of output is the same as the average variable cost of all output.

Variable cost c.f. economic concept of marginal cost.

The economic concept of marginal cost, ie, the cost of an additional unit, is based on curvilinear functions so that at certain activity levels marginal cost is falling and at other levels it is rising, whereas the accounting concept assumes a constant variable marginal cost. The above explanation covers a wide range of activity variations, but for limited activity variations, as in a typical short-run decision, the approaches are likely to give very similar results.

13. Variable cost c.f. direct costs

Direct costs are those costs directly identifiable with a product or saleable service, whereas variable costs are determined by their behaviour in relation to changes in activity levels. Thus it will be seen that variable costs and direct costs are determined by two quite distinct principles. Some variable costs, eg, material and wages, can often also be identified as direct costs.

14. Examples of variable costs

Examples of costs that are frequently variable in behaviour are raw materials, sales commissions, royalties, production wages, carriage and packing costs. Care should be taken not to pigeon hole costs too readily. It is the behaviour of a cost in relation to activity that determines whether or not it is variable, not some general assumption.

15. Fixed cost – definition

A fixed cost can be defined as:

'A cost which is incurred for a period, and which, within certain output and turnover limits, tends to be unaffected by fluctuations in the levels of activity (output or turnover). Examples are rent, rates, insurance and executive salaries.'*Terminology*

An alternative term for fixed costs is *period cost*.

The key parts of this definition are that fixed costs are time related and, within limits, are unaffected by changes in the level of activity. This does not mean that fixed costs do not change; rent and rates, for example, change quite frequently. The main point is that the change in the cost is not caused by changes in the volume of activity.

Fixed costs can be shown graphically as in figures 18.4 and 18.5:

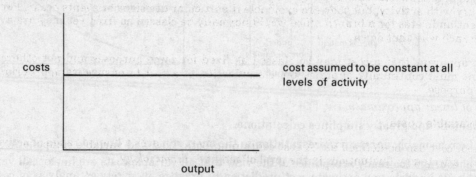

Figure 18.4 Fixed cost

Figure 18.4 is somewhat unrealistic in that it assumes that costs will be constant at all levels of activity from 0% to 100% which is not likely. More typically fixed costs could be graphed as in Figure 18.5:

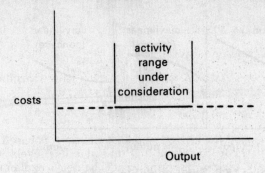

Figure 18.5 Fixed cost

Fixed costs can also be expressed algebraically:

$$COST = a$$

where a is a constant. It will be noted that v, the volume of output, does not appear in this expression, so that changes in activity are deemed not to affect the fixed cost.

16. Categories of fixed costs

It is important not to take too superficial a view of cost classification. The accountant must look at the actual and forecast behaviour of the cost and the purpose for which it is intended so that there is a realistic approach to the classification of costs.

For planning and decision making purposes the key point is that the classification must be *relevant for the intended purpose*. The concept of consistency of treatment which is a feature of financial accounting and cost ascertainment is **not** appropriate when applied to information for planning and decision making. So that the individual **characteristics** of cost are not overlooked and so dealt with incorrectly it is useful to sub-divide fixed costs into five categories

  i. The *time period classification*. Those types of cost which are not likely to change significantly in the short term, usually a year. In the long term all costs may change or become avoidable.

  ii. The *volume classification*. Costs which are fixed for small, but not large changes in output or capacity.

  iii. The *joint classification*. Where a cost is incurred jointly with another cost and is only capable of being altered jointly. For example, if an organisation leases a showroom which has a warehouse attached then the fixed cost element applies to both parts of the asset acquired whether or not they are both wanted.

  iv. The *policy classification*. These are costs which are fixed by management policy and bear no causal relationship to volume or time. They are usually items which are dealt with by appropriation budgets, eg, expenditure on advertising, research and development. These types of costs are sometimes known as programmed fixed costs and typically are reviewed annually.

  v. The *avoidable classification*. These are costs which are fixed in the normal sense ie, they do not vary with activity, but they are avoidable if particular decisions or events occur. For example, the rent and rates for a branch office would normally be classed as fixed yet they are avoidable if the branch was shut down.

It will be apparent that a cost may be classed as fixed for some purposes and not others and the cost accountant must continually appraise the classification of a cost to ensure its appropriateness for the intended purpose.

17. Semi-variable costs

This type of cost can be defined as; 'A cost containing both fixed and variable components, and which is thus partly affected by fluctuations in the level of activity'. *Terminology*.

Rarely is a cost purely fixed or purely variable, frequently there are elements of both classifications in a cost. A typical example would be electricity charges containing a fixed element, the standing charge, and a variable element, the cost per unit consumed.

Semi-variable costs can be shown graphically thus:

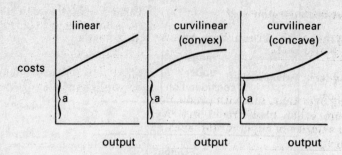

Figure 18.6 Semi variable cost patterns

In each case 'a' represents the fixed element of the cost.

Semi-variable costs can also be expressed algebraically by combining the previous expressions for variable cost (Para. 8) and fixed cost (Para. 15) thus

Linear semi-variable cost:

$$\text{COST} = a + bx$$

Curvilinear semi-variable cost:

$$\text{COST} = a + bx + cx^2 + dx^3 + \ldots + px^n$$

Example 3

Analysis of maintenance department costs shows that there is a fixed element of £500 per month and a variable element related to machine hours amounting to £2.25 per machine hour.

What is the expected cost for a month when the planned activity level is

    i. 1500 machine hours? **and**

    ii. 1800 machine hours?

Solution

    i. Total cost $= a + bx$

                         $= £500 + 2.25(1500)$

                         = £3875

    ii. Total cost $= £500 + 2.25(1800)$

                         = £4550

(Alternatively, as only the variable costs will alter between 1500 and 1800 hours, the second answer could be calculated as follows:

$$£3875 + 300 \,(2.25) = £4550.$$

The above example is for a clear cut linear cost, but, even when the underlying cost pattern is curvilinear, it is normal to make a linear approximation which greatly simplifies subsequent calculations.

Note: Alternative terms for semi-variable costs are: *semi-fixed* costs and *mixed costs*.

18. Alternative cost classifications

The classifications given above for variable, fixed and semi-variable costs are those conventionally used so must be thoroughly understood.

Professor Kaplan has suggested that these are less appropriate for classifying overheads when Activity Based Costing is used. As previously explained he has suggested a three-way classification; short-term variable costs; long-term variable costs and fixed costs. Table 18.1 compares the conventional classification to those suggested by Professor Kaplan.

Kaplans' Classification for use with ABC	Comments
Short-term variable cost defined as varying with production volume Typical example: Power costs	These would also be classified as *variable* using the conventional classification
Long-term variable cost defined as varying over time, not with production volume, but some other measure of activity. Typical example: salaries of support staff such as inspectors, engineers	Most of these would be conventionally classified as *fixed*
Fixed cost defined as not varying, over the given period, with any activity indicator. Typical examples: rates, executive salaries.	These would be conventionally classified as *fixed*

Table 18.1

19. Establishing the appropriate cost characteristics

So far in the examples the value of the fixed and variable elements have been provided, but in practice these characteristics have to be established. One way this can be done is by analysis of past cost and activity data. There are a number of techniques available for this purpose, three of which are dealt with below – the High/Low method, the scattergraph and the statistical technique known as the least squares method of linear regression analysis.

20. High/low method

This is a simple, crude technique which uses only the highest and lowest values contained in a set of data and, graphically or arithmetically, determines the rate of cost change and hence the variable cost. The variable costs so established are then used to estimate the fixed element.

The following data will be used to illustrate the technique.

Activity Level (units)	Costs (£)
36	800
48	700*
48	820
49	970
55	790
57	1050
59	900
65	880
66	1020
67	1180
72	950
75	1170
76	1020
82	1200
86	1060
92	1100
94	1310*
97	1250

* It will be seen that the high/low cost points are

48 units at a cost of £700

94 units at a cost of £1310

The difference between the two is a range of 46 units and £610. From this the rate of cost change per unit (ie, the variable cost) can be established thus

$$\frac{£610}{46} = \textbf{£13.26 per unit.}$$

From this value of variable cost the fixed element of cost can be deduced.

Cost at 48 units =		£700
less 48 × 13.26 =		636
∴ Fixed costs		**£64**

The values of the fixed and variable elements have been found above using arithmetic. The points could also be plotted on a graph and a line drawn joining the high/low points which could be extrapolated to zero units to provide an indication of the fixed element. This has been done in Figure 18.7. It will be apparent that, whether arithmetic or graphical methods are used, the high/low method is inaccurate and the results are directly effected by the extreme values which may be quite unrepresentative.

21. Scattergraph technique

This is simple visual technique which can be employed with as few as two previous observations, but obviously there is some gain in accuracy if a number of previous cost and activity readings are available. Figure 18.7 shows the plotting of the cost and activity data given in Para 19 above.

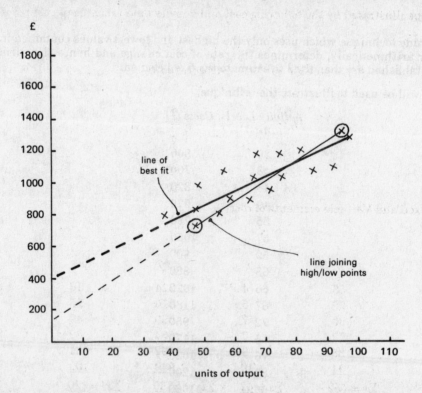

Figure 18.7 Scattergraph showing visual line of best fit and high/low points

The solid line is drawn at an angle adjudged to be the best representation of the slope of the points. The dotted line is drawn to show the intersection with the vertical axis and thus gives an estimate of the fixed content of the cost being considered, in this case £400. The slope of the line, ie, the variable element, is found as follows:

$$\text{cost @ zero activity} = \quad £400$$

$$\text{cost @ 100 units activity} = \quad £1250$$

Thus:
$$\text{variable element} = \frac{1250 - 400}{100 - 0} = \quad £8.5$$

∴ the estimated cost function using the line of best fit = **£400 + 8.5x,** where x = units of output.

The scattergraph technique is simple and convenient, but clearly no claims can be made for its accuracy.

22. Least squares *

* Note: This technique is dealt with in more detail in Quantitative Techniques. T. Lucey, D.P. Publications

This is a statistical method for calculating a line of best fit to data and has a variety of uses including the present one of establishing a cost function. The linear cost function can be represented by

$$y = a + bx,$$

where y equals cost and the other symbols are as previously defined. To find the values of the constants, a and b, two simultaneous equations need to be solved. These are

$$\sum y = an + b \sum x \dots\dots\dots\dots \text{Equation I}$$
$$\sum xy = a \sum x + b \sum x^2 \dots\dots \text{Equation II}$$

where n = number of pairs of cost and activity figures.

(Note: These equations are known as the *Normal Equations*).

The calculation will be illustrated by the following cost and activity data taken from past records.

Example 4

Cost (y)	Activity (units) (x)
£	
56	4
62	5
80	7
72	7
88	9
94	10

Calculate the Fixed and Variable elements of cost

Solution

y	x	xy	x^2
56	4	224	16
62	5	310	25
80	7	560	49
72	7	504	49
88	9	792	81
94	10	940	100
$\sum y = \underline{452}$	$\sum x = \underline{42}$	$\sum xy = \underline{3330}$	$\sum x^2 = \underline{320}$

and $n = 6$

Substituting in the equations given above we obtain

$$452 = 6a + 42b \qquad \dots\dots\dots\dots \text{I}$$
$$3330 = 42a + 320b \qquad \dots\dots\dots\dots \text{II}$$

Solving in the normal manner, ie, eliminating one of the constants (in this case multiply Equation I by 7 and deduct from Equation II) we obtain:

$$3330 = 42a + 320b \quad \dots\dots\dots\dots\text{II}$$

$$3164 = 42a + 294b \quad \dots\dots\dots 7 \times \text{I}$$

$$166 = 26b$$

∴ b = 6.385 and substituting in either equation the value of a is found to be 30.6

∴ the linear cost function is: $\underline{y = 30.6 + 6.385x}$

ie

$$y = \text{Total cost}$$

£30.6 = the Fixed costs

and

£6.385 = Variable cost per unit of activity.

How is the calculated cost function used?

Assume we wish to forecast what the total cost would be when the Activity was 12 units. The required value of, x, the Activity, is inserted into the cost function, thus:

$$\text{Total cost} = £30.6 + 6.385 \,(12)$$

$$= £107.22$$

This represents the estimate of total cost, assuming that the past cost behavioural characteristics continue to apply. Forecasting *outside* the range of the supplied data values (ie in this example, 4–18) is known as *extrapolation*. If we wished to estimate a value *within* the range, say 8 units in this example, this is known as *interpolation*.

Notes:

a.   The above is an outline of finding the constants *a* and *b* by the method of least squares which is sometimes known as *regression analysis*.

b.   The least squares method should only be applied to cost and activity data which show evidence of real correlation. This can be tested, for example, by a '*t*' test of the basic data.

c.   After the regression line has been calculated, its accuracy can be assessed by calculating its coefficient of determination (r^2).

23 . The effects of inflation

When we are trying to find the cost characteristics from past data, as shown above, a recurring problem is the effect of inflation on the costs. Over time, inflation affects all costs, both fixed and variable and to be able to get at the 'real' underlying cost characteristics the effects of inflation must be allowed for. This has to be done whatever technique of cost analysis is used ie high/low, scattergraph, least squares or whatever.

The general principles are illustrated by the following example

Example 5

Production and cost data have been recorded over two years thus:

	Last year	Current year
Production	50,000 units	54,000 units
Total costs	£1,700,000	£1,835,400

Between last year and the current year there has been 5% cost inflation.

Required

a.   Calculate the 'real' fixed and variable costs

b.   Estimate what the total costs will be next year when it is expected there will be 4% cost inflation and output will be 56,000 units.

Solution

a.   Eliminate the inflation effects from data supplied:

$$\text{Current year costs in 'real' terms} = \frac{\text{Current year Actual Costs}}{\text{Inflation rate} + 1} = \frac{£1,835,400}{1.05} = £1,748,000$$

Find the fixed/variable costs from the real cost and production differences

	Production units	Costs £
Current year	54,000 units	1,748,000
Last year	50,000 units	1,700,000
Difference =	4,000 units	£48,000

$$\therefore \text{'Real' variable cost/unit} = \frac{£48,000}{4000} = £12$$

'Real' Fixed costs = £1,748,000 − (54,000 × £12) = **£1.1m.**

[The actual costs in the current year are thus made up as follows:

$$(£1.1m \times 1.05) + (54,000 \times £12 \times 1.05) = £1,835,400$$

b. Cost estimate for the next year when there is expected to be 4% cost inflation and 56,000 units output = (£1.1m × 1.05 × 1.04) + (56,000 × £12 × 1.05 × 1.04)

$$= £1,935,024$$

If the inflation effects between periods are not allowed for, the cost breakdown into fixed and variable cannot be accurate.

24. Past and future costs

The analysis of past cost behaviour may be of help in predicting future cost behaviour, but care should be taken with any extrapolation into the future. The past will only be a guide to the future if conditions remain more or less the same. Conditions rarely remain the same, so judgement will always be required in cost prediction. Because many factors other than changes in activity levels influence costs, eg, changes in organisation, technology, methods, climatic influences etc, etc, care should be taken not to adopt a too simplistic view of cost behaviour.

On occasions no past data are available on which to base predictions. This is often the case with a new product and in such cases, or where significant changes in methods are anticipated for an existing product, cost estimates should be based on engineering and work study estimates.

The environment in which firms operate is highly volatile and change is ever present. There may be new products, new competitors, changes in methods and technology, changes in market conditions and a host of other factors. The effect of this is that past behaviour and patterns are highly unlikely to be applicable in the future.

Accordingly, *any* form of extrapolation of the past into the future, however sophisticated it may appear, is unlikely to produce accurate results. The further into the future we are trying to forecast, the less reliance we should place our past behaviour and results. Remember, the only thing we know for certain about the future is that it will not be the same as the past.

25. Alternative cost patterns

So far, all of the cost patterns, whether linear or curvilinear, fixed, variable or semi-variable, have had regular, continuous characteristics. This is not always the case and various other patterns exist, examples of which follow.

26. Step costs

These are costs which remain constant for a range of activity; then, when activity increases still further, the cost has to be increased by a significant amount. A typical example would be supervision costs. For a range of activities one supervisor will be sufficient, but there comes a point when an additional supervisor has to be appointed, so costs increase discretely. This can be shown graphically as in Figure 8.8.

There is not a simple algebraic expression which describes step costs as there is for continuous linear or curvilinear functions. Analysis involving step costs can be dealt with graphically or by either of the following methods.

i. If the range of activities being considered lies within one step, eg, between output levels v1 and v2 in Figure 18.8, then for analysis purposes the step cost can be treated as a fixed cost at level 2.

ii. Continuous approximation of step costs.

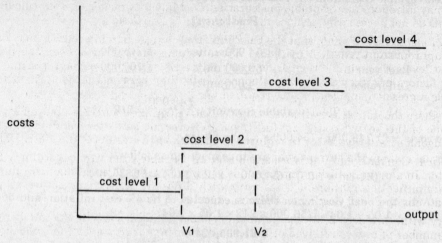

Figure 18.8 Illustration of step costs

Many costs in the aggregate do increase by discrete amounts so that they are strictly step costs. In many cases the steps are frequent and relatively small so that approximation by continuous functions is reasonably accurate and facilities subsequent analysis. This can be shown as in Figure 18.9:

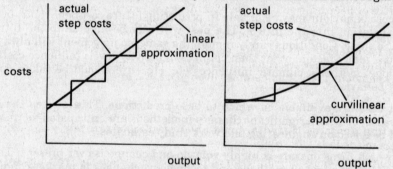

Figure 18.9 Continuous approximations of step costs

Because salaries and administrative costs comprise a large proportion of total cost in both private and public sector organisations, step costs are frequently encountered. For example, within the Education Service there are published bands which produce a stepped element in the salaries cost (which comprises about 80% of total costs).There are bands of pupil numbers which determined the number of teachers a school should have and also the salary of the head teacher. These are easily calculated step costs being based on published bands but many others exist in less obvious forms.

26. Problems of cost behaviour prediction

It is important to be aware of the pitfalls and problems in cost prediction so that where possible they can be avoided. Typical of these are the following:

a. *Tendency to classify costs for all time.* There is a tendency to classify costs, without too much regard to their actual behaviour, as fixed or variable according to conventions. An example of this is the tendency to classify labour costs as purely variable, whereas labour costs may have a substantial fixed element. Any classification of costs into fixed and variable needs to be continually reviewed in the light of their actual behaviour and in relation to the purpose for which the classification is intended to serve.

b. *Uncritical use of historical data.* If past cost data are to be used for prediction purposes, care must be taken to ensure that they are reasonably representative and not subject to special conditions. Ideally, past cost variations which are to be used for predictions, should be those which occurred as a result of volume changes only. Many factors other than changes in volume cause cost changes (ie, technology changes, product mix changes, method and tooling changes, seasonal and climatic changes) and if past data are not adjusted to take account of non-volume factors there is the implicit assumption that the non-volume factors will act upon costs in the future in the same manner and proportions as in the past. This is a somewhat sweeping assumption.

c. *Linearity assumption.* Costs display a variety of forms and the too ready assumption of linearity for all variable costs may introduce unacceptable inaccuracies. Cost linearity makes for easy calculations, but easy calculations do not necessarily produce the best results.

d. *Use of statistical methods.* Providing that the base data are sound, a gain in accuracy may be obtained by the use of appropriate statistical methods. Where volume changes have been the major factor influencing cost levels then simple regression analysis, as described in the chapter, can be of value. Where several factors are known to have influenced costs, then more advanced statistical methods, such as multiple regression analysis may be required.

Alternatively, where the data is curvilinear, statistical curve fitting should be employed to establish if the data fits one of the known statistical functions. However, no statistical method should be used uncritically, judgement will invariably be required in addition to the results of the statistical exercise.

e. *Oversimplification.* Conventionally it is assumed that all variable costs vary accordingly to a single activity indicator. In a manufacturing company this is typically taken to be production volume. This is a gross over-simplification. Different costs vary with different activity indicators as previously explained when Activity Based Costing was discussed.

Some costs vary with, (are driven by) the number of clients handled, some by the number of set-ups, others by the number of orders received or material movements or by some other cost driver. If the assumption is that all variable costs vary at the same rate accordingly to, say, production volume, it is illogical and ignores reality. In spite of this students should be aware that the assumption is frequently encountered in examination questions.

f. *Cost unit definition.* Ideally the cost units used for product and service costing and cost behaviour prediction should be standardised units; each identical with one other. In some cases this presents few problems. Each litre of beer brewed or tonne of cement produced or nuts manufactured are identical. However there are often problems especially within Service and Not-for-Profit organisations. For example, in the National Health Service 'Patient-Days' and "Out-patient Attendance's' are frequently used as cost units for internal and National comparative purposes. But patients, their illnesses their treatments, and times taken vary considerably and make the use of such units less valid. As a consequence cost behaviour prediction becomes even more of a problem.

27. Summary

a. For many accounting purposes it is vital to be able to estimate accurately the behaviour of cost in relation to changes in the level of activity.

b. Generally the situations being studied are for a limited time period and for a limited range of activity variations ie, short run.

c. Variable cost may be linear or curvilinear.

d. Linear approximations of curvilinear functions are frequently made.

e. Fixed or period costs are time, not activity related.

f. Semi-variable costs contain fixed and variable elements.

g. When past data are available, cost characteristics can be established visually by the scattergraph technique or by the method of regression analysis known as least squares.

h. Some cost patterns are not continuous, for example, step costs.

i. Many problems exist in accurately predicting cost behaviour and these include: inappropriate cost classifications, poor historical data, using linear approximation in inappropriate circumstances etc.

28. Points to note

a. Flexible budgeting, marginal costing, cost/volume/profit analysis have as their basis, predictions about cost behaviour.

b. It has been said with some truth that in the short run all costs are fixed and in the long run all costs are variable.

c. In practice costs do not behave in regular, predictable fashions. One example is that different types of variable costs vary with different activity indicators. One cost may vary with production another with sales, another one with orders received. In examinations there is frequently the simplifying assumption that all variable costs are related to one indicator, say sales volume. This makes for simpler questions but it is not necessarily realistic.

d. On occasions it is necessary to resolve a total cost into its fixed and variable elements. This can be done, somewhat crudely, by using the scattergraph technique or by using regression analysis based on the least squares method.

Student self-testing

Self Review Questions

1. What are the major reasons for the study of cost behaviour? (2)
2. What is normally assumed to be the major factor influencing the level of costs? (3)
3. Can statistical techniques be of value in predicting costs? (S)
4. Define a variable cost (6)
5. What is a curvilinear variable cost? (9)
6. What is the formula for the cost function known as a Parabola? (10)
7. What is a linear approximation? (11)
8. Distinguish between variable cost and the economic concept of marginal cost.(12)
9. What is a direct cost? (12)
10. Define a fixed cost (15)
11. What is a semi-variable cost? (17)
12. What is the formula for a linear semi-variable cost? (17)
13. What is the scattergraph technique? (21)
14. What are the least square Normal Equations? (22)
15. Why is it necessary to allow for the effect of inflation in cost analyses? (23)
16. Why is judgement required in cost prediction? (24)
17. What are step costs? (26)

Exercises and examination questions with answers

Exercises

A18.1   The behaviour of a cost can be expressed algebraically as:

$$\text{Cost} = bx + cx^2 + dx^3$$

       where b = labour hours
                  c = material in Kgs
                  d = machine hours
      and x = output in units

You are required to:

a. Explain what type of cost is depicted

b. Calculate the cost at output levels of 80 and 100 units when $b = 6$ $c = 0.7$ and $d = 0.04$

A18.2   Using the results obtained in Exercise 1 calculate the cost at 85 units using linear interpolation. What is the extent of the error caused by linear interpolation?

A18.3   The following cost and activity data were taken from factory records.

Cost incurred	Activity (units)
£	
656	80
692	86
683	87
698	94
707	95
703	97
712	104

Using the least squares method of linear regression calculate the fixed and variable elements of the cost.

A18.4   Draw a scattergraph of the data in A18.3 and show the calculated regression line.

Examination questions

A18.5 A company is reviewing the purchasing policy for one of its raw materials as a result of a reduction in production requirement. The material, which is used evenly throughout the year, is used in only one of the company's products, the production of which is currently 12,000 units per annum. Each finished unit of the product contains 0.4 kilos of the material, 20% of the material is lost in the production process. Purchases can be made in multiple of 500 kilos, with a minimum purchase order quantity of 1,000 kilos.

The cost of the raw material depends upon the purchase order quantity as follows:

Order Quantity (kilos)	Cost per kilo (£)
1,000	1.00
1,500	0.98
2,000	0.965
2,500	0.95
3,000 and above	0.94

Costs of placing and handling each order are £90, of which £40 is an apportionment of costs which are not expected to be affected in the short-term by the number of orders placed. Annual holding costs of stock are £0.90 per unit of average stock, of which only £0.40 is expected to be affected in the short-term by the amount of stock held.

The lead time for the raw material is one month, and a safety stock of 250 kilos is required.

Required:

a. Explain, and illustrate from the situation described above, the meaning of the terms 'variable', 'semi variable', and 'fixed' costs.

b. Calculate the annual cost of pursuing alternative purchase order policies and thus advise the company regarding the purchase order quantity for the material that will minimise cost.

(ACCA, Costing)

A18.6 The following graphs reflect the pattern of certain overhead cost items in a manufacturing company in a year. The vertical axes of the graphs represent the total cost incurred, whilst the horizontal axes represent the volume of production or activity. The zero point is at the intersection of the two axes.

You are required to:

a. identify which graph represents the overhead cost items shown below: (N.B. a graph may be used more than once.)

Ref.	Brief description	Details of cost behaviour
1.	Depreciation of equipment	When charged on a straight line basis.
2.	Cost of a service	£50 annual charge for subscription, £2 charge for each unit taken, with a maximum total charge of £350 per annum.
3.	Royalty	£0.10 per unit produced, with a maximum charge of £5,000 per annum.
4.	Supervision cost	When there is one charge hand for every eight men or less, and one foreman for every three charge hands, and when each man represents 40 hours of production, thus:

Hours

Under 320	one charge-hand
321-640	two charge-hands
641-960	three charge-hands,
etc.	

plus one foreman.

| 5. | Depreciation of equipment | When charged on a straight line basis. |
| 6. | Cost of a service | Flat charge of £400 to cover the first 5,000 units: |

Per unit:

£0.10 for the next 3,000 units
£0.12 for the next 3,000 units
£0.14 for all subsequent units

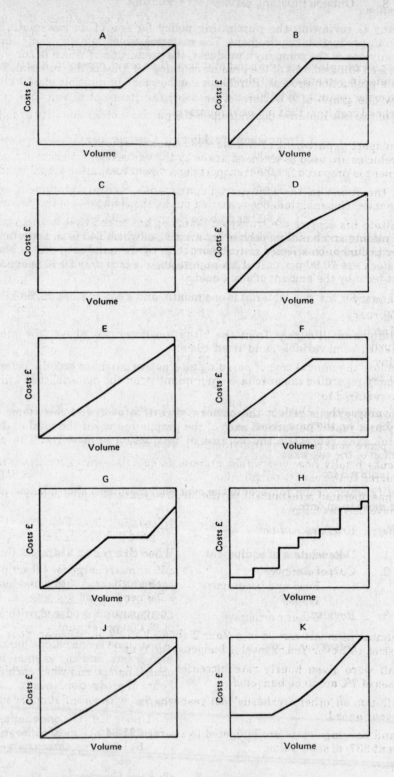

7.   Storage/carriage service

Per ton

£15 for the first 20 tons
£30 for the next 20 tons
£45 for the next 20 tons

No extra charge until the service reaches 100 tons; then:

£45 per ton for all subsequent tonnage.

8. Outside finishing service   Per unit

£0. 75 for the first 2 000 units
£0.55 for the next 2 000 units
£0.35 for all subsequent units

b. give an example of an overhead cost item that could represent those graphs to which you do not refer in you answer (a) above;

c. draw one graph of a pattern of an overhead item not shown and give an example of an overhead cost item that it would represent.

(CIMA, Cost Accounting 2)

A18.7 The transport department of the Norwest Council operates a large fleet of assorted vehicles. These vehicles are used as the need arises by the various departments of the Council. Each month a statement is prepared for the transport department comparing actual results with budget.

One of the items in the transport department's monthly statement is the cost of vehicle maintenance. This maintenance is carried out by the employees of the department.

To facilitate his control the transport manager has asked that future statements should show vehicle maintenance costs analysed into fixed and variable costs. Data for the six months from January to June inclusive are given below:

	Vehicle maintenance cost	*Vehicle running hours*
	£	
January	13,600	2,100
February	15,800	2,800
March	14,500	2,200
April	16,200	3,000
May	14,900	2,600
June	15,000	2,500

You are required to:

a. i. analyse the vehicle maintenance costs into fixed and variable costs, by means of a graph, based on the data given;

   ii. prove your results by utilising the least squares method;

b. discuss briefly how you would propose to calculate rates for charging out the total costs incurred to the user departments.
(CIMA, Cost Accounting 2)

A18.8 W Ltd has operated a restaurant for the last two years. Revenue and operating costs over the two years have been as follows:

	Year 1	Year 2
	£000	£000
Revenue	1,348,312	1,514,224
Operating costs:		
Food and beverages	698,341	791,919
Wages	349,170	390,477
Other overheads	202,549	216,930

The number of meals served in a Year 2 showed an 8% increase on Year 1 level of 151,156. An increase of 10% over Year 2 level is budgeted for Year 3.

All staff were given hourly rate increases of 6% last year (ie, in Year 2). In Year 3 hourly increases of 7% are to be budgeted.

The inflation on 'other overheads' last year was 5%, with an inflationary increase of 6% expected in the year ahead.

Food and beverage costs are budgeted to average £5.14 per meal in Year 3. This is expected to represent 53% of sales value.

Required:

a. From information given above, and using the high low method of cost estimation, determine the budgeted expenditure on wages and other overhead for Year 3. (round your final answer for each to the nearest £000).

b. Calculate the gross profit (ie, sales less food and beverage costs) percentage of sales, and the net profit percentage of sales, for each of the three years, and comment on the change in these percentages over the period. (Round all figures to the nearest £000 or 1 decimal place of a %).
(ACCA Cost and Management Accounting)

Exercises and examination questions without answers

Exercises

B18.1 The following cost and activity data were recorded for Department Y.

	Output (units)	
	1,800	2,400
Costs	£	£
Labour	9,000	11,400
Materials	12,600	16,800
Admin. salaries	6,000	6,000
Power	1,300	1,550
Depreciation	9,000	12,000
Rates	850	850
Indirect labour	1,460	1,460
Selling costs	6,100	7,300

You are required to:

a. Classify each type of cost with a brief explanatory note where necessary.

b. Where appropriate separate the fixed and variable elements of each cost.

c. Assuming that the pattern of cost behaviour remains the same calculate the expected cost for each item for 2,000 units.

B18.2 Cost and activity data were recorded as follows:

	Output (%)	Cost (£)
Period 1	55	2,300
Period 2	70	2,800
Period 3	58	2,650
Period 4	85	2,960
Period 5	95	3,580
Period 6	75	2,900
Period 7	67	2,410
Period 8	78	2,800
Period 9	92	3,460
Period 10	96	3,720

You are required to:

a. Draw a Scattergraph of the above data.
b. Draw a line of best fit.
c. Estimate the fixed and variable content of the cost from the graph.
d. Use the high/low points to estimate the fixed and variable contents of the cost.

B18.3 Use the least squares method to calculate the fixed and variable elements of the cost and activity data given in the previous exercise.

B18.4 For many purposes in accounting it is assumed that variable costs vary linearly. Is this assumption a realistic one?

Examination questions

B18.5 Data:

	£
Cost of motor car	5,500
Trade-in-price after 2 years or 60,000 miles is expected to be	1,500
Maintenance - 6 monthly service costing	60
Spares/replacement parts, per 1,000 miles	20
Vehicle licence, per annum	80
Insurance, per annum	150
Tyre replacements after 25,000 miles, four at	37.50 each
Petrol, per gallon	1.90

Average mileage from one gallon is 25 miles.

a. From the above data you are required:

   i. to prepare a schedule to be presented to management showing for the mileages of 5,000, 10,000, 15,000 and 30,000 miles per annum:

     1. total variable cost

     2. total fixed cost

     3. total cost

     4. variable cost per mile (in pence to nearest penny)

     5. fixed cost per mile (in pence to nearest penny)

     6. total cost per mile (in pence to nearest penny) If, in classifying the costs, you consider that some can be treated as either variable or fixed, state the assumption(s) on which your answer is based together with brief supporting reason(s).

   ii. on the graph paper provided, to plot the information given in your answer to (i) above for the costs listed against 1, 2, 3 and 6.

   iii. to read off from your graph(s) in (ii) and state the approximate total costs applicable to 18,000 miles and 25,000 miles and the total cost per mile (in pence) at these two mileages.

b. 'The more miles you travel, the cheaper it becomes. ' Comment briefly on this statement.

(CIMA, Cost Accounting 1)

B18.6 The following data relate to a company:

Sales £000	Delivery costs £000
80	16
85	11
115	21
160	16
205	23
280	18
290	27
330	32
390	30
450	37
470	25
550	35

You are required to:

a. i. plot these costs on a graph;

   ii. draw on the graph the 'line of best fit';

   iii. state the approximate level of fixed costs.

b. state and explain a formula which may be used for predicting future delivery costs for any level of sales. (Note: figures are not required.)

CIMA (Cost Accounting 1)

B18.7 Remix plc. makes ready-mixed cement and operates a small fleet of vehicles which delivers the product to customers within its delivery area. Maintenance records for the previous five years reveal:

Year	Mileage of vehicles	Maintenance cost £
1.	170,000	13,500
2.	180,000	14,000
3.	165,000	13,250
4.	160,000	13,000
5.	175,000	13,750

Transport statistics reveal:

Vehicle	Number of journeys each day	Average tonnage carried to customers tonnes	Average distance to customers miles
1	6	4	10
2	4	4	20
3	2	5	40
4	2	6	30
5	1	6	60

There are five vehicles operating a five-day week, for 50 weeks a year

Inflation can be ignored.

Standard cost data include:

Drivers' wages are £150 each per week

Supervisor/relief driver's wage is £200 per week

Depreciation, on a straight-line basis with no residual value:

	Cost	Life
Loading equipment	£100,000	5 years
Vehicles	£30,000 each	5 years

Petrol/oil costs 20p per mile

Repairs cost $7\frac{1}{2}$p per mile

Vehicle licences cost £400 p.a. for each vehicle

Insurance costs £600 p.a. for each vehicle

Tyres cost £3,000 p.a. in total

Miscellaneous costs, £2,250 p.a. in total

You are required to:

a. calculate a standard rate per tonne/mile of operating the vehicles;

b. comment on the use of a standard rate per tonne/mile, out-lining its limitations in decision making.

(CIMA Cost Accounting 2)

19: Marginal costing and absorption costing

1. Topics covered in this chapter

> 1. Marginal costing defined
>
> 2. Marginal costing and absorption costing compared
>
> 3. Marginal costing statements
>
> 4. Stock valuation using marginal and absorption costing.

2. Marginal costing - definition

Marginal costing distinguishes between fixed costs and variable costs as conventionally classified. The *marginal cost* of a product is its variable cost. This is normally taken to be; direct labour, direct material, direct expenses and the variable part of overheads. Marginal costing is formally defined as:

> 'the accounting system in which variable costs are charged to cost units and the fixed costs of the period are written-off in full against the aggregate contribution. Its special value is in decision making'. *Terminology.*

The term 'contribution' mentioned in the formal definition is the term given to the difference between Sales and Marginal cost. Thus

MARGINAL COST = VARIABLE COST =   DIRECT LABOUR
+
DIRECT MATERIAL
+
DIRECT EXPENSE
+
VARIABLE OVERHEADS

CONTRIBUTION = SALES – MARGINAL COST

The term marginal cost sometimes refers to the marginal cost per unit and sometimes to the total marginal costs of a department or batch or operation. The meaning is usually clear from the context.

Note: Alternative names for marginal costing are the '*contribution approach*' and '*direct costing*'.

3. Alternative concepts of marginal cost

To the economist, marginal cost is the additional cost incurred by the production of one extra unit. To the accountant, marginal cost is average variable cost which is presumed to act in a linear fashion, ie, marginal cost per unit is assumed to be constant in the short run, over the activity range being considered.

These views can be contrasted in the following graphs:

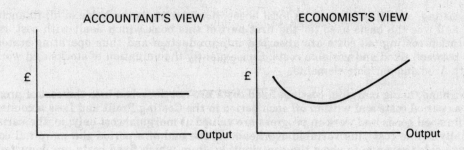

Figure 19.1 Marginal cost per unit

This difference of viewpoint regarding marginal cost per unit results in the following alternative views of a firm's total cost structure.

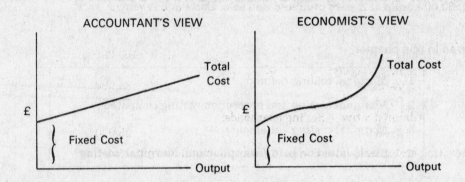

ACCOUNTANT'S VIEW   ECONOMIST'S VIEW

The economic model is an explanation of the cost behaviour of firms in general, whereas the accounting model is an attempt to provide a pragmatic basis for decision making in a particular firm. However, it is likely that differences between the two viewpoints are more apparent than real.

A number of investigations have shown that marginal costs are virtually constant per unit over the range of activity changes studied. Accordingly for short run decision making purposes the marginal cost per unit should be assumed to be constant. Thus if the marginal cost per unit was £5 per unit, the total marginal cost for

100 units would be £500

150 units would be £750

200 units would be £1000

and so on.......

Note:

The assumption of linearity should only be made in appropriate conditions. Where the question or facts of the situation indicate that variable costs behave in some other way, for example, curvi-linearly or in a stepped fashion, then the actual behaviour pattern should be used.

4. Uses of marginal costing

There are two main uses for the concept of marginal costing:

a. As a basis for providing information to management for planning and decision making. It is particularly appropriate for short run decisions involving changes in volume or activity and the resulting cost changes. This is an important area of study for students and it is dealt with in detail in the following chapter.

b. It can also be used in the routine cost accounting system for the calculation of costs and the valuation of stocks. Used in this fashion, it is an alternative to total absorption costing. This facet of marginal costing is dealt with below.

5. Marginal costing and absorption costing

Absorption costing, sometimes known as total absorption costing, is the basis of all financial accounting statements and was the basis used for the first part of this book which dealt with cost ascertainment. Using absorption costing, all costs are absorbed into production and thus operating statements do not distinguish between fixed and variable costs. Consequently the valuation of stocks and work-in-progress contains both fixed and variable elements.

On the other hand, using marginal costing, fixed costs are not absorbed into the cost of production. They are treated as period costs and written off each period in the Costing Profit and Loss account. The effect of this is that finished goods and work-in progress are valued at marginal cost only; ie, the variable elements of cost, usually Prime cost plus variable overhead. At the end of a period the marginal cost of sales is deducted from sales revenue to show the contribution, from which fixed costs are deducted to show net profit.

The two approaches are illustrated below using the following data:

Example 1

In a period, 20,000 units of Z were produced and sold. Costs and revenues were:

	£
Sales	100,000
Production costs:	
variable	35,000
fixed	15,000
Administrative + Selling overheads:	
fixed	25,000

Prepare operating statements based on both Absorption and Marginal Costing

Solution

Operating Statements

Absorption Costing Approach		Marginal Costing Approach		
	£		£	£
Sales	100,000	Sales		100,000
less Production Cost of Sales	50,000	*less* Marginal cost		35,000
= Gross Profit	50,000	= Contribution		65,000
less Admin. + Selling Overheads	25,000	*less* Fixed costs		
		Production	15,000	
		Admin. S+D	25,000	40,000
= Net Profit	£25,000	= Net Profit		£25,000

The above illustration, although simple, illustrates the general characteristics of both approaches.

The key figure arising in the Marginal statement is the Contribution of £65,000. The total amount of contribution arising from Product Z (and other products, if any) forms a pool from which fixed costs are met. Any surplus arising after fixed costs are met becomes the Net Profit.

6. Changes in the level of activity

When changes occur in the level of activity, the absorption costing approach may cause some confusion. In Example 1 the activity level was 20,000 units and using the absorption approach, the profit per unit and cost per unit can be calculated as follows:

	£
Selling Price per unit	5
less Total cost per unit $= \dfrac{£75000}{20000}$	3.75
Profit per unit	£1.25

If these figures were used as guides to results at any activity level other than 20,000, they would be incorrect and may mislead. For example, if the level of activity of Example 1 changed to 25,000 units, it might be assumed that the total profits would be 25,000 × £1.25 = £31,250. However, the results are likely to be as follows:

Operating Statement (Absorption approach)

	£
Sales (25,000 × £5)	125,000
less Production Cost (£35,000 × 125% + 15,000)	58,750
= Gross Profit	66,250
less Admin + Selling overheads	25,000
= Net Profit	£41,250

The difference is, of course, caused by the incorrect treatment of the fixed cost. In such circumstances the use of the marginal approach presents a clearer picture. Based on the data in Example 1 the marginal cost per unit and the contribution per unit is calculated as follows:

$$\text{Marginal cost/unit} = \frac{\text{Marginal Cost}}{\text{Quantity}} = \frac{35,000}{20,000}$$

$$= \pounds1.75$$

$$\therefore \text{contribution/unit} = \text{Sale Price} - \text{Marginal cost/unit} = \pounds5 - \pounds1.75$$

$$= \pounds3.25$$

If, once again, the activity is increased to 25,000 units, the expected profit would be:

$$(25,000 \text{ units} \times \text{Contribution/unit}) - \text{Fixed costs}$$

$$= (25,000 \times \pounds3.25) - \pounds40,000 = \pounds41,250$$

and the operating statement on marginal costing lines would be

	£
Sales	125,000
less Marginal cost (25,000 × 1.75)	43,750
= Contribution	£81,250
less Fixed costs	40,000
Net Profit	£41,250

Note:

Students will note that the marginal cost and contribution per unit have been assumed to be constant and that it has been assumed that fixed costs remain unchanged.

7. Stocks and marginal costing

Although the method of presentation was different, both marginal and absorption costing produced the same net profit for the data in Example 1. This was because there was no stock at the beginning or end of the period. Because the two methods differ in their valuation of stock, they produce different profit figures when stocks arise. This is illustrated below.

Example 2

Assume the same data as Example 1 except that only 18,000 of the 20,000 units produced were sold, 2000 units being carried forward as Stock to the next period.

Produce operating statements based upon marginal costing and absorption costing principles.

Solution

Operating Statements

Absorption Costing	£	£	Marginal Costing	£	£
Sales (18,000 × £5)		90,000	Sales		90,000
less Production Cost of sales	50,000		*less* Marginal cost	35,000	
– Closing stock (2000 × £2.50)	5,000	45,000	– closing stock (2000 × £1.75)	3,500	31,500
= Gross profit		45,000	= Contribution		58,500
less Admin + selling Overheads		25,000	*less* Fixed costs Production		15,000
			Admin S + D	25,000	40,000
= Net profit		£20,000	= Net profit		£18,500

a. The closing stock valuations using the two approaches are:

Absorption Costing = Average Production Cost (including fixed costs)

$$= \frac{£50,000}{20,000}$$

$$= £2.50$$

Marginal Costing = Marginal cost ie, variable costs only

$$= \frac{£35,000}{20,000}$$

$$= £1.75$$

b. By including fixed costs in stock valuation, absorption costing transfers some of this period's fixed costs into next period when they will be charged against the revenue derived from the stock carried forward (assuming it is sold). Marginal costing always writes off *all* fixed costs in the period they are incurred.

c. In a period with increasing stocks (as the one illustrated) absorption costing will show higher profits than marginal costing. Conversely in a period of decreasing stocks marginal costing will show the higher profits. The difference is, of course, entirely due to the different treatment of fixed costs in the stock valuation.

8. Typical marginal costing statements

Wherever marginal costing is used in the routine accounting system, similar principles to those described above will apply. Some examples of marginal costing statements in typical situations are the following;

a. Where Multiple Products or Multiple departments exist

Marginal Costing Operating Statement

Product or Department 1	Product or Department 2	Product or Department 3	...	Total
Sales l	Sales 2	Sales 3	etc	Total sales
less Marginal Cost 1 of Sales	Marginal Cost 2 of Sales	Marginal Cost 3 of Sales	...	Marginal Cost of Sales (Total)
= Contribut. 1	Contribut. 2	Contribut. 3		Total Contribution *less* Fixed Costs for whole organisation
				NET PROFIT

Notes:

i. Using Marginal Costing no attempt is made to apportion fixed costs arbitrarily across products or departments.

ii. With such a presentation the effects of eliminating a product or department or altering the level of activity can be shown more clearly. Care must be taken in assessing the effect of a product or department elimination to ensure that any effect on fixed costs is allowed for.

b. *Process Costing*

Where marginal costing is used in process accounting, the normal accounts and statements will be produced, as described in Chapter 15 except that:

    i. Process accounts will contain variable costs only.

    ii. Transfers from one process to another will be at marginal cost.

    iii. Losses, abnormal and normal, will be valued at marginal cost only.

    iv. All fixed costs will be written off, each period, to costing profit and loss.

9. Marginal costing or absorption costing

The arguments below relate to the use of these techniques in the *routine cost accounting system* of the organisation and not to their use for decision making or control. Arguments for the use of marginal costing in routine costing:

a. Simple to operate.

b. No apportionments, which are frequently on an arbitrary basis, of fixed costs to products or departments. Many fixed costs are indivisible by their nature, eg, Managing Director's Salary.

c. Where sales are constant, but production fluctuates (possibly an unlikely circumstance) marginal costing shows a constant net profit whereas absorption costing shows variable amounts of profit.

d. Under or over absorption of overheads is almost entirely avoided. The usual reason for under/ over absorption is the inclusion of fixed costs into overhead absorption rates and the level of activity being different to that planned.

e. Fixed costs are incurred on a time basis, eg, salaries, rent, rates etc, and do not relate to activity. Therefore it is logical to write them off in the period they are incurred and this is done using marginal costing.

f. Accounts prepared using marginal costing more nearly approach the actual cash flow position.

Arguments for the use of total absorption in routine costing.

a. Fixed costs are a substantial and increasing proportion of costs in modern industry. Production cannot be achieved without incurring fixed costs which thus form an inescapable part of the cost of production, so should be included in stock valuations. Marginal costing may give the impression that fixed costs are somehow divorced from production.

b. Where production is constant but sales fluctuate, net profit fluctuations are less with absorption costing than with marginal costing.

c. Where stock building is a necessary part of operations, eg, timber seasoning, spirit maturing, firework manufacture, the inclusion of fixed costs in stock valuation is necessary and desirable. Otherwise a series of fictitious losses will be shown in earlier periods to be offset eventually by excessive profits when the goods are sold.

d. The calculation of marginal cost and the concentration upon contribution may lead to the firm setting prices which are below total cost although producing some contribution. Absorption cost makes this less likely because of the automatic inclusion of fixed charges.

e. SSAP 9 (Stocks and Work in Progress) recommends the use of absorption costing for financial accounts because costs and revenues must be matched in the period when the revenue arises, not when the costs are incurred. Also it recommends that stock valuations must include production overheads incurred in the normal course of business even if such overheads are time related, ie, fixed. The production overheads must be based upon normal activity levels.

10. Conclusions regarding marginal and absorption costing

No generalised, all embracing answer can be given as to which technique should be used. Having regard to all the factors, the accountant should make a judgement as to which technique is more appropriate for the requirements of a particular organisation. Although any technique can be used for internal purposes, SSAP 9 is quite clear that absorption costing must be the basis of the financial accounts. It would appear that the use of a full marginal costing system in the routine cost ascertainment procedures of an organisation is relatively rare.

This does not mean that marginal costing principles are unimportant. An understanding of the behaviour of costs and the implications of contribution is vital for accountants and managers. The use of marginal costing principles in planning and decision making, dealt with in the following chapter, is universal and is of considerable importance.

11. Multi period example of marginal and absorption costing

To bring together the various points covered in the chapter, a fully worked example is shown below.

Example

Stock, production and sales data for Industrial Detergents Ltd. are given in the following.

	Period 1	Period 2	Period 3	Period 4
Production (litres)	60,000	70,000	55,000	65,000
Sales (litres)	60,000	55,000	65,000	70,000
Opening Stock (litres)	–	–	15,000	5,000
Closing Stock (litres)	–	15,000	5,000	–

The company has a single product, for which the financial data, based on an activity level of 60,000 litres/period, are as follows:

	Cost per litre £
Direct Material	2.50
Direct Labour	3.00
Production Overheads = 200% of direct labour	6.00
= Total cost/litre	£11.50
Selling price per litre	£18.00

Administrative overheads are fixed at £100,000 per period and half of the production overheads are fixed.

From the above information prepare operating statements on marginal costing and absorption costing principles.

Solution

The first step is to establish the amount of fixed production overheads per period. The cost data shown above are based on 60,000 litres.

Labour for 60,000 litres	=	60,000 × £3	=	£180,000
Total production overheads	=	200% × £180,000	=	£360,000
∴ Fixed production overheads	=	$\frac{£360,000}{2}$	=	£180.000

The variable overhead recovery rate is accordingly 100% of direct wages so that marginal cost per litre can be established as follows:

	£
Material	2.50
Labour	3.00
Variable overhead 100% of wages	3.00
	£8.50

Operating Statement using Marginal Costing

	Period 1 £		Period 2 £		Period 3 £		Period 4 £
Sales	1,080,000		990,000		1,170,000		1,260,000
Marginal cost of Production	510,000		595,000		467,500		552,500
+ opening stock					127,500		42,500
– closing stock			127,500		42,500		
= Marginal cost of Sales		510,000		467,500		552,500	595,000
Contribution		570,000		522,500		617,500	665,000
Fixed Costs (Admin + Prod'n)		280,000		280,000		280,000	280,000
Net profit		£290,000		£242,500		£337,500	£385,000

Note:

Stocks are valued at marginal cost.

Operating Statement using Absorption Costing in Accordance with SSAP 9

	Period 1 £		Period 2 £		Period 3 £		Period 4 £
Sales		1,080,000		990,000		1,170,000	1,260,000
Total cost of Production	690,000		805,000		632,500	747,500	
+ opening stock					172,500	57,500	
– closing stock			172,500		57,500		
= Total cost of Sales		690,000		632,500		747,500	805,000
Gross Profit		390,000		357,500		422,500	455,000
Administration Costs		100,000		100,000		100,000	100,000
Net profit		£290,000		£257,500		£322,500	£355,000
Planned activity Level		60,000		60,000		60,000	60,000
Actual activity Level		60,000		70,000		55,000	65,000
Difference		–		+ 10,000		– 5,000	+ 5,000
Overhead Over or (under) Absorption		–		+ £30,000		(£15,000)	+ £15,000

Notes:

a. Stocks are valued at full production cost including fixed production overheads ie, in this example £11.50 per litre. This represents the cost at normal activity levels in accordance with SSAP 9 recommendations.

b. The amount of over or under absorbed overhead represents the over or under recovery of fixed overheads caused when activity is above or below the planned activity level. In this example the fixed overheads are recovered at £3 per litre eg, in period 2 production was 70,000 litres as compared with 60,000 planned so the over absorption was 10,000 litres at £3 per litre = £30,000.

c. As explained in Chapter 9, the over/under absorption could be taken direct to P & L a/c or, more usually, taken to a suspense account from which the net balance at the end of the year would be written off to P & L.

d. The amount over absorbed would be deducted from total cost, the amount under absorbed would be added to total cost.

e. Because in this example, production and sales were equal over the periods concerned the profits using the two techniques can be reconciled thus:-

Profits using Marginal Costing

	£
Period 1	290,000
Period 2	242,500
Period 3	337,500
Period 4	385,000
	£1,255,000

Profits using Absorption Costing

	£
Period 1	290,000
Period 2	257,500
Period 3	322,500
Period 4	355,000
+ Net over absorption	30,000
	£1,255,000

12. Summary

a. Marginal costing is a costing technique where fixed and variable costs are differentiated. Only variable costs are charged to cost units and fixed costs are written off in full each period.

b. Contribution is the difference between sales and variable cost. The pool of contribution is available to cover the fixed costs and, when the fixed costs have been covered, the balance remaining is profit.

c. Marginal costing can be used as the basis of the routine cost accounting system or for management decision making.

d. Total absorption costing incorporates both fixed and variable costs into production and consequently into stock valuation. Stocks under marginal costing are valued at marginal cost only.

e. Because of the different methods of stock valuation the two approaches produce differing profit figures when stocks exist at the beginning or end of a period.

f. When used as a basis of the routine cost accounting system marginal costing avoids the sometimes arbitrary apportionment of fixed overheads to products or departments, charges period costs when they are incurred, and is claimed to show a more realistic situation.

g. Absorption costing recognises that fixed costs are an inescapable part of production costs and consequently includes fixed elements in stock valuation. SSAP 9 recommends absorption costing principles for stock valuation.

13. Point to note

Under examination conditions if the questions emphasises the use of cost statements for planning or decision making purposes, it is likely that a marginal cost approach is required.

Student self-testing

Self Review Questions

1. What is marginal costing? (2)
2. What is contribution and how is it calculated ? (2)
3. Distinguish between the accountant's and economist's view of marginal cost. (3)
4. What are the main uses of marginal costing? (4)
5. What is the essential difference between marginal and absorption costing? (5)
6. How does the method of stock valuation differ between marginal and absorption costing? (7)
7. What arguments are there for the use of marginal costing principles in the routine costing system of an organisation? (9)
8. What are the arguments for absorption costing? (9)

Exercises and examination questions with answers

Exercises

A19.1 The following data were taken from the past records of a company at two output levels.

The company has three departments and all fixed costs have been apportioned to the departments on the basis of sales turnover.

	Dept A £	Dept B £	Dept C £	Total £
Sales	50,000	75,000	125,000	250,000
less Costs	45,000	60,000	106,250	211,250
= Profit	5,000	15,000	18,750	38,750
Sales	60,000	90,000	150,000	300,000
less Costs	50,000	66,000	117,500	233,500
= Profit	10,000	24,000	32,500	66,500

You are required to recast the above statements using the Marginal Costing approach showing contribution per department and in total.

A19.2 The following data were taken from the records of a company.

	Period 1	Period 2	Period 3
Production	30,000	38,000	27,000
Sales	30,000	27,000	38,000
Opening Stock	–		11,000
Closing Stock		11,000	

All the above in Kgs

The firm makes a single product the financial details of which are as follows (based on a normal activity level of 30,000 Kgs.)

	Cost per Kg. (£)
Direct material	1.50
Direct labour	1.00
Production overheads = 300% of labour	3.00
	5.50

Selling price per Kg. £9

Administrative overheads are fixed at £25,000 and one third of the production overheads are fixed. Prepare separate operating statements on marginal costing and absorption costing principles.

A19.3 A firm has 3 departments and prepares operating statements using a marginal costing approach as follows (£000):

	A	B	C	Total
Sales	650	480	1420	2550
less Marginal costs	475	220	850	1545
= contribution	175	260	570	1005
less Fixed costs				850
= Profit				155

Recast the above statement using a total cost approach assuming that fixed costs are apportioned on the basis of marginal costs.

Examination questions

A19.4 X Limited commenced business on 1st March making one product only, the standard cost of which is as follows:

	£
Direct labour	5
Direct material	8
Variable production overhead	2
Fixed production overhead	5
Standard production cost	20

The fixed production overhead figure has been calculated on the basis of a budgeted normal output of 36,000 units per annum.

You are to assume that there were no expenditure or efficiency variances and that all the budgeted fixed expenses are incurred over the year. March and April are to be taken as equal period months.

Selling, distribution and administration expenses are:

Fixed	£120,000 per annum
Variable	15% of the sales value.

The selling price per unit is £35 and the number of units produced and sold were:

	March Units	April Units
Production	2,000	3,200
Sales	1,500	3,000

You are required to:

a. prepare profit statements for each of the months of March and April using:

   i. marginal costing; and

   ii absorption costing;

b. present a reconciliation of the profit or loss figures given in your answers to (a) (i) and (a) (ii) accompanied by a brief explanation;

c. comment briefly on which costing principle, ie, marginal or absorption, should be used for what purposes(s) and why, referring to any statutory or other mandatory constraints.

(CIMA, Cost Accounting)

A19.5 The following budgeted information relates to a company that sells one product.

	January 1992	February 1992
Sales	18,000	32,000
Production	25,000	25,000

	£
Selling price per unit	16
Cost per unit: Material	5
Direct labour	3
Variable production cost	2

Fixed production costs £75,000 per month

There is no opening stock and company policy is to absorb fixed overheads on the basis of direct labour cost

Required:

a. Prepare profit and loss statements for the months of January and February on the basis of:

  i.   Marginal costing
  ii. Absorption costing.

b. Calculate the stock valuation at the end of January under each method.

c. Account for the differences in profit figures between the two methods.

d. Explain the advantages of absorption costing over marginal costing in profit reporting.

(AAT Cost Accounting & Budgeting, part question)

A19.6 A company manufactures a single product with the following variable costs per unit.

Direct materials	£7.00
Direct labour	£5.50
Manufacturing overhead	£2.00

The selling price of the product is £36.00 per unit. Fixed manufacturing costs are expected to be £1,340,000 for a period. Fixed non-manufacturing costs are expected to be £875,000. Fixed manufacturing costs can be analysed as follows:

Production Department 1	Production Department 2	Service Department	General Factory
£380,000	£465,000	£265,000	£230,000

'General Factory' costs represent space costs, for example rates, lighting and heating. Space utilisation is as follows:

Production department 1	40%
Production department 2	50%
Service department	10%

60% of service department costs are labour related and the remaining 40% machine related.

Normal production department activity is:

	Direct labour hours	Machine hours	Production units
Department 1	80,000	2,400	120,000
Department 2	100,000	2,400	120,000

Fixed manufacturing overheads are absorbed at a predetermined rate per unit production for each production department, based upon normal activity.

Required:

a. Prepare a profit statement for a period using the full absorption costing system described above and showing each element of cost separately. Costs for the period were as per expectation except for additional expenditure of £20,000 on fixed manufacturing overhead in Production Department 1. Production and sales were 116,000 and 114,000 units respectively for the period.

b. Prepare a profit statement for the period using marginal costing principles instead.

c. Contrast the general effect on profit of using absorption and marginal costing systems respectively. (Use the figures calculated in (a) and (b) above to illustrate your answer.)

(ACCA Cost & Management Accounting 1)

A19.7   RH Ltd makes and sells one product, the standard production cost of which is as follows for one unit:

			£
Direct labour	3 hours at £6 per hour		18
Direct materials	4 kilograms at £7 per kg		28
Production overhead	Variable		3
	Fixed		20
Standard production cost			69

Normal output is 16,000 units per annum and this figure is used for the fixed production overhead calculation.

Costs relating to selling, distribution and administration are

Variable	20 per cent of sales value
Fixed	£180,000 per annum

The only variance is a fixed production overhead volume variance. There are no units in finished goods stock at 1 October 1992. The fixed overhead expenditure is spread evenly throughout the year. The selling price per unit is £140.

For the two six-monthly periods detailed below, the number of units to be produced and sold are budgeted as:

	Six months ending 31 March 1993	Six months ending 30 September 1993
Production	8,500	7,000
Sales	7,000	8,000

You are required

a. to prepare statements for management showing sales, costs and profits for each of the six-monthly periods, using

   i.   marginal costing,

   ii.   absorption costing;

b. to prepare an explanatory statement reconciling for each six-monthly period the profit using marginal costing with the profit using absorption costing;

(CIMA Cost Accounting, part question)

A19.8   A manufacturer of glass bottles has been affected by competition from plastic bottles and is currently operating at between 65 and 70 per cent of maximum capacity.

The company at present reports profits on an absorption costing basis but with the high fixed costs associated with the glass container industry and a substantial difference between sales volumes and production in some months, the accountant has been criticised by reporting widely different profits from month to month. To counteract this criticism, he is proposing in future to report profits based on marginal costing and in his proposal to management lists the following reasons for wishing to change:

1. Marginal costing provides for the complete segregation of fixed costs, thus facilitating closer control of production costs.

2. It eliminates the distortion of interim profit statements which occur when there are seasonal fluctuations in sales volume although production is at a fairly constant level.

3. It results in cost information which is more helpful in determining the sales policy necessary to maximise profits.

From the accounting records the following figures were extracted:

Standard cost per gross (a gross is 144 bottles and is the cost unit used within the business.):

	£
Direct materials	8.00
Direct labour	7.20
Variable production overhead	3.36
Total variable production cost	18.56
Fixed production overhead	7.52*
Total production standard cost	26.08

* The fixed production overhead rate was based on the following computations:

Total annual fixed production overhead was budgeted at £7,584,000 or £632,000 per month.

Production volume was set at 1,008,000 gross bottles or 70 per cent of maximum capacity.

There is a slight difference in budgeted fixed production overhead at different levels of operating:

Activity level % of maximum capacity	Amount per month £000
50 – 75	632
76 – 90	648
91 – 100	656

You may assume that actual fixed production overhead incurred was as budgeted.

Additional information:

	September	October
Gross sold	87,000	101,000
Gross produced	115,000	78,000
Sales price, per gross	£32	£32
Fixed selling costs	£120,000	£120,000
Fixed administrative costs	£80,000	£80,000

There were no finished goods in stock at 1 September.

You are required

a. to prepare monthly profit statements for September and October using

    i.   absorption costing; and

    ii. marginal costing;

b. to comment briefly on the accountant's three reasons which he listed to support his proposal.

(CIMA Cost Accounting)

Exercises and examination questions without answers

Exercises

B19.1   During a period 50,000 units were produced and sold. Costs and revenues were as follows:

	£
Sales	200,000
Production	120,000
Selling and Administration Costs	65,000

Based on an anticipated production level of 55,000 units fixed production costs were £1.50 per unit and fixed selling and administrative costs were 80p per unit. Using the above data prepare operating statements using:

a. Absorption Costing; and

b. Marginal Costing.

B19.2   Using the same data as in Exercise Bl, except that 10,000 units were unsold and carried forward to the next period, prepare operating statements using:

a. Absorption Costing; and

b. Marginal Costing.

B19.3   The following data are available regarding an organisation that makes a single product.

	Period 1	Period 2	Period 3
Production (units)	15,000	18,000	20,000
Sales	14,000	16,500	22,500
Opening Stock	–	1,000	2,500
Closing Stock	1,000	2,500	–

The following cost structure applies (based on a budgeted level of 17,000 units per period)

	Cost per unit £
Direct Material	2.00
Direct Labour	6.00
Production Overheads	3.00
	11.00

Selling price = £17 per unit

Administrative overheads are £15,000 per period and the budgeted production overheads are £51,000 per period of which £34,000 are fixed.

Prepare separate operating statements using absorption costing and marginal costing.

Examination questions

B19.4   The budget for JZ company for next year is for 20,000 units of product Z to be produced each month. The standard cost of each unit is as follows.

	£
Direct material	4.50
Direct Labour	1.50
Fixed overhead	3.00
The standard selling price is	15.00

For the first two months of the year

	Month 1	Month 2
Actual sales were –	18,000	22,000
Actual production was as budgeted	20,000	20,000

Required:

a.   Prepare profit and loss accounts for Month 1 and Month 2 assuming the firm uses

   i.   Marginal costing

   ii.   Full or total absorption costing.

b.   Calculate the stock valuation under each of the two costing methods.

(AAT Cost Accounting & Budgeting, part question)

B19.5   A distribution and marketing organisation sells three products named A, B and C in two areas which are designated as Area 1 and Area 2. The information given below is for 1990.

Data:	Product A	Product B	Product C
Selling price per unit	£40	£48	£60
Purchase price per unit	£32	£36	£44
Sales, in units:			
Area 1	92,000	40,000	28,000
Area 2	30,000	40,000	40,000
Number of orders:			
Area 1	40,000	20,000	10,000
Area 2	6,000	10,000	8,000
Volume in cubic metres per unit	2.0	1.5	1.0

Costs:	Variable	Fixed	Basis of apportionment
	£	£	
Selling	188	376	Number of orders
Warehousing/distribution	432	648	Volume sold
Advertising	270	540	Units sold
Administration	64	256	Sales value

You are required to

a.   prepare a budget for 1990 showing the profit or loss for each area and in total, using absorption costing;

b.   prepare a budget for Area 1 only, using marginal costing and showing relevant information for each product and the total profit or loss for that area;

c.   comment on the result shown in your answer to (b) above and suggest action which management ought to take.

(CIMA Cost Accounting)

B19.6 X Ltd manufactures and sells two varieties of a particular product. Selling prices and variable costs are budgeted for the following period as:

	Variety A	Variety B
	£/unit	£/unit
Retail selling price	5.00	6.00
variable production cost	1.50	1.90
Other variable costs	0.30	0.30

The two varieties are sold by X Ltd direct to retailers at a basic price sufficient to provide the retailers with a gross margin of 30% of sales (before discounts received). Discounts off basic price are given to retailers depending upon quantities purchased. Discount of 4% is expected on Variety A, and 5% on Variety B, in the following period.

Fixed production costs, jointly incurred by the two varieties of the product, are budgeted to total £225,000. Other fixed costs, also jointly incurred, are budgeted at £73,500.

Budgeted production and sales quantities are:

	Variety A	Variety B
	000 units	000 units
Production	100	150
Sales	105	140

The fixed production costs are absorbed into product costs using a predetermined rate per unit of product, based on budgeted quantities and budgeted costs. The same rate is applied to each variety of the product. Other fixed costs are shared amongst the two varieties on a similar basis ie, a rate per unit of product, based on budgeted quantities and costs.

Required:

a. Calculate the total revenue, gross profit and net profit that will occur in the following period:

   i.   if actual results in all respects are as per budget,

   ii. if actual results are as per budget apart from production of Variety A of 105,000 units.

b. Contrast the effect, on stock valuation and period profit reporting, of using absorption and marginal costing systems respectively.

(ACCA Cost & Management Accounting 1, part question)

20: Marginal costing and decision making

1. Topics covered in this chapter:

1.	Short run decision making
2.	Key or limiting factors
3.	Decision rules using marginal costing
4.	Differential Costing
5.	Opportunity costs
6.	Throughput accounting.

2. Decision making

Decision making is concerned with the future and involves a choice between alternatives. Many factors, both qualitative and quantitative, need to be considered and for many decisions financial information is a critical factor. It is therefore important that *relevant information* on cost and revenues is supplied. But what is relevant information? It is information about:

a. *Future costs and revenues*. It is the expected future costs and revenues that are of importance to the decision maker. This means that past costs and revenues are only useful in so far as they provide a guide to the future. Costs already spent, known as *sunk costs*, are irrelevant for decision making..

b. *Differential costs and revenues*. Only those costs and revenues which alter as a result of a decision are relevant. Where factors are common to all the alternatives being considered they can be ignored; only the differences are relevant. In many short run situations the fixed costs remain constant for each of the alternatives being considered and thus the marginal costing approach showing sales, marginal cost and contribution is particularly appropriate.

3. Short run tactical decisions

These are decisions which seek to make the best use of existing facilities. Typically, in the short run, fixed costs remain unchanged so that the marginal cost, revenue and contribution of each alternative is relevant. In these circumstances the selection of the alternative which maximises contribution is the correct decision rule.

In the long term (and sometimes in the short term) fixed costs do change and accordingly the differential costs must include any changes in the amount of fixed costs. Where there is a decision with no changes in fixed cost, normal marginal costing principles apply. Where the situation involves changes in fixed cost a more fundamental aid to decision making called differential costing is used. Marginal costing is covered first in this chapter and then differential costing.

4. Key factor

Sometimes known as *limiting factor* or *principal budget factor*. This is a factor which is a binding constraint upon the organisation ie, the factor which prevents indefinite expansion or unlimited profits. It may be sales, availability of finance, skilled labour, supplies of material or lack of space. Where a single binding constraint can be identified, then the general objective of maximising contribution can be achieved by selecting the alternative which *maximises the contribution per unit of the key factor*. It will be apparent that from time to time the key factor in an organisation will change.

For example, a firm may have a shortage of orders, it overcomes this by appointing more salesmen and then finds that there is a shortage of machine capacity. The expansion of the productive capacity may introduce a problem of lack of space and so on.

Note:

The 'maximising contribution per unit of the limiting factor' rule can be of value, but can only be used where there is a single binding constraint and where the constraint is continuously divisible ie, it can be altered one unit at a time. Where several constraints apply simultaneously, the simple maximising rule given above cannot be applied. This is not usually a problem for examination purposes, but real life is rarely that simple.

5. Examples of decisions where marginal costing can be used

Several typical situations in which marginal costing can provide useful information for decision making are given below. Once the general principles are understood, they can be applied in any other similar circumstances.

The steps in analysing such problems are:

a. Check that fixed costs are expected to remain unchanged.

b. If necessary, separate out fixed and variable costs.

c. Calculate the revenue, marginal costs and contribution of each of the alternatives.

d. Check to see if there is a limiting factor which will be a binding constraint and if so, calculate the contribution per unit of the limiting factor.

e. Finally, choose the alternative which maximises contribution.

The examples shown below are decisions about the acceptance of a special order, dropping a product, choice of product where a limiting factor exists, and make or buy.

6. Acceptance of a special order

By this is meant the acceptance or rejection of an order which utilises spare capacity, but which is only available if a lower than normal price is quoted. The procedure is illustrated by the following example.

Example 1

Zerocal Ltd. manufacture and market a slimming drink which they sell for 20p per can. Current output is 400, 000 cans per month which represents 80% of capacity. They have the opportunity to utilise their surplus capacity by selling their product at 13p per can to a supermarket chain who will sell it as an 'own label' product.

Total costs for the last month were £56,000 of which £16,000 were fixed costs. This represented a total cost of 14p per can.

Based on the above data should Zerocal accept the supermarket order? What other factors should be considered?

Solution

The present position is as follows

	£
Sales (400,000 × 20p) =	80,000
less Marginal cost (= 10p/can)	40,000
= Contribution	40,000
less Fixed Costs	16,000
= Net profit	£24,000

On the assumption that fixed costs are unchanged, the special order will produce the following contribution.

		£
Sales (100,000 × 13p)	=	13,000
less Marginal cost (100,000 × 10p)	=	10,000
= Contribution		£3,000

However, there are several other factors which would need to be considered before a final decision is taken.

a. Will the acceptance of one order at a lower price lead other customers to demand lower prices as well?

b. Is this special order the most profitable way of using the spare capacity?

c. Will the special order lock up capacity which could be used for future, full price business?

d. Is it absolutely certain that fixed costs will not alter?

Notes:

a. Although the price of 13p is less than the total costs of 14p per can, it does provide some contribution, so may be worthwhile.

b. The process of marginal cost pricing to utilise spare capacity is widely used, eg, hotels provide cheap weekend rates, railways and airlines have cheap fares for off peak periods, many manufacturers of proprietary goods produce own label products and so on.

c. The contribution from the special order can also be calculated by multiplying the quantity by the contribution per can ie, $100,000 \times 3p = £3,000$.

7. Dropping a product

If a company has a range of products one of which is deemed to be unprofitable, it may consider dropping the item from its range.

Example 2

A company produces three products for which the following operating statement has been produced:

	Product X £	Product Y £	Product Z £	Total £
Sales	32,000	50,000	45,000	127,000
Total costs	36,000	38,000	34,000	108,000
Net Profit (Loss)	(£4,000)	£12,000	£11,000	£19,000

The total costs comprise $\frac{2}{3}$ variable $\frac{1}{3}$ fixed.

The directors consider that as Product X shows a loss it should be discontinued.

Based on the above cost data should Product X be dropped?

What other factors should be considered?

Solution

First calculate the fixed costs, ie,

$$\tfrac{1}{3}(36,000) + \tfrac{1}{3}(38,000) + \tfrac{1}{3}(34,000) = £36,000$$

Rearranging the operating statement in marginal costing form produces:

	Product X £	Product Y £	Product Z £	Total £
Sales	32,000	50,000	45,000	127,000
less Marginal Cost	24,000	25,333	22,667	72,000
= Contribution	£8,000	£24,667	£22,333	£55,000
less fixedcosts				36,000
= Net profit				£19,000

From this it will be seen that Product X produces a contribution of £8,000. Should Product X be dropped the position would be:

	£
Contribution Product Y	24,667
Contribution Product Z	22,333
Total Contribution	47,000
less Fixed Costs	36,000
= Net profit	£11,000

Thus dropping product X with an apparent loss of £4000 reduces total profits by £8000 which is, of course, the amount of contribution lost from Product X.

Other factors which need to be considered:

a. Although Product X does provide some contribution, it is at a low rate and alternative, more profitable products or markets should be considered.

b. The assumption above was that the fixed costs were general fixed costs which would remain even if X was dropped. If dropping X resulted in the elimination of fixed costs originally apportioned to X, then the elimination would be worthwhile. However, this is unlikely.

8. Choice of product where a limiting factor exists

This is where a firm has a choice between various types of products which it could manufacture and where there is a single, binding constraint.

Example 3

A company is able to produce four products and is planning its production mix for the next period. Estimated cost, sales, and production data follow.

Product		W		X		Y		Z
		£		£		£		£
Selling Price/unit		29		36		51		51
	£		£		£		£	
Labour (@ £5/hr)	15		10		35		25	
Materials (@ £1/kg)	6	21	18	28	10	45	12	37
Contribution		£8		£8		£16		£14
Resources/Unit								
Labour (hours)		3		2		7		5
Materials (Kgs.)		6		18		10		12
Maximum Demand (Units)		5000		5000		5000		5000

Based on the above data, which is the most appropriate mix under the two following assumptions?

a. If labour hours are limited to 50,000 in a period or
b. If material is limited to 110,000 Kgs in a period.

Solution

Wherever products have a positive contribution and there are no constraints, there is a prime facie case for their production.

However, when, as in this example, constraints exist, the products must be ranked in order of contribution per unit of the constraint and the most profitable product mix established.

Accordingly, the contribution per unit of the inputs is calculated.

Product	W	X	Y	Z
	£	£	£	£
Contribution/Unit	8	8	16	14
Contribution/Labour Hour	2.67	4	2.29	2.8
Contribution/Kg of Mat'l	1.33	0.44	1.6	1.17

Labour hours restriction:

a. To make all the products up to the demand limit would require:

$(5000 \times 3) + (5000 \times 2) + (5000 \times 7) + (5000 \times 5) = 85,000$ labour hours but as there is a limit of 50,000 hrs in a period all the products cannot be produced up to their demand potential. Accordingly the products should be manufactured in order of attractiveness related to labour hours which is X, Z, W and finally Y.

Produce   5000 units X using 10,000 labour hours

5000 units Z using 25,000 labour hours

5000 units W using 15,000 labour hours

and no units of Y which uses the total of 50,000 hours available

Materials restriction:

b. If the constraint is 110,000 kgs of material, then a similar process produces a ranking of Y, W, Z and finally X which will be noted is the opposite of the ranking produced if labour is the constraint.

When material is the constraint, the optimum production mix is:

> 5000 units of Y using 50,000 Kgs material
>
> 5000 units of W using 30,000 Kgs material
>
> 2500 units of Z using 30,000 Kgs material

and no units of X, which uses the total of 110,000 Kgs of material

Notes:

a. The above process of maximising contribution per unit of the limiting factor can only be used where there is a single binding constraint.

b. Most practical problems have various constraints and many more factors than the example illustrated. In such circumstances, if linearity can be assumed, linear programming* will indicate the optimum solution. An outline of the graphical method of solving Linear Programming (LP) problems is given as an appendix to this chapter.

c. In general where no constraint is identified, a reasonable decision rule is to choose the alternative which maximises contribution per £ of sales value.

Example 4

You have been engaged as a consultant to Acme Manufacturing Company to provide advice on the most profitable production plan for the company.

The company makes three products X, Y and Z and the appropriate data are as follows:

	Costs per unit		
	Product X	Product Y	Product Z
	£	£	£
Direct materials	15	45	30
Direct Labour Process A	36	30	45
Process B	15	18	30
Process C	18	9	36
Variable overheads	30	20	50
Fixed costs	20	20	20
Total costs	£134	£142	£211
Selling price	£150	£190	£260

The rates of pay for the direct labour are Process A £3 per hour, Process B £6 per hour and Process C £3 per hour and you are advised that the labour in Process B is in short supply and cannot be increased*.

Fixed costs are recovered on a unit basis and the current production and forecasts for the three products are shown below.

	Product X Units	Product Y Units	Product Z Units
Current production	10000	5000	6000
Forecast of maximum sales possible	12000	7000	9000

It is required to advise the company on the most profitable mix of production showing what improvement in profitability is possible.

---

* A fuller discussion of LP is given in Quantitative Techniques, T. Lucey, DP Publications.

Solution

The total fixed costs can be ascertained from the current production levels and the cost per unit ie,

$$(10000 \times £20) + (5000 \times 20) + (6000 \times 20) = £420,000$$

The hours involved in each process for each product can be derived from the data supplied thus:

	Product X Hours	Product Y Hours	Product Z Hours
Direct Labour			
Process A (£3/hr)	12	10	15
Process B (£6/hr)	$2\frac{1}{2}$	3	5
Process C (£3/hr)	6	3	12

From the above table the total number of Process B hours (the limiting factor) can be calculated using the current production figures:

$$(10000 \times 2.5) + (5000 \times 3) + (6000 \times 5)$$

= 70,000 hours.

Based on the above data a profitability statement for current production levels can be prepared.

	Product X	Product Y	Product Z	Total
Production (units)	10,000	5,000	6,000	21,000
	£	£	£	£
Sales	1,500,000	950,000	1,560,000	4,010,000
less				
Marginal Costs				
Direct Materials	150,000	225,000	180,000	555,000
Direct Labour A	360,000	150,000	270,000	780,000
B	150,000	90,000	180,000	420,000
C	180,000	45,000	216,000	441,000
Variable Overheads	300,000	100,000	300,000	700,000
Total Marginal Cost	1,140,000	610,000	1,146,000	2,896,000
= Contribution	360,000	340,000	414,000	1,114,000
			less Fixed Costs	420,000
			= Net Profit	£694,000
Contribution per unit	£36	£68	£69	
Contribution per hour of type B Labour	£14.4	£22.67	£13.8	

This means that production should be ranked in the sequence YXZ up to the limits of the sales forecast given earlier having regard to the 70,000 limit of Type B hours. This results in a production plan as follows:

Product				
Y	7000	units (max)	using	21,000 hours
X	12000	units (max)	using	30,000 hours
Z	3800	units (balance)	using	19,000 hours
				70,000 hours

The projected profit statement is

	Product X	Product Y	Product Z	Total
Revised Plan (units)	12000	7000	3800	22800
	£	£	£	£
Total Contribution	432,000	476,000	262,200	1,170,200
			less Fixed Costs	420,000
			= Net Profit	£750,200

The usual reservations must be expressed regarding any such production revision, for example:

a. Can the new production quantities actually be sold?

b. Will the shortfall in production of Z (6000 – 3800 = 2200 units) cause problems with under utilisation of labour and machines previously used in making Product Z?

c. If customers buy combinations of the products will the reduction in availability of Product Z cause reductions in the sales of X and Y?

9. Make or buy

Frequently management are faced with the decision whether to make a particular product or component or whether to buy it in. Apart from overriding technical reasons, the decision is usually based on an analysis of the cost implications.

In general the relevant cost comparison is between the *marginal cost of manufacture* and the *buying in price*. However, when manufacturing the component displaces existing production, the lost contribution must be added to the marginal cost of production of the component before comparison with the buying in price. The two situations are illustrated below.

Example 5

A firm manufacturers component BK 200 and the costs for the current production level of 50,000 units are:

COSTS / UNIT

	£
Materials	2.50
Labour	1.25
Variable overheads	1.75
Fixed overheads	3.50
TOTAL COST	£9.00

Component BK 200 could be bought in for £7.75 and, if so, the production capacity utilised at present would be unused. Assuming that there are no overriding technical considerations, should BK 200 be bought in or manufactured?

Solution

Comparison of the buying in price of £7.75 and the full cost of £9.90 suggest that the component should be bought in.

However, the correct comparison is between the MARGINAL COST of manufacture (ie, £5.50) and the buying in price of £7.75. This indicates that the component should be manufactured, not bought in.

The reason for this is that the fixed costs of £175,000 (ie, 50,000 units at £3.50) would presumably continue and, because the capacity would not be used, the fixed overheads would not be absorbed into production.

If BK 200 was bought in, overall profits would fall by £112,500, which is the difference between buying in price and the marginal cost of manufacture, ie, (£7.75 – 5.50) × 50,000.

Example 6

A firm is considering whether to manufacture or purchase a particular component 2543. This would be in batches of 10,000 and the buying in price would be £6.50. The marginal cost of manufacturing Component 2543 is £4.75 per unit and the component would have to be made on a machine which was currently working at full capacity. If the component was manufactured, it is estimated that the sales of finished product FP97 would be reduced by 1000 units. FP97 has a marginal cost of £60/unit and sells for £80/unit.

Should the firm manufacture or purchase component 2543?

Solution

A superficial view, based on the preceding example, is that because the marginal cost of manufacture is substantially below the buying in price, the component should not be bought in and thus further analysis is unnecessary. However, such an approach is insufficient in this more realistic situation and the loss of contribution from the displaced product must also be considered.

Cost analysis - Component 2543 in batches of 10,000

	£
Marginal Cost of manufacture = £4.75/unit × 10,000	47,500
+ Lost contribution for FP97 = £20/unit × 100	20,000
	67,500
Buying in price = £6.50/unit × 10,000	65,000

∴ There is a saving of £2,500 per 10,000 batch by buying in rather than manufacture.

Note:

The lost contribution of £20,000 is an example of an *opportunity costs*. This is defined as the value of a benefit sacrificed in favour of an alternative course of action. This is a highly important concept and examples frequently occur in practice and in examination questions. Whenever there are scarce resources, there are alternative uses which must be foregone and the benefit sacrificed is the opportunity cost. Where there is no alternative use for the resource, as in Example 5, the opportunity cost is zero and it can thus be ignored.

10. Differential costing

Differential costing is a broader and more fundamental principle than marginal costing and therefore has a much wider application. Differential costing examines *all* the revenue and cost differences between alternatives so as to determine the most appropriate decision.

Marginal costing assumes that the only differences between alternatives are changes in variable costs and revenues, ie, that fixed costs do not alter. Because differential costing examines all differences, it is suitable for situations where fixed costs do alter and thus becomes appropriate for both short run and long run decisions. The process by which costs are divided into fixed and variable is still necessary so as to reflect more easily changes in activity levels.

11. Approach using differential costing

The general approach to decision making outlined in the preceding chapters is still relevant with the proviso that even more care should be taken to identify all the cost changes, both fixed and variable, because there is no assumption that fixed costs will remain unchanged.

A useful way of presenting differential cost statements is as follows:

Alternative A	Alternative B	Difference A – B
–	–	–
–	–	–
–	–	–

The following illustration uses this approach.

12. Differential cost example

Example

A company, currently operating at full capacity, manufactures and sells saucepans at £2 each. Current volume is 100,000 pans per annum with the following cost structure.

Operating Statement for year

	£	
Sales (100,000 at £2)		200,000
less Marginal Cost		
Labour	80,000	
Material	50,000	130,000
= Contribution		70,000
Fixed Costs		30,000
= Net profit		£40,000

An opportunity has arisen to supply an additional 30,000 pans per annum at £1.8 each.

Acceptance of this order would incur extra fixed costs of £8000 per annum for the hire for additional machinery and the payment of an overtime premium of 20% for the extra direct labour required. Should this order by accepted? What other factors need to be considered?

Solution

Differential Cost Statement

		Present Production Level 100,000 Pans £		Projected Production Level 130,000 Pans £		Difference 30,000 Pans £	
Sales			200,000		254,000		54,000
Less Marginal Cost	£		£		£		
Labour	80,000		108,800		28,800		
Materials	50,000	130,000	65,000	173,000	15,000	43,800	
= Contribution		70,000		80,200		10,200	
less Fixed costs		30,000		38,000		8,000	
= Net Profit		£40,000		£42,200		£2,200	

Thus purely on the cost figures the special order would appear to be worthwhile. Additional factors that would need to be considered include:

a. Will the special order disturb the existing full price market?

b. How accurate are the projected extra costs? The additional profit is small and could easily be wiped out by slight cost increases.

c. Can administration, despatch and other service departments cope with the 30% increase in throughput without extra costs?

13. Implications of differential cost

The only relevant costs for decision making are those which will change as a result of the decision.

If costs are not expected to alter, then they are irrelevant to the decision. Particular examples of cost that are irrelevant are the following:

a. Sunk costs, ie, costs which have already been incurred are irrelevant.

b. Book values of assets.

c. Cost of fully utilised resource, ie, if a limiting factor exists it will be used to the full and will therefore cost the same whatever alternative is considered. The differential cost between alternatives is therefore zero.

d. Conventionally prepared depreciation is not a differential cost and is therefore irrelevant.

e. Fixed costs. Any item which is genuinely fixed and will remain the same whichever alternative is chosen is not a differential cost and can be ignored in choosing alternatives.

14. Opportunity cost

Opportunity cost is an important concept for decision making purposes. It can be defined as the value of the best alternative foregone. Although often difficult to measure, the concept is of great importance because it emphasises that decisions are concerned with alternatives and that the cost of the chosen plan of action is the profit foregone from the best available alternative. Examples follow which will help to make the idea more concrete.

Example 7

A firm rents a small workshop for £50 per week. but at present does not use it.

They could sub-let the workshop for £80 per week, but they are considering using it themselves for a new project.

In assessing whether the new project it worthwhile, what is the appropriate cost to use for the workshop?

Solution

The recorded historical cost of £50 is inappropriate for this purpose. If the project is initiated the firm will forego the £80 rent they could obtain. This is the opportunity cost of the workshop and is the value to be included in the project appraisal.

Example 8

An unexpected order has been received for a product for which the labour and machine time is available and which requires three types of material A, B and C.

Material A. This material is used regularly within the firm for various products. The new order will require 1500 kgs. The present stock is 21,000 kgs purchased at £2.50 per kg. The current replenishment price is £2.65 per kg. and it is estimated that if 1500 kgs is used on the new order the normal stock replenishment order for A will have to be brought forward 3 weeks at which time it is estimated that the replenishment price will be £2.70 per kg.

*Material B.*1000 kgs of this material are in stock purchased at 85p per kg and the new order requires 800 kgs. The current replacement price is 95p per kg. This material is used on no other product and recent enquiries revealed that the material in stock could be sold at 55p per kg.

Material C. 5000 kgs are required for the order and large quantities are in stock purchased at 18p per kgs. Because of heavy usage the materials is purchased weekly and the current price is 21p per kg.

What is the relevant cost for decision making purposes of each of the three materials?

Solution

Material A. Relevant Cost: £2.70 per kg

The original purchase price is irrelevant and, as it is not intended to purchase immediately, so is the current replenishment price. The relevant cost is the replenishment cost at the expected purchase time.

Material B. Relevant Cost: 55p per kg

Once again the historical purchase price is not relevant and as there is adequate in stock for current needs there is no question of replenishment. The only alternative use for the material is sale at 55p per kg.

Material C. Relevant Cost: 21 per kg

As the material will be replenished within a week the current replenishment price is relevant

It will be noted that the recorded historical cost, which is the cost for normal cost ascertainment purposes, is not the relevant figure in any of the above examples. This is typical of decision making situations and means that great care must be taken to ascertain the intended purpose for any cost which is supplied so that relevant information can be provided at all times.

15. Marginal costing and advanced manufacturing technology (AMT)

A number of criticisms have been made about marginal costing applied to AMT factories where Just-in-Time principles are used to organise production. For example it is claimed that contribution, as conventionally calculated (ie sales – variable cost) is not a good guide to profitability because capacity factors and the rate of production are ignored. Also, marginal costing treats direct labour as a variable cost whereas in many factories, in the short term, direct labour is effectively a fixed cost along with most other costs. It is because of these problems and others that alternative systems have been developed to deal with the requirements of modern factories. One of these is *throughput accounting*.

16. Throughput accounting

Throughput accounting is a system of performance measurement and costing which traces costs to throughput time. It is claimed that it complements JIT principles and forces attention to the true determinants of profitability; the rate at which goods can be produced to satisfy customers' orders.

Throughput accounting is defined as follows: 'A method of performance measurement which relates production and other costs to throughput. Throughput accounting product costs relate to the usage of key resources by various products.' *Terminology.*

Throughput Accounting (TA) is based on three concepts:

Concept 1

With the exception of material costs, in the short-run, most factory costs (including direct labour) are fixed. These fixed costs can be grouped together and called Total Factory Costs (TFC).

Concept 2

With JIT, products should not be made unless there is a customer waiting for them because the ideal inventory level is zero. The effect of this is that there will be unavoidable idle capacity in some operations, except for the operation that is the bottleneck of the moment. Working on output just to increase WIP or finished goods stocks creates no profit and so would not be encouraged.

As Galloway and Waldron have stated 'If the resource cannot be exploited fully because of the bottleneck's limited capacity then letting it stand idle when it has completed the work required, costs nothing'.

This means that profit is inversely proportional to the level of inventory in the system. This can be expressed thus:

$$\text{Profit} = f\left(\frac{1}{MRT}\right)$$

where   *MRT*   is the manufacturing response time.

Concept 3

Profitability is determined by how quickly goods can be produced to satisfy customers orders. Producing for stock does not create profits. Improving the throughput of bottleneck operations will increase the rate at which customer demand can be met and will thus improve profitability.

Contribution in its traditional from (sales – variable costs) is not a good guide to profitability because capacity factors and the rate of production are ignored.

Using TA, product returns should be measured thus:

$$\textbf{Return per factory hour} = \frac{\text{Sales Price} - \text{Material Cost}}{\text{Time on key resource (ie the bottleneck)}}$$

Product costs are measured thus:

$$\textbf{Cost per factory hour} = \frac{\text{Total factory costs (TCF)}}{\text{Total time available on the key resource}}$$

The Returns and Cost per Factory hour are combined into the Throughput Accounting (TA) ratio thus:

$$\textbf{TA ratio} = \frac{\text{Return per Factory Hour (or minute)}}{\text{Cost per Factory Hour (or minute)}}$$

The TA ratio should be greater than 1. If it is less than 1 the product will lose money for the company and the company should consider withdrawing it from the market.

Using TA, value is not created until products are sold. Thus items made for stock produce no return and depress the TA ratio. This should encourage managers to use their limited bottleneck resource to produce products for which customer demand exists.

The TA ratio can also be considered in total terms and compares the total return from the throughput to the TFC ie

$$\text{Primary TA ratio} = \frac{\text{Return from total throughput (ie Sales – Material Costs)}}{\text{TFC (ie all costs other than materials)}}$$

17. Bottlenecks and overhead attribution

A bottleneck is an activity that places a restriction on a production line or factory. A typical bottleneck being the capacity of a key machine. On occasions there may be a 'wandering' bottleneck. This means that the identified key bottleneck is not fully utilised because of a temporary limitation elsewhere, caused by poor production planning and control. If there is a wandering bottleneck the actual time on the key resource is used, not the actual time on the wandering bottleneck.

TA suggests that overheads be attributed to product costs according to their usage of bottleneck resources:

$$\text{Throughput Cost} = \text{Standard minutes of throughput (usage of bottleneck resource)} \\ \times \text{Budgeted TFC cost per minute of bottleneck resource.}$$

Based on this, an efficiency percentage can be calculated thus:

$$\text{Efficiency \%} = \frac{\text{Throughput cost}}{\text{Actual TFC}} \%$$

This will fall below 100% if:

a. actual output is less than budgeted eg if there was a wandering bottleneck in production or poor quality *or*

b. actual factory costs exceed budget.

Labour efficiency can be measured as:

$$\text{Labour efficiency \%} = \frac{\text{Throughput cost}}{\text{Actual total labour cost}} \%$$

18. Examples using throughput accounting

The following examples illustrate various aspects of throughput accounting.

Example 8

A factory has a key resource (bottleneck) of Facility A which is available for 6260 minutes per period. Budgeted Factory costs and data on two products, X and Y, are shown below.

Product	Selling price/unit £	Material cost/unit £	Time in Facility A Mins
X	7	4	1
Y	7	3.50	2

Budgeted Factory costs per week

	£
Direct Labour	5,000
Indirect Labour	2,500
Power	350
Depreciation	4,500
Space costs	1,600
Engineering	700
Administration	1,000

Calculate:

- ❑ Total Factory Costs (TFC)
- ❑ Cost per Factory Minute
- ❑ Return per Factory Minute for both products
- ❑ TA ratios for both products

Solution

$$\text{Total Factory Costs} = \text{Total of all costs except materials}$$

$$= 5,000 + 2,500 + 350 + 4,500 + 1,600 + 700 + 1,000$$

$$= \textbf{£15,650}$$

$$\text{Cost per Factory Minute} = \frac{\text{TFC}}{\text{Minutes available in bottleneck}}$$

$$= \frac{15,650}{6,260}$$

$$= \textbf{£2.5}$$

$$\text{Return per bottleneck minute for product X} = \frac{\text{Selling Price} - \text{Material cost}}{\text{Minutes in bottleneck}}$$

$$= \frac{£7 - 4}{1}$$

$$= \textbf{£3}$$

$$\text{Return per bottleneck minute for Product Y} = \frac{\text{Return per minute}}{\text{Cost per minute}}$$

$$= \frac{£3}{£2.5}$$

$$= \textbf{1.2}$$

$$\text{TA ratio for Product Y} = \frac{£1.75}{£2.5}$$

$$= \textbf{0.7}$$

The TA ratios show that if we only made Product Y we would make a loss as its TA ratio is` less than 1; when we make Product X we make money.

Example 9

Based on the data in Example 1 above during a week actual production was 4,750 units of Product X and 650 units of Product Y. Actual factory costs were £15,650.

Calculate:

- ❑ Throughput cost for the week
- ❑ Efficiency percentage

and comment on the possible reason(s) for the efficiency percentage calculated.

Solution

Workings

$$\text{Standard minutes of throughput for the week} = (4,750 \times 1) + (650 \times 2)$$

$$= \textbf{6,050}$$

$$\text{Throughput cost for week} = 6,050 \times £2.5 \text{ per min (from Example 1)}$$

$$= \textbf{£15,125}$$

$$\text{Efficiency \%} = \frac{\text{Throughput cost}}{\text{Actual TFC}} \% = \frac{£15,125}{£15,650} \%$$

$$= \textbf{96.6\%}$$

The bottleneck resource of Facility A is available for 6,260 minutes per week but produced only 6,050 standard minutes. This could be due to:

a. the presence of a 'wandering' bottleneck causing Facility A to be under-utilised or

b. inefficiency in Facility A.

19. Throughput accounting – conclusion

It will be seen that the TA approach has certain similarities with the principle covered earlier in the chapter of maximising contribution per unit of the limiting factor.

However there are important differences. In TA, return is defined as sales less material costs in contrast to contribution which is sales less all variable costs (material labour and variable overheads). TA directs attention to bottlenecks and forces management to concentrate on the key elements in making profits namely; reducing inventory and the responsible time to customer demand.

Professors Kaplan and Shanks have criticised TA for its short-term emphasis but TA does appear to be helpful in JIT environments and complements the key principles of JIT.

Note: The outline of throughput accounting given above has been based mainly on the series of articles by Waldron and Galloway in Management Accounting (November 1988 to February 1989). For further details students are recommended to read all the articles themselves.

20. Summary

a. Decision making is concerned with the future and with the choice between alternatives.

b. Relevant information for decision making is concerned with future costs and revenues that will alter as a result of a decision.

c. Marginal costing is most appropriate for short run tactical decisions.

d. A key factor (or limiting factor or principal budget factor) is a binding constraint upon the organisation eg, shortage of labour, machine time or space.

e. Where a single limiting factor exists which is binding, then the decision rule is to maximise contribution per unit of the limiting factor.

f. Evaluate the sales, marginal cost and contribution of the various alternatives and, if fixed costs remain unchanged, choose the alternative which maximises contribution.

g. Differential costing is a broader concept than marginal costing and examines all the revenue and cost difference between alternatives.

h. The only relevant costs for decision making are those which will change as a result of the decision, ie, future costs. It follows that sunk costs are irrelevant.

i. Opportunity costs are the value of the best alternative forgone and are critical for decision making.

j. Throughput Accounting treats all costs as fixed except materials and calculates Return as Sales – Materials

k. Returns are related to the time available on the 'bottleneck' resource. Maximising the surplus of return per minute of the bottleneck over the cost per minute maximises profit.

21. Points to note

a. In practice the classification of costs into fixed and variable is extremely difficult. Cost do not behave in simple, general fashions. Some costs, eg, wages, are variable in nature when activity is rising, but may become fixed when activity reduces.

b. The concept of opportunity cost is all important for decision making. A relevant factor in choosing any alternative is the benefit sacrificed by not choosing some other alternative.

c. Past costs are not of themselves relevant for decision making. Their only value is that they may be of value in predicting future cost levels.

d. Always examine all the cost changes between alternatives. Do not be misled into assuming that because a cost is classified as fixed, it will always remain the same. So called 'fixed' costs can and do change quite frequently.

Student self-testing

Self Review Questions

1. What is relevant information for decision making? (2)
2. Distinguish between marginal costing and differential costing. (2)
3. What is a key factor? (4)
4. What is the decision rule if there is a single binding constraint? (4)
5. What are the steps in analysing a problem where the use of marginal costing is being considered? (5)
6. What are the general rules for dealing with an order at lower than normal prices? (6)
7. If a firm has a choice between various products and there is a simple binding constraint how should it choose which products to manufacture? (8)
8. What is the general rule in 'make or buy' decisions? (9)
9. Is differential costing suitable for long run decisions? (10)
10. Give examples of costs which are irrelevant for decision making. (13)
11. What is opportunity cost? (14)
12. What is Throughput Accounting? (16)
13. What is the Throughput Accounting ratio and what is its value to management? (16)
14. What is a bottleneck in TA? (17)
15. What is the relationship between maximising contribution per unit of the limiting factor and the principle behind TA? (19)

Exercises and examination questions with answers

Exercises

A 20.1 A firm makes a single product with a marginal cost of 15p. Up to 40, 000 units can be sold at 30p per unit but additional sales can only be made by reducing the selling price to 20p per unit. Fixed costs are £2,500 per period and there is a planned profit of £4,000 per period. How many units must be made and sold?

A20.2 The following details are available regarding three products.

Product	X	Y	Z
	£	£	£
Selling Price	200	300	400
Direct Materials (£4 per Kg)	20	112	90
Direct Labour (£8 per hour)	80	44	120
Variable Overheads	40	22	60

Variable overheads are recovered at the rate of £4 per hour. Total fixed overheads are £120,000.

You are required to calculate the priority ranking of the products when the limiting factor is:

    a. Sales
    b. Labour
    c. Materials

A20.3 A firm makes 150,000 electric thermostats selling at £12 each. Their last operating statement was:

	£	£
Sales (150,000 × £12)		1,800,000
less Labour	650,000	
Materials	525,000	1,175,000
= Contribution		625,000
less Fixed Costs		450,000
= Profit		175,000

A contract has been offered to sell an additional 50,000 thermostats at £10 each. Acceptance of this contract would increase fixed costs by £50,000 and would mean paying an overtime premium of 20% for the extra labour required. However, because of bulk purchasing a discount of 3% could be obtained for all material purchases.

Prepare a Differential Cost Statement for the above.

A20.4 A factory has a bottleneck, Machine Z, available for 10,000 minutes per period. Two products are made and the data are

Per unit

Product	Selling price £	Material cost £	Time in Z minutes
Mini	15	8	2
Micro	12	4	3

Total factory costs (excluding material) = £30,000

Calculate the Throughput Accounting Ratios for the products and state which earns money.

Examination questions

A20.5 A cinema chain, based in Oxford, owns three cinemas in the towns of Newbury, Reading and Basingstoke. It has prepared budgets for the coming year based upon a ticket price of £4.

	Reading £	Newbury £	Basingstoke £	Total £
Budgeted ticket receipts	1,600,000	1,200,000	800,000	3,600,000
Costs: Film hire	500,000	400,000	390,000	1,290,000
Wages and Salaries	300,000	250,000	160,000	710,000
Overheads	500,000	400,000	350,000	1,250,000
	1,300,000	1,050,000	900,000	3,250,000

Included in the overhead figures are the Oxford Head Office fixed costs that amount to £720,000, these have been allocated to each cinema on the basis of budgeted ticket receipts. All other costs are variable.

The management are concerned about the Basingstoke cinema and the fact that it is showing a budgeted loss and is considering closing the cinema and selling the site to a Property Developer.

Required:

a. Prepare marginal costing statements to show contributions for each cinema and contribution and profit for the overall chain on the basis of:

   i.   The original budget.

   ii. If the Basingstoke cinema is closed.

b. On the grounds of profitability do you think that the Basingstoke cinema should be closed? Give a reasoned explanation of your decision.

c. What is the contribution per ticket sale at each cinema?

d. If the Basingstoke cinema is kept open management want an increase in profitability. One suggestion is that receipts at the cinema can be increased by 50% by an advertising campaign directed at Basingstoke that will add £40,000 to the chains fixed costs.

Required:

Do you think that the advertising campaign should be undertaken to improve the cinema's profitability? Give reasons for your decision.

(AAT Cost Accounting & Budgeting, part question)

A 20.6 The management of an engineering company manufacturing a range of products is considering next year's production, purchase and sales budgets. Shown below are the budgeted total unit costs for two of the components and two of the products manufactured by the company.

	Component 12 £ per unit	Component 14 £ per unit	Product VW £ per unit	Product XY £ per unit
Direct Material	18	26	12	28
Direct Labour	16	4	12	24
Variable Overhead	8	2	6	12
Fixed Overhead	20	5	15	30
	£62	£37	£45	£94

Components 12 and 14 are incorporated into other products manufactured and sold by the company, but not the two products shown above. It is possible to purchase Components 12 and 14 from another company for £60 per unit and £30 per unit respectively.

The anticipated selling prices of Products VW and XY are £33 and £85 respectively.

Required:

a. Advise the management of the company whether it would be profitable to:

   i.   purchase either of the above components,

   ii. sell either of the above products.

b. State clearly, and where appropriate comment upon, the assumptions you have made in answering (a) above.

c. Consider how the following additional information would affect your advice in (a) above.

   i.   Next year's budgeted production requirements for the two components are 7,000 units of Component 12 and 6, 000 units of Component 14. Next year's budgeted sales for the two products are Product VW 5,000 units and Product XY 4,000 units.

   ii. A special machine is used exclusively by the above two components and two products and for technical reasons the machine can only be allowed to operate for 80,000 machine hours next year.

The budgeted usage of the machine is:

     Component 12 - 8 machine hours   Product VW- 6 machine hours

     Component 14 - 2 machine hours   Product XY- 12 machine hours

The operating costs of the machine have been included in the unit costs shown in (a) above.

(ACCA, Costing)

A20.7   In making its products the company uses a special component – which could be purchased from an outside firm.

The accountant of JZ Company has calculated that the 40,000 components needed have the following unit costs if manufactured.

	£
Direct Material	1.20
Direct Labour	2.25
General Fixed overhead	1.00
	4.45

The fixed overhead is absorbed on the basis of direct labour hours. The components could be purchased for £3.65 each from the outside supplier.

Required:

   i.   calculate the annual benefit of either purchasing or manufacturing the components, stating any assumptions.

   ii. What other factor would the firm need to consider before finalising a decision on whether to make or buy.

The sales and profit figures of Company A for two consecutive years are given below.

	Year 1	Year 2
Sales	£220,000	£280,000
Profit	£21,000	£36,000

   i.   Calculate the sales necessary to earn a profit of £42,000.

   ii. What would the profit be if sales were £188,000.

(AAT Cost Accounting & Budgeting, part question)

A20.8   A company is currently manufacturing at only 60% of full practicable capacity, in each of its two production departments, due to a reduction in market share. The company is seeking to launch a new product which it is hoped will recover some lost sales.

The estimated direct costs of the new product, Product X, are to be established from the following information:

Direct Materials:

   Every 100 units of the product will require 30 kilos net of Material A. Losses of 10% of materials input are to be expected. Material A costs £5.40 per kilo before discount. A quantity discount of 5% is given on all purchases if the monthly purchase quantity exceeds 25,000 kilos. Other materials are expected to cost £1.34 per unit of Product X.

Direct Labour (per hundred units):

  Department 1: 40 hours at £4.00 per hour.

  Department 2: 15 hours at £4.50 per hour.

Separate overhead absorption rates are established for each production department. Department 1 overheads are absorbed at 130% of direct wages, which is based upon the expected overhead costs and usage of capacity if Product X is launched. The rate in Department 2 is to be established as a rate per direct labour hour also based on expected usage of capacity. The following annual figures for Department 2 are based on full practical capacity:

  Overhead, £5,424,000

  Direct labour hours, 2,200,000.

Variable overheads in Department 1 are assessed at 40% of direct wages and in Department 2 are £1,980,000 (at full practical capacity).

Non-production overheads are estimated as follows (per unit of Product X):

  Variable, £0.70

  Fixed, £1.95

The selling price for Product X is expected to be £9.95 per unit, with annual sales of 2,400,000 units.

Required:

a. Determine the estimated cost per unit of Product X.

b. Comment on the viability of Product X.

c. Market research indicates that an alternative selling price for Product X could be £9.45 per unit, at which price annual sales would be expected to be 2,900,000 units.

Determine, and comment briefly upon, the optimum selling price.

(ACCA Cost and Management Accounting 1)

A20.9   A company in the civil engineering industry with headquarters located 22 miles from London undertakes contracts anywhere in the United Kingdom.

The company has had its tender for a job in north-east England accepted at £288,000 and work is due to begin in March 1993. However, the company has also been asked to undertake a contract on the south cost of England. The price offered for this contract is £352,000. Both of the contracts cannot be taken simultaneously because of constraints on staff site management personnel and on plant available. An escape clause enables the company to withdraw from the contract in the north-east, provided notice is given before the end of November and an agreed penalty of £28,000 is paid.

The following estimates have been submitted by the company's quantity surveyor:

Cost estimates

	North-east £	South coast £
Materials:		
In stock at original cost, Material X	21,600	
In stock at original cost, Material Y		24,800
Firm orders placed at original cost, Material X	30,400	
Not yet ordered- current cost, Material X	60,000	
Not yet ordered- current cost, Material Y		71,200
Labour - hired locally	86,000	110,000
Site management	34,000	34,000
Staff accommodation and travel for site management	6,800	5,600
Plant on site- depreciation	9,600	12,800
Interest on capital, 8%	5,120	6,400
Total local contract costs	253,520	264,800
Headquarters costs allocated at rate of 5% on total contract costs	12,676	13,240
	266,196	278,040
Contract price	288,000	352,000
Estimated profit	21,804	73,960

Notes:

1. X ,Y and Z are three building materials. Material X is not common use and would not realise much money if re-sold; however, it could be used on other contracts but only as a substitute for another material currently quoted at 15% less than the original cost of X. The price of Y, a material in common use, has doubled since it was purchased; its net realisable value if re-sold would be its new price less 15% to cover disposal costs. Alternatively it could be kept for use on other contracts in the following financial year.

2. With the construction industry not yet recovered from the recent recession, the company is confident that manual labour, both skilled, could be hired on a sub-contracting basis to meet the needs of each of the contracts.

3. The plant which would be needed for the south coast contract has been owned for some years and £12,800 is the years depreciation on a straight line basis. If the north-east contract is undertaken, less plant will be required but the surplus plant will be hired out for the period of the contract at a rental of £6,000.

4. It is the company's policy to charge all contracts with notional interest at 8% on estimated working capital involved in contracts. Progress payments would be receivable from the contractee.

5. Salaries and general costs of operating the small headquarters amount to about £108,000 each year. There are usually ten contracts being supervised at the same time.

6. Each of the two contracts is expected to last from March 1993 to February 1994 which, coincidentally, is the company's financial year.

7. Site management is treated as a fixed cost.

You are required, as the management accountant to the company,

a. to present comparative statements to show the net benefit to the company of undertaking the more advantageous of the two contracts;

b. to explain the reasoning behind the inclusion in (or omission from) your comparative financial statements, of each item given in the cost estimates and the notes relating thereto.

(CIMA Cost Accounting)

A20.10 The directors of a family-owned retail department store were shocked to receive the following profit statement for the year ended 31 January:

		£000	£000	£000
Sales			5,000	
Less: Cost of sales			3,398	
				1,602
Wages –	Departments	357		
	Office	70		
	Restaurant	26	453	
Delivery cost			200	
Departmental expenses			116	
Salaries – directors and management			100	
Director's fees			20	
Sales promotion and advertising			120	
Store capacity costs ie, rent, rates and energy			488	
Interest on bank overdraft			20	
Discounts allowed			25	
Bad debts			15	
Miscellaneous expenses			75	
				1,632
Net loss				(30)

Management accounting has not been employed but the following breakdown has been extracted from the financial records:

	Departments				
	Ladies wear	Men's wear	General	Toys	Restaurant
	£000	£000	£000	£000	£000
Sales	800	400	2,200	1,400	200
Purchases	506	220	1,290	1,276	167
Opening stock	90	70	200	100	5
Closing stock	100	50	170	200	6
Wages	96	47	155	59	26
Departmental expenses	38	13	35	20	10
Sales promotion and advertising	10	5	30	75	–
Floor space occupied	20%	15%	20%	35%	10%

The directors are considering two separate proposals which are independent of each other:

1. Closing the Toys Department

2. Reducing selling prices on Ladies' Wear and Men's Wear by 5% in the hope of boosting sales.

You are required

a. to present the information for the year to 31 January 1990 in a more meaningful way to aid decision making. Include any statistics or indicators of performance which you consider to be useful;

b. to show and explain the change in profit for a full year if the Toys department were closed and if all other costs remain the same;

c. to show for the Ladies' Wear and Men's Wear Departments, if selling prices are reduced by 5% and unit costs remain the same,

   i. the increase in sales value (to the nearest thousand pounds) that would be required for a full year to maintain the gross profits, in £s, earned by each of these Departments; and

   ii. the increase in (i) above expressed as a percentage of the sales for each Department to 31 January 1990;

d. to state your views on both the proposals being considered by the directors and recommend any alternative action you think appropriate.

(CIMA Cost Accounting)

Exercises and examination questions without answers

Exercises

B20.1 During a month when 1,000 units were made costs and sales per unit were as follows:

	£	£
Sales		48
less Prime Cost	22	
Fixed Costs	14	36
Profit		12

A proposal has been made to reduce the selling price to £45 per unit at which price sales would be 1,300 units. This volume would necessitate paying overtime to the labour which would result in an increase of £1 in the labour costs.

Is the proposal worthwhile?

What other factors should be considered?

B20.2 A firm makes three products from a common raw material. The costs are as follows:

Product	X	Y	Z
	£	£	£
Material	21	14	19
Labour	6	9	3
Variable Overheads	3	4	1
Total	30	27	23

Fixed costs are £300,000 per year.

The maximum forecast sales were as follows:

X	6,000 units at £50 each
Y	10,000 units at £45 each
Z	8,000 units at £40 each

The company is unable to make all the sales forecast because there is a shortage of 20% on the amount of material available.

What should be the production plan? What profit results?

B20.3 A product is made on a special milling machine. It uses 20 minutes of machine time and has a selling price of £12 and a total marginal cost of £8. The milling machine can also be used to make a component (used elsewhere in the firm) taking 30 minutes with a total marginal cost of £7. The component could be bought in at a price of £12.

Should the component be made or purchased? What other factors should be considered?

B20.4 What is the relationship between marginal cost and opportunity cost?

Examination questions

B20.5 What is meant by 'Differential Cost Analysis?'

A.B.C. Company Limited manufactures a single product which is sold only in the Home Market. A recent market survey undertaken on behalf of the company has revealed that the selling price for each unit of production should be fixed in accordance with the levels of output and their associated costs as follows:

Expenditure Head	Fixed, Variable or Semi-variable	Output ('000 units)						
		10	20	30	40	50	60	70
		£	£	£	£	£	£	£
Materials	Variable	6,000	9,000	13,500	18,000	22,500	27,000	31,500
Labour	Variable	12,000	18,000	27,000	36,000	45,000	60,000	63,000
Overhead:								
Factory	Variable	2,000	3,000	4,500	6,000	7,500	9,000	10,500
Factory	Semi-variable	4,000	4,000	5,000	5,000	5,000	5,000	5,500
Factory	Fixed	30,000	30,000	30,000	30,000	30,000	30,000	30,000
Selling	Semi-variable	4,000	4,000	7,000	7,000	7,000	7,000	8,500
Selling	Fixed	12,000	12,000	12,000	12,000	12,000	12,000	12,000
Administration	Fixed	8,000	8,000	8,000	8,000	8,000	8,000	8,000
Total cost		78,000	88,000	107,000	122,000	137,000	158,000	169,000
Selling price per unit		£20	£18	£15	£12	£9	£6	£3

Prepare a Budget Statement which will indicate to Management the total unit cost, the net profit per unit and the total net profit at each level of output. Indicate the level of output that you are recommending.

(CIPFA, Management Accounting)

B20.6 JEN Ltd manufactures three products, J E and N which undergo similar production processes and use similar materials and types of labour. The company's forecasted Profit Statement for the forthcoming year, as submitted to the Board, is as follows:

	Product J	Product E	Product N	Total
	£	£	£	£
Sales	1,344,000	840,000	680,000	2,864,000
Direct Materials	336,000	294,000	374,000	1,004,000
Direct Labour	201,600	168,000	136,000	505,600
Variable Overhead	268,800	168,000	204,000	640,800
	806,400	630,000	714,000	2,150,400
Contribution	537,600	210,000	(34,000)	713,600
			Fixed Overhead	113,600
			Profit	£600,000

At a Board meeting, a decision was made to discontinue the production of Product N as demand was falling and there was no possibility of increasing the selling price. Prospects for the other two products, however, were bright and the company had, in the past, been unable to meet the demand. It was decided, therefore, that the labour force released should be used to increase production of Products J and E; 60% of the budgeted labour for Product N being transferred to J and the remainder to E. The increased production of J and E is not expected to change their cost/selling price relationships.

You are required to prepare the revised forecast Profit Statement and to comment briefly upon the effect of the Board's decision.

(ACCA, Costing)

B20.7   a. Explain how the Cost Accountant distinguishes between: (i) Scrap and, (ii) Waste, by definition and recording.

b. A Company manufacturing three different electrical components has estimated its costs and selling prices as follows:

	Product X	Product Y	Product Z
Direct Materials			
Direct Labour	£3	£4	£8
Dept. I (Rate £2 hour)	2	4	2
Dept. 2 (Rate £1.50 hour)	3	6	9
	8	14	19
Selling Price	15	25	40
Quantities - units	10,000	20,000	5,000

It is anticipated that 5% of products are rejected by final inspection, and transferred to a small repair department. It takes 15 minutes to repair an X, 6 minutes each Y, and 12 minutes every Z.

Operators are paid £2.40 per hour.

Overheads are budgeted as follows, and are allocated on the basis of direct labour hours:

	Variable	Fixed
	£	£
Dept.1	110,000	55,000
Dept.2	130,000	65,000
Repair Dept.	550	2,750

The Management is not satisfied with the projected profit margin and have negotiated with another company who will purchase all rejected units for £3 per item for all products. The Repair Department would be closed down saving £2,000 Fixed Costs and £500 Variable Costs. Required:

   i.   Calculate the total unit cost for each product excluding any repair costs.

   ii.   Calculate the total repair cost only per product for the period.

   iii.   The profit projected from the information given utilising the repair dept.

   iv.   The profit projected if the Management's proposal is enforced.

   v.   Your report on the comparison of the alternatives and recommendation.

(AAT, Cost Accounting and Budgeting)

B20.8   Mrs Johnston has taken out a lease on a shop for a down payment of £5,000. Additionally, the rent under the lease amounts to £5,000 per annum. If the (lease is cancelled, the initial payment of £5,000 is forfeit. Mrs Johnston plans to use the shop for the sale of clothing and has estimated operations for the next twelve months as follows:

	£	£
Sales	115,000	
Less: Value added tax (VAT)	15,000	
Sales less V.A.T.		100,000
Cost of goods sold	50,000	
Wages and wage related costs	12,000	
Rent including the down payment	10,000	
Rates, heating, lighting and insurance	13,000	
Audit, legal and general expenses	2,000	87,000
Net profit before tax		13,000

In the figures no provision has been made for the cost of Mrs Johnston but it is estimated that one half of her time will be devoted to the business. She is undecided whether to continue with her plans because she knows that she can sub - let the shop to a friend for a monthly rent of £550 if she does not use the shop herself.

You are required to:

a. i. explain and identify the 'sunk' and 'opportunity' costs in the situation depicted above;

   ii. state what decision Mrs Johnston should make according to the information given, supporting your conclusion with a financial statement;

b. explain the meaning and use of 'notional' (or 'imputed') costs and quote two supporting examples.

(CIMA, Cost Accounting 1)

B20.9 Domestic political trouble in the country of an overseas supplier is causing concern in your company because it is not known when further supplies of raw material 'x' will be received The current stock held of this particular raw material is 17,000 kilograms which cost £136,000. Based on raw material 'x', your company makes five different products and the expected demand for each of these, for the next three months, is given below together with other relevant information:

Product code	Kilogram of raw material 'x' per unit	Direct labour hours per unit of finished product	Selling price per unit	Expected demand over three months
	Kg	Hours	£	Units
701	0.7	1.0	26	8,000
702	0.5	0.8	28	7,200
821	1.4	1.5	34	9,000
822	1.3	1.1	38	12,000
937	1.5	1.4	40	10,000

The-direct wages rate per hour is £5 and production overhead is based on direct wages cost - the Variable overhead absorption rate being 40% and the fixed overhead absorption rate being 60%.

Variable selling costs, including sales commission, are 15% of selling price.

Budgeted fixed selling and administration costs are £300,000 per annum.

Assume that the fixed production overhead incurred will equal the absorbed figure.

You are required to:

a. show what quantity of the raw material on hand ought to be allocated to which products in order to maximise profits for the forthcoming three months;

b. present a brief statement showing contribution and profit for the forthcoming three months, if your suggestion in a. is adopted;

c. comment briefly on the analysis you used to aid the decision-making process in a. and give three other examples of business problems where this type of analysis can be useful.

(CIMA, Cost Accounting)

B20.10 a. 'Discretionary costs are troublesome because managers usually find it difficult to separate and quantify the results of their use in the business, as compared with variable and other fixed costs.' (Synopsis extract – Management Accounting – December 1982)

You are required to discuss the above statement and include in your answer the meaning of discretionary costs, variable costs and fixed costs; give two illustrations of each of these three.

b. A drug company has initiated a research project which is intended to develop a new product. Expenditures to date on this particular research total £500,000 but it is now estimated that a further £200,000 will need to be spent before the product can be marketed. Over the estimated life of the product the profit potential has a net present value of £350,000.

You are required to advise management whether they should continue or abandon the project. Support your conclusion with a numerate statement and state what kind of cost is the £500,000.

c. Opportunity costs and notional costs are not recognised by financial accounting systems but need to be considered in many decisions taken by management.

You are required to explain briefly the meanings of opportunity costs and notional costs; give two examples of each to illustrate the meanings you have attached to them.

(CIMA Cost Accounting)

B20.11 A one-off order for 3,000 garden chairs has been received from an overseas customer for the coming period. Your budgeted production for the period is for 16,000 chairs, which represents 80% of your capacity to manufacture garden chairs. Budgeted data for the period is as follows:

	£	£
Sales		672,000
Materials	192,000	
Labour	196,000	
Overheads	200,000	
		588,000
Net profit		84,000

You ascertain that £20,000 of labour and 20% of overheads are fixed in nature and all the other costs are variable.

Required:

prepare a cost statement to show whether the order should be accepted if the customer was prepared to pay:

    i. £30 per chair

    ii. £36 per chair.

Give reasons for your decisions.

    b. What other factors need to be taken into consideration before the order is accepted or rejected?

(AAT Cost Accounting & Budgeting, part question)

B20.12 The Strategic Planning Department of your company has suggested that a separate division be created in order to enter the market providing a fast repair service for cars.

Enquiries made suggest that one typical fast repair service centre* would have sales and costs as follows, for one year:

	£	£
Sales		540,000
Components and consumable stores	301,600	
Wages and salaries	78,160	
Bonuses (profit sharing scheme)	30,400	
Pension scheme costs	5,600	
Staff health scheme	2,840	
National Insurance contributions	7,000	
A Rent	14,000	
B Rates on business premises	8,000	
C Power, heating and lighting	6,000	
D Advertising	10,000	
E Telephones and stationary	1,600	
F Customer ' creature comforts' (waiting room with coffee and magazines)	2,000	
Depreciation on plant and equipment – 10% straight -line method with Nil residual value	13,280	
Charges from Head Office for (i) financing costs	4,000	
(ii) administration and share of divisional expenses	10,000	
Total cost		494,480
Net profit before tax		45,520

Note: VAT is excluded from the above figures.

* It is envisaged that such a centre would provide for replacement tyres, batteries, exhausts, clutches, brake pads, sparking plugs, filters and oil changes. Mechanics of semi-skilled grades would be employed.

The following data are based on information published by a public company with a nationwide chain of the centres which specialises in supplying replacement tyres and exhaust systems

The figure relate to the supply and fitting of four tyres and an exhaust system for a small family car:

	£	%	£	%
Sales (excluding VAT)			154.60	100.00
Stocks: spent on buying replacement stocks from suppliers	77.48	50.12		
Staff: wages, pensions, staff health scheme and employer's National Insurance contributions	30.96	20.03		
Operating costs: the costs of running the business – rent, rates, heating, lighting, stationary, advertising and the like	27.38	17.71		

	£	%
Depreciation	3.33	2.15
Interest paid on money borrowed	1.33	0.86
Taxes – paid to the government	3.04	1.97
Dividends	3.80	2.46
Retained profits	7.28	4.70

You are required

a. to compare the cost structure of one typical fast repair service centre with the information given by the public company specialising in tyre and exhaust replacements. Comment on significant differences and state possible reasons for these differences;

b. to indicate which two of the six costs listed above (A-F) for the typical fast service repair centre should be classified as discretionary fixed costs;

c. to state if the costs you have identified as your answer to (b) above could be avoided and if so, to comment on the likely effect on profitability.

(CIMA Cost Accounting, part question)

B20.13 The Board of Mainaction Ltd have had a planning meeting for 1993. The company produces three main products and a draft budgeted Income Statement as follows:

	Product X £	Product Y £	Product Z £	Total £
Sales				
100,000 units @ £15	1,500,000			
80,000 units @ £25		2,000,000		
120,000 units @ £10			1,200,000	4,700,000
Material	300,000	400,000	480,000	
Labour	700,000	800,000	750,000	
Overheads	225,000	360,000	330,000	
	1,225,000	1,560,000	1,560,000	4,345,000
Profit/(Loss)	275,000	440,000	(360,000)	355,000

You are told the following:

i.   All material costs are available and all production is to be sold.

ii. The fixed cost element of labour is:

Product X – £100,000

Product Y – £160,000

Product Z – £90,000

iii. Overheads are a mixture of variable and fixed cost. The fixed cost element has been absorbed on the basis of machine hours at the rate of £5 per machine hour. One unit of each product takes the following machine time:

Product X – 15 minutes

Product Y – 30 minutes

Product Z – 15 minutes

iv. The Board are concerned about the loss on Product Z.

v.   The following separate proposals have been put forward for 1993:

1. Allow the budgeted level of activity for all products to stand but cut the labour supervision on Product Z, which will reduce labour fixed costs by £75,000 but increase the variable element of overheads for Product Z by 10%. In addition a cheaper material costing 75p per unit less would be introduced for Product Z.

2. Increase the selling price of Product Z by £1 per unit and assume demand will remain constant.

3. Stop making Product Z, which will incur redundancy payments of £50,000 but will also eliminate the fixed labour costs for Product Z.

Required:

a. Prepare a marginal costing statement to show the budgeted contribution per unit.

b. Prepare a statement to show the total contribution and profit at the budgeted level of production.

c. Show what effect each separate proposal made by the Board will have on the budgeted contribution and profitability of the firm.

d. Outline which strategy proposal you would recommend to the Board taking both monetary and non-monetary considerations into account. Bear in mind that the current outlook for future sales is likely to be depressed and that the firm has a reputation for the quality of its products.

(AAT Cost Accounting & Budgeting)

B20.14 Three products – X,Y and Z – are made and sold by a company; information is given below.

		Product X	Product Y	Product Z
Standard costs:		£	£	£
Direct materials		50	120	90
Variable overhead		12	7	16
Direct labour:	Rate per hour	Hours	Hours	Hours
	£			
Department A	5	14	8	15
Department B	6	4	3	5
Department C	4	8	4	15

Total fixed overhead for the year was budgeted at £300,000.

The budget for the current financial year, which was prepared for a recessionary period, was based on the following sales:

Product	Sales in units	Selling price per unit
		£
X	7,500	210
Y	6,000	220
Z	6,000	300

However, the market for each of the products has improved and the sales Director believes that without a change in selling prices, the number of units sold could be increased for each product by the following percentages:

Product	Increase
X	20%
Y	25%
Z	$33\frac{1}{3}\%$

When the Sales Director's views were presented to a management meeting, the Production Director declared that although it might be possible to sell more units of product, output could not be expanded because he was unable to recruit more staff for Department B: there being a severe shortage of the skills needed by this department,

You are required

a. i. to show in the form of a statement for management, the unit costs of each of the three products and the total profit expected for the current year based on the original sales figures;

ii. to state the profit if the most profitable mixture of the products was made and sold, utilising the higher sales figures and the limitation on Department B;

iii. to identify and to comment on three possible problems which may arise if the mixture in (a) ii. above were to be produced;

b. to describe briefly a technique for determining optimum output levels when there is more than one input constraint.

(CIMA Cost Accounting)

APPENDIX

1. Linear programming (LP)†

LP is a mathematical technique concerned with the allocation of scarce resources. It is a procedure to optimise the value of some objective (for example, maximise contribution) when the factors involved are subject to constraints (for example, only 500 machine hours and 200 labour hours are available in a week). LP can be used to solve problems which:

    a.   can be stated in numeric terms,
    b.   all factors have linear relationships,
    c.   have one or more restrictions on the factors involved,
    d.   have a choice between alternatives.

2. Standard formulation

Before attempting a solution, it is necessary to express the problem in a standard manner. This means determining the *Objective Function* and the *Constraints*. This is shown below using the following example.

A firm makes two products A and B which have a contribution of £15 and £10 per unit respectively. The production data are as follows:

	Machining Hours	Per Unit Labour hours	Materials (Kgs)
Product A	4	4	1
Product B	2	6	1
Availability per week	100	180	40

It is required to determine the production plan which maximises contribution.

This is a problem with 2 unknowns (ie, number of units A and B) with three constraints (ie, availability of machine hours, labour hours and material).

The first stage is to express the problem in the standardised format.

i e maximise	$15A + 10B$		(The objective function expressed in contribution per unit)
subject to:	$4A + 2B$	≤ 100	(machining hours constraint)
	$4A + 6B$	≤ 180	(labour hours constraint)
	$A + B$	≤ 40	(materials constraint)

Because this is a problem with only 2 unknowns, a graphical solution is possible:

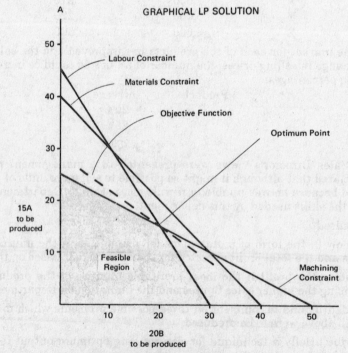

Graphical LP solution

---

† This subject is dealt with in detail in 'Quantitative Techniques', T. Lucey, DP Publications.

Notes:

a. The solution is always obtained on the edge of the feasible region and in this case is 15 units of A and 20 units of B giving a contribution of:

$$£(15 \times 15) + £(20 \times 10) = £425 \text{ TOTAL}$$

b. This solution uses the following quantities of the resources:

Machining hours	$(15 \times 4) + (20 \times 2) = 100$	(all utilised)
Labour hours	$(15 \times 4) + (20 \times 6) = 180$	(all utilised)
Material	$(15 \times 1) + (20 \times 1) = 35$	(5 Kgs spare)

c. The materials constraint is non binding, ie, it is redundant. This can be seen from the graph as it does not touch the feasible region and also from the calculation in b. which shows that there is 5 Kgs spare.

d. Where there are more than 2 unknowns, graphical solution is not possible and problems have to be solved using what is known as the *simplex* method.

21: Break even analysis

1. Topics covered in this chapter:

1. Uses and assumptions of cost-volume-profit analysis
2. C-V-P analysis by formulae
3. Traditional and Contribution Break-Even Charts
4. Multi-product Break-Even Charts
5. Limitations of Break-Even Charts.

2. Break-even analysis

This is the term given to the study of the interrelationships between costs, volume and profit at various levels of activity. Frequently these relationships are depicted by graphs, but this is not essential.

The term break-even analysis is the one commonly used, but it is somewhat misleading as it implies that the only concern is with that level of activity which produces neither profit nor loss – the break even point – although the behaviour of costs and profits at other levels is usually of much greater significance. Because of this an alternative term, cost-volume-profit analysis or C-V-P analysis, is frequently used and is more descriptive.

3. Uses of C-V-P analysis

C-V-P analysis uses many of the principles of marginal costing and is an important tool in short-term planning. It explores the relationship which exists between costs, revenue, output levels and resulting profit and is more relevant where the proposed changes in the levels of activity are relatively small. In these cases the established cost patterns are likely to continue, so C-V-P analysis may be useful for decision making. Over greater changes of activity and in the longer term existing cost structures, eg, the amount of fixed costs and the marginal cost per unit, are likely to change, so C-V-P analysis becomes less appropriate.

Typical short run decision where C-V-P analysis can be useful include; choice of sales mix, pricing policies, multi-shift working, and special order acceptance.

4. Assumptions behind C-V-P analysis

Before any formulae are given or graphs drawn, the major assumptions behind C-V-P analysis must be stated. These are:

a. All costs can be resolved into Fixed and Variable elements.
b. Fixed costs will remain constant and Variable costs vary proportionately with activity.
c. Over the activity range being considered costs and revenues behave in a linear fashion.
d. That the only factor affecting costs and revenues is volume.
e. That technology, production methods and efficiency remain unchanged.
f. Particularly for graphical methods that the analysis relates to one product only or to a constant product mix.
g. There are no stock level changes or that stocks are valued at marginal cost only.

It will be apparent that these are over simplifying assumptions for many practical situations. It is because of this that C-V-P analysis can only be an approximate guide for decision making. Nevertheless, by highlighting the interaction of costs, volume, revenue and profit, useful guidance can be provided for managers making short run, tactical decisions.

5. C-V-P analysis by formula

C-V-P analysis can be undertaken by graphical means which are dealt with later in this chapter, or by simple formulae which are listed below and illustrated by examples.

a. Break-even-point (in units) = $\dfrac{\text{Fixed costs}}{\text{Contribution/unit}}$

b. Break-even point (£ sales) = $\dfrac{\text{Fixed costs}}{\text{Contribution/unit}} \times \text{Sales Price/unit}$

$$= \text{Fixed Costs} \times \dfrac{1}{\text{C/S ratio}}$$

c. C/S ratio: $\dfrac{\text{Contribution/unit}}{\text{Sales Price per unit}} \times 100$

d. Level of Sales to result in target profit (in units) = $\dfrac{\text{Fixed costs+Target Profit}}{\text{Contribution/unit}}$

e. Level of sales to result in target profit after tax (units) = $\dfrac{\text{Fixed cost} + \left(\dfrac{\text{Target profit}}{1 - \text{Tax rate}}\right)}{\text{Contribution / unit}}$

f. Level of Sales to result in Target profit (£ sales) = $\dfrac{(\text{Fixed Cost} + \text{Target Profit}) \times \text{Sales price/unit}}{\text{Contribution/unit}}$

Note:

The above formulae relate to a single product firm or one with an unvarying mix of sales. With a multi product firm it is possible to calculate the break even point as follows:

$$\text{Break-even-point (£ sales)} = \dfrac{\text{Fixed Costs} \times \text{Sales Value}}{\text{Contribution}}$$

Example 1

A company makes a single product with a sales price of £10 and a marginal cost of £6. Fixed costs are £60,000 p.a.

Calculate

a. Number of units to break even
b. Sales at break-even point
c. C/S ratio
d. What number of units will need to be sold to achieve a profit of £20,000 p a.
e. What level of sales will achieve a profit of £20,000 p.a.
f. Because of increasing costs the marginal cost is expected to rise to £6.50 per unit and fixed costs to £70,000 p.a. If the selling price cannot be increased what will be the number of units required to maintain a profit of £20,000 p.a.?
g. If the taxation rate is 40% how many units will need to be sold to make a profit of £ 20,000 p. a.?

Solution

Contribution	= Selling price – marginal cost
	= £10 – 6
	= **£4**
a. Break-even point (units)	= $\dfrac{£60,000}{£4}$
	= **£15,000**
b. Break-even point (£ sales)	= 15,000 × £10
	= **£150,000**
c. C/S ratio	= $\dfrac{£4 \times 100}{£10}$
	= **40%**

d. Number of units for target profit $= \dfrac{£60,000 + 20,000}{£4}$

= 20,000

e. Sales for target profit $= 20,000 \times £10$

= £200,000

(Alternatively, the sales for target profit can be deduced by the following reasoning. After break-even point the contribution per unit becomes net profit per unit, so that as 15,000 units were required at break-even point, 5000 extra units would be required to make £20,000 profit,

∴ total units = 15,000 + 5000 = 20,000 × £10 = £200,000)

f. Note that the fixed costs, marginal cost and contribution have changed

No. of units for target profit $= \dfrac{£70,000 + 20,000}{£3.50}$

= 25,714 units

g. Number of units for target profit after tax $= \dfrac{£60,000 + \left(\dfrac{20,000}{1 - 0.4}\right)}{£4}$

= 23,333 units.

6. Graphical approach

This may be preferred

a. Where a simple overview is sufficient.

b. Where there is a need to avoid a detailed, numerical approach when, for example, the recipients of the information have no accounting background. The basic chart is known as a Break Even Chart which can be drawn in two ways. The first is known as the *traditional approach* and the second the *contribution approach*. Whatever approach is adopted, all costs must be capable of separation into fixed and variable elements, ie, semi-fixed or semi-variable costs must be analysed into their components.

7. The traditional break-even chart

Assuming that Fixed and Variable costs have been resolved, the chart is drawn in the following way:

a. *Draw the axes*
   ☐ Horizontal showing levels of activity expresses as units of output or as percentages of total capacity.
   ☐ Vertical showing values in £'s or £000s as appropriate, for costs and revenues.

b. *Draw the cost lines*
   ☐ Fixed cost.
   This will be a straight line parallel to the horizontal axis at the level of the fixed costs.
   ☐ Total cost. This will start where the fixed cost line intersects the vertical axis and will be a straight line sloping upward at an angle depending on the proportion of Variable cost in total costs.

c. *Draw the revenue line*
   This will be a straight line from the point of origin sloping upwards at an angle determined by the selling price.

Example 2

A company makes a single product with a total capacity of 400,000 litres p.a. Cost and sales data are as follows :

Selling price	£1 per litre
Marginal cost	£0.50 per litre
Fixed costs	£100,000

Draw a traditional break-even chart showing the likely profit at the expected production level of 300,000 litres.

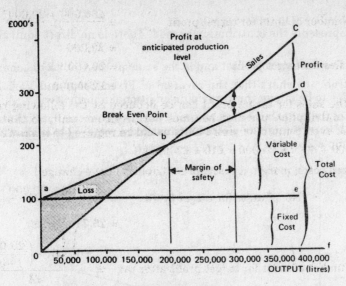

Figure 21.1

From the graph it will be seen that break-even point is at an output level of 200,000 litres and that the width of the profit wedge indicates the profit at a production level of 300,000. The profit is £50,000.

Note:

The 'margin of safety' indicated on the chart is the term given to the difference between the activity level selected and break-even point. In this case the margin of safety is 100,000 litres which in the more normal multi-product firm would be expressed in sales value.

8. The contribution break-even chart

This uses the same axes and data as the traditional chart. The only difference being that Variable Costs are drawn on the chart before Fixed Costs resulting in the contribution being shown as a wedge.

Example 3

Repeat Example 2 except that a contribution break-even chart should be drawn.

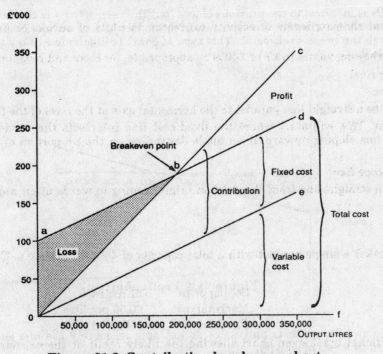

Figure 21.2 Contribution break even chart

Notes on figure 21.2:

a. The area c.o.e. represents the contribution earned. There is no direct equivalent on the traditional chart.

b. The area d, a, o, f represents total cost and is the same as the traditional chart.

c. It will be seen from the chart that the reversal of Fixed Costs and Variable Costs enables the contribution wedge to be drawn thus providing additional information.

An alternative form of the contribution break-even chart is where the net difference between sales and variable cost, ie, total contribution, is plotted against fixed costs. This is shown once again using the same data from Example 2.

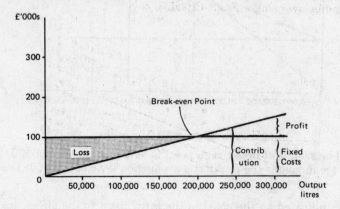

Figure 21.3 Alternative form of contribution break even chart

Notes on Fig. 21.3:

a. Sales and Variable costs are not shown directly.

b. Both forms of contribution chart, Figures 21.2 and 21.3, show clearly that contribution is first used to meet fixed costs and when these costs are met the contribution becomes profit.

9. Profit chart

This is another form of presentation with the emphasis on the effect on profit at varying levels of activity. It is a simpler form of chart to those illustrated so far because only a line showing profit is drawn.

The horizontal axis is identical to the previous charts, but the vertical axis is continued below the point of origin to show losses. A contribution line is drawn from the loss at zero activity, which is equivalent to the fixed costs, through the break-even point. This type of chart is illustrated below using, once again, the data from Example 2.

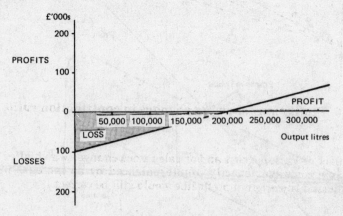

Figure 21.4 Profit chart

Note:

Lines for Variable and Fixed Costs and Sales do not appear, merely the one summary line showing contribution at various levels of activity.

10. Changes in costs and revenues

Several of the main types of chart have been described and it should be apparent that they are all able to show cost/revenue/volume/profit relationships in a simple, effective form. It is also possible to show the effect of changes in costs and revenues by drawing additional lines on the charts. The changes are of two types:

a. Fixed cost changes. Increases or decreases in fixed costs do not change the slope of the line, but alter the point of intersection and thus the break-even point.

b. Variable cost and sales price changes. These changes alter the slope of the line thus affecting the break-even point and the shape of the profit and loss 'wedges'.

These changes are illustrated below using a Profit-Chart.

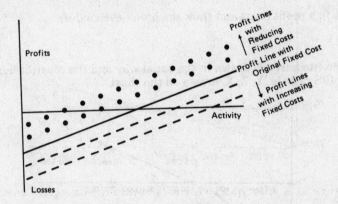

Figure 21.5 Profit chart showing changes in fixed costs

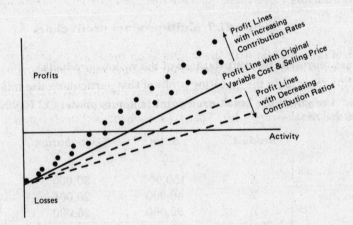

Figure 21.6 Profit chart showing changes in contribution ratio

Note:

The above chart shows the effect of Variable cost and/or sales price changes which alter the contribution. If, say, an increase in Variable costs was exactly counterbalanced by an increase in sales price, the contribution would be the same and the original profit line would still be correct.

11. Multi-product chart

All of the charts illustrated so far have assumed a single product. Equally they could have illustrated a given sales mix resulting in an average contribution rate equivalent to a single product. An alternative method is to plot the individual products each with their individual C/S characteristics and then show the resulting overall profit line. This is shown below.

Example

A firm has fixed costs of £50,000 pa. and has three products, the sales and contribution of which are shown below.

Product	Sales	Contribution	C/S ratio
	£	£	
X	150,000	30,000	20%
Y	40,000	20,000	50%
Z	60,000	25,000	42%

Plot the products on a profit chart and show the break-even sales.

Solution

The axes on the profit chart are drawn in the usual way and the contribution from the products, in the sequence of their C/S ratio ie, Y, Z, X, drawn on the chart.

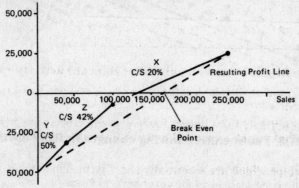

Figure 21.7 Multi-product profit chart

Notes:

a. The solid lines represent the contributions of the various products.

b. The dotted line represents the resulting profit of this particular sales mix and C/S ratios.

c. Reading from the graph the break-even point is approximately £170,000. The exact figure can be calculated as follows:

Product	Sales	Contribution
	£	£
X	150,000	30,000
Y	40,000	20,000
Z	60,000	25,000
Totals	£250,000	£75,000

$$\text{overall C/S ratio} = \frac{£75,000}{£250,000} = 30\%$$

$$\therefore \text{Break-even point} = \frac{\text{Fixed Costs}}{\text{C/S}}$$

$$= \frac{£50,000}{.3}$$

$$= £166,667$$

12. Limitations of break-even and profit charts

The various charts depicted show cost, volume and profit relationships in a simplified and approximate manner. They can be useful aids, but whenever they are used the following limitations should not be forgotten.

a. The charts are reasonable pointers to performance within normal activity ranges, say 70% 120% of average production. Outside this relevant range the relationship depicted almost certainly will not be correct. Although it is conventional to draw the lines starting from zero activity, as they have been drawn in this chapter, relationships at the extremes of activity cannot be relied upon. A typical relevant range of activity could be shown as follows.

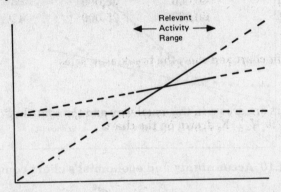

Figure 21.8 Break-even chart showing relevant activity range

b. Fixed costs are likely to change at different activity levels. A stepped fixed cost line is probably the most accurate representation.

c. Variable costs and sales are unlikely to be linear. Extra discounts, overtime payments, special delivery charges etc, make it likely that variable cost and revenue lines are some form of a curve rather than a straight line.

d. The charts depict relationships which are essentially short term. This makes them inappropriate for planning purposes where the time scale stretches over several years.

e. The charts, and C-V-P analysis make the assumption that all variable costs vary accordingly to the same activity indicator, usually sales or production. This is a gross over-simplification and reduces the accuracy of the charts and C-V-P analysis.

13. The accountants' and economists' view of break-even charts

The break-even chart used by accountants has been dealt with earlier in the chapter, Figure 21.1. The chart drawn by economists is shown below.

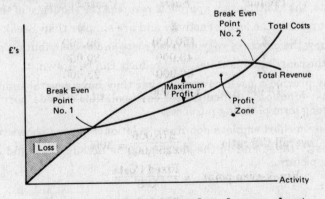

Figure 21.9 Economists break-even chart

Notes on figure 21.9:

a. More correctly this is a chart showing the point of profit maximisation.

b. BEP No. 2 is at the point where declining aggregate revenues equal increasing aggregate costs. BEP No. 1 is similar, but not exactly equivalent, to the single BEP shown on a typical accounting chart. The reason for the discrepancy is that the costs included in the economists chart include an allowance for a normal level of profit, which is deemed to be an economic cost, whereas the break even point on an accounting chart is simply the balancing of accounting costs and revenues.

c. The cost line shows economies of scale at first, then turns upwards as diminishing returns set in.

d. The revenue line curves downward on the assumption that selling prices will have to be reduced to increase sales volume.

Within the relevant activity range the differences between the economist's and accountant's chart are not great. The two types of charts are superimposed below.

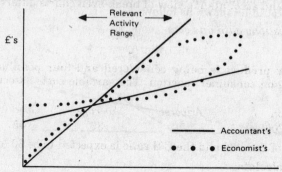

Figure 21.10 Accountants and economist's chart compared

14. Summary

a. Break-even analysis, or more descriptively, cost-volume-profit analysis studies the relationship between costs, volume, sales and profit.

b. C-V-P analysis is most appropriate for short run tactical decisions.

c. The major assumptions behind C-V-P analysis are that all costs are resolvable into Fixed and Variable, linearity is assumed, technology and efficiency remain constant and that volume is the only determinant of cost and revenue changes.

d. The main C-V-P formulae are

$$\text{Break-even point} = \frac{\text{Fixed costs}}{\text{contribution/unit}}$$

$$\text{C/S ratio} = \frac{\text{Contribution/unit}}{\text{Selling price/unit}}$$

e. The C/S ratio is an important ratio. An alternative term is the P/V ratio.

f. Break-even charts can be drawn in two different ways. The 'traditional approach' graphs the fixed cost first, then variable costs, the 'contribution approach' reverses the sequence of the cost lines.

g. Profit charts plot profit against the level of activity and are simpler than Break-even charts.

h. All of the charts can show the effects of varying fixed costs and/or contribution ratios.

i. Profit charts showing the contributions of various products can be drawn.

j. Break-even charts may provide a useful overview, but they have several limitations including: non-linear and stepped cost functions, difficulties of extrapolation outside normal activity levels and inappropriateness for long term planning purposes.

k. The economist's break-even chart employs non-linear relationships and shows two break even points.

l. Over the relevant activity range and in the short-run, the accountant's and economist's charts are likely to show a similar picture.

Student self-testing

Self Review Questions

1. What is an alternative term to break even analysis? (2)

2. What is the major purpose of C-V-P analysis? (3)

3. What are the major assumptions behind C-V-P analysis? (4)

4. What is the formula for: the Break even point (£ sales)? Break even point (units)? (5)

5. What is the C/S ratio? (5)

6. How is the traditional break-even chart drawn? (7)

7. What is a contribution break-even chart? (8)

8. How is a Profit chart drawn? (9)

9. What is a multi-product profit chart and how is it drawn? (11)

10. What are the major limitations of break-even and profit charts? (12)

11. How does the economist's and accountant's view of break-even charts differ? (13)

Exercises and examination questions with answers

Exercises

A21.1 The launch of a new product is being considered and four possible output levels are being considered depending on consumer reaction, The variable costs associated with these levels are shown below.

Consumer reaction	Adverse	Average	Good	Excellent
Variable Costs (£000's)	20	30	45	70

There are fixed costs of £36,000 and the C/S ratio is expected to be 60%.

You are required to calculate:

a. the profit or loss at each of the four levels.
b. the break even point in sales value.
c. the level of sales at which a profit of £10,000 would be made.

A21.2 The fixed costs of a company are £15,000 and the contributions from the three products are:

> Contribution per unit
> Product D £5
> Product E £2.50
> Product F £3.00

The sales forecast is

> Product D 1,000 units at £10 each
> Product E 5,000 units at £6.50 each
> Product F 2,500 units at £7 each

Assuming that the products are always sold in the same proportions you are required to:

a. Plot the above data on a Contribution Break Even Chart and
b. Show the break even point for the company as a percentage of budgeted activity.

A21.3 A manufacturer incurred the following costs in a period for his sole product:

	£
Labour (25% Variable)	8,000
Materials (100% Variable)	12,000
Selling Costs (10% Variable)	2,000
Other Costs (Fixed)	7,000
Total Costs	£29,000

A normal period's sales are 500 units at £70 each, but up to 650 units could be made in a period. Various alternatives are being considered:

i. Reduce the price to £63 each and sell all that could be made.

ii. Increase the price to £80 each at which price sales would be 400 units.

iii. Keep the present plan. What is the most profitable plan? What are the C/S ratios? What is the break even point for each alternative?

A21.4 A firm has fixed costs of £25,000 p.a. and has three products, the details of which are:

Product	Sales (£)	Marginal Cost (£)
A	80,000	40,000
B	130,000	90,000
C	60,000	36,000

Plot the above products on a single profit chart and show the breakeven sales.

Examination questions

A21.5 The following details relate to a shop which currently sells 25,000 pairs of shoes annually:

Selling price per pair of shoes	£40
Purchase cost per pair of shoes	£25

Total annual fixed costs:

	£
Salaries	100,000
Advertising	40,000
Other fixed expenses	100,000

Required:

Answer each part independently of data contained in other parts of the requirement.

i. Calculate the break even point and margin of safety in number of pairs of shoes sold.

ii. Assume that 20,000 pairs were sold in a year. Calculate the shop's net income/ loss.

iii. If a selling commission of £2 per pair of shoes sold was to be introduced, how many pairs of shoes would need to be sold in a year in order to earn a net income of £10,000?

iv. Assume that for next year an additional advertising campaign costing £20,000 is proposed, whilst at the same time selling prices are to be increased by 12%. What would be the break even point in number of pairs of shoes?

(AAT, Cost Accounting & Budgeting part question)

A21.6 A manufacturing company with a single product has the following sales and production results over three financial periods:

	Period 1 000 units	Period 2 000 units	Period 3 000 units
Sales	50	60	40
Production	70	40	60

The selling price per unit has remained at £10, and direct material and direct labour costs per unit at £5. All manufacturing overheads are absorbed into product cost at predetermined rates per unit of output. Any under/over absorbed balances are transferred to profit and loss in the period in which they arise. Variable manufacturing overhead absorption was predetermined at a rate of £1 per unit in each period. Fixed manufacturing overheads were expected to be £180,000 per period. Normal capacity is 60,000 units of output per period.

Manufacturing overheads actually incurred were as follows:

	Period 1 000 units	Period 2 000 units	Period 3 000 units
Variable	68	45	60
Fixed	180	180	180

Assume that no further overheads are incurred (ie, other than manufacturing overheads).

Required:
a. Calculate the expected break-even point per period.
b. Calculate the profit/loss that arose in each of the three periods.
c. Reconcile your answers to (a) and (b) above, clearly demonstrating, explaining fully the reasons for, and commenting briefly upon, any differences encountered. *(ACCA, Costing)*

A21.7 The summarised profit and loss statement for Exewye share p. l.c. for the last year is as follows:

	£000	£000
Sales (50,000 units)		1,000
Direct materials	350	
Direct wages	200	
Fixed production overhead	200	
Variable production overhead	50	
Administration overhead	180	
Selling and distribution overhead	120	
		1,100
Profit/(loss)		(100)

At a recent board meeting, the directors discussed the year's results, following which the chairman asked for suggestions to improve the situation.

You are required, as management accountant, to evaluate the following alternative proposals and to comment briefly on each:

a. Pay salesman a commission of 10% of sales and thus increase sales to achieve break-even point.

b. Reduce selling price by 10% which it is estimated would increase sales volume by 30%.

c. Increase direct wage rates from £4 to £5 per hour, as part of a productivity/pay deal. It is hoped that this would increase production and sales by 20%, but advertising costs would increase by £50,000.

d. Increase sales by additional advertising of £300,000, with an increased selling price of 20%, setting a profit margin of 10%.

(CIMA, Cost Accounting 2)

A21.8 A friend of yours has come to you for financial advice. He is about to set up in business manufacturing and selling personal computers. He provides you with the following budgeted information concerning his total costs:

	£
Material costs	280,000
Labour costs	300,000
Production overhead	150,000
Selling & Distribution overhead	140,000
Administration overhead	60,000

The above figures are based upon production of 3,500 computers, although there is production capacity for 4,000 computers. The budgeted selling price is £300 per computer.

You ascertain that £125,000 of labour costs, 100% of administration overheads. 30% of production overheads and 50% of selling and distribution overheads are fixed in nature.

All other costs are variable with the level of production.

Required:

a. Prepare a cost statement showing the contribution per computer and for the budgeted level of production.

b. What is the profit at the budgeted level of production?

c. construct a breakeven chart in good format, clearly showing the breakeven point in units and sales revenue as well as the margin of safety in units at the budgeted level of production.

d. List and comment upon the major assumptions upon which breakeven charts are based.

e. Your friend has had an offer to utilise his existing spare capacity by making 500 computers for a price of £225 per computer. He intends to reject this offer as the price is well below his total cost for making a computer. Advise him upon this course of action, giving reasons for your advise.

(AAT Cost Accounting & Budgeting)

A21.9 PE Limited produces and sells two products P and E. Budgets prepared for the next six months give the following information:

	Product P per unit £	Product E per unit £
Selling price	10.00	12.00
Variable costs: production and selling	5.00	10.00

Common fixed costs: production and selling - for six months £561,600

a. You are required, in respect of the forthcoming six months,

i. to state what the breakeven point in £s will be and the number of each product this figure represents if the two products are sold in the ratio 4P to 3E;

ii. to state the breakeven point in £s and the number of products this figure represents if the sales mix changes to 4P to 4E (ignore fractions of products);

iii. to advise the sales manager which product mix should be better, that in (a) i. above or that in (a) ii. above, and why;

    iv. to advise the sales manager which of the two products should be concentrated on and the reason(s) for your recommendation – assume that whatever can be made can be sold, that both products go through a machining process and that there were only 32,000 machine hours available, with product P requiring 0.40 hour per unit and product E requiring 0.10 hour per unit.

b. You are required to compare and contrast the usefulness of a conventional breakeven chart with a contribution breakeven chart. Your explanation should include illustrative diagrams drawn within your answer book and not on graph paper.

(CIMA Cost Accounting)

A21.10 A building company constructs a standard unit which sells for £30,000. The company's costs can be readily identifiable between fixed and variable costs.

Budgeted data for the coming six months includes the following:

	Sales (in units)	Profit £
January	18	70,000
February	20	100,000
March	30	250,000
April	22	130,000
May	24	160,000
June	16	40,000

You are told that the fixed costs for the six months have been spread evenly over the period under review to arrive at the monthly profit projections.

Required:

a. Prepare a graph for total sales, costs and outputs for the six months under review that shows:

    i. The breakeven point in units and revenue.

    ii. Total fixed costs

    iii. The variable cost line.

    iv. The margin of safety for the total budgeted sales.

Note: Marks will be awarded for workings.

b. The company is worried about the low level of sales. The sales director says that if the selling price of the unit was reduced by £5,000 the company would be able to sell 10% more units. All other costs would remain the same you are told.

Determine whether the company should reduce the selling price to attract new sales in order top maximise profit. Clearly show any workings.

c. Evaluate whether the assumption that costs are readily identifiable as either fixed or variable throughout a range of production is realistic. Give examples of any alternative classification.

(AAT Cost Accounting & Budgeting)

A21.11 a. Budgeted information for A Ltd for the following period, analysed by product, is shown below:

	Product 1	Product 2	Product 3
Sales units (000s)	225	376	190
Selling price (£ per unit)	11.00	10.50	8.00
Variable costs (£ per unit)	5.80	6.00	5.20
Attributable fixed costs (£000s)	275	337	296

General fixed costs, which are apportioned to products as a percentage of sales, are budgeted at £1,668,000.

Required:

    i. calculate the budgeted profit of A Ltd, and of each of its products.

    ii. Recalculate the budgeted profit of A Ltd on the assumption that Product 3 is discontinued, with no effect on sales of the other two products. State and justify other assumptions made.

    iii. Additional advertising, to that included in the budget for Product 1, is being considered.

Calculate the minimum extra sales units required of Product 1 to cover additional advertising expenditure of £80,000. Assume that all other existing fixed costs would remain unchanged.

iv. Calculate the increase in sales volume of Product 2 that is necessary in order to compensate the effect on profit of a 10% reduction in the selling price of the product. State clearly any assumptions made.

b. Discuss the factors which infuence cost behavior in response to changes in activity.

(ACCA Cost & Management Accounting 1)

A21.12 JK Limited has prepared a budget for the next twelve months when it intends to make and sell four products, details of which are shown below:

Product	Sales in units (thousands)	Selling price per unit £	Variable cost per unit £
J	10	20	14.00
K	10	40	8.00
L	50	4	4.20
M	20	10	7.00

Budgeted fixed Costs are £240,000 per annum and total assets employed are £570,000.

You are required

a. to calculate the total contribution earned by each product and their combined total contributions;

b. to plot the data of your answer to(a) above in the form of a contribution to sales graph (sometimes referred to as a profit-volume graph)

c. to explain your graph to management, to comment on the results shown and to state the breakeven point;

d. to describe breifly three ways in which the overall contribution to sales ratio could be improved.

(CIMA Cost Accounting)

Exercises and examination questions without answers

Exercises

B21.1 The following data relate to three products of a company with fixed costs of £60,000 per period.

Product	W	V	U
Unit selling price	£8	£12	£30
Unit marginal cost	£6.50	£6.50	£14
Sales volume (units)	20,000	5,000	1,000

You are required to draw a multi-product profit chart using the above data.

B21.2 A firm makes a single product with a marginal cost of £3.50 and a selling price of £5.50. Fixed costs are £30,000 per period.

You are required to calculate:

a. The C/S ratio

b. Sales at break even point

c. Number of units to break even

d. Sales to achieve a profit of £10,000

B21.3 A firm wishes to achieve a return on its capital of £500,000 of between 5% and 10%. The single product in the last period achieved a profit of £6 per unit when sales were 5,000 units at £40 each and Variable costs were £20 per unit.

a. How many units will need to be sold to achieve 5% return?, 10% return?

b. What is the firm's break even point?

c. What is the margin of safety (in units) if last periods sales were 95% of normal sales?

B21.4 A firm has a single product which sells at £4 per litre. Its results for the last two periods were:

	£	£
Sales	220,000	240,000
Total Costs	165,000	172,500
Profit	£55,000	£67,500

Calculate:

a. Sales at break-even.

b. Number of litres to break-even.

c. The margin of safety given that the budgeted sales are £230,000.

Examination questions

B21.5 The following information is extracted from the budgets of two manufacturing companies:

	Company A	Company B
	£'000s	£'000s
Sales	800	1,200
Manufacturing Costs:		
Materials	200	420
Direct labour	80	180
Fixed Factory Expenses	120	60
Variable Factory Expenses	20	120
Fixed Administration Costs	80	60
Variable Administration Costs	40	120
Fixed Selling Costs	120	60
Variable Selling Costs	60	120
Total Cost	720	1,140
Profit	80	60

Using the information stated above:

a. Prepare a contribution sales graph for each company.

b. Compare and comment on significant conclusions which can be derived from the graphs.

c. Explain the possible effects for each company of a 25% reduction in the availability of materials used, clearly stating any assumptions made.

(CIPFA, Management Accounting)

B21.6 A company located in London acts as a distributor for a range of specialist products that it sells to retailers throughout the United Kingdom.

The products vary considerably, and orders from retailers consist typically of a mixture of the products in the range. All despatches are made to retailers by hired road transport.

Hitherto the company has sent goods to retailers without charging for delivery, but due to increases in carriage costs it now proposes to place a bottom limit on free delivery orders. The limit proposed is £20 per order.

Data on the company's products are as follows:

Product	Selling price	Direct cost	Per pack Weight
	£	£	kilograms
A	1.50	0.75	1.0
B	7.50	5.50	6.0
C	6.50	4.20	13.5
D	15.00	8.50	12.0
E	16.00	11.60	16.0
F	4.50	3.50	4.0
G	3.50	3.00	5.0

Carriage costs per delivery, for an average distance of 150 miles, are:

Weight kilograms	Cost
	£
10 or less	1.3
over 10 but not above 15	1.5
over 15 but not above 20	1.8
over 20 but not above 25	2.0
over 25 but not above 30	2.2
over 30 but not above 35	2.4
over 35 but not above 40	2.7
over 40 but not above 45	2.9

The company is considering making all sales to retailers in the North (200 or more miles from London) through a sub-distributor who has his own sales force. The company would make bulk deliveries fortnightly to the sub-distributor, but would continue to collect payment of accounts from retailers.

You are required to:

a. show the percentage contribution to sales for each product and rank them in descending order;

b. calculate to one decimal place, the profits that would result from each of seven free delivery orders (for an average distance of 150 miles), the first being for £20's worth of product A, the second for £20's worth of B, the third for £20's worth of C, and so on through to the seventh order for £20's worth of G; (NB: Assume that packs can be split to make a £20 order).

c. state for which products £20 would be a suitable limit for free delivery if the company's criterion is that carriage costs (for an average distance of 150 miles) should not exceed one-third of the contribution provided by that product;

d. List the cost that the company would need to consider if it wished to decide what commission it could afford to pay to the sub-distributor in the North.

(CIMA, Cost Accounting 2)

B21.7 IS Limited produces an industrial solvent by means of a process through which various ingredients are mixed and changed in form, the output being in containers of 50-litre volume which have a selling price of £15 per container.

The input ingredients cost £10 per 50-litre container; wages, which are regarded as fixed costs amount to £2,000 per week. The production rate is 60 containers per hour; theoretical production time 40 hours per week. For some time plant breakdowns have results in a loss of ten hours per week on average and the production manager has suggested that preventive maintenance would reduce this idle time and the consequent lost production. Two alternatives have been suggested, viz.:

a. to have preventive maintenance carried out by a team of engineers working in the evenings, the cost being £800 per week which it is expected would reduce breakdown time to 20% of its current level;

b. to contract out the preventive maintenance to a firm which would carry out the work on Sunday mornings for a weekly fee of £300. A saving of half the breakdown time could be expected to result from this arrangement.

You are required to:

i. prepare a statement which would assist management to decide whether to continue as at present or to adopt one or other of the two alternatives suggested;

ii. state any other considerations management would probably have in mind in making its decision.

(ACCA, Costing)

B21.8 a. Define and illustrate by means of simple arithmetical examples:

i. contribution/sales ratio

ii. margin of safety

b. Demonstrate the relationship between a firm's contribution/sales ratio, its percentage margin of safety, and its profit/sales ratio.

c. What is the significance of a firm's margin of safety?

d. The following details relate to product X

	£	£
Selling Price		120
Costs:		
Material	60	
Labour	15	
Variable Overhead	5	
Fixed Overhead	10	
		90
Profit		£30

During the forthcoming year it is expected that material costs will increase by 10%, wages by $33\frac{1}{3}$% and other costs by 20%.

You are required to calculate the percentage increase in the selling price of X which would maintain the firm's contribution/sales ratio.

(ACCA, Costing)

B21.9 B Ltd is investigating the likely sales prospects for next year. The projection is that. 75,000 units will be sold at £10.60 each. Variable costs are £4.20 per unit and the relevant fixed costs, £220,000.

Three possible alternatives have been suggested. The managing director thinks that more could be sold if the price was reduced by 5%. The production manager thinks that the price could be increased by 10% with only a small loss in sales The sales manager proposes that the Variable cost should be increased by 20p per unit as commission to the sales force, with a consequent saving in fixed costs of £15,000.

You are required:

a. to calculate the levels of sales required under the first two proposals to maintain the projected profit at its original level before the proposals were considered;

b. to show the break even point if the sales manager's proposal was accepted, and to compare this with the break even point before the proposals were considered.

(AAT, Cost Accounting and Budgeting)

B21.10 a. Identify and discuss briefly five assumptions underlying cost-volume-profit analysis.

b. A local authority, whose area includes a holiday resort situated on the east coast, operates, for 30 weeks each year, a holiday home which is let to visiting parties of children in care from other authorities. The children are accompanied by their own house mothers who supervise them throughout their holiday. From six to fifteen guests are accepted on terms of £100 per person per week. No differential charges exist for adults and children.

Weekly costs incurred by the host authority are:

	£ per guest
Food	25
Electricity for heating and cooking	3
Domestic (laundry, cleaning etc) expenses	5
Use of minibus	10

Seasonal staff supervise and carry out the necessary duties at the home at a cost of £11,000 for the 30-week period. This provides staffing sufficient for six to ten guests per week but if eleven or more guests are to be accommodated, additional staff at a total cost of £200 per week are engaged for the whole of the 30-week period.

Rent, including rates for the property, is £4,000 per annum and the garden of the home is maintained by the council's recreation department which charges a nominal fee of £1,000 per annum.

You are required to:

i. tabulate the appropriate figures in such a way as to show the breakeven point(s) and to comment on your figures;

ii. draw, on the graph paper provided, a chart to illustrate your answer to b) i. above.

(CIMA, Cost Accounting)

B21.11 a. Distinguish between 'opportunity cost' and 'out of pocket cost' giving a numerical example of each using your own figures to support your answer.

b. Jason travels to work by train to his 5-day week job. Instead of buying daily tickets he finds it cheaper to buy a quarterly season ticket which costs £188 for 13 weeks.

Debbie, an acquaintance, who also makes the same journey, suggests that they both travel in Jason's car and offers to give him £120 each quarter towards his car expenses. Except for weekend travelling and using it for local college attendance near his home on three evenings each week to study for his CIMA Stage 2, the car remains in Jason's garage.

Jason estimates that using his car for work would involve him, each quarter in the following expenses:

	£
Depreciation (proportion of annual figure)	200
Petrol and oil	128
Tyres and miscellaneous	52

You are required to state whether Jason should accept Debbie's offer and to draft a statement to show clearly the monetary effect of your conclusion.

c. A company with a financial year 1 September to 31 August prepared a sales budget which resulted in the following cost structure:

		% of sales
Direct materials		32
Direct wages		18
Production overhead:	variable	6
	fixed	24
Adminmistrative and selling costs:	variable	3
	fixed	7
Profit		10

After ten weeks, however, it became obvious that the sales budget was too optimistic and it has now been estimated that because of a reduction in sales volume, for the full year, sales will total £2,560,000 which is only 80% of the previously budgeted figure.

You are required to present a statement for management showing the amended sales and cost structure in £s and percentages, in a marginal format.

(CIMA Cost Accounting)

B21.12 The production manager of your organisation has approached you for some costing advice upon project X, a one-off order from overseas that he intends to tender for. The costs associated with the project are as follows:

	£
Material A	4,000
Material B	8,000
Direct labour	6,000
Supervision	2,000
Overheads	12,000
	32,000

You ascertain the following:

i. Material A is in stock and the above was the cost. There is now no other use for Material A, other than the above project, within the factory and it would cost £1,750 to dispose of. Material B would have to be ordered at the cost shown above.

ii. Direct labour costs of £6,000 relates to workers that will be transferred to this project from another project. Extra labour will need to be recruited to the other project at a cost of £7,000.

iii. Supervision costs have been charged to the project on the basis of $33\frac{1}{3}$% of labour costs and will be carried out by existing staff within their normal duties.

iv. Overheads have been charged to the project at the rate of 200% on direct labour.

v. The company is currently operating at a point above break-even.

vi. The project will need the utilisation of machinary that will have no other use to the company after the project has finished. The machinary will have to be purchased at a cost of £10,000 and then disposed of for £5,250 at the end of the project.

The production manager tells you that the oversaes customer is prepared to pay up to a maximum of £30,000 for the project and a competitor is prepared to accept the order at that price. He also informs you the minimum that he can charge is £40,000 as the above costs show £32,000 and this does not take into consideration the cost of the machine and profit to be taken on the project.

Required:

a. Cost the project for the production manager clearly stating how you have arrived at your figures and giving reasons for the exclusion of other figures.

b. Write a report to the production manager stating whether the organisation should go ahead with the tender for the project, the reasons why and the price, bearing in mind that the competitor is prepared to undertake the project for £30,000.

Note: The project should only be undertaken if it shows a profit.

c. State four non-monetary factors that should be taken into account before tendering for this project.

d. What would be your advice if you were told that the organisation was operating below break-even point? Give reasons for your advice.

(AAT Cost Accounting & Budgeting)

B21.13 A company markets a range of products, which are sold through agents on a commission basis. Selling costs comprise the commision which is paid at 10% of selling price. The company is considering the introduction of its own sales force to replace the selling of products via agents.

Estimates of sales and costs (excluding selling costs) per period have been made three different levels of activity as follows:

	Low £000	Medium £000	High £000
Sales	600	700	800
Manufacturing costs	350	380	410
Administration costs	160	160	160

Sales and costs (excluding selling costs) are expected to be unaffected by the decision regarding method of selling. If the company's own sales force is introduced, selling costs per period would be expected to total £60,000.

Required:

i. Calculate the break-even point per period if selling via agents is continued.

ii. Calculate the break-even point per period if the company introduces its own sales force.

Note that for (i) and (ii) above you do not have to provide a break-even chart.

iii. Advise management on the decision regarding method of selling.

(ACCA Cost and Management Accounting 1, part question)

B21.14 a. The owners of a chain of retail petrol filling stations are considering opening an additional station. Initially one grade of petrol only would be sold and the normal selling price would be £0.44 per litre. Variable charges – cost of petrol, delivery and Excise Duty – total £0.40 per litre.

The fixed costs for a 4- week period are estimated to be:

	£
Rent	2,000
Rates on business premises	1,000
Wages – 5 people on shifts	3,000
Wage-related costs	400
Electricity for continuous opening (24-hour)	300
Other fixed costs	110

After establishing the site for petrol, it is intended at a later stage to develop on the same site a 'motorists' shop' selling the numerous small sundry items often required by motorists. There would be no increase in staff and one cash till only would be operated.

Throughout this question, Value Added Tax is ignored.

You are required

i. to calculate the breakeven point in number of litres and also in £s for a four-week period if

    (I)   the above costs applied,

    (II)   the rent was increased by 75%,

    (III) the rent remained at £2,000 but commission of £0.002 was given to the employees as a group bonus for every litre sold,

    (IV) the selling price was reduced to £0.43 and no commission was paid(with the rent at £2,000);

ii. to state how many litres would need to be sold per four-week period at £0.44 if costs were as in the original data (that is, with rent at £2,000) to achieve a profit or £700 per week;

iii. to advise the management about the following proposal, assuming sales for a four week period at a price of £0.44 per litre are normally

    (I)   275.000 litres, and

    (II)   425,000 litres.

The possibility of operating from 07.00 to 23.00 hours is being considered. The total savings for a four-week period on the original data would be £120 for electricity and one night-shift person paid £200 per week (wage related costs £25 per week) would no longer be required.

Sales would, however, reduce by 50,000 litres over a four-week period.

iv. to explain what would be required of the accounting system if the 'motorists' shop' idea was proceeded with.

b. Explain briefly what you understand by the terms 'contribution to sales ratio' and 'margin of safety', illustrating your answer with a diagram or graph (which is not expected to be on graph paper).

(CIMA Cost Accounting)

22: Capital investment appraisal*

1. Topics covered in this chapter:

1.	Long-run decision making
2.	Accounting Rate of Return and Payback
3.	Discounted Cash Flow (DCF)
4.	Net Present Value (NPV)
5.	Internal Rate of Return (IRR)
6.	Cost of Capital
7.	Risk and Uncertainty
8.	Post-Audit of investment decisions.

2. Long run decision making

The last two chapters have been concerned with decision making in the short run, but capital expenditure decisions are decisions where a longer term view must be taken. There are a number of similarities between short-run and long-run decision making; for example, the choice between alternatives, the need to consider *future* costs and revenues, the importance of incremental changes in costs and revenues and the irrelevance of sunk costs but there is the additional requirement for investment decisions that, because of the time scale and amount of money involved, the *time value of money* must be considered. In addition, because of the long term nature of the investments the treatment of uncertainty and inflation becomes of even greater importance than when considering short run decisions.

3. Investment decisions and the accountant

Capital expenditure decision making is invariably a top management exercise. This is because of the scale and long term nature of the consequences of such decisions. Typically a major capital investment decision, for example, launching a new product, buying a subsidiary or new factory or similar venture, will be the subject of months or even years of investigation and analysis before the final decision is made.

The accountant's task is to gather the essential data from various sources (marketing, engineering, production etc,) from both within and external to the organisation, consider the financing and taxation implications, analyse the data using one or more of the appraisal techniques and present the decision maker with the results of the analysis so that the decision maker will be able to take a more informed decision.

No method or technique of investment appraisal is a panacea. All decision making relates to the future where uncertainties abound; there may be material shortages, new competitors and products may arise, there may be strikes, changes in tastes, wars or floods – the list is endless. This means that overly sophisticated appraisal methods and pedantic, decimal point accuracy in the results presented probably serve little purpose.

It must be remembered that the accountant does not take the investment decision nor does he provide all the basic information. He performs an essential role in collating and analysing the data and presenting the results to the decision maker.

4. The decision to invest

Assuming that finance is available the decision to invest will be based on three main factors.

a. The investor's beliefs about the future. Surveys have consistently shown that confidence in the future is a more important influence than such factors as marginal taxation and interest rates.

---

* This chapter provides a simple introduction to the topic. It is covered in more detail in 'Management Accounting' by T. Lucey, DP Publications.

b. The alternatives available in which to invest. The various techniques covered in the rest of this chapter help to decide whether *any* of the alternatives being considered are worthwhile and, if so, which of the competing investment opportunities is the most favourable.

c. The investor's attitude to risk. The potential return from investment is conventionally expected to be proportional to the risk involved. The risk associated with individual projects and with combinations of projects and the decision makers attitude to risk are all key factors in investment decisions.

Numerous investment appraisal techniques are available to assist with investment decisions but, however sophisticated, they have the common characteristics that they *compare* the *returns expected* with the *investment* required.

The techniques covered in this manual are the two 'traditional' techniques of Accounting Rate of Return and the Payback method and the two most common Discounted Cash Flow (DCF) techniques, Net Present Value and Internal Rate of Return.

5. Accounting rate of return (ARR)

This can be defined as the ratio of average profits, after depreciation, to the capital invested. This is a basic definition only and various interpretations are possible ie,

a. Profits may be before or after tax.

b. Capital invested may be the initial capital invested or the average capital invested over the life of the project

$$\text{ie. } \frac{\text{Initial investment}}{2}$$

c. Capital may or may not include working capital.

Example 1

A firm is considering three projects each with an initial investment of £2,500 and a life of 5 years. The estimated profits are as follows:

After Tax and Depreciation Profits

Year	Project A £	Project B £	Project C £
1	250	500	100
2	250	450	100
3	250	100	100
4	250	100	450
5	250	100	500
	1,250	1,250	1,250

Calculate the ARR based on:

a. Initial capital invested.

b. Average capital invested.

Solution

	Project A	*Project B*	*Project C*
Average profits	$\dfrac{£1,250}{5}$	$\dfrac{£1,250}{5}$	$\dfrac{£1,250}{5}$
	= £250 pa.	= £250 pa.	= £250 pa.

∴ ARR (based on initial capital of £2,500)

$$= \frac{250}{2,500} = 10\% \qquad = \frac{250}{2,500} = 10\% \qquad = \frac{250}{2,500} = 10\%$$

ARR (based on average capital of £1,250)

$$= \frac{250}{1,250} = 20\% \qquad = \frac{250}{1,250} = 20\% \qquad = \frac{250}{1,250} = 20\%$$

6. Advantages and disadvantages of ARR

The only advantage that can be claimed for ARR is simplicity of calculation but the disadvantages are more numerous. Disadvantages:

a. Ignores the timings of outflows and inflows. The three projects in Example1 are ranked equally yet there are clear differences in the timings involved.

b. Uses a measure of return the concept of accounting profit. Profit has subjective elements, is subject to accounting conventions and is not as appropriate for investment decision making as the cash flows generated by the project.

c. There is no universally accepted method of calculating ARR.

Note: Alternative names for the ARR are; Return on Capital Employed and Return on Investment.

7. Payback

This is commonly used technique which can be defined as:

'The time it takes the cash inflows from a capital investment to equal the cash outflows, usually expressed in years'. *Terminology*.

The usual decision rule is to accept the project with the shortest payback period.

Example 2

Calculate the payback period for each of the following three projects.

Years	Project A Annual Cash Flow	Project A Cumulative Cash Flow	Project B Annual Cash Flow	Project B Cumulative Cash Flow	Project C Annual Cash Flow	Project C Cumulative Cash Flow
0	–2,000	–2,000	–2,000	–2,000	–2,000	–2,000
1	+800	–1,200	+500	–1,500	+600	–1,400
2	+700	–500	+700	–800	+700	–700
3	+500	Nil	+800	Nil	+500	–200
4	–		–		+200	Nil
5	–		–		+300	+300
6	–		–		+500	+800

Payback periods   Project A = 3 years

Project B = 3 years

Project C = 4 years

Note:

The usual investment appraisal assumptions are adopted for the above table and all subsequent examples; that Year 0 means now, Year 1 means at the end of one year, Year 2 the end of two years and so on and that a negative sign represents a cash outflow and a positive sign represents a cash inflow.

8. Advantages & disadvantages of payback

Advantages:

a. Simple to understand and calculate.

b. Is more objectively based because it uses project cash flows rather than accounting profits.

c. Favours quick return projects which may produce faster growth for the firm and enhance liquidity.

d. Choosing projects which payback quickest will tend to minimise time related risks. However not all risks are related merely to time elapsed.

Disadvantages:

a. Payback is a rough measure of liquidity not overall project worth. In Example 2, Project C is ranked after Project A and B even though it produces cash flows over a six year period.

b. Payback provides only a crude measure of the timing of project cash flows. In Example 2, Project A and B are ranked equally even though there are clear differences in the timings of cash flows.

Various surveys have shown that Payback, either used by itself or in conjunction with some other technique, is the most popular appraisal technique so it is important that its strengths and weaknesses are fully understood by the student.

9. Discounted cash flow (DCF)

All DCF measures use *cash flows* and make due allowance for the *time value of money*. These two features are expanded below:

Use of cash flows

All DCF methods use cash flows and not accounting profits. Accounting profits are invariably calculated for stewardship purposes and are period orientated thus necessitating accrual accounting with its conventions and assumptions.

For investment appraisal purposes a project orientated approach using cash flows is preferred because it is more objective and the accounting conventions regarding such matters as revenue/capital expenditure and stock valuation become largely redundant. The cash flows to be included are the *net after tax incremental cash flow effect* of the project ie, the difference in cash flow between having and not having the project.

Time value of money

There is general acceptance that any serious attempt at investment appraisal must make due allowance for the time value of money. Money has a time productivity ie, money received earlier can be put to use, for example, it can be invested to earn interest. This means that sums arising at different times cannot be compared directly, they must be reduced to equivalent values at some common date. The common date may be at any time but discounting methods typically use *now*, ie, the present time, as the common date.

The two main DCF methods of Net Present Value (NPV) and Internal Rate of Return (IRR) are described below.

10. Net present value

The NPV is the value in present day terms of the various cash inflows and outflows expected to arise at differing periods in the future.

To find the NPV it is necessary first to calculate or estimate a discounting rate which is known as the *cost of capital*. The calculation of the cost of capital is a complex process but for the stage of studies with which we are concerned the cost of capital is normally provided.

The formula for NPV is as follows:

$$NPV = \sum \frac{C_i}{(1+r)^i}$$

where C is the cash flow (+ or –).

   i is the period number.

   r is the cost of capital.

The discount factor $\frac{1}{(1+r)^i}$ can be found using a calculator but it is normal to use discount tables (see Table A). The Table shows the discount factors for discount rates ranging from 1% to 30% and for periods (usually years) from 1 to 25. For example, the discount factors for 10% for the first five years are:

0.909, 0.826, 0.751, 0.683 and 0.621

Example 3

The following cash flows have been estimated for a project:

Year	0	1	2	3	4	5
	–2,000	+ 400	+ 600	+ 700	+ 600	+ 500

It is required to calculate the project NPV and state whether the project is acceptable assuming that the cost of capital is either,

    a.   10% or

    b.   20%.

Solution

a. NPV when cost of capital is 10%

$$NPV = -£2,000 + (400 \times 0.909) + (600 \times 0.826) + (700 \times 0.751) + (600 \times 0.683) + (500 \times 0.621)$$

$$= + £105.$$

As the project NPV is *positive* at the cost of capital the project is *acceptable* (given the assumptions inherent in the basic NPV model)

b. NPV when cost of capital is 20%

$$NPV = -£2,000 + (400 \times 0.833) + (600 \times 0.694) + (700 \times 0.579) + (600 \times 0.482) + (500 \times 0.402)$$

$$= - £355.$$

As the NPV is *negative* at the cost of capital the project is *unacceptable* (given the usual DCF assumptions)

Notes:

a. The capital investment of –£2,000 at year 0 does not need discounting because it is already in present day terms.

b. It will be seen that the *higher the discounting rate the lower the NPV*. In this case the higher rate (20%) makes the project unacceptable.

c. The present value of a project, if positive, can be interpreted as the potential increase in consumption made possible by the project, valued in present day terms.

11. Internal rate of return (IRR)

The IRR can be defined as the discount rate which gives zero NPV. If the answers to Example 3 are studied it will be seen that they range from a positive NPV at 10% to a negative NPV at 20%. It follows that at some discount rate between the two the NPV will be zero, ie,

Discount rate	10%	? %	20%
NPV	+105	0	–355

The value of the IRR can be found graphically or more normally, by linear interpolation thus:

$$IRR = \underset{(a)}{10\%} + \underset{(b)}{10\%} \underset{(d)}{\left(\frac{105}{460}\right)}^{(c)} = 12.3\%$$

where

a. is the discount rate which gives a positive NPV (ie, 10% in this example)

b. is the difference between the discount rates chosen to give positive and negative NPV's (ie, 20% – 10% in this example)

c. is the value of positive NPV (£105 in this example)

d. is the range of NPV values (from + 105 to – 355 ie, a range of 460 in this example).

The IRR is used to determine whether the project is acceptable or not by comparing the calculated IRR with the cost of capital. Thus in Example 3, where two possible costs of capital were considered, the comparison is as follows:

Project IRR 12.3%

☐ When cost of capital is 10 %, the project is *acceptable* because IRR of 12.3% is *greater than* the cost of capital.

☐ When cost of capital is 20%, the project is *not acceptable* because IRR of 12.3% is *less than* the cost of capital.

Notes:

a. It will be seen that both NPV and IRR give the same accept or reject decision. For most projects this is always the case but note that the *ranking* of a group of projects may differ using NPV as opposed to IRR.

b. For normal decision making purposes it is sufficient to calculate either NPV or IRR and base the decision on the chosen criterion.

c. Although NPV has certain technical advantages over IRR, IRR is more commonly used in practice.

12. Cost of capital

The cost of capital is the name given to the discount rate used in NPV calculations and for the rate against which the calculated IRR is compared. In many examination questions the cost of capital is supplied but, on occasion, it is necessary to make an estimate of its value. There are various ways of making this estimate. One frequently used method produces what is known as the *Weighted Average Cost of Capital* (WACC).

The WACC recognises that companies are complex entities and that they are funded from a number of sources. The WACC is found by calculating the average of the costs of each component of the firms finances eg equity, preference shares, debentures and so on. The average is found by weighting the various sources by their proportionate share of the total pool of capital available.

Example 4

Multi-Source Ltd. has the following long-term sources of capital

☐ 8 million £1 Ordinary Shares with a market value of £1.80 per share and an estimated cost of 18%.

☐ 3 million £1 Preference Shares with a market value of 80p and an estimated cost of 12%.

☐ £10 million of Debenture Stock with a market value of £90 per £100 nominal value and an estimated cost of 7%.

Calculate the WACC

Solution

Component	Market Value		Proportion	Individual cost	Weighted cost		
		£					
Ord Shares	8m × £1.8 =	14.4m	56%	18%	0.56 × 18%	=	10.08%
Pref. Shares	3m × 80p =	2.4m	9%	12%	0.09 × 12%	=	1.08%
Debentures	10m × 0.9 =	9m	35%	7%	0.35 × 7%	=	2.45%
Total		25.8m	100%				13.61%

∴ The weighted average cost of capital = 13.61%. It is likely that this would be rounded up to 14% for discounting use.

Notes:

a. The proportions are based on market values not nominal values.

b. Further coverage of WACC and other methods of calculating the Cost of Capital is given in 'Management Accounting by T. Lucey, DP Publications.

13. Risk and uncertainty in investment appraisal

As pointed out earlier in the chapter it is important to make some form of appraisal of the risk and uncertainty associated with a project as well as the basic NPV or IRR calculation. This is so that the decision maker is provided with more information about a critical aspect of the project. It can be positively misleading to produce just a single NPV value or IRR percentage when many of the factors involved in the project (eg, the sales volume and price, labour rates, material prices and so on) are subject to uncertainty. There are many approaches to the problems of assessing risk and uncertainty in project appraisal and two simple approaches (payback and sensitivity analysis) are outlined below. More sophisticated methods are discussed in detail in 'Management Accounting' Ibid.

14. Payback as a measure of risk

Payback has already been described in Para. 7 as a possible way of appraising whether or not to accept a project. The technique can also be used in conjunction with NPV or IRR, to provide a simple measure of the risk associated with a project. For example if two projects both had an NPV of approximately £10,000 but one had a payback period of $4\frac{1}{2}$ years and the other 6 years, the former project would be preferred.

Used in this way Payback can provide some assistance in assessing time related risks but obviously factors other than elapsed time influence risk.

15. Sensitivity analysis

This is a technique which, although simple in principle, requires numerous calculations. It is a practical way of showing the effects of uncertainty by varying the values of key factors (eg, sales price, sales volume, rates of inflation, cost per unit) *one at a time* and showing the effect of the variation on the project outcome. The objective is to identify which of the factors affects the outcome the most.

For example, assume that a project (using single value estimates) has a positive NPV of £50,000 with a 15% cost of capital. Once this basic value of NPV has been obtained, the sensitivity analysis is carried out by flexing, both upwards and downwards, each of the project factors in turn. Part of the sensitivity analysis is given below relating to two of the project elements; sales price per unit and cost per unit.

Sensitivity Analysis Abstract

Basic NPV Value £50,000

A Element to be varied	B Alteration from basic value	C Revised NPV	D Increase /Decrease	E Percentage change	F Sensitivity Factor $\frac{E}{B}$
Sales price	+15	90,000	40,000	+80%	5.33
(Basic value	+10%	65,000	15,000	+30%	3
£10 per unit)	−10%	32,000	−18,000	−36%	3.6
	−20%	18,000	−32,000	−64%	3.2
Cost per unit	+20%	−21,000	−71,000	−142%	7.1
(Basic value	+10%	15,000	−35,000	−70%	7
£5.5 per unit)	−10%	76,000	+26,000	+52%	5.2
	−20%	94,000	+44,000	+88%	4.4

Sensitivity analysis is a useful way of identifying the most sensitive variables but it gives no indication of the likelihood of a given variation occurring and the process of flexing one factor at a time and holding others constant is almost certainly an unrealistic representation of reality where multiple and interacting changes occur.

16. Post audit of investment decisions and appraisals

The various approaches to investment appraisal covered in this chapter are aids to the process of investment decision making and naturally take place before the actual investment decision.

Useful information can also be obtained from carrying out a post audit review after the investment decision has been taken and the project initiated. It is usual to carry out such a post audit during the life of a project and at its conclusion. Most value will be obtained when, like all forms of audit, the investment post audit is carried out by different people to those involved in the original appraisal and decision.

The objectives of the post audit are to derive information which will improve future appraisal and forecasting methods, refine the decision process and to develop and extend good practices revealed by the post audit whilst, hopefully, eliminating poor practice. The objective is NOT to be negative and to attach blame to individuals for judgements and decisions honestly made which turn out to be incorrect.

The various factors covered in a typical post audit include:

a. Comparison of forecast and actual results for each of the project elements ie, sales price, volume, costs, inflation and so on.

b. Review of the forecasting methods used to assess their accuracy and appropriateness.

c. Review of the sources of information used for the appraisal.

d. Review of the appraisal and analysis carried out. For example, was Payback or DCF used in an appropriate manner? Was any form of risk analysis employed?

e. Review of the unforeseen factors which arose. Could these have been foreseen by a more rigorous appraisal?

f. Review of the decision process. Was the decision reasonable in the light of the evidence available at the time? Could the decision process be improved?

17. Extensions of basic investment appraisal

The contents of this chapter are merely a simple introduction to a field which is a specialisation in its own right. More advanced investment appraisal includes such matters as; dealing with inflation, the problem of combinations of projects, capital rationing, the factors governing the choice of the cost of capital and many other problems. Many of the more advanced aspects are covered in 'Management Accounting' Ibid.

18. Summary

a. There are similarities between short run and long run decision making but the time value of money must be considered in long run decision making.

b. The accountant's role in investment appraisal is to collate data, consider the financing and taxation implications, analyse the data and present the information to the decision maker.

c. The decision to invest is based on the investor's beliefs in the future, the alternatives available and the decision maker's attitude to risk.

d. The Accounting Rate of Return (ARR) is the ratio of average profits, after depreciation, to the capital invested.

e. Payback is the period, usually in years, in which it takes for the project's cash flows to recoup the original investment.

f. Discounted Cash Flow (DCF) techniques are based on cash flows, not profits, and take due allowance for the time value of money.

g. Net Present Value (NPV) is a DCF technique which calculates the value in present day terms of the cash inflows and outflows. If the NPV is positive at the company's cost of capital the project is acceptable.

h. Internal Rate of Return (IRR) is the discount rate which gives zero NPV. If the calculated IRR is greater than the cost of capital the project is acceptable.

i. The Weighted Average Cost of Capital is the weighted cost of the individual sources of capital.

j. Risk and uncertainty are ever present in project appraisals and the decision maker should be provided with information about expected project risk.

k. Two simple ways of assessing risk and uncertainty are Payback and Sensitivity Analysis.

l. A post audit review is a useful way of improving forecasting, appraisal and decision methods.

19. Points to note

a. It will be apparent that a critical factor in investment appraisal is the quality of forecasting.

b. Arguably of more importance than the particular method of appraisal is the existence of a stream of profitable investment opportunities. These do not automatically arise – they have to be sought out and developed.

c. Regular cash flows commonly occur, for example, lease and rent payments and a short cut discounting method is possible using Present Value Annuity Factors, Table B.

For example, assume that there is a regular cash flow of £500 p.a. for 3 years and it is required to calculate the present value when the discounting rate is 10%. This could be calculated by multiplying the yearly cash flows by the separate discount factors from Table A ie,

$$£(500 \times .909) + (500 \times .826) + (500 \times .751) = £1243$$

or alternatively the annuity factor can be found from Table B for 3 years at 10% ie, 2.487.

$$\therefore \text{ Present value} = £500 \times 2.487 = £1243$$

Student Self-Testing

Self Review Questions

1. What is the additional factor to be considered in long run decision making? (2)
2. What is the accountant's role in investment appraisal? (3)
3. What are the main factors involved in the decision to invest? (4)
4. Define the ARR. What variations are possible? (5)
5. What are the drawbacks of ARR? (6)
6. What is Payback and what is the normal decision rule when Payback is used? (7)
7. What are the advantages and disadvantages of Payback? (8)
8. What are the key features of all DCF methods? (9)
9. What is NPV and how is it calculated? (10)
10. Define IRR and describe how it is calculated. (11)
11. What is the decision rule using IRR? (11)
12. What is the WACC? (12)
13. Why is it important to consider risk and uncertainty in investment appraisal? (13)
14. How can Payback be used as a measure of risk? (14)
15. What is the purpose of sensitivity analysis and how is it carried out? (15)
16. What are the objectives of a post-audit and what factors would be covered in such an audit? (16)

Exercises and examination questions with answers

Exercises

A22.1 The cash flows for two projects are given below:

	Project X	Project Y
Year 0	− 5,000	− 8,000
1	+ 2,500	+ 1,500
2	+ 1,000	+ 2,000
3	+ 1,000	+ 2,500
4	+ 500	+ 1,000
5	+ 1,500	+ 1,000
6	+ 1,000	+ 2,500

Calculate the Payback period for the above projects and their NPV assuming that the cost of capital is 12%.

A22.2 Find the Internal Rates of Return of the projects in Exercise 1 using graphical methods.

A23.3 A firm with a cost of capital of 10% has estimated that it will have to pay its Sales Manager the following amounts of commission at the end of each of the next 5 years:

Year	1	2	3	4	5
	£4000	£2000	£8000	£3000	£10,000

The Sales Manager would prefer to receive a regular amount at the end of each year. Calculate this amount.

Examination questions

A22.4 Information relating to a proposed investment project 1 whose initial cost is £80,000, is as follows:

Year	Profit (loss)
	£
1	35,000
2	30,000
3	25,000
4	(10,000)
5	5,000

Included in the annual figures of profit and loss is a depreciation charge which is based on the assumption that at the end of five years the projea would be terminated, with £8,000 scrap value.

Required:

Calculate the payback period in years to 1 decimal place.

(AAT, Cost Accounting & Budgeting) part question

A22.5 a. With reference to the authorisation and control of capital expenditure, briefly explain what you understand by the following:
   i.   capital expenditure proposal;
   ii. capital expenditure authorisation;
   iii. post audit review.

b. The management of a laundry is considering whether to purchase a new piece of equipment which would cost £200,000.

40,000 items are expected to be laundered in each of the 5 years of the equipment's life.

The expected revenue from each item laundered is £4, and expected operating costs are £2.

General fixed overheads will be assigned to the equipment each year as follows:

Depreciation – £40,000

General fixed overheads – £80,000, based on 100% of operating costs.

Required:

   i. Calculate the payback period for the equipment.
   ii. Calculate the net present value for the equipment.

Note: The management expect that the cost of capital will remain constant at 20% p.a.

	Discount factor
Year 1	0.833
Year 2	0.694
Year 3	0.579
Year 4	0.482
Year 5	0.402

   iii. If the number of units to be laundered each year was to be increased by 10%, calculate the percentage increase in net present value.

(AAT, Cost Accounting & Budgeting)

A22.6 A company has called upon you for advice. It has a capital investment budget for the year of £300,000 and there are 4 projects in which they are keen to invest over the coming year. However they can only invest in one project. They intend using the proceeds of a 12% debenture issue to fund the project investement. If any of the funds are not used they can be invested at 12%.

The company has no system for investment appraisal and called in a Management Consultant for guidance and recieved the following from him.

Project	Cost of Project	Payback period	Accounting Rate of Return	Net Present Value	Internal Rate of Return
	£			£	
A	300,000	1.5 yrs	30%	190,000	17%
B	300,000	2.0 yrs	40%	270,000	23%
C	300,000	3.0 yrs	50%	240,000	21%
D	300,000	2.5 yrs	20%	(10,000)	11%

Unfortunately the Management Consultant did not explain the above.

Required:

a. Explain to the company the mechanics of each investment appraisal method and how it is applied.

b. After your explanation the Sales Director says the company should invest in Project A as costs are recovered the quickest. The Production Director says that the company should invest in Project C as it gives the best results in terms of return. The Personnel Director says the company should invest in Project B as that gives the highest discounted present value and internal rate of return. The Managing director wants you to resolve the problem.

Required:

Advise the Managing Director as to which proposal you agree with, outlining the reasons for your decision and the reasons why you have rejected the other two proposals.

c. The board of the company are unclear why you are using the 12% rate associated with the debentures in your calculations for two of the methods outlined in (a) above. They maintain that the raising of finance has nothing to do with the investment of that finance.

Required:

Set out the reasons as to why the 12% figure has been used in your calculations in (a) above and identify which investment appraisal methods have used it.

d. It is conceivable that the risk attached to the projects will increase before the investment is undertaken. In these circumstances the main objective of the company would be to keep the risk in the project investment to a minimum.

Required:

Outline how this will change your answer to B) above, if at all, giving explanations for your decision.

e. The circumstances might arise that the company has funds to unvest in all projects.

Required:

A reasoned analysis as to whether investment in all projects should be undertaken.

(AAT Cost Accounting & Budgeting)

A22.7 a. Your organisation has no system for authorising and controlling capital expenditure. The Managing Director has asked you, as Cost Accountant, to review the situation.

Required:

Draft a memorandum to your Board of Directors detailing an scheme for capital expenditure authorisation and control, briefly explaining each stage in your system.

b. The following information relates to two possible capital projects of which you have to select one to invest in. Both projects have an initial capital cost of £200,000 and only one can be undertaken.

Project	X	Y
Expected profits	£	£
Year 1	80,000	30,000
2	80,000	50,000
3	40,000	90,000
4	20,000	120,000
Estimated resale value at the end of Year 4	40,000	40,000

i. Profit is calculated after deducting straight line depreciation.

ii. The cost of capital is 16%.

iii. Relevant discount factors are:

End of Year		
1	0.862	
2	0.743	
3	0.641	
4	0.552	
5	0.476	

Required:

For both projects calculate the following:

    i.   The pay back period to one decimal place.

    ii. The accounting rate of return using average investement.

    iii. The net present value.

c. Advise the board which project in your opinion should be undertaken, giving reasons for yopur decision.

d. The board have looked at your proposal and you have been asked to clarify a number of issues:

    i.   What is meant by the term 'cost of capital' and why is it important in coming to an investment decision?

    ii. State two ways in which risk can be taken into account when making a capital investment decision.

(AAT Cost Accounting & Budgeting)

Exercises and examination questions without answers

Exercises

B22.1 Calculate the NPV of the following two projects assuming that the cost of capital is 10%.

	Project A	Project B
Year 0	–10,000	–15,000
Year 1	+4,000	+7,500
Year 2	+2,000	+3,500
Year 3	+1,500	+4,000
Year 4	+2,500	+2,000
Year 5	+3,000	+4,00

B22.2 Calculate the IRR's of the projects in Exercise 1 arithmetically using linear interpolation.

B22.3 A project has a cash outflow now of – £8,000 and one inflow after 5 years. The company's cost of capital is 20% and the NPV has been calculated at £5,000. What is the cash inflow?

B22.4 What is the IRR of the project in B22.3?

Examination questions

B22.5 A company is trying to decide which of two investment projects it should choose. The following information is provided:

	Project 1	Project 2
Capital Expenditure	£75,000	£75,000
Profit – Year 1	£30,000	£25,000
Profit – Year 2	£30,000	£15,000
Profit – Year 3	£20,000	£20,000
Profit (or Loss) Year 4	(£10,000)	£20,000
(Loss) – Year 5	(£10,000)	(£15,000)

Notes:

1. Each project is expected to be operational for 5 years, at the end of which time there is not expected to be any scrap value.

2. Capital expenditure for both projects would be incurred immediately.

3. The profit figures are shown after including depreciation on a straight-line basis.

4. Taxation is to be ignored.

5. The company's cost of capital is 15%.

6. The present value of £1 received at the end of:

Year 1:	0.869
Year 2:	0. 756
Year 3:	0.657
Year 4:	0.571
Year 5:	0.497
Year 6:	0.432

Required:

a. Calculate for each project:

    i.   the payback period in years to 1 decimal place;

    ii. the net present value.

b. State the relative merits of the methods of evaluation mentioned in a. above.

c. Explain which project you would recommend for acceptance.

(AAT, Cost Accounting & Budgeting)

B22.6   A company is proposing to enter a new market and has collected the following data:

Capital expenditure on plant and machinery to produce Product X will total £1,500,000 to be paid immediately. During the first year whilst the plant is being erected and machinery installed no production or sales of Product X is expected

Sales of Product X are expected to be 12,500 units each year from Year 2 to Year 5 inclusive. At the end of Year 5 the plant and machinery will be sold for scrap with cash receipts estimated at £100,000.

Data per unit of Product X:

	£
Selling price	80
Variable cost	30
Fixed overheads	30
Profit	20

Cost and revenue data are expected to remain constant throughout the project's life. The fixed overhead of £30 per unit is made up of Depreciation (£28) and general overhead (£2). The general overheads are the company's fixed costs which are allocated to each product on the basis of an absorption rate of 6.66% of unit Variable cost. There are no fixed costs which are specific to this project. The company's cost of capital is 20% p.a.:

Year	Discount factor
1	0.833
2	0.694
3	0.579
4	0.482
5	0.402

Required:

i. Calculate:

    a. the average accounting rate of return on average capital employed to 1 decimal place,

    b. the net present value.

ii. Discuss the relative merits of the accounting rate of return and net present value methods of investment appraisal, and explain whether you would undertake the project.

(AAT, Cost Accounting & Budgeting)

B22.7   Your company is considering investing in its own transport fleet. The present position is that carriage is contracted to an outside organisation. The life of the transport fleet would be five years, after which time the vehicles would have to be disposed of.

The cost to your company of using the outside organisation for its carriage needs is £250,000 for this year. This cost, it is projected, will rise 10% per annum over the life of the project. The initial cost of the transport fleet would be £750,000 and it is estimated that the following costs would be incurred over the next five years:

	Drivers' costs	Repairs & Maintenance	Other costs
	£	£	£
Year 1	33,000	8,000	130,000
Year 2	35,000	13,000	135,000
Year 3	36,000	15,000	140,000
Year 4	38,000	16,000	136,000
Year 5	40,000	18,000	142,000

Other costs include depreciation. It is projected that the fleet would be sold for £150,000 at the end of year 5. It has been agreed to depreciate the fleet on a straight line basis.

To raise funds for the project your company is proposing to raise a long-term loan at 12% interest rate per annum.

You are told that there is an alternative project that could be invested in using the funds raided, which has the following projected results:

Payback = 3 years

Accounting rate of return = 30%

Net present value = £140,000.

As funds are limited, investement can only be made in one project.

Note: The transport fleet would be purchased at the begining of the project and all other expenditure would be incurred at the end of each relevant year.

Required:

a. Prepare a table showing the net savings to be made by the firm over the life of the transport fleet project.

b. Calculate the following for the transport fleet project:

   i. Payback period

   ii Accounting rate of return

   iii. Net present value.

The discount factors for 12% are as follows:

Year	
1	0.893
2	0.797
3	0.712
4	0.636
5	0.567

c. Write a short report to the Investment Manager in your company outlining whether investment should be committed to the transport fleet or the alternative project outlined. Clearly state the reasons for your decision.

(AAT Cost Accounting & Budgeting)

B22.8   a. Explain why Net Present Value is considered technically superior to payback and accounting Rate of Return as an investment appraisal technique even though the latter are said to be easier to understand by management. Highlight the strenghts of the Net Present Value methods and the weaknesses of the other two methods.

   b. Your company has the opinion to invest in Projects T and R but finance is only available to invest in one of them.

You are given the following projected data:

Project	T	R
	£	£
Initial Cost	70,000	60,000
Profits: Year 1	15,000	20,000
Year 2	18,000	25,000
Year 3	20,000	(50,000)
Year 4	32,000	10,000
Year 5	18,000	3,000
Year 6		2,000

You are told:

1. All cash-flows take place at the end of the year apart from the original investment in the project which takes place at the beginning of the project.

2. Project T machinery is to be disposed of at the end of year 5 with a scrap value of £10,000.

3. Project R machinery is to be disposed of at the end of year 3 with a nil scrap value and replaced with new project machinery that will cost £75,000.

4. The cost of this additional machinery has been deducted in arriving at the profit projections for R for year 3. It is projected that it will last for three years and have a nil scrap value.

5. The company's policy is to depreciate its assets on a straight line basis.

6. The discount rate is to be used by the company is 14% and appropriate discount factors are:

Year 1	0.877
2	0.769
3	0.675
4	0.592
5	0.519
6	0.465

Required:

i. If investment was to be made in project R determine whether the machinery should be replaced at the end of year 3.

ii. Calculate for projects T and R, taking into consideration your decision in i) above:

   a. Payback period

   b. Net Present Value

   and advise which project should be invested in, stating your reasons.

   c. Explain what the discount rate of 14% represents and state two ways how it might have been arrived at.

(AAT Cost Accounting & Budgeting)

B22.9 A district health authority requires temporary accommodation for the training of a group of student nurses for a period of five years. The existing accommodation is both overcrowded and parts of it have been closed due to structural defects. The district estates manager has located three alternative sites which would be available namely:

i. Crystal House which can be rented at the following annual rentals:

Year	1	2	3	4	5
£	180,000	188,000	196,000	206,000	206,000

The scheme would have annual heating cost of £150,000 per annum. The agreement also requires £24,000 to be paid with the first rental payment to cover legal and agency costs.

ii. Maxwell Building which requires £200,000 to be paid at the commencement of a lease and with an annual rental of £170,000 per annum. The annual heating costs etc. are estimated at £140,000 per annum.

iii. The Arndale Complex which would require an annual rental of £190,000 for three years rising by £15,000 thereafter. The annual heating costs are £130,000 per annum. The agreement would also require that the complex was redecorated at the end of the lease period; this would cost an estimated £120,000.

As an accounting technician employed by the health authority you are required to:

a. Compare and comment upon the cost of the three alternatives, using a discounting technique, for the 5 year period. Unless otherwise stated you should assume that cash flows arise at the end of the year. The authority's notional cost of borrowing is 14% and you have been given the following information:

Year	14% Discounting Factor
1	0.877
2	0.769
3	0.675
4	0.592
5	0.519

b. Outline briefly any further information you would require before making a final decision between the three alternatives.

c. Explain what you understand by statement 'the time value of money' in relation to investment appraisal.

(AAT Public Sector Organisations & Financial Control)

23: Budgets

1. Topics covered in this chapter

1. Definition and benefits of budgeting
2. Budgetary planning and budgetary control
3. Fixed and flexible budgets
4. Behavioural aspects of budgeting
5. Cash budgeting
6. Zero-Based Budgeting
7. Activity-Based Budgeting.

2. What is a budget?

A budget is a quantitative expression of a plan of action prepared in advance of the period to which it relates. Budgets may be prepared for the business as a whole, for departments, for functions such as sales and production, or for financial and resource items such as cash, capital expenditure, manpower, purchases etc. The process of preparing and agreeing budgets is a means of translating the overall objectives of the organisation into detailed, feasible plans of action.

The formal definition is as follows: 'A plan expressed in money. It is prepared and approved prior to the budget period and may show income, expenditure, and the capital to be employed. It may be drawn up showing incremental effects on former budgeted or actual figures or be compiled by zero-based budgeting'. *Terminology.*

Zero-based budgeting, mentioned in the above definition, is an alternative method of establishing a budget and is described later in the chapter after the principles of budgeting have been covered.

3. Planning and control

The budgetary process is an integral part of both planning and control. Too often budgets are associated with negative, penny-pinching control activities whereas the full process is much broader and more positive than that. Budgeting is about making plans for the future, implementing those plans and monitoring activities to see whether they conform to the plan. To do this successfully requires full top management support, cooperative and motivated middle managers and staff, and well organised reporting systems.

4. The benefits of budgeting

The following benefits are those that can be derived from the full budgetary process. They do not accrue automatically, they have to be worked for. Indeed some organisations have systems of budgeting which are narrowly conceived and consequently they do not obtain the range of advantages which are possible. The benefits are dealt with under the following headings: planning and coordination, clarification of authority and responsibility, communication, control, motivation.

5. Planning and coordination

The formal process of budgeting works within the framework of long term, overall objectives to produce detailed operational plans for different sectors and facets of the organisation. Planning is the key to success in business and budgeting forces planning to take place. The budgeting process provides for the coordination of the activities and departments of the organisation so that each facet of the operation contributes towards the overall plan.

This is expressed in the form of a Master Budget which summarises all the supporting budgets. The budget process forces managers to think of the relationship of their function or department with others and how they contribute to the achievement of organisational objectives.

6. Clarification of authority and responsibility

The process of budgeting makes it necessary to clarify the responsibilities of each manager who has a budget. The adoption of a budget authorises the plans contained within it so that *management by exception* can be practised, i.e. a subordinate is given a clearly defined role with the authority to carry out the tasks assigned to him and when activities are not proceeding to plan, the variations are reopened to a higher level. Thus the full budgetary process is an excellent example of management by exception in action.

7. Communication

The budgetary process includes all levels of management. Accordingly it is an important avenue of communication between top and middle management regarding the firm's objectives and the practical problems of implementing these objectives and, when the budget is finalised, it communicates the agreed plans to all the staff involved. As well as vertical communication, the budgetary process requires communication between functions to ensure that coordination is achieved, for example, there must be full liaison between the sales and production functions to ensure that coordinated budgets are developed.

8. Control

This aspect of budgeting is the most well known and is the aspect most frequently encountered by the ordinary staff member. The process of comparing actual results with planned results and reporting on the variations, which is the principle of budgetary control, sets a control framework which helps expenditure to be kept within agreed limits. Deviations are noted so that corrective action can be taken.

9. Motivation

The involvement of lower and middle management with the preparation of budgets and the establishment of clear targets against which performance can be judged have been found to be motivating factors. However, there are many factors to be considered in relation to the human aspects of budgeting and these are dealt with in greater detail later in this chapter.

10. The budget period

Planning and therefore budgeting must be related to a specific period of time. The general process of budgeting breaks down long range plans and objectives prepared for, say, the next five years into shorter, operation periods invariably of one year. Typically these are subdivided into monthly periods for the purpose of monitoring and control.

Budgets can be prepared for any length of time and longer periods may be appropriate for particular types of budget. For example, a research and development budget may be prepared for the next three years because the long term nature of the activity makes yearly budgets less appropriate. Because of rapidly changing conditions many organisations review and modify their budgets on a rolling basis. Typically, each quarter or half year, budgets are reviewed for the following twelve months. This process is known as *continuous or rolling budgeting*.

11. Limiting factor or key factor or principal budget factor

It will be recalled from chapter 20 that the limiting factor is that factor which, at any given time, effectively limits the activities of an organisation. It may be customer demand, production capacity, shortage of labour, materials, space or finance. Because such a constraint will have a pervasive effect on all plans and budgets, the limiting factor must be identified and its effect on each of the budgets carefully considered during the budget preparation process.

Frequently the principal budget factor is customer demand i.e. the company is unable to sell all the output it can produce. The limiting factor can and does change—when one constraint is removed some other limitation will occur—otherwise, of course, the organisation could expand to infinity.

12. Profit centres and budget centres

It will be recalled that a cost centre is an identifiable function or part of the organisation for which costs can be identified. A profit centre is an extension of this idea on a larger scale, where not only costs are identifiable but also profits. The formal definition is; 'A part of a business accountable for costs and revenues. It may be called a *business centre, business unit*, or *strategic business unit*'. *Terminology.*

A budget centre is defined as: 'A section of an entity for which control may be exercised and budgets prepared'. *Terminology*. Thus it will be apparent that a budget centre may be a cost centre, or group of cost centres or it may coincide with a profit centre. Because of its size it is likely that a typical profit centre would consist of a number of budget centres each of which would contain either a single cost centre or a group of related cost centres.

Figure 23.1 is a simplified outline of the budget preparation process. For ease of illustration it is shown as a sequential series of steps but in practice the procedure is less straightforward. There is considerable discussion and consultation, additional information is requested, revisions are made, steps are repeated and so on.

Notes on Figure 23.1

1. The budget committee is given responsibility for the task of developing and coordinating budgets. The membership varies between organisations but usually comprises people from various functions of the company. The committee would be serviced by the budget officer, usually the accountant. His responsibility is to administer the budget when agreed and to provide technical assistance and data during the budget preparation. The budget planning process takes place prior to the budget period and where budgets are prepared on a rolling basis, budget planning is a regular, continuous activity.

2. An essential preliminary to making plans and budgets is to prepare forecasts. A forecast is a prediction of future events which are expected to happen, whereas a budget is a planned series of actions to achieve a given result. Invariably the primary forecast, from which much of the subsequent planning derives, is the sales forecast. Forecasting is a large and complex field frequently involving advanced statistical and mathematical techniques.

3. These steps comprise the bulk of the planning process. Coordination and communication between functions is essential to ensure interlocking, feasible budgets which accord to company policies and objectives. Many of these steps need to be repeated during the budget development as inconsistencies become apparent. The testing of one budget against another for feasibility and practicability is a key element in coordinating the budget process.

4. The Budget, comprising the individual departmental and functional budgets and the master budget, is submitted to the Chief Executive of the Board of Directors for examination and approval after any revisions thought necessary. When approved, the budget becomes an executive order and shows for each budget centre an approved plan of action together with an appropriate level of expenditure. (A budget centre is a section of the organisation so designated for budgetary purposes. It may be a cost centre, a group of cost centres or a department. It will be the responsibility of a designated person, the budget holder).

5. The agreed budgets are published and distributed to all the budget holders and budget centres. In this way budgets serve as a means of communicating plans and objectives downwards. In addition, that part of the budgetary process concerned with monitoring results, known as budgetary control, provides upward feedback on the progress made towards meeting plans.

6. These are the main stages in budgetary control. They take place after the actual events, usually on a monthly basis. Speedy production of budgetary control statements and immediate investigation of revealed variances provide the best basis for bringing operations into line with the plan or ,where there have been substantial changes in circumstances, making agreed alterations to the plan.

7. The investigations into the variances and their causes provides the link between budgetary control and budgetary planning. The experience of operations, levels of performance and difficulties are fed to the budget committee so that the planning process is continually refined.

13. The interrelationship of budgets

Figure 23.2 shows the major budgets and their interrelationships for a typical manufacturing concern. In practice there would be more budgets than those shown, there would in fact be a budget for each budget centre.

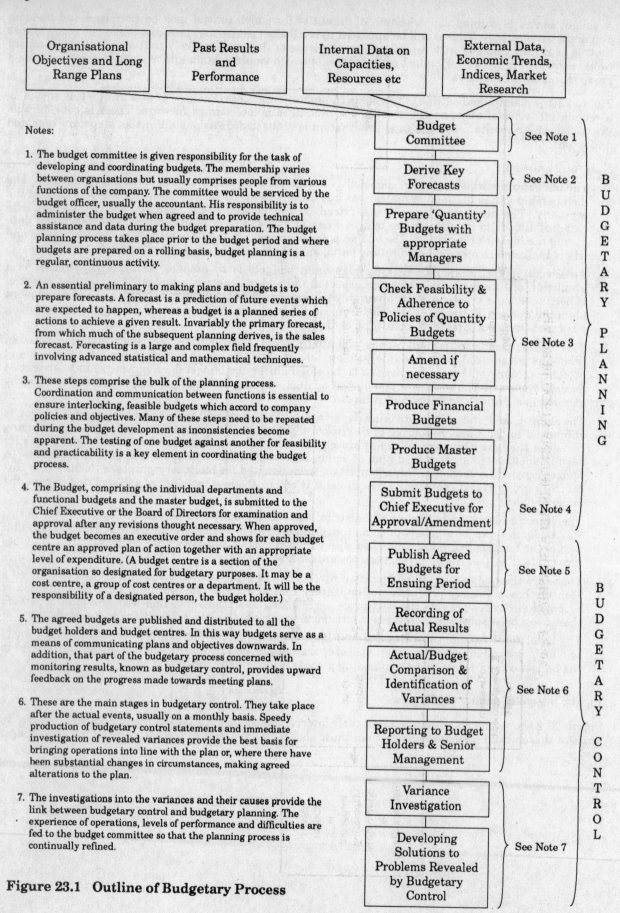

Notes:

1. The budget committee is given responsibility for the task of developing and coordinating budgets. The membership varies between organisations but usually comprises people from various functions of the company. The committee would be serviced by the budget officer, usually the accountant. His responsibility is to administer the budget when agreed and to provide technical assistance and data during the budget preparation. The budget planning process takes place prior to the budget period and where budgets are prepared on a rolling basis, budget planning is a regular, continuous activity.

2. An essential preliminary to making plans and budgets is to prepare forecasts. A forecast is a prediction of future events which are expected to happen, whereas a budget is a planned series of actions to achieve a given result. Invariably the primary forecast, from which much of the subsequent planning derives, is the sales forecast. Forecasting is a large and complex field frequently involving advanced statistical and mathematical techniques.

3. These steps comprise the bulk of the planning process. Coordination and communication between functions is essential to ensure interlocking, feasible budgets which accord to company policies and objectives. Many of these steps need to be repeated during the budget development as inconsistencies become apparent. The testing of one budget against another for feasibility and practicability is a key element in coordinating the budget process.

4. The Budget, comprising the individual departments and functional budgets and the master budget, is submitted to the Chief Executive or the Board of Directors for examination and approval after any revisions thought necessary. When approved, the budget becomes an executive order and shows for each budget centre an approved plan of action together with an appropriate level of expenditure. (A budget centre is a section of the organisation so designated for budgetary purposes. It may be a cost centre, a group of cost centres or a department. It will be the responsibility of a designated person, the budget holder.)

5. The agreed budgets are published and distributed to all the budget holders and budget centres. In this way budgets serve as a means of communicating plans and objectives downwards. In addition, that part of the budgetary process concerned with monitoring results, known as budgetary control, provides upward feedback on the progress made towards meeting plans.

6. These are the main stages in budgetary control. They take place after the actual events, usually on a monthly basis. Speedy production of budgetary control statements and immediate investigation of revealed variances provide the best basis for bringing operations into line with the plan or, where there have been substantial changes in circumstances, making agreed alterations to the plan.

7. The investigations into the variances and their causes provide the link between budgetary control and budgetary planning. The experience of operations, levels of performance and difficulties are fed to the budget committee so that the planning process is continually refined.

Figure 23.1   Outline of Budgetary Process

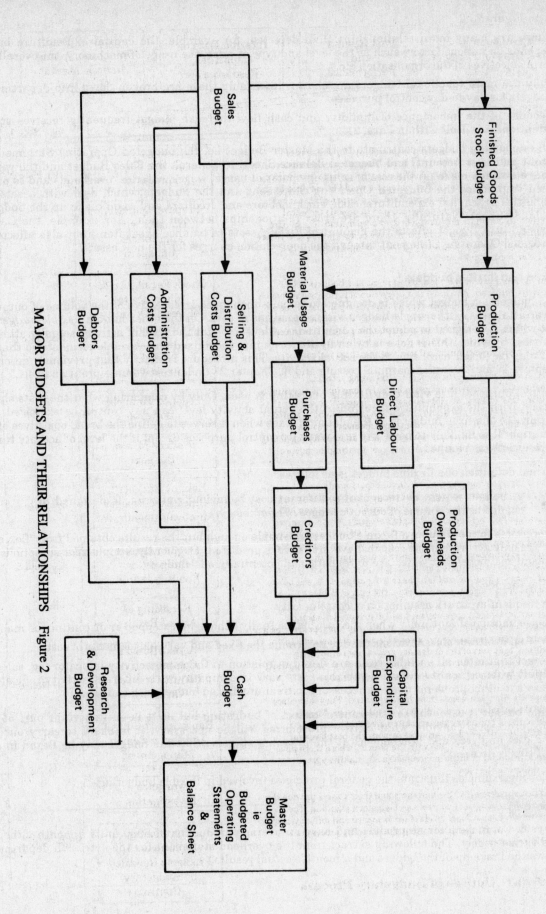

MAJOR BUDGETS AND THEIR RELATIONSHIPS   Figure 2

Notes on Figure 23.2:

a. There are many more relationships than depicted; for example, the capital expenditure budget depends on various factors such as the level and type of sales, the usage of machinery, the overall long term objectives of the organisation etc.

b. Only the main functional budgets are shown. Invariably these are broken down into departmental budgets for day-to-day control purposes.

c. Because of the importance of liquidity and cash flow the cash budget frequently receives special attention. It is dealt with in Para. 21.

d. All supporting budgets contribute to the Master Budget i.e. the budgeted Operating Statement (or Profit and Loss Account) and budgeted Balance Sheet. In general, the Sales Budget and the various budgets which make up the cost of sales eg, material usage, wages, salaries, overheads and so on are used to produce the budgeted Operating Statement and the budgets which deal with assets and liabilities eg, capital expenditure, cash, stock, debtors and creditors and so on make up the budgeted Balance Sheet. Naturally, there are cross relationships between them. For example, the Capital Expenditure Budget affects the amount of Fixed Assets (a balance sheet item) but also affects the budgeted Operating Statement through the depreciation charges for the new assets.

14. Fixed and flexible budgets

A fixed budget is a budget which is designed to remain unchanged irrespective of the volume of output or turnover attained i.e. it is single budget with no analysis of cost. On the other hand a *flexible budget* is a budget which is designed to adjust the permitted cost levels to suit the level of activity actually attained. The process by which this is done is by analysing costs into their fixed and variable elements so that the budget may be 'flexed' according to the actual activity. This procedure is exactly that previously described in Chapters 19 and 20 under marginal costing and in Chapter 21 under cost-volume-profit analysis.

For control purposes it is vital that flexible budgeting is used. Only by comparing what the costs should have been with the expenditure incurred at the actual activity level can any control be exercised. The major purpose of a fixed budget is at the planning stage when it serves to define the broad objectives of the organisation. It is unlikely to be of any real value for control purposes except if the level of activity turned out to be exactly as planned.

The formal definition of a flexible budget is as follows:

> 'A budget which, by recognising different cost behaviour patterns, is designed to change as the volume of output changes'. *Terminology*.

The procedures for developing a flexible budget are simple enough but the results obtained from 'flexing' a budget are only accurate if the costs behave in the ways predicted. Frequently, simplistic assumptions are made about cost behaviour which are unrealistic and potentially misleading.

Examples include

☐ the frequent arbitrary assumption of cost linearity

☐ the assumption of continuity when the cost may actually behave in a stepped or discontinuous manner

☐ the often arbitrary classifications used to determine the fixed and variable elements of costs

☐ the fact that often all variable costs are flexed in relation to the same activity indicator (eg, sales or output) when in reality different variable costs vary in sympathy with different activity indicators. These and other problems make it necessary to treat any flexed budget with caution.

A flexible budget is essential for the control aspect of budgeting but as it is an important part of the planning process to consider what control procedures will be necessary, it is usual to carry out the required cost analyses and breakdowns at the planning stage so that the budget may be flexed in due course if this is necessary.

The following examples illustrate the general principles involved in flexible budgeting.

Example 1

Ayres & Co. make a single product and have an average production of 5000 units a month although this varies widely. The following extract from the overhead statement for the extrusion department shows the make-up of the budget and a month's actual results.

	Budget for Average Production of 5000 Units	Actual Results for January Production 4650 Units
	£	£	£
Indirect Labour			
Fixed	3000		
Variable £1/Unit	5000	8,000	7,900
Consumables (all variable)		15,000	14,250
Variable overheads		20,000	18,200
Fixed overheads		12,500	12,500
		£55,500	£52,850

Show two budgetary control statements for January, one based on the fixed budget for 5000 units and one based on a flexible budget for the actual level of production.

Solution

Budgetary Control Statement 1
Fixed Budget c.f. Actual Results

Expense type	Fixed Budget	Actual results	Budget Variances Favourable (Adverse)
	£	£	£
Indirect Labour	8,000	7,900	100
Consumables	15,000	14,250	750
Variable overheads	20,000	18,200	1,800
Fixed overheads	12,500	12,500	–
	£55,500	£52,850	£2,650

Notes:

a. The variances are the differences between budget and actual. They are favourable when actual costs are BELOW budget and adverse when ABOVE.

b. When, as in this case, the activity level is different to that planned, the comparison of actual results with a fixed budget shows little or no useful information. We see that total costs are lower than budget, but so is the activity level. What is required is the appropriate *budgeted expenditure* for the *actual production level*. This is shown below.

Budgetary Control Statement 2
Flexed Budget c.f. Actual Results

Expense Type	Flexed Budget for 4650 Units	Actual Results	Budget Variances Favourable (Adverse)
	£	£	£
Indirect Labour £			
Fixed 3000 Variable £1 /Unit 4650	7,650	7,900	(250)
Consumables @ £3 Unit	13,950	14,250	(300)
Variable overheads @ £4/Unit	18,600	18,200	400
Fixed overheads	12,500	12,500	–
	£52,700	£52,850	£(150)

335

The values above in the Flexed Budget for 4650 units are calculated as follows:

Indirect Labour This comprises a fixed element (£3000) and a variable element at £1 per unit thus,

$$£3000 + 4650 \times £1 = £7650$$

Consumables These costs are wholly variable at the rate of £3 per unit thus,

$$4650 \times £3 = £13950$$

Variable Overheads As the name suggests, these are fully variable at the rate of £4 per unit, thus,

$$4650 \times £4 = £18600$$

Fixed Overheads These overheads remain the same regardless of changes in the level of activity and will thus be the same value as in the original budget ie, £12500.

Note:

The above example has a number of simplifying assumptions which, although not necessarily realistic, are widely used, especially in examination questions. These assumptions include;

a. All variable costs are deemed to vary in accordance with a single activity indicator, in this case production volume.

b. The variable costs are assumed to behave in a regular, linear way.

c. Fixed costs are deemed to remain unchanged.

The next example removes some of these assumptions and includes semi-variable and curvi-linear costs.

Example 2

After study of planned activities, forecast cost levels and the pattern of cost behaviour the following budget has been prepared based on an anticipated activity level of 8,000 labour hours.

Nature of expense	Budgeted Costs for 8,000 labour hrs.	Cost Classification	Cost Function (x = activity level)
	£		
Direct Wages	55,500	Linear semi-variable	£3,500 + 6.5x
Direct Materials	84,000	Linear variable	£10.5x
Salaries	22,000	Fixed	£22,000 + 0x
Depreciation	9,500	Fixed	£9,500 + 0x
Other overheads	19,200	Curvi-linear variable	£0.0003x²

Based on the above data it is required to prepare budgets for activity levels of 7,800 and 8,400 labour hours.

Solution

Expense	Cost Function	Budget for activity of 7,800 hrs.	Budget for activity of 8,400 hrs
		£	£
Direct Wages	£3,500 + 6.5x	54,200	58,100
Direct Materials	£10.5x	81,900	88,200
Salaries	£22,000 + 0x	22,000	22,000
Depreciation	£9,500 + 0x	9,500	9,500
Other overheads	£0.0003x²	18,252	21,168

The values in the flexed budgets for 7800 hours and 8400 hours are calculated by flexing or adjusting the expense according to the given cost functions thus,

Budgets for:	7800 hours			8400 hours		
Direct Wages (semi variable)	£3500 + 6.5 (7800)	=	£54,200	£3500 + 6.5 (8400)	=	£58,100
Direct Materials (fully variable)	£10.5 (7800)	=	£81,900	£10.5 (8400)	=	£88,200
Salaries (all fixed) ∴ no adjustment necessary		=	£22,000		=	£22,000
Depreciation (all fixed) ∴ no adjustment necessary		=	£9,500		=	£9,500
Other overheads (fully variable)	£0.0003² × 7800	=	£18,252	£0.0003² × 8400	=	£21,168

Notes:

a. Using a flexible budget the planned expenditure level for the actual activity can be compared with the actual expenditure so highlighting discrepancies.

b. A budget analysed to fixed and variable elements can be flexed to produce realistic budgeted expenditure for any given activity level, even where the activity changes month by month.

c. A word of caution. The expenditure levels obtained by flexing the budget are only as accurate as the initial analysis into fixed and variable elements. The difficulties inherent in that analysis have been dealt with in Chapter 18.

d. For control to be effective the actual expenditure must always be compared with a realistic budget allowance and care taken with the design of control reports.

15. Effective control reports

The budgetary control report is a major vehicle in the feedback process and to ensure maximum effectiveness it is important that its design, content, timing and general impact is given careful consideration. It is *actions* which produce benefits whilst information only produces costs. In consequence it follows that a budgetary control report which is ignored or misunderstood will not lead to effective actions and so will be useless.

The key items which should be shown are:

a. The budgeted level of costs and revenues for the period and year to date.

b. The actual level of costs and revenues for the period and year to date.

c. The variances between (a) and (b) together with the trends in variances.

d. An indication of what variances are significant together with, where possible, analysis and comment which can be used to bring the variances under control.

The recipients of budgetary control reports should be encouraged to make constructive criticisms of all aspects of the reporting procedure so that it is improved and made more effective.

A typical budgetary control report is shown in figure 23.3. It should be noted that the budgeted amounts would be the flexed budget allowances appropriate to the actual level of activity achieved.

Note: The problems of deciding what variances are significant are discussed in chapter 26.

16. Human aspects of budgeting

The behavioural aspects of budgeting are of supreme importance but, as with many aspects of human behaviour, they are complex, often contradictory and imperfectly understood. Considerable research has been carried out on this aspect of budgeting, but broad generalisations are difficult to make. On one point there does seem to be agreement.

That is, that budgeting is not considered by participants as a neutral, objective, purely technical process which is a view adopted by many accountants. The human, subjective aspects cannot be overemphasised and these are dealt with below under the following headings: goal congruence, participation, motivation, goal definition and communication.

```
┌─────────────────────────────────────────────────────────────────────────────┐
│                    BUDGETARY CONTROL REPORT NO                                │
│                                                                               │
│   BUDGET CENTRE _____      DATE PREPARED _____   │
│                                                                               │
│   BUDGET HOLDER _____        BUDGETED ACTIVITY LEVEL _____     │
│                                                                               │
│                          UP _____                                         │
│   REPORT RELATIONSHIP                 ACTUAL ACTIVITY LEVEL _____     │
│                          DOWN _____                                         │
│                                                                               │
│              ACCOUNTING PERIOD _____                                │
│                                                                               │
```

BUDGETED ITEM		CURRENT PERIOD			YEAR TO DATE			TREND OF VARIANCE	SIGNIFICANT? (Yes/No)	COMMENTS
CODE	DESCRIPTION	BUDGET	ACTUAL	VARIANCE	BUDGET	ACTUAL	VARIANCE			

Figure 23.3 Typical budgetary control report

17. Goal congruence

The ideal budgeting system is one which encourages goal congruence. This simply means that the goals of individuals and groups should coincide with the goals and objectives of the organisation as a whole. This is an ideal which is difficult to achieve completely but recognition must be given to the fact that organisational objectives cannot be imposed through the budgeting system without consideration of the influences of local group and departmental objectives.

There is growing evidence that authority imposed from above is less effective than authority accepted from below and that goal congruence is enhanced when there is a more participative management style rather than the traditional style of management with its emphasis on hierarchy and authority.

18. Participation

Budgets can be imposed by top management upon the budget holders or they may be evolved following participation of the budget holders in the budget preparation. Participation promotes common understanding regarding objectives and makes the acceptance of organisational goals by the individual much more likely. The control process is also assisted by participation of the budget holders into the investigation of solutions to the problems which arise. If people are genuinely involved they feel part of the team and become more highly motivated.

19. Motivation

The whole process of budget preparation and subsequent performance evaluation by budgetary control needs to be carried out so as to motivate managers rather than create resentment and adverse reactions. If the process is designed to be participative, encourages initiative and responsibility, is not seen merely as a pressure device, then the motivation of individuals will be strengthened. An emphasis on impossible targets, over emphasis on the short run, imperfectly set and understood objectives will cause motivation to be stifled.

Research has shown that motivation is increased when the reward-penalty system of the organisation is consistent with the organisational control systems of which budgetary control is a primary example. If the control system is seen to be unconnected to the reward-penalty system (ie, promotions, salary increases, bonuses, 'perks') then the control system will be perceived to be of little importance by the managers concerned and consequently it will be ignored and so, by inference, will the organisation's objectives.

20. Goal definition

In general, people work more efficiently when they have clearly defined targets and objectives. In a perfect world personal goals would coincide with organisational goals so that individual motivation would be at its highest and targets would be totally accepted and completely defined. Such an ideal is unattainable, but the importance of goal definition and of ensuring that individual aspirations and goals are considered is an important part of enlightened budget preparation. Clearly defined goals, agreed and accepted by the individuals concerned, will encourage goal congruence and increase motivation.

21. Communication

The process of communication, between and across the layers in the organisation, is an important factor in all planning and control systems. If any control system, including budgetary control, is not accepted by the people who have to operate it they will hamper and obstruct the flow of information so that realistic planning and control decisions will be difficult to take. Research has shown that frequent, up to date feedback of information to a manager regarding his performance has a motivating effect. Undue delay, inaccurate data, reports containing details of items over which the manager has no control, all reduce motivation and severely restrict the usefulness of the information system.

22. Cash budgets

A cash budget is one of the most important budgets prepared in an organisation. It shows, in summary form, the expected cash receipts and expected cash payments during the budget period. Liquidity and cash flow management are key factors in the successful operation of any organisation and it is with good reason that the cash budget should receive close attention from both accountants and managers.

The cash budget shows the effect of budgeted activities – selling, buying, paying wages, investing in capital equipment and so on – on the cash flow of the organisation. Cash budgeting is a continuous activity with budgets being rolled forward as time progresses. The budgets are usually subdivided into reasonably short periods – months or weeks.

Cash budgets are prepared in order to ensure that there will be just sufficient cash in hand to cope adequately with budgeted activities. The cash budget may show that there is likely to be a deficiency of cash in some future period – in which case overdraft or loans will have to be arranged or activities curtailed – or alternatively the budget may show that there is likely to be a cash surplus, in which case appropriate investment or use for the surplus can be planned rather than merely leaving the cash idle in a current account.

23. What is in a cash budget?

A cash budget must contain every type of cash inflow or receipt and every type of cash outflow or payment. In addition to the *amounts*, the *timings* of receipts and payments must also be forecast. Some examples of typical receipts and payments follow together with comments on the difficulties found in practice with the various items.

Typical receipts include: Cash Sales Receipts from debtors Sales of fixed assets Receipts of interest and dividends, Issues of new shares and loan stock. Any fees, royalties or other income, Receipts from loan repayments and so on.

Typical payments include: All payments to creditors for stock and material purchases. Wage, salary and bonus payments. Payments for overhead and expense items. Purchase of fixed assets, Payments of dividends, interest and taxation. Loan repayments and so on.

It is of the utmost importance to realise that cash receipts and payments are not the same as sales and the costs of sales found in the firm's Profit and Loss Account, because:

a. not all cash receipts affect profit and loss account income eg, the issue of new shares results in a cash inflow but would not be shown in the profit and loss account.

b. not all cash payments affect the costs shown in the profit and loss account eg, the purchase of a fixed asset or the payment of VAT.

c. some profit and loss items are derived from accounting conventions and are not cash flows eg, depreciation and the loss or profit on the sale of fixed assets.

d. the timing of cash receipts and payments does not coincide with the profit and loss accounting period eg, a sale is recognised in the profit and loss account when the invoice is raised yet the cash payment from the debtor may not be received until the following period or even later.

Although there are numerous items in a typical cash budget the major flows usually result from the following: cash receipts from debtors, payments to suppliers, payments for expense items and payments for (or receipts from) major non-trading items such as the purchase (or sales) of fixed assets and tax and dividend payments (or receipts). Some guidelines for these items are given below.

24. Guidelines for cash budget preparation

Establishing cash receipts from debtors:

a. Forecast the expected credit sales period by period, taking account of seasonal factors, promotions, sales trends and so on.

b. Forecast the typical payment pattern of debtors. This would usually be based on a detailed analysis of experience with the existing Sales Ledgers adjusted for any expected changes in the pattern.

c. Based on a, and b, calculate when the budgeted sales revenue will be received as cash, taking care to deduct any discounts allowed for prompt payment and making an appropriate allowance for bad debts.

d. Take care to allow for the cash receipts from the opening debtors.

Establishing cash payments to suppliers:

a. Based on the Production Quantities Budget, calculate the production quantities and material usage quantities, period by period.

b. Based on opening stock levels, the required closing stock levels and the production quantities from a. calculate the quantity and cost of material purchases, period by period.

c. Decide upon the length of credit period to be taken from suppliers and using b. calculate when the cash payments will be made to suppliers.

d. Take care to allow for the cash payments to the opening creditors.

Establishing payments for other expense items. (Note: These include, wages, salaries, bonuses, all types of overheads and so on.)

a. Forecasts of wages to be paid will, to some extent, depend on the Production Budget mentioned previously. Allow for any bonus payments, cost of living increases, holiday pay, the delay in settling PAYE and N.I. payments and so on.

b. Salaries can usually be forecast accurately but take care to allow for commissions, bonuses, part-time assistance and so on.

c. The amount and timing of many overhead items can often be forecast very accurately eg, Rates, Insurance, Electricity, Telephones etc. Take care to exclude any non-cash items which may be included in the general term 'overheads' eg, depreciation is a notional cost, and not a cash flow.

Payments and receipts of major non-trading items. These include:

a. Purchases or Sales of Fixed Assets. It is the amount and timing of the cash payment(s) or receipt(s) that is of importance for cash budgeting not the way the item is dealt with in the normal accounts. For example, the sale of a Fixed Asset for £5000 which has a written down value of £8000 will produce a notional loss in the normal accounts of £3000. In the cash budget it will, of course, be shown as a cash receipt of £5000 in the appropriate period.

b. Tax payments and dividends to be paid or received can usually be forecast accurately.

c. Similarly special transactions such as share issues, loan repayments and so on are usually known well in advance.

25. Format for cash budgets

The typical cash budget has the general form shown below.

Cash Budget	Period 1	Period 2	Period 3	etc.
Opening Cash Balance b/f	XXX	YYY	ZZZ	AAA
+ Receipts from Debtors				
+ Sales of Capital Items				
+ Any Loans Received				
+ Proceeds for Share Issues				
+ Any other Cash Receipts				
= Total Cash Available				
− Payments to Creditors				
− Cash Purchases				
− Wages and Salaries				
− Loan Repayments				
− Capital Expenditure				
− Dividends				
− Taxation				
− Any other cash Disbursements				
= Closing Cash Balance c/f	YYY	ZZZ	AAA	

Cash budgets are good examples of *rolling budgets* ie, where the process of continuous budgeting takes place whereby regularly each period (week, month, quarter as appropriate) a new future period is added to the budget whilst the earliest period is deleted. In this way the rolling budget is continually revised so as to reflect the most up to date position. The process of continuous budgeting could, of course, be carried out for any type of budget, not just cash budgets.

26. Cash budget example

The opening cash balance on 1st Jan was expected to be £30,000. The sales budgeted were as follows:

	£
November	80,000
December	90,000
January	75,000
February	75,000
March	80,000

Analysis of records shows that debtors settle according to the following pattern:

60% within the month of sale, 25% the month following, 15% the month following.

Extracts from the Purchases budget were as follows:

December	60,000
January	55,000
February	45,000
March	55,000

All purchases are on credit and past experience shows that 90% are settled in the month of purchase and the balance settled the month after.

Wages are £15,000 per month and overheads of £20,000 per month (including £5,000 depreciation) are settled monthly.

Taxation of £8,000 has to be settled in February and the company will receive settlement of an insurance claim of £25,000 in March.

Prepare a cash budget for January, February and March.

Solution

Workings

The receipts from sales are as follows:

	January Cash
November (15% × 80,000	£12,000
December (25% × 90,000)	22,500
January (60% × 75,000)	45,000
	£79,500

	February Cash
December (15% × 90,000)	£13,500
January (25% × 75,000)	18,750
February (60% × 75,000)	45,000
	£77,250

	March Cash
January (15% × 75,000)	£11,250
February (25% × 75,000)	18,750
March (60% × 80,000)	48,000
	£78,000

Payments for Purchases:

	January Cash
December (10% × 60,000)	£6,000
January (90% × 55,000)	49,500
	£55,500

	February Cash
January (10% × 55,000)	£5,500
February (90% × 45,000)	40,500
	£46,000

	March Cash
February (10% × 45,000)	£4,500
March (90% × 55,000)	49,500
	£54,000

Cash Budget

		January £	February £	March £
	Opening balance	30,000	24,000	17,250
	Receipts from sales	79,500	77,250	78,000
	Insurance claim			25,000
=	Total Cash Available	109,500	101,250	120,250
	Payments			
	Purchases	55,500	46,000	54,000
	Wages	15,000	15,000	15,000
	Overheads (less dep'n)	15,000	15,000	15,000
	Taxation		8,000	
=	Total Payments	85,500	84,000	84,000
	Closing balance c/f	24,000	17,250	36,250

27. Reconciliation of cash balance and profits

Organisations prepare both cash budgets and operating budgets which show the budgeted profits for each period. These two forms of statements are prepared on totally different bases; the cash budget on the practical, objective basis of measuring positive and negative cash flows whereas budgeted profits are based on the normal conventions of accounting. These include, for example, the accruals concept, the charging of cost which do not create a cash flow – eg, depreciation, the distinctions between capital and revenue expenditure and so on.

It is sometimes required to reconcile the budgeted cash and profit figures and the simplest approach to this is to use the Bank Reconciliation Statement approach and commence with one of the figures, say the budgeted cash balance, and then add or subtract the various elements in the budgets so as to agree with the figure of budgeted profit.

In practice there are innumerable items which cause differences between the two figures but the following examples include the major categories:

Sales/Purchases used in profit calculation whereas actual receipts from debtors and payments to creditors used in cash budgets.

Various items in cash budgets which do not appear in profit calculations, eg, capital expenditure, taxation and dividends, increases and decreases in loans, sales or fixed assets etc.

Notional cost items such as depreciation and imputed charges appear in profit statements but not in cash budgets.

Changes in credit policies and stock levels affect cash budgets but not profit statements.

Accruals and prepayments are normal features of profit statements but do not appear in cash budgets.

28. Commitment Accounting

One problem that managers have with conventional cash and expenditure budgeting is that they do not know what level of expenditure has been committed but not yet reflected in the financial information they are presented with. This is a problem in all types of organisations but is particularly acute in Public Sector organisations where they may be strict cash limits which cannot be exceeded.

One answer to this is to have a formal system of *commitment accounting* where the accounting system recognises a transaction and its impact on the budget, as soon as a contract or purchase or other financial commitment is entered into. If such a system was used the information available would be more up-to-date and more relevant thus helping budgetary control.

However whilst such a system has appeal there are some practical problems. These include;

1. Administrative problems caused by contracts and orders being amended and cancelled and the problems of year end accruals.
2. The difficulty of measuring the exact amount of the commitment in any periods as many orders and contracts are only estimates and deliveries are not always in accordance with the original order or contract.
3. The lack of security caused by numerous accesses to the financial information system.

Because of these and other problems a full system of commitment accounting would rarely be used. Instead many Public Sector organisations show commitments in memorandum form without making entries in the financial records.

29. Forecasting and budgets

It will be apparent from a study of the chapter so far that forecasting is an essential part of the budgeting process. Indeed it has been said with considerable truth that the budgetary process is more a test of forecasting skill than anything else.

To establish realistic budgets it is important to forecast a wide range of factors including; sales volume and prices, wage rates and earnings, material availabilities and prices, rates of inflation, the costs of bought in services, the cost of overhead items such as rates, electricity, telephones and many other such variables. It is not sufficient merely to add a percentage on to last year's budget and hope that this will produce a realistic result.

There is a wide range of forecasting techniques available ranging from simple linear regression analysis using least squares, through time series analysis, exponential smoothing systems, multiple regression analysis methods to specialised mathematical models such as Box Jenkins.

Some of the elements of forecasting have been covered in Chapter 18 but this is a vast and complex field and professional statistical and computer expertise should be sought to ensure that appropriate methods are employed. (Students requiring an introduction to quantitative and qualitative techniques of forecasting are recommended to read 'Quantitative Techniques', T. Lucey, D.P. Publications.)

30. The budget manual

As one of the objectives of budgeting is to improve communications it is important that a manual is produced so that everyone in the organisation can refer to the manual for guidance and information about the budgetary process. The budget manual does not contain the actual budgets for the ensuring period—it is more of an instructional/information manual about the way budgeting operates in the particular organisation and the reasons for having budgeting. Contents obviously vary from organisation to organisation but the following are examples of the information such a manual should contain.

Manual Contents

Foreword

☐ preferably by Chief Executive/Managing Director

Objectives/explanation of the budgetary process

☐ explanation of budgetary planning and control

☐ objectives of each stage of the budgetary process

☐ relationship to long term planning

Organisation Structures and responsibilities

☐ structure of the organisation showing titles, responsibilities and relationships

☐ titles and names of current budget holders

Main budgets and relationship

☐ outline of all main budgets and their accounting relationships

☐ explanation of key budgets (eg, Master Budget, Cash Budget, Sales Budget)

Budget development

☐ Budget committee, membership and terms of reference

☐ sequence of budget preparation

☐ timetable for budget preparation and publication.

Accounting procedures

☐ name and terms of reference of the budget officer (usually the accountant)

☐ coding lists

☐ sample forms

☐ timetable for accounting procedures, production of reports, closing dates.

31. Benefits and problems of budgeting

Properly planned and administered budgeting systems can bring benefits but these benefits do not automatically accrue; they have to be worked for. Problems can arise and intending accountants should have an awareness of the factors which could prevent the organisation gaining the maximum advantage from its budgeting system.

Typical benefits of budgeting:

a. It provides clear guidelines for managers and supervisions and is the major way in which organisational objectives are translated into specific tasks and objectives related to individual managers.

b. The budgetary process is an important method of communication and coordination both vertically and horizontally.

c. Because of the 'exception principle,' which is at the heart of budgetary control, management time can be saved and attention directed to areas of most concern.

d. The integration of budgets makes possible better cash and working capital management.

e. Better control of current operations is helped by regular, systematic monitoring and reporting of activities.

f. Provided there is proper participation, goal congruence is encouraged and motivation increased.

Typical problems which may arise with budgeting:

a. Variances are just as frequently due to changing circumstances and poor forecasting as due to managerial performance.

b. Budgets are developed round existing organisation structures which may be inappropriate for current conditions.

c.   The existence of well documented plans may cause inertia and lack of flexibility in adapting to change.

d.   Badly handled budgetary systems with undue pressure or lack of regard to behavioural factors may cause antagonism and may lower morale.

To overcome some of the problems of conventional budgeting systems and to make budgeting more effective various other approaches have been developed. Two of these; zero-based budgeting and activity-based budgeting are dealt with below.

32. Zero-based budgeting (ZBB)

ZBB is a cost-benefit approach whereby it is assumed that the cost allowance for an item is zero, and will remain so until the manager responsible justifies the existence of the cost item and the benefits the expenditure brings. In this way a questioning attitude is developed whereby each cost item and its level has to be justified in relation to the way it helps to meet objectives and how the expenditure benefits the organisation. This is a forward looking approach as opposed to the all too common method of extrapolating past activities and costs, which is a feature of the incremental budgeting approach.

ZBB is formally defined by the CIMA thus; 'A method of budgeting whereby all activities are re-evaluated each time a budget is formulated. Each functional budget starts with the assumption that the function does not exist and is at zero cost. Increments of cost are compared with increments of benefit, culminating in the planning maximum benefit for a given budgeted cost' *Terminology*.

The use of ZBB was pioneered by P Phyrr in the United States in the early 1970s and has gained wide acceptance probably because it is a simple idea obviously based on common-sense. ZBB is concerned with the evaluation of the costs and benefits of alternatives and, implicit in the technique, is the concept of opportunity cost.

33. Where can ZBB be applied?

ZBB can be applied in both profit seeking and non-profit seeking organisations. The technique gained wide publicity when the then President Carter directed that all US government departments adopt ZBB.

In a manufacturing firm, ZBB is best applied to service and support expenditure including; finance and accounting, production planning and so on. These activities are less easily quantifiable by conventional methods and are more discretionary in nature. Manufacturing costs such as direct materials and labour andproduction overheads can be more easily controlled by well established methods which compare production outputs with resource inputs rather than using ZBB.

ZBB can successfully be applied to service industries and to a wide range of non-profit seeking organisations. For example local and central government departments, educational establishments, hospitals and so on. ZBB could be applied in any organisation where alternative levels of provision for each activity are possible and the costs and benefits can be separately identified. ZBB is concerned with alternatives and means that established activities have to be compared with alternative uses of the same resources. ZBB takes away the implied right of existing activities to continue to receive resources, unless it can be shown that this is the best use of those resources.

34. Implementing ZBB

There are several formal stages involved in implementing a ZBB system but of greater importance is the development of an appropriate questioning attitude by all concerned. There must be a 'value for money' approach which challenges existing practices and expenditures and searching questions must be asked at each stage; typical of which are the following:

a.   Does the activity need to be carried out at all? What would be the effects, if any, if it ceased?

b.   How does the activity – existing or proposed – contribute to the organisation's objectives?

c.   What is the correct level of provision? Has too much or too little been provided in the past?

d.   What is the best way to provide the function? Have all alternative possibilities been considered?

e.   How much should the activity cost? Is this expenditure worth the benefits achieved?

f.   Is the activity essential or one of the frills?

and so on.

35. Stages in Implementing ZBB

The overall process of implementing a ZBB system can be sub-divided into three stages thus:

a. *Definition of decision packages*

A decision package is a comprehensive description of a facet of the organisation's activities or functions which can be individually evaluated. The decision package is specified by the managers concerned and must show details of the anticipated costs and results expected expressed in terms of tasks accomplished and benefits achieved.

Two types of decision package are possible:

❐ Mutually-exclusive decision packages

These are alternative forms of activity, tasks and expenditure to carry out the same job. The best option among the mutually exclusive packages is selected by comparing costs and benefits, and other packages are then discarded. Naturally, mutually exclusive packages would only be prepared when there are quite clearly different approaches for dealing with the same function.

As an example, an organisation with a distribution problem might consider two alternative decision packages: Package 1 might be an in-house fleet of lorries, whereas Package 2 could involve contracts with independent hauliers.

❐ Incremental decision packages

These packages reflect different levels of effort in dealing with a particular activity. There will be what is known as the *base package*, which represents the minimum feasible level of activity, and other packages which describe higher activity levels at given costs and resulting benefits.

As an example, a base package for a Personnel Department might provide for staff engagement and termination procedures and payroll administration. Incremental packages might include; education and training, welfare and social activities, pension administration, trade union liaison and negotiations etc. Each package would have its costs and benefits clearly tabulated.

b. *Packages are evaluated and ranked*

When the decision packages have been prepared, management will then rank all the packages on the basis of their benefits to the organisation. This is a process of allocating scarce resources between different activities, some of which already exist and others that are new.

Minimum requirements which are essential to get the job done and activities necessary to meet legal or safety obligations will naturally receive high priority. It will be found that the ranking process focuses management's attention on discretionary or optional activities.

Because of the large number of packages prepared throughout the organisation the ranking process can become onerous and time consuming for senior management. One way of reducing this problem is for lower level managers to rank the packages for their own budget centre and for these rankings to be consolidated, with others, at the next level up in the hierarchy. Alternatively, these could be ranked within the department and need not be referred higher.

c. *Resources allocated*

When the overall budgeted expenditure level is decided upon the packages would be accepted in the ranked priority sequence up to the agreed expenditure level.

Where the ranking of lower cost packages has been delegated to departments the proportion of the expenditure budget remaining after the more expensive packages have been ranked would be allocated to individual departments. The departments would then rank their own small packages up to their allocated expenditure level.

36. Advantages of ZBB

a. Properly carried out, it should result in a more efficient allocation of resources to activities and departments.

b. ZBB focuses attention on value for money and makes explicit the relationship between the input of resources and the output of benefits.

c. It develops a questioning attitude and makes it easier to identify inefficient, obsolete or less cost effective operations.

d. The ZBB process leads to greater staff and management knowledge of the operations and activities of the organisation and can increase motivation.

e. It is a systematic way of challenging the status quo and obliges the organisation to examine alternative activities and existing cost behaviour patterns and expenditure levels.

37. Disadvantages of ZBB

a. It is a time consuming process which can generate volumes of paperwork especially for the decision packages.

b. There is considerable management skill required in both drawing decision packages and for the ranking process. These skills may not exist in the organisation.

c. It may encourage the wrong impression that all decisions have to be made in the budget. Circumstances change and new opportunities and threats can arise at any time and organisations must be flexible enough to deal rapidly with these circumstances when they occur.

d. ZBB is not always acceptable to staff or management or trade unions who may prefer the cosy status quo and who see the detailed examination of alternatives, costs and benefits as a threat not a challenge.

e. There are considerable problems in ranking packages and there are inevitably many subjective judgements. Political pressures within organisations also contribute to the problem of ranking different types of activity, especially where there are qualitative rather than quantitative benefits.

f. It may emphasis short term benefits to the detriment of longer term ones which in the end may be more important.

Undoubtedly the major drawback to ZBB is the amount of time the system takes. One way of obtaining the benefits of ZBB is to apply it selectively on a rolling basis throughout the organisation. This year Marketing, next year, Personnel, the year after Research and Development and so on. In this way, over a period, all activities will receive a thorough scrutiny, the benefits of which should last for years.

ZBB is particularly appropriate for non-profit making organisations where quality of service is all important. These types of organisation do not necessarily apply all the detail of ZBB but try to follow its basic philosophy by undertaking reviews of base estimates rather than using the simple incremental approach. As an example, a survey by Skousen in 1990 found that 54% of UK local authorities claimed to challenge base estimates each year.

38. Activity based budgeting (ABB)

ABB, sometimes termed Activity Cost Management, is a planning and control system which seeks to support the objective of continuous improvement. It is a development of conventional budgeting systems and is based on activity analysis techniques. It will be recalled that these were described when Activity Based Costing (ABC) was covered previously. In outline this required the identification of the activities in *cost pools*.

ABB recognises that:

a. It is activities which drive costs and the aim is to control the causes (drivers) of costs directly rather than the costs themselves. In the long-run, costs will be managed and better understood.

b. Not all activities add value so it is essential to differentiate and examine activities for their value-adding potential.

c. The majority of activities in a department are driven by demands and decisions beyond the immediate control of the budget holder. Conventional budgets, expressed in financial terms against established cost headings, ignore this causal relationship.

d. More immediate and relevant performance measures are required than are found in conventional budgeting systems. These consist exclusively of traditional financial measures which are insufficient to fulfil the objectives of continuous improvement. Additional measures are required which should focus on the factors which drive activities, the quality of the activities undertaken, the responsiveness to change and so on.

It is claimed that ABB provides a link between the organisations strategic objectives and the objectives of individual activities.

39. Illustration of ABB

A Purchasing Department has two main activities; investigating and liasing with suppliers and issuing purchase orders. Two major cost drivers have been identified: the number of suppliers and the number of purchase orders placed.

The resources and costs of the department have largely been spread over the two main cost drivers. The balance of costs have been termed 'Department sustaining costs'. These include some general clerical costs and part of the manager's costs. Based on the activity expected for the period, cost driver volumes of 270 suppliers and 1,850 purchase orders have been forecast. Using these volumes and cost analysis, cost driver units and resource item costs have been budgeted for the department after discussion with the Departmental manager. The budget is as follows:

Budget for purchasing department

Cost drivers:	No of suppliers	No of purchase orders	Dept sustaining cost	Total
Cost	£	£	£	£
Management salaries	12,000	2,000	18,000	32,000
Clerical salaries	3,000	21,500	6,500	31,000
Space costs	1,000	14,500	2,000	17,500
Consumables, travelling etc	17,500	3,000	4,500	25,000
Information technology	3,000	8,500	1,000	12,500
Other costs	4,000	6,000	7,500	17,500
Total	40,5000	55,500	39,500	135,500
Activity volumes	270	1,850	–	–
Cost/unit of cost driver	**£150**	**£30**	**£39,500**	

Notes:

a. The apportionment of costs to activities will, of course, be partly subjective. The object however is that the resource has to be justified in supporting one or more of the activities or the sustaining function. There is no place to hide the costs.

b. ABB highlights the cost of activities and thus encourages new thinking.

c. ABB enables a more focused view of cost control because the activity level is taken into account. Trends can be monitored and comparison with other organisations can be made. This is known as *benchmarking*.

d. The cost driver rates £150 and £30 are used in calculating the product costs in the Activity Based Costing system.

e. The identification of activities and their costs helps to focus attention on those activities which add value and those that do not.

40. Possible problems with activity based analysis

An activity based approach may not be always suitable for month-to-month monitoring because of short-term fluctuations. If, for example, the number of purchase orders goes up by 20% in a month and resources stay the same the cost per order will decrease. However, if the increase in activity lasts long enough there is likely to be the need for more staff, overtime and so on. The inevitable variability in the cost per activity directs attention to whether resources are being used effectively and what levels may be required in the future.

There is also the need to guard against the notion that a selected cost driver provides a comprehensive basis for controlling costs. The cost levels of most activities behave in a more complex manner than can be explained by a single work load measure. Over-concentration on one performance measure can produce adverse consequences. In the Purchasing Department illustration above, the staff can decrease the cost per purchase order simply by splitting large orders into several smaller ones yet this could well have adverse longer-term effects.

41. Summary

a. A budget is a quantitative expression of a plan and the full budgetary process includes planning and control.

b. Budgeting can bring a number of real advantages including coordination, clarification of responsibility, improved communication, increased control and the motivation of personnel.

c. The limiting factor (or key factor or principal budget factor) is the factor which limits the activities of the organisation. Typical limiting factors include: sales, shortage of materials or production capacity or skilled labour, lack of finance etc.

d. The budget is prepared by the budget committee having regard to the organisation's objectives and is submitted to the Board of Directors or the Chief Executive for approval. When approved it becomes an executive order.

e. When the budget is approved it is issued so that the budgetary control process can be carried out when actual results are to hand. The investigation of variances and the development of solutions to problems discovered is the key to controlling expenditure.

f. A fixed budget is a budget for a single level of activity whereas a flexible budget, because of the analysis of costs into fixed and variable elements, can be adjusted or flexed for various activity levels.

g. The attitude of the people who have to operate the budgetary system is of critical importance. Budgets are frequently seen as pressure systems imposed by top management.

h. To avoid adverse reactions from the people involved there should be full and genuine participation, clear goal definition and good communications all of which will contribute to the budgetary process being a motivating rather than a disruptive force.

i. Zero-based budgeting means that each activity starts with a nil budget. Each increment of the budget has then to be justified in terms of costs related to the benefits achieved. The idea is to contain or reduce costs especially in public sector organisations. The idea is simple and appealing but the system is cumbersome and subject to political pressure.

j. Activity Based Budgeting or Activity Cost Management means budgeting is related to activities rather than conventional departments. ABB recognises that it is activities which cause costs and is a more focused method of budgeting.

42. Points to note

a. A master budget is the summary of all other budgets and is expressed as a Budgeted Profit and Loss account and Balance Sheet.

b. Too much attention is paid, particularly by accountants, to the mechanics of budgeting. Of far greater importance are the behavioural aspects, ie, is the process acceptable to those who have to operate it? Does it motivate them? Do they feel threatened by it?

c. Remember it is the quantities/volumes/units etc which are budgeted and the converted into financial terms as a common measure. Money figures are not directly budgeted.

d. Budgets can be used for both planning and for control. Frequently too much attention is paid to the control aspects of budgeting and the positive planning and coordinating activities of budgetary planning are not given the attention they deserve.

e. The problems of *budgetary slack* are frequently encountered. This is the term used to describe the way some managers obtain a budget larger than strictly necessary so that they either can spend more liberally up to the budget or appear to be containing costs very efficiently by beating their budget. An attempt to overcome this and other problems, particularly in public sector organisations, is the concept of zero-base budgeting.

   The zero base refers to the idea of starting with a nil budget to which is added an agreed budget allowance for each planned activity. In this way it is hoped that tighter limits will be set and that there should not be a perpetuation of past anomalies and inefficiencies which occur when the budget amount is arrived at by adding a percentage to last year's amount. Unfortunately experience suggests that such a concept has at least as many problems as other methods and has as many subjective elements and is just as susceptible to political pressure.

f. Budgeting and Budgetary control are dealt with in more detail in 'Management Accounting', T. Lucey, DP Publications.

Student self testing

Self Review Questions

1. What is a budget? (2)

2. What are the benefits to be gained from budgeting? (4)

3. How does the budgetary process assist communication? (7)

4. What is the budget period? (10)

5. What is the principal budget factor? (11)

6. Describe the major steps in the budget process. (12)

7. Distinguish between fixed and flexible budgets. (14)

8. Why are the behavioural aspects of budgeting so important? (16)

9. What is a Cash Budget and what does it contain? (22 & 23)

10. What is the format for a cash budget ? (25)

11. What is the Budget Manual? (30)

12. What are the benefits and problems associated with budgeting? (31)

13. Define and explain Zero-based Budgeting (ZBB). (32)

14. What are the objectives of ZBB? (34)

15. What are decision packages? (35)

16. What are the advantages and disadvantages of ZBB? (36 & 37)

17. What is Activity based budgeting ? (38)

Exercises and examination questions with answers

Exercises

A23.1 A company produces two domestic appliances, the Starfrig and Starfreezer. The following details have been estimated:

	Year 19-1
Sales	Starfrig 40,000 @ £75 each
	Starfreezer 80,000 @ £90 each

Total costs are estimated to be:

	£
Direct materials	2,400,000
Direct Labour	4,200,000
Variable Overheads	2,100,000
Fixed Overheads	800,000

Each Starfreezer requires the same material as a Starfrig but twice as much labour. Variable overheads are absorbed on direct labour. The demand for the Starfrig has been falling and a new model, the Starfrig II is to be introduced for 19-2 incorporating a freezer compartment which will sell at £115 each.

The estimated costs of the new model are (per unit) Direct Labour £46. Variable overheads £23 and Direct Materials £25. Because of the new model fixed overheads will increase by £200,000. Sales for 19-2 are forecasted to be: Starfreezer 80,000 units Starfrig 32,000 units Starfrig II 15,000 units

You are required to prepare budgeted profit statements for 19-1 and 19-2 showing the contribution from each model.

A23.2 A firm has produced the following budgets for two activity levels:

Expense	Budget for 5000 units £	Budget for 6000 units £
Wages	16,000	17,200
Materials	25,000	30,000
Salaries	22,500	23,000
Depreciation	18,000	18,000
Other Overheads	18,500	21,000

Prepare a budget for an activity level of 6,200 units.

A23.3 A company has a cash balance of £27,000 at the beginning of March and you are required to prepare a cash budget for March, April and May having regard to the following information.

Creditors give 1 month credit

Salaries are paid in the current month

Fixed costs are paid one month in arrears and include a charge for depreciation of £5,000 per month.

Credit sales are settled as follows: 40% in month of sale, 45 % in next month and 12 % in the following month. The balance represents bad debts.

Month	Cash Sales	Credit Sales	Purchases	Salaries	Fixed Overheads
	£	£	£	£	£
Jan		74,000	55,200	9,000	30,000
Feb		82,000	61,200	9,000	30,000
March	20,000	80,000	60,000	9,500	30,000
April	22,000	90,000	69,000	9,500	32,000
May	25,000	100,000	75,000	10,000	32,000

A23.4 a. Explain what you understand to be the objectives of budgetary control.

b. Write brief notes on TWO of the following:

  i. Budget manual;

  ii. budget committee;

  iii. master budget.

Examination questions

A23.5 On 1 January the summary Balance Sheet of CH Ltd, was as follows:

	£		£
Share capital	40,000	Machinery at cost	80,000
Reserves	20,000	less	
Loan 15%	40,000	Accum. depreciation	(19,200)
Proposed dividends	1,000	Stocks	24,200
Overdraft	9,000	Debtors	25,000
	110,000		110,000

The following are expected during the next three months:

	Sales	Purchases	Expenses
	£	£	£
January	150,000	100,000	20,000
February	200,000	150,000	25,000
March	300,000	280,000	30,000

All sales are on credit and the collections have the following pattern:

  During the month of sale   80% (a 4% discount is given for payment in this period)
  In the subsequent month   20%

Payment for purchase is made in the month of purchase in order to take advantage of a 10% prompt settlement discount, calculated on the gross purchase figures shown above. Stock levels are expected to remain constant throughout the period. Depreciation of machinery is calculated at a rate of 12% p.a. on cost. The appropriate portion for each month January – March is included in the expenses figures above. Expenses are paid for in the month in which they are incurred The proposed dividend will be paid in January. Loan interest for the three months will be paid in March.

Required:

  i. Prepare a cash budget for each of the three months January to March.

  ii. Prepare a forecast Trading Profit and Loss Account for the period.

  iii. Prepare a forecast Balance Sheet as at 31 March.

  iv. Briefly explain why the change in cash balance between 1 January and 31 March is not the same as the profit (or loss) figure for the period.

(AAT, Cost Accounting & Budgeting)

A23.6 Shown below are extracts from next year's budget for a company manufacturing two products using only one grade of direct labour.

		1st Quarter	2nd Quarter	3rd Quarter	4th Quarter
		Units	Units	Units	Units
Sales :	Product M	9,000	20,000	14,000	8,000
	Product N	10,000	16,500	11,000	7,000

Finished goods stocks have been provisionbally budgeted for each quarter end as follows:

Sales :	Product M	5,000	5,000	4,000	4,000
	Product N	4,000	4,000	2,000	2,000

The stock of finished goods at the beginning of the first quarter is expected to be 3,000 units of Product M and 1,000 units of Product N. Stocks of work-in-progress are not carried.

Inspection is the final operation for Product M and it is budgeted that 20% of production will be scrapped. Product N is not inspected and no rejects occur.

The company employs 210 direct operatives working a basic 40 hour week for 12 weeks in each quarter and the maximum overtime permitted is 12 hours per week for each operative. The company has an agreement with the union that operatives will not be made redundant, temporarily paid off, or any more recruited for the next two years.

The standard direct labour content of product M is 5 hours per unit and for product N 3 hours per unit. The budgeted productivity (or efficiency) ratio for the direct operatives is 90%.

It should be assumed that both products are profitable.

Required

a. Calculate the budgeted direct labour hours required in each quarter of next year and show the extent to which the direct labour hours available can meet these budgeted requirements.

b. i. Examine alternative courses of action which may minimise the shortfall or surplus of labour hours available and which also allows the company to achieve each quarters sales budget whenever possible. Where appropriate, calculations should be shown to support your analysis. Use only the information available in the question.

   ii. Assuming that the budgeted sales cannot be achieved in every quarter, explain how you could minimise the effect of the labour shortfall on the company's profits. Briefly comment upon any reservations you may have concerning your recommendations.

(ACCA, Costing)

A23.7 Forecasting is a crucial element in a budgetary control system.

You are required, in the context of a budgetary control system, to:

a. Discuss briefly the major problems in forecasting;

b. List and state the purpose of five techniques that can be used in forecasting.

(CIMA, Cost Accounting 2)

A23.8 The need for effective zero base budgeting... is increasingly apparent in both industry and government today, since all institutions must adapt to an environment in which the allocation of limited resources presents a constantly deepening challenge. (Peter Pyhrr)

You are required to:

a. discuss this statement in the context of the control of overhead;

b. describe the limitations of traditional budgetary control of overhead.

(CIMA, Cost Accounting 2)

A23.9 a. Exe plc. manufacturers one standard product and in common with other companies in the industry is suffering from the current depression in the market. Currently it is operating at a normal level of activity of 70% which represents an output of 6,300 units, but the sales director believes that a realistic forecast for the next budget period would be a level of activity of 50%.

	Level of activity		
	60%	*70%*	*80%*
Direct materials	37,800	44,100	50,400
Direct wages	16,200	18,900	21,600
Production overhead	37,600	41,200	44,800
Administration overhead	31,500	31,500	31,500
Selling and distribution overhead	42,300	44,100	45,900
Total cost	£165,400	£179,800	£194,200

Profit is 20% of selling price.

You are required, from the data given in the current flexible budget above, to prepare a budget based on a level of activity of 50%, which should show clearly the contribution which could be expected.

b. Discuss briefly three problems which may arise from such a change in level of activity.

(CIMA, Cost Accounting 2)

A23.10 A company is preparing budgets for the year ahead for two of its raw materials that are used in various products which it manufactures. Current year material usage standards are as follows:

Kilos per thousand units of product

	Product 1	*Product 2*	*Product 3*	*Product 4*	*Product 5*
Material A	25	70	15	–	55
Material B	30	5	–	20	–

It has been decided to change standards on Material B for the following year to reflect the favourable usage variances that are occuring for that material on all products. Usage variances on Material B are 10% of standard costs.

Budgeted sales quantities for the following year are:

	Product 1	*Product 2*	*Product 3*	*Product 4*	*Product 5*
(thousand units)	600	350	1850	1200	900

Production quantities are to be budgeted in line with sales, apart from Product 5 where an increase in stock of 30% is required by the end of the budget year. Stocks of the five products at the beginning of the budget year are expected to be:

	Product 1	*Product 2*	*Product 3*	*Product 4*	*Product 5*
(thousand units)	140	80	260	180	100

Stocks of Materials A and B at the end of the budget year are to be 10% of the year's budgeted usage. Stocks at the end of the current year are expected to be:

Material A	10,030 kilos
Material B	4,260 kilos

Required:

a. Describe the benefits that can be derived from a budgeting system.

b. Prepare material usage and purchases budgets (kilos only) for each of Materials A and B for the year ahead.

c. Prepare summary journal entries for the Material A stock account for the current periuod.

The following additional information is provided for the current period:

Material A purchases:

116,250 kilos at a cost of £280,160

(standard purchase price = £2.40 per kilo).

Production:	*Product 1*	*Product 2*	*Product 3*	*Product 4*	*Product 5*
(thousand units)	580	330	1900	1200	800

Material A usage has been at standard.

(ACCA Cost & Management Accounting 1)

A23.11 There is a continuing demand for three sub-assemblies – A, B, and C – made and sold by MW Limited. Sales are in the ratios of A 1, B 2, C 4 and selling prices are A £215, B £250, C £300.

Each sub-assembly consists of a copper frame onto which are fixed the same components but in differing quantities as follows:

Sub-assembly	Frame	Component D	Component E	Component F
A	1	5	1	4
B	1	1	7	5
C	1	3	5	1
Buying in costs per unit	£20	£8	£5	£3

Operation times by labour for each sub-assembly are:

Sub assembly	Skilled hours	Unskilled hours
A	2	2
B	$1\frac{1}{2}$	2
C	$1\frac{1}{2}$	3

The skilled labour is paid £6 per hour and the unskilled labour in an assembly department. A five-day week of $37\frac{1}{2}$ hours is worked and each accounting period is four weeks.

Variable overhead per sub-assembly is A £5, B £4 and C £3.50.

At the end of the current year, stocks are expected to be as shown below but because interest rates have increased and the company utilises a bank overdraft for working capital purposes, it is planned to effect a 10% reduction in all finished sub-assemblies and bought-in-stocks during Period 1 of the forthcoming year.

Forecast stocks at current year end:

Sub-assembly		Copper frames	1,000
A	300	Component D	4,000
B	700	Component E	10,000
C	1,600	Component F	4,000

Work-in-progress stocks are to be ignored.

Overhead for the forthcoming year is budgeted to be Production £728,000, Selling and Distribution £364,000 and Administration £338,000. These costs, all fixed, are expected to be incurred evenly throughout the year and are treated as period costs.

Within Period 1 it is planned to sell one thirteenth of the annual requirement which are to be the sales necessary to achieve the company profit target of £6.5 million before tax.

You are required

a. to prepare budgets in respect of period 1 of the forthcoming year for

   i. sales, in quantities and value;

   ii. production, in quantities only;

   iii. materials usage, in quantities;

   iv. materials purchases, in quantities and value;

   v. manpower budget, ie, numbers of people needed in each of the machining department and the assembly department;

b. to discuss the factors to be considered if the bought-in-stocks were to be reduced to one week's requirements – this has been proposed by the purchasing officer but resisted by the production director.

(CIMA Cost Accounting)

A23.12 An organisation is constructing its budget for the coming year. It makes three products: Alpha, Beta and Gamma. Sales forecasts for the year are as follows:

	Alpha	Beta	Gamma
Northern region (in units)	3,000	5,000	4,000
Southern region (in units)	5,000	7,000	6,000
	8,000	12,000	10,000

Selling prices are as budgeted

Alpha	£60
Beta	£110
Gamma	£90

You are given the following standard cost data to make one unit:

	Alpha	Beta	Gamma
Material X (in kilos)	2.00	3.00	2.5
Material Y (in kilos)	3.00	4.00	1.5
Labour hours – Department 1	0.75	1.25	2.0
– Department 2	1.50	2.00	2.5
Machine hours – Department 1	1.00	1.50	2.5
– Department 2	2.00	2.00	3.0

You are told:

		X	Y
i.	material cost per kilo	£3	£2

		Dept 1	Dept 2
	Labour rate per hour	£4	£3
ii.	Production overheads are:	Dept 1	Dept 2
		£415,000	£567,200

Overheads in Dept 1 are absorbed on a labour basis and in Dept. 2 on a machine hour basis.

iii. Administration overheads are £350,950 and are to be absorbed on the basis of labour cost.

iv. Opening and closing stocks are budgeted as follows:

	In units			In kilos	
	Alpha	Beta	Gamma	X	Y
Opening stock	1,000	1,200	1,500	5,000	7,500
Closing stock	1,200	1,000	1,800	8,000	10,000

Required:

Prepare the following budgets:

  i.   Sales budget in revenue.
  ii. Production budgets in units for each product.
  iii. material purchase budget.
  iv. Departmental labour cost budgets.
  v.   budgeted overhead absorption rates for Departments 1 and 2.
  vi. Standard Product cost and standard profit for each product.

(AAT Cost Accounting & Budgeting)

A23.13 A science-based contract research company is concerned that its research and development budget is not being utilised effectively, either for planning or control ourposes. Currently the budget is prepared on the basis of approved annual amounts for expenditure under the following departmental headings:

  Chemistry
  Physics
  Biology
  Experimental
  Adminisration

Usually, three seperate and unrelated projects are being worked on simultaneously but not necessarily in all departments.

You are required

a. to describe briefly what procedures should be introduced to aid control of expenditure on the projects;

b. to draft a form, to aid project control, to be prepared by the management accounting department each quarter end, to show the forecast and actual expenditure in each department for each project. The form is for presentation to senior managment and should also include additional information which you think would be useful to them.

(CIMA Cost Accounting)

A23.14 Freewheel is in the process of preparing its master budget for the 6 months ending December 1992. The Balance sheet for the year ended 30 June 1992 is estimated to be as follows:

	Cost	Deprec. Prov.	Net Book Value
	£	£	£
Fixed Assets	140,000	14,000	126,000
Current Assets:			
Stock	25,000		
Trade Debtors	24,600		
Bank	3,000		
Net Current Liabilities		52,600	
Creditors:			
Amounts falling due within one year			
Trade Creditors	25,000		
Other Creditors	9,000		
		34,000	
Net Current Assets			18,600
Total Assets less current liabilities			144,600
Capital and reserves:			
Share Capital			100,000
Profit and Loss Account			44,600
			144,600

The budget committee have derived the forecasts below for six months ended 31 December 1992:

	Sales Units	Purchases	Wages and salaries	Overheads Exc. deprec.	Purchase of fixed Assets	Issue of 20,000 £1 shares	Dividends
		£	£	£	£	£	£
May	4,000	12,000	8,000	7,000			
June	4,200	13,000	8,000	7,000			
July	4,500	14,000	8,000	7,000			
August	4,600	18,000	10,000	7,000			
September	4,800	16,000	10,000	7,000		20,000	
October	5,000	14,000	10,000	8,000			10,000
November	3,800	12,000	12,000	8,000	30,000		
December	3,000	12,000	12,000	8,000			

You are given the following information:

1. The selling price in May 1992 was £6 per unit and this is to be increased to £8 per unit in October. 50% of sales are for cash and 50% on credit to be paid two months later.

2. Purchases are to be paid for two months after purchase.

3. Wages and salaries are to be paid 75% in the month incurred and 25% in the following month.

4. Overheads are to be paid in the month after they are incurred.

5. The fixed assets are to be paid for in three months after they are declared and the receipts from the share issue are budgeted to be received in the month of issue.

7. Fixed assets are depreciated 10% per annum on a straight line basis on those assets owned at 31 December 1992.

8. Closing stock at the beginning of the period under review was equal to the previous two months purchases. At 31 December 1992 it was equal to three months purchases.

Required:

a. Prepare the following budgets for the 6 months ended 31 December 1992:

  i.   Cash Budget
  ii. Budgeted Profit and Loss Account
  iii. Budgeted Balance Sheet

b. Comment upon the results, highlighting those are that you wish to draw to the attention of the Budget Committee.

(AAT Cost Accounting & Budgeting)

A23.15 The following is an extract from a budget statement for the catering department in a public sector organisation; the statment covers the nine months to December 1991:

	Annual Budget	Budget for Period	Expenditure for period	Variance
	£	£	£	£
Salaries & Wages	146,236	109,677	107,632	2,045
Provisions	65,455	49,092	53,815	4,723

You are required to:

a. Comment on the format of the statement indicating, with reasons, four additions you would make to the statment in order to improve its usefulness to budget holders.

b. Identify six possible reasons for each of the variances.

c. Distinguish between the terms virement and supplementary estimate, indicating how financial control might be exercised over the application.

d. Comment on the following information; the budget for a period was set at £20,000 to produce 15,000 X-Rays wheras in the period the department produced 12,000 X-Rays at a total cost of £18,000..

(AAT Public Sector Organisation & Financial Control)

Exercises and examination questions without answers

Exercises

B23.1 The following budget was prepared for the overheads of a department for a period.

Budgeted Activity Level 90%

Overhead Item	Fixed	Variable	Total
	£	£	£
Rent	1,000	–	1,000
Power	–	540	540
Indirect Labour	2,200	1,350	3,550
Heat & Light	50	270	320
Salaries	1,200	–	1,200
Maintenance	700	225	925
	5,150	2,385	7,535

The actual results for the period when activity was 95% were as follows:

	Expenditure
Rent	1,000
Power	585
Indirect Labour	3,575
Heat & Light	340
Salaries	1,230
Maintenance	1,080

You are required to prepare an appropriate budget against which to compare actual results and show any variances which arise.

B23.2 The budgetary process is simply carried out by adding a percentage on to last year budgets to arrive at the budgets for next year'. Discuss this statement.

B23.3 A company has an opening cash balance of £32,500 and it is required to prepare a cash budget for October, November and December having regard to the following information:

Wages and salaries are paid in the current month.

Credit sales are settled as follows: 60% in month of sale, 30% in the next month and 8% in the month following.

Creditors give 1 month credit.

Overheads are paid 1 month in arrears and includes a £6,000 depreciation charge.

	Cash sales	Credit sales	Purchases	Wages & salaries	Overheads
	£	£	£	£	£
August	–	64,000	48,000	12,500	25,000
September	–	71,000	57,500	12,500	25,000
October	27,500	77,000	60,000	13,100	27,000
November	31,000	69,000	43,500	13,600	27,000
December	22,500	58,000	51,500	16,700	28,000

B23.4 A firm has a single product with a C/S ratio of 30% and a selling price of £10. The variable costs are materials and wages in the proportion of 2:1 and the firm has fixed costs of £35,000. Prepare a budget for an output level of 20,000 units.

Examination questions

B23.5 a. What do you understand by the term 'limiting factor' when considering production budgets?

b. A company manufactures three products A, B and C with the following annual production budget:

	A	B	C
Unit of output	6,000	3,000	5,000
Machine hours per output unit	3	4	2
	£	£	£
Direct materials	40,000	36,000	30,000
Direct labour	17,850	18,600	16,300
Direct expense	2,150	3,400	3,700
Variable Overhead	6,000	8,000	4,000
Unit setting price	17.50	32	16

Production is restricted by a storage of materials common to all three products, this shortage is expected to last for a further two years and the factory is operating below full capacity.

Fixed overhead for the year is estimated at £42,000 and is apportioned to each product on the basis of machine hours used.

Prepare a statement showing, in terms of the limiting factor, the profitability of each product, and calculate the effect on contribution if production is concentrated on the product showing the highest profitability.

(CIPFA, Management Accounting.)

B23.6 Budgetary control is the establishment of budgets relating the responsibilities of executives to the requirements of policy, and the continuous comparison of actual, with budgeted results, either to secure by individual action the objective of that policy or to provide a basis for its revision. In the above statement explain what is meant by:

a. Responsibilities of executives.

b. Requirements of a policy.

c. Continuous comparison.

d. A basis for its (policy) revision.

(AAT, Cost Accounting and Budgeting)

B23.7 The management of Beck plc. have been informed that the union representing the direct production workers at one of their factories, where a standard product is produced, intends to call a strike. The accountant has been asked to advise the management of the effect the strike will have on cash flow. The following data has been made available:

	Week 1	Week 2	Week 3
Budgeted Sales	400 units	500 units	400 units
Budgeted Production	600 units	400 units	Nil

The strike will commence at the beginning of week 3 and it should be assumed that it will continue for at least four weeks. Sales at 400 units per week will continue to be made during the period of the strike until stocks of finished goods are exhausted. Production will stop at the end of week 2. The current stock level of finished good is 600 units. Stocks of work-in-progress are not carried.

The selling price of the product is £60 and the budgeted manufacturing cost is made up as follows:

	£
Direct Materials	15
Direct wages	7
Variable Overheads	8
Fixed Overheads	18
	£48

Direct wages are regarded as a variable cost. The company operates a full absorption costing system and the fixed overhead absorption rate is based upon a budgeted fixed overhead of £9,000 per week. Included in the total fixed overheads is £700 per week for depreciation of equipment. During the period of the strike direct wages and variable overheads would not be incurred and the cash expended on fixed overheads would be reduced by £1,500 per week.

The current stock of raw materials are worth £7,500; it is intended that these stocks should increase to £11,000 by the end of week I and then remain at this level during the period of the strike. All direct materials are paid for one week after they have been received. Direct wages are paid one week in arrears. It should be assumed that all relevant overheads are paid for immediately the expense is incurred. All sales are on credit, 70% of the sales value is received in cash from the debtors at the end of the first week after the sales have been made and the balance at the end of the second week.

The current amount outstanding to material suppliers is £8,000 and direct wage accruals amount to £3,200. Both of these will be paid in week 1. The current balance owing from debtors is £31,200, of which £24,000 will be received during week 1 and the remainder during week 2. The current balance of cash at bank in hand is £1,000.

Required:

a. i. Prepare a cash budget for weeks 1 to 6 showing for balance of cash at the end of each week together with a suitable analysis of the receipts and payment during each week.

ii. Comment upon any matters arising from the cash budget which you consider should be brought to management's attention.

b. Explain why the reported profit figure for a period does not normally represent the amount of cash generated in that period.

(ACCA, Costing)

B23.8 You are required, from the data given below, to prepare next year's budgets for:

a. production;

b. purchases;

c. production cost.

Standard cost data are as follows:

		Product	
		Aye	Bee
		£	£
Direct materials:			
X	24 kilos at £2.0	48	
	30 kilos at £2.0		60
Y	10 kilos at £5.0	50	
	8 kilos at £5.0		40
Z	5 kilos at £6.0	30	
	10 kilos at £6.0		60
Direct wages:			
Unskilled	10 hours at £3.0 per hour	30	
	5 hours at £3.0 per hour		15
Skilled	6 hours at £5.0 per hour	30	
	5 hours at £5.0 per hour		25

Production overhead is absorbed on a basis of direct labour hours, while other overhead is recovered on the basis of 20% of production cost. Profit is calculated at 20% of sales price.

Budgeted data for the year:

	Material		
	X	Y	Z
	£	£	£
Stock at standard price			
1st January	60,000	125,000	72,000
31st December	70,000	135,000	75,000

Production overhead £900,000

Labour hours 75,000

	Product	
	Aye	Bee
	£	£
Finished goods stock at production cost		
Opening stock	152,000	256,000
Closing stock	190,000	352,000
Sales at standard sales price	1,368,000	1,536,000

(CIMA, Cost Accounting 2)

B23.9 You are required to:

a. compare the operation of fixed budgets (or cash limits) within public sector organisations or local government authorities with the budgeting procedures normally used in commercial organisations, listing *three* advantages and *three* disadvantages from the public sector or local government point of view;

b. explain the use of a budget manual and give an indication of the likely contents. Your explanation must be related to *one* of the following:

  i. a private sector organisation;
  ii. a public sector organisation;
  iii. a local government authority.

(CIMA, Cost Accounting)

B23.10 a. A transport company owns six lorries which cost £14,000 each. In preparing data for the budget for the year, the following is ascertained:

Each driver receives a basic pay of £8,500 p.a. and can expect overtime earnings amounting to 10% of basic pay.

The lorries are depreciated at a rate of 25% p.a. straight line.

Each lorry is expected to operate for 44,000 kilometres during the budget period.

Vehicle licence per lorry is £2,500 and insurance per vehicle is £1,000.

Average fuel consumption is 10 km, per litre, with fuel costing £0.4 per litre.

Replacement cost of a full set of tyres is £0. 02 per kilometre.

Required:

Prepare a statement for the budget period for a single lorry showing:

  i. total wages cost;
  ii. total standing costs;
  iii. total running costs;
  iv. total cost;
  v. total running costs and total cost in £ per kilometre, to 4 decimal places.

b. The following standard data is available:

		Product	
		Able	Baker
Direct Materials per unit		£10	£30
Direct Labour:	Rate per hour		
Grinding	£5.0	7 hours	5 hours
Finishing	£7.5	15 hours	9 hours
Selling price – per unit		£206.5	£168
Budgeted Production		1,200	600 units
Maximum sales for the period		1,500	800 units

Notes:

1. No closing stocks are anticipated.

2. The skilled labour used for the grinding processes is highly specialised and in short supply, although there is sufficient to meet the budgeted production. However, it will not be possible to increase the supply for the budget period.

Required:

i. Prepare a statement showing the contribution from each product based on the budgeted production.

ii. Prepare a statement showing the total contribution that could be obtained if the best use was made of the skilled grinding labour.

(AAT, Cost Accounting & Budgeting)

B23.11 The VX Company has produced the following information from which a cash budget for the first six months of next year is required.

The company makes a single product which sells for £50 and the variable cost of each unit is:

Material	£26
Labour	£8
Overhead	£2

Fixed costs excluding depreciation are budgeted at £5,500 per month payable on the 23rd of each month.

Other details:

i. Sales for the last two months of this year

November	December
1,000	1,200

ii. Budgeted sales for next year.

January	February	March	April	May	June
1,400	1,600	1,800	2,000	2,200	2,600

iii. Production quantities for the last two months of this year:

November	December
1,200	1,400

iv. Budgeted production units for next year:

January	February	March	April	May	June
1,600	2,000	2,400	2,600	2,400	2,200

v. Wages are paid in the month when output is produced.

vi. Variable overhead is paid 50% in the month when the cost is incurred and 50% the following month.

vii. Suppliers of material are paid 2 months after the material is used in production.

viii. Customers are expected to pay at the end of the second month following sale.

ix. A new machine is scheduled for January costing £34,000. this is to be paid for in February.

x. An old machine is to be sold for cash in January for £1,200.

xi. The company expects to have a cash balance of £35,500 on 1st January.

Required:

a. A month by month cash budget for the first six months of next year.

b. Comment on the action management might take in the light of the cash budget you have prepared.

c. Explain how depreciation would affect:

i. A cash budget and

ii. The calculation of profit in a business.

d. Explain the term 'Flexible Budget' and describe the uses and benefits that can be derived from a system that uses flexible budgets. *(AAT Cost Accounting & Budgeting)*

B23.12 a. Planning is expressed by the budgets which are prepared, but, prior to this, it is necessary to go through a forecasting exercise.

You are required to discuss briefly five problems which are likely to arise when forecasting for a business.

b. C Limited employs 300 people and has sales of £9 million. It has five producing departments, two service departments and manufactures one product.

No effective planning or financial control system ha been established but after one of the directors had attended a CIMA course on 'Finance for Non-Financial Managers' he decided to introduce a budget system and performance reports related to responsibilities. Other Directors and management had some reservations about the introduction of this system but they were persuaded to allow its introduction.

After the end of April, which was the first month of the current financial year, departmental performance reports were issued to all departmental supervisors. Thes took the form of that illustrated below for Production Department'D' which was produced by the office manager – the senior person on ths administrative staff. (A separate report was issued relating to direct material and direct labour.)

Monthly report: Department 'D' – April 1990

	Actual	Planning budget	Variance
Units produced	1,100	1,000	100
	£	£	£
Salaries and wages	10,000	10,500	500
Indirect labour	8,000	7,000	1,000*
Maintenance	3,500	2,750	750*
Overhead allocated	3,000	2,750	250*
Consumable stores	1,600	1,500	100*
Depreciation	2,500	2,500	0
Insurance	1,100	1,000	100*
Sundries	1,000	500	500*
	30,700	28,500	2,200

* Note: Considerable inefficiency: action should be taken to improve cost control in this department. J, the supervisor for department D, was not pleased on receiving her report and declared she did not have time to bother with such paperwork and, in any case, the report was inaccurate and unfair. Her comment was typical of others who had received similar reports.

You are required

i. to state what changes ought to be made to the report and why;

ii. to assess the situation as it now stands in May and indicate what should be done ion respect of the budget system and the departmental performance reports.

(CIMA, Cost Accounting)

B23.13 You are required

a. to state and explain the conditions which ought to be present within an organisation for a system of budgeting and budgetary control to be sucessful;

b. to discuss briefly *four* points related to the behaviour of people which management needs to take into consideration when a system of budgeting and budgetary contriol is introduced.

(CIMA Cost Accounting)

B23.14 Secondline Ltd. aware of the uncertain nature of their market for the coming year have prepared budgeted forecasts based on 90%, 100% and 105% activity as follows.

	90%	100%	105%
	£	£	£
Revenue	1,350,000	1,500,000	1,575,000
Less			
Material costs	337,500	375,000	393,750
Labour costs	440,000	485,000	507,500
Production overhead costs	217,500	235,000	243,750
Administration costs	120,000	130,000	135,000
Selling and distribution costs	70,000	75,000	77,500
	1,185,000	1,300,000	1,357,500
Net profit	165,000	200,000	217,500

In fact actual activity has turned out far worse than expected and only 37,500 units have been sold, with the following results:

	£	£
Revenue		1,075,000
Less expenses		
Material costs	311,750	
Labour costs	351,500	
Production overhead costs	171,250	
Administration costs	117,500	
Selling and Distribution costs	66,500	1,018,500
Net profit		56,500

You are also told that:

i.   The budgeted selling price is £30 per unit.

ii. All production is sold.

iii. The fixed element of the budgeted costs will remain unchanged to all levels of production.

Required:

a. Prepare a statement for the year showing the flexed budget at the actual level of activity, the actual results and the variance for each item of revenue and cost.

b. Examine the variances of £20,000 or greater, analysing the possible reasons for such variance and follow up action management can take.

Secondline Ltd. had seen that sales were likely to be depressed for the coming year and its sales team had secured a potential order for all the spare capacity from actual activity up to 100% activity. For this order a special selling price of £25 per unit had been agreed and budgeted variable administration costs would increase by 25%, budgeted variable production overhead costs by 20% and budgeted variable labour costs by £1 per unit. All other costs would remain the same.

Required:

c. Recommend whether Secondline should have maintained 100% activity for the year by accepting the order detailed above. Clearly state the reasons for your decision and show any workings.

(AAT Cost Accounting & Budgeting)

B23.15 You have been approached by a Principal of an accountancy college, that is going to teach the A.A.T. to advise them on the financial implications of their plans for their first year of operation.

You ascertain that the college staff will consist of the Principal, an administration department under the control of a Deputy Principal and two departments; accounting and business studies, each of these under a Head of Department. The teaching will be provided by staff within the departments.

The Principal gives you the following projected information for the first year. He is rather proud of his estimates, having referred to no-one else in the college.

Level	Number of students	Fee per student £
Preliminary	400	2,000
Intermediate	300	3,000
Final	250	4,000

For the Preliminary and Intermediate stages you are told that there are to be 20 students in each class and for the final level there are to be 10 students in each class. The college year will consist of 30 weeks tuition and each class will have the following:

Level	Hour tuition per week	Tuition cost per class hour £
Preliminary	16	20
Intermediate	20	22
Final	22	24

Required:

a. Prepare budgets showing the following information to the Principal for the college's first year of operation:

   i.   College revenue by level and total.

   ii. Number of classes required at each level.

   iii. Tuition costs for each level and total.

b. You are also told that other costs include the following:

	£
Rental of college	500,000
Administration salaries	132,000
Administration costs	800,000
Welfare expenses	400,000
Examination fees	100,000

All the tuition fees are collectable with the exception of 2% that are expected to turn out to be bad debts and 5% of the administration costs are for depreciation. All the remaining expenses are budgeted to be paid.

Required:

Prepare a cash budget for the year advising him upon the outcome and possible course of action open to him.

c. Acting upon the information given, evaluate the Principal's method of budgeting and advise him of any alternative course of action for Year 2 so that he maximises the benefit that a system of budgeting and budgetary control can bring.

(AAT Cost Accounting & Budgeting)

24: Standard costing introduction

1. Topics covered in this chapter

> 1. Types of standard
> 2. Principles of setting standards
> 3. Standard cost card
> 4. Behavioural aspects of standard costing.

2. Standard costing defined

Standard costing is a technique which establishes predetermined estimates of the costs of products and services and then compares these predetermined costs with actual costs as they are incurred. The predetermined costs are known as *standard costs* and the difference between the standard cost and actual cost is known as a *variance*. The process by which the total difference between actual cost and standard cost is broken down into its different elements is known as *variance analysis*.

Standard costing in practice is a detailed process and requires considerable development work before it is a useful tool. For standard costing to be successful requires reasonable stability and the existence of repetitive work. These conditions can be found across many sectors of the economy. For example in manufacturing, in Service Industries such as transport, computing and banking, in parts of the Public Sector (eg street cleaning, refuse disposal) and so on. Its major application in practice is in manufacturing and repetitive assembly work.

3. Standard cost

This can be formally defined as

'A standard expressed in money. It is built up from an assessment of the value of cost elements. Its main uses are providing bases for performance measurement, control by exception reporting, valuing stock and establishing selling prices'. *Terminology*. A standard cost is a target cost which should be attained. The build-up of a standard cost is based on sound technical and engineering studies, known production methods and layouts, work studies and work measurement, material specifications and wage and material price projections.

A standard cost is not an average of previous costs. These are likely to contain the results of past inefficiencies and mistakes. Furthermore changes in methods, technology and costs make comparisons with the past of doubtful value for control purposes.

4. Types of standards

There are three types of standard; basic, ideal, and attainable.

a. *Basic standards*. These are long term standards which would remain unchanged over the years. Their sole use is to show trends over time for such items as material prices, labour rates and efficiency and the effect of changing methods. They cannot be used to highlight current efficiency or inefficiency and would not normally form part of the reporting system except as a background, statistical exercise.

The formal definition of a basic standard is; a standard established for use over a long period from which a current standard can be developed.

b. *Ideal standards*. These are based on the best possible operating conditions, ie, no breakdowns, no material wastage, no stoppages or idle time, in short, perfect efficiency. Ideal standards, if used, would be revised periodically to reflect improvements in methods, materials and technology. Clearly ideal standards would be unattainable in practice and accordingly are rarely used. However, their use could be considered worthwhile for investigative and development purposes, but not for normal day-to-day control activities.

The formal definition of an ideal standard is; 'a standard which can be attained under the most favourable conditions with no allowance for normal losses, waste and machine breakdown. Also as a potential standard'. *Terminology*.

c. *Attainable standard.* This is by far the most frequently encountered standard. It is a standard based on efficient (but not perfect) operating conditions. The standard would include allowances for normal material losses, realistic allowances for fatigue, machine breakdowns etc. It must be stressed however that an attainable standard must be based on a high performance level so that its achievement is possible, but has to be worked for. Attainable standards provide a tough, but realistic target and thus can provide motivation for management. They can be used for product costing, for cost control, for stock valuation and as a basis for budgeting.

Attainable standards would be revised periodically to reflect the conditions expected to prevail during the ensuing period when the standards would apply. Unless otherwise stated, all subsequent references in this manual to standards mean *attainable standards*.

The formal definition of an attainable standard is; 'a standard which can be attained if a standard unit of work is carried out efficiently, a machine properly operated or material properly used. Allowances are made for normal losses waste and machine downtime'. *Terminology.*

Notes on the types of standard:

a. The type of standard used (basic, ideal, attainable) directly affects the level of the variances which can arise and the meaning which can be attached to the variances.

b. There are real problems in determining the level of attainment in standards so it follows that, to a greater or lesser extent, all standards contain a subjective element.

c. Like budgets the setting of standards, particularly relating to price and wage levels, is dependent on forecasting skill. This means that variances can arise from both differences in efficiency levels and from forecasting errors. This fact should be remembered when interpreting any variance.

5. Standards and budgets

Both standards and budgets are concerned with setting performance and cost levels for control purposes. They therefore are similar in principle although they differ in scope. Standards are a unit concept, ie, they apply to particular products, to individual operations or processes.

Budgets are concerned with totals; they lay down cost limits for functions and departments and for the firm as a whole. As an illustration the standard material cost of the various products in a firm could be as follows:

		Standard Material cost/unit	Planned Production	Total Material Cost
		£		£
Product	X321	3.50	5000 units	17,500
Product	Y592	7.25	1500 units	10,875
Product	Y728	1.50	2400 units	3,750
etc	etc	etc	etc	etc
etc	etc	etc	etc	etc

OVERALL TOTAL = MATERIALS BUDGET= £275,000

In this way the detailed unit standards are used as the basis for developing realistic budgets. This is particularly so for direct material and direct labour costs which are more amenable to close control through standard costing whereas overheads would normally be controlled by functional and departmental budgets. Further differences are that budgets would be revised on a periodic basis, frequently as an annual exercise, whereas standards are revised only when they are inappropriate for current operating conditions. Such revisions may take place more or less frequently than budget revisions.

The accounting treatment of standards and budgets also differs. Budgets are memorandum figures and do not form part of the double entry accounting system whereas standards and the resulting variances are included. The double entry treatment of standards and variances is explained in Chapter 25.

6. Setting standards

Realistic standards which can be used for control purposes rest on a foundation of properly organised, standardised methods and procedures and a comprehensive information system. It is little point trying to develop a standard cost for a product if the production method is not decided upon. A standard cost implies that a target or standard exists for every single element which contributes to the product; the types, usage and prices of materials and parts, the grades, rates of pay and times for the labour involved, the production methods and layouts, the tools and jigs and so on. Considerable effort is involved in establishing standard costs and keeping them up to date.

Traditionally, the standard cost for each part or product was recorded on a standard cost card and an example is given later in this chapter. With the increased usage of computers for costing purposes frequently nowadays there is no physical cost card. When a computer is used, the standard costs are recorded on a magnetic disc or tape file and can be accessed and processed as required. Whether a computer or manual system is used, there are no differences in the principles of standard costing, although there are many differences in the method of day to day operation. The following paragraphs explain some of the detailed procedures involved in setting standards.

7.Setting standards – materials

The materials content of a product; raw materials, sub-assemblies, piece parts, finishing materials etc, is derived from technical and engineering specifications, frequently in the form of a Bill of Materials. The standard quantities required include an allowance for normal and inevitable losses in production, that is, machining loss, evaporation, and expected levels of breakages and rejections. The process of analysis is valuable in itself because savings and alternative materials and ways of using materials are frequently discovered.

The responsibility for providing material prices is that of the buying department. The prices used are not the past costs, but the forecast expected costs for the relevant budget period. The expected costs should take into account trends in material prices, anticipated changes in purchasing policies, quantity and cash discounts, carriage and packing charges and any other factor which will influence material costs.

8. Setting standards – labour

Without detailed operation and process specifications it would be impossible to establish standard labour times. The agreed methods of manufacture are the basis of setting the standard labour times. The techniques of work measurement are involved, frequently combined with work study projections based on elemental analysis when a part is not yet in production.

The labour standards must specify the exact grades of labour to be used as well as the times involved. Planned labour times are expressed in *standard hours* (or *standard minutes*). The concept of a standard hour/minute is important and can be defined as, 'the quantity of work achievable at standard performance in an hour of minute' *Terminology*.

It will be noted that a standard hour represents a given work content. Indeed, production for a given period is frequently described as 'so many standard hours' rather than a quantity of parts. Once the times a grades of labour have been established, a forecast can be made of the relevant wage rates for the appropriate future period. This is usually done by the Personnel Department.

Note:

It must be understood that a standard hour or minute is a *measure of work content*, not a measure of time.

An alternative name for a standard hour is an *output hour*.

9. Setting standards – overheads

It will be recalled from earlier in the manual how overhead absorption rates are established. These predetermined overhead absorption rates become the standards for overheads for each cost centre using the budgeted standard labour hours as the activity base. For realistic control, overheads must be analysed into their fixed and variable components and separate absorption rates calculated for both fixed and variable overheads thus:

$$\text{Standard Variable O A R} = \frac{\text{Budgeted variable overheads for cost centre}}{\text{Budgeted standard labour hours for cost centre}}$$

and $$\text{Standard fixed O A R} = \frac{\text{Budgeted fixed overheads for cost centre}}{\text{Budgeted standard labour hours for cost centre}}$$

The level of activity adopted, expressed in standard labour hours, is the budgeted expected annual activity level which is the basis of the Master Budget. For reporting and control purposes this would be classed as 100% capacity.

10. Setting standards – sales price and margin

Fundamental to any form of standard costing, budgeting and profit planning is the anticipated selling price for the product. The setting of the selling price is frequently a top level decision and is based on a variety of factors including: the anticipated market demand, competing products, manufacturing costs, inflation estimates and so on.

Finally, after discussion and investigation, a selling price is established at which it is planned to sell the product during the period concerned. This becomes the standard selling price. The standard sales margin is the difference between the standard cost and the standard selling price. Where a standard marginal costing system is used, the standard contribution is calculated following the normal marginal costing principles explained in Chapter 19.

Note:

Normally when 'standard cost' is mentioned it means *total standard* cost, ie, total absorption cost principles are used incorporating fixed and variable costs. Standard marginal costing is also employed, but students should assume that total absorption cost principles are involved whenever the term standard cost is used without qualification. This nomenclature is adopted in this book. When marginal costing principles are used the term *standard marginal cost* is employed.

11. Responsibility for setting standards

The line managers who have to work with and accept the standards must be involved in establishing them. These managers and their superiors have the ultimate responsibility for setting the standards. Work study staff, accountants and other specialists provide technical support and information, but do not make the final decisions upon standards and performance levels.

12. The standard cost card

The process of setting standards results in the establishment of the standard cost for the product. The makeup of the standard cost is recorded on a standard cost card. In practice there may be numerous detail cards together with a summary card for a given product, or the standard cost details may be on a computer file. The principles, however, remain the same. A simple standard cost card is shown on the following page.

13. Revision of standards

To show trends and to be able to compare performance and costs between different periods, standards would be rarely changed. On the other hand, for day to day control and motivation purposes standards which reflect the most up to date position are required and consequently revisions would need to be made continually.

The above positions reflect the extremes of the situation. There is not doubt that standards which are right up to date provide a better target and are more useful for the foremen and managers concerned, but the extent and frequency of standard revision is a matter of judgement. Minor changes in rates, prices and usage are frequently ignored for a time, but their cumulative effect soon becomes significant and changes need to be made.

Prior to computer maintained standard cost files, standard cost revisions were a time consuming chore as it was necessary to ensure that all the effects of a change were recorded. For example, a change in the price of a common raw material would necessitate alterations to

a. the standard cost cards of all products, parts and assemblies using the material;

b. any price lists, stock sheets and catalogues involving the material and products derived from the material.

Because of such factors, it is common practice for all standard costs to be revised together at regular, periodic intervals such as every six or twelve months, rather than on an individual, random basis.

Standard Cost Card

PART NO: X291   DESCRIPTION: Stub Joint   BATCH QTY: 100

TOOL REF: T5983   WORK STUDY REF: WS255   DRAWING NO: D592/5

REVISION DATE: 3/12/92   REVISED BY: G.R.P.

Cost Type and Quantity	Standard Price or Rate		Dept 7	Dept 19	Dept 15	Total
			£	£	£	£
Direct Materials						
2.5 Kg P101	£14.80	Kg	37.00			37.00
1000 units A539	£3.75	100		37.50		37.50
						74.50
Direct Labour						
Machine operation						
Grade 15						
4.8 hrs	£2.5	hr	12.00			12.00
9.2 hrs	£2.5	hr		23.00		23.00
Assembly						
Grade 8						
16.4 hrs	£1.75	hr			28.70	28.70
						63.70
Production Overhead						
Machine Hour Rate	£11 hr		52.80	101.12		153.92
Labour Hour Rate	£6 hr				98.40	98.40
			101.80	161.62	127.10	252.32

Standard Cost Summary

	£
Direct Materials	74.50
Direct Labour	63.70
Production Overheads	252.32
Standard Cost per 100	£390.52

Standard cost card

14. Behavioural aspects of standards

The points made in the previous chapter regarding the importance of the human aspects of budgeting apply equally to standard costing. Both techniques employ similar principles and both rely absolutely upon the people who have to work to the budgets and standards. Because of the detailed nature of standard costing and its involvement with foremen and production workers, communication becomes of even greater importance. Production workers frequently regard any form of performance evaluation with deep suspicion and if a cost-conscious, positive attitude is to be developed, close attention must be paid to the behavioural aspects of the system.

Appropriate participation, realistic standards, prompt and accurate reporting, no undue pressure or censure – all contribute to an acceptable system. Remember: if the system is not accepted by the people involved it will be unworkable.

15. Advantages of standard costing

a. Standard costing is an example of 'management by exception'. By studying the variances, management's attention is directed towards those items which are not proceeding according to plan. Management are able to delegate cost control through the standard costing system knowing that variances will be reported.

b. The process of setting, revising and monitoring standards encourages reappraisals of methods, materials and techniques so leading to cost reductions.

c. Standard costs represent what the parts and products should cost. They are not merely averages of past performances and consequently they are a better guide to pricing than historical costs. In addition, they provide a simpler basis of inventory valuation.

d. A properly developed standard costing system with full participation and involvement creates a positive, cost effective attitude through all levels of management right down to the shop floor.

16. Disadvantages of standard costing

a. It may be expensive and time consuming to install and to keep up to date.

b. In volatile conditions with rapidly changing methods, rates and prices, standards quickly become out of date and thus lose their control and motivational effects. This can cause resentment and loss of goodwill.

c. There is research evidence to suggest that overly elaborate variances are imperfectly understood by line managers and thus they are ineffective for control purposes.

d. Standard costing concentrates only on a narrow range of financial factors but many other items are of importance eg quality, lead times, service, customer satisfaction and so on. By ignoring these, standard costing, at best, only controls part of operations.

17. Motivation and standards

One of the hoped for effects of standards is that people will be motivated to achieve the targets represented by the standards. In general people are likely to be motivated by standards if they accept them and do not feel threatened by the system.

There are numerous factors which affect the way that standards motivate, or do not motivate, the people responsible foe achieving the standards.

Three important factors are examined below; participation, attainment level and feedback.

Participation

Participation means that the people responsible for achieving the standards are consulted and are part of the standard setting process. Common sense would appear to suggest that people would prefer participation and that their performance would improve.

However the empirical studies show that the position is not so straight forward. Some studies (eg Kenis, Argyris and others) found that participation improved performance whilst others (eg. Milani, Bryan and Locke) found that participation tended to lead to lower performance levels. Vroom found that participation was not suitable for certain types of people, especially those who preferred directive leadership and clear cut unambiguous situations. In another study Brownell found that where people felt they had a large degree of control over their own destinies then there were positive effects from participation.

Thus it would appear that participation may have beneficial effects but has to be used selectively with due regard to the personalities of the people concerned.

Attainment Levels

The attainment level is the level of difficulty at which the standard is set. The various studies indicate that very difficult targets are not likely to be accepted. The person may give up and produce a performance worse than if a less demanding target had been set. Conversely if undemanding targets are set they will be achieved but the individuals are not motivated to achieve their full potential.

Hofstede conducted considerable research on the effect that targets set at different levels of difficulty have on aspiration levels (ie, an individual's personal goals).

In summary he found that setting targets does not always lead to improved performance. Very loose or very tight targets were particularly ineffective and the target level which motivates the best actual performance is unlikely to be met most of the time. This means that when targets are set at a level which motivates the best performance, adverse variances will often occur. If such variances are used in a punitive fashion this is likely to make individuals press for easier targets. These may produce fewer adverse variances but at the expense of lower actual performance.

Feedback

Feedback is part of the control cycle whereby information on actual performance against budget or standard and the resulting variances is reported to the individual concerned. It has been found that prompt accurate feedback of results has a positive motivational effect. Where feedback is delayed or is not understood or is inaccurate confidence in the system is undermined and motivation reduced. Accordingly, it is of considerable importance that the costing system produces speedy, relevant feedback otherwise its effectiveness will be reduced.

18. Summary

a. Standard costing compares actual costs with predetermined costs and analyses the differences, known as variances.

b. There are three main types of standard: basic standards, ideal standards, and attainable standards.

c. Basic standards are long-term standards which unchanged for long periods; ideal standards represent perfect working conditions and performances; attainable standards are standards based on high but not impossible performance levels. Attainable standards are the most common.

d. Standards relate to individual items, processes and products; budgets relate to totals.

e. Setting standards is detailed, lengthy process usually based on engineering and technical studies of times, materials and methods. Standards are set for each of the elements which make up the standard cost: labour, materials and overheads.

f. Accountants, work study engineers and other specialists provide technical advice and information, but do not set the standards. This is the responsibility of the line managers and their superiors.

g. The culmination of the standard setting process is the preparation of a standard cost card for the product showing the target cost for the following periods.

h. Difficulties arise with the too frequent revision of standards. Consequently it is common practice to revise them on a periodic basis, half yearly or yearly.

i. The behavioural aspects of standard costing, like budgeting, are all important. The system must be acceptable to the people who will have to operate it.

19. Points to note

a. A standard cost, like any cost, is made up from two components; the usage of materials, labour etc, and the price or rate of these elements. This cost makeup plays a significant part in variance analysis covered in the next chapter.

b. Standard costing and variance analysis are important examination topics. Because examiners are always seeking novel applications a thorough understanding of basic principles is vital for all students.

Student self testing

Self Review Questions

1. What is standard costing? (2)

2. Describe the three main types of standard. (4)

3. What is the relationship between standards and budgets? (5)

4. How are standards relating to materials set? (7)

5. What is a standard hour? (8)

6. How are overhead standards established? (9)

7. What is the standard sales margin? (10)

8. Who sets standards? (11)

9. What is a standard cost card? (12)

10. Why are the behavioural aspects of standard costing so important? (14)

11. What are the advantages and disadvantages of standard costing? (15 & 16)

12. How can standard costing enhance motivation? (17)

Exercises and examination questions with answers

Exercises

A24.1   There is a subjective element involved in the setting of all standards'. Discuss.

A24.2   From the following data prepare the Standard Cost Card for one unit of the sole product manufactured.

Direct Materials:

20Kgs 'A' @ £0.80 per Kg

15Kgs 'B' @ £2.49 per Kg

Direct Labour:

Preparation 14 hours at £3. 75 per hour

Assembly 5 hours at £2.50 per hour

The budgeted total overheads for year:

	£	Hours
Preparation dept.	88,000	21,000
Assembly dept	150,000	24,000

The fixed overheads (included in the above figures) are £25,000 and £48,000 respectively.

The standard cost card should show sub totals for:

a. Prime cost
b. Variable production cost
c. Total production cost

A24.3 'Standard Costing can only be applied in factories.' Discuss.

Examination questions

A24.4 A company manufactures three products, extracts from the standard cost data relating to which are as follows:

		Units of Material in Final Product		
Material	Unit Cost	ProductA	Product B	Product C
V	55p	5	4	–
W	50p	3	2	6
X	35p	–	3	5
Y	60p	–	1	4
Z	80p	1	1	–

No losses occur in the use of materials V, W, X and Y. The standard yield on Material Z is 90%. This is an ideal standard. The expected yield is 80%. During the first four-week period budgeted sales are:

Product	Sales Units
A	12,000
B	15,000
C	10,000

It is anticipated that 5% of the production of Product B will not pass inspection and will be disposed of immediately.

The stocks on hand at the beginning of the period are expected to be:

		Units
Finished goods	A	1,800
	B	2,000
	C	1,600
Materials	V	20,000
	W	30,000
	X	15,000
	Y	5,000
	Z	9,000

It is planned to increase finished goods stocks in order to satisfy orders more quickly. Production in period 1 will be sufficient to increase stocks by 10% by the end of the period. Materials stocks, however, are considered to be too high and a reduction of 10% is planned by the end of period 1.

Required:

a. Prepare budgets for:

i. Production (in quantity);

ii. Materials usage (in quantity);

iii. Materials purchases (in quantity and value).

b. Distinguish between 'ideal' and 'attainable' standards, and consider briefly the factors influencing the choice between them.

(ACCA Costing)

A24.5 From the information given below you are required to:

    a. Prepare a standard cost sheet for one unit and enter on the standard cost sheet the cost to show sub-totals for:
       i. prime cost;
      ii. variable production cost;
      iii. total production cost;
      iv. total cost;

    b. Calculate the selling price per unit allowing for a profit of 15% of the selling price.

The following data are given:

Budgeted output for the year 9,800 units

Standard details for one unit: Direct materials 40 square metres at £5.30 per square metre

Direct wages:

    Bonding department   48 hours at £2.50 per hour

    Finishing department 30 hours at £1.90 per hour

Budgeted costs and hours per annum:

	£	hours
Variable overhead:		
Bonding department	375,000	500,000
Finishing department	150,000	300,000
Fixed overhead:		
Production	392,000	
Selling and distribution	196,000	
Administration	98,000	

(CIMA, Cost Accounting 1)

Exercises and examination questions without answers

Exercises

B24.1 Your company is considering the introduction of a standard costing system but, somewhat to management's surprise, the production workers are suspicious and are threatening industrial action.

What can be learned from the situation described above?

B24.2 A perennial problem which arises in standard costing is to decide the frequency with which standards are revised.

Discuss the problems of standards revision particularly regarding their frequency.

B24.3 From the following data prepare a standard cost card for one unit of the sole product manufactured.

    Direct Materials
      30 Kgs @ £1.75 Kg

    Direct Wages
      Blanking 12 hours @ £4 hr.
      Finishing 8 hours @ £3.50 hr.

    Budgeted total overheads for year:

	£	Hours
Blanking Dept.	150,000	32,000
Finishing	110,000	21,000

When the output is as budgeted the fixed overhead per unit is £11.25 in the Blanking Dept and £10.67 in the Finishing Dept. The standard cost card should show sub-totals for:

    a. Prime Cost

    b. Variable Production Cost

    c. Total Production Cost

B24.4 The simplest way of setting standards is to calculate the average cost per unit in the last period and use this value as the standard cost.' Comment on this statement.

25: Standard costing variance analysis (material, labour and overheads)

1. Topics covered in this chapter

1. Definition and purpose of Variance Analysis
2. Relationship of common variances
3. Basic Material Variances
4. Labour Variances
5. Overhead Variance Analysis
6. Variable Overhead Variances
7. Fixed Overhead Variances
8. Mix and Yield Material Variances.

2. Variance analysis defined

It will be recalled from the previous chapter that a variance is the difference between standard cost and actual cost. The term variance is rarely used on its own. Usually it is qualified in some way, for example; direct materials cost variance, direct labour efficiency variance and so on. The process by which the total difference between standard and actual costs is sub-divided is known as variance analysis which can be defined as: The analysis of performance by means of variances. Used to promote management action at the earliest possible stages.'*Terminology.*

Variances arise from differences between standard and actual quantities and/or differences between standard and actual prices. These are the *causes* of variances; the *reasons* for the differences have to be established by management investigation.

Note:

Variances may be ADVERSE, ie, where actual cost is greater than standard, or they may be FAVOURABLE ie, where actual cost is less than standard. Alternatively they may be known as MINUS or PLUS variances respectively.

3. The purpose of variance analysis

The only purpose of variance analysis is to provide practical pointers to the causes of off-standard performance so that management can improve operations, increase efficiency, utilise resources more effectively and reduce costs. It follows that overly elaborate variance analysis which is not understood, variances that are not acted upon and variances which are calculated too long after the event do not fulfil the central purpose of standard costing.

The types of variances which are identified must be those which fulfil the needs of the organisation. The only criterion for the calculation of a variance is its usefulness – if it is not useful for management purposes, it should not be produced.

4. Responsibility for variances

Ideally, variances should be detailed enough so that responsibility can be assigned to a particular individual for a specific variance. Cost control is made much more difficult if responsibility for a variance is spread over several managers. In such circumstances it is all too easy to 'pass the buck'.

Because of the importance of this principle, standard costing and budgetary control are known in America as *responsibility accounting*. A simple example of the process of calculating variances in accordance with responsibilities is the subdivision of the direct materials cost variance, that is, the total difference in material costs between actual and standard.

This is composed of a usage component, which is usually deemed the responsibility of a foreman, and a price component which is usually deemed the responsibility of the buyer. Accordingly, a usage variance and a price variance need to be calculated to show how much of the total difference is attributable to either person. This example is at the most basic level; frequently more variances are calculated than those given above.

Note:

The assignment of clear cut responsibilities for variances is an ideal which is difficult to achieve in practice. Interrelationships and interdependencies make the process much more complex than the basic theory.

For example, it is conventional to assume that material usage and labour efficiency variances are within the control of the departmental manager concerned. However, where a department receives inputs from another department the receiving department's operations are greatly influenced by the quality and delivery of its inputs. This is but one example of an interdependency, many others exist in a typical organisation.

5. The relationship of variances

The overall objective of variance analysis is to subdivide the total difference between budgeted profit and actual profit for the period into the detailed differences (relating to material, labour, overheads and sales) which go to make up to total difference. The particular variances which are computed in any given organisation are those which are relevant to its operations and which will aid control.

Figure 25.1 on page 376 shows typical variances which are generally found useful, but it must be emphasised that relevance and appropriateness to management are the only criteria, not the fact that a variance is mentioned in textbooks and on examination paper 6. The chart shows a hierarchy of frequently encountered variances and should be studied carefully together with the notes which follow:

Notes to Figure 25.1:

a. Each variance and sub-variance is described in detail in the paragraphs which follow.

b. For simplicity the full title of each variance is not shown in each box. The full titles are easily derived from the chart. For example, under the *Direct Materials* Total Variance is found the *Direct Materials* Price Variance, the *Direct Materials* Usage Variance and so on.

c. The chart is arithmetically consistent, ie, the total of the linked variances equals the senior variance shown. For example,

Variable Overhead Expenditure Variance + Variable Overhead Efficiency Variance = Variable Overhead Variance

d. The price and quantity aspects of each variance are shown clearly on the chart and can be summarised as shown in the table below.

Cost Element	Price Variances	Quantity Variances
Direct Labour	Rate	Efficiency
Direct Materials	Price	Usage
Variable Overheads	Expenditure	Efficiency
Fixed Overheads	Expenditure	Volume

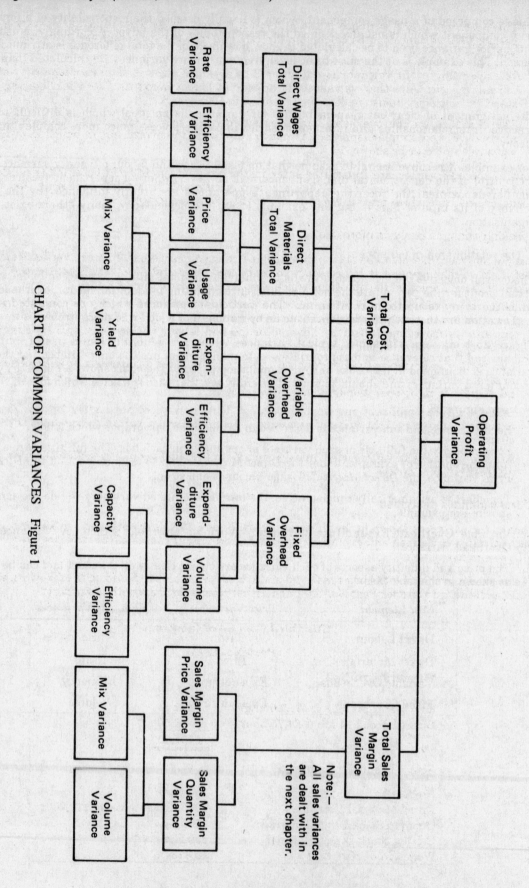

CHART OF COMMON VARIANCES Figure 1

Figure 25.1 Chart of common variances

e. The *'operating profit'* variance is the difference between budgeted and actual operating profit for a period. This variance can be calculated directly and it is the sum of all variances, ie, cost variances and sales variances.

The operating profit variance is not entered in a ledger account because budgeted profit does not appear therein. All other variances do appear in ledger accounts. The book keeping entries for standard costing systems are described in detail in Chapter 26.

f. The chart shows the overhead variances sub-divided into Fixed and Variable components. An alternative, and simpler, approach is not to sub-divide the overheads, in which case the overhead variances would be as shown.

Both of the approaches are illustrated later in the chapter but it must be emphasised that neither approach is 'correct' or 'incorrect' – they are merely different. It is worth repeating that the 'correct' variances are those which provide *relevant information for management*.

6. Making variance analysis more useful

It is not sufficient merely to be able to describe and calculate variances. To make variance analysis into a useful aid to management it is necessary to probe and investigate the variances and the data used to calculate them. Typical of the questions which should be asked are the following:

a. Is there any relationship between the variances? For example, there may be pleasure in observing a favourable materials price variance caused by purchase of a job lot of material, but if this favourable variance is more than offset by adverse usage and labour variances caused by the poor quality material, then there is little cause for rejoicing.

b. Can further information than merely the variance be provided for management? Remember, variance analysis is but a means to an end. Management's task is to find the reasons for the variances and to take action to bring operations into line with the plan.

c. Is the variance significant and worth reporting? This is an important matter for both the accountant and the manager and the ways of assessing the significance of variances are dealt with in the next chapter.

d. Are the variances being reported quickly enough, to the right people, in sufficient or too much detail, with explanatory notes?

7. The variances described

Each of the variances shown in the Variance Chart, Figure 25.1, is described in the following paragraphs. Each variance is defined and explained, a formula and typical causes of the variance are given together with a worked example.

The worked examples for the basic material and labour variances are based on the following abstract from the Standard Cost Card for Part No. 100X and actual results for the month of January.

Standard Cost Card (abstract)	
Part No. 100X	
Standard Cost/Unit	
	£
Raw Materials 50 Kgs @ £2.50/Kg.	125
Direct Labour 14 hrs @ £4.75/hour	66.50
	£191.50
Actual Result for January	
Production	150 units
Direct Material Purchases	7000 Kgs at a cost of £18,200
Opening Stock Direct Material	1300 Kgs
Closing Stock Direct Material	850 Kgs
Wages paid (2020 hrs)	£9,898

8. The basic materials variances

This paragraph deals with the Direct Materials Total Variance, the Direct Materials Price Variance and the Direct Materials Usage Variance. A particular problem arises with Materials variances in that materials can be charged to production at either actual prices or standard prices. This affects when the price variance is calculated, ie, either at the time of purchase or at the time of usage. Although both these approaches are possible, the procedure where materials are charged to production at standard price has many advantages and will be adopted in this manual.

This method means that variances are calculated as soon as they arise, (ie, a price variance when the material is purchased) and that they are more easily related to an individual's responsibility (ie, a price variance would be the buyer's responsibility). Accordingly for materials variances (and ALL other variances), price variances are calculated *first* and thereafter the material is at *standard price*. The individual material variances can now be considered:

Direct Materials Total Variance – definition:

> 'The difference between the standard direct material cost of the actual production volume and the actual cost of direct material.'

> (Alternatively the direct materials total variance can be considered as the sum of the Usage and Price Variances.)

Direct Materials Price Variance – definition:

> 'The difference between the standard price and actual purchase price for the actual quantity of material.'

> (This variance may be calculated at the time of *purchase* or the time of *usage*. It is generally preferable to calculate the variance at the time of purchase).

Direct Materials Usage Variance – definition:

> 'The difference between the standard quantity specified for the actual production and the actual quantity used, at standard purchase price.'

Formulae

Actual purchase quantity × Actual price (ie Total purchase cost) *minus* Actual purchase quantity × STANDARD PRICE	Price variance
Actual quantity used for actual production × STANDARD PRICE *minus* STANDARD QUANTITY FOR ACTUAL PRODUCTION × STANDARD PRICE	Usage variance

Price variance + Usage variance = Total direct material variance

Example 1

(based on data from Para. 7)

		£	
	Total purchase price	18,200	Price variance **£700 Adverse**
minus	7000 Kgs @ £2.50	17,500	
	7450 Kgs @ £2.50	18,625	Usage variance **£125 Favourable**
minus	(150 × 50) @ £2.50	18,750	

Total material variance **£575 Adverse**

It will be seen in this case that *usage* was lower than planned (a gain) but the *price* paid was higher than planned (a loss).

Notes:

a. Although rules can be given regarding the sequence of the formula so that a minus variance is always adverse and a plus is favourable, it is easier and less error prone to determine the direction of the variance by common sense, ie, if the price/usage is less than standard the variance is *favourable*, if more, then the variance is *adverse*.

b. The price variance is based on the actual quantity purchased and is extracted first. Thereafter the actual price is never used for variance calculations.

c. In the above example, the actual usage (7450Kgs) was calculated as follows:

Opening Stock + Purchases – Closing Stock = Usage   ie. 1300 + 7000 – 850 = 7450 Kgs

d. It follows from the above calculations that a price variance could arise even if there was no usage, provided that there were purchases during the period.

e. Students should note how the formulae develop from actual values (in lower case) progressively to STANDARD VALUES (in capitals). This layout is used throughout the book.

Typical causes of material variances

Price variances

a. Paying higher or lower prices than planned.

b. Losing or gaining quantity discounts by buying in smaller or larger quantities than planned.

c. Buying lower or higher quality than planned.

d. Buying substitute material due to unavailability of planned material.(both (c) and (d) may affect usage variances).

Usage Variances

a. Greater or lower yield from material than planned.

b. Gains or losses due to use of substitute or higher/lower quality than planned.

c. Greater or lower rate of scrap than anticipated.

Note:

As can be seen from the variance chart, Figure 25.1, the usage variance can be further divided into mix and yield variances. This is only done when useful information can be thus provided. These variances are dealt with later in the chapter.

9. Labour variances

This paragraph deals with the Direct Labour Total Variance, the Direct Labour Rate Variance (the 'price variance') and the Direct Labour Efficiency Variance (the 'usage' variance). These are defined below:

Direct Labour Total Variance – definition.

> The difference between the standard direct labour cost and the actual direct labour cost incurred for the production achieved.

Direct Labour Rate Variance – definition.

> The difference between the standard and actual direct labour hour rate per hour for the total hours worked.

Direct Labour Efficiency Variance – definition.

> The difference between the standard hours for the actual production achieved and the hours actually worked, valued at the standard labour rate'.

The formulae are given below and it should be noted that they follow a similar pattern to the material variances described in the previous paragraph.

Formulae

Actual labour hours × Actual rate (ie Total labour cost) *minus* Actual labour hours × STANDARD RATE	Rate variance
Actual labour hours × STANDARD RATE *minus* STANDARD LABOUR × STANDARD RATE	Efficiency variance

Total direct labour variance

a. It will be seen that the second line of the rate variance and the first line of the efficiency variance are identical.

b. As with the material variances the price (rate) variance is dealt with first; thereafter all calculations use the standard rate.

c. Where appropriate records exist, an idle time variance can be calculated by multiplying the hours of idle time by the standard rate. The variance so calculated, together with the efficiency variance, forms the labour usage variance. Where no idle time variance is calculated, as in the example above, the efficiency variance is equivalent to the labour usage variance. As with labour efficiency, the effect of idle time on variable and fixed overheads can also be calculated.

Example 2

(based on data from Para. 7)

		£	
	Actual wages paid	9,898	Rate variance £303 Adverse
minus	2020 hrs @ £4.75	9,595	
minus	(150 × 14) hrs @ £4.75	9,975	Efficiency variance £380 Favourable

Total direct labour variance £77 Favourable

The total variance can be verified by calculating the difference between actual wages, £9898, and the standard labour cost of the actual production, £9975, ie,

£9975 – £9898 = **£77 Fav.**

In this case a higher rate was paid than planned but efficiency was better than anticipated. 2020 actual hours were used to produce 150 units. The standard allowed was 14 hours per unit; a total standard allowance of 150 × 14 = 2100 hrs.

∴ 80 hrs (2100 – 2020) at a standard rate of £4.75 were saved,

ie a favourable efficiency variance of 80 × £4.75 = £380.

Typical causes of labour variances:

Rate

a. Higher rates being paid than planned due to wage award.

b. Higher or lower grade of worker being used than planned.

c. Payment of unplanned overtime or bonus.

Efficiency

a. Use of incorrect grade of labour.

b. Poor workshop organisation or supervision.

c. Incorrect materials and/or machine problems.

d. Unexpectedly favourable conditions.

10. Basic variance analysis

So far only the basic material and labour variances have been dealt with. The illustrations have been deliberately kept simple in order to emphasise the major principles of variance analysis. There is considerable similarity between the methods of calculating all types of variance and students are advised to master the first part of this chapter before proceeding to the overhead and other variances which follow.

An important general principle which should be apparent at this stage is that actual prices or rates are never used in variance analysis, except to calculate the price or rate variance which is *always done first*.

11. Introduction to overhead variance analysis

Before dealing with the individual variances it is necessary to recall some of the earlier material in the book. Overheads are absorbed into costs by means of predetermined overhead absorption rates (OAR) which are calculated by dividing the budgeted overheads for the period by the activity level anticipated. The activity level can be expressed in various ways (units, weight, sales etc,), but by far the most useful concept is that of the Standard hour. It will be recalled that the 'Standard hour' is a unit measure of production and is the most commonly used measure of activity level. Thus:

$$\text{Total overhead absorbed} = \text{OAR} \times \text{SHP}$$

where SHP is the number of Standard Hours of Production.

Where the Standard costing system uses total absorption costing principles (ie, where both fixed and variable overheads are absorbed into production costs) the total overheads absorbed can be subdivided into Fixed Overhead Absorption Rates (FOAR) and Variable Overhead Absorption Rates (VOAR) thus:

$$\text{Fixed overheads absorbed} = \text{FOAR x SHP}$$

$$\text{Variable overheads absorbed} = \text{VOAR x SHP}$$

$$\text{and Total overheads absorbed} = (\text{FOAR} + \text{VOAR}) \text{ x SHP.}$$

Where standard *marginal* costing is used, only variable overheads are absorbed into production costs and thus only variances relating to variable overheads arise; fixed overheads being dealt with by the budgetary control system. Thus it will be seen that overhead variance analysis is considerably simplified when standard marginal costing is employed.

All the overhead variances depicted in Figure 25.1 and the Notes are described and illustrated below. Firstly where the overheads are sub-divided into Fixed and Variable elements and then the simpler approach where overheads are considered in total.

The following data will be used for the examples:

Budget for February Department No. 82

	£
Fixed Overheads	11,480
Variable Overheads	13,120
Labour Hours	3280 hrs
Standard Hours of Production	3280 hrs

Actual results for February Department No. 82

	£
Fixed Overheads	12,100
Variable Overheads	13,930
Actual Labour Hours (ie, clock hrs)	3,150
Standard Hours Produced	3,230

Based on the budgeted figures the predetermined overhead absorption rates can be calculated:

$$\text{F.O.A.R.} = \frac{\text{Budgeted fixed overheads}}{\text{Budgeted activity level}} = \frac{£11,480}{3280 \text{ Std. hrs}} = \textbf{£3.5/hour}$$

$$\text{V.O.A.R.} = \frac{\text{Budgeted variable overheads}}{\text{Budgeted activity level}} = \frac{£13,120}{3280 \text{ Std. hrs}} = \textbf{£4/hour}$$

The total overhead absorption (O.A.R.) is the total of the F.O.A.R. and the V.O.A.R. ie, **£7.5/hour**

Notes:

a. It will be seen that *budgeted* labour hours and the *budgeted* standard hours production are the same. This is the normal planning basis. If actual labour hours and the standard hours actually produced also were the same, then efficiency would be exactly as planned and no efficiency variances would arise. It will be seen from the data that this is not the case on this occasion.

b. It will be apparent that because absorption rates for fixed overheads have been calculated the examples will be based on total absorption costing principles.

c. The absorption base is the standard hours of production.

12. Variable overhead variances

This paragraph describes the variable overhead variance, the variable overhead expenditure variance and the variable overhead efficiency variance.

Definitions:

❑ **Variable overhead variance**

   The difference between the actual variable overheads incurred and the variable overheads absorbed. (This variance is simply the over or under absorption of overheads).

❑ **Variable overhead expenditure variance**

   The difference between the actual variable overheads incurred and the allowed variable overheads based on the actual hours worked.

❑ **Variable overhead efficiency variance**

   The difference between the allowed variable overheads and the absorbed variable overhead.

Formulae

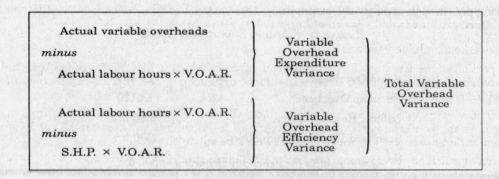

Example 3

(Based on data from para 11)

		£		
minus	Actual variable overheads	13,930	Variable Overhead Expenditure Variance **£1,330 Adv**	Total Variable Overhead Variance **£1,010 Adv**
	Actual labour hours × V.O.A.R. (3,150 × £4)	12,600		
minus	Actual labour hours × V.O.A.R.	12,600	Variable Overhead Efficiency Variance **£320 Fav**	
	S.H.P × V.O.A.R. (3,230 × £4)	12,920		

Note:

The total variance can be confirmed by calculating the difference between what variable overheads actually cost and what the actual production absorbed in variable overheads.

$$£13,930 - £12,920 = £1010 \text{ (Adv)}.$$

13. Fixed overhead variances

This paragraph describes one approach to fixed overhead variance analysis and covers the fixed overhead variance, the fixed overhead expenditure variance, the fixed overhead volume variance and its sub-variances the capacity variance and the efficiency or productivity variance.

Definitions

❑ Fixed overhead variance

The difference between the standard cost of fixed overhead absorbed in the production achieved, whether completed or not, and the fixed overhead attributed and charged to that period.

Note:

As with the variable overhead variance, the fixed overhead variance simply represents under or over absorption.

❑ Fixed overhead expenditure variance

The difference between the budget cost allowance for production for a specified control period and the actual fixed expenditure attributed and charged to that period.

Note:

More simply, though somewhat less precisely, this variance can be defined as the difference between actual fixed overheads and allowed or budgeted fixed overheads.

❑ Fixed overhead volume variance

That portion of the fixed production overhead variance which is the difference between the standard cost absorbed in the production achieved, whether completed or not, and the budget cost allowance for a specified control period.

Note: The volume variance arises from the actual volume of production differing from the planned volume. As shown in the variance chart, Figure 25.1, the volume variance can be subdivided because the total difference in the volume of production can be due to either

i. Labour efficiency being greater or less than planned (the efficiency variance).
ii. Hours of work being greater or less than planned (the capacity variance) or some combination of both. The formal definitions of these variances follow.

❑ Fixed overhead efficiency variance.

That portion of the fixed production overhead volume variance which is the difference between the standard cost absorbed in the production achieved, whether completed or not, and the actual direct labour hours worked (valued at the standard hourly absorption rate).

❑ Fixed overhead capacity variance.

That portion of the fixed production overhead volume which is due to working at higher or lower capacity than standard. Capacity is often expressed in terms of average direct labour hours per day, and the variance is the difference between the budget cost allowance and the actual direct labour hours worked (valued at the standard hourly absorption rate).

The formulae for these variances are given below:

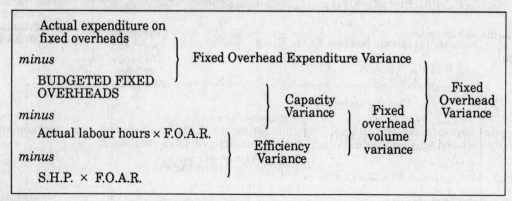

Example 4

(based on data from Para. 11)

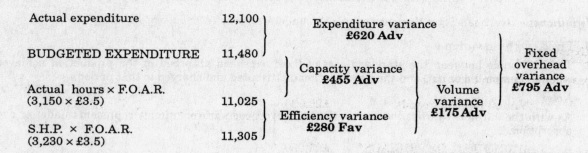

14. Total overhead variances

As previously explained there is a simpler approach to overhead variances whereby the overheads are not sub-divided into fixed and variable elements. In such circumstances the following variances can be calculated.

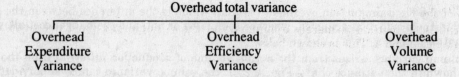

Definitions:

Overhead total variance –

'The difference between the standard overhead cost specified for the production achieved, and the actual cost incurred'.

Overhead expenditure variance –

'The difference between budgeted and actual overhead expenditure'.

Overhead efficiency variance –

> 'The difference between the standard overhead rate for the production achieved and the standard overhead rate for the actual hours taken'.

Overhead volume variance –

> 'The difference between the standard overhead cost of the actual hours taken and the flexed budget allowance for the actual hours taken'.

The formulae are as follows.

Formulae

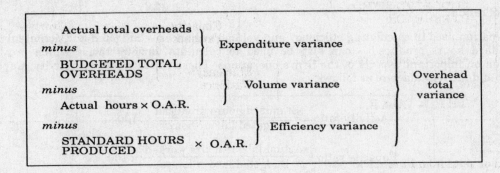

Note that the Overhead Total Variance equals the under/over absorption of overheads.

Example 5

(based on data from Para. 11)

Actual total overheads	£26,030	Expenditure variance £1,950 Adv
minus		
BUDGETED OVERHEADS*	£24,080	Volume variance £455 Adv
minus		
Actual hours × O.A.R. (3,150 × £7.5)	£23,625	Efficiency variance £600 Fav
minus		
STANDARD HOURS × O.A.R. PRODUCED (3,230 × £7.5)	£24,225	Overhead total variance £1,805 Adv

It will be seen that this method is merely a summary of the variable and fixed overhead variances calculated in Examples 3 and 4. This is shown below.

	Expenditure £	Efficiency £	Capacity £	Total £
Variable overhead variances (Ex. 3)	1330 (Adv)	320 (Fav)		1010 (Adv)
Fixed overhead variances (Ex.4)	620 (Adv)	280 (Fav)	455 (Adv)	795 (Adv)
Total overhead variances (Ex. 5)	1950 (Adv)	600 (Fav)	455† (Adv)	1805 (Adv)

It will be seen that what was previously entitled 'capacity variance' is directly equivalent to 'volume variance' when the Total Overhead approach is used.

---

* The budgeted overheads are found from the usual process of flexing a budget, ie, fixed overheads + the actual hours at the VOAR. Thus: £11,480 + (3150 × £4) = £24,080

† It will be seen that what was previously entitled 'capacity variance' is directly equivalent to 'volume variance' when the Total Overhead approach is used.

15. Reasons for overhead variances

Overhead variances are somewhat more complex than basic labour and material variances, mainly because of the conventions of the overhead absorption process. Overhead absorption rates are calculated from estimates of expenditure and activity levels and variances arise from differences in both of these factors. In addition, because overheads are frequently absorbed into production by means of labour hours, overhead variances can also arise when labour efficiency is greater or less than planned.

Overhead variances are essentially a book balancing exercise providing an arithmetic reconciliation between standard and actual costs. Apart from the expenditure variance the calculation of the other overhead variances provides little real control information being related more to the conventions of overhead absorption than to operational reality. This aspect of overhead variances is developed in more detail in 'Management Accounting' ibid.

16. Control ratios

The information used in calculating efficiency and volume variances – budgeted and actual labour hours and standard hours produced – can also be used to calculate various ratios which provide clear information on important aspects of the firm's operations. These ratios relate to Activity, Capacity and Efficiency and the formulae are as follows:

$$\text{Activity ratio} = \frac{\text{Standard hours produced}}{\text{Budgeted labour hours}} \times 100$$

$$\text{Capacity ratio} = \frac{\text{Actual labour hours worked}}{\text{Budgeted labour hours}} \times 100$$

$$\text{Efficiency ratio} = \frac{\text{Standard hours produced}}{\text{Actual labour hours worked}} \times 100$$

Example

Using the data from Para. 11, reproduced below, calculate the three control ratios.

Data:		
	Budgeted labour hours	3280
	Actual labour hours	3150
	Standard hours produced	3230

Solution

$$\text{Activity ratio} = \frac{3230}{3280} \times 100 = \textbf{98\%}$$

$$\text{Capacity ratio} = \frac{3150}{3280} \times 100 = \textbf{96\%}$$

$$\text{Efficiency ratio} = \frac{3230}{3150} \times 100 = \textbf{102\%}$$

The control ratios are directly related to variances and can provide a useful relative measure rather than the absolute measure provided by variances.

The Activity ratio is equivalent to the Fixed Overhead Volume variance.

The Capacity ratio is equivalent to the Fixed Overhead Capacity variance.

The Efficiency ratio is equivalent to the Fixed and Variable Overhead and Labour Efficiency variances.

17. More detailed material variances

The basic material variances were described earlier in the chapter. In certain circumstances it is conventional for sub-variances to be calculated, known as the *Direct Materials Mix Variance* and the *Direct Materials Yield Variance*. Typical circumstances in which such calculations are considered appropriate are those where the production process involves mixing different material inputs to make the required output. Examples include: the manufacture of fertilisers, steel, plastics, food products and so on. A feature of such processes is the existence of process losses through impurities, evaporation, breakage's, machinery failures and other such factors which affect the yield from the process.

There are several methods of calculating mix and yield variances; some treat the mix variance as part of the price variance, others that there should be a combined mix/price variance, whilst another approach is that the mix and yield variances are sub-variances of the usage variance. This latter approach is illustrated in Figure 25.1 and is included in the CIMA *Terminology* of *Management Accounting*.

There are two alternative ways of sub-dividing the usage variance. One uses the individual standard prices of the ingredients whilst the other uses a weighted average price for all ingredients. For the variance calculations these prices are applied to slightly different ingredient quantities. Both methods produce the *same mix and yield variances* in total; all that differs is the amount attributed to each constituent ingredient.

For identification the methods will be termed the 'individual price' and the 'weighted average price' methods and both are defined and illustrated below using the same data for comparative purposes. The individual price method (which is that in the CIMA *Terminology*) is illustrated first.

Definitions (Individual price method)

Direct Materials Mix Variance

> The difference between total quantity in standard proportion, priced at the standard price and the actual quantity of material used priced at the standard price.

Direct Material Yield Variance

> The difference between the standard yield of the actual material input and the actual yield, both valued at the standard material cost of the product.

18. Mix and yield formulae (individual price method)

Formulae

Direct Materials Mixture Variance	=	STANDARD COST of the actual quantity of the actual mixture	minus	STANDARD COST of the actual quantity of the STANDARD MIXTURE
Direct Materials Yield Variance	=	STANDARD COST of the actual quantity of the STANDARD MIXTURE	minus	STANDARD COST of the STANDARD QUANTITY of the STANDARD MIXTURE

Notes:

a. Because the price variance is always dealt with first, the mix and yield variances use only standard prices.

b. Note how the expressions move from actual to STANDARD values and that the second part of the mix variance is the same as the first in the yield variance.

c. The yield variance measures abnormal process losses or gains.

Example 6

A fertiliser is made by mixing and processing three ingredients, P, N and Q. The standard cost data are as follows:

		Standard Proportions	Standard cost
Ingredient	P	50%	£20 per tonne
	N	40%	£25 per tonne
	Q	10%	£42 per tonne

A standard process loss of 5% is anticipated.

In a period the output was 93.1 tonnes and the inputs were as follows:

		Actual usage	Actual price	Actual Cost
Ingredient	P	49 tonnes	£16 per tonne	£784
	N	43 tonnes	£27 per tonne	£1,161
	Q	8 tonnes	£48 per tonne	£384
				£2,329

Calculate all relevant material variances using the individual price method.

Solution

The total variance is calculated thus:

Standard cost for 1 tonne

Ingredient	P	0.5 tonne @ £20	=	£10
	N	0.4 tonne @ £25	=	£10
	Q	0.1 tonne @ £42	=	£4.2
				£24.2

1 tonne of input at standard produces 0.95 tonnes of output so the standard cost per tonne of output is:

$$£24.2 \times \frac{100}{95} = £25.473684$$

∴ Standard cost of actual output = 93.1 × £25.473684 = £2371.6

Actual cost of output = £2329

∴ Total Variance = £42.6 **(Fav)**

The three relevant variances are: Price, Mix and Yield which are to be calculated in that order. The usage variance is merely the total of the mix and yield variances.

The summary of the variance calculations is given below followed by explanatory notes for a. to d.

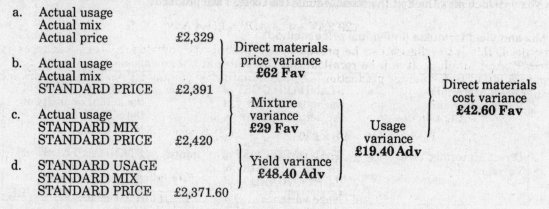

It will be seen how the factors involved, usage-mix-price, start all at actual and move stage by stage to become all at STANDARD. This is the key to remembering the method of calculation.

Notes:

a. Actual usage, actual mix, actual price is the cost given in the question, ie, **£2,329**.

b. The actual usage in the actual proportions is evaluated at the standard price, ie,

$$£(49 \times 20) + (43 \times 251) + (8 \times 42) = \textbf{£2,391}$$

c. The standard mix is found by putting the actual total quantity (100 tonnes) into the standard proportions (50%, 40% and 10%), ie, 50P, 40N and 10Q. These are evaluated at the standard prices and compared with the values from b.

Ingredient	Actual usage	Total usage in standard proportions	Difference	Standard	Variance
	Tonnes	*Tonnes*	*Tonnes*	*£*	*£*
P	49	50	+1	20	20 Fav
N	43	40	−3	25	75 Adv
Q	8	10	+2	42	84 Fav
	100	100		Total Mix Variance	**29 Fav**

d. The standard usage is found by working back from the actual output (93.1 tonnes) to determine what the standard total quantity of inputs should be, assuming a normal process loss of 5%.

ie, standard output quantity = 95 % of standard input quantity

$$\therefore \text{Standard input quantity} \quad = \frac{100}{95} \times \text{actual output quantity}$$

$$= \frac{100}{95} \times 93.1$$

$$= \textbf{98 tonnes}$$

This value is pro rated in the standard proportions, calculated at the standard price and compared with the values from c. thus:

Ingredient	Total usage in standard proportions		Standard usage for output in standard proportions	Difference	Standard Price	Variance	
	Tonnes		*Tonnes*	*Tonnes*	£	£	
P	50	(98 x 50%)	49	−1	20	20	Adv
N	40	(98 x 40%)	39.2	−0.8	25	20	Adv
Q	10	(98 x 10%)	9.8	−0.2	42	8.4	Adv
	100		98		Total Yield Variance	48.4	**Adv**

The Mix variance plus the Yield variance equals the Usage variance, thus:

£29 FAV + 48.4 ADV = **£19.4 Adv**

If required, this latter figure can be proved by calculating the individual Usage variances for each ingredient and totalling. It will be recalled that the Material Usage variance is calculated as follows: (Standard quantity for actual production—Actual quantity) × Standard Price = Usage variance This formula gives:

Ingredient			
P	(49 − 49) × £20	=	NIL
N	(39.2 − 43) × £25	=	£95 Adv
Q	(9.8 − 8) × £42	=	£75.6 Fav
	Total Usage variance	=	**£19.4Adv** as above

The alternative weighted average price method is now defined and illustrated.

19. Alternative method for mix and yield variances

Definitions (weighted average price method)

Direct Materials Mix Variance

> The difference between the standard quantity of inputs for the output achieved and the actual quantity used priced at the difference between individual standard prices and weighted average standard price.

Direct Materials Yield Variance

> The difference between the standard quantity of inputs for the output achieved and the actual quantity used priced at the weighted average standard price.

Example 6 is reworked below based on these alternative definitions.

Example 6 (reworked)

The Total Variance is £42.6 ADV and the Price Variance is calculated in exactly the same manner and is, as previously, £62 Favourable.

To calculate the weighted average mix and yield variances the input quantity differences and the weighted average standard ingredient price have to be calculated.

Ingredient	Standard usage for output in std. proportions	Actual usage	Input differences
	Tonnes	Tonnes	Tonnes
P	49	49	–
N	39.2	43	–3.8
Q	9.8	8	+1.8
	98	100	–2.0

Weighted Average Standard ingredient price.

From the original data the standard cost of 1 tonne is:

£

Ingredient	P	0.5 × £20	=	10
	N	0.4 × £25	=	10
	Q	0.1 × £42	=	4.2
				24.2

∴ Weighted average ingredient cost is **£24.2 per tonne.**

These values are used in the variance calculations.

Mix variance:

Ingredient	Input differences	×	Standard price less weighted average price	=	Variance
	Tonnes		£		£
P	–				–
N	–3.8		(£25 – 24.2) = 0.80		3.04 Adv
Q	+1.8		(£42 – 24.2) = 17.80		32.04 Fav
			Total mix variance		**29.00 Fav**

Yield variance:

Ingredient	Input differences Tonnes	×	Weighted average standard price	=	Variance
	Tonnes		£		£
P	–				–
N	–3.8		24.2		91.96 Adv
Q	+1.8		24.2		43.56 Fav
			Total yield variance		**48.40 Adv**

Thus it will be seen that the alternative approaches produce the same total mix and yield variances but differ in the amount attributed to each ingredient. Which is the correct method?

No one method of calculating variances or any given variance is more correct than any other. The 'correct' variances are those which assist management to make the right decisions. Accordingly, management would use whichever of the above methods is deemed to provide the most relevant information if, in fact, mix and yield variances are thought to provide any useful information.

However, students should be aware that there are serious doubts about the usefulness and meaning of conventionally prepared mix and yield variances. These doubts are explored in 'Management Accounting' ibid.

20. Summary

a. Variance analysis is the process of analysing the total difference between planned and actual performance into its constituent parts.

b. Variance analysis must be useful to management otherwise it is pointless.

c. Variances should be calculated in accordance with responsibilities.

d. Although there are different names, each type of variance, materials, wages and overheads has a *price element* and a *quantity element*.

e. The relationship between variances must be considered. Variances should not be considered in isolation.

f. The basic materials variances measure the differences between actual and standard price and actual and standard usage.

g. Price variances are *always* extracted first. Thereafter all variance calculations use standard price.

h. The basic labour variances measure the difference between actual and standard wage rates and actual and standard labour efficiency.

i. An important factor in overhead absorption and overhead variance analysis is the activity level. Frequently this is measured in standard hours. A standard hour is a unit measure of production, not of time.

j. Using total absorption principles, both fixed and variable overheads are absorbed into production, so variances relating to both fixed and variable overheads will arise. Using standard marginal costing only variable overheads are absorbed into production overheads so that fixed overhead variances cannot arise.

k. Variable overhead variances reflect differences in variable overhead expenditure and labour efficiency.

l. The basic materials usage variance can be subdivided into a mix variance and a yield variance. These variances measure differences due to mixing in non standard proportions and to yields (ie, process losses) being different to those planned.

m. The Total Cost Variance, shown in Figure 1, is merely the total of all the variances ie, the Direct Materials Cost Variance, the Direct Labour Cost Variance and the Variable and Fixed Overhead Variances.

21. Points to note

a. Variances are related to responsibilities. It follows, therefore, that a manager should only be held responsible for a variance when he has control over the resource or cost element being considered.

b. It must be stressed that variance analysis merely directs attention to the cause of off-standard performances. It does not solve the problem, nor does it establish the reasons behind the variance. These are management tasks.

c. The variance described are ones commonly found, but many others exist. It would be impossible to describe or remember all the possible variances, but of far greater importance is to understand the principles underlying variance analysis; once this is done any given variance can be calculated easily.

d. The relationships between variances must always be considered. Rarely is a single variance of great significance. Is a favourable variance offset by a larger adverse one?

e. Although budgetary control and standard costing are techniques which use the same underlying principle, an important difference is that standard costs and variances form part of the double entry system, whereas budgetary control is in memorandum form.

f. The overhead volume variances can be criticised because information which is intended for product costing purposes (ie, absorption of fixed overheads into cost units) is used as a basis for control information. Fixed overheads are based more on time than activity so that it becomes very difficult to trace responsibility for an adverse volume variance. Because of this, the fixed overhead expenditure variance is probably the most relevant fixed overhead variance for control purposes.

Student self-testing

Self Review Questions

1. What is variance analysis? (2)

2. What is its purpose? (3)

3. Should variances be related to responsibilities? Why? (4)

4. In what ways can variance analysis be made more useful for management? (6)

5. What are the main sub-divisions of the Materials Cost Variance? (8)

6. Define the Direct Labour Efficiency Variance. (9)

7. What role does the number of standard hours produced have in overhead variance analysis? (11)

8. What are the main Variable Overhead Variances? (12)

9. What is the Fixed Overhead Volume Variance? (13)

10. What are the formulae for the – Activity Ratio, Capacity Ratio, and Efficiency Ratio? (15)

11. When are Mix and Yield variances calculated? (17)

12. How are the Mix and Yield variances calculated using the individual price method ? (18), using the weighted average price method? (19)

Exercises and examination questions with answers

Exercises

A25.1   The following details were extracted from the standard cost card of a component:

Raw Materials

2.82 Kgs @ £4.80 Kg

Direct Labour

Type I   6.5 hrs @ £3.75

Type II   3.85 hrs @ £4.25

During a period actual results were as follows:

Production 1,100 components.

Direct Material Purchase and usage

3,200 Kgs at a cost of £15,100

Wages Paid

Type I (7,120 hrs) £27,056

Type II (4,235) £ 18,210

You are required to calculate what variances have arisen.

A25.2   The following figures relate to the Milling Department:

Budget		£
Fixed overheads		2,500
Variable overheads		1,550
Hours		650

Actual		£
Fixed overheads		2,625
Variable overheads		1,710
Clock hours		625
Standard hours produced		680

Calculate the variances using the simpler, combined overhead recovery rate approach.

A25.3   Using the data in Exercise A25.2. calculate the variances relating to variable and fixed overheads.

A25.4   The standard mix of a product is as follows:

Material	% of input	Standard cost per Kg
X	30%	£1.20
Y	50%	£2.95
Z	20%	£1.15

The standard process loss is 15% of input weight. During a period 2,450 Kgs of good output were produced from the following inputs:

Material	Input Kgs	Price per Kgs
X	815	£1.25
Y	1,500	£2.90
Z	585	£1.15

You are required to calculate the relevant variances.

A25.5   In a period results were as follows:

Output 6250 units

Wages paid £33,680 for 10,400 hours

Material £17,059 for 3,850 Kgs.

Variances:

Labour Rate £1 720 (Adv)
Labour Efficiency £525 (Fav)
Material Price £1400 (Fav)
Material Usage £890 (Adv)

Calculate the Standard Prime Cost per unit.

Examination questions

A25.6 You have been asked to examine the performance of a subsidiary company for May. The subsidiary supplies kitchen units to the building industry. The standard cost of one unit for May was as follows:

		£
Direct Material	5 kilos at £4 per kilo	20
Direct Labour	4 hours at £6 per hour	24
Overheads (based upon an Overhead Absorption Rate of £4 per labour hour)		16
		60

The standard selling price of one unit was £100 and budgeted sales were 1,200 units. All overheads are fixed in nature.

The actual results were:

1. 1,300 units were made and sold for a total of £130,000.
2. Direct material used was 6,600 kilos at a total cost of £25,080.
3. Direct labour was 5,330 hours at a cost of £32,513.
4. Actual fixed overheads were £22,000.

Required:

Calculate the following:

a. i. Material price variance

 ii. Material usage variance

 iii. Labour rate variance

 iv. Labour efficiency variance

 v. Fixed overhead expenditure variance

 vi. Fixed overhead capacity variance

 vii. Fixed overhead efficiency variance

b. Prepare a variance report for management for May reconciling the standard profit expected at actual production with actual profit, clearly showing the total variance for each element of cost.(Note: sub-variances are not required).

c. Using your results from (a) and (b) above, comment upon the performance of the subsidiary company for May. *(AAT Cost Accounting & Budgeting)*

A25.7 Shown below is the standard prime cost of a tube of industrial adhesive, which is the only product manufactured in one department of Gum plc.

Industrial Adhesive

	£ per tube	£ per tube
Materials: Powder	1.50	
Chemicals	0.60	
Tube	0.30	2.40
Labour – Mixing and pouring		1.80
Total Standard Prime Cost		£4.20

The standard material allowance for each tube of adhesive is 2 lbs of powder, $\frac{1}{4}$ litre of chemical and one tube. The standard wage rate for mixing and pouring is £4.50 per hour.

During the previous month 4,500 tubes of adhesive were produced, there were no work-in-progress stocks at the beginning or end of the month, and the receipts and issues of materials during the month are shown below:

	Powder	Chemicals	Tubes
Opening Stock	1,500 lbs	200 litres	100 tubes
Purchases:	10,000 lbs at 70p per lb	600 litres at £2.30 per litre 600 litres at £2.50 per litre	5,000 tubes at 30p each
Issues:	9,800lbs	1,050 litres	4,520 tubes

The above materials are used exclusively in the production of the adhesive and it is the policy of the company to calculate any price variance when the materials are purchased.

The direct employees operating the mixing and pouring plant worked a total of 2,050 hours during the previous month and earned gross wages of £8,910.

Required:

a. Calculate for the previous month the following variances from standard cost: Materials Price Variance, analysed as you consider appropriate. Materials Usage Variance, analysed as you consider appropriate. Direct Labour Efficiency Variance. Direct Wages Rate Variance.

b. Discuss the possible causes of the material variances and the direct labour efficiency variance.
(ACCA, Costing).

A25.8 A manufacturing company has the following budgeted costs for one month which are based on a normal capacity level of 40,000 hours. A departmental overhead absorption rate of £4.40 per hour has been calculated, as follows:

Overhead item	Fixed	Variable per hour
	£000	£
Management and supervision	30	–
Shift premium	–	0.10
National insurance and pension costs	6	0.22
Inspection	20	0.25
Consumable supplies	6	0.18
Power for machinery	–	0.20
Lighting and heating	4	–
Rates	9	–
Repairs and maintenance	8	0.15
Materials handling	10	0.30
Depreciation of machinery	15	–
Production administration	12	–
	120	

Overhead rate per hour:	Variable	1.40
	Fixed	3.00
	Total	£4.40

During the month of April, the company actually worked 36,000 hours producing 36,000 standard hours of production and incurred the following overhead costs:

	£000
Management and supervision	30.0
Shift premium	4.0
National insurance and pension costs	15.0
Inspection	28.0
Consumable supplies	12.7
Power for machinery	7.8
Lighting and heating	4.2
Rates	9.0
Repairs and maintenance	15.1
Materials handling	21.4
Depreciation of machinery	15.0
Production administration	11.5
Idle time	1.6
	175.3

You are required to:

a. prepare a statement showing for April the flexible budget for the month, the actual costs and the variance for each overhead item;

b. comment on each variance of £1,000 or more by suggesting possible reasons for the variances reported;

c. state, for control purposes, with reasons to support your conclusions:

    i.   whether (b) above is adequate; and

    ii. whether the statement prepared in respect of the request in (a) above could be improved, and if so, how;

d. calculate:

    i.   the overhead absorbed;

    ii. the total amount under/over spent;

    iii. the overhead volume variance.

(CIMA, Cost Accounting)

A25.9 This diagram reflects material costs within a standard costing system. Assume that all the variances are unfavourable.

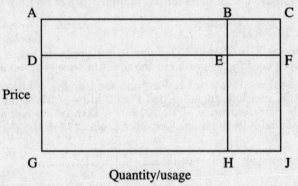

You are required to:

a. state which rectangle(s) represent the:

    i.   standard cost;

    ii.   actual cost;

    iii. material price variance;

    iv. material usage variance;

    v. material cost variance.

Note: Your answer should be stated in the form of the letters representing each corner of each rectangle; it is not necessary to draw the diagram.

b. give a short explanation of:

    i.   principal budget factor;

    ii. the membership and functions of a budget committee.

(CIMA, Cost Accounting 1)

A25.10 The following data relate to actual output, costs and variances for the four-weekly accounting period number 4 of a company which makes only one product. Opening and closing work-in-progress figures were the same

Actual production of Product XY	18,000 units
Actual costs incurred:	£000
Direct materials purchased and used 150,000 kilograms	210
Direct wages for 32,000 hours	136
Variable production overhead	38
Variances:	£000

Direct materials price	15 Favourable
Direct materials usage	9 Adverse
Direct labour rate	8 Adverse
Direct labour efficiency	16 Favourable
Variable production overhead expenditure	6 Adverse
Variable production overhead efficiency	4 Favourable

Variable production overhead varies with labour hours worked. A standard marginal costing system is operated.

You are required to:

a. present a standard product cost sheet for one unit of Product XY;

b. describe briefly three types of standard that can be used for a standard costing system, stating which is usually preferred in practice and why.

(CIMA, Cost Accounting)

A25.11 AB Ltd manufactures a range of products. One of the products, Product M, requires the use of Materials X and Y. Standard material costs for the manufacture of an item of Product M in Period 1 included:

Material X: 9 kilos at £1.20 per kilo.

Total purchases of Material X in Period 1, for use in all products, were 142,000 kilos costing £171,820. 16,270 kilos were used in the period in the manufacture of 1,790 units of Product M.

In Period 2 the standard price of Material X was increased by 6%, whilst the standard usage of the material in Product M was left unchanged. 147,400 kilos of Material X were purchased in Period 2 at a favourable price variance of £1,031.80. A favourable usage variance of 0.5% of standard occurred on Material X in the manufacture of product M in the period.

Required:

a. Calculate:

    i.   the total price variance on purchases of Material X in Period 1;

    ii. the Material X usage variance arising from the manufacture of Product M in Period 1;

    iii. the actual cost inflation on Material X from Period 1 to Period 2. Calculate as a percentage increase to one decimal place.

    iv. the percentage change in actual usage of Material X per unit of Product M from Period 1 to Period 2. Calculate to one decimal place.

b. Describe, and contrast, the different types of standards that may be set for raw material usage and labour efficiency.

(ACCA Cost and Management Accounting 1)

A25.12 RS Ltd makes and sells a single product, J, with the following standard specification for materials:

	Quantity	Price per Kilogram
	Kilograms	£
Direct material R	10	30
Direct Material S	6	45

It takes 30 direct hours to produce one unit of J with a standard direct labour cost of £5.50 per hour.

The annual sales/production budget is 1,200 units evenly spread throughout the year.

The budgeted production overhead, all fixed, is £252,00 and expenditure is expected to occur evenly over the year, which the company divides into twelve calendar months. Absorption is based on units produced.

For the month of October the following actual information is provided. The budgeted sales quantity for the month was sold at the standard selling price.

	£	£
Sales		120,000
Cost of sales:		
Direct Material used	58,136	
Direct wages	17,325	
Fixed production overhead	22,000	
		97,461
Gross profit		22,539
Administration costs	6,000	
Selling and distribution costs	11,000	
		17,000
Net profit		£5,539

Costs of opening stocks, for each material, were at the same price per kilogram as the purchases made during the month but there had been changes in the materials stock levels, viz:

	1 October	30 October
	Kgs	*Kgs*
Material R	300	375
Material S	460	225

Material R purchases were 1,100 Kgs for £35,000.

Material S purchases were 345 Kgs for £15,180.

The number of direct labour hours worked was 3,300 and the total wages incurred £17,325.

Work-in-progress stocks and finished goods stocks may be assumed to be the same at the beginning and end of October.

You are required:

a. to present a standard product cost for one unit of product J showing the standard selling price and standard gross profit per unit;

b. to calculate appropriate variances for the materials, labour, and fixed production overhead, noting that it is company policy to calculate material price variances at time of issue to production;

c. to present a statement for management reconciling the budgeted gross profit with the actual gross profit;

d. to suggest a possible cause for each labour variances you show under (b) above, stating whether you believe each variance was controllable and, if controllable, the job title of the responsible official. Please state the name and amount of each variance about which you write and explain the variance, quantifying it, where possible, in non-financial terms which might be better understood by line management.

(CIMA Cost Accounting)

Exercises and examination questions without answers

Exercises

B25.1   From the following data extract all the overhead variances.

Budgeted production	60 batches
F.O.A.R.	£12 per hour
Standard hours per batch	100
Budgeted variable overheads	£17,500
Actual results:	
Hours worked	7,150
No. of batches	75
Variable overheads	£24,250
Fixed overheads	£67,750

B25.2 The following details were obtained from the standard cost card:

Per Assembly:

Material	6 Kgs at £7.50
Skilled labour	10.5 hours at £4.00 per hour
Unskilled labour	5 hours at £2.50 per hour

Actual results:

Assemblies produced	425
Material purchased and used	2,750 Kgs at £7.25 Kg
Skilled labour	4,370 hours wages paid £18,150
Unskilled labour	2,100 hours wages paid £6,200

Calculate all variances

B25.3 The standard mix of an industrial plastic is as follows:

Input material	Percentage of input	Standard cost
A	45%	£6.50 per Kg
B	35%	£7.50 per Kg
C	20%	£15.25 per Kg

The standard process loss is 20% of input weight. During a period 850 Kgs of good output were produced from the following inputs:

Material	Input weight (Kgs)	Cost per Kg
A	390	£5.75
B	340	£7.80
C	220	£16.00

Calculate all relevant variances.

B25.4 Data

Budget for period

	£	
Overheads	26,520	(60% Fixed)
Labour hours	4,500	
Standard hours of production	4,500	

Actual results for period

	£
Expenditure on overheads	28,570
Labour hours	4,350
Standard hours of production	4,400

Calculate the overhead variances using the total overhead method.

Examination questions

B25.5 The NWA Plastic Company decides to manufacture 2 products and to implement a system of standard costing in respect of them. The standard costs are based on the following information for a standard week:

a. Expected output – Product A 20,000 units Product B 10,000 units

b. Materials required – Product A 800 kilos Product B 600 kilos

c. Price per kilo – both products £7.50

d. Wages – Product A 0.25 standard hours per unit

Product B 0.50 standard hours per unit

e. Total cost of labour is expected to be £20, 000 and labour grades are identical

f. Variable overhead is recovered at 40% of direct labour on both products

g. Fixed overhead is £10,000 allocated 60% to Product A and 40% to Product B

h. At the end of a week's production the following information was available:-

Actual output	– Product A	20,500 units
	– Product B	9,800 units
Materials used	– Product A	860 kilos @ £8.00 per kilo
	– Product B	560 kilos @ £8.00 per kilo
Labour used	– Product A	5,000 hours @ £1.90 per hour
	– Product B	5,000 hours @ £1.90 per hour

Variable overheads were fully recovered and total overheads incurred amounted to £19,020.

Using the information stated above:-

a. Prepare a statement of standard cost per unit for each product.

b. Calculate the variances and present them in the form of a statement for production management.

c. Comment briefly on the variances you have calculated and suggest any remedial action required.

(CIPFA, Management Accounting)

B25.6 You are given the following information in relation to the month just finished:

Budget Production	3,200 units	Actual Production	3,050 units
Actual hours worked	25,250	Actual labour cost	£60,600
Standard labour rate per hour	£2.60	Standard hours per unit	8

You are required:

a. to calculate:

   i. the efficiency ratio;

   ii. the capacity ratio;

   iii. the activity ratio;

b. to calculate:

   i. the labour efficiency variance;

   ii. the labour rate variance;

   iii. the labour cost variance;

c. the comment on the results.

(AA T, Cost Accounting and Budgeting.)

B25.7 a. Discuss in general the ways in which variance analysis helps management to control a business.

(*Note* – there is no need to refer to specific variances.)

b. NC Limited uses flexible budgets and standard costing for its single product P which it makes and sells. Three kilograms of material, having a standard cost of £4.40 per kilogram, are required for each unit of P. Actual material purchased and used in April cost £336,000 with the actual purchase price being £4.20 per kilogram. Each unit of P requires thirty minutes of direct labour time and the standard wages rate per hour is £5. The actual wages rate in April was £5.40 per hour. Sufficient direct labour time was utilised to produce 28,000 units of P although actual production in April was 25,000 units.

The company has a normal operating capacity of 15,000 hours per month and flexible overhead budgets are:

Hours of operation	12,500	14,000	15,000
	£	£	£
Variable production overhead	150,000	168,000	180,000
Fixed production overhead	270,000	270,000	270,000
	420,000	438,000	450,000

Actual overhead incurred in April was £430,000 of which £270,000 was fixed. You are required to:

   i. calculate the appropriate variances for material, labour and overhead;

   ii. show the variances in a statement suitable for presentation to management, reconciling the standard cost with the actual cost of production.

(CIMA, Cost Accounting)

B25.8   a.   A company manufactures and sells Product Beta.

The following information is available for a reporting period:

	Budget	Actual
Production of Beta	1,000 units	1,000 units
Sales of Beta	1,000 units	800 units
Sales revenue	£90,000	£95,000
Raw materials consumed	8,000 kilos	9,000 kilos
Cost of raw materials	£40,000	£36,000
Direct labour hours	5,000 hours	6,000 hours
Direct labour cost	£30,000	£37,200
Administration fixed costs	£10,000	£12,000

Included in the actual labour hours are 200 hours which were paid for, although no work was possible because of machine breakdown. There are no opening or closing stocks of raw materials, and no opening stocks of Product Beta.

Stocks are valued at standard production cost.

Required:

i.   Calculate the actual profit for the period.

ii.   Calculate appropriate variances for material and labour.

(AAT, Cost Accounting & Budgeting) part question

B25.9   A labour intensive production unit operating a standard absorption cost accounting system provides the following information for period 10:

Normal capacity, in direct labour hours	9,600
Budgeted variable production overhead	£3 per direct labour hour
Budgeted fixed production overhead per four-week financial period	£120,000

To produce one unit of output takes two hours of working.

Actual figures produced for the four-week period 10 were:

Production, in units	5,000
Variable production overhead incurred	£28,900
Fixed production overhead incurred	£118,000
Actual direct labour hours worked	9,300

You are required

a.   to calculate, in accordance with the 1991 edition of the Institute's Terminology, the variances for

i.   variable production overhead expenditure variance,

ii.   variable production overhead efficiency variance,

iii.   fixed production overhead expenditure variance,

iv.   fixed production overhead volume variance;

b.   to sub-divide your volume variance produced for (a) (iv) above into two sub-variances and explain the meaning of these in the form of a brief report to management.

(CIMA Cost Accounting)

B25.10   A company has two departments, A and B. Its budget and standards for last year included the following data:

	A	B
Units of production	8,000	10,000
Standard labour cost per hour	£4.00	£3.50
Standard labour hours per unit	2.0	1.5
The actual results were:		
Units of production	7,500	9,000
Labour cost	£70,875	£56,700
Labour hours	216,875	15,750

The company is unhappy with these results and wants to relate wage payments to labour effort and hopefully cut its own costs for the coming year.

Using the actual results above as a basis you are told that the two labour payment schemes under review would have the following features.

Scheme 1

A full time employee in Department A works 45 hours whilst in Department B a full-time employee works 42 hours. They will be paid the actual hourly rate which was paid last year in each department.

Scheme 2

Piecework rates are to be paid on the basis of £8 per unit in department A and £6 per unit in department B.

You are told that there will be an even flow of work over a 50 week year and the company has a policy of engaging full and part-time employees.

Required:

a. Calculate labour rate, labour efficiency and total labour cost variances for departments A and B for last year.

b. Analyse the results achieve in (a) suggesting reasons for any variances.

c. Calculate the weekly wage that would be paid to a full time employee in department A and department B under Schemes 1 and 2 for the coming year.

d. Recommend which scheme the company should contemplate using clearly stating your reasons.

(AAT Cost Accounting & Budgeting)

B25.11 A manufacturing company has recently introduced a system of standard costing and you, as the assistant management accountant, wish to demonstrate the value of the system to the management. The following data apply to period 4 which was a four-week financial period.

Direct Materials

Purchases:	Material A 50,000 kilograms for £158,750
	Material B 25,000 kilograms for £105,000
Used:	Material A 4,800 kilograms
	Material B 1,800 kilograms

Direct labour

	Actual hours worked	Wages paid £
Department 1	3,000	11,800
Department 2	2,400	13,250

Budgeted normal capacity expressed in direct labour hours

| Department 1 | 3,400 hours |
| Department 2 | 2,600 hours |

Other information

Standard cost for 1 unit of finished product

	Quantity	Price £	£
Direct material A	10 kgs	3.25	32.50
Direct material B	5kgs	4.00	20.00
Direct wages Dept 1	8 hours	4.00	32.00
Direct wages Dept 2	5 hours	5.00	25.00
			109.50

It had been decided to extract material price variances at the time of receipt.

400 finished goods units were produced in the period.

You are required

a. to calculate price and usage variances for each of the direct materials A and B;

b. to calculate rate and efficiency variances for the direct labour employed by each of Departments 1 and 2;

c. to suggest one possible reason for each of the variances shown in your answers to (a) and (b) above without stating the same reason more than once;

d. to calculate for Department 1 and Department 2

    i.   the production volume ratio,

    ii. the efficiency ratio;

e. to appraise critically the decision to calculate and extract material price variances at the time of receipt.

(CIMA Cost Accounting)

26: Standard costing variance analysis (sales and standard marginal costs) and special applications

1. Topics covered in this chapter

1. Sales margin variances
2. Standard Marginal Costing
3. Standard costing in process industries
4. Standard costing in the Public Sector
5. Significance of variances
6. Accounting for standard costing
7. Standard accosting and Advanced Manufacturing Technology
8. Appendix of Variance formulae.

2. Sales margin variances

The previous chapter described the various cost variances and it will be recalled that the objective of that analysis was to help management to control costs. To achieve planned profits management also wish to control sales, or more correctly, to control the profit (or margin) from sales.

This is the overall objective of calculating sales margin variances. Because cost variance analysis extracts all the differences between planned and actual costs, the products are *treated at standard manufacturing cost for the purpose of sales margin variance analysis*. Part of Figure 25.1, Chapter 25, is given below to show the variances dealt with in this chapter.

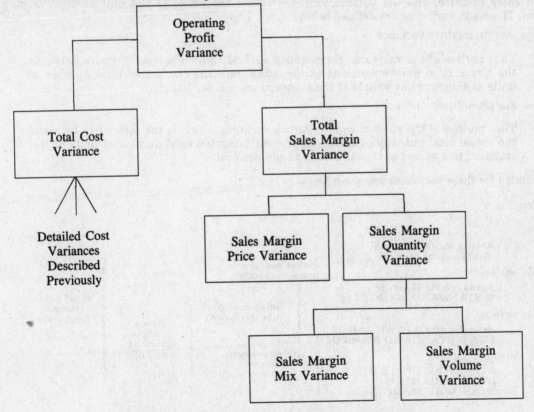

Figure 26.1 Extract from Figure 25.1, Chapter 25

3. Standard sales margin

This is the difference between the standard selling price of a product and its standard cost and it is the same as the standard profit for the product.

Note: The 'standard cost' referred to above is the 'total standard cost', ie, it includes both fixed and variable costs. When fixed costs are excluded it becomes the standard marginal cost and the difference between standard selling price and standard marginal cost is known as the *standard sales contribution.*

4. Sales margin variances – definitions

❒ Total sales margin variance

The difference between the budgeted margin from sales and the actual margin when the cost of sales is valued at the standard cost of production.

❒ Sales margin price variance

That portion of the total sales margin variance which is the difference between the standard margin per unit and the actual margin per unit for the number of units sold in the period.

Note: This is a normal price variance and could equally well be described as the 'sales turnover price variance'.

❒ Sales margin quantity variance

That portion of the total sales margin variance which is the difference between the budgeted number of units sold and the actual number sold valued at the standard margin per unit.

Note: This is a normal usage variance, analogous to the direct materials usage variance described in the previous chapter.

Where more than one product is sold, the Sales Margin Quantity Variance can be subdivided into a Mix Variance and a Volume Variance. The mix variance shows the effect on profits of variations from the planned sales mixture, and the volume variance shows the effect of the unit volume varying from standard. These sub-variances are defined below.

❒ Sales margin mixture variance

That portion of the sales margin quantity variance which is the difference between the actual total number of units at the actual mix and the actual total number of units at standard mix valued at the standard margin per unit.

❒ Sales margin volume variance

That portion of the sales margin quantity variance which is the difference between the actual total quantity of units sold and the budgeted total number of units at the standard mix valued at the standard margin per unit.

The formulae for these variances are given below.

Formulae

Note: There is considerable similarity in approach between these variances and the direct materials variances shown in Example 6 in the previous chapter.

Example 1

A company makes and sells three products, W, X and Y. During a period, budget and actual results were as follows:

Product	Budget				Budgeted Total Margin	Actual				Actual Total Margin
	Total Sales	Unit				Total Sales	Unit			
		Volume	Price	Margin			Volume	Price	Margin	
	£		£	£	£	£		£	£	£
W	5,000	500	10	2	1,000	5,500	550	10	2	1,100
X	4,500	300	15	3	900	4,000	250	16	4	1,000
Y	4,000	200	20	4	800	1,900	100	19	3	300
	13,500	1,000			£2,700	£11,400	900			£2,400

Calculate all relevant sales margin variances.

Solution

The summary of the variance calculations is shown below followed by explanatory notes.

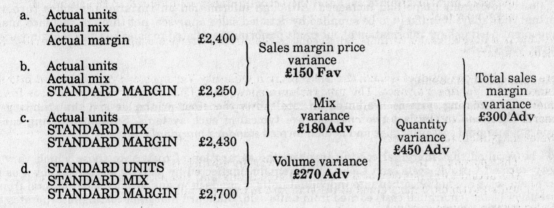

Notes:

a.   This is the actual total margin achieved as shown in the question, ie,

$$£(550 \times 2) + (250 \times 4) + (100 \times 3) = £2,400$$

b.   This is the actual units in the actual proportions, but at the budgeted margins ie,

$$£(550 \times 2) + (250 \times 3) + (100 \times 4) = £2,250$$

c.   This is the actual total number of units sold (900), but at the standard proportions, ie, 50%, 30% and 20%, valued at standard.

$$£(450 \times 2) + (270 \times 3) + (180 \times 4) = £2,430$$

d.   Finally the total budgeted margin is required. This is given in the question ie,

$$£(500 \times 2) + (300 \times 3) + (200 \times 4) = £2,700$$

The total variance can be verified by comparing the budgeted position with the actual position ie,

Total budgeted margin – Actual margin = Total sales margin variance

$$£2700 + 2400 = £300 \text{ Adv.}$$

By this stage the student should be totally familiar with the pattern of variance calculation and should be in a position to calculate an unfamiliar variance(s) from first principles. Get into the habit of cross-checking the detailed variances by calculating the total variance in the manner shown in each example in this book.

5. Limitations of sales margin variance analysis

The purpose of all variance analysis is to aid management control. To do this variances must be relevant and within a manager's control. Because there are so many external factors involved, the control of sales volume, sales margins and sales mix is extremely difficult and it is somewhat doubtful whether full variance analysis in this area is useful.

In certain circumstances however, some of the variances may provide useful information; for example, where the sales price is under the control of the selling organisation and prices are stable, then the sales margin price variance could be useful, alternatively when a manager is responsible for two or more products which are substitutes for one another (different qualities of paint) then the mix variance would show the effect of changes in demand and therefore might be useful.

Note:

In the above example the standard proportions were based on the number of units. On occasions where there are substantial differences in the selling prices of the various products within a firm (eg bicycle tyres and tractor tyres) standardising on the number of units could product distortions.

In such cases the proportions for the standard mix would be based on sales turnover, not units. This procedure would only alter the balance between the mix and volume variances. The overall quantity variance would remain unchanged.

6. Sales variance c.f. sales margin variances

Historically variance analysis in the sales area commenced with variances based on sales turnover, ie, if actual sales were above budget there was a favourable sales variance even if profits fell, perhaps because the sales of low profit items had increased. Although information on variations in sales turnover is important, nowadays it is likely to be supplied by detailed sales analyses, not through variance analysis. Management need to have information about profit performance related to sales so sales margin variances have been described.

7. Standard marginal costing

Most standard costing systems are based on total absorption cost principles and the standards and variances described in the last two chapters are typical of such systems. Standard costing can also incorporate marginal cost principles and is then termed *standard marginal costing*.

It will be recalled that marginal costing involves the separation of costs into those which vary with activity, termed variable costs, and those which remain unaffected by activity changes, known as fixed costs. Fixed costs are not absorbed into individual units of production and are deducted in total from the contribution (sales – marginal cost) earned from units sold. Standard marginal costing incorporates these principles and has the following characteristics.

a. Standards are developed in the normal manner and entered as usual on the standard cost card, except that fixed costs do not appear. The standard cost card includes:

> Direct materials
> Direct labour
> Direct expenses
> Variable overheads (ie, no fixed costs)

b. A standard contribution is set for each product and added to the standard marginal cost. This sets the standard selling price. The standard contribution becomes the standard sales margin.

c. A budgeted profit statement is prepared for the next period with budgeted levels of sales and fixed overheads. Typically this would appear as follows:

Budgeted Profit Statement for Period

	£
Budgeted sales (Budgeted no. of units × standard selling price)	XXX
less Budgeted cost of sales (Budgeted no. of units x standard marginal cost per unit)	XXX
= Budgeted Contribution	XXX
less Budgeted fixed costs	XXX
= Budgeted profit	XXX

d. Variance analysis is simplified because of the disappearance of the fixed overhead volume variance and its sub-variances, the capacity and volume productivity variances. All other variances are identical or very similar. The different categories are listed below.

Types of variance	Characteristics of standard marginal cost variances
Direct materials Direct labour Variable overheads	Identical to absorption standard cost variances
Fixed overheads	Only variance is the fixed overhead expenditure variance. All other fixed overhead variances disappear
Sales variances	With the exception that the standard sales margin is now the standard contribution, the variances are calculated in an identical manner. The new titles are: ❏ Sales contribution variance (was sales margin variance) ❏ Sales contribution price variance (was sales margin price variance) ❏ Sales contribution quantity variance (was sales margin quantity variance) ❏ Sales contribution mixture variance (was sales margin mixture variance) ❏ Sales contribution volume variance (was sales margin volume variance)

Standard marginal cost example

Example 2

The following data relate to the budget and actual results of a firm which makes and sells a single product and which employs standard marginal costing.

	Budget			*Actual*		
Production		10,000 units	Production			10,600 units
Sales		10,000 units	Sales			10,600 units
		£				£
Sales		180,000	Sales			180,200
less						
Standard Marginal Cost	£		Actual Marginal Cost		£	
– Materials	10,000		– Materials		11,600	
– Labour	60,000		– Labour		63,000	
– Var. Overheads	80,000	150,000	–Var. Overheads		83,000	157,000
= Contribution		30,000	= Contribution			22,600
less			*less*			
Fixed Costs		15,000	Fixed costs			15,600
= Budgeted Profit		£15,000	= Actual Profit			£7,000

The Standard cost card for the product is as follows:

	£
Materials 5 Kgs @ 20p/Kg.	1.00
Labour 4 hrs @ £1.50/hour	6.00
Var. Overheads 4 hrs @ £2/hour	8.00
= Standard marginal cost	15.00
Standard contribution	3.00
Standard selling price	£18.00

During the period material usage was 55,000 Kgs and 41,300 labour hours were worked.

Calculate all relevant variances.

Solution

The total variance is the Operating Profit variance, ie, the difference between budgeted and actual profit ie,

$$£15,000 - £7,000 = £8000 \text{ Adv.}$$

All other variances will in total equal the operating profit variance and will account for the difference between budgeted and actual profit.

The cost variances are as follows:

Materials variances:

Actual quantity Actual price	£11,600	}	Price variance **£600 Adv**	}	Direct materials variance **£1,000 Adv**
Actual quantity STANDARD PRICE (55,000 × 20p)	£11,000	}			
			Usage variance **£400 Adv**		
STANDARD PRICE STANDARD QUANTITY (53,000 × 20p)	£10,600	}			

Labour variances:

Actual hours Actual rate	£63,000	}	Rate variance **£1,050 Adv**	}	Direct labour variance **£600 Fav**
Actual hours STANDARD RATE (41,300 × £1.50)	£61,950	}			
			Efficiency variance **£1,650 Fav**		
STANDARD HOURS STANDARD RATE (42,400 × £1.50)	£63,600	}			

Variable overhead variances:

Actual variable overheads	£83,000	}	Expenditure variance **£400 Adv**	}	Variable overhead variance **£1,800 Fav**
Actual labour hours × V.O.A.R. (41,300 × £2)	£82,600	}			
			Efficiency variance **£2,200 Fav**		
S.H.P (ie 4 per unit) × V.O.A.R. (10,600 × 4 × £2)	£84,800	}			

Note: All the above variances are calculated exactly as described in the previous chapter.

Fixed overhead variance

Actual fixed overheads – Budgeted fixed overheads = £15,600 – £15,000

$$= £600 \text{ (Adv.)}$$

Note: This is the fixed overhead expenditure variance and is the only variance for fixed overheads.

Summary of cost variances

Direct materials	1,000 Adv.
Direct wages	600 Fav.
Variable overheads	1,800 Fav.
Fixed overheads	600 Adv.
∴ Total cost variance =	**£800 Fav.**

The sales variances are as follows:

Standard contribution = £3/unit and standard cost is £15/unit.

Actual contribution when sales
are valued at standard cost   £21,200
(£180,200 − (10,600 × £15))

Actual units @ STANDARD
CONTRIBUTION   £31,800
(10,600 @ £3)

BUDGETED UNITS @
STANDARD CONTRIBUTION   £30,000
(10,000 × £3)

Contribution
price variance
£10,600 Adv

Contribution
quantity variance
£1,800 Fav

Sales
contribution
variance
£8,800 Adv

Overall variance summary

Total cost variance	3800 Fav.
Total sales variance	£8,800 Adv.
= Operating Profit Variance	£8,000 Adv.

The variances could be used to show the change from budgeted to actual profit, ie,

	£	£
Budgeted profit		15,000
less Adverse variances	£	
Contribution Price Variance	10,600	
Direct Materials Variance	1,000	
Fixed overheads variance	600	12,200
		2,800
plus Favourable variances	£	
Contribution quantity variance	1,800	
Direct wages variance	600	
Variable overhead variance	1,800	4,200
Actual profit =		£7,000

8. Standard costing in process industries

Standard costing lends itself to continuous and repetitive methods of production so it follows that it can be applied most effectively in process industries. Where standard costing is used the process account is maintained at standard cost throughout and the problems and potential conflicts between the FIFO and average price methods are eliminated entirely.

The following example illustrates the technique.

Example 3

A company operates a standard process costing system and it is required to prepare the Process Account for Department 2, the necessary supporting expense accounts and show the variances which arise. The relevant data are as follows:

The opening WIP was 1000 units which had the following element values:

	Value £	% age complete
Input material (from Process 1)	5,000	100
Material B (introduced)	1,500	50
Labour	1,800	30
Overheads	3,000	30
	£11,300	

During the period 3800 units were received from Process 1 and 4000 completed units were transferred to Process 3.

The closing WIP was 800 units which were at the following stages of completion:

	% age completion
Input material	100%
Material B	60%
Labour	40%
overheads	40%

The following standard costs have been established for Process 2.

	Standard Cost per unit £
Input material (std. cost Process 1)	5
Material B	3
Labour	6
Overheads	10
Total standard cost	£24

During the period actual costs for Process 2 were:

Material B	£12,350
Labour	£23,800
Overheads	£42,000

Solution

All entries in the process account are at standard cost so all that is necessary is to calculate the effective units and multiply by the appropriate standard cost to obtain the values of transfers and closing WIP.

Cost Element	Completed Units	+	Equivalent Units in closing WIP	–	Equivalent Units in Opening WIP	=	Total Effective Units
Input Material	4000	+	800	–	1000	=	3800
Material B	4000	+	480	–	500	=	3980
Labour	4000	+	320	–	300	=	4020
Overheads	4000	+	320	–	300	=	4020

Transfers out of completed units

$4000 \times £24 = £96,000$

Closing WIP

Input Material	$800 \times £5$	=	£4,000
Material B	$480 \times £3$	=	£1,440
Labour	$320 \times £6$	=	£1,920
Overheads	$320 \times £10$	=	£3,200
			£10,560

Cost transfers to Process 2 account

Material B	$3980 \times £3$	=	£11,940
Labour	$4020 \times £6$	=	£24,120
Overheads	$4020 \times £10$	=	£40,200

The process account and the supporting expense accounts can now be prepared.

Process 2 A/C

	Units	£		Units	£
Opening WIP	1,000	11,300	Transfers to Process 3	4,000	96,000
Transfers from Process 1	3,800	19,000	Closing WIP	800	10,560
Material B		11,940			
Labour		24,120			
Overheads		40,200			
	4,800	106,560		4,800	106,560

Departmental Material B A/C

Stores	12,350	Process 2 A/C		11,940
		Material Variance A/C		410
	12,350			£12,350

Departmental Wages A/C

Wages	23,800	Process 2 A/C	24,120
Labour Variance A/C	320		
	£24,120		£24,120

Departmental Overhead A/C

Overheads	42,000	Process 2 A/C	40,200
		Overhead Variance A/C	1,800
	£42,000		£42,000

Thus it will be seen that the total variances are:

Total Material Variance £410 (Adv

Total Labour Variance £320 (Fav)

Total Overhead Variance £1,800 (Adv)

Given the requisite data on hours, rates, usage and prices these total variances could be analysed into their sub-variances in exactly the same manner as previously described.

9. Standard costing in the public sector

As previously stated where appropriate conditions exist (ie stability and repetition) standard costing can be used in the Public Sector. It can provide more detailed control information and is probably best suited to the parts of the sector where competition has been introduced. For example, where there has been competitive tendering for Refuse Collection, Street cleaning, Routine House Maintenance and so on.

Example 4

The Direct Service Organisation of Loamshire District Council have been awarded the street cleaning contract against competition from private firms. The contract price is £6.2 per kilometre of road and the budget and actual results for Period 1 are as follows:

Period 1

Budget

	£	£
12,500 kilometres of cleaning @ £6.20 km		77,500
Direct Labour (3200 hours @ £7)	22,400	
Direct materials (1250 kgs @ £5)	6250	
Variable Overheads (3200 hrs @ £4.5)	14,400	
Fixed Overheads	25,600	68,650
= Budgeted surplus		8,850

Actual

	£	£
11,750 kilometres cleaned @ £6.2 km		72,850
Direct Labour (3050 hours @ £7.1)	21,655	
Direct materials (1160 kgs @ £5)	5800	
Variable Overheads	13,945	
Fixed Overheads	25,100	66,500
= Actual surplus		6,350

Required

a. Calculate the variances in as much detail as possible

b. Reconcile the budgeted and actual surpluses.

Solution

a. *Sales Variances*

Sales Margin Price Variance = Nil

Sales Margin Quantity Variance

= Quantity Shortfall × Standard Margin

= (12500 − 11750) × 0.708 = **£531 (A)**

Note:

	£
Standard price per km =	6.20
less Standard cost (£68,650 ÷ 12500) =	5.492
= Standard Margin =	0.708

Cost Variances

Labour:

	Actual cost	£21,655	Rate variance **£305 (A)**
less	Actual hours × Std rate (3,050 × £7)	£21,350	
less	Std hrs × Std rate (3,008[1] × £7)	£21,056	Efficiency variance **£294 (A)**

Material:

	Actual cost	£5,800	Usage variance **£75 (F)**
less	Std usage × Std price (1,175 × £5)	£5,875	

Variable overheads:

	Actual cost	£13,945	Expenditure variance **£220 (A)**
less	Actual hours × V.O.A.R. (3,050 × £4.5)	£13,725	
less	Std hrs × V.O.A.R (3,008 × £4.5)	£13,536	Efficiency variance **£189 (A)**

Fixed overheads:

Actual cost	£25,100	Expenditure variance **£500 (F)**
less		
Budgeted cost	£25,600	Capacity variance **£1200 (A)**
less		
Actual hours × F.O.A.R. (3,050 × £8)	£24,400	
less		Efficiency variance **£336 (A)**
Std hrs × F.O.A.R (3,008 × £8)	£24,064	

Notes:

1. Standard hours required for 11750 km $= \dfrac{3200}{12500} \times 11750$

   $= \textbf{3008}$

2. Fixed Overhead Absorption Rate $= \dfrac{£25,600}{3200}$

   $= \textbf{£8}$

b. *Reconciliation*

	£
Budgeted Surplus	8850
less Sales quantity Margin Variance	531
	8319

Cost Variances

		ADV £	FAV £
Labour :	Rate	305	
	Efficiency	294	
Materials :	Usage		75
Var. Overheads :	Expenditure	220	
	Efficiency	189	
Fixed Overheads :	Expenditure		500
	Capacity	1200	
	Efficiency	336	
		2544	575

less Net Cost Variance	1969
= Actual Surplus	6350

10. The significance of variances

Standard costing is an example of management by exception. It is hoped that the. The majority of items will progress according to plan (ie, at standard or budget) and only a few will show significant variances. It is of important to decide what is a 'significant variance' both for the accountant and the manager.

From a practical viewpoint a variance can be considered significant when it is of such a magnitude, relative to the standard or budget, that it will influence management's actions and decision. Variances may arise for a number of reasons of which the following three are the most important:

    a.   Failure to meet a correctly set and agreed standard.

    b.   An incorrectly set or out of date standard.

    c.   Random deviations.

Variances arising from reasons a. and b., if of sufficient magnitude, are variances which require further investigation and possibly management action. Random deviations, ie, fluctuations which have arisen by chance are, by definition, uncontrollable. The problem remains of how to determine whether a variation from standard is attributable to chance and not significant or whether it is due to a controllable cause and therefore significant. The discussion on the significance of variances and setting control limits applies both to standard costing and budgetary variances.

11. Standard costs as a range

Typically a standard cost is shown as a single figure, but more correctly it should be considered as a band or range of values with the standard cost as the central value. This is illustrated below by a graph representing the times taken for a number of batches of an assembly.

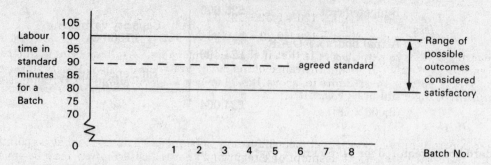

Figure 26.2 Standard Labour time for Assembly 100 X

If the actual result falls within the band it is considered satisfactory and the variance would not be deemed to be significant. If the actual result was outside this band it would be considered significant and would be reported and possibly a fuller investigation mounted. When used in this fashion, the range of values shown on the graph is known as a *control band* and the upper and lower limits known as *control limits*.

12. Setting control limits

The control limits may be set by estimation or statistical analysis.

a. *Estimation*

   This approach is the most commonly used and bases the control limits on judgement or experience. Typically a figure of ± 5% is used and variances within this range would be deemed insignificant. Although obviously lacking any statistical rigour, this approach is practical and implicitly uses the same concepts as more rigorous methods.

b. *Statistical analysis*

   Up until now the term 'significant' has been used in a general sense. More precisely, a variance which is statistically significant is one which is of such a magnitude that it is unlikely to have arisen purely by chance. Statistical probability tests based on the properties of normal distributions can be used to determine whether differences from standard arise from chance (ie, not significant) or from controllable causes (ie, significant).

   To set control limits which can be used to determine statistical significance is dependent upon certain statistical assumptions regarding costs and upon being able to calculate or estimate the standard deviation of the costs. (The statistical techniques alluded to above are covered in most statistics textbooks and would form part of Foundation Level Studies for all accounting students). Based on the properties of the normal distribution, control limits at any level can be set, for example:

   5% control limits are set at mean ± 1.96 standard deviations

   2% control limits are set at mean ± 2.33 standard deviations

   1% control limits are set at mean ± 2.57 standard deviations

   0.2% control limits are set at mean ± 3.09 standard deviations

Example 4

   The standard usage of a part is 120 per assembly and analysis of past usage indicates that the standard deviation of usage is 4 items.

   a. What are the 2% control limits?

   b. What is the meaning of such control limits?

   c. Show the control limits graphically.

Solution

a. 2% control limits are set at the mean ± 2.33 s.d.

ie, 120± 2.33 (4)

ie, **120 ± 9.32**

Upper control limit = 120 + 9.32 = **129.32**

Lower control limit = 120 – 9.32 = **110.68**

b. The meaning of these control limits is that if chance alone cause variations from standard, then 98% of variances should fall within the range of the mean (standard) ± 2.33 standard deviations. If a variance falls outside these limits ie, above 129.32 or below 110.68, then the variance is said to be *significant at the 2% level.*

Note:

Although setting control limits by statistical means appears to be more rigorous, it must be pointed out that some of the necessary statistical assumptions regarding the cost distribution may be invalid in practice and also that the calculation or estimation of the standard deviation may be difficult.

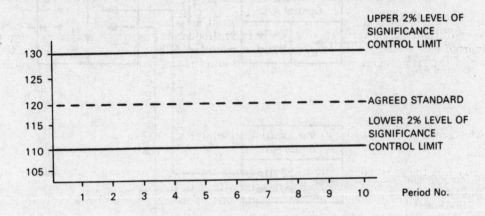

Figure 26.3 Graph of Control Limits

13. Variance control charts

Whether the control limits are set by statistical analysis or by estimation, a variance control chart can be a useful device, particularly for the identification of trends in the variance. A series of increasing adverse variances, although still within the control limits, may point to a growing problem which perhaps may be rectified before it becomes significant. Not all variances which are significant, ie, outside the control limits, require detailed investigations. Often the cause is already known or readily ascertainable. The likely benefits of a detailed investigation must be compared with the costs involved.

14. Accounting for standard costing systems

Standard costs and the resulting variances form part of the double entry accounting system. Whether the accounting system is an integrated one or separate financial and cost records are kept, there are common features in the way standard costing is normally dealt with in the accounts.

a. Variances are isolated as early as possible, ie, as near as possible to the point of occurrence or when the element of cost is charged to production by being debited to the Work-in-Progress A/c.

b. Variance accounts are maintained for each type of variance. Each period these accounts are closed down and the balances transferred to the Costing P + L account.

c. Transfers between the Work-in-Progress, Finished Goods, and Cost of Sales accounts are at standard.

d. Stocks of W.I.P., Finished Goods, and Raw Materials are the balances on the respective accounts and are automatically valued at standard.

A diagram of typical entries in a standard costing system is shown in Figure 26.4.

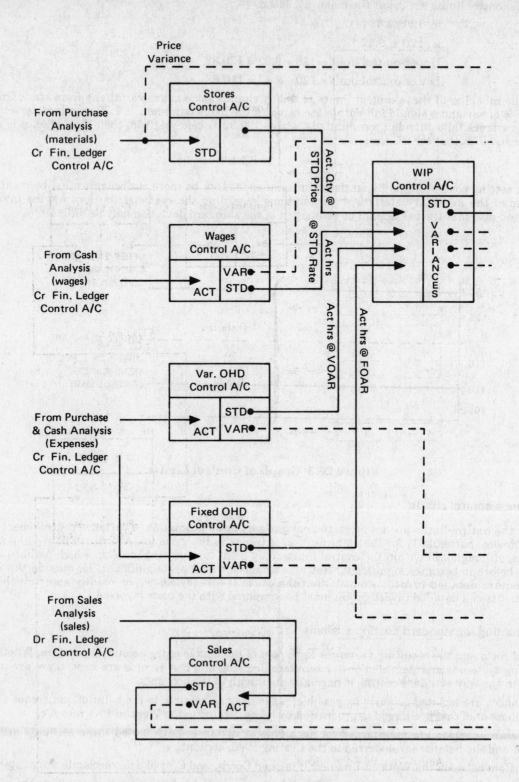

Figure 26.4 Typical accounting entries in a standard absorption costing system

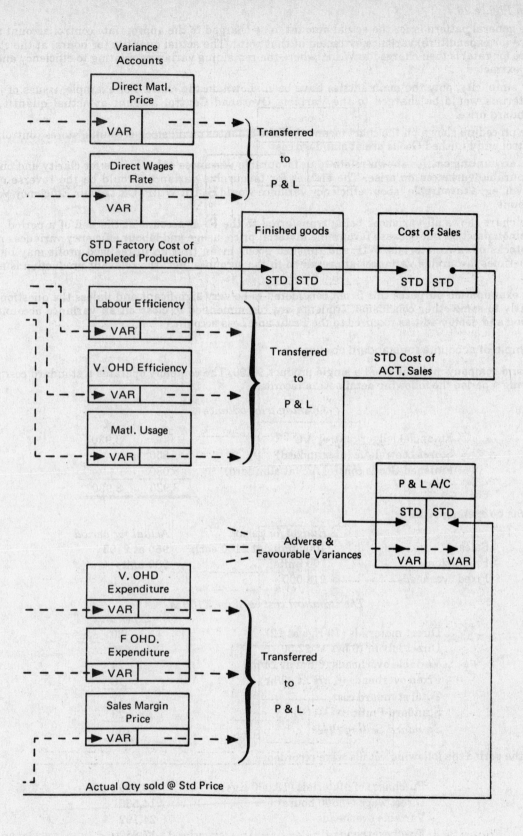

Figure 26.4 Typical accounting entries in a standard absorption costing system

Notes on Figure 26.4:

a. The general pattern is for the actual amount to be charged to the appropriate control account and the price (or expenditure) variance extracted at that point. The actual quantity (or hours) at the standard price (or rate) is then charged to W.I.P. where the remaining variances relating to efficiency and usage are extracted.

b. For simplicity, only the main entries have been shown on the chart. For example, issues of indirect materials would be charged to the Variable Overhead Control account at actual quantity times standard price.

c. The procedure shown on the chart means that the balances on all stock accounts, stores control, W.I.P. control and Finished Goods are at standard cost.

d. The accounting entries shown relate to unfavourable variances only. This is for clarity and obviously favourable variances do arise. The entries for favourable variances would be the reverse of those shown, eg, a favourable labour efficiency variance would be DR W.I.P. CR Labour Efficiency Variance account.

e. The chart shows all variances being transferred to the P+ L account at the end of a period. This is common practice, but because favourable material price, usage and labour efficiency variances relating to stocks of raw materials, WIP and finished goods mean that an unrealised profit may be taken, sometimes favourable variances are retained in the accounts until the relevant production is actually sold.

For examination purposes this is not considered to be very significant and unless the question points clearly to some other conclusion, students are recommended to close off all variance accounts each period and debit/credit as required to the Profit and Loss account.

15. Example of accounts for standard costing

Dalton and company make and sell a single product, X100. The company operates a standard cost system and during a period the following details were recorded.

Opening trial balance

	£	£
Financial ledger control A/C		3,930
Stores control A/c (at standard)	850	
Finished Goods control A/c (at standard)	3,080	
	3,930	3,930

There was no opening W.I.P.

	Budget for period	Actual for period
Sales	1000 units at £100 each	950 at £103
Production	100 units	980 units
Fixed overheads	£18,000	

The standard cost card for X100 is.

	£ per unit
Direct materials (10 Kgs at £2)	20
Direct labour (6 hrs at £2.50)	15
Variable overheads (6 hrs at £4/hr)	24
Fixed overheads (6 hrs at £3/hr)	18
Total standard cost	77
Standard Profit	23
Standard Selling Price	100

During the period the following details were recorded:

	£
Purchases of materials (13,000 Kgs)	26,500
Direct wages (5600 hours)	14,560
Variable overheads	24,192
Fixed overheads	17,850
Material issues to production were 9810 Kgs	

Using the above information it is required to prepare all cost and variance accounts and a profit and loss account and a closing trial balance.

Solution

The first stage is to calculate the variances.

Cost Variances

Material Price = $(13000 \times £2) - £26,500$	= £500 Adv.
Material Usage = $(9810 - (980 \times 10)) \times £2$	= £20 Adv.
Labour Rate = $(14560 - (5600 \times £2.50))$	= £560 Adv.
Labour Efficiency = $(5600 - (980 \times 6)) \times £2.50$	= £700 Fav.
Variable Overhead Expenditure $(£24192 - (5600 \times £4))$	= £1792 Adv.
Variable Overhead Efficiency $(5600 - (980 \times 6)) \times £4$	= £1120 Fav.
Fixed Overhead Expenditure = $£18000 - £17850$	= £150 Fav.
Fixed Overhead Volume = 20 units $\times £18$	= £360 Adv.

Sales Margin Variance

Standard sales margin = £23 and actual margin	= £26
$\therefore$ Sales margin price variance = $(£26 - £23) \times 950$	= £2850 Fav.

Stores Control

Balance	850	WIP	19,620
F.L. Control	26,000	Balance	7,230
	26,850		26,850
Balance	7,230		

Wages Control

F.L. Control	14,560	Labour Rate Variance	560
		WIP	14,000
	14,560		14,560

Variable Overhead Control

F.L. Control	24,192	Expens. Variance	1,792
		WIP	22,400
	24,192		24,192

Sales Control

Marg Price Variance	2,850	F.L. Control	97,850
P + L	95,000		
	97,850		97,850

Cost of Sales

Fin. Goods	73,150	P + L	73,150

Financial Ledger Control A/c

Sales	97,850	Balance	3,930
		Purch (std)	26,000 (a)
		Purch Variance	500
		Wages	14,560
		Variable Ohds.	24,192
Balance	12,620	Fixed Ohds.	17,850
		Profit	23,438
	110,470		110,470
		Balance	12,620

Finished Goods Control

Balance	3,080	Cost of Sales	73,150 (b)
WIP	75,460	Balance c/f	5,390
	78,540		78,540
Balance	5,390		

Fixed Overhead Control

F. L control	17,850	Volume	360
Expen. Var.	150	WIP	17,640
	18,000		18,000

WIP Control

Wages	14,000	Material usage var.	20
Labour efficiency var.	700	Finished goods	75,460 (c)
Material	19,620		
Var. Overhead	22,400		
Vr, Ohd. Eff. variance	1,120		
Fixed overhead	17,640		
	75,480		75,480

Variance Accounts

Material Price

F.L. Control	500	P + L	500

Labour Rates

Wage control	560	P + L	560

Variable Overhead Expenditure

Ohd. control	1,792	P + L	1,792

Fixed Overhead Expenditure

P + L	150	Ohd. control	150

Sales Margin Price

P + L	2,850	Sales Cont	2,850

Material Usage

WIP	20	P + L	20

Labour Efficiency

P + L	700	WIP	700

Variable Overhead Efficiency

P + L	1,120	WIP	1,120

Fixed Overhead Volume

Ohd. control	360	P + L	360

Profit Statement

		£
	Sales (at standard)	95,000
Less	Cost of sales (at standard)	73,150
	Standard Profit on actual sales	21,850
+	Sales margin price variance	2,850
		24,700

Add	Favourable cost variances		
	Fixed Overhead Expenditure	150	
	Labour Efficiency	700	
	Variable Ohd efficiency	1,120	1,970
			26,670

Less	Unfavourable cost variances		
	Materials price	500	
	Labour rate	560	
	Material usage	20	
	Fixed overhead volume	360	
	Variable Ohd efficiency	1,792	3,232
			23,438 (to Fin. Ledg. Con)

Closing Trial Balance

	£	£
Financial ledger control		12,620
Stores Control	7,230	
Finished Goods Control	5,390	
	12,620	12,620

Notes on accounts:

a. Price variance segregated so all materials carried at standard.

b. This is standard cost of 950 sales.

c. This is standard cost of 980 production.

In addition to the accounts and profit statement shown above management would also require an explanation of the difference between the actual results and the original budget.

16. Accounting for standard marginal costing

This follows very similar lines to standard absorption costing as previously described. Because fixed overheads are not included in the production accounts (WIP, Finished Goods and Cost of Sales) the following differences are necessary.

a. No fixed overheads are charged to WIP, finished goods and cost of sales.

b. The valuations of all types of stock, WIP, finished goods etc, will be at standard marginal cost.

c. Budgeted fixed overheads will be transferred directly from fixed overhead control to P+L, ie, Cr Fixed Overhead control Dr P+L, whilst any balance on the Fixed overhead control in comparison to actual fixed overheads, represents the Fixed Overhead Expenditure variance.

d. The standard sales margin becomes the standard sales contribution.

17. Standard costing and AMT

Standard costing originated in the early years of this century. It was a control system designed to serve the industrial conditions of the time and proved to be a sound management tool. Conditions, however have changed dramatically and doubts have been roused about the usefulness of standard costing in today's industrial environment.

Nowadays, world class manufactures use computer assisted Advanced Manufacturing Technology (AMT) and Just-in -Time (JIT) production and purchasing methods. There is a constant drive for improvement and excellence, the elimination of all forms of waste, a move towards zero defects and inventories, and production according to demand rather than for stock. As a consequence of these and other developments there have been major changes in cost patterns. These can be summarised thus:

❏ Direct labour now constitutes only a small proportion of costs– typically 5 – 15% in modern factories.

❏ Most costs are now fixed in the short run, including labour. In many factories, materials and power costs are the only variable costs.

❏ Overheads are a much higher proportion of total costs and need to be monitored and controlled much more closely than in the past.

18. Problems of standard costing in AMT factories.

It is argued that traditional standard costing and variance analysis is of limited value in these new circumstances. Some specific criticisms are:

a. By concentrating on a narrow range of financial factors, variance analysis ignores many other vital matters such as quality, lead times and customer satisfaction and encourages short-termism.

b. In a mainly fixed cost environment many variances are of little or no value for short-term cost control. For example, where labour costs are largely fixed, labour variances provide little information. Where overhead expenditure is unrelated to production volume, which is the case for many overheads, most overhead variances do not provide managers with realistic control information.

c. There is an over-emphasis on direct labour which is nowadays a small, and declining, proportion of total cost.

d. In traditional Standard Costing a Standard represents a target to be achieved and maintained whereas JIT has a philosophy of continuous improvement. This is best served by reporting a range of actual performance measures (eg lead and delivery times, defects found, quality and so on) over time so that trends in performance can be measured.

e. Some variances and traditional performance measures produce incorrect signals and work against AMT and JIT objectives. For example, if material price variances were used the buyer would be motivated to buy on price alone and thus avoid adverse variances. This may lead to larger inventories, poorer quality and irregular deliveries. JIT purchasing concentrates on quality, reliability and integrated deliveries not merely price.

Some traditional measures such as fixed overhead volume variances encourage maximising output even though this increases inventories, uses space and increases finance charges. JIT is demand led and aims to produce the required quantities only when they are actually needed. This may mean that there is idle time on occasions, which is considered preferable to producing for stock. Maximising output to move into stock does not maximise long-term profitability.

f. Much variance reporting is done weekly or even monthly. In consequence there is a significant delay between the actual event or operation and information about its performance. In fast moving JIT factories with short production cycles delays of this nature are unacceptable.

As a consequence more direct, non-financial performance measures are supplanting traditional standard costing reports and there is greater emphasis on control by production workers themselves. This is done by training workers to monitor continuously production flows, quality, set-up times, defects and so on.

19. Developments in control and performance measurement

In order to overcome some of the deficiencies outlined above and to make control and performance measurement systems more relevant to today's needs, numerous developments are taking place. These include:

a. Standards are being revised more frequently and allowances for scrap, waste and reworks eliminated. Standards are progressively tightened in line with the JIT philosophy of continuous improvement.

b. More use of on-line data capture and computing systems to process and display information continuously in real time.

c. Labour efficiency and material quantity variances are reported immediately in physical rather than financial terms. This is speedier and the physical values (hours taken, units produced, material and component usage) have more impact on production personnel than money values.

d. A broader range of performance measures are used, most of which are non-financial. Examples include ratios and data connected with; Manufacturing cycle times and efficiency, In-coming quality, customer satisfaction, delivery performance, Process times, Set-up times, Distance parts travel, No of defects and so on.

e. As discussed earlier in the book, changes in the level of many overheads are unrelated to short-term changes in production volume. These are, the costs described, by Kaplan as long-run variable costs. There is a growing realisation that these types of cost are best managed in the long-term by controlling the activities which drive them.

Accordingly Activity Based Costing and Activity Based Budgeting Systems are increasingly being used in factories with AMT and JIT systems. Activity cost management is of course equally applicable to service industries and the Public Sector as well as manufacturing firms.

20. Summary

a. The objective of Sales Margin Variance is to help to control the profit, ie margin, on sales.

b. The standard sales margin is the difference between the standard selling price and the standard cost of an item.

c. The total sales margin variance can be subdivided into Price and Quantity variances. Where more than one product is sold, the Quantity variance can be subdivided into Mixture and Volume variances.

d. The method of calculating the sales margin variances is similar to the methods used for calculating materials variances.

e. Standard costing can employ marginal costing principles and becomes known as Standard Marginal costing. Fixed costs are not absorbed into individual units of production.

f. A standard marginal cost is the total of all standard variable costs. A standard contribution is added to give a standard selling price.

g. Using standard marginal costing variance analysis is simplified because all fixed overhead variances disappear, except for the fixed overhead expenditure variance.

h. Material, labour and variable overhead variances are identical and, with the exception that the standard contribution becomes the sales margin, so are the sales variances.

i. Standard costing is particularly appropriate for process industries and where standard costing is employed all entries in the process account are at standard.

j. Significant variances are those which are of such a magnitude that management action will be called for.

k. The determination of what is a significant variance can be done by comparison with control limits.

l. Control limits can be set by judgement, for example plus or minus 5%, or by statistical analysis based on the properties of the normal distribution.

m. Where standard costing is used the variances form part of the double entry system.

n. Typically variances are isolated as early as possible and flows through the main accounts (WIP, Finished Goods, Process) are at standard cost.

o. The usefulness of standard costing in modern AMT factories has been questioned. Many variances are of little value when most costs are fixed and labour is a small proportion of total cost.

p. More immediate and relevant reporting on performance is required and a range of non-financial measures are used. These cover quality, process and lead times, set-up times, defects and so on. In addition cost management relating to activities is being more widely used.

21. Points to note

Variances calculated using traditional standards, as described in the last two chapters, are of value for control purposes only if the standard is still a realistic, attainable target in current conditions. If there have been uncontrollable changes in internal or external conditions then the standard may not now be a realistic one and it follows that the calculated variances will be of little or no value for control purposes and may even be misleading.

This is a real problem particularly in volatile conditions and one attempt to deal with this problem is to separate the traditional variances into *planning variances* and *operational variances*.

Planning variances seek to explain the extent to which the original standard needs to be revised in order to reflect current conditions. In effect the original standard is brought up to date so that it is a realistic, attainable target in current conditions. Operating variances indicate the extent to which attainable targets (ie, the adjusted standards) have been achieved. Operational variances are calculated after the planning variances have been derived and are thus a realistic way of assessing current performance.

Planning and operational variances are described more fully in 'Management Accounting' Ibid.

Student self-testing

Self Review Questions

1. What product cost is used in sales margin variance analysis? (2)

2. What is the standard sales margin? (3)

3. What is the standard sales contribution? (3)

4. What are the sub divisions of the total sales margin variance? (4)

5. What drawbacks are there in sales margin variance analysis? (5)

6. Distinguish between sales variances and sales margin variances. (6)

7. What are the major differences between standard marginal costing and standard costing based on total absorption costing principles? (7)

8. What are the features of standard process costing? (8)

9. What is a significant variance? (9)

10. What are control limits? (10)

11. In what ways can control limits be set? (11)

12. How are variances dealt with in the accounting records? (13)

13. What accounting differences arise when standard marginal costing is used? (15)

14. What problems are encountered using standard costing in AMT factories? (17)

15. Give examples of non-financial measures used for Performance Appraisal. (19)

APPENDIX – SUMMARY OF VARIANCE FORMULAE

Basic material variances

Materials Total Variance:

$$(\text{Standard Units} \times \text{Standard Price}) - (\text{Actual Units} \times \text{Actual Price})$$

Materials Price Variance:

$$(\text{Standard Price} - \text{Actual Price}) \times \text{Actual Quantity}$$

Materials Usage Variance:

$$(\text{Standard quantity for actual production} - \text{Actual quantity}) \times \text{Standard Price}$$

Note:

Price + Usage Variances = Total Variance

Basic labour variances

Labour Total Variance:

$$(\text{Standard labour hours produced} \times \text{Standard rate}) - (\text{Actual hours} \times \text{Actual rate})$$

Labour Rate Variance:

$$(\text{Standard rate} - \text{Actual rate}) \times \text{Actual hours}$$

Labour Efficiency Variance:

$$(\text{Standard hours produced} - \text{Actual hours}) \times \text{Standard rate}$$

Note: Rate + Efficiency Variances = Total Variance

Overhead variances

a. The following abbreviations are used:

> SHP = Standard Hours Produced
>
> VOAR = Variable Overhead Absorption Rate
>
> FOAR = Fixed Overhead Absorption Rate
>
> OAR = Overhead Absorption Rate (ie, Fixed + Variable)

b. Overhead variances can be calculated in different ways depending on the requirements of the firm and whether the overheads have been separated into fixed and variable components. The formulae that follow show the variances which could be calculated when the overheads are sub-divided into fixed and variable components and, alternatively, when a total overhead approach is used. The assumption throughout is that overheads are absorbed on labour hours.

Variable overhead variances

Variable Overheads Total Variance:

> Actual variable overheads – SHP × VOAR

Variable Overheads Expenditure Variance:

> Actual variable overheads – Actual hours × VOAR

Varisble Overhead Efficiency Variance:

> (Actual hours – SHP) × VOAR

Note:

Expenditure + Efficiency variances = Total variance

Fixed overhead variances

Fixed Overhead Total Variance:

> Actual fixed overheads – SHP × FOAR

Fixed Overhesd Capacity Variance:

> Budgeted fixed overheads – Actual hours × FOAR

Fixed Overhead Efficiency Variance:

> (Actual hours – SHP) × FOAR

Notes:

1. Capacity + Efficiency variances = Volume variance
2. Volume + Expenditure Variances = Total variance

Total overhead variances (ie, including both fixed and variable)

Total Overhead Variance:

> Actual total overheads – SHP × OAR

Total Overhead Expenditure Variance:

> Actual total overhead – Budgeted total overheads

Total Overhead Volume Variance:

> Budgeted total overheads – Actual hours × OAR

Total Overhead Efficiency Variance:

$$(\text{Actual hours} - \text{SHP}) \times \text{OAR}$$

Note:

Expenditure + Volume + Efficiency variances = Total variance

Material mix and yield variances (as sub-divisions of Usage Variance)

Materials Mix Variance:

(Actual quantity in Actual proportions – Actual quantity in Standard proportions) × Standard price

Materials Yield Variance:

(Actual quantity in Standard proportions – Standard quantity in Standard proportions) × Standard price

Note:

Mix + Yield variances = Usage variance

Sales margin variances

Note:

For sales margin variance analysis products are valued at standard manufacturing cost.

Sales Margin Total Variance:

$$\text{Budgeted total margin} - \text{Actual total margin}$$

Sales Margin Price Variance:

$$(\text{Actual units} \times \text{Actual margins}) - (\text{Actual units} \times \text{Standard margins})$$

Sales Margin Mix Variance:

(Actual units × Standard margins) – (Actual total units in Standard proportions × Standard margins)

Sales Margin Volume Variance:

(Actual total units in Standard proportions – Standard total units in Standard proportions) × Standard margins

Notes:

1. Mix + Volume variances = Quantity variance
2. Price + Quantity variances = Total variance

Exercises and examination questions with answers

Exercises

A26.1   A firm makes and sells three products, A, B and C. For period 9 the budgeted and actual results were as follows:

Budget

Product	Total Sales Value	Units	Price per unit	Standard Manufacturing Cost
	£		£	£
A	10,000	2,000	5	3.50
B	12,000	4,000	3	1.80
C	6,000	500	12	8.50
	£28,000	6,500		

Actual

Product	Total Sales Value £	Total Sales Units	Actual Margin £
A	10,500	2,100	1.35
B	12,920	3,800	1.20
C	6,844	580	3.35

Calculate all relevant sales margin variances.

A26.2 A firm employing standard marginal costing has the following actual results for a period:

Production 7,200 units

Material used	8,450 (420 Kgs)
Labour costs	35,280 (9,100 hours)
Variable overheads	34,200
Fixed costs	28,500
Direct Material Price Variance	370 (Fav)
Direct Material Usage Variance	252 (Fav)
Direct Labour Rate Variance	1,120 (Fav)
Direct Labour Efficiency Variance	1,040 (Fav)
Variable Overhead Expenditure Variance	2,350 (Adv)
Variable Overhead Efficiency Variance	910 (Fav)
Fixed Overhead Variance	500 (Adv)

Unfortunately the standard cost card has been lost together with the budget for the period but the accountant recalls that the budgeted output was 7,000 units.

You are required to derive the standard cost card for the item and the budget for the period.

A26.3 The standard labour cost of a component is £5 and a standard deviation of 20p has been estimated.

a. Calculate the 2% control limits.

b. In a period the output was 480 units and the labour cost was exactly on the upper 2% limit. What was the actual labour cost in the period and what was the labour cost variance?

A26.4 A firm operates a Standard Process Costing system and three partially complete accounts are given below:

Materials A/c

Stores Control	42,800	Process A/c	44,750
①			
	44,750		44,750

Wages A/c

Wages Control	21,407	Process A/c	18,480
		②	
	21,407		21,407

Overhead A/c

Overhead Control	34,906	Process A/c	31,521
		③	
	34,906		34,906

Required:

a. Complete the entries ①, ②, ③.
b. Explain their meaning.
c. Where would the double entries be?

Examination questions

A26.5 Your company's Sales division is split on a regional basis, north and south. The sales budget had been set at the following levels for the current year. Your company sells only one product with the budgeted price set higher in the south than in the north.

	Budgeted Units	Price	Budgeted Revenue
Northern Region	150,000	£10	£1,500,000
Southern region	180,000	£12	£2,160,000
Total	330,000		£3,660,000

Actual sales for the year turned out to be 350,000 units of which 40% were in the northern region. The total revenue for the northern region was £1,470,000 and for the southern region was £2,310,000. The budgeted and actual cost was £9 per unit.

The Sales Director has asked you to analyse the above figures before he has a meeting with the Sales Managers of the Northern and Southern regions.

Required:

a. Prepare profit statements to show budgeted profit, actual profit and total sales margins variance for each region and the company as a whole for the year under review.

b. Prepare sales margin price variances and sales margin quantity variances for each sales region and reconcile to the total sales margin variances calculated in a. above.

c. Analyse the above results for the Sales Director highlighting possible reasons for the variances and action that should be taken.

d. Outline the methods by which the standards set in a budget for sales volume and sales price will be arrived at.

(AAT Cost Accounting & Budgeting)

A26.6 a. A company is preparing its factory labour budget for the year ahead. In Department X a single product is manufactured. The following information is available about the product:

1. Stocks at the beginning of the budget period are expected to be 48,600 units.

2. Budgeted sales for the year ahead (including 49,000 units in Month 1) are 567,300 units.

3. Stocks at the end of the budget period are required to be sufficient to meet the first month's sales in the following period, when a 10% year-on-year increase is expected.

4. Standard efficiency for direct operatives is 112 units per hour.

5. The standard rate per hour for direct operatives in the budget period is £5.20 per hour.

Required:

Prepare the labour budget for direct operatives (hours and £) for the year ahead.

b. In the first month of the budget year, actual results in Department X were as follows:

1. Production of the single product was 50,400 units compared with a budget of 49,700 units.

2. Direct operatives worked 458 hours, including overtime of 6 hours. Overtime is paid at 50% above the basic wage rate. Overtime premium is charged to overhead.

3. Total labour cost of direct operatives was £2,420.25 including employee deductions of £565.35.

4. Indirect labour costs (excluding the overtime premium relating to direct operatives) totalled £1254.85, including employee deductions of £303.90.

Required:

i. Reconcile the budgeted and actual direct labour costs for Month 1, identifying variances from budget in as much detail as possible.

ii. Prepare Department X's wages control account for Month 1, assuming that efficiency variances are identified in the work in progress account.

c. Explain briefly the role of the following in the costing of labour:

i. Time Sheets.

ii. Piecework tickets.

(ACCA Cost and Management Accounting)

A26.7 B Limited operates an integrated accounting system and the following details given relate to one year.

You are required from the details given to:

a. enter in the appropriate ledger accounts the transactions for the year;
b. prepare a profit and loss account for the year; and
c. prepare a balance sheet as at the end of the year.

Trial balance at beginning of the year:	£000's	£000's
Capital	–	1,000
Reserves	–	200
Creditors	–	150
Expense creditors	–	20
Freehold buildings, at cost	500	–
Plant and machinery, at cost	300	–
Provision for depreciation of plant and machinery	–	100
Stock of: raw materials	220	–
work-in-progress	40	–
finished goods	60	–
Debtors	200	–
Bank	150	–
	1,470	1,470

The following data for the year are given:

		£000's
Materials:	purchased on credit	990
	returned to suppliers	40
	issued to production	850
Production:	wages incurred	250
	salaries	60
	expenses incurred	320
Carriage inwards		45
Provision for depreciation of plant and machinery		50
Production: Overhead absorbed		425
Production, at standard cost		1,600
Administration:	salaries	100
	expenses incurred	260
	overhead absorbed in finished goods	380
Selling and distribution:	salaries	80
	expenses incurred	120
	absorbed in cost of sales	210
Finished goods sold		2,000
Sales on credit		2,500
Sales returns		60
Variance: direct material:	price (adverse)	35
	usage (favourable)	20
direct wages rate (favourable)		15
direct labour efficiency (favourable)		30
production overhead: expenditure (adverse)		25
	efficiency (favourable)	40
Abnormal loss of raw material stock, insurance claim agreed and cash received		60
New machinery purchased, paid by cheque		50
Paid: creditors		895
expense creditors		730
Cash discount received from trade creditors		25
Paid wages and salaries		425
Deduction from wages and salaries		50
Received cheques from debtors		2,350
Cash discount allowed		35
Bad debts written off		25

All 'price' variances (ie, direct material price, direct wages rate, production overhead expenditure) are recorded in the relevant expenditure accounts; 'quantity variances (ie, direct material usage, direct labour efficiency, production overhead efficiency) are recorded in the work-in-progress account.

(CIMA, Cost Accounting 2)

A26.8   a.   Discuss the uses and limitations of standard cost, ignoring inflation.

b.   'A high rate of inflation tends to make standard costing a waste of time' said the production manager to her managing director.

You are required, as the assistant accountant, to draft a brief memorandum to the production manager in reply to her statement.

Notes:

1.   Do not repeat any part of your answer to a. above.

2.   Do not refer to planning and operational variances because such variances are outside the CAC syllabus.

c.   The following information relates to the standard cost and selling price of product Y:

		£ per unit (kg)
Direct materials	1 kilogramme	8.00
Direct labour	2 hours at £6 per hour	12.00
Variable overhead	2 hours at £1.20 per hour	2.40
Fixed overhead		4.00
Production royalty, per kg		0.80
		27.20
Selling and distribution costs at £2 per kg.		2.00
Total cost		29.20
Sales margin		5.80
Standard selling price		35.00

Variable overhead is deemed to vary with hours worked.

The budget for Period 9, on which the fixed overhead rate per kilogramme was based, was 10,000 kilograms. Sales Budget was 7,000 kg. After the standard had been set, the royalty was increased to £1 per kilogramme.

Actual sales, production and costs for Period 9 were as follows:

Sales	7,000 kilogrammes at £37 per kg
Production	8,000 kilogrammes
Costs:	
Direct materials, purchased and used	8,300 kilograms at £7.90 per kg
Direct wages incurred	17,000 hours at a cost of £107,000
Variable overhead	£18,800
Fixed overhead	£39,000
Royalties	£8,000
Selling and distribution costs	£12,000

Assume opening finished goods stock to be nil and the closing stock for both the statements required for i. and ii. below is to be valued at standard cost.

You are required to present in columnar format, using two facing pages in the answer book,

i.   actual revenues and costs;

ii.   standard revenues and costs;

iii.   variances analysed into price and usage/efficiency.

(CIMA Cost Accounting)

Exercises and examination questions without answers

Exercises

B26.1   The following data relate to a department for a single period.

	Budget
Labour hours	2,650
Standard hours production	2,650
Variable overheads	£8,480

	Actual
Labour hours	2,550
Standard hours produced	2,500
Variable overheads incurred	£8,650

You are required to plot the above data on a graph showing all variances.

B26.2   a. Why is it necessary to decide whether a variance is 'significant'?

b. Assuming that statistical methods are used to determine the signifcance of variances what are the 5% control limits when the standard usage is 250 and the standard deviation of usage is 8?

c. 2% control limits have been set by statistical methods and are 157.96 and 102.04. What is the standard usage and what is the standard deviation of the usage?

B26.3   A Firm operates a standard cost system and the following variances have been calculated:

	£	
Material price	350	FAV
Material usage	130	ADV
Labour rate	627	FAV
Labour efficiency	303	ADV
Variable overhead expenditure	804	FAV
Variable overhead efficiency	921	ADV
Fixed overhead expenditure	486	FAV
Fixed overhead volume	173	ADV

(Ignore sales variances)

The opening trial balance was as follows:

	£	£
Financial ledger control A/C		6,620
Stores Control A/C (at standard)	2,150	
Finished Goods (334 units)	4,470	

There was no opening or closing WIP.

The budget and actual results for the period were as follows:

	BUDGET	ACTUAL
Sales	4,900 units at £30	5,000 units at £30
Production	4,900 units	4,800 units
Fixed overheads	£8,500	

The following information was also available on the period's expenditure:

	£
Material purchases	23,250
Direct wages	19,480
Variable overheads	13,724
Fixed overheads	8,014

The closing stock of materials was £3,200 (at standard).

Using the above information prepare all necessary accounts and a profit and loss statement for the period clearly showing the final trial balance.

B26.4   No meaning can be attributed to any variance unless the basis of the standard is clearly understood.

Discuss this statement.

Examination questions

B26.5   The following standard costs apply in a business that manufactures a single product.

Standard weight to produce one unit	12 kilos
Standard price per kilo	£9
Standard Hours to produce one unit	10
Standard rate per hour	£4

Actual production and costs for one accounting period.

Material used	3,770 kilos
Material cost	£35,815
Hours worked	2,755
Wages paid	£11,571

The actual output was 290 units.

Required:

a. Calculate relevant material and labour cost variances, and present these in a format suitable for presentation to the management of the company.

b. Explain how standard costs for material and labour might be compiled.

c. Present the accounts for:

i.   Stores Ledger - assuming the price variance is calculated on receipt of materials.

ii. Wages.

iii. Work in progress.

(AAT Cost Accounting and Budgeting)

B26.6   a. Q Limited operates a system of standard costing and in respect of one of its products which is manufactured within a single cost centre, the following information is given.

For one unit of product the standard material input is 16 litres at a standard price of £2.50 per litre. The standard wage rate is £5 per hour and 6 hours are allowed in which to produce one unit. Fixed production overhead is absorbed at the rate of 120% of direct wages cost.

During the last four-week accounting period:

The material price variance was extracted on purchase and the actual price paid was £2.45 per litre.

Total direct wages cost was £121,500.

Fixed production overhead incurred was £150,000.

Variances	Favourable	Adverse
	£	£
Direct material price	8,000	
Direct material usage		6,000
Direct labour rate		4,500
Direct labour efficiency	3,600	
Fixed production overhead expenditure		6,000

You are required to calculate for the four-week period:

i.   budgeted output in units,

ii. number of litres purchased,

iii. number of litres used above standard allowed,

iv. actual units produced,

v.   actual hours worked,

vi. average actual wage rate per hour.

b. 'Physical measures of output and technical measures of production efficiency are often more useful than financial measures, particularly at the lower levels of an organisation.'

You are required, in the context of variance analysis, to discuss and expand on the above statement.

(CIMA Cost Accounting)

B26.7 JC Limited produces and sells one product only, Product J, the standard cost for which is as follows for one unit.

	£
Direct material X - 10 kilogrammes @ £20	200
Direct material Y - 5 litres @ £6	30
Direct wages - 5 hours @ £6	30
Fixed production overhead	50
Total standard cost	310
Standard gross profit	90
Standard selling price	400

The fixed production overhead is based on an expected annual output of 10,800 units produced at an even flow throughout the year; assume each calendar month is equal. Fixed production overhead is absorbed on direct labour hours.

During April, the first month of the financial year, the following were the actual results for an actual production of 800 units.

	£	£
Sales on credit: 800 units at £400		320,000
Direct materials: X 7,800 kilogrammes	159,900	
Y 4,300 litres	23,650	
Direct wages: 4,200 hours	24,150	
Fixed production overhead	47,000	
		254,700
Gross profit		65,300

The material price variance is extracted at the time of receipt and the raw materials stores control is maintained at standard prices. The purchases, bought on credit, during the month of April were: X 9,000 kilogrammes at £20.50 per kg from K Limited

Y 5,000 litres at £5.50 per litre from C plc.

Assume no opening stocks.

Wages owing for March brought forward were £6,000.

Wages paid during April (net) £20,150.

Deductions from wages owing to the Inland Revenue for PAYE and NI were £5,000 and the wages accrued for April were £5,000.

The fixed production overhead of £47,000 was made up of expense creditors of £33,000, none of which was paid in April, and depreciation of £14,000.

The company operates an integrated accounting system.

You are required to

a. i. calculate price and usage variances for each material,

   ii. calculate labour rate and efficiency variances,

   iii. calculate fixed production overhead expenditure, efficiency and volume variances;

b. show all the accounting entries in T accounts for the month of April - the work-in-progress account should be maintained at standard cost and each balance on the separate variance accounts is to be transferred to a Profit and Loss Account which you are also required to show:

c. explain the reason for the difference between the actual gross profit given in the question and the profit shown in your profit and loss account.

(CIMA Cost Accounting)

B26.8 B Ltd manufactures a single product in one of its factories. Information relating to the month just ended is as follows:

i.   Standard cost per hundred:

		£
Raw materials: 15 kilos at £7 per kilo		105
Direct labour: 10 hours at £6 per hour		60
Variable production overhead: 10 hours at £5 per hour		50
		215

ii.   226,000 units of the product were completed and transferred to finished goods stock.

iii. 34,900 kilos of raw material were purchased in the month at a cost of £245,900.

iv.   Direct wages were £138,545 representing 22,900 hours work.

v.   Variable production overheads of £113,800 were incurred.

vi.   Fixed production overheads of £196,800 were incurred.

vii. Stocks at the beginning and end of the month were:

	Opening Stock	Closing Stock
Raw materials	16,200 kilos	16,800 kilos
Work in progress	-	4,000 units, (complete at to raw materials but only 50% complete as to direct labour and overhead)
Finished goods	278,000 units	286,000 units

Raw materials, work in progress, and finished goods stocks are maintained at standard cost. You should assume that no stock discrepancies or losses occurred during the month just ended.

Required:

a. Prepare the cost ledger accounts relating to the above information in B Ltd's interlocking accounting system. Marginal costing principles are employed in the cost ledger.

b. Explain and contrast the different types of standards that may be set as a benchmark for performance measurement.   *(ACCA Cost and Management Accounting)*

B26.9   The financial and cost accounts of the MA Manufacturing Company for the year ended 30th September, have been reconciled as below.

Financial profit and loss account for the year ended 30th September.

Raw materials:					
Opening stock	56,450		Cost of goods manufactured		810,000
Purchases	324,560				
	381,010				
Closing stock	58,060	322,950			
Direct wages		247,320			
Production salaries		86,465			
Indirect wages		42,321			
Depreciation		50,000			
Power		10,642			
Telephone		8,742			
Rates		16,400			
Insurance		6,475			
Miscellaneous		18,325			
		809,640			
Work –in – progress:					
Opening stock	18,620				
Closing stock	18,260	360			
		810,000			810,000
Finished goods:			Sales		1,103,500
Opening stock	142,350				
Manufactured	810,000				
	952,350				
Closing stock	146,850	805,500			
Gross proft c/d		298,000			
		£1,103,500			£1,103,500

	£		£
Administration expenses	124,620	Gross profit b/d	298,000
Selling and distribution expenses	87,380	Discount received	1,600
Discount allowed	1,240		
Debenture interest	6,360		
Net profit c/d	80,000		
	£299,600		£299,600

Reconciliation of Financial and Cost Accounts Year ended 30th September.

	£		£
Profit as per financial accounts	80,000	Profit as per cost accounts	84,550
Discounts allowed	1,240	Discount received	1,600
Debenture interest	6,360	Difference in stock valuation	
Difference in stock valuation:		Raw materials:	
Work-in-progress:		Opening	700
Closing	480	Raw materials:	
Finished goods:		Closing	750
Opening	720	Work-in-progress	
		Opening	620
		Finished goods:	
		Closing	580
	£88,800		£88,800

Data in the cost accounts include:

	£
Direct material price variance	3,120 Adverse
Direct material usage variance	1,280 Adverse
Direct labour rate variance	4,160 Favourable
Direct labour efficiency variance	4,470 Favorable
Production overhead expenditure variance	4,880 Favourable
Production overhead volume variance	1,680 Adverse

You are required, from the above data, to show the following accounts as they should appear in the cost ledger:

a. stores ledger control;

b. work-in-progress ledger control;

c. finished goods ledger control;

d. profit and loss

(CIMA Cost Accounting 2)

27: Uniform costing

1. Topics covered in this chapter

> 1. Objectives of uniform costing
> 2. Features of uniform costing
> 3. Advantages and disadvantages.

2. Uniform costing defined

This can be defined as, 'the use by several undertakings of the same costing systems ie, the same basic costing methods, principles and techniques'. *Terminology*.

Uniform costing systems do not, in general, contain novel or advanced features. Rather they ensure that there are similar costing foundations and reports in a number of organisations. Uniform costing may be employed by members of the same group, various local authorities, or members of the same trade association. Examples of the application of uniform costing systems include: the printing, hotel and dairy industries, retail and wholesale groups with multiple outlets etc.

3. Objectives

The major objectives of uniform costing are,

a. To promote uniformity of costing methods so that valid cost comparisons can be made between organisations.

b. To serve as a basis for competitive but non destructive bidding.

c. To eliminate inefficiencies and promote good practices revealed by the cost comparisons.

d. To serve as a basis for government subsidies or grants which need similar costing systems to ensure equitable distribution.

4. Features of uniform costing systems

There is no hard and fast rule which determines what is a uniform costing system. However, it would be generally accepted that systems which follow agreed guidelines in the areas given below would be classed as uniform systems.

a. *Cost statements and reports.*

These should be organised and laid out in a similar fashion so that each element of cost revenue can be compared easily.

b. *Accounting periods.*

There must be agreement on whether calendar months or 4 week months will be used. Invariably there will be a standard accounting calendar.

c. *Cost classification.*

An agreed classification system must be used so that similar items will be classified in the same manner by all concerned. This will avoid an item being classified by some as indirect and others as direct.

d. *Valuation basis.*

There must be agreement of the methods of valuing stocks and W.I.P. and of the methods of charging stores issues eg, will FIFO, LIFO etc be used.

e. *Asset valuation.*

These must be agreement on the basis for fixed asset valuations eg, pure historical cost or revaluation at agreed periods.

f. *Depreciation.*

Both the method (reducing balance or straight line) and the actual rates for each type of asset must be agreed.

g. *Costing principles and techniques.*

There will need to be full agreement on the methods of cost build-up and whether marginal / absorption / standard costing or Activity Based Costing will be used.

h. *Bases of apportionment and absorption.*

When the type of system (marginal, absorption) is agreed, then there will have to be agreement on the way costs are apportioned to cost centres and on the way overheads will be absorbed into products. For example, will overheads be absorbed on units of production, labour hours, machine hours? What will be the basis of apportioning service costs to production cost centres? If ABC is used what cost pools and cost drivers will be used?

5. Advantages of uniform costing

a. *Cost comparability.*

This is the prime advantage. Because similar principles, bases and valuations are used, genuine cost comparisons can be made between different firms or organisations.

b. *Professional expertise.*

Frequently uniform costing systems are designed by consultants or senior, experienced accountants employed by an association. In this way the systems are soundly developed to high professional standards in a manner which would be too expensive for a single organisation, particularly one operating on a small scale.

c. *Basis for data processing.*

Uniform costing systems make it easier to computerise the accounting system of the various organisations. Similar cost classifications and report layouts considerably reduce the systems and programming effort required.

d. *Staffing costs and staff flexibility.*

Because of the similar nature of the costing systems it may be possible to use lower grade staff in the separate organisations with qualified, senior personnel at headquarters. Also transferability between organisations may be facilitated.

6. Disadvantages of uniform costing

a. *Inappropriateness to the individual organisation.*

Where members of a trade association use uniform costing, the chosen system may not suit every firm, particularly where there is a range of sizes and structures. Frequently a tailor made system would be better for particular organisations.

b. *Inflexibility.*

Uniform costing systems, like most centralised systems, are slow to adapt to changing conditions and demands upon them.

7. Summary

a. Uniform costing is the use by a number of undertakings of the same costing methods, principles and techniques.

b. The major objectives are to enable cost comparisons to be made, to serve as a basis for competitive bidding and to eliminate inefficiencies.

c. The major features of uniform costing include: similar cost statements, standard accounting periods, agreed cost classifications and valuation bases and agreed costing principles and techniques.

d. The major advantages are: genuine cost comparability, high professional standards, possibly lower staff costs and greater staff interchangeability.

e. The disadvantages are: possible inappropriateness to particular organisations and possible inflexibility in relation to changing circumstances.

Student self-testing

Self Review Questions

1. What is uniform costing? (2)

2. What are the objectives of uniform costing? (3)

3. What are the major features which determine whether a system can be classed as uniform? (4) 4. What are the advantages and disadvantages of uniform costing? (5 & 6)

Exercise with answer

A27.1   A firm of printers is contemplating joining the uniform costing system operated by its Trade Association but the Managing Director is dubious about the advantages of becoming involved in the scheme.

    Prepare a report to the Managing Director describing the advantages that the firm is likely to gain.

28: Costing and computers

1. Topics covered in this chapter

1. Features of computers useful for costing
2. Data processing or Transaction Processing
3. Decision Support Systems
4. Software and Application Packages
5. Spread sheets.

2. Background computer knowledge

All students taking costing examinations will either be concurrently studying computers and data processing or will be exempt from the subject because of their previous studies.

Accordingly no attempt will be made in this book to explain what computers are or how they operate. The emphasis will be on highlighting some of the ways they can be used for costing purposes and the resulting advantages and disadvantages. It is assumed that students are familiar with the more common terms used in data processing; for example, hardware, software, files, VDU, disc storage, terminal, on-line, application packages, printers, program, and so on.

Students unfamiliar with these terms or who wish to study computers and data processing in more detail are advised to consult a comprehensive book on the subject, for example Data Processing by Oliver and Chapman, D P Publications Ltd. Any questions in a costing examination which involve computers are thought unlikely to require much detailed technical computer knowledge, rather it is expected that they will test understanding of the application of computers to various facets of costing.

3. Why are computers useful for costing?

Computers can be valuable tools for costing purposes for the same reasons as they are for all other applications, namely, speed, accuracy, filing and retrieval abilities, calculating and decision making capabilities, input and output facilities.

These points are expanded below:

Speed

Relative to manual methods, all aspects of computer operations (except the initial manual input of data via the keyboard) take place at very high speeds. Whether the computer is calculating an overhead variance, making an entry on a job cost file, printing an actual/budget statement or carrying out some other costing task the computer does this in a minute fraction of the time it would take manually.

Accuracy

All computers incorporate inbuilt checking features which ensure for all practical purposes 100% accuracy in following a program. If a program has been thoroughly tested and produces the required output or performs the correct calculations, then this will be followed faithfully time after time after time.

On occasions computer systems do produce errors but investigations invariably show that these errors arise from such factors as errors contained in the data input or programming errors or an unforeseen combination of circumstances not allowed for in the program and not from computer malfunction.

Filing and retrieval abilities

Computer files, nowadays invariably maintained on some type of disc storage, and the associated software file handling systems, permit the rapid updating, amendment, cross-referencing and retrieval of huge volumes of data that would be virtually impossible using any manual system. Computer backing storage systems are becoming physically smaller, cheaper and permit faster access. These developments mean that accountants and managers can have more and more information readily available for instantaneous display on their terminal.

Calculating and decision making capability

Computer calculating speeds are measured in millionths of a second and are the heart of their power. In computer terms, the calculations required for costing purposes are very modest yet these same calculations done manually are tedious and time-consuming. Take for example the calculations required for apportioning various items of overhead expenditure over cost centres, which is a routine but necessary task. Each calculation is simple but the overall task, including cross and down totalling, can be lengthy when done manually, yet is ideally suited to the computer where it would be done virtually instantaneously.

Allied to the calculating power of the computer is its ability to test different values or conditions and depending on the results, take different actions. It is this ability which enables the computer to make decisions and makes it qualitatively different from other machines. The speed, calculating power and decision-making ability of the computer enables the accountant to extend the scope of his analysis beyond that which would be feasible manually, except for a special once-off exercise.

As an example, manually-prepared variance statements typically highlight variances above a certain value (say, £1000) or those more than a given percentage (say ± 5%) away from standard. The computer could be programmed to do this and also to analyse the variance and its significance by statistical methods including the calculation of the standard deviation – and, where a significant variance is detected, to retrieve the history of this variance for comparison and to ascertain trends. In short, a more detailed analysis could routinely be undertaken, where required, without extra effort on the part of the accountant who would know that all truly significant variances would be highlighted so leaving more time for any personal investigations felt necessary.

This, incidentally, is the key to effective use of computers for costing (or any other) purposes. They should be used, where feasible, for all forms of routine ledger keeping, calculating, searching, periodic statements, report production and so on in order that there is more time for activities requiring the human touch; for example interpretation of results, special investigations, planning, interviewing and so on.

Input and Output facilities

Computers can read and search files, print results or display information on VDU's at very high speeds. With modern software, report layouts can be altered at will, results can be displayed using a range of diagrammatic and graphical displays, often in full colour, and displays can be interrogated and manipulated by the user without leaving his desk. Taken together, the various facilities provide a far more flexible and speedy service than would be possible using manual means.

4. What applications should the computer be used for?

Because of the dramatically falling real cost of computer systems, their increasing power and the ever growing availability of software, more and more facets of costing and of other commercial tasks are worthwhile computer applications. In the early days of computers they were very expensive indeed and only a few large applications were economically worthwhile. Chip technology and miniaturisation has changed that situation dramatically.

As an example, 25 years ago a computer typically would cost £100,000 (say, 200 times the then cost of a Mini car or 100 times the salary of a cost clerk) yet today a machine with greater power and capacity which is infinitely more flexible and adaptable, can be purchased for £2000 or less (a quarter of the cost of a mini car or about a month's salary for a cost clerk).

Computer power has now become much cheaper than clerical power and this fact will cause significant changes in the way that all administrative work, including costing, is carried out. No longer is it necessary for all computer jobs to be high volume, repetitive tasks in order for them to be economically worthwhile. Smaller volume, more varied jobs and even one-off analyses and investigations using the 'what if' facility incorporated in much application software, have become a feasible proposition.

This means that virtually any costing task is now an economic application and indeed in an increasing number of organisations – even very small ones – the desk top micro linked to disc backing storage maintains all the costing records and produces all the required reports except those resulting from special one-off investigations.

Typical of the costing tasks now routinely dealt with by computer is the following list, which is by no means exhaustive.

☐ Job and Contract Costing and associated reporting.

☐ Stores and material control, including issues pricing, WIP and Finished Goods valuation, EOQ calculations etc.

☐ All aspects of labour costing.

☐ Nominal ledger including cost centre analysis, apportionment's, overhead calculations.

☐ Budgetary Control including comparative reporting, calculation of variances.

☐ Standard costing including control reports, variance calculations, testing variances by statistical means.

☐ Cash budgeting and reporting.

☐ Cost accounting using either integrated or separate ledgers.

☐ Forecasting cost and revenue behaviour using regression analysis or more sophisticated statistical techniques.

☐ Fixed asset recording including depreciation calculations.

... and so on.

In addition to dealing with the above and other basic costing tasks, computers are also being widely used for work which is generally regarded as Management Accounting. Examples include: investment appraisals, financial modelling, decision analysis and so on which can be grouped under the term 'Decision Support Systems'.

Thus it will be seen that there are two main areas of the application of computers in organisations although there are, of course, overlaps between the categories.

☐ Data processing (or Transaction Processing)

☐ Decision Support Systems (or End user computing)

These are shown in Figure 28.1

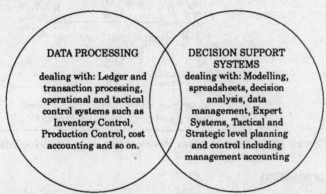

Figure 28.1 Computers and Information Systems

Both categories contribute to the overall Management Information System (MIS) of the organisation of which cost and management accounting information systems are a part. The two categories are developed below:

5. Data processing systems

These systems perform the essential role of collecting and processing the daily transactions of the organisation, hence the alternative term, *transaction processing*. Typically these include: all forms of ledger keeping, accounts receivable and payable, invoicing, credit control, rate demands, stock movements, cost recording and analysis etc.

These types of systems were the first to harness the power of the computer and originally were based on centralised mainframe computers. In many cases this still applies, especially for large volume repetitive jobs, but the availability of micro and mini computers has made distributed data processing feasible and popular. Distributed data processing has many variations but in essence means that data handling and processing are carried out at or near the point of use rather than in one centralised location.

Transaction processing is substantially more significant in terms of processing time, volume of input and output than say, information production for tactical and strategic planning. Transaction processing is essential to keep the operations of the organisation running smoothly and provides the base for all other internal information support. This is shown in Figure 28.2.

6. Characteristics of data processing systems

These systems are 'pre-specified'; that is their functions, decision rules and output formats cannot usually be changed by the end user. These systems are related directly to the structure of the organisation's data. Any change in the data they process or the functions they perform usually requires the intervention of information system specialists such as system analysts and programmers.

Some data processing systems have to cope with huge volumes and a wide range of data types and output formats. As an example consider the Electricity and Gas Board Billing and Payment Handling systems, the Clearing Bank's Current Accounting Systems, the Motor Policy handling systems of a large insurer and so on. The systems and programming work required for these systems represents a major investment. For example, the development of a large scale billing system for a public utility represents something like 100 man years effort.

Of course, data processing also takes place on a more modest scale and the ready availability of application packages – ie software to deal with a particular administrative or commercial task – means that small scale users have professionally written and tested programs to deal with their routine data processing. The better packages provide for some flexibility and the user can specify – within limits – variations in output formats, data types and decision rules.

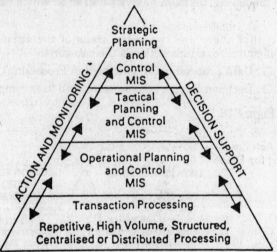

Figure 28.2 Transaction Processing as a base for MIS

7. Scope of transaction processing

Transaction processing is necessary to ensure that the day to day activities of the organisation are processed, recorded and acted upon. Files are maintained which provide both the current data for transactions; for example the amount invoiced and cash received during the month for statement preparation, and which also serve as a basis for operational and tactical control and for answering enquiries.

Transaction processing can be sub-divided into:

    a.   Current activity processing

    b.   Report processing

    c.   Inquiry processing

Figure 28.3 shows in outline these sub-divisions with examples of the various processing types drawn from inventory control and materials processing.

A routine data processing system is not in itself an MIS because it does not support all the management functions of the organisation nor does it have the decision focus which is the primary objective of MIS. Nevertheless it should be apparent that routine transaction processing is essential for day-to-day activities and provides the indispensable foundation upon which the organisation's MIS is built.

For example, there would be little point in developing a sophisticated flexible budgeting system complete with detailed variance analysis if the routine, but essential, cost analysis and recording system was not working perfectly.

8. Decision support systems (DSS)

DSS are alternatively termed *end-user computing systems*. Their objective is to support managers in their work, especially decision making.

DSS tend to be used in planning, modelling, analysing alternatives and decision making. They generally operate through terminals operated by the user who interacts with the computer system. Using a variety of tools and procedures the manager (ie the user) can develop his own systems to help perform his work more effectively. It is this active involvement and the focus on decision making which distinguishes a DSS from a data processing system. The emphasis is on support for decision making not an automated decision making which is a feature of transaction processing.

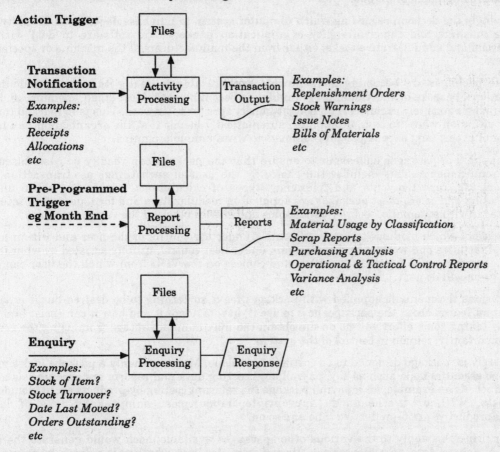

Figure 28.3 Sub-divisions of Transaction Processing with Inventory Control examples

DSS are especially useful for semi-structured problems where problem solving is improved by interaction between the manager and the computer system. The emphasis is on small, simple models which can easily be understood and used by the manager rather than complex integrated systems which need information specialists to operate them.

The main characteristics of DSS are:

a.   The computer provides support but does not replace the manager's judgement nor does it provide predetermined solutions.

b.   DSS are best suited to semi-structured problems where parts of the analysis can be computerised but the decision maker's judgement and insight is needed to control the process.

c.   Where effective problem solving is enhanced by interaction between the computer and the manager.

Typical of the functions and facilities available to support managers are the following:

a. Modelling and simulation
b. Spreadsheets
c. Statistical analyses of all types
d. Forecasting
e. Non-linear and Linear programming
f. Regression analysis
g. Financial modelling
h. Sensitivity and risk analysis
i. Activity cost management.

9. Software and application packages

Increasingly the decision regarding which computer system to purchase depends on the software support for the machine and the availability of application packages (ie software to deal with particular commercial and administrative tasks) either from the manufacturers of the machine or specialist software suppliers.

Because packages are becoming more flexible and are able to deal with an ever-widening range of applications, bespoke or individual programming is becoming rare. Most small, medium, and quite a few large organisations rely exclusively on bought-in packages for their work. This is in marked contrast to the earlier situation when, to own a computer, automatically meant that the organisation had to employ an number of expert (and expensive!) programmers to write unique programs.

The suppliers of packages endeavour to ensure that the package can readily be customised to suit the user's requirements. This includes the choice by the user of such things as: transaction types, data requirements, report layouts and frequency, types of calculations – including those unique to the organisation and so on. Most packages are supplied in modular form and form part of an integrated suite of packages with automatic, secure relationships and entries between the various modules.

The choice of which modules to use is, of course, under the control of the user and within a module the choice of facilities and work to be done is again under user control, usually assisted by what is termed the 'menu'. This is simply a display of options and choices on the VDU from which the user can decide what the program will do next.

On occasions the manuals supplied with packages leave something to be desired but it is vital that the accountant learns about the package, how to use it, how to adapt it and how it can assist him in his work. Only by taking some effort will he or she obtain the maximum advantage from using the computer and, most importantly, remain in control of the system.

Only rarely is package designed to do costing work alone. More commonly a package is designed to carry out some essential task, such as say, payroll, and costing data and reports are produced as an automatic by-product. As an example, for a payroll package the relevant costing by-products could include: entries for job costs, WIP, or overheads as appropriate, labour cost analyses by type of labour / cost-centre / productive / non-productive time and so on.

Similar principles apply to the various other packages available; each would generate the routine, but essential source data on which the costing system depends whether it relates to wages, materials, performance levels, waste and scrap, expenditure by cost centre and so on.

It will be realised that the same procedure is followed even when the system is dealt with by manual means. For example, a manual production control system provides data to the cost department on such matters as: output and performance levels, down time, scrap and re-work levels and so on. This data is usually transferred on a form or docket and would then be worked upon in the cost department to produce costing information by pricing, extending, calculating, making ledger entries and so on. Using a computer system the transfers, calculations and ledger updating would take place automatically with total accuracy and at high speed with obvious time savings.

It would clearly be impossible to describe the detailed capabilities of all the various packages available but students are strongly advised either to gain first-hand experience of using different packages or, failing this, to study articles in the technical journals which describe the facilities available or to read the suppliers' leaflets.

One particular type of software, the spread sheet package, is described below because of its particular usefulness for accounting and costing purposes.

10. Spread sheet packages

Most packages are designed to deal with a single specific application, for example, stock control, sales ledger and so on, but the concept of the electronic worksheet, which is the heart of a spread sheet package is so flexible and versatile that it can be used for innumerable tasks and applications. Once the principles have been mastered a spread sheet package is arguably the most useful type of package available to the accountant. The two pioneering spread sheet packages, VISICALC and SUPERCALC are by far the best selling software packages of all; clear evidence of the usefulness of spreadsheets.

The basic concept of spread sheets is that both alphabetic data (for labels, headings and titles) and numeric data can be stored and manipulated on an electronic worksheet arranged as a grid of say 64 columns, labelled alphabetically and a number of rows, say 256, which are numbered.

Each cell within the grid is referred to by its co-ordinates D3, E15, H182 etc and cell contents can be manipulated in virtually any fashion required, eg rows or columns added or subtracted, or worked upon by more complex formulae as required including any type of special calculations required by the user.

Because of the limit set by size of the VDU only part of the worksheet can be seen at any one time but all the data stored in the worksheet remains in the computer memory and can be recalled to the screen on the user's command, in a horizontal or vertical movement, by the process known as *scrolling*. A small part of a spread sheet grid pattern is show in Figure 28.4 with the cursor in position B6.

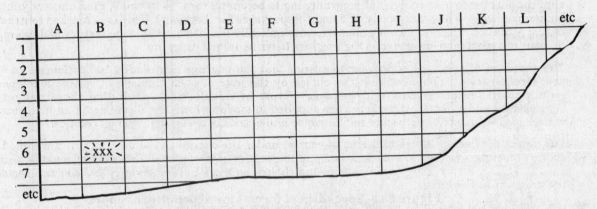

Figure 28.4 Part of spread sheet display

The key feature of a spread sheet package is its ability to change all elements in the matrix automatically when one or more of the key assumptions are changed. As an example the accountant may have prepared on the spreadsheet a series of detailed interlocking departmental operating statements culminating in an overall projected profit and loss account. If one or more of the variables (rates of pay, output levels, sales, absorption rates and so on) needs to be altered then the new value needs only to be entered once and the whole of the matrix is recalculated virtually instantaneously with all relationships, sub-totals and totals automatically catered for.

This facility allows a series of outcomes to be explored, providing answers to the 'what if' questions which are so essential to the accountant. For example, what would be the effect on profit of a change in inflation rate/cost per unit contribution margin/scrap rates or whatever factor need to be explored. Used in this way spread sheet packages perform a modelling function and this facility is greatly expanded in the latest spread sheet packages.

A few typical applications of spread sheet packages are briefly described below but it must be emphasised that the potential range of applications is enormous and is only limited by the imagination of the user.

11. Some applications of spreadsheets

Monthly expenditure reports

A format, ie the layout of the report with appropriate headings, is set up initially including the necessary simple formulae for calculating variances, percentages, subtotals, totals, etc. Various files of the data to be used on the spreadsheet display are maintained and updated each month by the current months actual figures.

Typically the files would include: cumulative actual, monthly budget, cumulative budget, previous year cumulative. On command, the necessary budget and actuals are copied into the spreadsheet model of the monthly report. The model is then automatically recalculated producing all the necessary percentages, variances and totals. A further command prints out the completed budget report ready for distribution.

A typical layout for such a report is shown in figure 28.5.

EXPEN-DITURE		CURRENT MONTH					YEAR TO DATE					CUMULATIVE LAST YEAR	
		% to Sales					% to Sales					Actual to Date	% to Sales
Type	Code	Actual	Budget	Actual	Budget	Variance	Actual	Budget	Actual	Budget	variance		
		%	%	£	£	£	%	%	£	£	£	£	%
OVERHEADS													
RATES 1012													
SALARIES 1020													
INSURANCE 1031													
etc.													

EXPENDITURE REPORT MONTH ....

BUDGET HOLDER ....   **DEPARTMENT** ....

Figure 28.5 Spreadsheet format for expenditure report

Cash budgets

Cash budgets are examples of routine but highly essential reports which need frequent updating to reflect current and forecast conditions, changes in credit behaviour, anticipated gains or expenditures and so on. In a similar manner to that already described the format, relationships and formulae required are set up initially and files maintained for brought forward information.

Each period (weekly, monthly, quarterly, as required) changes and up-to-date information are input and, in combination with the brought forward file data, the cash budget will be automatically projected forward by the spread sheet program with highlighted surpluses and/or deficiencies, balances carried forward from one period to another and all the usual contents of a cash budget. The budget could be shown in both an abbreviated and detailed format and could also be displayed in a graphical form.

Figure 28.6 shows the possible output of a Summary Cash budget and a corresponding graphical display, the facility for which is increasingly being included in modern spread sheet packages.

Maintaining standard cost records

Using traditional systems, standard costs were kept on individual cards with the standard amounts and standard prices of materials, labour and overheads extended and totalled on the card. Problems occur when there is a change in say the price of material, used in numerous components which are in turn incorporated into numbers of assemblies. A single price change might require hundreds or even thousands of amendments making standard cost revision a very lengthy and tedious manual task.

Using a spread sheet package, after the necessary once-off initial formatting and set-up procedures, the input of a material price change – or any other change – would cause the automatic reworking of the costs of all components, assemblies and finished items containing that material. This means that costs can be updated more frequently thus making the subsequent variance analysis more useful and, where standard costs are used in estimating, may mean that selling prices are more realistic. Overall the process becomes more accurate and considerable routine clerical work is avoided.

The above brief outline of spreadsheets and typical applications is, of necessity, at a basic level. Packages are becoming ever more comprehensive and thus the possible range of applications is increasing all the time. More integrated packages are becoming available where spreadsheets, modelling, data base management and word processing facilities are all included in the same package, greatly increasing the power and flexibility.

Spread sheet packages and integrated packages which include spread sheet facilities are widely available. Examples include: Visicalc, Supercalc, Practicalc, Mulitplan, Lotus 1-2-3, Symphony, and so on.

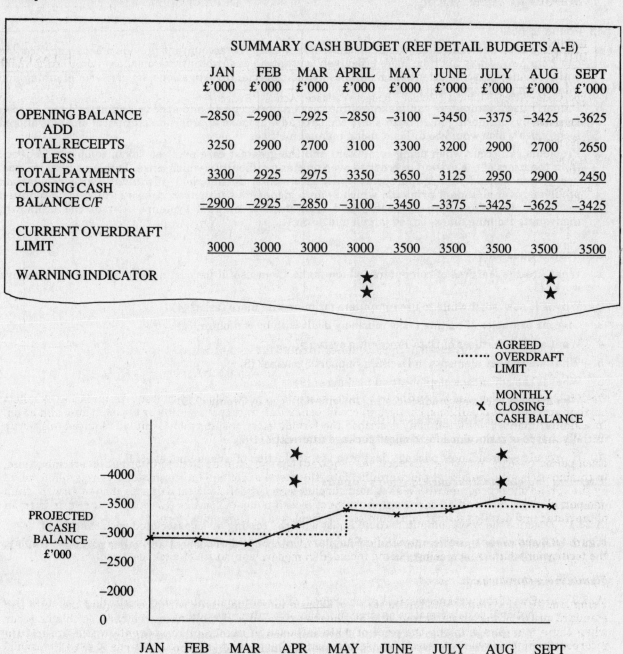

SUMMARY CASH BUDGET (REF DETAIL BUDGETS A-E)

	JAN £'000	FEB £'000	MAR £'000	APRIL £'000	MAY £'000	JUNE £'000	JULY £'000	AUG £'000	SEPT £'000
OPENING BALANCE ADD	−2850	−2900	−2925	−2850	−3100	−3450	−3375	−3425	−3625
TOTAL RECEIPTS LESS	3250	2900	2700	3100	3300	3200	2900	2700	2650
TOTAL PAYMENTS	3300	2925	2975	3350	3650	3125	2950	2900	2450
CLOSING CASH BALANCE C/F	−2900	−2925	−2850	−3100	−3450	−3375	−3425	−3625	−3425
CURRENT OVERDRAFT LIMIT	3000	3000	3000	3000	3500	3500	3500	3500	3500
WARNING INDICATOR				★★				★★	

AGREED OVERDRAFT LIMIT
········

MONTHLY CLOSING CASH BALANCE
✗

Figure 28.6 Tabular and graphical cash budget

12. Summary

a. Computers are useful for costing purposes because of their speed, accuracy, filing and retrieval abilities, calculating power and input and output capabilities.

b. Because of the low cost of computing power, more and more accounting and costing applications are worthwhile.

c. Software support for the computer system is vitally important especially the availability of application packages. Most packages are designed to do an essential task, such as stock control, and produce costing data as a by-product.

d. Spread sheet packages are based on an electronic worksheet and have a vast range of applicability in accounting and costing work.

13. Points to note

a. Properly used and controlled, computer systems can help the accountant provide a better service and can help him utilise his time more effectively so that he can concentrate on those non-routine tasks which require personal attention. Examples include: special investigations, longer term planning and interviewing managers and staff.

b. Properly used, computers can make routine tasks more accurate and speedy, can extend and deepen analysis by considering more factors and can take advantage of appropriate statistical and operational techniques which would be difficult using manual methods.

c. Problems can occur when using computers and the greatest care must be taken to obtain feedback from the users of the system in order to overcome any difficulties which arise. Problems may include: use of generalised and inappropriate packages which do not deal adequately with specialised problems, over-abundant printouts which swamp managers with paper, delays in producing required results, antagonism from managers and staff used to manual systems, fear of the unknown, inadequate training, unexplained jargon and so on.

Self-review questions

1. What are the features of computers- which make them useful for costing and other administrative work? (3)

2. Why is it now worthwhile to use computers for more and more tasks? (4)

3. Give six examples of costing tasks routinely dealt with by computer. (4)

4. What are the features of Data Processing systems? (5)

5. What are the key elements in Decision Support Systems? (8)

6. What is the advantage of application packages? (9)

7. Why do most packages produce costing information as a by-product? (9)

8. What is a spread sheet package? (10)

9. What type of tasks can spread sheet package deal with? (10)

10. How could a spreadsheet package deal with the production of a cash budget? (11)

Exercises and examination questions with answers

Exercises

A 28.1 Describe the ways computers could assist with the costing tasks associated with overheads.

A28.2 Give 6 areas in which the 'what if' facility available in spreadsheet and other packages could be useful to the cost accountant.

Examination questions

A28.3 a. One of the weaknesses, it is often argued, of operating an integrated accounting system is that 'notional costs' cannot be entered in to the accounting records.

You are required to discuss the above statement, to explain the meaning of notional costs and to illustrate with two examples why their inclusion in cost accounts may be desirable.

b. Knowing that you are studying for the CIMA examinations, a friend seeks your advice on the following problem. He owns and manages a small unincorporated business and is concerned at the high level of charges made by his bank for the business account even though it is seldom overdrawn. Querying the charge with his bank manager, he was told that the charge was based on the costs of handling his business account. Your friend does not see how the bank can possibly arrive at a cost of handling his business account.

You are required to explain to your friend the problems faced by the bank in arriving at a cost, as suggested by the bank manager, including any limitations attaching to such a cost.

c. The reduced price of personal computers has undoubtedly led to a growth in their use for cost and management accounting purposes.

You are required to list and explain very briefly four benefits which have followed from this increased use of personal computers.

(CIMA Cost Accounting)

A28.4 Describe briefly the benefits to cash budgeting from the use of a particular type of software package.

(CIMA, Cost Accounting, part question)

Exercises and examination questions without answers

Examination questions

B28.1 An expanding retailing organisation which currently has 90 shops selling shirts, sweaters, suits and shoes for both males and females in the age range of 15 to 30 years, has asked you to recommend a user oriented cost/management accounting information system which will assist management in the control of the business.

You are required, as the Assistant Management Accountant, to:

a. suggest how you would approach the task;

b. recommend an appropriate information system including performance indicators;

c. draft a suitable form of weekly profit statement which could be used for each shop;

d. indicate in what way computers would be used for the system recommended in your answers to b. above. *(CIMA, Cost Accounting)*

B28.2 A rapidly expanding medium-sized business, manufacturing and selling small electrical appliances used in household kitchens (toasters, can openers, food mixers, kettles, jugs), requires better information than is currently being provided for the control of its selling, warehousing and distribution activities.

The sales director currently has responsibility for all aspects of selling, warehousing and distribution; he has a sales manager, a warehouse manager and a transport manager reporting directly to him. The home market is served by a territorial sales force and overseas sales are executed by agencies in the countries to which the appliances are exported.

The sales director has his own staff who keep budgets of sales and monitor actual results for comparison with these budgets but there is no costing information about the activities under his control other than that contained within nominal ledger accounts for the following:

Salespersons' salaries and commissions
Salespersons' expenses
Warehouse labour
Own transport, including maintenance
Hired transport
Packing materials
Overseas agencies' expenses and commissions
Advertising

The salaries of the three managers reporting to the sales director are included, with other staff, in a salaries account.

You are required, as the assistant management accountant, to write a report to the sales director showing

a. the general principles which would be followed in planning a system for the control of the costs of the activities under his control;

b. in relation to functional budgets, a list of twenty accounts which ought to be provided from the company's chart of accounts;

c. i. how the sales ought to be analysed, and

ii. the way in which a computer could be useful to aid this analysis;

d. the cost and sales information that could be given to the salespersons and for what purpose.

(CIMA Cost Accounting)

Case exercises

Case study based teaching is increasingly used for accountancy and business education. The system encourages learning by doing and enables students to see business problems and techniques in a variety of realistic contexts. Accordingly a number of cases have been included in this book. They can either be tackled individually or used as the basis of group or assignment work. The cases cover a wide range of costing applications and vary in length and complexity. They can be profitably studied by all readers but will be found to be of most value when used under the direction of a lecturer.

The cases include:

	page
BETA ENGINEERING *Cost ascertainment and overhead absorption*	450
MULTI-MANUFACTURING GROUP *Overhead analysis and product costing using conventional and ABC methods*	451
DOLLBEE ELECTRONICS *Budgeting including behavioural aspects*	453
HOMAID PICKLES *Cost control and standard costing*	454
CORDON BLEU *Activity level changes and treatment of fixed and variable costs*	455
BRIMFORD GENERAL HOSPITAL *Costing and performance analysis in a hospital.*	457
ALTERNATIVE CARS *Job and Batch costing, cash budgeting, cost-volume-profit analysis*	459

Special note to lecturers:

Guidelines to solutions are given in the Lecturers' Supplement which is available free to lecturers adopting this book as a course text.

Beta Engineering Ltd

A case dealing with job costing in a jobbing engineering company and various methods of absorbing overheads.

Beta Engineering are manufacturers of small metal fabrications. All items are made to order and quantities range from a single fabrication up to batches of 1000. Some fabrications require a substantial amount of machining or welding, others are largely hand made using simple hand tools. Because of the varying applications for the fabrications, the materials used vary widely; including special purpose alloy and stainless steels, non-ferrous metals and ordinary mild steel.

Sara Hall has recently commenced work at Beta Engineering as a Cost Clerk and is given the task of calculating the cost of each job. This is done by using the Estimate Sheet, prepared at the Quotation stage, and adjusting this for the actual materials used so as to find the actual job cost. The amount of material used is found from the Stores Issue notes.

Extracts from the Estimate Sheet for 50 stainless steel fuse holders and the subsequent Job Costs are shown below:

Estimate Sheet

		£
Labour:	500 hours @ £4 =	2,000
Materials:	150 Kgs @ £8 kg =	1,200
Overheads:	400% of materials =	4,800
=	Total cost	8,000
+	20% profit	1,600
=	Selling price for batch	9,600

When this batch was made Sara totalled the Issue Notes and found that 173 Kgs of material had been used and accordingly prepared the following Job Cost:

Job Cost

		£
Labour:	(as estimate)	2,000
Materials:	173 Kgs @ £8	1,384
Overheads:	40% of materials	5,536
=	Total cost	8,920
	Selling Price	9,600
	Actual Profit	£680

After only a few weeks of doing this work, Sara had serious misgivings about the systems used which seem to have numerous problems.

Possible questions and tasks

1. Do you think that the method used for absorbing overheads is a good one? If not, why not?
2. What are some of the problems with the method used for calculating Job Costs?
3. What other methods of overhead absorption might be appropriate for this firm?
4. What are the main costing problems found in firms like Beta Engineering?
5. What features would you expect to find in a good Job Costing system for Beta Engineering?
6. Design a more appropriate Job Cost form.

Multi-Manufacturing group

A case dealing with Overhead analysis and product costing using traditional absorption costing and Activity Based Costing.

The Multi-Manufacturing group consists of a number of manufacturing companies. They have recently acquired a new company, Total Fabrication Ltd and are considering the system of product costing to be used in the company.

During the purchase negotiations the Group received a considerable amount of raw data which is being studied by the Group Management Accountant. A summary of the information is as follows.

Total Fabrications produces sophisticated control and weighing units for use on conveyors in quarries and mines in four main types; A, B, C and D. There are three production departments; Machining, Fabrication, Assembly (which includes calibration) and two service departments; Production Services and Stores. The latest available financial and production data are as follows:

General Overhead Costs

	£'000
Power	25
Rent & Rates	40
Purchase department	28
Insurance	14
Canteen Deficit	11
Inspection	40
Set-up Costs	12
Maintenance	20
Heating	10
Engineering Design(tooling etc)	24
Materials Control	14
	238

Directly Allocated Overheads

£'000

Department	Indirect Labour	Indirect Material
Machinery	16	7
Fabrication	8	11
Assembly	4	8
Production Services	12	14
Stores	10	12
	50	52

Production Data

Departments:	Machining	Fabrication	Assembly	Prod.Services	Stores
Area (sq metres)	8,000	12,000	10,000	2,000	3,000
No of employees	75	40	80	25	30
Machine hours	13,000	4,500	6,000	–	–
Plant Valuation £	140,000	45,000	55,000	60,000	50,000
Direct Labour Hours	11,000	7,500	15,000	6,000	7,000
Machine Power rating (Kw Hrs)	1,650	450	550	250	300
Material Requisitions	1,200	800	600	800	100

The data relating to the products are as follows:

		Products		
	A	B	C	D
Production Volume (units)	800	600	1000	1400
Machine hours per unit				
Machining	3	3	4	3
Fabrication	1	2	1	1
Assembly	2	2	1	$1\frac{1}{2}$
Direct Labour hours per unit				
Machining	1	2	3	4
Fabrication	2	2	2	1
Assembly	2	3	5	4
Direct Material per unit £	160	220	190	80

Activities traceable to products:

Per unit	A	B	C	D
Inspections	4	3	2	5
Purchase Orders	4	4	2	3
Machine Set-ups	5	8	2	1
Tool changes	1	4	3	2
No. of material movements	1	5	2	2

The demands on Service Departments are:

	Machining	Fabrication	Assembly	Prod Serv.	Stores
Prod. Services	40%	10%	30%	–	20%
Stores	20%	30%	40%	10%	–

Direct wages are £7 per hour.

The Group Management Accountant decides to carry out further analysis before deciding what type of product costing system he will recommend.

Possible questions and tasks

1. Prepare an overhead analysis based on conventional absorption costing using traditional apportionment bases.

2. Calculate the product cost per unit of the four products assuming that overhead absorption is based on machine hours.

3. Prepare an overhead analysis and appropriate cost driver rates assuming ABC will be used. Make what judgements and assumptions you feel necessary

4. Calculate the product costs based on ABC.

5. Compare the product costs prepared by conventional absorption costing and those using ABC and comment on the likely reasons for any differences.

6. What other factors do you think will need to be considered before a decision is made on which product costing system will be used?

7. What further analysis will be needed if a full ABC system is to be used?

Dollbee Electronics Plc

A case involving the behavioural aspects of budgeting and the problems caused by preparing budget statements on incorrect principles.

Dollbee Electronics are manufacturers of high quality audio amplifiers and loudspeakers. The company has recently been taken over by Electronics International Inc. (EII) a multi-national company operating on all continents. Hyram K. Cross of EII has been sent to review the budgeting and reporting systems used by Dollbee and finds that monthly budgets are prepared for each department. He asks to see the last budget statement for a typical department and is shown the statement for the Loudspeaker Department; whose manager is Jack Bell.

The budget statement for the last period was:

Budget Statement for period......
Department: Loudspeaker Department
Actual Results: 12500 units produced with 35350 labour hours

	Actual results £'000s	Budgeted Results £'000s	Budgeted Variances £'000s
Direct Materials	252	240	−12
Direct Labour	123	120	−3
Variable Prod. Overhead	79	72	−7
Fixed Prod. Overhead	59	56	−3
Variable Admin. Overhead	41	40	−1
Fixed Admin. Overhead	50	48	−2
Total costs	604	576	−28
Sales value of Production	775	744	+31
Profit	171	168	+3

Hyram found that the budget was based on 12,000 units with a standard labour content of 2.85 hours and went to Jack Bell to find out his reactions to the budget and what use he makes of the budgeting system.

To Hyram's surprise, Jack Bell was not enthusiastic about the system and thought it of little value to a departmental manager. Jack said, 'It was introduced about a year ago by consultants who only spent about 10 minutes with me, then the budgeting system was introduced without any explanation. Frankly I think they put in a ready made system developed elsewhere. It doesn't seem to help me to run my department. For example, last month's statement showed a positive variance on profit yet I know costs have risen, though nothing like as much as the statement shows, so I would have expected to be down on budgeted profit yet according to this I am £3000 up! It just doesn't make sense so I tend to ignore it altogether.'

After leaving Jack Bell, Hyram visited several other departments and had similar reactions from the departmental managers. Hyram decided, as a matter of urgency, to try to make the budgeting system more useful and more acceptable to the departmental managers.

Possible questions and tasks

1. What behavioural problems are brought out in the case?
2. What was wrong with the approach of the consultants who installed the system?
3. Do you think the present system fulfils the behavioural objectives of budgetary control systems? If not, why not?
4. Criticise the way the budget statement has been prepared.
5. Redraft the budget statement in a more informative manner and give an explanation of your reasoning.
6. What steps do you think Hyram should take now?

Homaid Pickles

This case deals with the control of costs in a process industry and the possible introduction of a standard costing system.

Homaid Pickles was started by Mary Hyde some years ago and has developed rapidly. The emphasis is on fresh, high quality ingredients and unusual flavours. The main outlets are high class departmental stores, mail order and delicatessens and trade is booming. In the early days, Mary was able to oversee every stage in the manufacturing process and was thus able to control costs in a direct and personal way. Those times have long since gone and over the last few years she has concentrated on marketing the products. As a consequence control over manufacturing has slipped and Mary feels sure that yields and costs could be improved if only she could obtain up-to-date and relevant control information.

All products follow the same processes which can be shown as follows:

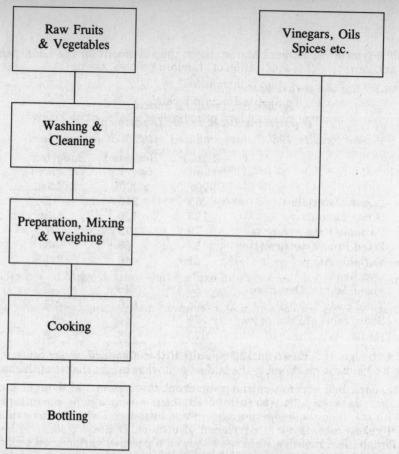

The key process is that of Preparation, Mixing and Weighing because at that stage, costs, yields and quality are determined.

She discusses the problem with Bob Allen, her newly appointed Factory Manager. He thinks that some form of Standard Process costing would provide useful information but Mary is far from convinced. She suggests that Bob prepares some information for her based on last week's production of one of their best selling lines, 3L Pickle; which is made from Lemons, Leeks and Loganberries.

With the assistance of a friend, who is an accountant, Bob sets to work. A summary of what he found follows:

The recipe card for the 3L Pickle showed that it is made in batches. Each batch is expected to produce 2000, 250 gram jars of pickle from the following ingredients:

300 kgs of leeks at a target cost of	£0.45 kg
50 kgs of lemons at a target cost of	£1.30 kg
40 kgs of loganberries at a target cost of	£0.95 kg
290 litres of spiced vinegar at a target cost of	£0.53 litre
(the vinegar price is the equivalent of £0.59 kg)	

Typically a batch is expected to take the Pickle Team seven hours. The team comprises a Chargehand paid £4.25 per hour and four Operatives paid £3.10 per hour.

Bob found that five batches of 3L Pickle were made in the week and after analysing the wages paid and invoices he found that the actual costs were:

Leeks	1568 kgs	costing	£752
Lemons	243 kgs	costing	£335
Loganberries	222 kgs	costing	£211
Vinegar Mix	1362 litres	costing	£817

39 hours were worked by the Pickle Team at a total cost of £682. The output of pickles for the week was 9340 jars.

Bob was fairly sure he now had sufficient data to produce an example of the type of control information that could be made available.

Possible questions and tasks

1. Does this seem to be a reasonable application of standard process costing?
2. What are the likely benefits if a system is introduced?
3. Outline how a system could be installed in Homaid Pickles.
4. What is a reasonable estimate of the standard prime cost of a batch of 3L Pickle?
5. What is the percentage expected loss?
6. What is the standard prime cost of a 250 gram jar of pickle?
7. Calculate the following variances for the week:

> Materials price variance
> Materials mixture variance
> Materials yield variance
> Labour rate variance
> Labour efficiency variance

8. What was the actual percentage loss in yield?
9. Interpret the meaning of these variance and explain how control would be assisted by their preparation.
10. Do you think that there are any alternative methods of maintaining control over costs and yields? If so, what?

Cordon bleu – Catering Packs Ltd

This is a multi-part case covering different forms of operating statements, the treatment of fixed and variable costs and the effects of advertising and product substitutability.

Part A

Cordon Bleu are rapidly expanding specialist food suppliers to restaurants, wine bars, pubs and similar outlets. They buy, prepare and cook the ingredients which are then packaged, deep frozen and supplied to their customers who microwave or boil the meals before serving to their clients who are usually unaware that they are eating pre-packaged meals. Cordon Bleu have five main lines; Chicken Supreme, Boeuf Bourguignon, Duck a l'orange, Chili Con Carne and Chicken Kiev.

Mike Commer has recently been appointed as Managing Director of Cordon Bleu after many years experience as a Director of a major national food manufacturer. He is in the process of reviewing all aspects of operations, especially the financial and sales side which he suspects have been neglected in the formative years of Cordon Bleu, when production and packaging difficulties absorbed most of the attention of John Watson, the founder, who is now Chairman of the company.

Mike asks Bill Hope, who is the Accountant and Office Manager, to prepare a Budgeted Operating Statement for the next period showing the profitability of the main product lines. Up to now there has been no attempt to show separately the profitability of the product lines and the exercise causes Bill a great deal of work. Finally he produces the following statement which, he admits, shows a surprising result and as a consequence he recommends to Mike that he should give serious consideration to cutting out the Boeuf Bourguignon and Duck a l'orange packs to avoid the losses.

The statement produced by Bill Hope was as follows:

Cordon Bleu
Budgeted Operating Statement (£'000s)

Product	Chicken Supreme	Boeuf Bourguignon	Duck a l'orange	Chili con Carne	Chicken Kiev	Total
Sales	1600	1400	2100	950	1900	7950
Production costs:						
Materials	290	280	370	145	265	1350
Labour	350	260	390	90	310	1400
Overheads	368	366	567	122	377	1800
	1008	906	1327	3	952	4500
Packaging & Transport	183	168	227	83	164	825
Advertising & Office Costs	322	406	550	207	415	1900
	505	574	777	290	579	2725
Total cost	1513	1480	2104	647	1531	7275
Profit (Loss)	87	(80)	(4)	303	369	675

Mike Commer studied the operating statement and suspected that there was more to the problem than the statement showed. Before coming to any decision he felt he needed more detail and sent for Bill Hope. After a lengthy meeting it was agreed that Bill Hope would supply the following additional information:

a. an analysis of the fixed and variable elements of the various costs
b. clear guidance on the methods of allocation and apportionment used in the statement.

Fortunately Bill Hope had kept his working papers and was able to produce the required detail quite quickly. This was as follows:

Supplement to the Budgeted Operating Statement

1. Both labour and material costs are a combination of variable costs and a surcharge of 15% and 10% respectively to absorb general fixed costs. In the case of labour this is for general production supervision and general storage and ordering costs for materials.

2. Production overheads are a combination of variable overheads recovered on the total labour cost, general fixed overheads of £830,000 recovered on labour costs and directly attributable fixed costs as follows:

Chicken Supreme	Boeuf Bourguignon	Duck a l'orange	Chili con Carne	Chicken Kiev	Total
£70,000	145,000	235,000	55,000	115,000	620,000

The directly identifiable fixed overheads would cease if the product was discontinued.

3. Packaging and transport costs consist of £150,000 general fixed overheads absorbed on labour costs, the balance being variable costs absorbed on total material costs.

4. Advertising and Office costs have three elements: Advertising costs absorbed on sales value, general fixed overheads of £100,000 also absorbed on sales value and directly attributable fixed costs as follows:

Chicken Supreme	Boeuf Bourguignon	Duck a l'orange	Chili con Carne	Chicken Kiev	Total
£40,000	160,000	180,000	40,000	80,000	500,000

Once again the identifiable fixed costs would cease if the product was discontinued.

Possible questions and tasks

1. Comment on the position shown in the budgeted operating statement produced by Bill Hope.
2. Should the decision be taken at this stage to discontinue the two products shown making a loss? If not, why not?
3. What other information, additional to that in the Supplement, might be useful to Mike Commer in assessing the budgeted position ?
4. Redraft the budgeted operating statement in a more informative manner assuming that all five products will continue.
5. Comment on your redrafted operating statement explaining why it is more informative.
6. Prepare a new budgeted operating statement assuming that Boeuf Bourguignon and Duck a l 'orange are discontinued and sales of the other products continue as budgeted.
7. Comment on the new statement.
8. What decisions should be taken about the product range?

Part B

After his study of the financial aspects of Cordon Bleu's operation, Mike turned his attention to the problems of Sales and Advertising. He commissioned a study from Rowe and Devenish, a market research agency specialising in the food and catering industry, to examine the impact of special product marketing and the extent of product substitutability.

Rowe and Devenish's report was long and detailed but fortunately they provided a succinct summary as follows:

☐ Sales of any individual product could be increased by selective advertising, by up to 30% of the existing sales figures. An approximately linear relationship between sales increase and advertising expenditure was found eg, a 10% increase in sales required 100% increase on existing advertising expenditure, a 20% increase a 200% increase and so on.

☐ Limited product substitutability is possible. For example, if Chili con Carne is offered as a substitute for Boeuf Bourguignon, each £1 reduction in sales of Boeuf Bourguignon causes a 60p increase in sales of Chili con Carne. If Chicken Kiev is the substitute, the increase is 50p more sales for each £1 reduction in Boeuf Bourguignon.

Possible questions and tasks

1. Investigate whether selective advertising is worthwhile.
2. Which products would be worthwhile advertising?
3. If advertising costs are limited to £150,000 which products should be advertised?
4. Should alternative products be substituted for Boeuf Bourguignon ? If so, is Chicken Kiev or Chili con Carne a more profitable substitute.

Brimford General Hospital

A multi-part case dealing with costing and performance analysis in a hospital

Part 1

The Brimford General Hospital is a Trust Hospital and operates within the market for healthcare in the National Health Service. As a consequence much greater attention is now being paid to costs and operational efficiency. The management is in the process of developing a full Profit Centre System within the hospital. One of the consequences of this is that specialist departments such as Orthopaedics; Paediatrics, Surgery and so on make charges internally for their services. The specialist departments in turn are charged for the services they use, for example, General Nursing, Maintenance, Pharmacy, Laundry and so on. Some of these services are charged according to patient-days whilst others are on a fixed yearly basis.

In order to assess how the system is working and to gain information about the costs and operations of the Specialist Departments it has been decided to examine each Department in turn. The first to be examined is the Orthopaedics Department and the following information was obtained relating to the last year.

Orthopaedics Department

No of beds	50
Gross Revenue Received	£1,533,000
Charging rate	£125 per patient day

Expenses charged by the Hospital to Orthopaedics for last 12 months

	Basis of Charging	
	Patient-Days	Yearly charge
	£	£
Meals	50,700	
Pharmacy	128,000	
Laundry	43,250	
Laboratory	142,800	
Maintenance	18,500	32,000
General Admin		408,500
Porters		23,560
Rent/Heating/Space		47,940
	383,250	512,000

General Nursing Staff are supplied from a general pool. Each nurse costs £20,000 per year and at the end of the year the specialist Departments are charged according to the following schedule:

Annual Patient-Days	Number of Nurses Charged
6000 – 10,000	15
10,000 – 14,000	20
14,000 – 18,000	25

The Consultants and Registrars in Orthopaedics cost a total of £172,000 for the year.

Possible questions and tasks

1. Calculate the number of patient days in Orthopaedics last year.
2. What was the Bed-Occupancy percentage?
3. How many Nurses will be charged for the year? At what cost?
4. What was the cost per patient-day for the year.
5. Excluding consultants' fees how many patient-days were required to break-even last year.
6. Including consultants' fees how many patient-days were required to break even?
7. What was the margin of safety percentage for last year? Comment on the value you have calculated.

Part 2

The budget for next year is being considered and the following cost increases have been forecast:

Meals	7%
Pharmacy	12%
Laundry	4%
Admin.	5%

All other costs are expected to increase by 6%.

It is anticipated that the number of patient days will increase by 15% over last year.

Possible questions and tasks

1. Calculate the anticipated Bed-Occupancy percentage for next year.

2. Calculate the anticipated cost per patient day.

3. Calculate the Break-Even point in patient days, assuming that the same price per day is charged as last year.

4. What is the margin of safety percentage? Comment on your result.

5. How many patient-days would be required next year to achieve the same profit as last year assuming the anticipated costs and last year's charging price?

6. A possibility is being considered of charging Nursery Costs to the specialist Departments at £35 per patient-day instead of the 3-tier system used at present. Evaluate the position for Orthopaedics if this proposal is adopted for next year.

Alternative Cars

A comprehensive multi-part case dealing with numerous aspects of costing including: consideration of costing methods, overhead analysis, apportionment and absorption, cash budgeting, break-even analysis and so on.

This case has been devised by G.S. Clinton, M.Soc.Sc, FCMA, ACIS, MBIM, Principal Lecturer in Accounting at the University of Wolverhampton. © G.S. Clinton.

Part 1– Overhead Analysis, Absorption and Batch Costing

The Waltburys lived at Treefain in the Rea Valley. A closeknit, lively and enterprising family, they had been in business as agricultural engineers for eighty years. The present generation consisted of the parents and three children, the daughter who looked after the business records and two sons who had studied agricultural engineering. It did look until recently that such a small business would not be able to support all the children, but now the future looked very different.

It all began so simply and in a small way. Robert, the youngest, inherited the Volkswagon Beetle. It had been 'handed down' through the children, and had been the means whereby they all had learnt their car mechanics. The idea was born to put a new body on the old floorpan (chassis), and they experimented with various forms of bodywork: alloy panels secured to a frame with rivets, fibre glass (G.R.P.) moulded to an old Packard sports car shape. Mark I was amusing, Mark II primitive, Mark III unusual, Mark IV... well, remarkably good, resembling a 1930's sports car, distinctive and attractive. The 'Waltbury' soon became well known in the area, and when featured in the Northbridge Journal, the local newspaper, enquiries rolled in and a steady flow of orders ensued. It immediately became apparent that there were many types of customer, those who wanted a complete car perhaps modified to their taste, and then enthusiasts who wished to build their own car from a kit. These latter enthusiasts often already had a chassis and engine, but there were some who looked to the business to supply this running gear as well. Others required a car to the point of application of the first coat of primer paint... There was a demand for cars at all stages of completion and for all types of popular running gear modification.

There were inevitably many technical problems in the early days to which the family involved themselves with enthusiasm, often working well into the night. Just as inevitably there were financial, administrative and clerical problems which the male Waltbury's avoided unless forced to by some crisis. The 'admin' side was Susan's ran the argument, and usually she did cope well. It should be added that Susan was 'perfectly liberated', capable now of tackling most of the engineering jobs around the business just as she had been able to bowl a respectable leg cutter when times had demanded.

Midway through the fourth year of manufacture, the business experienced a surge of demand for both their kits and cars. It seemed that all of a sudden Alternative Cars were the vehicles to have and the 'Waltbury' had by then developed a sound and enviable reputation. It was clear that as they were presently organised, they could neither cope with this increased demand in terms of production space nor with the finance necessary to support such expansion... there was money for mig welders, presses, pipe benders etc. to be found. The eventual solution was new rented premises on the Treefain Industrial Estate, backed with funds from the Small Business Finance Corporation (S.B.F.C.). Part of the terms of financing was regular financial returns backed by a sound costing system. The S.B.F.C. offered help and advice in the installation of these systems, but were adamant that procedures were adhered to and gone were the cavalier days when paperwork was ignored or postponed. The business still remained job and batch oriented, but every effort was made to standardise components.

The costing system followed the geographical layout of the new premises and natural departments were created, viz.

> Stores
>
> Chassis repair and modifications
>
> G.R.P. mouldings
>
> Panel and special parts
>
> Assembly and finishing

Susan set about organising a job and batch costing system with enthusiasm, striving to attain the same satisfaction from her efforts as did her brothers in the production of Alternative Cars. There was a woeful lack of information available with every statistic collected from scratch. The following information (Figure 1), although not perfect, did allow for a more scientific approach to the costing of jobs and the preparation of more reliable estimates for customers. As the business expanded it was intended of course to add on new centres as necessary, and already it was proposed that a service centre for maintenance be created.

	Service Centre				
	Stores	Chassis	G.R.P	Panels	Assembly
Area (square feet)	600	2,000	1,800	600	3,000
No. of employees	2	6	12	4	6
No. of hours on direct production		1,000	2,000	550	760
Plant values (year end)	£360	13,920	12,000	6,600	9,120
Insurance cost	£100	20	250	20	10
Stores issue notes		350	200	200	230

Figure 1 Business statistics (based on an average month)

A new four-stage procedure was adopted in an attempt to tighten administrative control

1. A formal estimate would be prepared for each customer requiring complete or partially complete cars. No more Ad Hoc quotations to be given verbally.

2. When confirmed an order to be raised detailing all the parts necessary and the dates when required.

3. A proper job cost card to be kept.

4. Each job to be costed out and compared with the original estimate. A post mortem to be held on each completed job at the regular production meetings.

This new procedure required the creation of many forms and an underpinning coding system. It sounded simple enough, but the creation of the coding system itself proved a headache... it either was too complicated as to be unusable or so brief as to create ambiguity. The job cost card was more successful and immediately pinpointed areas of weakness within the business where the greatest discrepancies between estimates and actuals took place. It was not long before certain personnel who had hitherto taken form filling light-heartedly were brought to heel in no uncertain manner... Susan ruled supreme. There were times when her brothers looked back with nostalgia to the days when they made Alternative Cars for fun. The job cost card headings were shown below, together with an actual job cost summary for a Waltbury Mark IV (the job cost summary is kept on the back of the cost card).

JOB COST CARD												
Customer			**Waltbury Mark IV**				**Job No.**					
Estimate Ref.							**Started**					
							Completion Req.					
	Material				**Labour**					**Overheads**		
Date	Ref	Qty.	Price	Cost £ p	Date	Ref.	Centre	Hours	Rate	Cost £ p	Hours	OAR	Cost £ p

JOB COST SUMMARY – Job 672

	Estimate £	Actual £
Direct material	127.50	
Special expenses	–	
Direct labour	195.00	
Prime cost	322.50	
Production overhead	78.00	
Production cost	400.50	
Selling/Admin overhead		
10% on production cost	40.05	
Total cost	440.55	
Invoice price	528.66	
Profit/Loss	88.11	

Wherever possible it was business policy to adhere to the estimate price, and usually variation only took place if the customer made special requests after the estimate date. This philosophy had been pursued right from the beginning, and it had become part of their reputation that estimates could be relied upon. Some losses had been incurred consequently, particularly with the early cars, but at that time it was viewed as a cost of 'research and development'. Now with the S.B.F.C. looking over their financial affairs, they could not afford to 'get it wrong' too often. They certainly, in a matter of months, became more cost conscious, and in an attempt to achieve more efficient production wherever possible parts were standardised and manufactured in batches. For example the Mark V roll-over bars were now manufactured for stock in batches of 20's or 30's depending upon the space available in the finishing ovens, viz.

S.L.R. Bar Mark V Waltbury

Batch Quantities	20	30
Chassis Department		
Hours – Setting up	2 hrs. 30 mins	2 hrs. 30 mins
Bending	2 hrs	3 hrs
Welding	1 hr. 30 mins	2 hrs
Drilling	1 hr	1 hr. 30 mins
Material – M.M. Tube	£2.50 per length	
Flange brackets	5p each (2 per bar)	
End stops	1p each (2 per bar)	
Assembling and Finishing		
Hours – Preparation	2 hrs	2 hrs. 30 mins
Priming	1 hr	1 hr
Painting	1 hr	1 hr
Finishing	1 hr	1 hr 30 mins
Material – Paints	£1.55	£2. 10

The above cost information incidentally was compiled by Susan when demonstrating how much could be saved by batching the production of bars which when manufactured singly cost £11.50 each.

Possible questions and tasks

1.
   a. Why is job costing appropriate to the manufacture of Alternative Cars.
   b. Why would process costing not be suitable.
   c. Which basic records and forms must be completed to ensure a sound job costing system.
   d. Name 3 other manufacturing situations that might use job costing.
   e. Contrast job costing with batch costing.

2. The following overhead is appropriate to one month for Alternative Cars:

   i. Maintenance and repair of equipment (by centres) Stores £78, Chassis £309, G.R.P. £346, Panels £77, Assembly £90.
   ii. Depreciation 10% of plant values.
   iii. Rent £800.
   iv. Indirect labour £960.
   v. Labour costs £600.
   vi. Indirect materials £490.

Using the information contained in Figure 1:

  a. Prepare an overhead analysis sheet.
  b. Calculate overhead absorption rates based on direct production hours.
  c. Calculate a blanket absorption rate.

3. Assume that because of the growth in business, Alternative Cars create a separate maintenance department. The business now has two service departments, maintenance (M) and Stores (S) and four production departments Chassis (C), Mouldings (GRP), Panels (P) and Assembly (A). The service departments provide services for each other as well as for the production departments.

The overheads for a period after analysis are:

    M £1,000   S £500   C £1,400   GRP £1,600   P £700   A £1,200

The data for apportionment of service department overheads:

	M	S	C	GRP	P	A
Plant investment	£6,000	£3,000	£15,000	£14,000	£7,000	£11,000
Proportion		6%	30%	28%	14%	22%
Stores issues	400	–	400	200	300	300
Proportion	25%	–	25%	12.5%	18.75%	18.75%

Reapportion the service centre overhead to production centres on:

  a. The continuous allotment method

  b. The elimination (or 1 step) method.

4. Job 672 was the conversion of an Alfasud Saloon to accept a Waltbury Mark V body kit. This involved stripping the Alfa and fitting a multi-tubular chassis based on box section steel members. The chassis was to be constructed with a top wishbone, front suspension and shock absorbers. In addition the propeller shaft and steering column had to be modified.

Most of the parts were standard from the normal Escort conversion, but adjustments were necessary compared with the orthodox chassis building. In particular a special precision jig tool had to be hired to ensure exact matching with the body kit. Actual figures were:

    Chassis Centre

    91 labour hours at £3 per hour

    Total direct material Chassis unit and suspension etc. £92.80

    Jig hire £30

  a. Calculate the cost of Job 627.

Assume that the target profit on labour intensive work is 20% of total cost. Overhead should be absorbed on the rates calculated in 2b.

  b. In the light of the result if the estimate invoice price is maintained, what advice would you give to Alternative Cars both for this and future orders.

  c. Recalculate the invoice price using the blanket absorption rates calculated in 2c.

  d. Comment upon the two prices you have now calculated (4a. and 4c.). Which approach is the more reliable and why?

5. What is the cost per roll-over bar when produced in batches of 20 as compared with batches of 30. Assume overhead data is as calculated in 2b. and the wage rate currently being paid is £3 per hour.

6. For the month of October the overhead below was budgeted for Alternative Cars. Using the information contained in Figure 1 prepare an overhead analysis sheet for the month together with the *cost centre* absorption rates and the blanket rate.

	Month of October	£
i.	Indirect materials	588
ii.	Labour costs	660
iii.	Indirect labour	1,680
iv.	Rent	1.200
v.	Depreciation 20% of plant values	
vi.	Maintenance and repair of equipment by centres:	

        Stores   £42
        Chassis   £85
        GRP   £214
        Panels   £108
        Assembly   £123

7. Refer back to Question 3. Now reapportion the service centre overhead to production centres on the direct method (where all inter-service servicing is ignored).

8. a. Assume that an immediate *repeat* order for a Job 672 is received from that customer's brother. The actual figures for Job 672 R are as follows:

   Chassis centre 45 labour hours at £3 per hour
   Total direct material chassis unit and suspension £72. 80
   Jig hire £20

   Cost methods and pricing remain as Question 4.a.

   What would be the invoice price to the customer?

   b. Do you feel this invoice price should be the one to be charged to the new customer?

9. What is the cost per roll-over bar when produced in batches of 40 as compared with batches of 20 and 30.

   Hours for 40's

Chassis	Setting up	2 hours 30 mins
	Bending	3 hours 30 mins
	Welding	2 hours 15 mins
	Drilling	1 hour 45 mins
Finishing	Preparation	3 hours
	Priming	1 hour
	Painting	1 hour
	Finishing	2 hours
	(Paint cost £2.65)	

   Assume overhead data is as calculated in 2.b. and the wage rate currently being paid is £3 per hour.

Part 2 – The Planning of Cash, Production and Profit

The remarkable growth of Alternative Cars from its humble beginnings at Treefain to one of Europe's largest kit manufacturers merits every respect and admiration. Behind the technical and creative drive of the two brothers lay a very firm and sound financial control influence. The Small Business Finance Corporation (S.B.F.C.) understood from the beginning that they were backing a winner if only they could curb some of the wilder over-imaginative dreams of the technical boys who assumed that an infinite supply of money was available. In Susan they found a willing and able administrator whose rulings and judgements were accepted, not necessarily without a fight, but eventually accepted they were. The S.B.F.C. could afford to control from a distance. Take for instance the new Body/Chassis Plant at Warburton.

The Waltbury Mark IV was a major design breakthrough in a number of ways. It retained the rugged sportscar style of the 30's but was able to seat 4 people in comfort. Fixed chassis tubes were placed along the outer cockpit sides to give protection against side impact. Another feature from the kit market angle, was that the body/chassis was precision jig-drilled and designed to accept the mechanical components from estates, vans and cars of 8 of Europe's most widely sold vehicles. In nearly all of these cases no modifications would be necessary to suspension, engine, gearbox or propeller shaft.

New premises, different methods of production, more sophisticated machinery, greater advertising, enthusiasm and expectation ran very high and the sky seemed the limit.

The S.B.F.C. did not wish to dampen these enthusiasms but clearly there were dangers, particularly from the cash flow point of view. Through Susan they were able to instil some measure of planning, crude perhaps and little more than forecasts, but they did help. Looking back it is surprising just how accurate some of these guesses were. Take for example that first demand schedule shown in Figure 2.

Body/Chassis Mark VI

	For Kits	*For cars*
June	5	
July	18	12
August	30	15
September	45	30
October	45	45
November	45	15

Figure 2 Forecast Demand

A stock level of 15 to be held at the end of November.

It was the cash requirements of the venture that gave the greatest concern and Susan was grateful for the support given to her by the S.B.F.C. staff. Alternative Cars was to be no longer the small happy-go lucky jobbing business of the past; money and finance were now to rule over all the major decisions. In a summary form Figure 3 shows the conclusions that were reached for those early months of the body plant venture which was to prove a watershed in the life of that family business.

The selling price for each body/chassis kit would be £1,500 each. A raw material stock of £20,000 would always need to be held. The cost of producing each body/chassis was calculated as:

> Material £700;   Labour £400;   Variable overhead £100

Running costs of the Warburton plant in terms of fixed overheads *per month* were assessed at £11,500. The plant and machinery would cost £100,000.

> Payable July £50,000;   September £25,000;   November £25,000

The Trade terms: Sales 50% deposit with order – the balance payable 2 months later on average.

Labour: Cash

All other expenditure 2 months credit.

Figure 3 Summary form

Possible questions and tasks

10. Prepare a production schedule for the period June to November. This schedule must take into account that no more than 60 body/chassis can be manufactured each month.

11. Prepare a cash budget monthly June to November to indicate to the S.B.F. C. the level of funding required

12. Assuming that the plant has a life of 5 years and a resale value of £10,000, what is the normal profit per month from the body/chassis centre when maximum production is sold. (Ignore any interest charges.)

13. How many body/chassis must Alternative Cars sell *each year* to break even.

14. Prepare an alternative production schedule for the period June to November. This schedule must take into account that other than the first month (June*) production must be in each month either 60 or 65 body/chassis to achieve efficient working.

    *In June it is planned to produce 10 only.

15. On the basis of this revised production schedule, prepare a new cash budget for the first *4 months* of this period.

16. Assuming that the plant has a life of 10 years and a resale value of £10,000, what is the profit/loss per month when:

    a. Producing and selling at 10 per month
    b. Producing and selling at 65 per month

17. How many body/chassis must Alternative Cars sell each year to achieve a profit of:

    a. £93,000
    b. £3,000
    c. £153,000

Progress Tests

Four test papers follow, each containing a number of Multiple Choice Questions.

The tests follow the sequence of the book and should be attempted at appropriate points such as:

Progress Test 1 after completing Chapters 1 – 8

Progress Test 2 after completing Chapters 9 – 16

Progress Test 3 after completing Chapters 17 – 21

Progress Test 4 after completing Chapters 22 – 28

Each Test should take the average student 45 minutes – 1 hour.

Always make a determined effort to complete each question *before* you look at the answers. (The answer key is at the end of the Tests)

Good luck!

Test 1

1. Cost accounting is mainly concerned with providing information to:
   a. Government agencies such as the Inland Revenue.
   b. Managers within the firm.
   c. Shareholders.
   d. Trade Unions on behalf of the workers.

2. Direct costs are costs that:
   a. are incurred directly the factory is open
   b. are directly charged to a department.
   c. can be directly identified with a product or service
   d. are directly under the control of a manager.

3. Prime cost includes:
   a. Direct labour, direct materials and direct expenses
   b. All direct costs plus factory overheads
   c. Direct materials plus total overheads
   d. Direct labour plus factory overheads.

4. A cost centre is:
   a. A unit of production in relation to which costs are ascertained
   b. A location which is responsible for controlling direct costs
   c. Part of the overhead system by which costs are gathered together
   d. Any location or department which incurs cost.

5. Cost apportionment is carried out by:
   a. Charging each cost unit a realistic proportion of overheads
   b. Charging whole items of cost to cost centres
   c. Ensuring that each period carries its fair amount of costs by making accruals or prepayments
   d. Dividing common costs among cost centres in proportion to the benefit received.

6. Overhead absorption is done so that:
   a. Common costs are shared among cost centres, in proportion to the benefit received
   b. The total amount of overheads for the firm can be calculated
   c. The total overheads for a cost centre can be calculated
   d. Each unit of the product carries a share of overheads.

7. Expenditure on steel used in the product would be classified into which of the following categories:
   a. direct material/cost unit
   b. direct material/production overheads
   c. indirect material/cost unit
   d. prime cost/production overhead.

8. Product costing is mainly concerned with:
   a. finding the cost of sales and valuing stock
   b. analysing cost behaviour
   c. finding the total of production overheads
   d. controlling product costs.

9. Check digit variation is:
   a. the process of checking invoices for correct calculations
   b. a method of making code numbers self checking
   c. to enable codes to be self-indexing
   d. the encoding of invoices with internal codes.

10. The Perpetual Inventory System is:
    a. where the stock levels are checked on a continuous basis
    b. where stocks are always available to meet production demands
    c. where the different stock records are continually compared to ensure agreement
    d. where the stock balance is shown after each movement.

11. There are 525 units of Part No Y612 in stock and 3750 are on order from the suppliers. Customers' orders outstanding total 1810. What is the Free Stock?
    a. 2335
    b. 2460
    c. 1940
    d. 6080

The following information on Part No X250 is to be used for the next three questions:

Lead time 6 – 8 weeks
Reorder quantity   2000 units
Average demand   300 units per week
Maximum demand 430 units per week
Minimum demand 220 units per week

12. What is the level at which Part No X250 would be reordered?
    a. 2580
    b. 2810
    c. 3440
    d. 2400

13. What is the minimum level for Part No X250?
    a. 1340
    b. 1640
    c. 1080
    d. 2580

14. What is the maximum level for part No X250?
    a. 5440
    b. 3440
    c. 4120
    d. 5580

15. What is the EOQ when demand is 10,000 units per year, ordering costs are £100 and it costs £10 to keep an item in stock for year?
    a. 1414
    b. 447
    c. 316
    d. 10,000

16. The EOQ is the order quantity that:
    a. minimises the total of carrying costs and order costs
    b. minimises the total of carrying costs and stockout costs
    c. minimises the total of ordering costs and stockout costs
    d. minimises carrying costs.

17. Which of the following is not a relevant cost in determining the EOQ?
    a. the cost of insurance based on the average level of stocks
    b. the opportunity cost of capital invested in stocks
    c. quantity discounts for purchases over specified quantities
    d. the salary of the buyer.

18. The First in First Out (FIFO) materials pricing system charges issues at:
    a. the price of the most recent batch in stock
    b. the price of the first component used in the period
    c. the average price of goods in stock
    d. the price of the oldest batch in stock.

19. The Last in First Out (LIFO) system will:
    a. value stocks at current values
    b. understate product costs in times of rising prices
    c. tend to produce realistic product costs
    d. make cost comparisons between jobs easier.

20. Using the Average Price issuing system:
    a. is more complicated than LIFO and FIFO
    b. the issue price is recalculated after each receipt
    c. is not recommended by SSAP 9
    d. exaggerates price fluctuations.

21. The double entry for an issue of indirect material for use in the factory is:
    a. DR Production overheads   CR Stores Control
    b. DR Stores Control   CR Production overheads
    c. DR Work in Progress   CR Production overheads
    d. DR Work in Progress   CR Stores Control

22. Direct wages should always be classified:
    a.   as variable costs
    b.   as fixed costs
    c.   as semi-fixed costs
    d.   according to their actual behaviour.

23. Both nationally and internationally the wages paid to production workers are:
    a.   an increasing proportion of total costs
    b.   always equal to production overheads
    c.   a decreasing proportion of total costs
    d.   none of these.

24. Job Evaluation can be described as:
    a.   a way of assessing how a person suits a job
    b.   a way of improving the methods by which a job is performed
    c.   a way of assessing the content of a job
    d.   a form of staff appraisal.

25. Labour turnover can be expressed as a ratio as follows:
    a.   Number of leavers   ÷   Numbers of starters
    b.   Number replaced   ÷   Average number of employees
    c.   Number of employees at the end   ÷   Number at the beginning
    d.   Number of leavers in a period   ÷   Number of weeks in period.

26. A cost driver is
    a.   the amount of overhead caused by an activity
    b.   a unit of activity which causes costs
    c.   a long term variable cost
    d.   equivalent to a cost centre

27. Activity Based Costing absorbs overheads into products
    a.   by treating most of them as long-term variable costs
    b.   by ignoring the volume of production
    c.   according to the usage of support overheads
    d.   by only producing on demand.

28. Significant Digit Codes are
    a.   where some of the digits are part of the description
    b.   only used for raw materials
    c.   to enable a code to be self-checking
    d.   a means of combining expenditure and location codes.

Test 2

1. A firm uses direct labour as a basis for overhead absorption.

    If large fluctuations in labour hours are experienced:
    a. this is a reason to use predetermined overhead rate
    b. this will mean that overheads will be under or over absorbed for the year
    c. different amounts of overhead will be charged to jobs with the same labour hours
    d. it will be better to use a machine hour rate.

2. A predetermined overhead rate using machine hours as a basis:
    a. is calculated by dividing actual overheads by budgeted machine hours
    b. results in the over absorption of overhead
    c. is inferior to a rate based on labour hours
    d. results in charging similar overheads to jobs with similar machine hours

3. A firm recovers overheads on labour hours which were budgeted at 3500 with overheads of £43,750.
    Actual results were 3620 hours with overheads of £44,535.
    a. Overheads were underabsorbed by £785
    b. Overheads were overabsorbed by £715
    c. Overheads were overabsorbed by £1,500
    d. Overheads were underabsorbed by £715

4. A firm that uses departmental overhead rates as opposed to a single blanket rate:
    a. might be better able to check the profitability of each job
    b. will charge about the same overhead to each job
    c. will make the departments more profitable
    d. is more likely to have under-absorbed overheads.

5. A firm that has underabsorbed overhead at the end of the period:
    a. has been working inefficiently
    b. would be better not using predetermined rates
    c. incorrectly budgeted the absorption base and/or the amount of overheads
    d. has overspent on overheads.

6. The simultaneous equation method of dealing with reciprocal servicing:
    a. is more sophisticated and produces more accurate results
    b. is a convention like all the other methods
    c. enables servicing department costs to be controlled
    d. needs a computer to work out the results.

7. An asset costs £65,000 and is expected to last 10 years when the scrap value will be £15,000.

    What is the appropriate percentage to use for depreciation using the reducing balance method (to nearest %):
    a. 50%
    b. 10%
    c. 15%
    d. 14%

8. A firm maintains separate cost and financial ledgers. The profit in the financial accounts was £64,275 where the closing stock was valued £850 lower than the cost accounts whilst the opening stock was £275 higher. What is the profit in the cost accounts?
    a. £65,400
    b. £63,150
    c. £64,850
    d. £63,700

9. Using interlocking cost and financial accounts, the Financial Ledger Control Account in the cost ledger:
    a. is a memorandum account only
    b. provides automatic reconciliation of the ledgers
    c. is part of the double entry of the Financial Ledger
    d. is part of the double entry system in the Cost Ledger.

10. Which of the following firms would be most likely to use job costing?
    a. a paint manufacturer
    b. a sugar refinery
    c. a firm of architects
    d. a car manufacturers.

The following data are the basis of the next 3 questions. A firm makes special switch gear to customers requirements and uses job costing. The data for a period are:

	Job No		
	X100	Y252	Z641
Opening WIP	£6,200	21,000	0
Material added in period	£15,250	0	9,000
Labour for period	£9,000	7,000	8,000

The overheads for the period were exactly as budgeted, £60,000.

11. What overhead would be added to Job No X100 for the period?
    a. £20,000
    b. £22,500
    c. £9,000
    d. £24,000

12. Job No Y252 was completed in the period and consisted of 30 identical switch units. The firm adds 25% on to total costs to calculate the selling price. What is the price of a switch unit?
    a. £1,167
    b. £2,292
    c. £1,896
    d. £1,517

13. Jobs X100 and Z641 are the only incomplete jobs. What is the value of closing WIP?
    a. £89,950
    b. £47,450
    c. £112,437
    d. £41,250

14. The costing associated with a typical site based contract:
    a. means that more costs can be identified as direct
    b. requires some estimate to be made of interim profits
    c. means that the contract account will be credited with materials at the end of the contract
    d. includes all of these.

15. Which of the following firms are most likely to use process costing?
    a. a car manufacturer
    b. a sugar refinery
    c. a builder
    d. a departmental store.

16. Using process costing the amount of cost transferred to Finished Goods stock is the cost of :
    a. the equivalent production for the period
    b. the units started and completed during the period
    c. the units completed during the period
    d. the units in the opening Finished Goods stock

The following data are the basis of questions 17 and 18.

Process 2 for period		
	Units	
Opening WIP	1,800	(80% complete)
Started in process	16,000	
Completed	15,000	
Closing WIP	2,800	(60% complete)

17. Using the FIFO method the equivalent production is:
    a. 15,240
    b. 15,760
    c. 16,680
    d. 15,000

18. Using the Average cost method the equivalent production is:
    a. 15,240
    b. 15,760
    c. 16,680
    d. 15,000

19. In a process costing system where there is no opening or closing WIP:
    a. current production costs equal costs transferred out
    b. weighted average and FIFO will give the same cost per unit
    c. units completed equals equivalent units of production
    d. all of the above.

20. A firm using process costing finds that production is steadily increasing by period. Substantial WIP stocks are held which remain about the same in equivalent units, period to period. A high proportion of manufacturing cost is fixed. In these circumstances the relationship between FIFO and weighted average cost per unit figures is that:
    a. FIFO will be higher than weighted average
    b. weighted average will be higher than FIFO
    c. both will be about the same
    d. it is not possible to tell what the relationship will be.

21. Let O = units in opening WIP, C = units in closing WIP, S = units stated in production. Then U = units completed and
    a. $U = O + S - C$
    b. $U = O + C - S$
    c. $U = O + S - C$
    d. $U = O + S + C$

22. A process department began with no opening stocks. A total of 8500 units was transferred in at a cost of £93,500. The cost of raw materials added was £3.50 per unit and labour costs were £5 per unit. If 6750 units were completed and transferred out the total cost transferred out was:
    a. £165,750
    b. 93,500
    c. £131,625
    d. £74,250

23. Apportioning joint costs over joint products on either the physical unit or sales value basis is useful for
    a. no purposes as the methods are conventions only
    b. decision making
    c. stock valuation and decision making
    d. stock valuation.

The following data are to be used for questions 24 and 25.

A process produces three products R, S and T. Total joint costs were £17,000 and outputs and selling prices were:

    R   250 kgs sold at £22 per kg
    S   550 kgs sold at £19 per kg
    T   450 kgs sold at £25 per kg

24. Apportioning the joint costs on the physical unit basis gives:
    a. R = £4,250   S = £9,350   T = £7,650
    b. R = £3,438   S = £6,531   T = £7,031
    c. R = £5,667   S = £5,667   T = £5,666
    d. R = £5,667   S = £4,894   T = £6,439

25. Apportioning the joint costs on the sales value basis gives:
    a. R = £4,250   S = £9,350   T = £7,650
    b. R = £3,438   S = £6,531   T = £7,031
    c. R = £5,667   S = £5,667   T = £5,666
    d. R = £5,667   S = £4,894   T = £6,439

26. When Activity Based Costing is used it is probable that
    a. all products will cost more
    b. high volume products will tend to be costed lower
    c. direct costs will be a smaller proportion of total costs
    d. more costs will be charged to products which are produced for stock.

27. The use of backflush accounting means that
    a. conversion costs cannot be carried forward in stock values
    b. stocks cannot occur
    c. raw material costs will be reduced
    d. costs are attributed to stock and cost of sales when the finished goods are made.

28. Unit costs are extensively used in the Public Sector. This is because
    a. they are a rough and ready guide to efficiency
    b. they are a good measure of the quality of service provided
    c. they allow for regional differences
    d. they enable Public Sector organisations to stay within the set cash limits.

Test 3

1. Information for decision making:
   a. concerns the alternatives possible
   b. deals with the future, not the past
   c. is concerned with the incremental costs and revenues
   d. is all of the above

2. Double loop feedback:
   a. is information designed to ensure that operations conform to plans
   b. is designed to assess how well the control system operates and how relevant current plans are.
   c. is information passed up two layers of the organisation
   d. is information that is double checked for accuracy.

3. If the total expenditure on Cost type X was expressed as a cost per unit of the product, X would be classified as variable if:
   a. the cost per unit changed with the level of activity
   b. the cost per unit was affected by inflation
   c. the cost per unit remained constant with changes in the level of activity
   d. the total expenditure on X remained the same.

4. Analysis has shown that the cost of a process is represented by the function:

   $$Cost = \pounds ax + bx^2 + cx^3$$

   where $a = 7; b = 0.6; c = 0.04$

   What will be the cost when output is 26 units? (nearest £)
   a. £628
   b. £1,291
   c. £199
   d. £1,523

5. What type of cost function is shown in Q4?
   a. curvi-linear variable
   b. semi-variable, curvi-linear
   c. linear approximation
   d. semi-variable, linear

6. Using the high/low method what is the value of the slope based on the following data?

Cost	Units
£12,650	6000
9,200	4520
8,800	3500
11,750	5200

   a. £1 per unit
   b. £2.11 per unit
   c. £2.51 per unit
   d. £1.54 per unit

7. In the regression result, $y = \pounds 280 + \pounds 2.6x$
   a. £2.6 is an estimate of the fixed costs per unit
   b. x is the dependent variable
   c. y is the dependant variable
   d. there are two independent variables.

8. Given that $\sum y = 694$, $\sum x = 72$, $\sum xy = 8210$ and $\sum x^2 = 936$ and $n = 9$, what is the regression equation?
   a. $y = \pounds 15.22 + 7.60x$
   b. $y = \pounds 72 + 9x$
   c. $y = \pounds 76 + 1.522x$
   d. none of the above.

9. Marginal costing gives a different profit to absorption costing when
   a. all production costs are fixed
   b. opening and closing stocks are different
   c. all production costs are variable
   d. there are no opening or closing stocks.

The following data relate to questions 10 to 13. A firm makes a single product and data for a period are:

No opening stock
Sales 65,000 units @ £60 each
Production 73,500 units
Variable costs £23 per unit
Total fixed costs for period £1.3m
Fixed overheads are recovered on a unit basis and the average production level is 70,000 units.

10. Using marginal costing the profit for the period is: (to nearest £'000)
    a. £2,445,000
    b. £1,293,000
    c. £1,145,000
    d. £1,295,000

11. Using absorption costing the profit for the period is?
    a. £2,445,000
    b. £1,293,000
    c. £1,145,000
    d. £1,295,000

12. Using marginal costing the closing stock valuation is?
    a. £353,357
    b. £80,500
    c. £345,840
    d. £195,500

13. Using absorption costing the closing valuation is?
    a. £353,357
    b. £80,500
    c. £345,840
    d. £195,500

14. Relevant information for decision making:
    a. can include sunk costs
    b. usually includes historical costs
    c. is incremental to the decision in hand
    d. includes all of the above.

15. Opportunity cost cannot be
    a. the replacement cost of an item
    b. the next best operating value of an item
    c. the net realisable values of the item
    d. the original cost of the item.

16. The formula for the sales at breakeven point for a multi-product firm is:

    a. $\dfrac{\text{Fixed costs}}{\text{Contribution/unit}} \times \text{sales price per unit}$

    b. $\dfrac{\text{Fixed costs} \times \text{Sale value}}{\text{Contribution}}$

    c. $\text{Fixed costs} \times \dfrac{1}{\text{CS ratio}}$

    d. None of these.

17. The margin of safety is:
    a. the difference between budgeted sales and the breakeven sales
    b. the difference between actual sales and budgeted sales
    c. sale minus variable costs
    d. the difference between zero sales and breakeven sales.

The following data are used for questions 18 to 20.

A firm makes a single product with a marginal cost of £3 at a selling price of £5 and fixed costs of £25,000.

18. What level of sales will produce a product of £15,000?
    a. £120,000
    b. £20,000
    c. £100,000
    d. £40,000

19. How many units will need to be sold to breakeven?
    a. 5,000
    b. 25,000
    c. 40,000
    d. 12,500

20. If the taxation rate is 30% how many units will need to be sold to obtain a £20,000 profit?
    a. 17,857
    b. 26,785
    c. 45,833
    d. 33,333.

21. Which of the following would increase the per unit contribution the most?
    a. a 5% decrease in total fixed costs
    b. a 5% decrease in unit variable costs
    c.. a 5% increase in selling price
    d. a 5% increase in unit volume

The graph below relates to questions 22 to 25

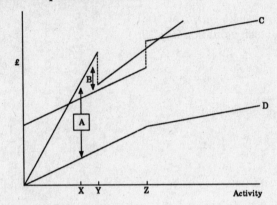

22. The distance A represents:
    a. contribution at activity level X
    b. profit at activity level X
    c. the amount of variable costs at activity level X
    d. the margin of safety.

23. The distance B represents
    a. contribution at activity level Y
    b. the amount of variable costs at activity level Y
    c. the level of sales at activity Y
    d. the amount of variable costs at activity level Y

24. Which of the following are possible causes of the changes in the graph at activity level Z?
    a. an increase in sales value causing an increase in contribution
    b. a decrease in fixed costs causing an increase in variable costs
    c. an increase in total fixed costs and a decrease in variable costs per unit
    d. an increase in total variable costs and a decrease in fixed costs per unit.

25. What do the lines C and D represent?
    a. Fixed costs and variable costs respectively
    b. Total costs and variable costs respectively
    c. Variable cost and fixed costs respectively
    d. Sales revenue and total costs respectively

The following data are to be used for questions 26 to 28.

	Last year	This year
Output (units)	15,000	17,000
Total costs	£112,500	128,525

Cost inflation this year was 6%

26. What is the underlying real variable cost per unit?
    a. £7.5
    b. £7.34
    c. £6.41
    d. £3.5

27. What is the underlying fixed cost?
    a. £60,000
    b. £112,500
    c. £16,025
    d. It is not possible to calculate without more information.

28. What are the expected total costs for next year if inflation is forecast at 4% and output 18,500 units?
    a. £141,304
    b. £135,869
    c. £137,524
    d. £138,750

Test 4

1. A project has an IRR of 13% and the firm's cost of capital is 15%. At the cost of capital the NPV will be:
   a. Positive
   b. Zero
   c. Negative
   d. equal to the IRR.

The following data are used for questions 2 and 3.

A firm with a cost of capital of 12% is considering a project with the following cash flows:

	0	1	2	3	4
	− 5000	+ 2500	+ 2000	+ 2000	+ 1500

2. What is the NPV of the project?
   a. 6204
   b. 1204
   c. 3896
   d. 5000

3. What is the project's IRR? (nearest %)
   a. 15%
   b. 28%
   c. 12%
   d. 23%

4. A flexible budget is:
   a. the only suitable budget for control purposes
   b. a budget analysed to fixed and variable elements
   c. designed to show the appropriate expenditure for the actual production level
   d. all of the above.

5. The total budgeted expenditure for 17,000 units was £58,500 and for £17,500 units £59,875. This means that fixed costs were estimated to be:
   a. £11,750
   b. £1,375
   c. £58,500
   d. £23,500

6. A firm exactly met its budgeted output of 42,500 litres but the total expenditure of £196,200 was £12,000 over budget. Analysis showed that fixed costs of £35,500 were exactly as budgeted. What was the budgeted variable cost per litre?
   a. £0.83
   b. £3.5
   c. £4.62
   d. £1.12.

7. In a budgeting system goal congruence is achieved when:
   a. the actual expenditure equals the budget
   b. the budgeted allowance is agreed by the manager
   c. management by exception is practised
   d. personal and organisational objectives coincide.

8. A standard hour:
   a. is one where operatives work for 60 minutes
   b. is the number of hours worked above normal time
   c. is a measure of work content
   d. is any hour in which standard labour rates are paid.

9. The operating profit variance is :
   a. the only variable not entered in a ledger account
   b. the total of all the cost variances
   c. always equal to the largest variance
   d. is the figure required to make the ledger accounts balance.

10. In a period 5220 hours were worked at a total cost of £22,185. The Labour Rate Variance was £1,566 (Adv) and the Labour Efficiency Variance was £711 (Fav). How many standard hours were produced?
    a. 5220
    b. 5400
    c. 5588
    d. 5421

11. The standard Material content of Part No Y252 is 27 kgs at £5.75 per kg. In a period 486 units of Part No Y252 were produced and actual material usage was 13,132 kgs at a cost of £74,852. The Material Price and Material Usage Variances were:
    a. £155 (FAV) and £295 (ADV)
    b. £657 (ADV) and £575 (FAV)
    c. £575 (FAV) and £657 (ADV)
    d. £657 (FAV) and £575 (ADV)

The data below are to be used for questions 12 to 16.

Budget for Period, Dept XXX

Fixed overheads	£27,495
Variable overheads	31,850
Labour hours	6,500
Standard hours of production	6,500

Actual for period

Fixed overheads	29,800
Variable overheads	31,850
Labour hours	6,450
Standard hours produced	6,550

12. What are the variable overhead expenditure and variable overhead efficiency variances for Dept XXX?
    a. £490 (FAV) and £245 (ADV)
    b. Nil and £245 (ADV)
    c. £245 (ADV) and £490 (FAV)
    d. Nil and £490 (FAV).

13. What are the fixed overhead expenditure and volume variances for Dept XXX?
    a. £2,305 (ADV) and £670 (FAV)
    b. £670 (FAV) and £2,305 (ADV)
    c. £2,305 (FAV) and £670 (FAV)
    d. none of the above.

14. What are the fixed overhead capacity and fixed overhead efficiency variances for Dept XXX?
    a. £430 (ADV) and £240 (ADV)
    b. £240 (FAV) and £430 (FAV)
    c. £430 (FAV) and £240 (FAV)
    d. £2,305 (ADV) and £670 (FAV)

15. Assuming a Total Overhead approach calculate the Volume and Efficiency Variances for Dept XXX.
    a. £240 (FAV) and £920 (ADV)
    b. £240 (ADV) and £920 (FAV)
    c. £240 (FAV) and £920 (FAV)
    d. £2,550 (ADV) and £920 (FAV)

16. Calculate the Efficiency Ratio for Dept XXX
    a. 99%
    b. 98%
    c. 101%
    d. 102%

17. To calculate Sales Margin Variances it is assumed that products are:
    a. at standard manufacturing cost
    b. valued at marginal cost only
    c. always sold in the budgeted proportions
    d. sold at standard prices

The data below are used for questions 18 to 20

A detergent called Kleenawl is made by mixing 3 ingredients and the standard cost data are:

	Proportions	Standard cost
Ingredient A	40%	£2 per litre
B	50%	£1.50 per litre
C	10%	£4 per litre

During a period 600 litres of Kleenawl were produced and inputs were:

	Actual consumption	Actual price per litre
Ingredient A	3,200	£2.1
B	3,950	£1.46
C	900	£4 .25

18. Calculate the Materials Price Variance for Kleenawl:
    a. £320 (ADV)
    b. £387 (FAV)
    c. £529 (ADV)
    d. £387 (ADV)

19. Calculate the Mixture Variance for Kleenawl (nearest £):
    a. £387 (ADV)
    b. £227 (ADV)
    c. £1,073 (ADV)
    d. £227 (FAV)

20. Calculate the Yield Variance for Kleenawl
    a. £1,073 (FAV)
    b. £1,300 (ADV)
    c. £1,073 (ADV)
    d. £387 (ADV)

21. When standard process costing is used:
    a. transfers out and WIP are valued at standard
    b. effective units = completed + units in closing WIP – units in opening WIP
    c. the total variances do not appear in the process account
    d. all of the above apply.

22. It is required to set control limits using statistical methods and analysis shows that the standard labour cost of an assembly averages £250 with a variance of £25. The 5% control limits are (nearest £):
    a. £240 to £260
    b. £225 to £275
    c. £201 to £299
    d. £245 to £255.

23. A firm uses standard costing and an integrated double entry accounting system. The double entry for a favourable Material Usage Variance is:
    a. DR WIP control a/c. CR Stores Control a/c
    b. DR WIP control a/c. CR Material Usage Variance a/c
    c. DR Store Control a/c. CR WIP Control a/c
    d. DR Material Usage Variance a/c. CR WIP Control a/c

24. In the accounting for Standard Costing, the costs recorded in the Factory Overhead account:
    a. must be at Standard
    b. may be at Actual or Standard
    c. must be at actual
    d. depend on whether there is over or under recovery.

25. An accountant wishes to be able to test a large number of possible conditions (level of sales, cost variations, collection periods for debtors and so on) to determine the range of cash requirements. He would be advised to use:
    a. a cash budget
    b. a budgeted balance sheet
    c. regression analysis
    d. a computer-based simulation model.

26. Participation by staff in standard and budget setting:
    a. always improves performance
    b. is liked by all staff
    c. needs to be done selectively
    d. can only be done when zero-base budgeting is used

27. The use of Standard costing in factories employing Advanced Manufacturing Technology
    a. concentrates on a narrow range of financial factors
    b. means that some variances have little or no control value
    c. over-emphasises direct labour
    d. has all the above features

28. Decision Support Systems
    a. consist of automatic decision making systems
    b. are best for semi-structured problems
    c. perform the routine data processing of the firm
    d. can only be used for accounting problems.

Answer key to multiple-choice tests

Question No	Test 1	Test 2	Test 3	Test 4
1	B	A	D	C
2	C	D	B	B
3	A	B	C	D
4	C	A	B	D
5	D	C	A	A
6	D	B	D	B
7	A	D	C	D
8	A	A	A	C
9	B	D	B	A
10	D	C	C	B
11	B	B	B	D
12	C	C	D	C
13	A	A	A	A
14	C	D	C	B
15	B	B	D	C
16	A	C	B	D
17	D	A	A	A
18	D	C	C	D
19	C	D	D	B
20	B	B	B	C
21	A	A	C	D
22	D	C	A	A
23	C	D	D	B
24	C	A	C	C
25	B	B	B	D
26	B	B	D	C
27	C	D	A	D
28	A	A	C	B

Table A

Present value factors. Present value of £1 $(1 + r)^{-n}$

Periods (n)	Interest rates (r)%								
	1%	2%	4%	6%	8%	10%	12%	14%	15%
1	0.990	0.980	0.962	0.943	0.926	0.909	0.893	0.877	0.870
2	0.980	0.961	0.925	0.890	0.857	0.826	0.797	0.769	0.756
3	0.971	0.942	0.889	0.840	0.794	0.751	0.712	0.675	0.658
4	0.961	0.924	0.855	0.792	0.735	0.683	0.636	0.592	0.572
5	0.951	0.906	0.822	0.747	0.681	0.621	0.567	0.519	0.497
6	0.942	0.888	0.790	0.705	0.630	0.564	0.507	0.456	0.432
7	0.933	0.871	0.760	0.665	0.583	0.513	0.452	0.400	0.376
8	0.923	0.853	0.731	0.627	0.540	0.467	0.404	0.351	0.327
9	0.914	0.837	0.703	0.592	0.500	0.424	0.361	0.308	0.284
10	0.905	0.820	0.676	0.558	0.463	0.386	0.322	0.270	0.247
11	0.0896	0.804	0.650	0.527	0.429	0.350	0.287	0.237	0.215
12	0.887	0.788	0.625	0.497	0.397	0.319	0.257	0.208	0.187
13	0.879	0.773	0.601	0.469	0.368	0.290	0.229	0.182	0.163
14	0.870	0.758	0.577	0.442	0.340	0.263	0.205	0.160	0.141
15	0.861	0.743	0.555	0.417	0.315	0.239	0.183	0.140	0.123
16	0.853	0.728	0.534	0.394	0.292	0.218	0.163	0.123	0.107
17	0.855	0.714	0.513	0.371	0.270	0.198	0.146	0.108	0.093
18	0.836	0.700	0.494	0.350	0.250	0.180	0.130	0.095	0.081
19	0.828	0.686	0.475	0.331	0.232	0.164	0.116	0.083	0.070
20	0.820	0.675	0.456	0.312	0.215	0.149	0.104	0.073	0.061
21	0.811	0.660	0.439	0.294	0.199	0.135	0.093	0.064	0.053
22	0.803	0.647	0.422	0.278	0.184	0.123	0.083	0.056	0.046
23	0.795	0.634	0.406	0.262	0.170	0.112	0.074	0.049	0.040
24	0.788	0.622	0.390	0.247	0.158	0.102	0.066	0.043	0.035
25	0.780	0.610	0.375	0.233	0.146	0.092	0.059	0.038	0.030

Periods (n)	Interest rates (r)%								
	16%	18%	20%	22%	24%	25%	26%	28%	30%
1	0.862	0.847	0.833	0.820	0.806	0.800	0.794	0.781	0.769
2	0.743	0.718	0.694	0.672	0.650	0.640	0.630	0.610	0.592
3	0.641	0.609	0.579	0.551	0.524	0.512	0.500	0.477	0.455
4	0.552	0.516	0.482	0.451	0.423	0.410	0.397	0.373	0.350
5	0.476	0.437	0.402	0.370	0.341	0.328	0.315	0.291	0.269
6	0.410	0.370	0.335	0.303	0.275	0.262	0.250	0.227	0.207
7	0.354	0.314	0.279	0.249	0.222	0.210	0.198	0.178	0.159
8	0.305	0.266	0.233	0.204	0.179	0.168	0.157	0.139	0.123
9	0.263	0.225	0.194	0.167	0.144	0.134	0.125	0.108	0.094
10	0.227	0.191	0.162	0.137	0.116	0.107	0.099	0.085	0.075
11	0.195	0.162	0.135	0.112	0.094	0.086	0.079	0.066	0.056
12	0.168	0.137	0.112	0.192	0.076	0.069	0.062	0.052	0.043
13	0.145	0.116	0.093	0.075	0.061	0.055	0.050	0.040	0.033
14	0.125	0.099	0.178	0.062	0.049	0.044	0.039	0.032	0.025
15	0.108	0.084	0.065	0.051	0.040	0.035	0.031	0.025	0.020
16	0.093	0.071	0.054	0.042	0.032	0.028	0.025	0.019	0.015
17	0.080	0.060	0.045	0.034	0.026	0.023	0.020	0.015	0.012
18	0.069	0.051	0.038	0.028	0.021	0.018	0.016	0.012	0.009
19	0.060	0.043	0.031	0.023	0.017	0.014	0.012	0.009	0.007
20	0.051	0.037	0.026	0.019	0.014	0.012	0.010	0.007	0.005
21	0.044	0.031	0.022	0.015	0.011	0.009	0.008	0.006	0.004
22	0.038	0.026	0.018	0.013	0.009	0.007	0.006	0.004	0.003
23	0.033	0.022	0.015	0.010	0.007	0.006	0.005	0.003	0.002
24	0.028	0.019	0.011	0.008	0.006	0.005	0.004	0.003	0.002
25	0.024	0.016	0.010	0.007	0.005	0.004	0.003	0.002	0.001

Table B

Present value annuity factors.

Present value of £1 received annually for n years $\left(\dfrac{1-(1+r)^{-n}}{r}\right)$

Periods (n)	Interest rates (r) %								
	1%	2%	4%	6%	8%	10%	12%	14%	15%
1	0.990	0.980	0.962	0.943	0.926	0.909	0.893	0.877	0.870
2	1.970	1.942	1.886	1.833	1.783	1.736	1.690	1.647	1.626
3	2.941	2.884	2.775	2.675	2.577	2.487	2.402	2.322	2.283
4	3.902	3.808	3.610	3.465	3.312	3.170	3.037	2.914	2.855
5	4.853	4.713	4.452	4.212	3.996	3.791	3.605	3.433	3.352
6	5.795	5.601	5.242	4.917	4.623	4.355	4.111	3.889	3.784
7	6.728	6.472	6.002	5.582	5.206	4.868	4.564	4.288	4.160
8	7.652	7.325	6.733	6.210	5.747	5.335	4.968	4.639	4.487
9	8.566	8.162	7.435	6.802	6.247	5.759	5.328	4.946	4.772
10	9.471	8.983	8.111	7.360	6.710	6.145	5.650	5.216	5.019
11	10.368	9.787	8.760	7.887	7.139	6.495	5.988	5.453	5.234
12	11.255	10.575	9.385	8.384	7.536	6.814	6.194	5.660	5.421
13	12.114	11.343	9.986	8.853	7.904	7.103	6.424	5.842	5.583
14	13.004	12.106	10.563	9.295	8.244	7.367	6.628	6.002	5.724
15	13 865	12.849	11.118	9.712	8.559	7.606	6.811	6.142	5.847
16	14.718	13.578	11.652	10.106	8.851	7.824	6.974	6.265	5.954
17	15.562	14.292	12.166	10.477	9.122	8.022	7.120	6.373	6.047
18	16.328	14.992	12.659	10.828	9.372	8.201	7.250	6.467	6.128
19	17.226	15.678	13.134	11.158	9.604	8.365	7.366	6.550	6.198
20	18.046	16.351	13.590	11.470	9.818	8.514	7.469	6.623	6.259
21	18.857	17.011	14.029	11.764	10.017	8.649	7.562	6.687	6.312
22	19.660	17.658	14.451	12.042	10.201	8.772	7.645	6.743	6.369
23	20.456	18.292	14.857	12.303	10.371	8.883	7.718	6.792	6.399
24	21.243	18.914	15.247	12.550	10.529	8.985	7.784	6.815	6.434
25	22.023	19.523	15.622	12.783	10.675	9.077	7.843	6.873	6.464

Periods (n)	Interest rates (r) %								
	16%	18%	20%	22%	24%	25%	26%	28%	30%
1	0.862	0.847	0.833	0.820	0.806	0.800	0.794	0.781	0.769
2	1.605	1.566	1.528	1.492	1.457	1.440	1.424	1.392	1.361
3	2.246	2.174	2.106	2.042	1.981	1.952	1.923	1.868	1.816
4	2.798	2.690	2.589	2.494	2.404	2.362	2.320	2.241	2.166
5	3.274	3.127	2.991	2.864	2.745	2.689	2.635	2.532	2.436
6	3.685	3.498	3.326	3.167	3.020	2.951	2.885	2.759	2.643
7	4.039	3.812	3.605	3.416	3.242	3.161	3.083	2.937	2.802
8	4.344	4.078	3.837	3.619	3.421	3.329	3.421	3.076	2.925
9	4.607	4.303	4.031	3.786	3.566	3.463	3.366	3.184	3.019
10	4.833	4.949	4.192	3.923	3.682	3.571	3.465	3.269	3.092
11	5.029	4.636	4.327	4.035	3.766	3.656	3.544	3.335	3.147
12	5.197	4.793	4.439	4.127	3.851	3.725	3.606	3.387	3.190
13	5.342	4.910	4.533	4.203	3.912	3.780	3.656	3.427	3.223
14	5.468	5.008	4.611	4.265	3.961	3.824	3.965	3.459	3.249
15	5.575	5.092	4.675	4.315	4.001	3.859	3.726	3.483	3.268
16	5.669	5.162	4.730	4.357	4.033	3.887	3.751	3.503	3.283
17	5.749	5.222	4.775	4.391	4.059	3.910	3.771	3.518	3.295
18	5.818	5.273	4.812	4.419	4.080	3.928	3.786	3.529	3.304
19	5.877	5.316	4.844	4.442	4.097	3.942	3.799	3.539	3.311
20	5.929	5.353	4.870	4.460	4.110	3.954	3.808	3.546	3.316
21	5.973	5.384	4.891	4.476	4.121	3.963	3.816	3.551	3.320
22	6.011	5.410	4.909	4.488	4.130	3.970	3.822	3.556	3.323
23	6.044	5.432	4.925	4.499	4.137	3.976	3.827	3.559	3.325
24	6.073	5.451	4.937	4.507	4.143	3.981	3.831	3.562	3.327
25	6.097	5.467	4.948	4.514	4.147	3.985	3.834	3.564	3.329

Examination technique

INTRODUCTION

If you are a genius and/or can calculate and reproduce facts and figures with the speed of a computer and/or know the examiner then there is no need for you to read this section. On the other hand if you do not fall into any of the above categories then you will stand more chance of passing your examinations first time if you study this section carefully and follow the simple rules.

WELL BEFORE THE EXAMINATION

No amount of examination room technique will enable you to pass unless you have prepared yourself thoroughly beforehand. The period of preparation may be years or months long. It is no use expecting to pass with a feverish last minute bout of revision. By this stage you should have worked through all of the book and you should be thoroughly familiar with your syllabus and the type of examination questions that you have been set in the past.

By the end of your study and revision you should be able to answer every question in this book.

IMMEDIATELY BEFORE THE EXAMINATION

a. Make sure you know exact time, date and location of examination.

b. Carefully check you travel arrangements. Leave yourself adequate time.

c. Check over your examination equipment: Calculator? Spare Battery? Pens? Pencils? Tables? Watch? Sweets? etc.

d. Check your examination number.

IN THE EXAMINATION ROOM

If you have followed the rules so far you are well prepared; you have all the equipment you need; you did not have to rush — *you are calm and confident.*

Before you start writing

a. Carefully read the whole examination paper including the rubric.

b. Decide what questions you are going to answer.

c. Decide the sequence you will tackle the questions. Generally, answer the easiest question first.

d. Decide the time allocation for each question. In general the time allocation should be in direct proportion to the marks for each question.

e. Read the questions you have decided to answer again. Do you know exactly what the examiner is asking? Underline the key words in the question and keep these in you mind when answering.

Dealing with the questions

a. Make sure you plan each question first. Make a note of the main points or principles involved. If you are unable to finish the question you will gain some marks from these points.

b. Attempt all questions required and each part of each question.

c. Do not let your answer ramble on. Be as brief as possible consistent with covering all the points you know.

d. Follow a logical sequence in your answers.

e. Write neatly, underline headings and if the question asks for a particular sequence of answer then follow that sequence.

f. If diagrams graphs or tables are required give them plenty of space, label them neatly and comprehensively, and give a key to symbols, lines etc used. A simple clear diagram showing the main points can often gain a good proportion of the marks for a question.

When you have finished writing

a. Check that you have followed the examination regulations regarding examination title, examination number, candidates number and sequence of answer sheets.

b. Make sure you include all the sheets you require to be marked.

c. If you have time carefully read each and every part of each answer and check each calculation.

General points

a. Concentrate on answering the questions set not some related topic which you happen to know something about.

b. Do not leave the examination room early. Use every minute for checking and rechecking or adding points to questions answered.

c. Always attempt every question set and every part of each question.

EXAMINERS' REPORTS

After every examination an Examiner's Report is prepared and you are urged to obtain a copy and thoroughly digest the contents. Much useful advice is given not only about the detail of individual questions, but about the general approach to be adopted.

Ever since examinations were invented examiners have complained, with justice, about similar problems and deficiencies. The more common ones include: – failure to read the question – failure to answer the question as set – careless work, especially with calculations – bad English – poor writing – poor charts/diagrams with no titles or keys – rote learning rather than real understanding – inadequate time planning resulting in the failure to answer all questions – inclusion of irrelevant material – failure to relate theory and practice

You are strongly advised to note carefully the above list of common failings and to make sure that you are not guilty of any of them.

Solutions to Exercises and Examination Questions
(Set at the end of chapters)

Chapter 1 Solutions

Exercises

A1.1

Hospitals
Transport undertakings
Departmental stores
Farms
Banks
Colleges
Power generation

A1.2

Typical examples include:-

Hospitals	– Budgetary control – Cost ascertainment eg, cost per patient night
Transport undertakings	– Cost ascertainment eg, cost per tonne mile or cost per passenger mile – Cost control of running costs
Departmental Stores	– Operating statements of departmental efficiency and profitability – Stock turnover and other efficiency ratios
Farms	– Crop/field operating statements – Decision making information perhaps utilising marginal costing
Banks	– Branch operating statements
Colleges	– Cost control – Cost ascertainment eg, cost per full time equivalent student
Power generation	– Cost ascertainment – Plant operating statements

Examination Questions

A1.3

Report No. CA1

Date...............................

To: MANAGING DIRECTOR

From: COST ACCOUNTANT

Subject – PROPOSED COST ACCOUNTING SYSTEM

As requested I give below the major aims of the system and give examples of specific information which could be provided by the system when installed.

Main Aims

a. In general to provide the basis of an internal financial information service to management which will be of assistance in planning, control and decision making.

b. To assist forward planning by providing cost information on such matters as the relative profitability of products and departments so that the level of production, mix of products and pricing strategies can be decided.

c. To aid control by regular reporting of product costs and profitability, the performance of the different types of labour, the departments and sections.

d. To aid decision making by regular and special cost reports on any facet of operations.

e. To provide motivation and to promote cost consciousness for all levels of staff by providing them with feedback on their performance in the form of cost reports, budget statements etc.

f. To provide a formal means of gathering detailed information on operations which is vital now that the firm is beyond the size where personal observation is sufficient. Typical information which would be available includes:

   i. Product costs per unit and in total.
   ii. Departmental operating statements showing performance, expenditure etc.
   iii. Efficiency statements on labour, machine and material utilisation.
   iv. Analysis of cost trends particularly in relation to changing levels of activity.
   v. Product profitability and contribution statements.
   vi. Periodic stock valuations.
   vii. Cash budgets.
   viii. Scrap and rectification costs.
   ix. Special order costs.

A1.4

There are several ways in which a cost accountant could contribute to the efficient and economic operation of the equipment. In general the contribution that can be made is by detailed reporting on costs, times, outputs and other data. To be effective the reports should:

a. Be produced at regular, appropriate intervals which may be per shift, day, week or more, depending on the nature of the item.
b. Show controllable matters only.
c. Show comparative figures against budget or standard and the resulting variances, both periodic and cumulatively.
d. Be produced promptly.
e. Should be in a format which is effective and agreed by the recipients.

Typical areas covered by the reports include:

Machine utilisation:
including Down Time suitably analysed to maintenance, breakdowns, idle time, set-up time. Production performance per hour/shift etc. compared with targets, capacity projections covering the next budget period showing potential overloads/under utilisation.

Operating costs:
including details of direct and indirect labour costs, Waste/Scrap and reworks, Power and consumable material consumption, Direct Material Consumption.

A1.5

Report No.
Date.............................

To: MANAGING DIRECTOR
From: A.N. OTHER, COST ACCOUNTANT
Subject – PRINCIPAL ITEMS OF INFORMATION FROM A COSTING SYSTEM

As requested I give below six items of information produced on a regular basis by the Costing System.

a. Statements on direct labour, machine and material utilisation showing trends and values.
b. Job costs broken down to material, labour and overheads showing a comparison with estimates.
c. Cost control statements for each section and department showing actual results compared with budget.
d. Periodic stock valuations enable interim operating statements to be prepared.
e. Scrap and rectification cost reports.
f. Budgets for planning and control purposes including cash budgets for monitoring liquidity.

Chapter 2 Solutions

Exercises

A2.1

a. Litres of paint
   Thousands of washers
   Tyres
   Garden forks
   Metres of cloth

b. Hours of chargeable work (for example, architects, accountants)
   Area ploughed (contract farm work)
   Kilograms plated or painted
   Sets repaired (service contractors)
   Tonnage transported

A2.1

Added value is the increase in market value of the product brought about by the organisation itself ie, it excludes bought out materials and services.

To deal with the requirement that a statement of added value should be included in cost accounting reports it would be necessary to classify (and code accordingly) all expenditures as to whether they are bought in or not. In addition, if statements of added value are required at all intermediate processing points (ie, before final sale) then a notional sales value would have to be imputed for each stage and process of manufacture. Clearly, this would be an onerous, subjective procedure which would have little to commend it.

However, the calculation of added value at the final stage of external sales could be done relatively easily and would provide a clear statement of the efficiency of the organisation to produce profits without the largely uncontrollable influences of bought in goods and services.

A2.3

The main effects from a costing viewpoint of increasing automation are:

a. reduction in direct labour costs per unit;
b. increase in overhead costs caused by purchasing, maintaining, depreciating and operating expensive equipment;
c. change in cost structures; reducing variable costs and increasing fixed costs. Generally this has the effect of raising a firm's break-even point;
d. usually greater throughput and thus reduced costs per unit;
e. makes labour hours increasingly unsuitable as an overhead absorption base; machine hours are likely to be more appropriate;

f.   probable reduction in production workers but an increase in support staff.

Examination questions

A2.4

Essential elements of effective cost control.

a.   Staff support at all levels.
b.   Mutually agreed budgets/standards where appropriate.
c.   Participation by staff in design and operation of system which should be seen as supportive not threatening.
d.   Adequate accounting system to analyse, record and monitor costs and to prepare regular and prompt reports.
e.   Adequate training for all staff.
f.   Top management support and involvement.

Possible problems with cost control systems.

a.   May be seen as divisive and threatening.
b.   Difficulties in setting standards and budgets.
c.   All standards and subjects contain subjective elements and thus there is no such thing as totally accurate standards or variances.

A2.5

a.   i.   Cost centre and cost unit are defined in the book.

ii.   Possible cost units

a hospital	– patient/night, operations, outpatient visits.
a road haulage business	– tonne/miles, miles.
a hotel	– guest/nights, beds occupied/nights, meals supplied.
public transport	– passenger/miles, miles travelled, passenger journeys, tickets issued.

A2.6

Key Points

❑   Absorption on direct labour hours developed because it was simple, labour hours were recorded automatically and labour was a high proportion of total cost.

❑   Nowadays labour is a small and declining proportion of total cost thus recovering overheads (which may be 60-90% of costs) on labour will cause distortions.

❑   Various methods to overcome this problem:

Absorption based on machine hours.
Activity Based Costing where overheads are traced to products using specific cost drivers (ie, measures of activity).

❑   Above points valid if objective is to obtain more accurate product costs. However if objective is to influence behaviour then absorption on labour may be useful as it influences firms to reduce direct labour. This is the reason why absorption on labour hours is still widely practised in Japan.

A2.7

This can be taken directly from the text.

Chapter 3 Solutions

Exercises

A3.1

		Subjective Classification	Likely Objective Classification
	a.	Indirect wages	Production overheads
	b.	Administrative salaries	Administrative overheads
	c.	Indirect expense	Production overheads
	d.	Indirect expense	Production overheads
	e.	Indirect materials	Production overheads
	f.	Indirect expense	Production overheads
	g.	Direct materials	Cost unit
	h.	Administrative salaries	Administrative overheads
	i.	Indirect wages	Production overheads
	j.	Indirect expense	Selling overheads
	k.	Direct wages	Cost unit
	l.	Indirect wages	Production overheads

A3.2

Possible Block Coding System.

Direct Materials	1000-1100
Indirect Materials	1101-1200
Direct Wages	1201-1300
Direct Expenses	1301-1400
Indirect Wages	1401-1500
Indirect Expenses	1501-1600
Salaries	1601-1700

Cost Centre Codes

Direct to cost unit	100
Production Cost Centres	101- 200
Admin Cost Centres	201- 300
S & D Cost Centres	301- 400

Using the above simple system the items could be coded as follows:

a. 1410-120 (and other C.C's as appropriate)
b. 1637-212
c. 1506-101 (and other C.C's as appropriate)
d. 1530-101 (and other C.C's as appropriate)
e. 1146-101 (and other C.C's as appropriate)
f. 1545- appropriate C.C in range 101-200
g. 1120-100
h. 1642-250
i. 1420-101 (and other C.C's as appropriate)
j. 1570-301
k. 1201-100
l. 1405-101 (and other C.C's as appropriate)

A3.3

Five likely effects of incorrectly coding direct wages as indirect:

a. Direct wages will be understated and indirect wages (and thus overheads) will be overstated.
b. Predetermined overhead absorption rates will be incorrect.
c. Job and product costs will be incorrect.
d. If substantial, stock valuations will be incorrect.
e. If prices are based on recorded costs then they will be incorrect and thus the firm will lose profits or orders.

Examination questions

A3.4

a. A functional classification is one that relates to the functions or tasks that need to be done. Accordingly within the marketing area the following functions can be found and the costs associated with each of the functions would be coded accordingly.

Typical functions include:

i. Sales Administration; eg, managerial and clerical salaries, head office and branch office costs, showroom costs.
ii. Sales Representation; Salaries, commission and bonus payments, travelling and car expenses, training costs.
iii. Sales Promotion; eg, advertising, printing and sample costs, exhibitions and demonstrations.
iv. Market Research; salaries, survey costs and fees, expenses of canvassers, computer costs (for analysis purposes).
v. Invoicing, credit control and debt collection; eg, salaries, fees, legal expenses, stationery.

Depending on the particular organisation other functions might also come under the control of marketing eg, warehousing, delivery, storage.

It should be realised that the functional classifications referred to above (Sales Representation, Sales Promotion etc.) are the OBJECTIVE classifications and the examples given of costs (salaries, bonus etc.) are the SUBJECTIVE classifications.

b. Analysis of marketing costs.

The costs mentioned in part (a) could be analysed (where possible and economically feasible) according to:

i. Product and product group
ii. Type of sales outlet
iii. By area
iv. By representative
v. By order size and similar sub-divisions.

The purpose of this analysis is to assist management control, to increase marketing effectiveness and to increase profitability. In all cases the analysis is enhanced by comparison of actual with budget or target.

A3.5

a. Report No. Date..............
To: STORES CONTROLLER
From: COST ACCOUNTANT
Subject: MATERIAL CLASSIFICATION AND CODING

Classification is the process of arranging items into groups according to their likeness and is a fundamental process in any form of stores control system. A materials classification system is an example of subjective classification ie, classification according to the nature of the material or item.

i. The major principles in designing a materials coding system area.
   a. Uniqueness of code for each material.
   b. Distinctiveness of appearance of code.
   c. Uniformity of code length and construction.
   d. Brevity. Codes should be as brief as possible.
   e. Exhaustiveness. The coding structure should encompass the full range of existing and proposed materials.
   f. No ambiguity.
   g. Adaptable for automatic data processing.

ii. The major advantages of a sound, well designed coding system for stores control are:

   a. Coding will enable items to be uniquely identified.
   b. Ambiguity arising from varying descriptions will be avoided.
   c. The coding system will aid communication between stores, purchasing, production control, costing and all departments concerned with materials.
   d. Identification of redundant or slow moving items will be facilitated.

b. It can be deduced from the examples given that the code is split into four parts, each of 2 digits ie,

Digit No's.	1 2	3 4	5 6	7 8
	Type of material	Length	Thickness	Width

It is also apparent that 02 = Brass and 04 = Stainless Steel

(ie, alphabetical order) and the length is in units of 6", thickness in units of $\frac{1}{16}$" and width in units of $\frac{1}{4}$".

i. Accordingly the codes required are as follows:

	Aluminium –	6'6" $\times$	$\frac{1}{4}$" $\times$	$3\frac{1}{2}$"
Code =	01	13	04	14
	Copper –	1' $\times$	$\frac{3}{8}$" $\times$	$4\frac{1}{4}$"
Code =	03	02	06	17

ii. Finally the bars defined by the given codes.

Code	03	11	29	03
	Copper	$5\frac{1}{2}$" $\times$	$1\frac{13}{16}$" $\times$	$\frac{3}{4}$"
Code	01	07	17	21
	Aluminium	$3\frac{1}{2}$" $\times$	$1\frac{1}{16}$" $\times$	$5\frac{1}{4}$"

A3.6

a. *Classification of Cost*

   This is defined in the chapter.
   There are numerous ways in which cost may be classified
   eg, by behaviour – fixed, variable or semi-variable
   　　　by function – marketing, production
   　　　by location – cost centre, department

b. To fulfil the functions required of an integrated coding system for both financial and cost accounting purposes the code would have to be in several segments each describing a characteristic of the expense. For example an eight digit coding system would permit considerable flexibility enabling the specification of the type and location of the expense and the destination of the expense for both financial and cost accounting purposes. Some examples follow:

First 2 digits
Expense used in the following final accounts
01 –	Operating Statements
04 –	Trading Account
06 –	Profit & Loss Account etc

Next 2 digits
Nature of expense
10 –	Steel
15 –	Stationery
20 –	Direct Wages
25 –	Salaries etc.

Next 2 digits
Cost centre
10 – 50	Factory Cost Centre
60	Sales Office
70	Works Administration

Last 2 digits
Cost classification
00 – 10	Direct Costs
10 – 20	Indirect Costs
50	Capital

Thus the code 06 – 15 – 60 – 20 would be stationery bought for the Sales Office, which is an overhead item which will eventually appear in the Profit and Loss Account.

c. Four advantages of using code numbers for materials:

   i. More precise than descriptions so there is less chance of error and ambiguity
   ii. Shorter than descriptions and more suitable for data processing
   iii. The codes facilitate accounting and costing
   iv. Can be preprinted on all works documentation.

A3.7

i. a. 11/20/202
   b. 12/24/204
   c. 06/21/208
   d. 07/25/210

New codes created as follows:

Singapore   06
Port of Spain   07
Research   25
Salaries   210

ii. Can be taken from the book.

Chapter 4 Solutions

Exercises

A4.1

Purchase order

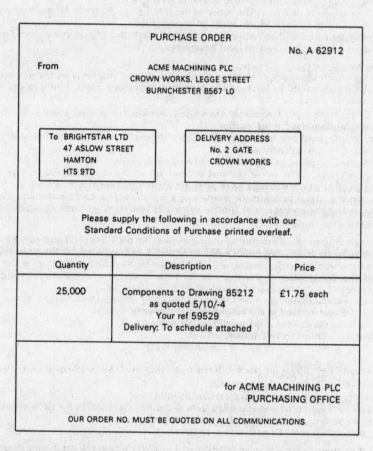

New codes created as follows:

	PURCHASE ORDER	

PURCHASE ORDER

No. A 62912

From

ACME MACHINING PLC
CROWN WORKS, LEGGE STREET
BURNCHESTER B567 LO

To BRIGHTSTAR LTD
47 ASLOW STREET
HAMTON
HTS 9TD

DELIVERY ADDRESS
No. 2 GATE
CROWN WORKS

Please supply the following in accordance with our
Standard Conditions of Purchase printed overleaf.

Quantity	Description	Price
25,000	Components to Drawing 85212 as quoted 5/10/-4 Your ref 59529 Delivery: To schedule attached	£1.75 each

for ACME MACHINING PLC
PURCHASING OFFICE

OUR ORDER NO. MUST BE QUOTED ON ALL COMMUNICATIONS

A4.2

Six advantages of Continuous Stocktaking

a. Continuous Stocktaking avoids the disruption caused by the large, annual stocktake.
b. Regular checking is likely to produce more accurate stock figures.
c. Discrepancies, losses, deterioration etc. will be discovered earlier.
d. Stock figures for interim operating statements and profit & loss accounts are readily available.
e. Better quality staff can be employed who will gain experience and expertise which would not be possible with annual stocktaking.
f. The continual presence of independent stock checkers may reduce pilferage and losses.

A4.3

Five reasons for stock-taking errors:

1. Errors in weighing, counting or measuring.
2. Part number errors.
3. Omitting whole groups of stock or including more than once.
4. Calculation errors on stock sheets.
5. Poor writing, illegible figures causing misreading.

A4.4

Differences of J.I.T. Purchasing to conventional purchasing.

a. Deliveries in accordance to Production Schedules not bulk deliveries moving into storage.
b. Likely to be fewer suppliers.
c. Usually no incoming quality checks which therefore must be done at the suppliers.

d. Components/materials delivered in production convenient form eg, on pallets, in packages etc sometimes directly onto the production floor.
e. Much closer liaison between Purchaser and Supplier.

Examination questions

A4.5

a. *Centralised or de-centralised stores.*
  i. *Stock levels.* Because duplication can be avoided overall stock investment can be reduced by a central stores.
  ii. *Control.* A centralised stores facilitates control by safeguarding high value items, better security measures, higher quality staff etc.
  iii. *Recording.* Certain aspects of paper work can be reduced eg, single stock records but other aspects may be increased eg, requests from remote locations.
  iv. *Equipment.* A centralised stores is likely to be able to justify the use of mechanised handling equipment, video displays, moveable racking etc.
  v. *Space.* In general a centralised stores is more economical on space.
  vi. *Convenience.* Decentralised stores at the scene of operations are likely to be more convenient. A remote central stores can introduce delays which might be unacceptable.
  vii. *Staff.* Theoretically less staff will be required in a central store and higher quality staff may be justifiable. However this might be offset by a lack of local knowledge.

b. *Continuous stocktaking*
This is the process by which the stock of items is checked at regular intervals by trained staff and compared with the stock record which would be kept on the perpetual inventory basis. This process has the following advantages:
  i. Stocks would be checked more frequently than the conventional annual stock take. Discrepancies and problems will thus be discovered much earlier.
  ii. Higher quality, trained staff can be employed so there should be fewer errors than on annual stock takes where untrained staff are frequently used.
  iii. There is no disruption or cessation of production during stock takes.
  iv. Continuous stocktaking and the investigations carried out on discrepancies found may deter pilferage or discover it earlier and should encourage more accurate documentation and recording.
  v. Because stock records are checked more frequently they should be more accurate. This will assist the ordering functions and the management control aspects of inventory systems eg, maximum and minimum levels.

c. *The layout of stores*
This is a technical subject for which engineering and work study advice would be required. Typical factors to be considered include:
  i. Access for deliveries and issues.
  ii. Well organised gangways large enough for loaders, fork lift trucks etc.
  iii. Logical distribution of stocked items with the most frequently required items adjacent to issue points.
  iv. Sufficient horizontal and vertical space for pallets, containers and racks.
  v. Good security features eg, external walls, ceilings, TV scanners etc.
  vi. Space for making up bulk orders and issues.

A4.6

Although there are innumerable reasons for stock differences arising they can be grouped into categories ie.
a. Quantity errors eg, miscounts during the stock take.
b. Classification errors eg, a stainless steel part classified as mild steel.
c. Pricing errors eg, a correctly counted and classified item might be priced at £56 for 1000 instead of £56 per 100.
d. Recording errors eg, an omission of the entry of a goods received note.
e. System errors eg, no adequate recording of returns to stores.

The steps to be taken for an investigation involve scrutiny and analysis within the categories given above.

Quantity errors
Examine the stock taking instructions and procedures. Sample count/weigh items and, allowing for subsequent stock movements, reconcile these balances with original stock sheets. Sample check prices and extensions on stock sheets.

Classification errors
Sample check classifications on stock sheets and stock ledgers. Check for compensating errors on raw material, W-I-P and Finished Goods. Analyse coding systems in use.

Pricing errors
Sample check prices on stock sheets. Check materials, labour and overhead books and valuations for W-I-P pricing. If standard costing is used check that all variances have been dealt with correctly.

Recording errors
Reconcile stock lists and stores ledger balances. If bin cards and stores records are kept reconcile the balances. Examine the prelisting or batch control system used for ledger posting. Check that recording is up to date; have all invoiced goods/returns/transfers from W-I-P to finished goods etc. been dealt with?

System errors
Are all issues to W-I-P recorded? - and returns? Was a common cut-off date used for all type of stocks? Is the scrap recording system effective? Can despatches be made without invoices being raised?

A4.7

Accountant's contribution to material cost control

This is a very wide ranging question indeed because material cost control can cover innumerable factors ranging from the design and specification of the product, ordering and reception, storage and handling, production methods, scrap control, rectification and so on.

Assuming that the accountant would not be responsible for the design of systems such as purchasing, inspection and the like his major role would be in the preparation of comparative cost data on all aspects of; materials handling and usage, the audit of procedures and results, the preparation of budgets and standards for purchasing, production and scrap.

Typical areas of involvement include: Material selection/product design. Although primarily a technical function cost estimates are involved.

Purchasing, ordering and materials reception
A purchase budget would need to be prepared and cost comparisons made of buying patterns, order costs etc. Variance reports may be prepared where standard costing is used.

Inventory control procedures
The monitoring of the effectiveness of inventory control procedures, EOQ calculations and provision of cost data on stock holding costs.

Storage and handling
Apart from routine cost reports on storage and handling there should be periodic reports on stocks held, perhaps using ABC or Pareto analysis, stock movements and turnover, obsolescence, stock losses, costs of pilferage etc.

Production
All aspects of material issues, pricing methods, material utilisation, scrap, rejects and reworked materials must be analysed and costed. Regular, detailed material cost reports produced for all levels of management from charge-hands upwards help to promote an awareness of material costs.

Chapter 5 Solutions

Exercises

A5.1

The situation described in the question is a common one where several records exist relating to the same item.

Typical of the reasons are the following:

a. Errors in entering, totalling or sub-totalling.
b. Delays in entering up the different records so that at any time they will show different balances.
c. Loss of source documents eg, Goods Inwards Notes, Material Requisitions etc.
d. Errors in source documents either of quantities or part numbers
e. Errors in physical issues of receipts.
f. Deliberate falsification perhaps to hide fraud.
g. Theft or breakage of materials and parts which is not recorded.
h. Stores transfers or goods returned not recorded.

A5.2

The perpetual Inventory System is a system of recording stocks so that the balance of stock is always available from the records whether manually maintained or by computer. To ensure that the stock balance is as accurate as possible the actual stock levels should be checked frequently, particularly for fast moving items, and discrepancies investigated using the procedures of Continuous Stocktaking.

A5.3.

$$\text{Demand p.a.} = 25 \times 250 = 6250$$

$$\text{EOQ} = \sqrt{\frac{2.Co.D}{Cc}}$$

$$= \sqrt{\frac{2 \times 150 \times 6250}{3 \times 0.12}}$$

$$= 2282$$

Examination questions

A5.4

a. Materials purchased as percentage of sales.

There are several possible causes of the percentage increase:

  i. More purchases causing an increase in stocks.
  ii. Higher purchase price with same volume of purchases.
  iii. Changes in mix of products sold.
  iv. Lower selling prices.
  v. Inaccurate recording or purchases/issues/sales.

b. There are numerous points in any system where wastes and losses could occur. These include:

  i. Over issues and/or excessive consumption. Remedies: better stores and production supervision, palletised and/or boxed issues.

ii. Obsolete and deteriorating materials. Remedies: proper stock control systems with calculated control points, regular review of stock, better storage conditions.

iii. Fraud, pilfering and damage. Remedies: better quality control, more invoice/GRN checks, better purchasing, better storage conditions, more supervision.

A5.5

a. The Economic Order Quantity (EOQ) is the order quantity which minimises the balance of cost between stock holding costs and reordering costs. The basic EOQ formula is,

$$EOQ = \sqrt{\frac{2.Co.D}{Cc}}$$

where   Co = ordering cost per order
D = Demand per annum
Cc = Carrying cost per item p.a.

The EOQ is illustrated below

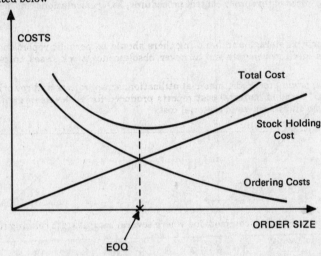

From the graph it will be seen that stock holding costs rise as the order size increases whilst total ordering costs fall as fewer orders of a larger quantity are placed during the year.

b. With a given annual usage (600 units) and from I to 6 orders being placed a year obviously the order size must vary.

ie,

No of orders p.a.	1	2	3	4	5	6
Order Size	600	300	200	150	120	100

Where there is no buffer stock (as in this example) average stock is $\frac{1}{2} \times$ reorder quantity.

Schedule of Costs for No. of orders Placed

		1	2	3	4	5	6
1	No of orders p.a.	1	2	3	4	5	6
2	Order size	600	300	200	150	120	100
3	Average stock $\left(\frac{\text{Line 2}}{2}\right)$	300	150	100	75	60	50
4	Average stock value (Line 3 × £2.4)	£720	£360	£240	£180	£144	£120
5	Average holding cost (Line 4 × 20%)	£144	£72	£48	£36	£28.8	£24
6	Order cost p.a. (Line 1 x £6)	£6	£12	£18	£24	£30	£36
	Annual Cost (Line 5 + Line 6)	£150	£84	£66	£60	£58.8	£60

∴ EOQ = 120 resulting in 5 orders p.a. and a total cost of £58.8.

c. Three problems involved in determining the EOQ are as follows:

i. The assumption that all costs are known and constant ie, ordering costs, unit cost etc. This is unlikely to be so.

ii. Determining the carrying cost is a subjective matter based on estimates of interest rates which may vary.

iii. Demand forecasting is notoriously difficult.

A5.6

a. Three control levels.

Reorder level = max. usage × lead time
= 1,350 kilos × 4 days
= 5,400 kilos

Maximum stock level = Reorder level + EOQ – minimum usage in lead time
= 5,400 + 9,000 – (800 × 4)

$$= 11,200 \text{ kilos}$$

Minimum stock level $= $ Reorder level $-$ Average usage in lead time
$$= 5,400 - (1,000 \times 4)$$
$$= 1,400 \text{ kilos}$$

b.

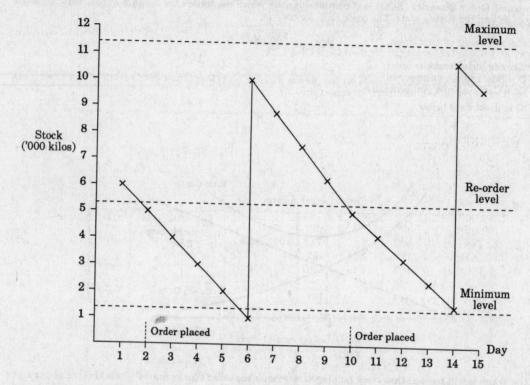

c. Actual level on Day 6 fell to 900 c.f. the calculated minimum level of 1,400. This was mainly due to the actual usage being 80 kilos per day greater than average. The minimum level is a warning level and acts as a signal when breached. Safety stock is carried to allow for minor fluctuations as in the example.

A5.7

Reorder level $=$ Maximum usage in lead time
$$= 100 \times 30$$
$$= 3000 \text{ units}$$

Reorder quality $= \sqrt{\dfrac{2.Co.D}{Cc}}$

$$= \sqrt{\dfrac{2 \times 400 \times (100 \times 48 \times 5)}{\pounds10 \times 10\%}}$$

$$= 4382 \text{ units}$$

Maximum level $=$ Re-order level $+$ order quantity $-$ minimum usage in lead time
$$= 3000 + 4382 - (100 \times 20)$$
$$= 5382 \text{ units}$$

Minimum level $=$ Re-order level $-$ Average usage in average lead time
$$= 3000 - (100 \times 25)$$
$$= 500 \text{ units}$$

A5.8

a. Can be answered from the book.

b.

Aug	Receipts units	Price £	Value £	Issues		Value £
1	2000	2	4000			
2	3000	2.2	6600			
3	2000	3	6000			
4				3000	{ 2000 @ £2	4000
					{ 1000 @ £2.2	2200
5	3000	2.5	7500			

6	6000	2000 @ £3	4400	
		2000 @ £3	6000	
		2000 @ £2.5	5000	
10,000	24100	9000		21600
	Balance	1000	@2.5	2500

c. The first step is to find the cause which might be:

i. Changes in usage or lead times.
ii. Incorrect values of order quantities or order levels.
iii. Unplanned purchases etc.

The action to be taken naturally depends on the reason found. Unless there have been errors in stock recording it is likely that no orders will be placed for some time.

Chapter 6 Solutions

Exercises

A6.1

Stores Ledger Account – LIFO

	Qty	Price £	£		Qty	Price £	£
1st Jan Bal	500	2	1000	2 Jan Issue	300	2	600
6 Jan Deliv	160	2.20	352	16 Jan Issue	[1]210		[2]452
20 Jan Deliv	180	2.25	405	Bal c/f	[3]330		[4]705
	840		1757		840		1757

Workings: [1] 160+50; [2] 160×£2.20 + 50×£2; [3] 180+150; [4] 180×£2.25 + 150×£2;

Stores Ledger Account – FIFO

	Qty	Price £	£		Qty	Price £	£
1st Jan Bal	500	2	1000	2 Jan Issue	300	2	600
6 Jan Deliv	160	2.20	352	16 Jan Issue	[1]210		[2]422
20 Jan.	180	2.25	405				
				Bal. C/F	[3]330		[4]735
	840		1757		840		1757

Workings: [1] 200+10; [2] 200×£2 + 10×£2.20; [3] 150+180; [4] 150×£2.20 + 180×£2.25

Stores Ledger Account – Average Price

	Qty	Price £	£		Qty	Price £	£
1st Jan Bal	500	2	1000	2 Jan Issue	300	2	600
6 Jan. deliv.	160	2.20	352	16 Jan.	210	[1]2.088	439
20 Jan.	180	2.25	405	Bal. C/F	330	[2]2.176	718
	840		1757		840		1757

Workings: [1] 200×£2 + 160×£2.20 = 752 and $\frac{752}{360}$ = £2.088; [2] 150×£2.086 + 180×£2.25 = 718 and $\frac{718}{330}$ = £2.176

A6.2

a. *Cash discount.* The consensus is that these would *not* be deducted from the invoice price.
b. *Trade discount.* The net value of materials after the trade discount would be used in the cost accounts.
c. *VAT.* This would *not* be included.
d. *Freight charges.* Are generally deemed to be part of the cost of obtaining materials.
e. *Unreturnable containers.* Classed as part of material costs.
f. *Returnable containers.* The cost of returnable containers would not be included in material costs although if the containers were returnable but at a reduced value then the net cost would be included in the material costs.

A6.3

The cost, after the 20% Trade Discount, is included. VAT is reclaimable so is not included. The pallets were non-returnable so the cost is included. The $2\frac{1}{2}$% discount is not included.

	£
Thus	
150 units net cost	600
+ Packing	25
	625

∴ cost per unit = $\frac{625}{150}$ = £4.17

Examination questions

A6.4

a. *Calculation of quantity of material issues:*

Timber:

Opening stock and receipts:	£
1/4 40,000 sq.ft. at £1.40 per sq.ft. =	56,000
5/4 125,000 sq.ft. at £1.50 per sq.ft =	187,500
19/4 70,000 sq.ft. at fl.70 per sq.ft =	119,000

Issues:

12/4 £120,000 ÷ £1.50 = 80,000 sq.ft

26/4 £164,000 ÷ £1.70 = 96,471 sq.ft, which is greater than the receipt on 19 April. Therefore all receipts on 19 must have been issued = 70,000 sq.ft at £1.70 = £119,000 leaving £45,000 which equals 30,000 sq.ft of previous issue ∴ total issue on 26/4 = 100,000 sq.ft.

Varnish:

Opening stock and receipts:	£
5/4 1,600 litres at £1.20 per litre =	1,920
19/4 400 litres £1.10 per litre =	440
1/4 1,800 litres at £1.30 per litre =	2,340

Issues:

12/4 £1,200 ÷ £1.20 = 1,000 litres
26/4 £1,550 which must contain 600 litres of remaining stock = £720
The balance of £830 contains the 400 litres received on 5/4 = £440
The balance of £390 ÷ price of receipt on 19/4 of £1.30 per litre = 300 litres

∴ total issue on 26/4 = 1,300 litres

Calculation of closing book stocks and comparison with physical stock-take:

	Timber	Varnish
Opening stocks	40,000 sq. ft	1,600 litres
Total receipts	195,000 sq. ft.	2,200 litres
	235,000 sq. ft.	3,800 litres
Issues:	180,000 sq. ft.	2,300 litres
Closing stock – book	55,000 sq. ft.	1,500litres
Closing stock – physical	55,000 sq. ft.	700 litres
'Stock Loss'	Nil	800 litres

b. *Calculation of material consumption during April per Works Manager's estimates*

Calculation of quantity of finished goods completed during month:

	Desks
Sales	4,600
Plus: Closing Stock	925
	5,525
Minus: Opening Stock	650
Total number completed	4,875

Calculation of quantity of equivalent desks produced during month:

	Timber Desks	Varnish Desks
No. of desks completed	4,875	4,875
Plus: Degree of completion of closing work-in-progress	120 (160 × 75%)	60 (160 × 37.5%)
	4,995	4,935
Minus: Degree of completion of opening stock	200 (300 × 66.67%)	75 (300 × 25%)
	4,795	4,860

Comparison of estimated and actual material consumption:

	Timber	Varnish
No. of equivalent desks	4,795 desks	4,860 desks
Estimated consumption per desk	30 sq.ft	0.47 litres
Total estimated consumption	143,850 sq. ft.	2,284 litres
Actual consumption:		
As shown by Issues	180,000 sq. ft.	2,300 litres
'Stock Loss	Nil	800 litres
Total material consumed	180,000 sq. ft.	3,100 litres
Material Consumption in excess of Manager's estimates	36,150 sq. ft.	816 litres

c. *Possible reasons for discrepancies.* Examination of figures above shows that the records for timber are accurate but the consumption is not under control. The converse applies to varnish as the consumption (after issue) appears to be under control but there are inaccuracies in the recording or losses in store.

Possible reasons for timber discrepancies:

i. Poor estimates of consumption
ii. Excessive usage and/or waste.

iii. Losses and/or pilferage in factory.
iv. Poor stock counts including WIP and finished goods.

Possible reasons for varnish discrepancies:

i. Poor record keeping in stores.
ii. Losses and/or pilferage in stores.
iii. Inaccurate stock counts.
iv. Fraud relating to non-delivery.

A6.5

Stores Ledger Records

Weighted Average method

Date	Receipts		Issues		Balance		Stock
	Quantity	Price	Quantity	Price	Quantity	Price	Value
		£		£		£	£
Opening					100	39	3,900
May	100	41			200	40	8,000
June	200	50			400	45	18,000
July			250	45	150	45	6,750
August	400	51.875			550	50	27,500
September			350	50	200	50	10,000
October			100	50	100	50	5,000

F.I.F.O method

Date	Receipts		Issues		Balance		Stock
	Quantity	Price	Quantity	Price	Quantity	Price	Value
		£		£		£	£
Opening					100	39	3,900
May	100	41			{100 {100	39 41	8,000
June	200	50			{100 {100 {200	39 41 50	18,000
July			250	{100@39 {100@41 {50@50	150	50	7,500
August	400	51.875			{150 {400	50 51.875	28,250
September			350	{150@50 {200@51.875	200	51.875	10,375
October			100	51.875	100	51.875	5187.5

L.I.F.O method

Date	Receipts		Issues		Balance		Stock
	Quantity	Price	Quantity	Price	Quantity	Price	Value
		£		£		£	£
Opening					100	39	3,900
May	100	41			{100 {100	39 41	8,000
June	200	50			{100 {100 {200	39 41 50	18,000
July			250	{200@50 {50@41	{100 {50	39 41	5,590
August	400	51.875			{100 {50 {400	39 41 51.875	26,700
September			350	51.875	{100 {50 {50	39 41 51.875	8,543.75
October			100	{50@51.875 {50@41	100	39	3,900

b.

Trading accounts for the period

Sales		Weighted average	FIFO	LIFO
	£	£	£	£
Sales		47,900	47,900	47,900
Opening stock	3,900			
+ Purchases	34,850	38,750	38,750	38,750
– Closing stock		5,000	5,187.5	3,900
= Cost of sales		33,750	33,562.5	34,850
= Gross profit		£14,150	£14,337.5	£13,050

c. In this example, with rising purchase prices, the most realistic profit will be found when the costs of material charged relate most closely to current prices. The method which does this is the LIFO system.

A6.6

a. i. Methods of Pricing of which 2 may be selected.

F.I.F.O.

Date	Receipts		Issues		Balance	
	Kilos	£	Kilos	£	Kilos	£
1 Nov.					20,000	60,000
3 Nov.	5,000	20,000			25,000	80,000
10 Nov.	12,000	60,000			37,000	140,000
17 Nov.			24,000	76,000	13,000	64,000
20 Nov.	17,000	76,500			30,000	140,500
27 Nov.			20,000	95,500	10,000	45,000

L.I.F.O.

Date	Receipts		Issues		Balance	
	Kilos	£	Kilos	£	Kilos	£
1 Nov.					20,000	60,000
3 Nov.	5,000	20,000			25,000	80,000
10 Nov.	12,000	60,000			37,000	140,000
17 Nov.			24,000	101,000	13,000	39,000
20 Nov.	17,000	76,500			30,000	115,500
27 Nov.			20,000	85,500	10,000	30,000

Averaged weighted cost

Date	Receipts		Issues		Balance	
	Kilos	£	Kilos	£	Kilos	£
1 Nov.					20,000	60,000
3 Nov.	5,000	20,000			25,000	80,000
10 Nov.	12,000	60,000			37,000	140,000
17 Nov.			24,000	90,720	13,000	49,280
20 Nov.	17,000	76,500			30,000	125,780
27 Nov.			20,000	83,853	10,000	41,927

ii. *JOB 124*

	F.I.F.O.	L.I.F.O.	W.A.
	£	£	£
Direct Material	171,500	186,500	174,573
Direct Labour	50,000	50,000	50,000
Overhead (110% on material)	188,650	205,150	192,030
Total Cost	410,150	441,650	416,603
Profit*	45,572	49,072	46,289
Selling Price	455,722	490,722	462,892

*Profit = 10% of selling price (which is unknown)

∴ cost = 90% of selling price

∴ selling price $= \dfrac{\text{cost}}{0.9}$

and profit = selling price – cost.

iii. If L.I.F.O. is used it results in this example, in the highest selling price which may be appropriate in periods of rising prices.

The method of overhead absorption (percentage of materials) which is used is a poor method and leads to gross distortions.

b. i. and ii. Continuous stock-taking and centralised store-keeping can be taken from the text.

c. i.
$$\text{EOQ} = \sqrt{\frac{2 \times (400 \times 50) \times 150}{£6 \times 33\frac{1}{3}\%}}$$

$= 1,732$ kilos

Reorder level $= 600 \times 3 = 1,800$ kilos

Minimum level = 1,800 − (2 × 400) = 1,000 kilos
Maximum level = 1,800 + 1,732 − (400 × 1) = 3,132 kilos

Chapter 7 Solutions

Exercices

A7.1

Graph of Earnings Per Hour

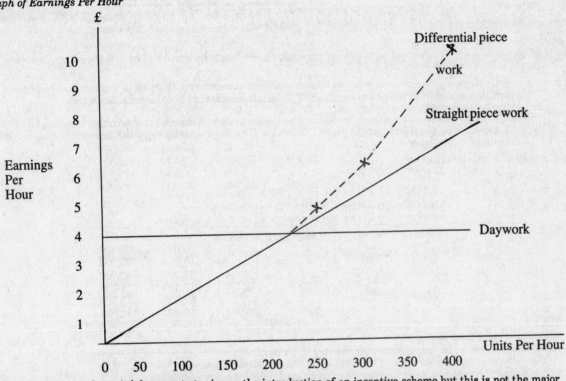

A

It is not uncommon for unit labour costs to rise on the introduction of an incentive scheme but this is not the major objective of such schemes. The main purpose of incentive schemes is to increase production (which has occurred in this case) so that the average overhead cost per unit falls. If the reduction is overhead cost per unit is greater than the increase in labour cost per unit then the scheme will be worthwhile.

A7.3

		£
DAY 1 68 units		
£(50 ×.5) + (18 × .6)	=	35.80
DAY 2 83 units		
£(50 ×.5) + (20 × .6) + (10 × .65) + (3 × .7)	=	45.60
DAY 3 59 units		
£(50 ×.5) + (9 ×.6)	=	30.40
DAY 4 94 units		
£(50 ×.5) + (20 × .6) + (10 × .65) + (14 × .7)	=	53.30
DAY 5 47 units		
£(47 ×.5)	=	23.50
		£188.60

Examination questions

A7.4

a. Four factors leading to changes in the labour cost percentage:

   i.   The increase in sales value may be due to selling price increases rather than the volume (no. of units) sold. If so the labour cost percentage is bound to fall.

   ii. Because fixed costs go to make up the sales value a variable cost such as direct labour would automatically become a smaller percentage.

   iii. The sales mix, and hence production mix, may be different in the two periods causing a change in the relative proportion of labour costs.

   iv. Although impossible to tell from the figures given there could be a genuine improvement in labour efficiency.

b. The report is not an effective means of controlling labour costs. Specifically it lacks detail, and most importantly no comparison is shown between the actual labour cost for the actual production and what the labour cost should have been. Furthermore it is unsatisfactory to group all labour costs together and relate them to one factor such as sales value. Each type of labour cost should be considered separately and controlled individually. In general the most appropriate control measures would be:

Best controlled by:

Direct labour – Standard costs based on engineering and work study investigations.

Control ratios.

Indirect labour – Flexible budgets relating to the most appropriate measure of activity for each cost.

Note: The latter part of this question uses some material covered later in the book. The answer is given for completeness, but, if desired, it can be ignored at this stage.

A7.5

a. Major factors are: guaranteed earnings agreements, in-lieu bonuses, growth of salaried workers, tendency to retain skilled workers when activity falls.

b. i. overtime premium – generally considered an indirect expense and charged to Production Overheads. If overtime specifically requested to finish a particular job then may be considered a direct cost.
   ii. incentive payments – direct wage cost.
   iii. sick pay and holiday pay – usually considered an indirect cost and charged to Production Overheads.
   iv. idle time – also considered an indirect Production Overhead usually reported separately because it is considered controllable.

c. Output in standard hours:

Operator

A $((15 \times 42) + (13 \times 60) + (11 \times 75)) \div 60 = 37.25$ hours
B $((15 \times 42) + (10 \times 60) + (8 \times 75)) \div 60 = 30.5$ hours
C $((15 \times 42) + (18 \times 60) + (16 \times 75)) \div 60 = 48.5$ hours

Gross pay Calculation

Operator	Attendance	Output	%	Rate £	Gross Pay £
A	38	37.5	98.7	2.80	106.40
B	39	30.5	78.2	2.40	93.60
C	42	48.5	115.4	3.40	142.80

A7.6

a. Ways of classifying wages.
Direct/indirect, ie, for prime cost or overhead calculation.
By behaviour, ie, whether fixed or variable according to volume of output or activity.
By payment method, ie, cash, cheque standing order. Useful for payroll purposes.
By controllability, ie, whether the wages are controllable or not by an individual within a given time period.
By location, ie, section/factory/branch useful for budgetary purposes.

b. Can be largely answered from book. Main Points.

Effect on output and cost per unit.
Effect on overhead recovery.
Effect on total wages bill.
Effect on quality of output.
Need for more supervision/inspection.
More rate/pay negotiations.

A7.7

i. Piecework

Guaranteed wages = 80% $(8 \times £5.5) = \underline{£35.2}$

80 units
Standard time = $80 \times 3 = 240$ mins.
∴ Piecework price = $240 \times £.1 = £24$
∴ Guarantee applies ie, £35.2

120 units
Piecework price = $120 \times 3 \times £.1 = £36$
£36 > £35.2 ∴ wage = $\underline{£36}$

210 units
Piecework price = $210 \times 3 \times £.1 = £63$
£63 > £35.2 ∴ wage = $\underline{£63}$

ii. Premium bonus

Units	Time taken mins.	Time allowed mins.	Saved mins.	Wages paid
80	480	240	–	$8 \times 5.5 = £44$
120	480	360	–	$8 \times 5.5 = £44$
210	480	630	150	$(\frac{3}{4} \times 2\frac{1}{2}) + 8 \times 5.5 = £54.31$

A7.8

a. There are several possible ways of dealing with the premium element of wages.
- ❏ Where the premium is payable because of a customer's request and is recoverable in the price then this should be charged direct to the job.
- ❏ Where it is accidental which job is done in overtime it is normal to charge the premium part of wages to overheads.
- ❏ Where there is always a premium element in wages but it is not possible to determine in advance which job will be worked on at a given time the day rate for wages could be grossed up to include the expected premium element.

b. The details of J.I.T. manufacturing and its benefits can be taken from the chapter.

The probable effects on the cost accounting system.
- ❏ Generally the system would be greatly simplified with less need to track production through production.
- ❏ Direct labour is likely to be treated as a fixed cost.
- ❏ More attention would be paid to non-financial measures of performance including; quality, lead-time, set-up times and so on.
- ❏ The need for standard costing would be questioned as many variances became irrelevant or misleading.

Chapter 8 Solutions

Exercises

A8.1

a. Where overtime is worked occasionally it would be normal cost accounting practice to charge the overhead premiums to production overheads and only normal time to the jobs thus:

	Job X321	Job X786	Job X114
Total hours	592	310	246
@£3 per hour =	£1,776	£930	£738

b. Where overtime is worked by request all of the wages (including overtime premiums) would be charged to the jobs.

Effective wage rates per hour:

Normal time	£3
Evenings	£4.50
Weekends	£6

	Job X321		Job X786		Job X114	
		£		£		£
Normal Time	480 × £3 =	1,440	220 × £3 =	660	150 × £3 =	450
Evenings	102 × £4.50 =	459	60 × £4.50 =	270	80 × £4.50 =	360
Weekends	10 × £6 =	60	30 × £6 =	180	16 × £6 =	96
		£1,959		£1,110		£906

A8.2

Typical reasons for inaccuracies in labour records (and many other types of data used for cost accounting purposes) are:

a. Difficulties in completing paperwork in factory conditions – lack of desks etc.
b. Inexperience of some production workers in clerical tasks.
c. Delays in completing paperwork so that data are entered from memory.
d. Deliberate falsification perhaps to improve bonuses.
e. Poor form design.

The implications for the cost accountant are:

a. Job/process labour costs will be inaccurate.
b. The overheads absorbed (if based on labour) will be incorrect.
c. Sales prices if cost based will be inaccurate.
d. Stock and work-in-progress valuations will be incorrect.
e. The profit figures shown in costing operating statements will differ from financial accounts based on physical stock takes.
f. If standard costing is used variances will be incorrect.

A8.3

If time spent working is classified as waiting time the likely effects are:

a. The direct costs of a job will be under-recorded.
b. The amount of overheads will be incorrect.
c. The amount of overheads absorbed (if based on direct labour) will be incorrect.
d. If cost based, the job price will be incorrect.
e. If the times involved are excessive production planning will be rendered more difficult and inaccurate.

A8.4

Remuneration of Employees

Employee	Hourly Rate		Basic Piece Rate		Bonus Scheme	
		£		£		£
Salmon	40 hrs @ £1.25 =	50.00	270 @ £0.2 =	54.00	Hourly £50 + Bonus $\frac{1}{9}\times$ £50 =	55.55
Roach	38 hrs @ £1.05 =	39.90	200 @ £0.25 =	50.00	Hourly £39.90 + Bonus $\frac{6}{25}\times$ £39.90 =	49.48
Pike	36 hrs @ £1.2 =	43.20	220 @ £0.24 =	52.80	Hourly £43.20 + Bonus $\frac{2}{11}\times$ 43.20 =	51.06

b. *Effectiveness of bonus scheme.*

Although such a bonus scheme has the theoretical advantage that time saved is shared between employer and employee it is likely to be unpopular to both. To the employer because it is more complicated to administer than straight piece work and to the employee because there is an inbuilt ceiling to earnings. Accordingly the normal piecework rate is likely to be preferred.

A8.5

a. This can be taken directly from the book.

Note that the cost implications include *replacement costs* eg, retraining, advertising and so on and *preventive costs* eg, welfare and costs of enlightened personnel policies.

b. The further information could include:

More detailed analysis into male/female, administrative/production, section and department and so on. There could be age profiles of leavers ie, age, length of service.

Trends could be identified.

Reasons for leaving could be specified perhaps in broad groups.

Special factors eg, more leavers from particular areas.

c. Five possible reasons for high labour turnover.

i. Relatively poor pay and conditions.
ii. Low morale perhaps caused by poor management.
iii. Attractiveness of other local firms.
iv. Incorrect recruitment policies and poor training.
v. High labour turnover may be normal in the industry eg, where there is a high proportion of women workers.

A8.6

a. Labour turnover percentage = $\dfrac{\text{No. leaving in period}}{\text{Average no. of employees}}$ % = $\dfrac{7}{42}$ % = 16.67%

b. Can be taken from the text and answers to other questions.

c. Efficiency ratio = $\dfrac{\text{Standard hours produced}}{\text{actual hours worked}} = \dfrac{5194}{4900} = 106\%$

∴ Labour rate = £4.6 + (4.6 × 3%) = £4.738 per hour

A8.7

		£	
Hours worked	(34 + 5) @ £5	195	direct cost
Overtime premium	5 @ £2.5	12.5	indirect cost
Idle time	6 @ £5	30	indirect cost
Group bonus		4	direct cost
		241.50	

Chapter 9 Solutions

Exercises

A9.1

Overhead absorption rates:

Basis	Calculation	Rate
Labour hours	$\dfrac{£12,900}{1,400}$	£9.21 per hour
Percentage on Wages	$\dfrac{£12,900}{3,600}\times 100\%$	358% of wages
Percentage on Prime Cost	$\dfrac{£12,900}{£3,600 + 7,500}\times 100\%$	116% of Prime Cost
Machine hours	$\dfrac{£12,900}{2,850}$	£4.53 per mc. hour
Unit	$\dfrac{£12,900}{535}$	£24.11 per unit

b. Prime Cost = £16.50 + 17.50 = £34.

The overheads and total cost using the various bases are as follows:

Basis	Calculation	=	Overheads £	+	Prime Cost £	=	Total Cost £
Labour hours	$(5\frac{1}{2} \times £9.21)$	=	50.65	+	34	=	84.65
Percentage on wages	(358% of £17.50)	=	62.65	+	34	=	96.65
Percentage on Prime Cost	(116% of £34)	=	39.44	+	34	=	73.44
Machine Hours	$(8\frac{1}{2} \times £4.53)$	=	38.5	+	34	=	72.5
Cost unit	$(£24.11 \times 1)$	=	£24.11	+	34	=	58.11

c. In the circumstances outlined the Machine Hour Rate would generally be considered to be the most appropriate so that the cost per unit would be £72.5 and £38.50 of overheads would be recovered on this unit.

A9.2

a. Overheads not as budgeted.

Activity level not as budgeted.
Changes in labour or machine efficiency.

b. *Based on labour hours*

$$\text{O.A.R.} = \frac{£57,500}{5,600} = £10.27 \text{ hour}$$

∴ Overheads absorbed by production = 5,925 × £10.27 = £60,850

∴ Under recovery = £61,257 − £60,850 = £407

Based on machine hours

$$\text{O.A.R.} = \frac{£57,500}{3,300} = £17.42 \text{ hours}$$

∴ Overheads absorbed by production = 3,418 × £17.42 = £59,542

∴ Under recovery = £61,257 − £59,542 = £1,715

Based on unit recovery

$$\text{O.A.R.} = \frac{57,500}{81,000} = £0.71 \text{ per unit}$$

Actual production 85,296 units

∴ Overheads absorbed = 85,296 × £0.71 = £60,560

∴ Under recovery = £61,257 − £60,560 = £697

A9.3

The only advantage of a blanket overhead rate is that of simplicity but the disadvantages are more numerous.

a. Does not reflect the varying characteristics and times spent in the various departments.

b. Products or jobs spending more time in departments or cost centres with high overheads will be under costed. Conversely where departments with lower overheads are involved the products or jobs will be over costed.

A single, blanket absorption rate is suitable when there is a single product which passes through all departments equally although it is unnecessary as total costs can be divided by total output.

A9.4

Net Asset Value = £20,000 + 8500 − 1500 = 27,000

$$\text{Depreciation charge p.a.} - \text{Straight Line} = \frac{27000}{12} = £2250$$

$$\text{Reducing Balance percentage} = \left(1 - \sqrt[n]{\frac{s}{a}}\right) \times 100 = \left(1 - \sqrt[12]{\frac{1,500}{28,500}}\right) \times 100 = (1 - 0.728) \times 100 \approx 22\%$$

∴ First year depreciation = 28500 × 22% = £6270

A9.5

a. Labour Hours

Product X = 6,000 units × 1	6,000	
Product Y = 8,000 units × 2	16,000	
	22,000	

$$\therefore \text{Labour hour O.A.R.} = \frac{264,000}{22,000} = £12 \text{ per hour}$$

Overheads absorbed on labour hours

	Product X	Product Y
Overheads absorbed =	1 × £12 =£12	2 × £12 = £24

∴ Total overheads = 6,000 × £12 = £72,000 8,000 × £24 = £192,000

b. Using ABC

Machine hours per period

Product X = 6,000 × 4 =	24,000
Product Y = 8,000 × 2 =	16,000
	40,000

Cost Driver Rates

Production Set-ups = $\dfrac{£179,000}{60}$ = £2983 per set-up

Order Handling = $\dfrac{£30,000}{72}$ = £417 per order

Machine Costs = $\dfrac{£55,000}{40,000}$ = £1.375 per hour

Overheads using ABC (rounded)

		Product X £		Product Y £
Set-ups	15 × £2,983 =	44,745	45 × £2,983 =	134,255
Orders	12 × £417 =	5,000	60 × £417 =	25,000
Machine Costs	24,000 × 1.375	33,000	16,000 × 1.375	22,000
Totals		£82,745		£181,255

A9.6

i. % direct material = $\dfrac{\text{Budgeted overheads}}{\text{Budgeted material}}$ = $\dfrac{£250,000}{100,000}$ = 250%

Direct labour = $\dfrac{\text{Budgeted overheads}}{\text{Budgeted labour hours}}$ = $\dfrac{£250,000}{50,000}$ = £5 per hour

ii. Overheads for job ZX

	£
Using material = £7000 × 250% =	17,500
Using labour hours = 800 × £5 =	4,000

		£
iii.	Overhead incurred	£350,000
	Overhead absorbed (55,000 × £5)	275,000
	= Under absorption	75,000

This amount would be written off to the P+L account either directly or via a suspense account.

iv. This can be taken from the book.

A9.7

The method of production overhead absorption given in the question is probably the worst that could be thought of in the circumstances described, (which is, no doubt, the reason it was selected by the Examiner!).

The main objections to it are as follows

a. The units are not standard but overheads would be shared equally.
b. No recognition is given to the differing nature of the production departments.
c. It makes no allowance for the differing demand the products make on the departments or the fact that some products do not pass through each department.
d. Product costs will be arbitrarily affected by the seasonal fluctuations.
e. Being calculated after the end of the period the advantages gained by the use of predetermined overheads will be lost.

The above objections include comments on the effect on product costs.

If the company bases its prices on costs then the absorption method used will influence prices in the following ways:

a. As costs are averaged, more complex and time consuming products will be under costed and thus under priced. This will mean that the company will tend to obtain more of this type of business to the detriment of profitability. The converse will apply to simpler and cheaper products.
b. Prices, if cost related, will be affected by the seasonable fluctuations resulting in higher prices when activity is low and lower prices when activity is high which is the exact opposite of a rational pricing policy.
c. There is also the real operational problem that if prices are cost related there will be delays in price fixing because predetermined O A R's are not used.

If prices are determined by market forces then the methods used in establishing costs will have no effect although the profitability shown for each of the products will have little basis in reality.

A9.8

a. The circumstances in which it would be appropriate to use the absorption methods shown in the question are:

Machine Hour Rate
In the first place it would be necessary for all products passing through the department or cost centre to spend some time on the machine/equipment in the department.

Time is chosen as the most appropriate base with which to charge overheads to products as it is considered that most overheads accrue on a time basis, eg, rent, salaries, depreciation etc and consequently, it is fair proportionately to charge overheads to the products in accordance with the amount of time each product spends in a department. However, a major determinant of the extent of the overheads incurred during a particular time period is the existence and operation of plant and equipment in a department and the consequent running and maintenance costs incurred. Therefore, if the major determinant of the extent of overheads in a department is the existence and operation of plant and equipment, then the length of time each product spends on the machine(s) would be the most appropriate basis by which overheads are charged to products.

Percentage of Direct Wages

This method is also an attempt to charge overheads to products on a time basis in that direct wages incurred on a particular job may reflect the amount of time the product spent in the department. However, it is suitable only when the direct wage cost does reasonably accurately reflect time, ie, when all employees in the department or cost centre earn the same or similar hourly rates of pay.

Rate per Unit

The assumption underlying this method is that all products consume a similar amount of overhead service, ie, where there is only one product type, or where different products pass through an identical operation.

This method may also be used where a particular department's overheads are considered to be a relatively minor part of the total cost.

b. Next year's budgeted overheads for each department

Department A

	Budgeted Production (Note 1)	Budgeted Overhead Rate £	Total Budgeted Overhead £
Product X	13,200	11.2	147,840
Product Y	27,500	8.0	220,000
Product Z	7,000	4.8	33,600
			£401,440

	Total Budgeted Overhead £
Department B	
Budgeted Wages × Budgeted Absorption Rate, ie, £717,900 × 50% (also could be obtained by a similar calculation to Department A) =	£358,950
Department C	
Total Number of Units of all products × Absorption Rate (13,200 + 27,500 + 7,000) = 47,700 × £2.50 =	£119,250

c. Department A,

Total Overhead over absorbed-all fixed = £840

Number of machine hours worked in excess of budget = $200 \times \dfrac{£4.8}{£1.6} = 600$ hours

Therefore fixed overhead absorption rate = $\dfrac{£840}{600} = £1.40$ per machine hr.

Total budgeted fixed overhead equals

	Machine Hours	Budgeted Production	Total Machine hours
Product X	$\dfrac{£11.2}{£1.6} = 7$	× 13,200	92,400
Product Y	$\dfrac{£8.0}{£1.6} = 5$	× 27,500	137,500
Product Z	$\dfrac{£4.8}{£1.6} = 3$	× 7,000	21,000
			250,900

Therefore total budgeted fixed overhead = 250,900 × £1.40 = £351,260
and variable overheads 250,900 × £0.20 = 50,180

£401,440

Note: One of the alternative methods of calculating the fixed overhead would be:

Total budgeted overhead £401,440 × $\dfrac{£1.40}{£1.60}$ = £351,260

Department B
Total overhead over absorbed – all fixed = £1,680
Wages incurred in excess of budget = £21 × 200 = £4,200
Therefore fixed overhead content of overhead absorption rate
= $\dfrac{£1,680}{£4,200} = 40\%$

∴ Fixed Overheads = 40% of £717,900 = £287,160
Variable Overheads = 10% of £717,900 = £71,790

£358,950

Note:1 There are alternative methods of calculating the fixed overhead content.

Note 2   *Calculation of Budgeted Production*

	Product X	Product Y	Product Z
Budgeted Wages in Department B	£158,400	£412,500	£147,000
Budgeted Wage Cost per product in Department B	£12	£15	£21
∴ Budgeted No. of Units	13,200	27,500	7,000

A9.9

a. See Overhead Analysis Sheet, Figure 1.

b. O.A.R. based on direct labour hours

i. Assembly department $= \dfrac{\text{Total overheads}}{\text{Direct labour hours}} = \dfrac{46,930}{32,000} = $ **£1.47 per labour hour**

ii. For finishing department $= \dfrac{£10,440}{4,000} = $ **£2.61 per direct labour hours**

c. The objective of apportioning costs over several cost centres is to share out common costs in an equitable fashion. In so far as it can be done the apportionment should reflect the incidence of usage or demand on the particular cost. In this question the cost items were dealt with as below.

Item of Cost	Basis of Apportionment	Comment
Occupancy Costs	Area occupied	The most realistic basis as most of these costs will vary with area.
Depreciation and Insurance on plant	Plant and equipment cost	From the information given the only reasonable basis. Probably a fair correlation with cost.
Wage related costs	Total wages	An accurate basis. Such costs will follow wages paid more closely than, say, number of employees.
Factory admin. and personnel	No. of employees	Personnel costs probably vary with no. of employees and because administration costs are grouped with personnel then these also would be spread on no. of employees. However this is probably a poor basis.
Stores Cost	Number of requisitions	A typical basis and is probably some reflection on the loading of the stores.

d. To improve the apportionments it would be necessary to have more details, split down to departments on values, times etc. Typical examples follow.

Overhead Analysis Sheet Four weeks ending..................

Cost item	Basis of Apportionment	Total	Machining Dept	Assembly Dept	Finishing Dept	Stores	Occupancy
Allocated costs		£	£	£	£	£	£
Indirect wages		34,000	9,000	15,000	4,000	6,000	
Indirect materials		2,400	400	1,400	600		
Maintenance		2,100	1,400	600	100		
Power		2,200	1,600	400	200		
Rent		2,000					2,000
Rates		600					600
Insurance on building		200					200
Lighting and heating		400					400
Cleaning of factory		800					800
Apportioned costs							
Depreciation on plant and equipment	Plant and equipment cost	16,700	14,000	2,000	600	100	
Wage related cost	Total wages	28,200	8,320	16,440	2,240	1,200	
Factory administration and personnel	No. of employees	7,100	2,000	4,000	1,000	100	
Insurance on plant and equipment	Plant and equipment cost	1,670	1,400	3200	60	10	
Occupancy costs	Area in sq. feet	–	1,200	1,800	800	200	(4,000)
Stores costs	No. of requisitions	–	1,680	5,090	840	(7,610)	
		98,370	41,000	46,930	10,440	–	–

Figure 1

Depreciation – either departmental analysis, machine by machine, or depreciation related to usage in which case records of utilisation would be required.

Plant insurance – departmental analysis based on insurance valuations.

Stores costs – where there are substantial variations in the times taken to handle requisitions then some form of activity on a sample basis might be better than the number of requisitions.

Factory administration – always a difficult cost to apportion but probably a better basis would be activity in each department.

As all apportionments are merely conventions there is no way to prove what is more accurate so that a common-sense approach must be adopted. If to develop a more accurate method of apportioning costs it is necessary to incur significant expenditure then it is probably not worthwhile.

A9.10

a.

	Production cost centres			Service cost centres	
	1 £	2 £	3 £	S £	T £
Overheads Allocated	20,000	24,000	36,000	13,500	9,500
Apportionment of S	–	(55) 8,250 (90)	(35) 5,250 (90)	–13,500	
Apportionment of T	(45) 4,500 (95)	(35) 3,500 (95)	(15) 1,500 (95)		–9,500
Chargeable Overhead	£24,500	£35,750	£42,750	–	–
b.					
Overheads Allocated	20,000	24,000	36,000	13,500	9,500
Apportionment of T	(45) 4,275 (100)	(35) 3,325 (100)	(15) 1,425 (100)	(5) 475 (100)	–9,500
Apportionment of S		(55) 8,540 (90)	(35) 5,435 (90)	–13,975	
Chargeable Overhead	£24,275	£35,865	£42,860	–	–
c.					
Overheads Allocated	20,000	24,000	36,000	13,500	9,500
1st Apportionment of S	–	7,425	4,725	–13,500	1,350
1st Apportionment of T	4,883	3,798	1,627	542	–10,850
2nd Apportionment of S	–	298	190	–542	54
2nd Apportionment of T	24	19	8	3	–54
Final Apportionment of S	–	2	1	–3	
Chargeable Overhead	£24,907	£35,542	£42,551	–	–

A9.11

a. Six O.A.R.s

i. Labour hour $= \dfrac{\text{Production overheads}}{\text{Labour hours}} = \dfrac{£300,000}{25,000} = £12$ per hour

ii. Machine hours $= \dfrac{\text{Production overheads}}{\text{Machine hours}} = \dfrac{£300,000}{150,000} = £20$ per hour

iii. Percentage of direct materials $= \dfrac{\text{Production overheads}}{\text{Direct materials}} \times 100\% = \dfrac{£300,000}{£100,000} \times 100\% = 300\%$

iv. Percentage of direct wages $= \dfrac{\text{Production overheads}}{\text{Direct wages}} \times 100\% = \dfrac{£300,000}{150,000} \times 100\% = 600\%$

v. Percentage of prime cost $= \dfrac{\text{Production overhead}}{\text{Prime cost}} \times 100\% = \dfrac{£300,000}{150,000} \times 100\% = 200\%$

vi. Per job (ie unit) $= \dfrac{\text{Production overhead}}{\text{No. of jobs}} = \dfrac{£300,000}{300} = £1,000$ per job

b. Comments on O.A.R.s

i. and ii. the time based methods are generally considered to be the most equitable as most overheads relate to time. Because of increasingly mechanisation/automation, machine hour rates are likely to be the most relevant in the future.

iii. Only suitable if all jobs are made from the same materials otherwise absurd results will occur.

iv. Simple to operate and where similar rates are paid it produces similar results to the labour hour method. Can produce anomalies where people earning different rates work on jobs.

v. This is a combination of the wages and materials rates so includes their anomalies.

vi. If all jobs (units) are the same then this is the best method. If they are different, as is likely, then this is the worst method as equal overheads will be charged to unequal jobs.

c. Job A 57 – COST ESTIMATES USING different O.A.R.S.

	Labour hour OAR £	Machine hour OAR £	Percentage of Materials £	Percentage of wages £	Percentage of prime cost £	Per job £
Prime Cost	450	450	450	450	450	450
Overhead	960	1000	750	1200	900	1000
Total Cost	1410	1450	1200	1650	1350	1450

A9.12

a.

Cost Statement for cost centres

	Accom-modation £	Catering £	Leisure £	Outings £	Total £
Labour	110,000	100,500	35,000	38,500	284,000
Materials	19,000	36,000	16,000	13,000	84,000
Power (kilowatt hour)	20,000	10,000	50,000	4,000	84,000
Rent and Rates (floor space)	36,000	12,000	18,000	6,000	72,000
Depreciation (market value)	5,000	10,000	30,000	15,000	60,000
Advertising (No. of customer days)	30,000	24,000	16,000	6,000	76,000
	220,000	192,500	165,000	82,500	660,000
	(8/24)	(7/24)	(6/24)	(3/24)	
Office expenses	80,000	70,000	60,000	30,000	240,000
Total cost	300,000	262,500	225,000	112,500	900,000
No. of customer days	15,000	12,000	8,000	3,000	
Cost per day	£20.00	£21.875	£28.125	£37.50	

b.

Price per person

	Cost per day		Days		£
Accommodation	20.00	×	7 =		140
Catering	21.875	×	7 =		153.125
Leisure	28.125	×	3 =		84.375
Outings	37.50	×	3 =		112.5
					490.00
	Profit 30% *				210.00
	Price per person				700.00
	Price for couple for one week				£1,400.00

* Profit is 30% on selling price. ∴ costs = 70% of selling price and selling price = $\dfrac{£490}{0.7}$ = £700

∴ profit = 30% of £700 = £210

c.

Cost centre	Costs absorbed £		Actual costs £	(Under)/ over absorption) £
Accommodation	20.000 × 15,250 =	305,000	320,000	(15,000)
Catering	21.875 × 13,000 =	284,375	275,000	9,375
Leisure	28.125 × 6,800 =	191,250	200,000	(8,750)
Outings	37.500 × 3,200 =	120,000	125,000	(5,000)

A9.13

a. Machine hour O. A. R. = $\dfrac{\text{Total overheads}}{\text{Total machine hours}}$ = $\dfrac{£26,000}{1300}$ = £20 per hour

Product costs

	A £	B £	C £	D £
Prime cost	68	71	44	81
Overheads	80	60	40	60
Cost per unit	148	131	84	141
Total cost	£17,760	13,100	6,720	16,920

b. Costs using ABC

Calculation of Cost Driver Rates

Cost	£	Driver		Cost/unit of driver
Set ups	5,250	Production runs	21	£250
Stores/receiving	3,600	Requisitions	80	£45
Inspection/quality	2,100	Production runs	21	£100
Handling/despatch	4,620	Orders	42	£110
Machine Dept.	10430	Machine hours	1300	£8.02

Product Costs

	A	B	C	D
Prime costs	8,160	7,100	3,520	9,720
Set ups	1,500	1,250	1,000	1,500
Stores/receiving	900	900	900	900
Inspection/quality	600	500	400	600
Handling/despatch	1,320	1,100	880	1,320
Machine dept costs	3,851	2,407	1,284	2,888
Total costs	16,331	13,257	7,984	16,928
Cost per unit	£136.09	£132.57	£99.8	£141.07

c. Cost per unit

Cost from (a)	148.00	131.00	84.00	141.00
Costs from (b)	136.09	132.57	99.80	141.07
Difference	(11.91)	1.57	15.80	0.07

The difference are due to the different conventions used for absorbing the overheads into products. These differences may influence

i. pricing if based on cost-plus
ii. Profits if pricing levels influence sales
iii. Profits if stock levels fluctuate between periods.

A9.14

a. i. <u>Overhead Absorption Bases</u>
Percentage of wages

$$\frac{£600,000}{£200,000} = 300\% \text{ on Direct Labour}$$

ii. Per labour hour

$$\frac{£600,000}{40,000} = £15 \text{ per labour hour}$$

iii. Per machine hour

$$\frac{£600,000}{50,000} = £12 \text{ per machine hour}$$

b. Predetermined overhead absorption rates are used so that each unit produced carries a share of overheads.

c. From the data given machine hours would seem to be a suitable convention to use.

d.
Job AX
Pricing calculations

	£
Direct material	3,788
Direct labour	1,100
Direct expenses	422
Prime cost	5,310
Production overheads 120 hours × 12	1,440
Factory cost	6,750
Admin overhead	1,350
Total cost	8,100
Profit	900
Price	9,000

Workings

Absorption of admin overheads
Budgeted total cost

Direct material	800,000
Direct labour	200,000
Direct expenses	40,000
Prime cost	1,040,000
Production overheads	600,000
Factory cost	1,640,000
Admin overhead	328,000

$$\text{OAR for admin overheads} = \frac{\text{Admin overheads}}{\text{Factory cost}} = \frac{£328,000}{£1,640,000} = 20\% \text{ on Factory cost.}$$

e. This can be taken from the text (Chapter 7).

Chapter 10 Solutions

Exercises

A10.1

Raw Material control A/c

Balance	9,318	WIP	36,291
FL control	41,286	Product ohds.	2,958
		Admin. ohds.	1,307
		Balance	10,048
	50,604		50,604
Balance	10,048		

W-l-P Control A/c

Balance	10,652	Fin. Goods	78,280
Wages	20,444		
Issues	36,291		
Overheads	19,800	Balance	8,907
	87,187		87,187
Balance	8,907		

Finished Goods Control A/c

Balance	4,313	Cost of Sales	92,500
Admin. ohds.	17,200	Balance	7,293
WIP	78,280		
	99,793		99,783
Balance	7,293		

Wages Control A/c

FL control	26,579	WIP	20,444
		Product ohds.	6,135
	26,579		26,579

Product Overheads Control A/c

Wages	6,135	Ohds. recovered	19,800
FL control	8,680		
Issues	2,958		
Overhead adj.	2,027		
	19,800		19,800

S & D Overhead Control A/c

FL control	5,217	Cost of Sales	10,100
Salaries	5,157	Ohd. adj. A/C	274
	10,374		10,374

Salaries Control A/c

FL control	14,263	Admin.	9,106
		S & D	5,157
	14,263		14,263

Cost of Sales A/c

S & D ohds.	10,100	P & L	102,600
Fin. Gds.	92,500		
	102,600		102,600

Admin. overheads

FL control	7,213	Fin. goods	17,200
Issues	1,307	Ohd. adj. A/C	426
Salaries	9,106		
	17,626		17,626

Costing P & L A/c

Cost of sales	102,600	Sales	143,650
Profit	42,377	Ohd.adj.	1,327
	144,977		144,977

Financial Ledger Control A/c

Sales	143,650	Balance	24,283
		Purchases	41,286
		Wages	26,579
Balance c/f	26,248	Salaries	14,263
		Admin. expenses	7,213
		Prod. expenses	8,680
		S & D expenses	5,217
		Profit	42,377
	169,898		169,898
		Balance	26,248

Closing Trial Balance

Raw mat. cont.	10,048	FL control	26,248
Fin. Gds. cont.	7,293		
WIP control	8,907		
	£26,248		£26,248

Overhead Adjustment A/c

S & D overheads	274	Product overheads	2,027
Admin. overheads	426		
P & L	1,327		
	2,027		2,027

A10.2

Memorandum Reconciliation A/c

	£		£
Profit as financial a/cs	11,287	Profit on Cost a/cs	2,704
Depreciation difference	694	Profit on sale of asset	850
		Dividend received	2,635
		Imputed rent charge	3,250
		Stock difference	2,010
		(opening)	
		(closing)	532
	11,981		11,981

A10.3

Financial Ledger Control A/c

Sales	37,529	Bal B/F	24,952
Bal C/F	21,242	Costs	29,286
		Profit	4,533
	£ 58,771		58,771
		Balance	21,242

Closing Trial Balance

Store ledger	3,916	Financial ledger	21,242
WIP	12,521		
Finished goods	4,805		
	21,242		21,242

A10.4

a. i.

		£
Financial Profit		50,000
less Dividend	1,000	
Interest	8,000	9,000
		2,000
add Loss on sale		43,000
Stock differences		
Raw materials	– 800	
Finished goods	+ 1,000	+ 200
+ Costing Profit		43,200

ii. Can be answered from the text.

A10.5

Assembly department's Control A/cs.

Before the entries can be made in the accounts it is necessary to calculate and analyse the wages.

Wages Calculations

	Direct £		Indirect £
Attendance payments	1,200	(350 × 1.00)	350
(800 × £1.50)			
Overtime premium	75	(40 × £0.50)	20
(100 × £0.75)			
Shift Premium	150		50
Bonus	160		70
= Gross Wage	1,585		490
Deductions			
Income Tax	250		100
NI	75 325		35 135
= Net Wages	£1,260		£355

Analysis of Direct workers Gross Wages

	Direct (charged to WIP) £		Indirect (charged to Overheads) £
Productive time	885	Balance	315
(590× £1.50)			
Overtime Premium	15	Balance	60
(20× £0.75)			
Shift Premium & Bonus	–		310
	900		685

Analysis of Indirect Gross Wages

	£		£
Attendance time 20% of 40 hours @ £1	8	Balance	342
Overtime Premium 8 hrs @ £0.50	4	Balance	16
Shift Premium & Bonus	–		120
Total Charge: to WIP	£912	Total Charge: to Production Overheads	£1,163

Using the various figures from above the accounts can be prepared.

Wages Control A/c

	£		£
Cash (Net direct Wages)	1,260	WIP	912
Cash (Net indirect Wages)	355	Production Overheads	1,163
Income Tax A/c (250 + 100)	350		
NI A/c (75 + 35)	110		
	2,075		2,075

W-I-P Control A/c

	£	
Wages Control	912	

Production Overhead Control A/c

	£	
Wages Control	1,163	
NI A/c (Employers)	180	

Bank A/c

			£
		Wages Control	1,260
		Wages Control	355

Income Tax A/c

			£
		Wages Control	350

NI A/c

			£
		Wages Control	110
		Production Overheads	180
			290

b. *Treatment of various costs.*

It is preferable to charge costs as directly as possible where this can be done without excessive administration and where direct charging to a product or batch does not cause anomalies.

i. *Employers NI Contribution.* This is not readily attributable to particular products or batches and so is normally charged to Production Overheads where it will be absorbed into products via the absorption rate.

ii. *Group Bonus.* Frequently a bonus can be identified with a particular batch and, if so, it should be classified as direct and charged to W-I-P. However there is insufficient information given in this question for this to be done and so it is charged to Production Overheads for eventual absorption into all products.

Overtime earnings. There are two elements which make up total overtime earnings, basic rate and overtime premium. The basic rate is readily identifiable to a product or batch and should be charged direct. The overtime premium is also readily identifiable to a batch but it is generally accepted that the premium should be charged to overheads and thus spread over all batches. The reason for this is that it is usually fortuitous which particular batch is actually dealt with during the overtime hours so it would create anomalies by charging the premium direct to that batch. The exception to this rule would be where, as in this question, there is a special reason such as a request from a customer for a batch to be produced during overtime. In such cases the premium could legitimately be charged direct.

A10.6

Stores Ledger Control A/c

	£		£
Balance B/D	24,175	WIP	26,350
Creditors	76,150	Production overhead	3,280
		Balance C/F	70,695
	100,325		100,325

WIP control

	£		£
Balance B/D	19,210	Finished goods	62,130
Stores ledger	26,350	Closing stock	24,360
Wages	15,236		
Production overhead	22,854		
P & L A/c – Stock again	2,840		
	86,490		86,490

Finished goods Control

	£		£
Balance B/D	34,164	Cost of goods sold	59,830
WIP Control	62,130	Closing stock	36,464
	96,294		96,294

Production Overhead control

	£		£
Payments	2,100	WIP control	22,854
		(15236 × 150%)	
Stores ledger	3,280	Capital under construction	4,005
		(2670 × 150%)	
Wages – Direct	5,230	P & L A/c under absorbed ohd.	183
– Indirect	4,232		
Cash	12,200		
	27,042		27,042

P & L A/C

	£		£
Cost of goods sold	59,830	Sales	75,400
Selling and Dist. ohd.	5,240	WIP Stock gain	2,840
Prod. ohd. under absorbed	183		
Profit	12,987		
	78,240		78,240

b. Aspects of accounts which should be investigated.
   1. Causes of WIP stock gain.
   2. Material stocks appear high in relation to usage and previous month's figures.
   3. There is a wages discrepancy– Gross earnings of direct workers = (£17646 + £4364) = £22010 but wage recordings total £23136 (ie 15236 + 5230 + 2670).

c. Stocks are valued so as to be able to calculate periodic profits and to provide a valuation of assets for balance sheet purposes.

   Expense items are included because they represent cash and resources expended during production. The costs thus attached to an item are matched with the sales value when sold.

A10.7

a. Control accounts in the Cost Ledger.

Raw Material stores

	£		£
Balance B/d	49,500	WIP	104,800
Purchases	108,800	Flood loss	2,400
		Balance c/f	51,100
	£158,300		£158,300
Balance b/d	51,100		

W-I-P

	£		£
Balance B/d	60,100	Finished goods	222,500
Raw materials	104,800	Balance c/f	56,970
Direct wages	40,200		
Prod. Overheads	74,370		
	£279,470		£279,470
Balance B/d	56,970		

Finished Goods

	£		£
Balance B/d	115,400	Cost of sales	212,100
WIP	222,500	Balance c/f	125,800
	£337,900		£337,900
Balance B/d	125,800		

Production Overhead

	£		£
Financial ledger control	60,900	WIP	74,370
Notional rent	12,000		
Overhead over absorbed	1,470		
	£74,370		£74,370

b. *Costing P and L*

	£	£
Sales		440,000
less Cost of sales	212,100	
Flood loss	2,400	214,500
		225,500
Add back		
Overhead over absorbed	1,470	
Notional rent	12,000	13,470
		£238,970

Reconciliation of Financial and Costing Profits

	£	£	£
Profit as financial accounts			230,000
Differences in Stock Valuations			
+ W-I-P opening	3,900		
+ Finished Goods opening	4,600		
+ Finished Goods closing	3,900	12,400	
– Raw Material opening	1,500		
– Raw Material closing	900		
– W-I-P closing	1,030	3,430	8,970
= Profit as Cost accounts			£238,970

c. The over absorption of overhead for the quarter can be credited to Costing P & L in the quarter, or the over/under absorption taken to an Overhead Adjustment Account each quarter with a final credit or debit as necessary to Costing P & L at the year end.

A10.8

a. The purpose of the Wages Control account is to act both as a control on the total payroll postings and as a manageable, summary account for the payroll details.

b. i.

		£	£
Wages control	Dr	122,300	
Bank			122,300
Wages control	Dr	58,160	
Employees' National Insurance			14,120
Employees' Pension Fund			
Contributions			7,200
Income Tax			27,800
Court Order Retentions			1,840
Trade Union Subscriptions			1,200
Private Health Plans			6,000
		180,460	180,460
Production Overhead Control Dr		18,770	
Employer's National Insurance			18,770
		18,770	18,770

ii.

		£	£
Work-in-Progress Control Dr (Wages)		77,460	
	(Overtime Wages – Direct)	16,800	
Production Overhead Control			
	(Overtime Premium)	9,000	
	(Shift Premium)	13,000	
	(Indirect Wages)	38,400	
	(Overtime Wages – Indirect)	10,200	
Assets in Course of Construction		2,300	
Statutory Sick Pay		9,000	
Idle Time		4,300	
Wages Control			180,460
		180,460	180,460

A10.9

a. *Raw materials:*

Date		Kilos	Total Value £	Average Price £/Kilo
Opening Balance		21,600	28,944	1.3400
1st	Issue	(7,270)	(9,742)	1.3400
7th	Purchase	17,400	23,490	1.3500
		31,730	42,692	1.3455
8th	Issue	(8,120)	(10,925)	1.3455
15th	Issue	(8,080)	(10,872)	1.3455
20th	Purchase	19,800	26,730	1.3500
		35,330	47,625	1.3480
22nd	Issue	(9,115)	(12,287)	1.3480
Closing Balance		26,215	35,338	1.3480

	£
Opening balance	28,944
+ Purchases	50,220
– Issues	(43,826)
= Closing Balance	35,338

Raw material stock control account

	£		£
Opening balance	28,944	Work in process	43,826
Purchases	50,220	Closing balance	35,338
	79,164		79,164

Production costs:

	£
Raw materials	43,826
Labour and overhead	35,407
	79,233

+17,150 units = £4.62 per unit

Opening stock of finished goods	16,960 units
+ Production	17,150 units
– Closing stock of finished goods	(17,080) units
= Sales	17,030 units

Cost of Sales:	£
= Opening stock (16,960 units)	77,168
+ 70 units from production × £4.62	323
	77,491

Summary:	£
Opening balance	77,168
+ Production costs for period	79,233
– Cost of sales	(77,491)
= Closing balance	
(ie, 17,080 × £4.62)	78,910

Finished Goods Stock Control Account

	£		£
Opening balance	77,168	Cost of sales	77,491
Raw materials	43,826	Closing balance	78,910
Labour and overhead	35,407		
	156,401		156,401

b. The financial ledger control account is in the Cost Ledger in a set of interlocking accounts. It has two purposes. One is to maintain the cost ledger as a self balancing ledger and the other is to be equal and opposite to the cost ledger account in the financial ledger.

A10.10

Calculation of Costing Profit

	£	£
Financial Profit		75,000
Stock adjustments		
Raw materials (– 5,000 + 7,000)	+ 2,000	
Finished Goods (+ 5,000 + 1,000)	+ 6,000	8,000
		83,000
Add back		
Debenture interest	13,000	
Goodwill write-off	20,000	
Discounts allowed	7,000	
Overhead adjustment	20,000	60,000
		143,000
Deduct		
Rent received	25,000	
Notional rent	14,000	
Discount received	5,000	
Profit on m/c sale	6,000	50,000
= Costing Profit		93,000

Chapter 11 Solutions

Exercises

A11.1

Key Points

Job Costing: Work is done to customer's requirements. The Job is the cost unit and is treated separately. Examples include; engineering, printing, architectural designs.

Batch Costing: Where a number of items are made as a batch. Similar to job costing except that a number of units are made. Examples; engineering, clothing, footwear.

Contract Costing: Usually site based and relatively long duration. Many similarities to Job Costing. Examples; bridge and road building, shipbuilding.

Process Costing: where a large number of homogeneous products or units are made from a series of operations. Examples; food manufacture, refining.

Service Costing: is the costing of services where the cost unit is some suitable homogeneous measure of the service or function. Examples; transport, canteens, hospitals.

The method of costing must suit the product or service and the organisation.

Chapter 12 Solutions

Exercises

A12.1

	Batch Cost		£	£
Labour				
Dept A	420 × £3.50		1,470	
B	686 × £3.00		2,058	3,528
Materials				3,280
		= Prime Cost		6,808
Overheads				
Dept A	420 × £8		3,360	
B	686× £5		3,430	6,790
		= Factory cost		13,598

∴ Factory cost should be 75% of sales value

∴ Sales value = $\dfrac{13,598}{0.75}$ = £18,131

∴ Administration overheads are £18,131 × 10% = £1,813

Summary for batch		£	£
Selling Price			£18,131
– Factory Cost		13,598	
– Admin. Overheads		1,813	15,411
= Net Profit			2,720
Selling price per unit	=		£18.13
Admin. overheads recovered	=		£1,813
Net profit per unit $\dfrac{2,720}{1,000}$	=		£2.720

A12.2

This is a problem which is encountered in many aspects of cost accounting not merely the example quoted. The cost accountant must always be aware of the 'cost of costing' and relate the costs incurred in producing any form of cost information to the benefits expected from the use of such information.

In the example cited in the question the cost accountant should investigate the uses and value obtained from the production of costs for all jobs and what would be the effect of producing individual costs only for jobs above a certain size. If such a system was adopted, costs for small jobs would be charged to a General Jobbing account which would be credited with their sales value. Although control over individual job costs would be lost if the new system was adopted, costs would be saved and a judgement must be made as to whether this cost saving would be worthwhile.

A12.3

This is commonly encountered problem especially when firms increase the amount of mechanisation and automation, yet do not update their costing systems. The likely effects would be:

a. Incorrect product costs which do not reflect the actual nature of the job.
b. As prices are based on cost the calculated selling prices will be incorrect – some too high, some too low.
c. Because of the incorrect selling prices the firm will tend to get jobs on which it will make a loss ie, those where the prices are too low.
d. Overhead rates and amounts under/over absorbed will be incorrect.

The remedy is to calculate both labour and machine hour rates and use them according to the nature of the job.

Examination questions

A12.4

a. If this is a normal procedure then all products should receive an appropriate proportion of the marginal scrap costs at normal levels. If the scrap level is abnormal the excess over normal levels would be charged direct to Costing P&L. If scrapping at final inspection is an abnormal event then all marginal costs would be written off to Costing P & L.

b. Generally such a salary would be regarded as a fixed cost and written off in period incurred.

c. Generally regarded as a variable cost and, if identifiable, the material basic cost would be increased – otherwise charged to Production Overheads.

d. Generally considered as a variable cost and if for one batch or job charged to that job– otherwise charged to Production Overheads.

e. Such costs are difficult to identify with particular orders and although there are variable elements, they would generally be treated as a fixed cost and charged to the Costing P & L in the period incurred.

A12.5

a. This can be answered directly from the book.

b. Typical elements of gross wages

> Basic time earnings
> Overtime earnings
> Shift allowances
> Bonus
> Piecework earnings
> In lieu/enforced idle time payments

In general directly identifiable and traceable items would be classed as prime cost.

Normally these include

> Basic time earnings (excluding non – productive time – classed as overheads)
> Basic time rates in overtime earnings (balance to overheads)
> Bonus/Piecework earnings. If traceable included as prime cost otherwise overheads.
> Shift allowances, in lieu or idle time payments. Generally not traceable so classed as overheads.

A12.6

Current overhead absorption rate

a. Percentage of direct wages $= \dfrac{\text{Budgeted production overhead}}{\text{Budgeted Direct Wages}} \times 100\% = \dfrac{£225,000}{£150,000} \times 100 = 150\%$

b. Production overhead – Production Cost and Gross Profit

Cost of Job No. 657

	£
Direct Materials	190,000
Wages	170,000
= Prime Cost	360,000
Production Overhead (150% of 170,000)	255,000
= Total Production Cost	615,000
Gross Profit ($\frac{1}{3}$ of 615,000)	205,000
	£820,000

c. i. A single overhead rate, as indicated in the first part of the question, is only likely to give accurate job costs when the incidence of overheads in each department is similar. From the data given it is apparent that this is not so. Department A with a quarter of the direct wages of B has four times the production overheads probably indicating a substantial amount of machinery related overheads. In such circumstances anomalies would arise between job costs because the rate used is an average of substantially different patterns of overheads.

   ii. Departmental rates.

   Department A. There are a considerable number of machine hours with a correspondingly high incidence of overheads. It is likely that a *machine hour rate* would be most appropriate ie,

   $$\frac{\text{Budgeted overhead}}{\text{Budgeted Machine Hours}} = \frac{£120,000}{40,000} = £3 \text{ per machine hours}$$

   Department B. In this department the large number of labour hours would indicate that a *labour hour rate* would be most appropriate ie,

   $$\frac{\text{Budgeted overhead}}{\text{Budgeted Labour Hours}} = \frac{£30,000}{50,000} = £0.6 \text{ per labour hour}$$

   Department C. A machine hour rate cannot be considered because there are apparently no machine hours involved. Accordingly a labour hour rate would be appropriate or, as there appears to be only a single wage rate of £1 per hour, a percentage on direct wages. Both absorption bases would give the same result.

Labour hour rate

$$\frac{\text{Budgeted overhead}}{\text{Budgeted Labour Hours}} = \frac{£75,000}{25,000} = £3 \text{ per labour hour}$$

or Direct Wages Percentage

$$\frac{\text{Budgeted Overheads}}{\text{Budgeted Wages}} \times 100\% = \frac{£75,000}{£25,000} \times 100\% = 300\%$$

d. Production overhead using departmental rates

Job 657

Dept		£
A	40 machine hours × £3 per hour	120
B	40 labour hours × £0.6 per hour	24
C	10 labour hours × £3 per hour	30
		£174

This compares with the £255 shown in part (b) above.

e. Over or (under) absorption

i. Using single rate of 150% on wages

Dept	Absorbed £	Actual £	Over (under) Absorption £
A	45,000	130,000	(85,000)
B	120,000	28,000	92,000
C	45,000	80,000	(35,000)
	£210,000	£238,000	(£28,000)

ii. Using departmental rates

A	135,000	130,000	5,000
B	27,000	28,000	(1,000)
C	90,000	80,000	10,000
	£252,000	£238,000	£14,000

A12.7

a. In general an overall uplift as shown is not recommended because it masks the individual characteristics, and hence their differences. These differences should be reflected in varying costs. A further problem with the system shown is that it is a general uplift on materials $\frac{2}{5}$ of Prime Cost) which is usually a poor indicator of overhead use.

b. It is conventionally considered that absorption of production overheads on labour or machine hours and the separate absorption of administration and selling costs produces more realistic product costs. Alternatively an Activity Based approach may be worthwhile.

Based on labour hour rates the following cost estimate could be prepared.

Job 878

	Note	£	£
Prime cost			12,800
Overheads:			
Grinding	1	1,750	
Finishing	2	1,440	3,190
Production cost			15,990
Admin.	3	1,028	
Selling	4	1,666	2,694
Total cost			18,684

Notes

1. Grinding labour hour rate $= \dfrac{£175,000}{40,000} = £4.375$ per hour

    ∴ Job 878 total $= 400 \times 4.375 = £1,750$

2. Finishing labour hour rate $= \dfrac{£208,000}{43,333} = £4.8$ per hour

    ∴ Job 878 total $= 300 \times £4.8 = £1440$

3. Admin overheads based on the relationships in the P & L account

    $= \dfrac{£118,500}{£1,843,000} = 6.43\%$ of production cost

    ∴ Job 878 charge $= £15,990 \times 6.43\% = £1,028$

4. Similarly for Selling Overheads $= \dfrac{192,000}{£1,843,000} = 10.42\%$ of production cost

    ∴ Job 878 charge $= £15,990 \times 10.42\% = £1,666$

    Assuming that $16\frac{2}{3}$ % of selling price is required the recommended selling price would be

$$\frac{£18,684}{100\% - 16\frac{2}{3}\%} = £22,421$$

and the Job Profit would be £3,737.

Note: Based on the same percentage on selling price the selling price and profit based on the figures in the question are £22,657 and £3,777 respectively. Thus the figures are very similar.

c. The accounting information could be improved as follows

   i. Using comparisons with previous periods
   ii. Using budgeted figures for the current period and tracking variances
   iii. by analysing costs into fixed and variable so as to examine the effects of altering prices and activity.

A12.8

Workings

Overhead	£
Supervisory Labour	3,760
Depreciation	585
Cleaning matls.	63
Stationary & telephone	275
Rent and Rates	940
Vehicle Costs	327
Other admin.	688
Overtime premium 1	522
Idle time 2	492
Wastage 3	345
Rectification 4	1,035
	9,032

Notes

		£
1.	Overtime premium = 290 × £1.80 =	522
2.	Idle time = 82 × £6 =	492
3.	Wastage = 60 kilos × £1.812 + £236 =	345
4.	Rectification = 37 hrs × £6 + 340 kilos × £1.812 + £197 =	1,035

Direct labour hours = 3,640 basic + 290 o'time – 82 idle time – 37 rectification = 3811

Overhead Absorption rate $= \dfrac{£9,032}{3,811} = £2.367$ per d.l.h.

Material P

	kilos		£
Opening Balance	3,100		5,594
Purchases	3,500	@£1.81	6,335
	3,800	@ £1.82	6,916
	10,400		18,845

Weighted average price $= \dfrac{£18,845}{10,400} = £1.812$ kilo

Job Cost No. 126

	Direct materials	£
P.	960 kilos @ £1.812	1,740
	other	2,030
		3,770
	less wastage & rectification	75
		3,695
	Labour 474 hrs @ £6	2,844
	= Prime cost	6,539
	+ overhead 474 @ £2.367	1,122
		7,661

b. Other information

	Job 126	All Jobs in month
Idle Time	$\dfrac{10}{474}$	$\dfrac{82}{3,811}$
	= 2.11%	= 2.15%
Wastage	$\dfrac{42}{3,770}$	$\dfrac{345}{32,220}$
	=1.11%	=1.07%
Rectification	$\dfrac{105}{6,539}$	$\dfrac{1,035}{53,928}$
	= 1.61%	= 1.92%

Performance on all jobs was below expectation. Job 126 was better than average on Idle Time and Rectification.

Chapter 13 Solutions

Exercises

A13.1

Contract A/cs

	Y282 £	Z650 £		Y282 £	Z650 £
Wages (incl. accrued)	52,660	39,460			
Materials	12,680	19,280	Materials C/F	2,100	6,400
Site expenses	6,500	8,620	WIP C/F	3,500	2,200
Plant depreciation	30,000	6,500	Cost of work certified	108,551	75,449
Head office charges*	12,311	10,189			
	114,151	84,049		114,151	84,049
Cost of work certified	108,551	75,449	Value certified	110,000	85,000
Profit for year	1,449	9,551			
	110,000	85,000		110,000	85,000
Materials B/F	2,100	6,400	Accrued wages B/F	4,217	2,242
WIP B/F	3,500	2,200			

*Prime costs		Y282		Z650
Materials	12,680		19,280	
– Stock	2,100	10,580	6,400	12,880
+ Wages		52,660		39,460
= Prime Cost		63,240		52,340
Head Office Charges apportioned on Prime Cost		£12,311		£10,189

A13.2

There are numerous problems associated with site and contract work, typical of which are the following:

a. Pilferage of materials, petrol, tools etc.
b. Unauthorised use of equipment and vehicles.
c. General difficulties of recording and paperwork.
d. Wasteful use of materials, high volumes of breakages.
e. Difficulties of supervision on dispersed sites.
f. Wasteful labour practices, incorrect labour bookings.

It must be recognised that it is extremely difficult to eradicate these problems entirely but the following practices will help to overcome excesses.

a. Good security procedures eg, perimeter fencing, lockable stores and vehicles and so on.
b. Well motivated and competent site management.
c. On site cost clerks providing rapid information.
d. Clear, simple records and forms.
e. Simple quantity budgets for materials usage with rapid feedback of discrepancies.

A13.3

Arguments for charging individual contracts with a proportion of Head Office costs:

a. The total contract cost can be calculated.
b. Head Office charges have to be recovered somewhere.
c. A net profit or loss can be calculated for each contract.
d. If prices are cost based a more realistic price can be calculated.
e. Head Office costs are inescapable and the services they represent are necessary for each contract so it is reasonable that each contract should bear a proportion.

Arguments against:

a. Any method of apportioning Head Office costs is arbitrary and thus may produce illogical results.
b. Head Office costs are not controllable at the contract level so may appear to be an unwanted burden to site management.
c. Apportioned costs may obscure the real operating results of individual contracts.
d. Having a large, uncontrollable apportioned cost may be a disincentive to site management.

Examination questions

A13.4

a. i. Shipbuilding
Civil engineering work such as road construction, bridge building office blocks.
   ii. Can be taken from the text.

b. i) ii) & iii) Can be taken from the text. Note particularly the uncertainties associated with contract work and the consequent need for prudence.

c. As the contract is nearing completion it is not necessary to take an excessively prudent view of profits.

A reasonable profit calculation is:

Anticipated Contract Result

		£'000s
Value on completion		1,400
Costs to date	900	
Costs to completion	150	1,050
= Overall profit		350

$$\therefore \text{Attributable profit} = \frac{\text{Costs to date}}{\text{Total costs}} \times \text{Final Profit} = \frac{900}{1,050} \times 350 = 300 \text{ ('000s)}$$

i.

Radley Contract account

	£		£
Materials issued from Store	600,000	Materials returned to store	50,000
Wages paid	250,000	Materials on site c/d	20,000
Wages accrued	30,000	Value of plant c/d	60,000
Sub- contractors charges	25,000	Cost of work certified to Profit and Loss a/c	900,000
Plant purchased at cost	100,000		
Overheads	25,000		
	1,030,000		1,030,000

Contractee account

	£		£
Value of work certified	1,200,000	Cash	1,000,000
		balance c/d	200,000
	1,200,000		1,200,000

ii.

Contract Profit and Loss Account

	£		£
Cost of work certified	900,000	Value of work certified	1,200,000
Profit and loss a/c	300,000		
	1,200,000		1,200,000

d. i. Under the old rules, which are now superseded, the WIP was valued as follows:

Costs to date + attributable profits – Progress payments received and receivable

ii. Under the rules which now apply the WIP is

Cost to date *less* costs allocated to cost of sales

Note: Although not asked for in the question the Contract balances for Balance Sheet purposes are calculated below

	£'000s
Costs to Date	900
Cost of sales	900
WIP balance	–
Amount taken as turnover	1200
less Progress payments	1000
Balance	200

Thus there is no WIP in this example and £200,000 will be grouped with Debtors as the amount taken for Turnover is greater than the Progress Payments received.

A13.5

a. This can be taken directly from the text.

b. Contract profitability.

	£'000
Costs of completed work	250
Materials (see note)	500
Wages	487
Plant hire	96
Other expenses	74
Material discrepancies (500 × 0.4%)	2
General overhead (1840 × 5%) – 13)	79
	1,488
Costs to completion	215
Estimated total costs	1,703
Contract price	2,100
Estimated profit	397

Note
Materials

Opening Stock	10
+ Site materials	512
	522
– Closing stock	18
	504
– Shortage	4
	500

A reasonable proportion of the profit can be taken (according to SSAP9). One method is to relate the profit to the cost to date compared with estimated total costs thus

$$\text{Proportion of profit} = 397 \times \frac{1488}{1703} = £347,000$$

This notional value would be taken unless this is greater than the actual profit to date on the work certified thus:

Actual profit to date = Value of work certified – cost of work certified = 1840 – (1488 – 35) = £387,000

Thus the figure of £347,000 could reasonably be taken.

c. If the contract price was £3.5m the contract is likely to run for longer and a more prudent view of profits would be taken. As there is no estimate of costs to completion, a reasonable method would be to take a proportion (say $\frac{2}{3}$) of the notional profit reduced by the retention percentage

ie, $\frac{2}{3}$(value – cost of work certified) – Retention percentage

Thus assuming a 20% retention percentage the profit would be

$$\tfrac{2}{3}(1840 - 1453) \text{ less } 20\% = £206,400 \text{ say } £206,000.$$

Chapter 14 Solutions

Exercises

A14.1

This is a very real practical problem which is faced by numerous service organisations. Probably the most obvious example is that of urban passenger transport. During the morning and evening rush hours there is extremely high demand yet during the day the demand falls dramatically.

This fluctuation means that the amount of capacity which has to be provided is much greater than average usage rates. The amount and type of capacity is a critical management decision for such organisations and the cost accounting system should provide appropriate information to assist decision making and control.

Typical of the information to be supplied is the following:

a. Detailed analysis of usage patterns, period by period, highlighting trends.
b. Operating cost breakdowns clearly differentiating between fixed and variable costs.
c. Revenue analysis showing the effects of demand patterns and projections of trends.
d. Cost and revenue projections showing the differential effects of changes in costs, rates of inflations, tariffs etc.
e. Detailed budgetary control statements showing operating costs, costs of idle facilities, maintenance etc.
f. Cash forecasting and budgeting.

A14.2

The costs in running a fleet of 20 lorries are substantial and a costing system is essential to maintain control.

The elements of a possible cost control system include the following:

a. Comprehensive cost classification and coding system enabling costs to be gathered, analysed and presented in various ways eg, per vehicle, repairs, running costs, labour costs and so on.

b. A regular reporting system covering each of the elements of cost/mileage travelled/tonnage carried/ hours of operation showing actual against budget and highlighting trends.

c. Ad hoc reports and analyses of major items of expenditure eg, replacements, major overhauls, tyre performance, etc.

There should be an investigation into the most relevant cost unit for the particular style of operation being undertaken. It might be tonne/mile, miles travelled, operating hour or day, tonnage or some combination of such cost units.

Without knowing more details of the organisation and its operation firm recommendations are not possible.

Examination questions

A14.3

Vehicle Operating Costs

a.

Vehicle Type........   Registration No...................

　　　Variable costs
　　　　fuel
　　　　oil
　　　　tyres
　　　　parts
　　　　repairs
　　　　maintenance
　　　　depreciation (part) etc　　　　　　　_____

　　　Fixed costs
　　　　driver's wages & N.I.
　　　　insurance and tax
　　　　depreciation (parts) etc　　　　　　_____

　　　Total direct cost　　　　　　　　　　_____

Miles run	cost per mile
No. of journeys	cost per journey
Tonnage carried	cost per tonne and tonne/mile
Items carried	cost per item

(*Note*: Operating costs, by definition will not include any general business overheads)

Bus Income and Expenditure

Date.......　　　　　　　　　Period............

　　　　　　　　　　　　　Route　1　2　3 ....　　Total

Fare income
　　Contract income (School, hiring etc.)
　　Advertising
　　Any other income

　　Variable costs
　　　Fuel
　　　Oil
　　　Tyres
　　　Parts
　　　Repairs
　　　Maintenance
　　　Depreciation (part) etc

　　Direct fixed costs
　　　Wages & N.I.
　　　Insurance and Tax
　　　Depreciation etc
　　　Total direct costs

　　Gross route income
　　Allocated & apportioned
　　General overheads
　　Net route income

b.　The general rules of allocation and appointment would thus apply and the passenger service manager would be allocated to that service and apportioned over the routes. The accountants costs would be apportioned over the three segments of the business.

A14.4

a.　i.　*30 seater coach*

	Total coaches	Per coach
No. of Miles	125,000	25,000
Gallons of fuel	10,000	2,000
	£	£
Cost of fuel	22,000	4,400
Driver's wages 52 × £220	57,200	11,440
Licence fees	1,750	350
Insurance	1,700	340
Repairs and maintenance	25,000	5,000
Admin expenses	28,600	5,720
Depreciation	15,000	3,000
	151,250	30,250

Cost per mile $= \dfrac{£30,250}{25,000} = £1.21$

ii. *50 seater coach*

	Total coaches	Per coach
No. of Miles	200,000	20,000
Gallons of fuel	25,000	2,500
	£	£
Cost of fuel	55,000	5,500
Driver's wages 52 × £250	130,000	13,000
Licence fees	5,000	500
Insurance	4,000	400
Repairs and maintenance	40,000	4,000
Admin expenses	65,000	6,500
Depreciation	40,000	4,000
	339,000	33,900

Cost per mile = $\dfrac{£33,900}{20,000}$ = £1.695

b. *Calculations of Tender Price*

	30 seater coach	50 seater coach
Passenger miles per week	50	75
Miles per year	2,000	3,000
Cost per mile	£1.21	£1.695
Cost per coach	£2,420	£5,085
	× 3	× 2
Total cost	£7,260	£10,170
Profit (40% of selling price)*	£4,840	£6,780
Contract price	£12,100	£16,950

This gives a Total tender price of £29,050

* A profit of 40% of selling price means that costs are 60% of selling price.

ie, £7,260 costs gives $\dfrac{£7,260}{0.6}$ = £12,100 selling price and £4,840 profit.

Note: The above tender price has been based, as required, on the cost per mile 'calculated'. For this to be valid it assumes that work will be found for the coaches for the remaining part of each day (assuming morning and evening runs for the students) and the for the other 10 weeks in the year. If the contract makes it impossible to achieve average mileage then this must be taken into account and a higher contract price charged.

c. Possible reasons for high staff turnover

   i.   poor conditions of work
   ii. poor management
   iii. bad initial selection
   iv. dissatisfaction over pay and advancement

The cost of high turnover include; loss of efficiency, extra selection and training costs, poor morale. The benefits of a stable workforce mean that all of the above will improve.

Chapter 15 Solutions

Exercises

A15.1

			Process 1			
	Units	£			Units	£
Material input	12,000	36,000	Process 2		9,000	61,290
Labour		32,000	WIP		3,000	14,710
Overheads		8,000				
	12,000	76,000			12,000	76,000

			Process 2			
Material input(Process 1)	9,000	61,290	Finished goods		7,600	96,892
Labour		28,500	Normal loss		600	
Overheads		14,000	WIP		800	6,898
	9,000	103,790			9,000	103,790

Workings for Cost per Equivalent Units

Process 1

Units	Material	Labour	Overheads	Total
Fully complete	9,000	9,000	9,000	9,000
W-I-P				
Material	3,000			3,000
Labour (50%)		1,500		
Overheads			1,500	
Equivalent Units	12,000	10,500	10,500	12,000
Costs	£36,000	£32,000	£8,000	£76,000
Cost/Unit (complete units)	£3	£3.048	£0.762	

$\therefore$ Cost of complete units = 9,000 × £6.81 = £61,290

Cost of W-I-P = (3,000 × £3) + (1,500 × £3.048) + (1,500 × £0.762) = £14,715 (rounded to £14,710)

Cost per Equivalent Units

Process 2

Units	Material	Labour	Overheads	Total
Fully complete	7,600	7,600	7,600	7,600
Normal Loss				600
W-I-P	800			800
Labour		200		
Overheads			200	
= Equivalent Units	8,400	7,800	7,800	9,000
Costs	£61,290	£28,500	£14,000	£103,790
Cost/Unit	£7.3	£3.654		

$\therefore$ Cost of complete units = 7,600 × £12.749 = £96,892

Cost of W l P = (800 × £7.3) + (200 × £3.654) + (200 × £1.795)

= £6,930 (rounded to £6,898)

A15.2

Process 1

	Units	£		Units	£
Allotted costs	60,000	122,900	Normal loss	3,000	–
Overheads app'd on wages		10,273	Abnormal loss	1,800	4,205
			Output to II	55,200	128,968
	60,000	133,173		60,000	133,173

Notes

a.
Input	60,000	units
Normal loss (5%)	3,000	
Notional output	57,000	
Actual output	55,200	
$\therefore$ Abnormal loss	1,800	

b. The abnormal loss is costed on the same basis as good production:

$$\frac{\text{Actual costs} - \text{expected scrap credit}}{\text{Notional output}} = \frac{£133,173}{57,000} = £2.336 \text{ per unit}$$

Process II

	Units	£		Units	£
Allotted costs		35,350	Normal loss	2,760	27,60
Overheads app'd		7,902	Output to III	53,800	173,855
Transfers from I	55,200	128,968			
Abnormal gain	1,360	4,395			
	56,560	176,615		56,560	176,615

a.
Input	55,200	units
Normal loss (5%)	2,760	
Notional output	52,440	
Actual output	53,800	
$\therefore$ Abnormal gain	1,360	

b. The abnormal gain is costed on the same basis as good production:

$$\frac{\text{Actual costs} - \text{expected scrap credit}}{\text{Notional output}} = \frac{£172,220 - 2,760}{52,440} = £3.2315$$

Process III

	Units	£		Units	£
Allotted costs		38,700	Normal loss	2,690	4,842
Overheads app'd		8,825	Abnormal loss	1,510	6,397
Transfers from II	53,800	173,855	Output	49,600	210,141
	53,800	221,380		53,800	221,380

Notes

a.

Input	53,800	units
Normal loss (5%)	2,690	
Notional output	51,110	
Actual output	49,600	
∴Abnormal gain	1,510	

b. The abnormal gain is costed on the same basis as good production $\frac{£221,380 - 4,842}{51,110} = £4.2367$ per unit.

Abnormal loss / Gain account

	£		£
Process I	4,205	Process II	4,395
Process III	6,397	Scrap Sales (Proc III)	2,718
Scrap sales (Proc II)	1,360		

(At the end of the year the balance on this account would be taken to the P&L account.)

Scrap Sales account

	£		£
Process II(normal)	2,760	Abnormal gains (Proc II)	1,360
Process III (normal)	4,842		
Abnormal losses (Proc III)	2,718		

(At the end of the year the balance on this account would be taken to the P&L account.)

A15.3

Input	250 Kgs
less Normal waste	20 Kgs
= Normal O/P	230 Kgs
Actual O/P	225Kgs
= Abnormal loss	5 Kgs

Process A/c

	Kgs	£		Kgs	£
Material	250	1,750	Good output	225	5097
Labour		3,500	Normal loss	20	40
			Abnormal loss	5	113
	250	5,250		250	5,250

Abnormal loss A/c

		£		£
Process A/c		113	P & L	113
		113		113

Scrap Sales

	£	
Process A/c	40	

A15.4

Cost Element	Equivalent Units in WIP	+	Complete Units	=	Total Effective Production	Total Costs £	Cost per unit £
Material	700 × 80% = 560	+	2,100	=	2,660	24,800	9.32
Labour	700 × 60% = 420	+	2,100	=	2,520	16,750	6.65
Overheads	700 × 50% = 350	+	2,100	=	2,450	36,200	14.78
				Totals £		77,750	30.75

∴ Value of completed production = 2,100 × £30.75

= £64,575

∴Value of WIP = Total costs – Value of completed production

= £77,750 – 64,575

= £13,175

Examination questions

A15.5

Workings

Process 1

Input		15,000 units
– Output	10,000	
WIP	4,400	14,400
= Actual loss		600 units
Normal loss =	5% of 15,000	750 units
∴ Abnormal gain of	150 units	

(This will be valued as good production)

Process 2

Input and opening WIP	=	12,000 units
– Output	9,500	
WIP	1,800	11,300
= Actual loss		700 units
Normal loss =	5% of 12,000	600 units
∴ Abnormal loss of	100 units	

(Valued as good production)

a. i.

Process 1

	Units	£		Units	£
Material	15,000	26,740	Transfer to Process 2	10,000	85,000
Labour		36,150	Closing WIP	4,400	19,800
Overheads		40,635	Normal	750	
Abnormal Gain	150	1,275			
	15,150	104,800		15,150	104,800

ii.

Process 2

	Units	£		Units	£
Opening WIP	2,000	26,200	Finished units	9,500	175,750
Transfer from Process 1	10,000	85,000	WIP	1,800	28,200
Labour		40,000	Normal loss	600	5,100
Overheads		59,700	Abnormal loss	100	1,850
	12,000	210,900		12,000	210,900

iii.

Normal Loss Account

	Units	£		Units	£
Process 2 Account	600	5,100	Cash	600	5,100

iv.

Abnormal Gain / Loss Account

	£		£
Process 2 Account	1,850	Process 1 Account	1,275
		Profits and Loss Account	575
	1,850		1,850

A15.6

Workings

Process A

Actual output =	1400	Kgs
Expected (80% of 200) =	1600	
∴ Abnormal loss	200	Kgs

Process B

Actual output	2620	
Expected (90% of 1400 + 1400)	2520	
∴ Abnormal gain	100	Kgs

The abnormal gain and loss are valued as the good production.

i.

Process A Account

	Kg	£		Kg	£
Direct material	2,000	10,000	Normal loss	400	200
Direct Labour		7,200	Process B	1,400	26,005
Process costs		8,400	Abnormal loss	200	3,715
Overhead		4,320			
	2,000	29,920		2,000	29,920

Notes

Normal loss sold @ 50p per Kg
Valuation of transferred output and abnormal loss:
(£29,920 − £200)/(1,400 + 200) = £18.575 per Kg.

ii.

Process B Account

	Kg	£		Kg	£
Process A	1,400	26,005	Finished goods	2,620	56,989
Direct material	1,400	16,800	Normal loss	280	511
Direct Labour		4,200			
Overhead		2,520			
Process costs		5,800			
Abnormal gain	100	2,175			
	2,900	57,500		2,900	57,500

Notes

Normal loss sold at £1.825 per Kg
Valuation of transferred output and abnormal gain: (£55,352 − £511)/(2,620 − 100) = £21.75 per Kg.

Normal Gain / Loss Account

	Kg	£			Kg	£	
Process A	400	200	Cash		600	300	2)
Process B	280	511	Cash		180	328.5	3)
Abnormal loss A/c	200	100	1)	Abnormal Gain A/c	100	182.50	4)
	880	811			880	811	

Notes

1) Transfer of scrap value of the 200 Kgs of abnormal loss in Process A.
2) Sale of 600 Kgs of Process A loss (ie 400 normal + 200 abnormal)
3) Sales of 180Kgs of Process B loss (ie 280 normal − 100 abnormal gain)
4) Transfer of Scrap value of Process B Abnormal gain of 100 Kgs.

Abnormal loss / gain Account

	Kgs	£		Kgs	£
Process A	200	3715	Process B	100	2175
Normal loss A/c	100	182.5	Normal loss A/c	200	100
			P & L (balance)	–	1622.50
	300	3897.50		300	3897.50

Finished Goods A/C

	Kg	£	
Process B	2620	56989	

P & L A/C (extract)

Abnormal loss/gain net effect	1622.50	

A15.7

a. i. Weighted average; all losses normal

	Raw materials kg	Conversion costs kg
Equivalent units:		
completed output	92,400	92,400
plus closing WIP	28,200	14,100
	120,600	106,500
Unit costs:	£	£
period costs	276,672	226,195
plus opening WIP	56,420	30,597
	333,092	256,792
less scrap value of normal loss*		
(6,700 kg × £0.45)	3,015	–
	330,077	256,792
+ equivalent units (kg)	120.600	106,500
	= £2.7370/kg	£2.4112/kg
	Total =	£5.1482/kg

*Loss calculated thus

	kg
Opening WIP	21,700
+ Input	105,500
	127,300
− Closing WIP	28,200
= Theoretical output	99,100
but Actual output	92,400
∴ Loss	6,700 kg

ii. FIFO; normal losses 5%

	Raw materials kg	Conversion Costs kg
Equivalent units:		
completed output	92,400	92,400
plus closing WIP	28,200	14,100
plus abnormal losses		
(6,700 – (105,600 × 5%))	1,420	–
	122,020	106,500
less opening WIP	21,700	13,020
	100,320	93,480
	£	£
Unit costs:		
period costs	276,672	226,195
less scrap value of normal loss		
(5,280 kg × £0.45)	2,376	–
	274,296	226,195
+ equivalent units (kg)	100,320	93,480
	= £2.7342/kg	£2.4197/kg
	Total =	£5.1539/kg

Process A/C

	kgs	£		kgs	£
Opening WIP			Completed units [1]	92,400	472,402
– Materials	21,700	56,420			
– Conversion costs		30,597	Abnormal loss [2]	1,420	3,883
Inputs in period			Normal loss [3]	5,280	2,376
– Materials	105,600	276,672			
– Conversion costs		226,195	Closing WIP [4]	28,200	111,223
	127,300	589,884		127,300	589,884

Notes

[1] Cost of completed units made up as follows:

	£
Opening WIP (£56,420 + 30,597)	87,017
Materials (92,400 – 21,700) × £2.7342	193,308
Conversion costs (92,400 – 13,020) × £2.4197	192,077
	472,402

[2] Abnormal loss

= 1,420 kgs @ £2.7342 = £3,883

[3] Normal loss

= 5,280 kgs @ £0.45 = £2,376

[4] Closing WIP

Materials 28,200 × £2.342	77,104
Conversion 14,100 × £2.4197	34,119
	111,223

A15.8

Note: This is an unusual and interesting question because in it there are two special features.

a. There is both an abnormal GAIN (from evaporation) and an abnormal LOSS (through toxic waste) in the one process account. They could, of course, be netted but less information would result.

b. The toxic waste has a disposal cost which increases normal manufacturing costs unlike the usual question where waste has a scrap value which reduces cost.

Cost of normal production/10000 kilos.

	£
Process costs	2830
Plus normal toxic waste disposal 600× £0.80	480
less net selling price of normal by – product 500 × £0.50	250
= Normal process cost	£3,060
Normal output = 8500 kilos	

$$\therefore \text{cost per kilo} = \frac{3,060}{8,500} = 36\text{p per kilo}$$

Process Account

	Kilos	£		Kilos	£
Material	10,000	1,500	Finished Prod. @ 36p	8,400	3,024
Conversion Cost		1,330	By-Product	500	250
Normal toxic waste cost		480	Normal Toxic Waste	600	
Abnormal gain – Evaporation	100	36	Normal evaporation	400	
			Abnormal loss – toxic waste @ 36p	200	72
	10,100	3,346		10,100	3,346

Notes.

1. Normal toxic waste is 600 kilos with a charge to process A/C of 600 × 80p = £480.
2. As there is an abnormal loss of toxic waste of 200 kilos this is credited to process account at normal output cost.
3. There should be 500 kilos lost through evaporation but there is only 400 kilos (10000 – (8400 + 500 + 800)) ∴. Abnormal gain of 100 kilos debited at normal output cost of 36p.

By-Product A/c

	Kilos	£		Kilos	£
Process A/C	500	250	Sales	30	22.50
Packing costs		125	Closing stock	470	352.50
	500	375		500	375

Normal toxic waste A/C

		£		£
Cash (disposal)		480	Process A/C	480

Abnormal toxic waste A/C

	£		£
Cash (disposal)	160	P & L A/C	232
Process A/C	72		
	232		232

Abnormal gain – Evaporation

	£		£
P & L A/C	36	Process A/C	36

b. Has been answered via the various notes above. In general abnormal loss/gain effects are separated from costs of normal manufacture.

A15.9

Input		Output		Equivalent units								Total
				Input from Process 2		Mat'ls added in process		Direct wages		Prod'n overhead		
Details	Units	Details	Units	Units	%	Units	%	Units	%	Units	%	
Opening stock	1,200	Opening stock	1,200	–	–	720	60	480	40	360	30	
Process 2	10,800	Normal loss	1,100	–	–	–	–	–	–	–	–	
		Abnormal loss	250	250	100	125	50	100	40	50	20	
		Fully processed	8,450	8,450	100	8,450	100	8,450	100	8,450	100	
		Closing stock	1,000	1,000	100	800	80	600	60	400	40	
	12,000		12,000	9,700		10,095		9,630		9,260		
Cost			£	£		£		£		£		£
			7,980									
		Less scrap	220	7,760		2,019		2,889		6,482		19,150
		per unit		0.8		0.2		0.3		0.7		2.0
Evaluation												
Opening stock				–		144		144		252		540
Normal loss				–		–		–		–		–
Abnormal loss				200		25		30		35		290
Fully processed				6,760		1,690		2,535		5,915		16,900
Closing stock				800		160		180		280		1,420
				£7,760		2,019		2,889		6,482		19,150

b.

Process 3 A/C

	Units	£		Units	£
Opening WIP	1,200	1,860	Normal loss	1,100	
Process 2	10,800	7,980	Scrap value – normal loss		220
Materials added		2,019	Transfers to Proc.4	9,650	19,300
Wages		2,889	Abnormal loss	250	290
Overhead		6,482	Closing WIP	1,000	1,420
	12,000	21,230		12,000	21,230

Abnormal loss A/C

	£		£
Process 3	290	Scrap value	50
		P & L	240
	290		290

Chapter 16 Solutions

Exercises

A16.1

Apportionment on Sales Value

Product	Sales Value £	Apportionment	Costs apportioned £
A	24,000	$\frac{24,000}{57,000} \times £35,000 =$	14,737
B	18,000	$\frac{18,000}{57,000} \times £35,000 =$	11,053
C	15,000	$\frac{15,000}{57,000} \times £35,000 =$	9,210
	£57,000		£35,000

Profit Statement

Product	A £	B £	C £	Total £
Sales Value	24,000	18,000	15,000	57,000
less Apportioned Costs	14,737	11,053	9,210	35,000
Selling Costs	3,500	4,500	1,000	9,000
= Profit	£5,763	£2,447	£4,790	£13,000

Apportionment on Physical Unit Basis

Product	Weight	Apportionment	Costs Apportioned
A	180	$\frac{180}{570} \times £35,000$	11,053
B	240	$\frac{240}{570} \times £35,000$	14,737
C	150	$\frac{150}{570} \times £35,000$	9,210
	570		£35,000

Profit Statement

Product	A £	B £	C £	Total £
Sales Value	24,000	18,000	15,000	57,000
less Apportioned Costs	11,053	14,737	9,210	35,000
Selling Costs	3,500	4,500	1,000	9,000
= Profit (loss)	£9,447	(£1,237)	£4,790	£13,000

A16.2

$$\text{Unit price of X} = \frac{\text{Sales}}{\text{Kgs sold}} = \frac{£52,500}{30,000} = £1.75$$

Market value at split off point of X is

Sales	£52,500
+ Closing Stock (15,000 × £1.75)	26,250
	£78,750

The joint costs to be apportioned are Process 1 costs which total £180,000.

The notional sales value at split off point is

	£
Product X	78,750 (from above)
Product Y (150,750– 28,000)	122,750
= Total notional sales value	£201,500

Using the values calculated above the apportionment of joint costs can be made as follows:

Product	Notional Sales Value	Joint Costs Apportioned	Post split off Costs	Total costs
	£	£	£	£
X	78,750	$\frac{78,750}{201,500} \times 180,000 = 70,347$	–	70,347
Y	122,750	$\frac{122,750}{201,500} \times 180,000 = 109,653$	28,000	137,653
	201,500	£180,000	£28,000	£208,000

A16.3

All methods of apportioning joint costs to individual joint products are arbitrary conventions totally unsuitable for any form of decision making. The Sales Manager is acting rationally in obtaining the best price for each of the individual products. Naturally, the *combined* price for all the products must be greater than the total joint costs.

Examination questions

A16.4

i. Total process costs of £400,000 to be apportioned on sales value.

	Sales Value	%	Cost Apportionment
A	£120,000	24	£96,000
B	80,000	16	64,000
C	300,000	60	240,000
	500,000		400,000

ii. The total sales value of £500,000 exceeds the costs of £400,000 so initial process is worthwhile.

	Final Output	Revenue Possible £	Original revenue £
Alpha	9,500 l	× 22 = 209,000	120,000
Beta	14,400 l	× 9 = 129,600	80,000
Gamma	18,400 t	× 24 = 441,600	300,000

	Revenue Increase	Extra Costs	Profit (loss)
Alpha	£89,000	£70,000	£19,000
Beta	49,600	48,000	1,600
Gamma	141,600	160,000	(18,400)

∴ Alpha and Beta should be produced but C sold without further processing.

A16.5

a.

Process 1 A/c

	Kgs	£		Kgs	£
Material	25,000	100,000	Normal loss	2,500	5,000
Wages		62,500	O/P to Process 2	23,000	207,000
Overheads		45,000			
Abnormal gain	500	4,500			
	25,500	212,000		25,500	212,000

Workings

Material	25,000	Kgs
less Normal loss	2,500	
	22,500	Kg
less O/P	23,000	
= Abnormal gain	500	

Cost per Kilo

$$= \frac{\text{Total cost} - \text{Scrap recovery}}{\text{Actual O/P} - \text{Abnormal gain}} = \frac{207,500}{23,000 - 500} = £9 \text{ Kg}$$

Normal Loss A/c

	£		£
Process 1	5,000	Bank	4,000
		Abnormal gain	1,000
	5,000		5,000

Abnormal Gain

	£		£
Normal loss A/c	1,000	Process 1 A/c	4,500
Costing P & L	3,500		
	4,500		4,500

b. Profit attributable to joint products by apportioning process costs:

    i.   according to weight of output:

Total cost of the two processes –	Process 1	£207,000	
	Process 2	£138,000	
		£345,000	
Weight of Production		23,000	Kilos

∴ cost per kilo = £15 per kilo

	A	B	C	Total
Selling price of joint products	£24	£18	£12	
Unit cost (*see above*)	£15	£15	£15	
Unit Profit/(Loss)	£9	£3	(£3)	
Quantity Produced	9,000	8,000	6,000	
Total Profit/(Loss)	£81,000	£24,000	(£18,000)	£87,000

    ii.   according to the market value of production:

	A	B	C	Total
Sales Value of Production	216,000	144,000	72,000	432,000
Proportions	50%	33.33%	16.67%	
Apportioning Costs according to above proportions	172,500	115,000	57,500	345,000
Total Profit/(Loss)	£43,500	£29,000	£14,500	£87,000

Note: The only meaningful figure in the above statements is the total figure of £87,000.

c. This has been dealt with in the chapter. For such purposes as inventory valuation a consistent method of joint cost apportionment is necessary (although arbitrary). For decision making purposes and for product income determination such apportionments are meaningless.

A16.6

a. Cost apportionment based on weights at split-off point.

Dept 1 produces PA, PB and QA

	Cost per batch
	£
Material 50 lbs P @ £0. 8 =	40
70lbs Q @ £0.6 =	42
30 lbs R @ £0.2 =	6
Conversion cost	32
	£120

	PA	PB	QA
Output proportions	30	20	50
Proportions of £120 cost	£36	£24	£60

	£
	Cost per Batch
Dept 2	
Material 20 lbs PB	24
50 lbs S @ £0. 30	15
Conversion Cost	10
= Cost of PX	49

	PA	PB	QA	PX
∴ Cost per Batch	£36	£24	£60	£49

b. Cost per lb of PAS

	Costs per Batch
Dept 3	
	£
30 lbs PA	36
20 lbs S @ £0. 30	6
Conversion Cost	24
	£66

which would be spread over the main product ie, 10 lbs of PAS

∴ Cost per lb of PAS = £60 = £6.6

When net revenue from PAS reduces departmental costs.

AZ Net revenue = (£0.40 − £0.05) × 40 lbs = £14

∴ Cost per lb of PAS = $\dfrac{£66 - 14}{10}$ = £5.20 lb

c. Total profit in Period 5

		£
Sales (Note 1)		27,564
less Departmental costs (Note 2)		

	£
Dept 1	9,600
Dept 2	2,000
Dept 3	2,400
Packing	128
	14,128

Less Closing Stocks (Note 3)	1,068	13,060
		14,504
Fixed costs		6,000
= Profit		£8,504

Note 1

	Sales		£
PAS	80 batches × 10 lbs = 800 lbs @ £15	=	12,000
PX	80 batches × 50 lbs × 85% = 3400 lbs @ £1.1	=	3,740
AZ	80 batches × 40 lbs × 80% = 2560 @ £0.40	=	1,024
QA	80 batches × 50 lbs × 90% = 3600 lbs @ £3	=	10,800
			£27,564

Note 2

	Costs		
Dept 1	80 × £120	=	£9,600
Dept 2	(80 × 50 lbs × £0.30) + conversion (80 × £10)	=	£2,000
Dept 3	(80 × 20 lbs × £0.30) + conversion (80 × £24)	=	£2,400

Note 3

Closing Stocks

QA $10\% \text{ of } (80 \times 50 \text{ lbs} \times \frac{£60}{50})$ = £480

PX $15\% \text{ of } (80 \times 50 \text{ lbs} \times \frac{£49}{50})$ = 588 = £1,068

Net sales value per lb of PB

	£
Sales 50 lbs PX @ £1.10/lb	55
Less Dept 2 costs (Net of PB cost)	25
	£30

∴ net sales value of PB per lb = $\frac{£30}{20}$ £1.50

Net sales value per batch

∴ Dept 1 costs pro rated

	£	%	£
PA 30 lbs @ £2	60	25	30
PB (from above)	30	12.5	15
QA 50 lbs @ £3	150	62.5	75
	£240	100	£120

A16.7

a. The first stage is to calculate the individual weight proportions of the products to the total weight of 240 tonnes.

Products	A	B	C
Weight proportion	$\frac{100}{240} = 41.67\%$	$\frac{60}{240} = 25\%$	$\frac{80}{240} = 33.33\%$

Profit Statement

Products

	A		B		C		Total	
		£		£	£		£	
Sales Revenue		50,000		48,000		48,000		146,000
	£		£		£		£	
Less Pre-separation Costs in weight proportions	40,000		24,000		32,000		96,000	
Post separation costs	20,000	60,000	12,000	36,000	8,000	40,000	40,000	136,000
= Profit (LOSS)		£(10,000)		12,000		8,000		10,000

b. This part of the question involves comparing the extra revenue obtained from further processing after the separation point with the costs of that processing.

Financial effects of further processing

| | Products | | |
	A £	B £	C £
Incremental Revenue from further processing. *	25,000	6,000	12,000
Less Post separation costs	20,000	12,000	8,000
= Incremental net revenue Profit (LOSS)	£5,000	(£6,000)	£4,000

The table shows that £6,000 additional profit would be gained if Product B was sold at separation point and was not further processed.

* The incremental revenue figures are obtained as follows:

Product   A   £500 – 250 = £250 tonne × 100 tonnes =   £25,000
            B   £800 – 700 = £100 tonne × 60 tonnes =   £6,000
            C   £600 – 450 = £150 tonne × 80 tonnes =   £12,000

A16.8

a.

	B £	K £	C £	Total £
Revenue	35,000	50,000	60,000	
Pre-separation costs (1)	17,500	12,500	10,000	
Post separation costs	20,000	10,000	22,500	
Profit/ (Loss)	(2,500)	27,500	27,500	52,500

i.   Joint costs = £40,000, total output 8000 litres $\therefore \dfrac{£40,000}{8,000}$ = £5 per litre.

ii.   To find if its worth selling at the split-off point it is necessary to calculate the incremental profits as follows.

Incremental costs	20,000	10,000	22,500
Incremental revenue	14,000	30,000	42,000
Incremental benefit	(6,000)	20,000	19,500

Therefore profit will increase by £6,000 if B is sold at split off point.

Revenue	21,000	50,000	60,000	
Pre-separation costs (1)	17,500	12,500	10,000	
Post separation costs	–	10,000	22,000	
Profit	3,500	27,500	22,500	58,500

b.   Joint cost apportionments can be done in various ways all of which are arbitrary conventions.

Accordingly they are of no value for planning decision making and control. Indeed they can mislead management so it is probably better not to make such apportionments.

A16.9

a.   Workings

First process:

i.   cost per kilo: $= \dfrac{£509,640}{744,000}$
                                     = £0.685 per kilo

ii.   cost of sales (W and X):
          W – 255,000 kilos × £0.685   =   £174,675
          X – 312,000 kilos × £0.685   =   £213,720
iii.   closing stock (W, X and Y):
          W –   21,000   kilos
          X –   22,000   kilos
          Y –   6,000   kilos
              49,000   kilos × £0.685   =   £33,565

Second process:

i.   cost per kilo:

		£
Y – 128,000 kilos × £0.685	=	87,680
labour and overhead		17,920
Less: By-product BP - 8,000 kilos × £0.12		(960)
		104,640
+		96,000 kilos
	=	£1.09 per kilo

ii.   cost of sales (Z):

			£
8,000 kilos		=	8,640
+ 86,000 kilos × £1.09		=	93,740
			102,380

iii.   closing stock (Z):

10,000 kilos × £1.09	=	£10,900

Profit and Loss Account

	W	X	Z	Total
	£	£	£	£
Sales	240,975	277,680	100,110	618,765
Production cost of sales	174,675	213,720	102,380	490,775
Selling and admin.	24,098	27,768	10,011	61,877
Total cost	198,773	241,488	112,391	552,652
Profit/(loss)	42,202	36,192	(12,281)	66,113

b.

		£
Revenue from Z per kilo	=	1.0650
Less: Opportunity cost of sales of		
Y = 1.33 kilos × £0.62	=	0.8266
= Additional revenue from further processing		0.2383
Additional costs of further processing		0.1766
(£17,920 – 960) ÷ 96,000		
Additional profit from further processing		0.0617

Notes

a.   The costs of the first process are common to both schemes so can be ignored.

b.   It is assumed that selling and Admin. costs are fixed.

c.   Can be taken from the text.

Chapter 17 Solutions

Exercises

A17.1

It is true that the cost accounting system of the firm records the costs incurred in the past and it is also true, as can be inferred from the statement, that decision making is concerned with the future. This would seem to mean that the statement is correct but this is not a realistic conclusion.

The records and information obtained from the cost accounting system are frequently of great value in decision making because they provide an excellent basis for judging future behaviour. The information obtained from the cost accounting system should not be used directly in decision making but should be examined critically so as to serve for a guide to the future behaviour of costs, revenues, efficiencies, outputs and so on.

It is important to realise that it is *future* costs and revenues which are relevant for decision making.

A17.2

Control is the process of ensuring that operations and performance conform, as far as practicable to the plan. If the plan has been properly developed in accordance with the objectives of the organisation then it is clearly of prime importance that a monitoring process is instituted so that actual performance is compared with plan and, if performance is different from that planned, corrections can be made. The control mechanism should be considered and designed at the planning stage otherwise the advantages of having a planned pattern of activities is unlikely to be realised.

A17.3

Examples of decision making:

    ❑   at the Strategic Level

        major investment decisions
        acquisitions or divestments
        senior management appointments
        decisions on organisation structures
        and so on

    ❑   at the Tactical Level

        pricing decisions
        middle and junior level appointments
        routine replacement decisions
        purchasing (materials, parts etc.) decisions
        production planning and scheduling
        and so on

◻ at the Operational Level
      production and clerical appointments
      shop floor work organisation
      staff allocation
      transport decisions
      and so on

Examination questions

A17.4

a. A broadly based question within which virtually every aspect of cost accounting could be mentioned.

There will be the general requirement of a rapid feedback of cost information to local store management and then, suitably summarised and analysed to Head Office. In addition there will need to be information on stock holding at store and regional level to ensure cost effective stocking and delivery policies.

Particular examples follow in the two categories mentioned.

Planning / Decision making activities

Information and analyses could be provided to assist in:

i. Investment appraisals regarding new stores or major developments of existing stores.
ii. Product line and selling price decisions.
iii. Stock level decisions.
iv. Transportation and stock location decisions.
v. Promotion and advertising plans.
vi. Budgetary planning information.
vii. Cash planning and working capital management. and so on

Controlling/Evaluating activities

Within this category would be a wealth of rapidly produced reports and analyses of current operations and efficiencies.

i. Budgetary control reports for all stores, departments, depots.
ii. Operating statements analysing performance and profitability of stores, departments, product lines.
iii. Depot operating returns showing costs, mileage's, cost per ton mile etc.
iv. Wages and labour returns showing costs/labour turnover etc.
v. Stock turnover reports. and so on

b. To provide the full range of cost accounting information which would be required the cost classifications would need to be detailed and flexible.

Typical of the ways costs might be classified are:

i. By Nature
ii. By location – cost centre, store, depot, department, vehicle etc.
iii. By period
iv. By behaviour – fixed, variable.

In addition to the above routine classification, for special planning and decision making purposes costs would also have to be classified as to relevancy, controllability and responsibility.

Chapter 18 Solutions

Exercises

A18.1

Cost function = $bx + cx^2 + dx^3$

a. A curvi-linear variable cost of parabolic form.

b. Cost at 80 units = $6(80) + 0.7(80^2) + 0.04(80^3) = £25,440$

Cost at 100 units = $6(100) + 0.7(100^2) + 0.004(100^3) = £47,600$

A18.2

Cost at 85 (using linear interpolation) = $£25,440 + \dfrac{5}{20} (47,600 - 25,440) = £30,980$

The error is the difference between the linear interpolation figure of £30,980 and the value using the formula.

Cost at 85 = $6(85) + 0.7(85^2) + 0.04(85^3) = £30,132$

∴ Error = $£30,980 - 30,132 = £848$

A18.3

The Normal Equations:

$$\Sigma y = an + b \Sigma x$$
$$\Sigma xy = a \Sigma x + b \Sigma x^2$$

y	x	xy	x²
656	80	52,480	6,400
692	86	59,512	7,396
683	87	59,421	7,596
698	94	65,612	8,836
707	95	67,165	9,025
703	97	68,191	9,409
712	104	74,048	10,816
4,851	643	446,429	59,451
Σy	Σx	Σxy	Σx²

and n = 7

$$4,851 = 7a + 643\,b \quad \text{Equation I}$$

$$446,429 = 643a + 59,451\,b \quad \text{Equation II}$$

less $\underline{445.599} = \underline{59.064\,b} \quad \text{Equation I} \times \dfrac{643}{7}$

$$= 830 = 387\,b$$

∴ b = £2.145 = variable cost

and substituting:

4,851 = 7a + 643 (2.145)

3,472 = 7a.

∴ a = £496 = Fixed cost.

A18.4

Scattergraph and Regression Line

x
x Scattergraph

– – – Regression Line = 496 + 2.145x

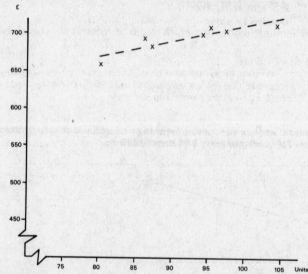

Examination questions

A18.5

a. In the data given there is not a truly variable cost. However if the raw material is consistently ordered in one of the order quantities shown (say in 1000 kilo lots) then the raw material cost could be deemed to be variable, according to the usual accounting criteria.

If order quantities vary then material costs are semi – variable. There are two examples of fixed costs: part of the order handling and part of the holdings costs.

Explanations of variable, semi-variable and fixed costs can be taken from the text.

b. Annual usage = 12000 units $\times \dfrac{0.4 \text{ kilos}}{0.8 \text{ yield}}$ = 6000 kilos.

Cost Summary.

Order Qty	No. of Orders p.a.	Purchase Cost	Ordering Costs		Holding Costs*		Total Costs	
			Short Term	Long Term	Short Term	Long Term	Short Term	Long Term
		£	£	£	£	£	£	£
1000	6	6000	300	540	300	675	6600	7215
1500	4	5880	200	360	400	900	6480	7140
2000	3	5790	150	270	500	1125	6440	7185
2500	2.4	5700	120	216	600	1350	6420	7266
3000	2	5640	100	180	700	1575	6440	7395
3500	1.71	5640	86	154	800	1800	6526	7594

* based on safety stock + $\frac{1}{2}$ purchase quantity.

Based on the cost summary an order quantity of 2500 in the short term is indicated. There is little to choose between 2000, 2500 and 3000 so if the estimates are incorrect there could easily be a change in the above recommendations.

Holding costs are high so that in the long term if the apportioned costs are avoidable it would be preferable to purchase 1500 kilos and thus reduce holding costs.

A18.6

a. Overhead cost patterns

Reference No.	Cost Description	Graph Reference
1	Depreciation of equipment	C
2	Cost of a service	F
3	Royalty	B
4	Supervision	H
5	Machine hour depreciation	E
6	Cost of a service	K
7	Storage/carriage service	G
8	Outside finishing	D

b. Graphs not used A & J.

Graph A

Any cost which has a standing charge covering usage up to a given volume and thereafter has an additional charge per unit. eg, Use of a photo copying machine with a standing charge of £500 which covers all copies up to 5,000. Above 5,000 copies would be charged at an extra cost of 10p per copy.

Graph J

Any scarce resource, with no standing charge, which has an increasing marginal cost eg engineer's services calls could be charged for the first 5 hours £10 per hour, from 5-15 hours £13 hour and so on.

c.

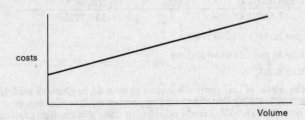

This graph could represent any cost which has a standing charge and then a linear variable cost eg, charges for power where there is a £1,000 per month standing charge and 10p per unit consumed.

A18.7

a. i

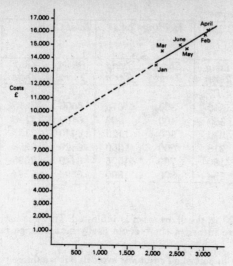

SCATTERGRAPH OF TRANSPORT COSTS

ii. **Least squares**

Costs	Hours	xy	x^2
(y)	(x)	'000s	'000s
13,600	2,100	28,560	4,410
15,800	2,800	44,240	7,840
14,500	2,200	31,900	4,840
16,200	3,000	48,600	9,000
14,900	2,600	38,740	6,760
15,000	2,500	37,500	6,250
$\Sigma y = 90,000$	$\Sigma x = 15,200$	$\Sigma xy = 229,540$	$\Sigma x^2 = 39,100$

Normal Equations

$$\Sigma y = an + b\,\Sigma x$$
$$\Sigma xy = a\,\Sigma x + b\,\Sigma x^2$$

90,000	=	6a	+	15,200b	I
229,540,000	=	15,200a	+	39,100,000b	II

Solving in the normal way, ie II − I $\left(\dfrac{15,200}{6}\right)$ gives:

229,540,000	=	15,200a	+	39,100,000b
− 228,000,000	=	15,200a	+	38,506,667b
1,540,000	=			597,773b

∴ b = £2.576 per hour (variable cost)

and substituting in one of the equations

a = £8,474 (fixed cost)

b. If it is required to charge out the whole of transport costs then this could be done by adding up the whole of the Departmental fixed costs (salaries, building costs etc.) and apportioning this amount over the various vehicles on some basis. To this would be added the fixed costs relating to each vehicle (eg, licence, insurance, depreciation etc.) and the variable running costs (eg, petrol, variable maintenance). The total would be divided by an estimated annual mileage and the total cost per mile calculated.

Alternatively the fixed charges could be directly allotted to departments on some agreed basis and a mileage charge made based on variable costs only.

A18.8

a. It is assumed that, apart from inflation, the only cost changes between Year 1 and Year 2 are variable cost changes. To find the underlying 'real' variable costs it is first necessary to eliminate the inflation effects thus:

	Year 2 Actual £	+ inflation	Year 2 at Year 1 prices £
Wages	390,477	+ 1.06	368,375
Other overhead	216,930	+ 1.05	206,600

Year 1 cost behaviour:

| | Year 2 – Year 1 | | Year 1 | | |
	Increase in units	Increase in costs (excl infl)	Variable Cost per unit	Total Variable cost	Fixed Cost
	1	2	3 = 2 ÷ 1	4 = 3 × 151,156	5 = Total cost – 4
Wages	12,092	£19,205	£1.5882	£240,066	£109,104
Other overhead	12,092	£4,051	£0.3350	£50,637	£151,912

Year 3 costs:

	At Year 1 prices Variable Cost (unit cost × 179,573 units)	Total cost	× 2 Years inflation	Budgeted expenditure Year 3
Wages	£285,198	£394,302	× 1.06 × 1.07	£447,217
Other overhead	£60,157	£212,069	× 1.05 × 1.06	£236,033

b.

	Year 1 £000	%	Year 2 £000	%	Year 3 £000	%
Sales	1,348	100.0	1,514	100.0	1,742	100.0
Food/beverage	698		792		923	
Gross profit	650	48.2	722	47.7	819	47.0
Wages	349		390		447	
Other overheads	203		217		236	
	552	40.9	607	40.1	683	39.2
Net profit	98	7.3	115	7.6	136	7.8

The Gross Profit percentage is steadily declining perhaps reflecting an increase in the bought-in costs of Food and Beverages which W Ltd are unable to pass on, in full, to their customers. However, the Net Profit percentage is increasing no doubt due to the higher throughput and the fixed element of costs.

Chapter 19 Solutions

Exercises

A19.1

Assuming that the only changes in cost between the two output levels are changes in variable costs then the costs can be analysed as follows:

Dept A

$$\text{Variable} = \frac{\text{Cost change}}{\text{Sales change}} = \frac{£5,000}{10,000} = \text{Costs per £ sales} = 50\text{p}$$

∴ Fixed costs = 45,000 – (50,000 × .5) = £20,000

and using a similar process the analysis for the other departments is as follows:

Dept B

Variable = 40p per £ sales
Fixed = £30,000

Dept C

Variable = 45p per £ sales
Fixed = £50,000

Using the above information the Statements can be shown in Marginal Costing form.

	Dept A £	Dept B £	Dept C £	Total £
Sales	50,000	75,000	125,000	250,000
less Variable Costs	25,000	30,000	56,250	111,250
= Contribution	25,000	45,000	68,750	138,750
less Fixed costs				100,000
= Profit				£38,750

	Dept A £	Dept B £	Dept C £	Total £
Sales	60,000	90,000	150,000	300,000
less Variable Costs	30,000	36,000	67,500	133,500
= Contribution	30,000	54,000	82,500	166,500
less Fixed costs				100,000
= Profit				£66,500

A19.2

Based on the data supplied the Production overheads can be analysed into fixed a elements thus:

$\frac{1}{3}$ of production overheads are fixed = £1 per Kg

∴ Fixed overheads = £1 × 30,000 = £30,000 and the marginal production cost is £4.50 per Kg.

Operating Statement Using Marginal Costing

	£	Period 1 £	£	Period 2 £	£	Period 3 £
Sales		270,000		243,000		342,000
Marginal Prod. Cost	135,000		171,000		121,500	
+ Opening Stock					49,500	
– Closing Stock	49,500					
= Marginal Cost of Sales		135,000		121,500		171,000
= Contribution		135,000		121,500		171,000
less Fixed Costs		55,000		55,000		55,000
= Profit		£80,000		£66,500		£116,000

Note: Stocks valued at Marginal Cost.

Operating Statement Using Absorption Costing

	£	Period 1 £	£	Period 2 £	£	Period 3 £
Sales		270,000		243,000		342,000
Total Cost of Prod.	165,000		209,000		148,500	
+ Opening Stock					60,500	
– Closing Stock			60,500			
= Total Cost of Sales		165,000		148,500		209,000
= Gross Profit		105,000		94,500		133,000
less Admin. Overheads		25,000		25,000		25,000
= Profit		£80,000		£69,500		£108,000
Over(under) recovery of fixed ohds.		–		8,000		(3,000)
= Profit		£80,000		£77,000		£105,000

Notes
a. Stocks valued at total cost at the normal production level of 30,000 kgs.
b. Alternatively the over(under) recovery of fixed overheads could be reconciled at the year end.

A19.3

Statement Using Total Cost
£'000s

	A	B	C	Total
Sales	650	480	1420	2550
less Total Costs	736	341	1318	2395
= Profit (loss)	(86)	139	102	155

Note: the fixed costs of £850 were apportioned as follows:

$$\frac{\text{Fixed costs}}{\text{Total Marginal Cost}} \times \text{Marginal cost of a dept} = \text{Fixed costs for the department.}$$

eg, Dept A

$$\frac{850}{1545} \times 475 = 261 \text{ fixed costs}$$

£261+ 475 marginal = <u>£736 Total Costs</u>

Examination questions

A19.4

a. i.

Profit statements using marginal costing
(Stocks valued at marginal cost)

	March £			£	April £
Sales (1500 @ £35)	52,500	(3,000 @ £35)			105,000
less Marginal Cost of Sales					
Opening Stock	–			7,500	
Marginal Mfg. cost	30,000			48,000	
	30,000			55,500	
less Closing Stock (500 × £15)	7,500	(700 @£15)		10,500	
	22,500			45,000	
Variable Selling Costs (15% of sales)	7,875	30,375		15,750	60,750
= Contribution		22,125			44,250
less Fixed costs					
Production and selling		25,000			25,000
Profit (loss)		(£2,875)			£19,250

ii. Profit statements using Absorption costing

(Stocks valued at full production cost at normal output level)

	March £			April £	
Sales		52,500			105,000
less Cost of Sales					
	£			£	
Opening Stock				10,000	
Mfg. cost @ £20 per unit	40,000			64,000	
	40,000			74,000	
less Closing Stock					
(500 × £20)	10,000		(700 × £20)	14,000	
	30,000			60,000	
Fixed Overhead					
Under absorption	5,000	35,000	Over absorption (1,000)	59,000	
(1000 × £5)			(200 × £5)		
= Gross profit		17,500		46,000	
less Variable Selling	7,875			15,750	
Fixed selling	10,000	17,875		10,000	25,750
Profit (Loss)		(£375)			£20,250

b. *Reconciliation of profits*

	March £		April £
Marginal cost result	(2,875)		19,250
Fixed overhead @ £5 per unit carried forward in 500 units	2,500	B/F	(2,500)
Fixed overhead in 700 units c/fwd			3,500
Absorption cost result	(£375)		£20,250

c. As pointed out in the text either system could be used for internal purposes but because of SSAP 9 recommendations, absorption costing is generally preferred for reporting purposes. For decision making marginal costing can be of value.

A19.5

a.

Profit and Loss Statements

Marginal Costing	Jan £	£		Feb £	£
Sales		288,000			512,000
less Marginal cost =	250,000		*less* Marginal cost op. stock	70,000	
– Stock	70,000	180,000	+ Prod.	250,000	320,000
= Contribution		108,000			192,000
– Fixed costs		75,000			75,000
= Profit		33,000			117,000

Absorption Costing	£	£		£	£
Sales		288,000			512,000
less Full Cost =	325,000		*less* o/stock	91,000	
– Stock	91,000	234,000		325,000	416,000
= Profit		£54,000			£96,000

b. Stock Valuations

Marginal Costing

7,000 units @ £10 each = £70,000

Absorption costing

Full cost = £10 variable + $\frac{75,000}{25,000}$ = £13

∴ Stock value = 7,000 × £13 = £91,000

c. The difference in profit is entirely due to the difference in stock valuation. The absorption costing method transfers £21,000 of January's fixed cost to February whereas using Marginal Costing, the fixed costs are written off each month.

d. This can be taken from the text.

A19.6

a. Workings:

Fixed manufacturing overhead absorption rate:

(£000)	Production Department 1	2	Service Department	General Factory	Total
Allocated	380	465	265	230	1,340
Share of general factory	92	115	23	(230)	
			288		
Share of service department	76.8	96.0	(172.8)		
	57.6	57.6	(115.2)		
	606.4	733.6			1,340
	+ 120,000	+ 120,000			
	= £5.053	= £5.053			
	per unit	per unit			

Total manufacturing costs per unit based on Normal activity.

	£
Direct materials	7.00
Direct labour	5.50
Variable overhead	2.00
Fixed overhead – Dept.1	5.053
Dept.2	6.113
	25.6

Profit Statement – Absorption Costing

	£000
Sales: 114,000 units × £36	4,104
Cost of sales: 114,000 units × £25.6	(2,926)
Gross profit	1,178
Non-manufacturing costs	(875)
Net profit (before adjustment)	303
Under-absorbed overhead:	
Dept. 1 £20,000 + (4,000 units × £5.053)	(40,213)
Dept. 2 4,000 units × £6.113	(24,453)
Net profit (after adjustment)	238.3

b.

Profit Statement – Marginal Costing

		£000
Sales: 114,000 units × £36		4,104
Variable cost of sales: 114,000 units × £14.50		1,653
Contribution		2,451
Fixed costs: manufacturing (1,340 + 20)	1,360	
non-manufacturing	875	
		2,235
Net profit		216

c. There is a £22,300 increase in profit shown by the Absorption Costing approach. This represents the fixed costs carried forward in stock ie, 2,000 × (£5.053 + 6.113).

A19.7

Workings:

	£
Marginal cost per unit = Production	49
+ selling (20% × 140)	28
	77

This figure is used for stock valuation when marginal costing is used.

Absorption production cost per unit = £69 which is used for the stock valuation when Absorption costing is used.

i. *Marginal costing format*

Six months to 31/3/93

	£'000	£'000
Sales		980
less Marg. Cost.		
Production	654.5	
– Closing stock	115.5	539
= Contribution		441
less Fixed costs (160 + 90)		250
= Profit		191

Six Months to 30/9/93

	£'000	£'000
Sales		1120
less Marg. Cost		
Opening stock	115.5	
+ Production	539	
	654.5	
– Closing stock	38.5	616
= contribution		504
less Fixed costs		250
= Profit		254

ii. *Absorption costing*

Six Months to 31/3/93

	£'000s	£'000s
Sales		980
less Production costs		
Product costs	586.5	
– Closing stock	103.5	483
		497
+ Over absorption (500 × £20)		10
		507
Selling & Distribution Costs		
Variable (20% of 980)	196	
Fixed	90	286
+ Profit		221

Six Months to 30/9/93

	£'000s	£'000s
Sales		1120
less Production Costs		
Opening stock	103.5	
Production	483	
	586.5	
– Closing Stock	34.5	552
		568
– Under absorption (1000 × £20)		20
		548
Selling and Distribution costs		
Variable (20% of 1120)	224	
Fixed	90	314
= Profit		234

b. The profit differences are caused by the differences in stock valuations under marginal and absorption costing.

Reconciliation

Six months to 31/3/93

	£'000s
Marginal costing Profit	191
+ Fixed production overheads	
C/F in Stock (1500 × 20)	30
= Absorption costing profit	221

Six months to 31/3/93

Marginal Costing Profit	254
– Fixed overheads in stock reduction (1000 × £20)	20
= Absorption costing profit	234

Note that because there is 500 units stock at 30/9/93 the profit from the two systems do not reconcile over the two periods.

ie, Marginal costing = £191 + 254 = £445
Absorption costing = £221 + 234 = £455

The difference is due to the fixed element being carried forward when absorption costing is used:
ie, 500 units × £20 = £10,000 difference.

A19.8

a. i. Workings:

100% Capacity production is 1,008,000/0.7 = 1,440,000 gross/annum

= 120,000 gross/month

	September	October
Production (units)	115,000	78,000
% capacity	96%	65%
Fixed Costs	656,000	632,000
Fixed overhead absorbed:		
115,000 × £7.52	864,800	–
78,000 × £7.52	–	586,560
Over/(under) absorption	208,800	(45,440)

Absorption Costing

	September		October	
	£000	£000	£000	£000
Sales		2,784.00		3,232.00
Opening stock			730.24	
Production cost	2,999.20		2,034.24	
	2,999.20		2,764.48	
Closing stock	730.24		130.40	
		2,268.96		2,634.08
		515.04		597.92
Over(under) absorption		208.80		(45.44)
		723.84		552.48
Fixed selling cost	120.00		120.00	
Fixed administrative cost	80.00		80.00	
		200.00		200.00
Net profit		523.84		352.48

ii. *Marginal Costing*

Unit contribution £32 – £18.56 = £13.44

	£000	£000	£000	£000
Contribution		1,169.28		1,357.44
Fixed Costs:				
Production	656		632	
Selling	120		120	
Administrative	80		80	
		856.00		832.00
Net profit		313.28		525.44

b. Where fixed and variable costs are clearly differentiated, as in marginal costing, then control may be enhanced. However, when production is fairly constant and sales fluctuate, marginal costing will produce greater profit variations than will absorption costing. It is doubtful whether a change from one conventional method of stock valuation to another will affect real operations.

Chapter 20 Solutions

Exercises

A20.1

Planned profit + fixed costs = contribution required.

£4,000 + 2,500 = £6,500

The first 40,000 units give (40,000 × 15p) £6,000 contribution leaving a balance of £500 which must come from the reduced price sales which have a unit contribution of 5p (20p – 15p).

Thus additional units required = $\frac{£500}{0.05}$ = 10,000 units.

Thus total number of units required is 40,000 + 10,000 = 50,000

A20.2

Contribution statement

	Product X	Product Y	Product Z
	£	£	£
Selling Price	200	300	400
– Marginal Cost	140	178	270
= Contribution	60	122	130
CS ratio	30%	41%	32%
Contribution/labour hours	£6	£22.18	£8.67
Contribution/Kg material	£12	£4.35	£5.78

Priority rankings

a. Based on sales – in order of CS ratios, Y, Z, X
b. Based on labour – in order of contribution per hr. Y, Z, X
c. Based on materials – in order of contribution per Kg X, Z, Y.

A20.3

Differential Cost Statement

	Existing Position	With Additional Contract	Difference
	£	£	£
Sales	1,800,000	2,300,000	500,000
less Labour	650,000	910,000*	260,000
Materials	525,000	679,000**	154,000
Variable costs	1,175,000	1,589,000	414,000
= Contribution	625,000	711,000	86,000
less Fixed costs	450,000	500,000	50,000
= Profit	175,000	211,000	36,000

* Labour Costs

$$£650,000 + (650,000 \times \frac{50}{150} \times 1.2) = £910,000$$

** Material Costs

$$(£525,000 + (525,000 \times \frac{50}{150}) \times .97 = £679,000$$

A20.4

$$\text{Cost per bottleneck minute} = \frac{£30,000}{10,000} = £3$$

Return per minute:

$$\text{Mini} = \frac{15.8}{2} = £3.5; \quad \text{Micro} = \frac{12.4}{3} = £2.67$$

∴ Throughput Accounting ratios:

$$\text{Mini} = \frac{£3.5}{3} = 1.16; \quad \text{Micro} = \frac{£2.67}{3} = 0.89$$

Mini earns money, Micro does not.

Examination questions

A20.5

a. i. Original budget in marginal form.

	Reading		Newbury		Basingstoke		Total
	£000		£000		£000		£000
Budgeted receipts		1,600		1,200		800	3,600
Variable costs							
Wages and Salaries	300		250		160		
Film Hire	500		400		390		
Overheads	180	980	160	810	190	740	2,530
Contribution		620		390		60	1,070
					less Fixed Costs		720
					Profit		350

ii. Budget if Basingstoke is closed, assuming that the closure of the cinema does not affect H.O. costs.

	Reading	Newbury	Total
	£000	£000	£000
Budgeted receipts	1,600	1,200	2,800
Variable cost	980	810	1,790
Contribution	620	390	1,010
	Less: Fixed costs		720
	Profit		290

b. If H.O. costs are unaffected (which in practice is unlikely) then Basingstoke should not be closed as it provides a contribution of £60,000 towards general fixed costs.

c. i.

	Reading	Newbury	Basingstoke
Revenue	£1,600,000	£1,200,000	£800,000
Cost per ticket	£4	£4	£4
Budgeted sales in seats	400,000	300,000	200,000
Contribution	£620,000	£390,000	£60,000
Contribution per seat	£1.55	£13.0	£0.30

d. *Proposed advertising campaign in Basingstoke*

Contribution per ticket at Basingstoke	30p
Present contribution in total	£60,000
Increase in contribution	£30,000
Extra fixed costs	£40,000
Effect upon profit	(£10,000)

The advertising campaign should not be undertaken in Basingstoke as the increased contribution of £30,000 is less than the increase in fixed costs of £40,000. Management should look at other options to increase profitability at the Basingstoke cinema.

A20.6

	Component 12	Component 14	Product VW	Product XY
	£/unit	£/unit	£/unit	£/unit
Variable Cost	42	32	30	64
Purchase Price	60	30		
Selling Price			33	85

Recommendations Make 12
Buy 14
Make and Sell VW and XY as both produce contribution.

b. Assumptions.

i.   Budgeted costs are accurate and variable costs are truly variable.
iii That no additional costs such as inspection, delivery etc will arise from buying Component 14.
iii. That there are no technical/production/limiting factor reasons why Component 14 should not be purchased.

c. Implications of additional information.

Machine Time requirements (component 12, Products VW and XY)

$= (7000 \times 8) + (5000 \times 6) + (4000 \times 12) = 134,000$ but only 80,000 available.

∴ 54000 shortfall.

Objective is to maximise contribution per unit of limiting factor ie, machine hours, thus:

	Component 12	Product VW	Product XY
Contribution (unit)	£18	£3	£21
Machine Hours required	8	6	12
Contribution/machine hour	£2.25	£0.50	£1.75
Ranking	1	3	2

Thus based on this ranking the best production plan would be to make all of Component 12 and use balance of hours on Product XY ie:

Component 12	7000 units	= 56000 hours
Product XY	2000 units	= 24000 hours
Total		80000 hours

The usual caveats must apply, ie will there be loss of goodwill from not having Product VW available, is the limiting factor a long or short term problem etc.

A20.7

Variable manufacturing cost = £3.45; Purchase price = £3.65
∴Worthwhile manufacturing
Annual benefits = 40,000 × 20p = £8,000

Assumptions:
a.   Manufacture does not displace more profitable production.
b.   Manufacture does not cause extra fixed costs.

Other factors:
a.   Possibility of higher contribution work arising.
b.   Security of supplies.
c.   Quality.

Sales and profit figures for Company A
Assuming that there are no fixed cost changes between the two sales levels, the profit increase of £15,000 is also the contribution increase.

∴ Contribution margin $= \dfrac{£15,000}{60,000} = 25\%$

∴ Sales to earn profit of £42,000 (assuming no more fixed costs) ie, an extra £6,000 over the highest sales in question.

To earn £6,000 contribution means that $(\frac{6,000}{0.25})$ £24,000 sales are required.

∴ To earn £42,000 profit means that £280,000 + 24,000 = £304,000 Sales required.

Profit @ £188,000 sales

Necessary to deduce fixed costs from data supplied thus:

Sales £220,000 at 25% contribution give £55,000 contribution but profit only £21,000.

∴ fixed costs = £34,000

∴ Profit @ £188,000 = (188,000 × 25%) − 34,000 = £13,000.

A20.8

a. Workings:

Material A purchase quantity:

(30 kilos ÷ 0.9) × (2,400,000 ÷ 100 ÷ 12) = 66,667 kilos per month

Therefore, 5% discount applies.

Department 2 overhead:

Variable	£1,980,000
Fixed	£3,444,000
	£5,424,000

Variable overhead rate $= \dfrac{1,980,000}{2,200,000} =$ £0.9 per direct labour hour

Fixed overhead rate:

Expected usage of capacity = (2.2 m hours × 60%) + (2.4 m units × 15/100) = 1.68 m direct labour hours

Rate $= \dfrac{3,444,000}{1,680,000} =$ £2.05 per direct labour hour.

Cost Statement

	£ per hundred units
Direct materials:	
Material A: 30 kilos + 0.9 × £5.13/kilo	171.00
Others: £1.34/unit × 100	134.00
	305.00
Direct labour:	
Department 1: 40 hours × £4.00/hour	160.00
Department 2: 15 hours × £4.50/hour	67.50
	227.50
Production overhead:	
Department 1: Variable, 40% × £160.00	64.00
Fixed, 90% × £160.00	144.00
Department 2: Variable, £0.9 per dlh × 15 hours	13.50
Fixed, £2.05 per dlh × 15 hours	30.75
	252.25
Other overhead:	
Variable: £0.70 per unit × 100	70.00
Fixed: £1.95 per unit × 100	195.00
	265.00
	1,049.75

∴ Cost per unit = £10.4975, say £10.50

b. On a full cost basis the selling price of £9.95 shows a loss of 55p. per unit. However, the new product does provide a contribution and this must be considered:

		£ per unit
Selling Price		9.95
less Variable costs	£	
Direct materials	3.05	
Direct labour	2.275	
Variable production overhead	0.775	
Other variable overhead	0.70	6.80
= Contribution		£3.15

∴ Total contribution = 2.4 m units × £3.15 = £7.56 m

The new product will utilise about a third of the existing 40% underutilised capacity and will thus make a valuable contribution to fixed costs (assuming that existing fixed costs are not increased unduly by the new product) so it would seem to be worthwhile.

c. At a selling price of £9.45, contribution is £2.65 per unit and total contribution becomes 2.9m × £2.65= £7.685m. This means that contribution increases by only (7.685 m − 7.56 m) £125,000. This is at the expense of reducing the spare capacity and possibly increasing fixed costs and working capital requirements. Thus the small increase may not be considered worthwhile.

A20.9

Comparative Statements

a.

		North East £000	South Coast £000
Materials			
X	(note 1.)	19,440	-----
X	(note 2.)	27,360	-----
X	(note 3.)	60,000	-----
		106,800	
Y	(note 4.)	-----	49,600
Z	(note 5.)	-----	71,200
Labour	(note 6.)	86,000	110,000
Accommodation and travel for site management	(note 7.)	6,800	5,600
Site management	(note 8.)	-----	-----
		199,600	236,400
Plant rental received	(note 9.)	(6,000)	-----
Relevant operational costs		193,600	236,400
Penalty clause	(note 10.)	-----	28,000
		193,600	264,400
Contract price		288,000	352,000
Contract surplus		94,400	87,600

The benefit from undertaking the more advantageous of the two contracts, in the North East, is £94,400. This is £6,800 greater than that from the contract in the South Coast.

b. Note 1. If the stock quantity of X is used for the contract it will be necessary to buy the cheaper materials for use elsewhere ie, (£21,600 × 90%) = £19,400.

Note 2. The actual cost of £30,400 is a committed cost so the correct cost is the current cost ie, £30,400 × 0.9 = £27,360.

Note 3. Normal relevant cost =£60,000.

Note 4. As the material is in common use it would not be resold but would have to be replaced ∴ price is the current replacement price = £24,800 × 2) = £49,600.

Notes 5, 6 and 7. Normal incremental costs ∴ relevant.

Note 8. Site management is a fixed cost and therefore presumably would be the same whether contract undertaken or not. Therefore not relevant.

Note 9. If the N.E. contract is undertaken there will be a £6,000 inflow.

Note 10. If the South Coast contract is undertaken there will be a penalty because the firm will be obliged to withdraw from the N.E. contract.

Note that Notional Interest is not a cash flow item neither is Depreciation so they have been excluded. Head Office costs are fixed so are not incremental and are thus excluded.

A20.10

a.

	Ladies' wear £000	%	Mens' wear £000	%	General £000	%	Toys £000	%	Restaurant £000	%	Total £000	%
Sales	800	100	400	100	2,200	100	1,400	100	200	100	5,000	100
Cost of Sales	496		240		1,320		1,176		166		3,398	
Gross profit	304	38	160	40	880	40	224	16	34	17	1,602	32
Direct fixed costs												
Wages	96		47		155		59		26		383	
Expenses	38		13		35		20		10		116	
Sales and Advertising	10		5		30		75		=		120	
	144		65		220		154		36		619	
Gross profit less direct fixed costs	160	20	95	24	660	30	70	5	(2)	(1)	983	20
General Fixed costs												
Delivery costs									200			
Salaries									100			
Directors' fees									20			
Capacity costs									488			
Interest									20			
Discounts allowed									25			
Bad debts									15			
Office wages									70			
Miscellaneous									75		1,013	
Net loss											£(30)	(1)
Gross profit/1% Area (£)	15,200		10,660		44,000		6,400		3,400			
Gross profit– direct fixed costs/1% Area (3)	8,000		6,333		33,000		2,000		(200)			
(1) Opening stock	90		70		200		100		5			
Purchases	506		220		1,290		1,267		167			
	596		290		1,320		1,376		172			
Closing stock	100		50		170		200		6			
Cost of sales	496		240		1,320		1,176		166			

b. If the Toy Dept closed there would be a loss of contribution of £224,000 and a gain from the decrease in specific costs of £154,000 making a total profit reduction of £70,000.

c.

	Ladies' wear	Mens' wear
Gross profit (£000)	304	160
Revised sales (£000)	760	380
Revised gross profit(£000)	264	140
Revised gross profit ratio	0.347	0.368
Required sales (£000)	875.15	434.29
Sales increase (£000)	75.15	34.29
Percentage increase	9.4	8.6

d. The toy Dept should only be closed if the space could be used productively. Mere closure would just reduce profits.

The price reductions would be worthwhile for ladies' and men's wear if there were corresponding revenue increases of at least 9.4% and 8.6% respectively.

The General Dept seems to be the most profitable and efforts should be made to expand this if possible or to gain higher margins elsewhere.

Chapter 21 Solutions

Exercises

A21.1

C/S ratio is 60% variable costs are 40% of sales. Given the variable costs, the sales for any level can be found as follows:

$$\frac{\text{Variable Costs}}{0.4} = \text{Sales}$$

Consumer reaction	Adverse £	Average £	Good £	Excellent £
Sales (£'000s)	50	75	112.5	175
less Variable Costs	20	30	45	70
= Contribution	30	45	67.5	105
less Fixed Costs	36	36	36	36
Profit (Loss)	(6)	9	31.5	69

b. Break even point in sales value = $\frac{36,000}{.6}$ = £60,000

c. Level of sales for profit of £10,000 = $\frac{36,000 + 10,000}{.6}$ = £76.667

A21.2

Sales will be made in constant proportions

	Forecasted sales value £	Proportion	Variable costs £	Contribution £
Product D	10,000	0.17	5,000	5,000
E	32,500	0.54	20,000	12,500
F	17,500	0.29	10,000	7,500
	60,000	1.00	35,000	25,000

∴ Overall C/S ratio = $\frac{25,000}{60,000}$ = 41.67%

a. & b. See graph.

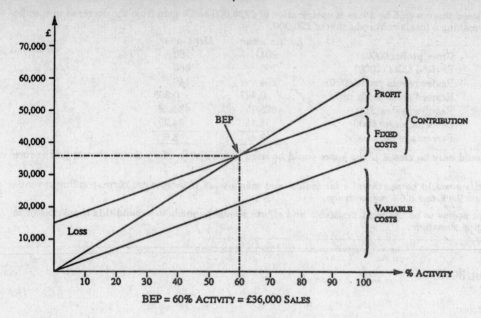

BEP = 60% ACTIVITY = £36,000 SALES

A21.3

	£
Variable Costs	
Labour	2,000
Material	12,000
Selling	200
	14,200

$$\therefore \text{Cost per unit} = \frac{14,200}{500} = £28.4$$

As the fixed costs remain the same the contributions of the three options can be considered directly.

    i.   Contribution $(63 - 28.4) \times 650 = £22,490$

    ii. Contribution $(80 - 28.4) \times 400 = £20,640$

    iii. Contribution $(70 - 28.4) \times 500 = £20,800$

    $\therefore$ Option 1 is preferable ie, reduce price to £63 and sell all output.

C/S ratios

    i. $= \dfrac{34.6}{63} = 55\%$

    ii. $= \dfrac{51.6}{80} = 64.5\%$

    iii. $= \dfrac{41.6}{70} = 59\%$

$$\text{Breakeven point (units)} = \frac{\text{Fixed costs}}{\text{Contribution/unit}}$$

Option

    i. $= \dfrac{4,800}{34.6} = 428$ units

    ii $= \dfrac{14,800}{51.6} = 287$ units

    III. $= \dfrac{14,800}{41.6} = 356$ units

A21.4

Multi-Product Profit Chart

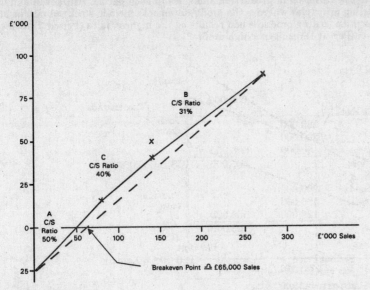

Breakeven Point ⟂ £65,000 Sales

Examination questions

A21.5

i.

Contribution = £15, Fixed costs = £240,000

$$\therefore \text{B.E.P.} = \frac{240,000}{15} = 16,000 \text{ pairs}$$

Margin of safety = 25,000 − 16,000 = 900 pairs

ii.

Sales of 20,000 pairs	£
Contribution = 20,000 × 15 =	300,000
less fixed cost	240,000
Profit	£60,000

iii.

After commission, the contribution is £13

$$\therefore \frac{240,000 + 10,000}{13} = 19,231 \text{ pairs}$$

iv.

Contribution = £44.8 − 25 = £19.8

$$\therefore \text{BEP} = \frac{260,000}{19.8} = 13,131 \text{ pairs}$$

A21.6

a.

$$\text{Breakeven point} = \frac{\text{Fixed Cost}}{\text{Contribution}} = \frac{180,000}{£4} = 45000 \text{ units.}$$

or £450000 sales.

b.

Profit/loss in each period.

At normal capacity $\text{FOAR} = \dfrac{£180,000}{60,000} = £3$ per unit.

∴ Total OAR = £3 + 1 = £4 per unit.

	Period 1		Period 2		Period 3	
	£		£		£	
Sales		500,000		600,000		400,000
Costs						
Labour and Materials	350,000		200,000		300,000	
Variable	68,000		45,000		60,000	
Fixed	180,000		180,000		180,000	
	598,000		425,000		540,000	
Stock adjustment			+180,000	605,000		
	−180,000	418,000			−180,000	360,000
= Profit/(loss)		£82,000		(5,000)		40,000

Profit reconciliation with breakeven point.

	Period 1	Period 2	Period 3
Breakeven profit	–	–	–
Actual contribution c.f. B/E	£20,000	60,000	(20,000)
Fixed overheads in stock	£60,000	(60,000)	60,000
Expenditure differences on variable overheads	20,000	(5,000)	–
Profits/(losses)	£82,000	(5,000)	40,000

c. Differences which arise are due to the variation in production and sales in each period. Breakeven and C/V/P analysis is based on marginal costing principles whereas the profit statements include stock valuations at full absorption cost. In this case absorption costing produces odd results eg the highest sales (Period 2) result in a loss and sales just above breakeven (Period 1) result in a high profit.

A21.7

Profit Statement recast into marginal form.

		£	
Sales		1,000,000	
less variable costs			
Materials	350,000		
Wages	200,000		
Overheads	50,000	600,000	
= Contribution		400,000	(CS ratio 40%)
less fixed costs			
Prod. overheads	200,000		
*Administration	180,000		
*S & D	120,000	500,000	
= Loss		(100,000)	

	Per unit
Selling Price	£20
less variable costs	12
= Contribution	8

a. 10% Commission.

To pay this commission would reduce C/S ratio to 30%.

$$\therefore \text{ Sales at B.E.P.} = \frac{\text{Fixed Costs}}{\text{C/S ratio}} = \frac{£500,000}{0.3} = £1.66 \text{ m}$$

This represents a $66\frac{2}{3}\%$ increase in sales which is a large increase unlikely to occur.

b. Reduce selling price by 10% (to £18) and increase volume by 30%.

	£
Sales (50,000 × 130% × £18)	1,170,000
less Marginal cost	780,000
= Contribution	390,000
less Fixed Costs	500,000
= Loss	£110,000

This is a poorer result than last year so, assuming that the estimates are reliable, would not be recommended.

c. Increase wages to £5 hr, increase sales by 20% and advertising costs by £50,000.

		£
Sales (60,000 × £20)		1,200,000
Materials	420,000	
Wages	250,000	
Variable overhead	60,000	730,000
= Contribution		470,000
less Fixed Costs		550,000
= Loss		(80,000)

This series of possibilities results in a slightly smaller loss so, assuming the estimates are reliable is to be preferred to the status quo.

d. Increased advertising of £300,000 with an increased selling price of 20%, with a 10% profit margin. Assuming 10% profit, the C/S ratio must be 50%.

$$\therefore \text{ Sales required} = \frac{\text{Fixed costs + Profit target of 10\% sales}}{\text{C/S ratio}}$$

$$= \frac{500,000 + 300,000 + 10\% \text{ sales}}{50\%}$$

$$= 1,000,000 + 20\% \text{ sales}$$

$$\therefore 80\% \text{ sales} = 1,600,000 \quad \therefore \text{ sales} = £2\text{m}$$

	£	
Sales	2,000,000	(ie 83,333 @ £24 each)
less Variable costs	1,000,000	
= Contribution (50%)	1,000,000	
less Fixed Costs	800,000	
= Profit	200,000	ie 10% of sales

Although this shows a profit there seems little likelihood of increasing sales at the rate required.

A21.8

a. Cost Analysis

	Total £	Fixed £	Variable £
Material	280,000		280,000
Labour	300,000	125,000	175,000
Production overhead	150,000	45,000	105,000
S & D overhead	140,000	70,000	70,000
Admin. overhead	60,000	60,000	–
	930,000	300,000	630,000

$\therefore$ Variable cost per unit $= \dfrac{£630,000}{3,500} = £180$

b. Profit @ 3,500 units

	£
= Revenue	1,050,000
– Variable cost	630,000
= Contribution	420,000
– Fixed cost	300,000
= Profit	120,000

c.

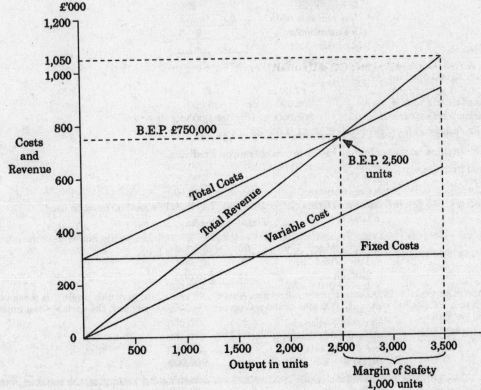

d. Can be taken from the text.

e. Order for additional 500 computers

	£
= selling price	225
– marginal cost	180
= contribution	45

$\therefore$ as all fixed costs are already absorbed this contribution is all profit.

ie, an addition of $500 \times £45 = £22,500$.

However there are many factors to be considered. For example, will this order cause other customers to demand a lower price?

A21.9

a. i.

Product	P £	E £
Unit contribution	5	2
Weighting	4	3
$\therefore$ Total contribution per group of 7	£20 +	£6 = £26

$$\therefore \text{BEP (groups of 7)} = \frac{£561,000}{26} = 21,600$$

$$\therefore \text{Sales BEP} = 21,000 \, (4 \times 10 + 3 \times £12) = £1,641,000$$

$$\therefore \text{Sales of P} = 21,000 \times 4 \times £10 = £864,000$$

$$\therefore \text{Sales of E} = 21,000 \times 3 \times £12 = £756,000$$

ii.   Change of mix to 4P, 4E

$$\therefore \text{Group of 8 contribution} = (4 \times £5) + (4 \times £2) = £28$$

$$\therefore \text{BEP} = \frac{£561,000}{28} = 20,036 \text{ groups.}$$

$$\therefore \text{BEP in sales} = 20,036 \times £88 = £1,763,168$$

iii.   Average contribution of 4P, 3E = £26 ÷ 7 = £3.71
Average contribution 4P, 4E = £28 ÷ 8 = £3.5
4P, 3E mix is better.

iv.   32,000 mc. hours available but BEP for 4P, 3E mix takes 41,040 hours and BEP for 4P, 4E mix takes 40,072 hours

∴ not possible to reach BEP with either of the groupings proposed. Better to concentrate on product which maximises contribution per machine hour:

	P £	E £
Contribution/unit	5	2
M/c hours/unit	0.4	0.1
Contribution/Mc hr.	12.5	20

Based on 32,000 machine hours.

	£		£
Total contribution =	400,000	*or*	640,000
– Fixed costs	561,000		561,000
= Profit(loss)	(161,000)		79,000

∴ where machine hours are limited better to concentrate on Product E.

b.   Can be taken from the text.

A21.10

a.   It is first necessary to derive fixed and variable elements of cost. The high/low method must be used.

	Units	Profit £
High - March 1993	30	250,000
Low - June 1993	16	40,000
Difference	14	210,000

Thus 14 units sales make £210,000 extra profit difference. Above BEP contribution equals profit this means that contribution/unit = £210,000 ÷ 14 = £15,000 and as the selling price is £30,000 per unit the variable cost must be also £15,000 per unit.

Using March 1993 data the monthly fixed costs can be derived.

	£
Sales (30 × £30,000)	900,000
less profit	250,000
= Total costs	650,000
less variable costs (30 × £15,000)	450,000
∴ Fixed costs	200,000

∴ 6 months fixed costs = 6 × £200,000 = £1,200,000

Six months statement (130 units)

	£'000
Sales	3,900
– Variable costs	1,950
= Contribution	1,950
– Fixed costs	1,200
= Profit	750

$$\therefore \text{BEP} = \frac{1,200,000}{15,000} = 80 \text{ units}$$

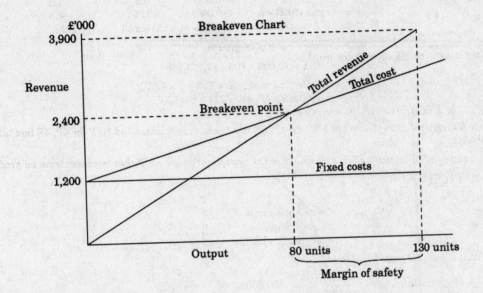

b. New contribution = £25,000 – 15,000 = £10,000

New sales = 130 + 10% =143

$$\therefore \text{Total contribution} = 143 \times £10,000 \quad = \quad \begin{array}{r} £ \\ 1,430,000 \end{array}$$

$$\begin{array}{rr}
- \text{Fixed costs} \quad - & \underline{1,200,000} \\
= \text{Profit} & \underline{\underline{230,000}}
\end{array}$$

Profits reduce by (750,000 – 230,000) £520,000 so option not worthwhile.

c. Cost behaviour, assumptions and so on can be taken from the text.

A21.11

a. i. BUDGETED PROFIT

	Product I £000	Product II £000	Product III £000	Total £000
Sales	2,475	3,948	1,520	7,943
Contribution	1,170	1,692	532	3,394
Attributable fixed costs	(275)	(337)	(296)	(908)
General fixed costs	(520)	(829)	(319)	(1,668)
	(795)	(1,166)	(615)	(2,576)
Profit	375	526	(83)	818
	= £1.6/unit	= £1.40/unit	= (£0.04/unit)	

ii. Product III discontinued.

Assumptions: Attributable fixed costs for Product III are saved but General Fixed costs continue unchanged.

New position	£'000
Contribution for I and II	2,862
less Attributable fixed costs	612
less General fixed costs	1,668
= Profit	582

Thus profit would be reduced from £818,000 to £582,000.

iii. Minimum extra sales of Product I (assuming all other costs relationships hold)

$$\frac{\text{Extra Expenditure}}{\text{Contribution per unit}} = \frac{£80,000}{£5.2} = 15,385 \text{ units}$$

iv. Effect of 10% reduction in sales price, Product II

= New selling price – Variable cost = New contribution = £9.45 – 6 = £3.45 per unit.

$$\frac{\text{Existing total contribution}}{\text{New contribution per unit}} = \frac{1,692,000}{3.4} = 490,435 \text{ units}$$

This is a 30.4% increase over the existing budget of 376,000 units.

b. This can be taken from the text.

A21.12

a.

Product	Unit Contribution	Total Contribution	C/S Ratio	Ranking
J	6	60,000	0.3	= 2nd
K	32	320,000	0.8	1st
L	(0.2)	(10,000)	(0.05)	4th
M	3	60,000	0.3	= 2nd
Total Contribution		£430,000		

b. *Multi-product contribution: Sales graph*

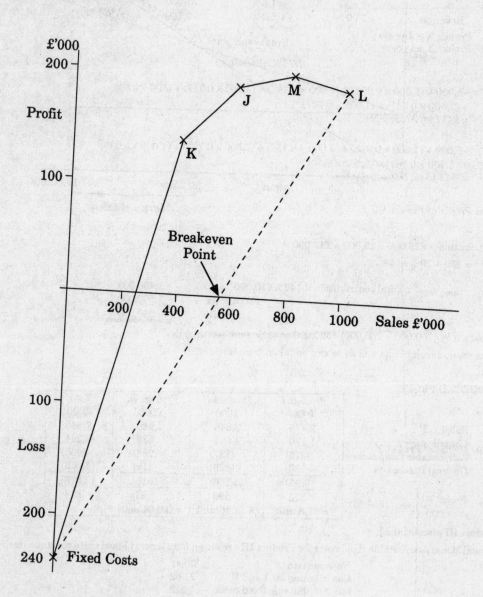

c. The BEP can be calculated thus:

$$\frac{\text{Fixed costs} \times \text{Sales Value}}{\text{Contribution}} = \frac{240 \times 1,000}{430} \text{ (£'000s)} = \underline{£558.140}$$

Note that Product L should be discontinued because it produces a negative contribution. If it was eliminated, contribution and profit would increase by £10,000.

d. Ways that overall C/S ratio could be improved.

 i. Eliminate L and concentrate on K with the highest C/S ratio, if possible.

 ii. Increase selling prices, if possible.

 iii. Reduce variable costs by greater efficiency, more mechanisation or better purchasing.

Chapter 22 Solutions

Exercises

A22.1

	Project X		Project Y	
	Cash Flow	Cumulative	Cash Flow	Cumulative
Year 0	–5,000	–5,000	–8,000	–8,000
1	+2,500	–2,500	+1,500	–6,500
2	+1,000	–1,500	+2,000	–4,500
3	+1,000	–500	+2,500	–2,000
4	+500		+1,000	–1,000
5	+1,500	+1,500	+1,000	–
6	+1,000	+1,000	+2,500	+2,500

Pay Back: Project X = 4 years
Project Y = 5 years

NPV Calculations

Project X

$$\text{NPV} = -5{,}000 + (2{,}500 \times 0.893) + (1{,}000 \times 0.797) + (1{,}000 \times 0.712) + (500 \times 0.636)$$
$$+ (1{,}500 \times 0.567) + (1{,}000 \times 0.507)$$
$$= £417 \text{ ie, Acceptable.}$$

Project Y

$$\text{NPV} = -8{,}000 + (1{,}500 \times 0.893) + (2{,}000 \times 0.797) + (2{,}500 \times 0.712) + (1{,}000 \times 0.636)$$
$$+ (1{,}000 \times 0.567) + (2{,}500 \times 0.507)$$
$$= -£816 \text{ ie, Not acceptable.}$$

A22.2

Present Value Profile of Project X

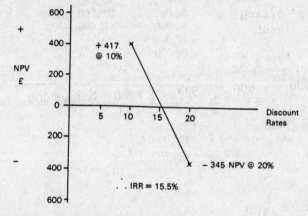

Present Value Profile of Project Y

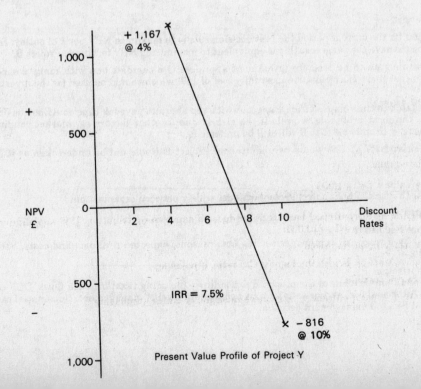

Present Value Profile of Project Y

A22.3

Present value of existing commission

$$= (4000 \times .909) + (2000 \times .826) + (8000 \times .751) + (3000 \times .683) + (10,000 \times .621)$$
$$= £19,555$$

Annuity factor for 5 years @ 10% = 3.791

$$\therefore \text{Regular amount} = \frac{19,555}{3.791} = £5,158$$

(ie, £5,158 received annually for 5 years at 10% discount has a present value of £19,555).

Examination questions

A22.4

Depreciation Charge is $\dfrac{80,000 - 8,000}{5} = 14,400$ p.a.

$\therefore$ Cash flows are:

Year	Profit & depreciation	Cumulative cash flow
1	£49,400	£49,400
2	44,400	93,800
3	39,400	133,200

$\therefore$ assuming even cash flows the payback is $1 + \dfrac{80,000 - 49,400}{44,400} = 1.7$ years

Assuming year end cash flows the payback is 2 years.

A22.5

a. i., ii. & iii.   Can be taken from the text.

b. i.

	Project Cash Flows	Cumulative
Year 1	40,000 × £2 = £80,000	80,000
2	80,000	160,000
3	80,000	240,000
4	80,000	
5	80,000	

$$\therefore \text{Payback} = 2\,\frac{40,000}{80,000} \text{ years} = 2.5 \text{ years}$$

Note: The above assume that cash flows occur evenly throughout the year. Depreciation and fixed overheads are excluded.

ii. $\text{NPV} = 80,000 \times A\,\overline{_{5}}|_{20\%} = 80,000 \times 2.991 =$

	£239,280
less investment =	200,000
$\therefore$ NPV =	£39,280

With 10% increase in revenue

NPV = 88,000 × 2.991 – 200,000 = £63,208

$$\text{Percentage increase} = \frac{63,208 - 39,280}{39,280} = 61\%$$

A22.6

a. Can be taken from the text.

b. Where funds are limited for the current period the best decision rule is to maximise NPV per £ of outlay. In this example as all the projects have the same cost this is equivalent to maximising NPV ie, choose Project B.

c, The choice of the discount rate to be used for investment appraisal is a complex one with many competing theories. In this simple case there is a clear cut opportunity cost of 12% which should be used for the investment appraisal.

d. If the risk is purely related to time elapsed then Project A with the shortest payback time could be considered even though it is not the most profitable project. If the risk is due to other factors eg, market conditions, consumer preferences etc. it is probable that B will still be preferred.

e. All projects with a positive NPV at 12% would be undertaken. Project D would not be undertaken as it has a negative NPV.

A22.7

a. Capital Expenditure Authorisation and control procedures vary widely between organisations.

Typical of the procedures are:

❑ Capital Expenditure Request
Usually submitted by a responsible manager setting out; reasons, expected revenues and costs, benefits hoped for and so on.

❑ Analysis and Authorisation
Detailed analysis of all implications of the proposed expenditure including taxation, cash flows, DCF calculations and so on. After analysis, authorisation by an appropriate level of management. Substantial capital expenditures would be a top management decision.

❏ Control
Actual expenditure will be compared to budget, project timing will be monitored.

❏ Post-Audit
(Usually after project has been running for some time.) Full review of project analysis, revenue and cost expectations, risks etc.

b. Depreciation p.a. $(200,000 – 40,000) \div 4 = £40,000$ to be added to profits to obtain cash flows:

Payback

	Project X	Project Y
Cash flows	120,000	70,000
	120,000	90,000
	80,000	130,000
	60,000	160,000

Capital cost £200,000

Payback $\quad X = 1 + \dfrac{80,000}{120,000} = 1.67$ years

$\qquad\qquad Y = 2 + \dfrac{40,000}{130,000} = 2.31$ years

Accounting Rate of Return (NB Based on profits not cash flows)

	Project X	Project Y
Total profits over the 4 years	£220,000	£290,000
	÷ 4	÷ 4
= Average profit p.a.	= £55,000	=£72,500

Average investment = $(200,000 – 40,000) \div 2 = £80,000$

∴ Accounting Rate of Return $\quad \dfrac{£55,000}{80,000} = 69\% \quad \dfrac{£72,500}{80,000} = 91\%$

iii. D.C.F. (uses cash flows)

$X = \ -200,000 + (0.862 \times 120,000) + (0.743 \times 120,000) + (0.641 \times 80,000)$
$\qquad + (0.552 \times 100,000)$
$\qquad = £99,080$

$Y = \ -200,000 + (0.862 \times 70,000) + (0.743 \times 90,000) + (0.641 \times 130,000)$
$\qquad + (0.552 \times 200,000)$
$\qquad = £120,940$

c. Normally the Project with the higher NPV should be chosen unless there is some other reason. Thus Y should be chosen.

d. i. Cost of capital can be taken from the text.

   ii. Two ways of considering risk.
   ❏ Use of expected values based on multiple output estimates and probabilities.
   ❏ Consideration of payback periods.

Chapter 23 Solutions

Exercises

A23.1

Budgeted Profit Statement for 19-1

	Starfrig		Starfreezer		Total
Sales (units)	40,000		80,000		
	£	£	£	£	£
Sales Revenue		3,000,000		7,200,000	
less Variable Costs					
Materials	800,000		1,600,000		
Labour	840,000		3,360,000		
Overheads	420,000	2,060,000	1,680,000	6,640,000	
= Contribution		940,000		560,000	1,500,000
less Fixed Costs					800,000
= Profit					£700,000

Budgeted Profit Statement for 19-2

	Starfrig			Starfrig II			Starfreezer		Total
Sales (units)	32,000			15,000			80,000		
		£	£		£	£		£	£
Sales Revenue	2,400,000			1,725,000			7,200,000		
less Variable costs									
Materials	640,000			375,000			1,600,000		
Labour	672,000			690,000			3,360,000		
Overheads	336,000	1,648,000		345,000	1,410,000		1,680,000	6,640,000	
= Contribution		752,000			315,000			560,000	1,627,000
							less Fixed costs		1,000,000
							= Profit		£627,000

A23.2

Budget for 6,200 units

Expense	Budget for 6,200 units £	Derived Cost Function
Wages	17,440	£10,000 + £1.20 unit
Materials	31,000	£5 per unit
Salaries	23,100	£20,000 + 0.50 per unit
Depreciation	18,000	Fixed
Other overheads	21,500	£6,000 + £2.50 per unit

A23.3

Cash Budget

	March	April	May
Opening Balance	27,000	29,000	38,340
+ Receipts from debtors*	77,700	81,840	90,100
+ Cash sales	20,000	22,000	25,000
= Total Cash Available	124,700	132,840	153,440
– Salaries	9,500	9,500	10,000
– Fixed overheads	25,000	25,000	27,000
– Purchases	61,200	60,000	69,000
Total disbursements	95,700	94,500	106,000
Balance c/f	29,000	38,340	47,440

The receipts from debtors are calculated as follows:

March	£	April	£	May	£
40% March	32,000	40% April	36,000	40% May	40,000
45% Feb	36,900	45% March	36,000	45% April	40,500
12% Jan	8,800	12% Feb	9,840	12% March	9,600
	£77,700		£81,840		£90,100

A23.4

There are many similarities between the preparation of conventional budgets and activity based budgets. These include; consideration of organisational objectives and long term plans; the need for co-ordination, the need to consider resources and possible limiting factors.

There are however some important differences which include:

Clarification of responsibilities:
Conventional budgets are usually developed around existing Departmental Structures with their managers being responsible for budgets. Budgets based on Activities are likely to cross conventional departmental barriers thus causing potential responsibility problems.

Difficulties of cost attribution:
Especially in the development stages of activity budgeting there may be difficulties in attributing costs to activities perhaps because the cost analysis/coding systems are more suited to gathering costs by department rather than activity.

Demand control and cost control separated.
The person designated as responsible for the cost control of an activity is not likely to be the same person who has control over the demand for the activity. This is a form of split responsibility which can cause friction.

Examination questions

A23.5

Cash Budget

	Jan	Feb	Mar
Opening Balance	(9,000)	21,000	45,400
+ Receipts	140,200	183,600	270,400
Cash Available	131,200	204,600	315,800
Payments			
Creditors	90,000	135,000	252,000
Expenses	19,200	24,200	29,200
Interest			1,500
Dividend	1,000		
Total Payments	110,200	159,200	282,700
Closing balance c/f	21,000	45,400	33,100

Workings:

Cash Receipts

Dec. Sales	25,000		
Jan. Sales	115,200	30,000	
Feb. Sales		153,600	40,000
Mar. Sales			230,400
	140,200	183,600	270,400

Payments to Creditors

Purchases	100,000	150,000	280,000
Discount	10,000	15,000	28,000
	90,000	135,000	252,000
Expenses	20,000	25,000	30,000
less Depn.	800	800	800
= Cash Flow	19,200	24,200	29,200

Discounts

			£
Jan	$150,000 \times 0.8 \times 0.04$	=	4,800
Feb	$200,000 \times 0.8 \times 0.04$	=	6,400
Mar	$300,000 \times 0.8 \times 0.04$	=	9,600
			20,800

Budgeted P + L A/c for period

	£	£
Sales		650,000
less Cost of sales		530,000
= Gross Profit		120,000
less Expenses		
General expenses	72,600	
Depreciation	2,400	
Discount Allowed	20,800	
Discount Received	(53,000)	
Loan Interest	1,500	44,300
	= Net Profit	75,700

Balance Sheet at end of period

	£	Fixed Assets		£
Share capital	40,000	Machinery at cost		80,000
P + L (20,000 + 75,700)	95,700	– Depreciation		21,600
	135,700			58,400
		Current Assets		
Loan	40,000	Stocks	24,200	
		Debtors	60,000	
		Cash	33,100	117,300
	£175,700			£175,700

iv. Differences between the change in cash of £42,100 and profit of £75,700 is due to some items being included in profit calculations but not cash, eg, depreciation and the different timing treatment of sales and cash from sales.

A23.6

a. Budgeted Labour Hours.

Product M	Qtr 1		Qtr 2		Qtr 3		Qtr 4	
Budgeted sales (units)	9,000		20,000		14,000		8,000	
Stock adjustment	+ 2,000		–		– 1,000		–	
Budgeted net production	11,000		20,000		13,000		8,000	
+ Scrap allowance $\frac{10}{8}$								
= Gross Production	13,750		25,000		16,250		10,000	
@ 5 std hours/unit =	68,750	hrs	125,000	hrs	81,250	hrs	50,000	hrs
Product N								
Budgeted sales (units)	10,000		16,500		11,000		7,000	
Stock adjustment	+ 3,000		–		– 2,000		–	
Production	13,000		16,500		9,000		7,000	
@ 3 std hours/unit	39,000	hrs	49,500	hrs	27,000	hrs	21,000	hrs
Total Std Hours (both products)	107,750		174,500		108,250		71,000	
+ efficiency allowance $\frac{10}{9}$	119,722		193,889		120,278		78,889	
Hours available (210 × 40 × 12) Normal	100,800		100,800		100,800		100,800	
With overtime	131,040		131,045		131,040		131,040	
Surplus (shortage)	Within Band		(62,849)		Within Band		21,911	

b. i. Examination of the figures shows a large shortage of labour hours in Quarter 2 and a surplus in Quarter 4.

Various possibilities could be examined.

   a. Rescheduling of production eg increasing production in Ql up to maximum possible ie 11318 hrs and carry forward larger stocks.
   b. Altering projected stock levels eg increase Ql – Q2 stocks and reduce Q2—Q3 stocks.
   c. If possible improve efficiency ratios of operatives and scrap rates. Maximum available hours available from these sources = (119,722 – 107,750) + (193,889 – 174,500) = 31,361 hours plus (68,750 + 125,000) × 20,000 = 38,750 = 70,111 hours total
   d. The surplus hours in Q4 (21911) are approximately equivalent to the overtime hours worked in Q3 ie (120278 – 100800) = 19478.

Approximately halving the Q3 closing stocks would smooth the production between the two quarters so that only basic time need be worked.

   ii. If budgeted sales are restricted because of the shortage of labour hours profit maximisation can be achieved by concentrating production on the product which achieves the greatest contribution per labour hour. The usual caveats would apply ie sales of other product not affected, only one binding constraint and so on.

A23.7

This can be answered largely from the text.

Particular points to note include; uncertainties, government actions and legislation, competitors actions, new products and technologies, inflation and numerous other such factors make any form of forecasting a problem.

Any forecasting technique may have a place in budgeting. Typical examples include:

❑ High/low methods and scattergraphs
Short run forecasting in stable conditions.

❑ Regression analysis using least squares
Short run forecasting.

❑ Time series analysis
Short/medium term forecasting.

❑ Moving average/exponential smoothing
Form of continuous or rolling forecasting.

Delphi method

Qualitative forecasting method where data are unavailable. Longer term forecasting system.

A23.8

a. Zero base budgeting is in principle a simple concept. Each type of overhead expenditure starts at zero and each item of expense is examined and has to be justified. There can be advantages in minutely examining each overhead category, perhaps on a rolling programme, and savings in public expenditure have been reported by using this principle. Obviously such an approach can be time consuming and cause friction so it must be used with caution.

b. Traditional budgetary control suffers from inertia and there is often concealed budgetary slack. All too often this year's budget is last year's plus an allowance for inflation which has the effect of making previous mistakes and inefficiencies a permanent feature.

A23.9

a. Examination of the figures shows that administration overheads are fixed but all other items are variable or semi-variable with regular differences for each 10% capacity change, ie

		Fixed Element
Materials	£6,300 Change	–
Wages	2,700 Change	–
Prod. overhead	3,600 Change	£16,000
Selling	1,800 Change	£31,500

as 70% = 6,300 units, each 10% change represents 900 units, thus the 50% activity level represents 4,500 units.

∴ Costs for 50% activity:

	£
Materials	31,500
Wages	13,500
Prod. Overhead	34,000
Selling	40,500
Admin.	31,500
Total Cost	151,000
20% profit on sales	
= 25% on cost	37,750
= Sales	188,750

Budget for 50% level of activity.

	£	£
Sales		188,750
Variable costs	£	
Materials	31,500	
Wages	13,500	
Var. Prod. ohd.	18,000	
Var. Selling ohd.	9,000	72,000
	Contribution	116,750
less		
Fixed costs		
Production ohd	16,000	
Admin.	31,500	
selling	31,500	79,000
	= Profit	£37,750

b. Problems arising from working at 50% capacity.
 i.   Possible redundancies and consequent labour/union problems.
 ii. Almost certain losses.
 iii. Under-utilised capacity.
 iv. Lack of cash flow.

A23.10

a. Can be taken from the text. Key points; planning, control, co-ordination and motivation.

b. Production = Sales, except Product 5 where production =

Sales	900,000 units
Plus stock increase	30,000 units (30% × 100,000)
	930,000 units

New standards for Material B (kilos per hundred units) are:

Product	1	2.7	(3.0 × 90%)
	2	0.45	(0.5 × 90%)
	4	1.8	(2.0 × 90%)

Material usage budget (kilos):

		Product				
	1	*2*	*3*	*4*	*5*	*Total*
Material A:						
kilos per hundred units	2.5	7.0	1.5	-	5.5	
× production (hundred units)	6,000	3,500	18,500	-	9,300	
= usage (kilos)	15,000	24,500	27,750	-	51,150	118,400
Material B:						
kilos per hundred units	2.7	0.45	-	1.8	-	
× production (hundred units)	6,000	3,500	-	12,000	-	
= usage (kilos)	16,200	1,575	-	21,600	-	39,375

Material purchases budget (kilos):

	Material A	*Material B*
Budgeted usage (kilos)	118,400	39,375
plus/minus change in stock	1,810	(322.5)
	120,210	39,052.5

c. Workings:

Material A usage =

Production (hundred units) × standard usage per hundred units:

Product			
1	5,800 × 2.5 =	14,500	
2	3,300 × 7.0 =	23,100	
3	19,000 × 1.5 =	28,500	
5	8,000 × 5.5 =	44,000	
		110,100	× £2.40 = £264,240

Material A price variance:

Actual cost	£280,160
Standard cost (116,250 × 2.40)	£279,000
	£1,160A

Journal entries:

		Dr £	Cr £
1.	Material A stock	280,160	
	Purchase ledger		280,160
	Purchases of Material A		
2.	Raw material price variance	1,160	
	Material A stock		1,160
	Price variance on purchases of Material A		
3.	Work in progress	264,240	
	Material A stock		264,240

Issues of Material A to production.

A23.11

a.

	A		B		C	Total
Sales mix	1	:	2	:	4	
Required annual profit						£6.5m
Required period 1 profit						£0.5m
	£		£		£	
Unit selling price	215		250		300	
Unit costs:						
Frame	20		20		20	
Component D	40		8		24	
E	5		35		25	
F	12		15		3	
	57		58		52	
Labour						
Skilled	12		9		9	
Unskilled	9		9		13.5	
	21		18		22.5	
Variable production overhead	5		4		3.5	
Contribution	112		150		202	
Weighted by Sales mix	×1		×2		×4	
	=112		= 300		= 808	1,220

Required period 1 contribution:	£m
Profit	0.500
Add fixed costs:	
Production	0.056
Selling and Distribution	0.028
Administration	0.026
	0.610

$$\therefore 500 \frac{£610,000}{£1,220} \text{ 'mixes' must be sold each period.}$$

		A	B	C	
i.	Sales quantities	500	1,000	2,000	
	Sales value	£107,500	£250,000	£600,000	
ii.	Sales quantities	500	1,000	2,000	
	Closing stock	270	630	1,440	
		770	1,630	3,440	
	Opening stock	300	700	1,600	
	Production	470	930	1,840	
iii.	Usage				Total Units
	Frame	470	930	1,840	3,240
	D	2,350	930	5,520	8,800
	E	470	6,510	9,200	16,180
	F	1,880	4,650	1,840	8,370

iv.	Purchases (units)	Frame	D	E	F
	Closing stock	900	3,600	9,000	3,600
	Add: used in production	3,240	8,800	16,180	8,370
		4,140	12,400	25,180	11,970
	Less opening stock	1,000	4,000	10,000	4,000
	Purchases (units)	3,140	8,400	15,180	7,970
	Cost	62,800	67,200	75,900	23,910

v. Manpower budgets

	Machining Hours	Assembly Hours
A (units produced × hour/unit)	940	940
B	1,395	1,860
C	2,760	5,520
	5,095	8,320
Divide by 4 × 37½ = 150 hours	34 people	56 people

b. Reducing stocks to 1 weeks requirements is moving towards JIT purchasing rather than traditional mass ordering. Some of the major implications are:

i.   Reduction in storage space required and of working capital needed
ii. Need to ensure that incoming quality is high
iii. Need to liaise more closely with suppliers over deliveries
iv. Need for production to be flexible and for there to be contingency plans.
v.   Need to ensure that goods inward and purchasing can cope with many smaller deliveries.

A23.12

i.

Revenue Budget (Value)

	Alpha £	Beta £	Gamma £	Total £
Northern Region	180,000	550,000	360,000	1,090,000
Southern Region	300,000	770,000	540,000	1,610,000
Total	480,000	1,320,000	900,000	2,700,000

ii.

Production Budget In Units

	Alpha	Beta	Gamma	Total
Opening Stock	1,000	1,200	1,500	3,700
Closing Stock	1,200	1,000	1,800	4,000
Increase (Decrease) In stock	200	(200)	300	300
Sales	8,000	12,000	10,000	30,000
Production	8,200	11,800	10,300	30,300

iii.

Material Purchase Budget (Value)

	X units	Y units	Total £
Opening stock	5,000	7,500	
Closing stock	8,000	10,000	
Stock increase	3,000	2,500	
Plus usage			
Alpha 8,200 × 2	16,400	× 3 24,600	
Beta 11,800 × 3	35,400	× 4 47,200	
Gamma 10,300 × 2.5	25,750	× 1.5 38,625	
Required Purchases	80,550	89,750	
	× £3	× £2	
Cost	= £241,650	= £179,500	421,150

iv.

Labour Cost Budget

	Alpha units	Beta units	Gamma units
Production (from ii above)	8,200	11,800	10,300

		Department 1 Labour hours		Department 2 Labour hours	
Alpha	8,200	× 0.75 =	6,150	× 1.5 =	12,300
Beta	11,800	× 1.25 =	14,750	× 2.0 =	23,600
Gamma	10,300	× 2.0 =	20,600	× 2.5 =	25,750
Budget Labour hours			41,500		61,650
× Labour rate			× £4		× £3
Labour cost			= £166,000		= £184,950

Total £350,950

v.

Overhead Absorption Rates

		Department 1		Department 2	
		Labour hours		*Machine hours*	
Alpha	8200 × 0.75 =	6,150	8,200×2 =	16,400	
Beta	11,800 × 1.25 =	14,750	11,800×2 =	23,600	
Gamma	10,300 × 2 =	20,600	10,300×3 =	30,900	
	Total	41,500	Lab hrs	70,900	Machine hrs
		£415,000	Overheads	£567,200	Overheads

$$\text{OAR} = \frac{£415,000}{41,500} = £10 \text{ per labour hour} \qquad \frac{£567,200}{70,900} = £8 \text{ per labour hour}$$

vi.

Standard Product Costs and Standard Profits per Unit

		Alpha £	Beta £	Gamma £
Material	X	6	9	7.5
	Y	6	8	3
Labour Dept	1	3	5	8
	2	4.5	6	7.5
Prime Cost		19.5	28	26
Production overhead				
Dept 1 (on Lab hrs)		7.5	12.5	20
Dept 2 (on mc. hrs.)		16	16	24
Production Cost		43	56.5	70
Admin Ohds.*		7.5	11	15.5
= Total Cost		50.5	67.5	85.5
Profit		9.5	42.5	4.5
Selling Price		60	110	90

$$* \text{ Admin overhead rate} = \frac{\text{Admin OHD}}{\text{Labour cost}} = \frac{£350,950}{£350,950} = £1 \text{ ohd per £1 labour.}$$

A23.13

a. Procedures to aid expenditure control include
   - ❏ Having budgets or estimates for each stage or each period for each project
   - ❏ Regular reporting of budget: actual costs and analysis of differences
   - ❏ Regular reporting of project degree of completion c. f. estimated dates
   - ❏ Requiring different levels of expenditure to receive the necessary authorisation
   - ❏ Clear lines of responsibility for each project and each type of cost
   - ❏ Involving Project Leaders and Project teams in budget setting

   and so on.

b.

Project control report for quarter ending....								
Project No.	1		2		....		Total	
Department	Budget £	Actual £	Budget £	Actual £	Budget £	Actual £	Budget £	Actual £
Chemistry								
Physics								
Biology								
Experimental								
Administration								
B/F from Last Quarter								
Total to date C/F								
Budgeted Total Cost								
Forecast costs to complete								
Forecast Total Cost								
Actual % Complete								
Budget % Complete								
Forecast Completion Date								
Budgeted Completion Date								

A23.14

a. i.

Freewheel Ltd.
Cash Budget July– December 1992

	July £	Aug £	Sept £	Oct £	Nov £	Dec £
Opening Balance	3,000	1,500	(1,600)	15,300	14,100	8,200
Receipts						
Sales						
Cash	13,500	13,800	14,400	20,000	15,200	12,000
Credit	12,000	12,600	13,500	13,800	14,400	20,000
Share Issue			20,000			
Cash Available	28,500	27,900	46,300	49,100	43,700	40,200
Expenses						
Purchases	12,000	13,000	14,000	18,000	16,000	14,000
Wages & Salaries 1)	6,000	7,500	7,500	7,500	9,000	9,000
2)	2,000	2,000	2,500	2,500	2,500	3,000
Overheads	7,000	7,000	7,000	7,000	8,000	8,000
Instalment						10,000
Cash payments	27,000	29,500	31,000	35,000	35,500	44,000
Closing Balance	1,500	(1,600)	15,300	14,100	8,200	(3,800)

ii.

Freewheel Ltd.

Budgeted Profit and Loss Account
6 months July – December 1992

		£	£
Sales	13,900 × £6	83,400	
	11,800 × £8	94,400	
			177,800
Less	Cost of sales		
	Opening stock	25,000	
+	Purchases	86,000	
–	Closing Stock	38,000	
			73,000
Gross Profit			104,800
Less expenses			
Wages & Salaries		62,000	
Overheads		45,000	
Depreciation		8,500	
			(115,500)
Net loss			(10,700)
Profit & Loss Account balance b/f			44,600
Profits available for appropriation			33,900
Less dividends			10,000
Balance c/f			23,900

Budgeted Balance Sheet
As at 31 December 1992

	Cost £	Deprec Prov. £	N.B.V £
Fixed assets	170,000	22,500	147,500
Current Assets			
Stock	38,000		
Trade Debtors	27,200		
Bank		65,200	
Creditors: Amounts falling within one year:			
Trade creditors	24,000		
Other creditors	41,000		
Bank overdraft	3,800		
		(68,800)	
Net Current Assets			(3,600)
	Net Assets		143,900
Represented by:			
Shares			120,000
Profit and Loss Account			23,900
			143,900

b. ❑ The cash Budget shows two small deficiencies (July and August). Arrangements with the bank will have to be made or activities curtailed

❏ There is a budgeted net loss of £10,700.
   Can sales be increased and/or costs reduced to avoid this?

❏ Sales in November and December are decreasing yet stocks have increased. Is this necessary or is it evidence of lack of control?

A23.15

a. Numerous improvements could be made to the budget including-

❏ the budget shown is simply $\frac{9}{12}$ of the annual budget. It is better to derive budgets which recognise the month by month variations which occur

❏ the budget should show

   Budget for month   Actual for Month   Variance (ADV or FAV)
   and similar headings for year to date.

❏ the expenditure should be analysed in more detail eg, various types of staff and salaries, wages by category, various types of provisions instead of totals.

❏ there should be details of activity and staff levels

❏ the variances should be identified as adverse or favourable and reasons given.

b. Possible reasons for variances

Gain variance of £2045 for salaries

❏ incorrect budget
❏ less activity than planned
❏ inflation less than budgeted
❏ staff vacancies
❏ different and cheaper mix of staff than budgeted
❏ greater efficiency in staff use

Adverse variance of £4,723 for provisions:

❏ incorrect budget
❏ increase in prices
❏ greater usage than budgeted
❏ inefficiencies in use
❏ pilfering
❏ lack of control

c. Virement is the transfer of an underspent amount on one budget heading to another budget heading.

A supplementary estimate is an approved increase in a budget heading during the year.

Control of virement is carried out by having limits laid down which have to be authorised by appropriate levels of management. A small virement say under £1,000 may only require the agreement of both budget holders. Above this limit more senior officials may have to give approval. There will naturally have to be all the necessary changes in budget levels expenditure codes etc, to take account of the virement.

A supplementary estimate has normally to be approved at a senior level as it sometimes means using contingency funds. There would be careful scrutiny of the reasons for a request for supplementary funds.

d. Activity fell from 15,000 budgeted to 12,000 actual , a drop of 20% yet costs have fallen by only 10%. As the breakdown into fixed and variable elements its not known it is not possible to say whether this was reasonable.

If all the costs were variable the cost for 12,000 X-rays should be £16,000 but it is not likely that all costs are variable. This illustrates the need to have a proper cost analysis in order to be able to flex budgets correctly.

Chapter 24 Solutions

Exercises

A24.1

The typical build up of a standard cost involves detailed engineering analysis of materials, methods, tools etc. and work study investigations of layouts, work flows and methods.

These procedures are detailed and have the appearance of total objectivity but examination shows that there are subjective factors involved.

For example, the precise amount of material contained in a product is an objective fact but the standard cost will include an additional amount for 'normal' waste. This amount must involve judgement. Also the labour method and type of labour can be objectively determined but the rate at which labour is deemed to work is a subjective assessment. The pricing factors (eg, labour rate, material price) also contain subjective factors as they relate to prices expected over the future period.

In short all standards involve some subjective elements and an awareness of this will avoid taking too pedantic a view of variances.

A24.2

Standard Cost card For One Unit

		£	£
Direct Materials			
	20 Kgs A @ £0.80	16.00	
	15 Kgs B @ £2.40	36.00	52.00
Direct Labour			
Preparation	14 hrs @ £3.75	52.50	
Assembly	5 hrs @ £2.50	12.50	65.00
= Prime Cost			117.00
Variable Overheads			
Preparation	14 hrs @ £3	42.00	
Assembly	5 hrs @ £4.25	21.25	63.25
= Variable Production Cost			180.25
Fixed Overheads			
Preparation	14 hrs @ £1.19	16.67	
Assembly	5 hrs @ £2	10.00	26.67
= Total Production Cost			£206.92

A24.3

Whilst it is true that most applications of standard costing are in factories the technique can be more widely applied. It could be used in offices, transport undertakings, computer departments, local authorities, indeed anywhere where suitable conditions exist. These include:

a. Some form of repetitive process or operation which is regularly carried out.
b. Where the process has been analysed in sufficient detail for methods and times to be established with reasonable accuracy.
c. Where it would be cost effective to monitor and control costs using a reasonably sophisticated technique such as standard costing.

Examination questions

A24.4

a. i. Production Budget (units)

	A	B	C
Sales	12,000	15,000	10,000
+ Stock increase	180	200	160
Net production	12,180	15,200	10,160
+ Inspection loss		800	
Gross Production	12,180	16,000	10,160

ii. Material Usage (units)

Material Requirements	V	W	X	Y	Z
Product A (12180)	60,900	36,540	–	–	12,180
Product B (16000)	64,000	32,000	48,000	16,000	16,000
Product C (10160)	–	60,960	50,800	40,640	–
	124,900	129,500	98,800	56,640	28,180
+ loss*					7,045
Usage	124,900	129,500	98,800	56,640	35,225

*28,180 ÷ 0.8 = 35,225.

iii. Materials Purchases (quantity and value)

	V	W	X	Y	Z
Usage (from ii)	124,900	129,500	98,800	56,640	35,225
– stock decrease	2,000	3,000	1,500	500	900
= Purchases	122,900	126,500	97,300	56,140	34,325
× Price	55p	50p	35p	60p	80p
= Value	£67,595	63,250	34,055	33,684	27,460

b. This can be taken directly from the book.

A24.5

Standard Cost Sheet (Per Unit)

		£	£
Direct materials 40 M² @ £5.30 per M²			212
Direct wages:			
Bonding dept. 48 hours @ £2.50 per hour		120	
Finishing dept. 30 hours @ £1.90 per hour		57	
			177
i.	*Prime cost*		389
	Variable overhead:		
	Bonding dept. 48 hours @ £0.75 per hour	36	
	Finishing dept. 30 hours @ £0.50 per hour	15	
			51
ii.	*Variable production cost*		440
	Fixed production overhead		40
iii.	*Total production cost*		480
	Selling and distribution cost	20	
	Administration cost	10	
			30
iv.	*Total cost*		510
	Profit 15% of selling price $= \dfrac{15}{100-15} \times 100$ of cost		90
b.	*Selling price per unit*		**600**

Workings

Variable overhead rates per hour

$$\text{Bonding dept.} = \frac{\text{£375,000}}{500,000} \text{ hours} = \text{£0.75}$$

$$\text{Finishing dept.} = \frac{\text{£150,000}}{300,000} \text{ hours} = \text{£0.50}$$

Rates per unit

$$\text{Fixed production overhead } \frac{\text{£392,000}}{9,800} = \text{£40}$$

$$\text{Selling and distribution cost } \frac{\text{£196,000}}{9,800} = \text{£20}$$

$$\text{Administration cost } \frac{\text{£98,000}}{9,800} = \text{£10}$$

Note:

The fixed overheads have been recovered on a unit basis and considering the round figures that result from this method, there is little doubt that the examiner intended this basis to be used. However, strictly speaking this is incorrect. It will be noted that the budgeted output is 9800 units. Using the labour hours given the total labour hours are:

    Bonding   470,400 hrs but budget 500,000 hrs
    Finishing 294,000 hrs but budget 300,000 hrs

Unless the discrepancy was unintended this can only mean that some other product(s) are being made, in which case they should bear their proportion of fixed overheads whereas all the fixed overheads are recovered on the 9800 units in the question. If there are other products then fixed overheads could be recovered on the total number of hours (800,000) resulting in the following overhead recoveries instead of the round figures previously obtained ie, £40, £20 and £10.

					Overhead Recovery
Fixed production overhead	$= \dfrac{392,000}{800,000}$	= £0.49	per hour × 78 =		£38.22
Selling & Distribution overhead	$= \dfrac{196,000}{800,000}$	= £0.245	per hour × 78 =		£19.11
Administration	$- \dfrac{98,000}{800,000}$	= £0.1225	per hour × 78 =		£9.55

Chapter 25 Solutions

Exercises

A25.1

The variances arising relate to Materials & Labour

Materials

Purchase cost	= £15,100	} Price variance £260 Fav	
less			} Total materials variance £210 Adv
Purchases at standard cost	= £15,360	}	
less		} Usage variance £470 Adv	
Standard quantity for actual production	= £14,890		

Labour (Type I)

Actual labour cost	= £27,056	} Rate variance £356 Adv	
less			} Total type I labour variance £244 Adv
Labour hours at std.	= £26,700	}	
less		} Efficiency variance £112 Fav	
Standard hours for actual production at std.	= £26,812		

Labour (Type II)

Actual labour cost	= £18,210	} Rate variance £211 Adv	
less			} Total type II labour variance £211 Adv
Actual labour hours at std	= £17,999	}	
less		} Efficiency variance NIL	
Standard hours for actual production at standard	= £17,999		

Note: The two labour types could be combined but as the details are available more information is supplied if they are dealt with separately.

A25.2

The variances to be calculated relate to overheads and, as usual, the absorption rates should be calculated using the budgeted figures.

$$FOAR = \frac{2,500}{650} = £3.846 \text{ per hour}$$

$$VOAR = \frac{1,550}{650} = £2.385 \text{ per hour}$$

and total OAR = £3.846 + £2.385 = £6.23 per hour

It will be recalled that the budgeted hours are both clock hours and standard hours produced.

The total overhead variance is:

$$\text{Actual overheads} - SHP \times (FOAR + VOAR)$$

$$\text{ie, } £4,335 - 4,236 = £99 \text{ ADV}$$

This can be analysed as follows using the simpler, combined approach covered in the chapter.

Actual overheads	= £4,335	} Expenditure variance £344 Adv	
less			} Total overhead variance = £99 Adv
Budgeted overheads	= £3,991	}	
less		} Volume variance £97 Adv	
Actual hours × OAR	= £3,894	}	
less		} Efficiency variance £342 Fav	
SHP × OAR	= £4,236		

A25.3

Variable overhead variances

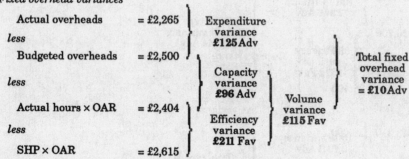

Actual variable overheads	= £1,710	
less		Expenditure variance £219 Adv
Actual hours × VOAR	= £1,491	
less		Efficiency variance £130 Fav
SHP × VOAR	= £1,621	

Total variable overhead variance = **£89 Adv**

Fixed overhead variances

Actual overheads	= £2,265	Expenditure variance £125 Adv
less		
Budgeted overheads	= £2,500	
less		Capacity variance £96 Adv
Actual hours × OAR	= £2,404	
less		Efficiency variance £211 Fav
SHP × OAR	= £2,615	

Volume variance £115 Fav

Total fixed overhead variance = **£10 Adv**

A25.4

There are three variances to be calculated; Price, Mix and Yield:

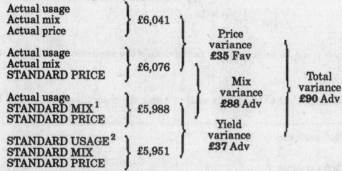

Actual usage Actual mix Actual price	£6,041
Actual usage Actual mix STANDARD PRICE	£6,076
Actual usage STANDARD MIX[1] STANDARD PRICE	£5,988
STANDARD USAGE[2] STANDARD MIX STANDARD PRICE	£5,951

Price variance £35 Fav

Mix variance £88 Adv

Yield variance £37 Adv

Total variance £90 Adv

[1] Standard mix ie, actual quantity, 2,900 Kgs into standard proportions ie, 30% , 50% and 20% ie,

X 30% = 870 tonnes @ £1.20
Y 50% = 1,450 tonnes @ £2.95   Total £5,988
Z 20% = 580 tonnes @ £1.15

[2] Standard Usage.
This is found from working back from the actual output of 2,450 Kgs.

$$\therefore \text{Standard input quantity} = \frac{100}{85} \times 2,450 = 2,882 \text{ Kgs}$$

which is evaluated in the standard proportions
$(2,882 \times .3 \times £1.20) + (2,882 \times .5 \times £2.95) + (2,882 \times .2 \times £1.15) = \underline{£5,951}$.

A25.5

Labour

		£	
	Actual wages	33,680	
less	Rate Variance	1,720	
=	Standard Wages	31,960	for 10,400 hours

∴ Standard rate per hour = £3.073

∴ Labour Efficiency variance represents $\frac{£525}{3.073} \approx 171$ hours

∴ Standard hours for 6250 units is 10,400 + 171 = <u>10,571</u>

∴ Standard hours per unit = 10571 ÷ 6250 = <u>1.69136</u>

Material

		£	
	Material Cost	17,059	
plus	Price Variance	1,400	
=	Standard Material Cost	18,459	for 3,850 Kgs

∴ Standard cost per Kg = 18,459 ÷ 3,850 = <u>£4.795</u>

∴ Usage variance represents $\frac{£890}{4.795} = 185.6$ Kgs

∴ Standard usage for 6250 units = 3,850 + 185.6 = 4035.6 Kgs

∴ Standard Kgs per unit = $\dfrac{4035.6}{6250}$ = 0.6457

Standard Prime Cost / Unit

			£
Labour			
1.69136 hours @ £3.073	=		5.198
Material			
0.6457 Kgs @ £4.795	=		3.096
= Standard Prime Cost	=		£8.294

Examination questions

A25.6

a. *Materials Variances*

	£	
Actual cost	25,080	Price variance £1,320 Fav
– AQ × SP (6,600 × £4)	26,400	
		Usage variance £400 Adv
– SQ × SP (1,300 × 5 × £4)	26,000	

Labour Variances

Actual wages	32,513	Rate variance £533 Adv
– AH × SR (5,330 × £6)	31,980	
		Efficiency variance £780 Adv
– SH × SR (1,300 × 4 × £6)	31,200	

Fixed Overhead Variances

Actual overheads	22,000	Expenditure variance £2,800 Adv
– Budgeted overheads (1200 × 4 × £4)	19,200	
		Capacity variance £2,120 Fav
– AH × OAR (5,330 × £4)	21,320	
		Efficiency variance £520 Adv
– SH × OAR (1,300 × 4 × £4)	20,800	

b.

Profit Reconciliation

			£
Budgeted Profit			48,000
+ extra production 100 × £40			4,000
= Budgeted profit for actual prod.			52,000
less Cost Variances			
Material Price	£1,320	F	
Material Usage	400	A	
Labour rate	533	A	
Labour efficiency	780	A	
Overhead Exp.	2,800	A	
Overhead Cap.	2,120	F	
Overhead Efficiency	520	A	1,593 A
= Actual Profit			50,407

c. Usual comments on reasons for the various adverse and favourable variances can be taken from the text.

A25.7

Material price variances (when purchased)

	Standard Cost	Actual Cost	Variances	
Powder	(100,000 ×.£0.74)	(10,000 × 0.70)		
	= £7500	= £7000	£500	(F)
Chemical (1200 × £2.40)		(600 × £2.30 + 600 × £2.50)		
	= £2880	= £2880	NIL	
Tubes (5200 × £0.3)	= £1560	(200 × £0.4 + 5000 × £0.3) = £1580	£20	(A)

Material Usage Variances

	Standard cost of standard usage	Standard cost of actual usage	Variances	
Powder (9,000 ×.£0.75)	= £6700	(9,800 × £0.75) = £7350	£600	(A)
Chemical (1,200 × £2.40)	= £2700	(1050 × £2.40) = £2520	£180	(F)
Tubes (5,200 × £0.3)	= £1350	(4520 × £0.3) = £1356	£6	(A)

Direct Wages Variance

Actual wages =	£8910
Actual hours @ std rate (2050 × £4.50) =	£9225
RATE VARIANCE =	£315 (F)

Efficiency variance

Standard cost of actual production – actual hours at standard = (4500 × £1.80) – £9225 = £1125 A

b.   Possible reasons for variances

Materials Price
Incorrect standards not reflecting current conditions.
Purchasing efficiency/inefficiency.
Purchase of lower quality powder perhaps causing the adverse usage variances.
Purchase of small quantities of tubes.

Materials Usage
Incorrect standards.
Poor quality materials.
Inefficient and careless operatives.
Excess Breakage/spillage.

Labour Efficiency
Incorrect standards.
Inefficient operatives.
Poor or ill-adjusted machinery.
Trainee workers.
Poor works organisation.

A25.8

a.

Budget statement for month

Overhead item	Flexed Budget			Actual Expenditure	Variances	
	Fixed £	Variable £	Total £	£	Adv. £	Fav. £
Management & Supervision	30,000	–	30,000	30,000	–	–
Shift premium	–	3,600	3,600	4,000	400	
N.I. and pension costs	6,000	7,920	13,920	15,000	1,080	
Inspection	20,000	9,000	29,000	28,000		1,000
Supplies	6,000	6,480	12,480	12,700	220	
Power	–	7,200	7,200	7,800	600	
Light and heat	4,000	–	4,000	4,200	200	
Rates	9,000	–	9,000	9,000		
Repairs	8,000	5,400	13,400	15,100	1,700	
Materials handling	10,000	10,800	20,800	21,400	600	
Depreciation	15,000	–	15,000	15,000		
Production Admin.	12,000	–	12,000	11,500		500
Idle time	–	–	–	1,600	1,600	
	120,000	50,400	170,400	175,300	6,400	1,500
				Total	(4,900)	

b.   Possible reasons for each variance of £1,000 or more.

N.I. and Pension Costs
From the information available it must be assumed that there has been an imposed N.I. increase which is outside management's control. It is not clear whether the variance relates to N.I. increases or 'pension costs' which are unspecified. It is surprising that there is a large variance in this predictable cost and care should be taken to make sure that changes in N.I. are known to those making the budget calculation.

Inspection
A substantial favourable variance which may be due to the incorrect budget, or different mix of production requiring less inspection, less wages paid to inspectors, poorer standards of inspection and so on. Needs further information/investigation.

Repairs
This may be due to: incorrect budgeting, unexpected repairs or breakdowns. This cost is difficult to forecast because of unpredictability.

Idle Time
It is assumed that this is abnormal idle time and may be due to machine breakdowns, poor production planning, material shortages, etc.

c. i. In general the absolute value of a variance is not as important as its relative significance compared with the budgeted allowance. More information would be supplied if variance which were greater than some percentage variation (say ± 5%) were identified. Significant variances can also be identified using simple statistical tests; for example 5% control limits are at ± 1.96 standard deviations away from the budgeted figure.

ii. More information would be provided for management control and to make future budgeting more accurate if the actual costs had been segregated into fixed and variable elements as was the budget.

d. i. Overhead absorbed.

= 36,000 standard hours × £4.40 = £158,400

ii. Total overspent is shown in the budget statement, ie £4,900.

iii. Overhead volume variance.

'The difference between the standard overhead cost of the actual hours taken and the flexed budget allowance for the actual hours taken.' – *Terminology*.

ie Actual hours × standard overhead rate – (budgeted fixed overhead + actual hours × variable overhead rate).

= 36,000 × £4.40 – (£120,000 + 36,000 × £1.40)) = £158,400-170,400 = £12,000 ADV.

A25.9

a. Assuming that price variances are extracted at the time of purchase the answers are as follows:

Standard Cost	DEHG
Actual Cost	ACJG
Price Variance	ACFD
Usage Variance	EFJH
Material Cost Variance	ACJG – DEHG or ACFD + EFJH

b. i. Principal budget factor. This can be taken directly from the text.

ii. Membership and functions of a budget committee.

Membership
    senior managers representing various functions in the organisation usually serviced by the accountant.

Typical functions
    Producing and updating the Budget Manual
    Co-ordinating the budgetary planning
    Liaising and communicating with budget holders
    Preparing a budget timetable
    Preparing budget summaries
    Producing operating rules and procedures
    Presenting budgets to management

A25.10

a. *Workings*

Materials	£
Actual cost 150,000 kg	210,000
+ Price variance	15,000
= Standard cost	225,000
= £1.5kg	

Usage variance 9000 ADV.÷1.5 = 6000 kg

$$\therefore \frac{150,000 - 6,000}{18,000} = 8Kg \ per \ unit$$

Labour	£
Actual cost 32000 hours	136,000
– rate variance	8,000
= Standard cost	128,000
= £4 per hour	

Efficiency variance £16,000 (FAV).÷ 4 = 4000 hours

$$\therefore \frac{36000}{18000} = 2 \ hours \ per \ unit$$

Overhead	£
Actual cost	38,000
– expenditure variance	6,000
= Standard cost	32,000
= £1 per hour	

Note: At £1 per hour the £4,000 efficiency variance is equivalent to 4,000 hours ie, as labour efficiency variance

£32,000 ÷ £1 = 32000 hours + 4000 hours

= 36000 hours

Summary: Standard cost 1 unit xy

	£
Materials 8 kgs @ £1.50 =	12
Labour 2 hours @ £4	8
Var. Ohds. 2 hours @ £1	2
	£22

b. Can be answered directly from the text.

A25.11

a. i. & ii.

Material X

	£	
Actual cost	171,820	Price variance
Actual purchases @ std (142,000 × £1.20)	170,400	£1,420 Adv
Actual usage @ std (16,270 × £1.20)	19,524	Usage variance
Standard usage @ std (1,790 × 9 × £1.20)	19,332	£192 Adv

(Actual cost = £1.21 per kilo)

iii. New standard price = £1.20 × 1.06 = £1.272

∴ Standard cost of purchases = 147,400 kilos × £1.272

= £187,492.80

∴ Actual cost = £187,492.8 − £1031.80 price variance

= £186.4611

and cost per kilo = £187,461 ÷ 147,400 = £1.265

∴ Actual cost inflation = $(\frac{1.265}{1.21} - 1)$ % = 4.5%

iv. Percentage change in usage

Period 1 = $\frac{16270 \text{ kilos}}{1790 \text{ units}}$ = 9.0894 kilos per unit

Period 2 = 9 kilos/unit × 0.995 = 8.955 kilos per unit

∴ Change in usage = $\frac{9.0894 - 8.955}{9.0894}$ % = 1.5% improvement

b. Can be taken from the text.

A25.12

a.

Standard product specification

Product J

		£	£
Selling price			1,200
Direct material	R (10 Kgs × £30)	300	
	S (6 Kgs × £45)	270	
		570	
Direct labour	(30 hrs × £5.50)	165	
	Prime cost	735	
Fixed production overhead (£252,000/1,200)		210	
	Total Production cost		945
	Profit		255

b. Variances

Price Variances (on Issue)

Material R. Issues × (Act − Std price)

1025 Kgs × (£31.82 − £30) = £1866 ADV

Material S 580 Kgs × (£44 − £45) = £580 FAV

Notes: Issues calculated thus

Material R = 300 + 1100 − 375 = 1025 Kgs

Material S = 460 + 345 − 225 = 580 Kgs

Usage variances

Material R (Issues − Std for output) × Std Price

(1025 − (100 × 10)) × £30 = £750 ADV

Material S (580 − (100 × 6)) × £45 = £900 FAV

Labour Variances

	£	
Actual cost	17,325	Rate variance £825 Fav
less		
− AH × SR (3,300 × £5.50)	18,150	Efficiency variance £1,650 Adv
less		
SH × Act Prod × SR (30 × 100 × £5.50)	16,500	

Overhead Variances

	£	
Actual cost	22,000	Expenditure variance £1,000 Adv
less		
Budget (100 units @ £21)	21,000	Capacity variance £2,100 Fav
less		
AH × OAR per hour (3,300 × £7)	23,100	Efficiency variance £2,100 Adv
less		
SH × Act Prod × OAR (30 × 100 × £7)	21,000	

Note the volume variance is capacity + Efficiency ie £2,100 FAV + £2,100 ADV = NIL

c.

Profit Reconciliation

	£ (F)	£ (A)	£
Budgeted gross profit			25,500
Operating variances:			
Material Price R		1,866	
S	580		
Material Usage R		750	
S	900		
Direct Labour rate	825		
efficiency		1,650	
Fixed overheads			
expenditure		1,000	
efficiency		2,100	
capacity	2,100		
	4,405	7,366	2,961 (A)
Actual gross profit			22,539

d.

Variance	Qty	Controllable	*Official*	*Possible causes*
Lab rate £825 (F)		yes	Personnel Manager	Reduced bonus, Different labour
Lab eff'y £1,650 (A)	300 hrs (A)	yes	Production manager	Poor training, wrong labour

---

Chapter 26 Solutions

Exercises

A26.1

The relevant variances are the Sales Margin Price, Mix and Volume Variances.

Actual units Actual mix Actual margin	£9,338	Sales margin price variance £402 Adv
Actual units Actual mix STANDARD MARGIN	£9,740	Mix variance £220 Fav
Actual units STANDARD MIX [1] STANDARD MARGIN	£9,520	Volume variance £30 Adv
STANDARD UNITS STANDARD MIX STANDARD MARGIN (ie budgeted margin)	£9,550	

Total sales margin variance £212 Adv

[1] Standard mix is the actual number sold (6,480) in the standard proportions ie,

$$\frac{2,000}{6,500}, \frac{4,000}{6,500} \text{ and } \frac{500}{6,500} \text{ thus}$$

$$
\begin{aligned}
A &= 1{,}994 @ £1.50 = & £2{,}991 \\
B &= 3{,}988 @ £1.20 = & £4{,}786 \\
C &= 498 @ £3.50 = & \underline{£1{,}743} \\
& & \underline{£9{,}520}
\end{aligned}
$$

A26.2

The Standard Cost Card is as follows:

Standard cost per unit

	£
Direct Materials 0.06 Kg at £21 Kg	1.26
Direct Labour 1.3 hours at £4 hr.	5.20
= Prime Cost	6.46
+ Variable overheads 1.3 hours at £3.5 hr.	4.55
= Total Variable Cost	£11.01

Budget for period – output 7,000 units

	£
Direct Materials	8,820
Direct Labour	36,400
Variable Overheads	31,850
= Total Variable Cost	£77,070
Fixed Costs	28,000
= Total Cost	£105,070

Proofs

Material variances

Actual cost	= £8,450	Price variance £370 Fav	
less			Total material variance £622 Fav
Standard cost of actual qty. (420 Kg × £21)	= £8,820		
less		£252 Fav	
Standard cost of std. qty. (432 Kg × £21)	= £9,072		

Labour variances

Actual cost	= £35,280	Rate variance £1,120 Fav	
less			Total labour variance £2,160 Fav
Actual hours at std. rate (9,100 × £4)	= £36,400		
less		£1,040 Fav	
Standard hours at std. rate (9,360 × £4)	= £37,440		

Variable overheads

Actual overheads	= £34,200	Expenditure variance £2,350 Adv	
less			Total variable overhead variance £1,440 Adv
Actual hours at VOAR (9,100 × £3.5)	= £31,850		
less		Efficiency variance £910 Fav	
Standard hours at VOAR (9,360 × £3.5)	= £32,760		

Fixed Overheads

Actual – Budget = £28,500—28,000 = **£500 Adv**

A26.3

a. 2% control limits are set at the mean ± 2.33 σ

∴ σ = 20. ∴ control limits are £5 ± 2.33 (0.20) = £5 ± 47p

b.
Labour cost per unit	=	£5.47
∴ Total labour cost	=	£2,625.60
Standard labour cost	=	2,400.00
∴ Labour cost variance	=	£225.60 ADV

A26.4

a. Entry 1. Total material variance £1,950 FAV
Entry 2. Total labour variance £2,927 ADV
Entry 3. Total overhead variance £3,385 ADV

b. Entry 1 – This indicates that the actual material cost of £42,800 was £1,950 below the standard for the output.

Entry 2 – This indicates that the actual wages of £21,407 were £2,927 above the standard labour cost for the output.

Entry 3 – This indicates that the actual overheads of £34,906 were £3,385 above the standard overhead cost for the output.

c. The double entries would be:

For Entry 1   CR Material Variance A/c   DR Materials A/c
For Entry 2   DR Labour Variance A/c   CR Wages A/c
For Entry 3   DR Overhead Variance A/c   CR Overhead A/c

Examination questions

A26.5

a.

Sales Statements

	North £	South £	Total £
Budget			
Budgeted sales	1,500,000	2,160,000	3,660,000
Budgeted costs	1,350,000	1,620,000	2,970,000
Budgeted profit	150,000	540,000	690,000
Actual			
Actual sales	1,470,000	2,310,000	3,780,000
Actual costs	1,260,000	1,890,000	3,150,000
Actual profit	210,000	420,000	630,000
Sales Margin Variances	60,000 (F)	120,000 (A)	60,000 (A)

b. *Northern Region*

Standard Margin = £10 – 9 = £1

Variances	£	
Actual margin (from (a))	210,000	Margin price variance **£70,000 Fav**
less		
Actual units @ std margin (350,000 × 40% × £1)	140,000	Margin mix variance **£17,500 Adv** / Margin quantity variance **£10,000 Adv**
less		
Actual units @ std mix* @ std margin (350,000 × 45% × £1)	157,500	Margin volume variance **£7,500 Fav**
less		
Standard margin (from (a))	150,000	

∴ £70,000 FAV – £10,000 ADV = £60,000 FAV as (a)

* This is the actual total quantity. 350,000 in the original budget proportions ie, 45% North, 55% south.

Note that the mix variance has been given for completeness

Southern region

Standard Margin = £12 – 9 = £3

Variances	£	
Actual margin (from (a))	420,000	Margin price variance **£210,000 Adv**
less		
Actual units @ std margin (350,000 × 60% × £3)	630,000	Margin mix variance **£52,500 Fav** / Margin quantity variance **£90,000 Fav**
less		
Actual units @ std mix @ std margin (350,000 × 55% × £3)	577,500	Margin volume variance **£37,500 Fav**
less		
Standard margin (from (a))	540,000	

∴ £210,000 ADV + £90,000 FAV = £120,000 ADV (as (a))

c. North shows an overall gain mainly because the actual margin was £1.50 instead of the standard margin of £1. Demand appears relatively inelastic.

South reduced the margin from £3 to £2 with adverse effects. Although more units were sold it was not enough to offset the substantial price decrease. Suggest prices increased.

d. Typical factors in setting sales budgets

❑ Market research

❏ Salesmens' forecasts
❏ Economic analyses
❏ Analysis of competitors' prices, models etc.
❏ Past sales patterns
❏ Consumer trends

and so on.

A26.6

a.

Sales	567,300 units
+ Closing stock	53,900 units
	621,200 units
– Opening stock	48,600 units
= Production	572,600 units

$$\text{Direct labour hours} = \frac{572,600}{112} = 5,112.5$$

∴ Labour budget = 5112.5 × £5.20 = £26,585

b. Equivalent hours at basic rate = 458 hours + 3 hours overtime premium 461 hours.
Basic rate = £2,420.25 + 461= £5.25 per direct labour hour

Direct labour charge = 458 × £5.25 = £2,404.50
Overtime premium (charged to overhead) = 3 × £5.25 = £15.75
Budgeted direct labour cost (Month 1) = 49,700 + 112 = 443.75 hours × £5.20 = £2,307.50
Standard direct labour cost (Month 1) = 50,400 + 112 = 450 hours × 5.20 = £2,340

Variances   £

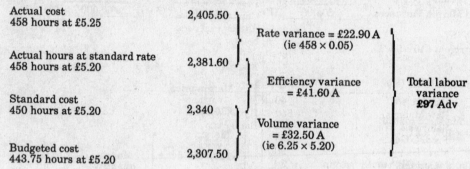

Actual cost
458 hours at £5.25   2,405.50

Rate variance = £22.90 A
(ie 458 × 0.05)

Actual hours at standard rate
458 hours at £5.20   2,381.60

Efficiency variance
= £41.60 A

Total labour
variance
£97 Adv

Standard cost
450 hours at £5.20   2,340

Volume variance
= £32.50 A
(ie 6.25 × 5.20)

Budgeted cost
443.75 hours at £5.20   2,307.50

Wages Control Account

	£		£
Cash /accrued wages	£2,805.85	Work in progress	£2,381.60
Employee deductions	869.25	Overhead*	1,270.60
		Rate variance	22.90
	£3,675.10		£3,3675.10

*Indirect labour cost of £1254.85 plus overtime premium of £15.75 = £1270.60.

c. Can be taken from text.

A26.7

a. The ledger accounts follow. All accounts are in £'000s.

Capital

		Balance b/d	1,000

Reserves

		Balance b/d	200

Creditors

Returns	40	Balance b/d	150
Bank	895	Raw materials	990
Discount Rec'd	25		
Balance c/f	180		
	1140		1140
		Balance	180

Raw material Control

Balance b/d	220	Returns	40
Creditors	990	WIP	850
		Price Variance	35
		Bank(ins. claim)	60
		Balance c/f	225
	1,210		1,210
Balance	225		

Finished Goods Control

Balance b/d	60	Cost of Sales	2,000
WIP	1,600	balance c/f	40
Admin O'Head	380		
	2,040		2,040
Balance	40		

Debtors Control

Balance b/d	200	Returns	60
Sales	2,500	Bank	2,350
		Cash Discount	35
		Bad Debts	25
		Balance c/f	230
	2,700		2,700
Balance	230		

Freehold Building (Cost)

Balance b/d	500		

Plant & Machinery (Cost)

Balance b/d	500		
Bank	50		

Expense Creditors

Bank	730	Balance b/d	20
Balance c/f	35	Prod'n Expenses	320
		Carriage inwards	45
		Admin. expenses	260
		Selling expenses	120
	765		765
		Balance	35

W-I-P Control

Balance b/d	40		
Raw Material	850	Finished Goods	1,600
Salaries & Wages	250	Balance c/f	55
Prod. O'Head	425		
Mat'l Usage var.	20		
Labour Eff var.	30		
O'head Eff.Var	40		
	1655		1655
Balance	55		

Depreciation Provision Plant & M/c

		Balance b/d	100
		Prod'n Overhead	50
			150

Production O'Head Control

Salaries & Wages	60	WIP	425
Expenses CRS	320	Expenditure Var.	25
Carriage	45	Overhead Adj. (under absorbed o'hd)	25
Depreciation	50		
	475		475

Bank

Balance b/d	150	Plant &mach.	50
Mat'l (Ins. claim)	60	Creditors	895
Debtors	2350	Expense Crs.	730
		Salaries & Wages	425
		Balance c/f	460
	2560		2560
		Balance	460

Administration Overhead Control

Salaries & Wages	100	Finished goods	380
Expense Crs.	260		
Over absorbed o/h	20		
	380		380

Cost of Sales

S & Dist.	210	P & L	2210
Fin. goods	2000		
	2210		2210

Material Price Variance

Materials	35	P & L	35

Wage Rate Variance

P & L	15	Salaries & Wages	15

Production O'Head Efficiency variance

P & L	40	WIP	40

Salaries & Wages Deductions

		Salaries & Wages	50

Discount Received

P & L	25	Creditors	25

Overhead Adjustment A/c

Prod'n o/h	25	Admin overhead	20
P & L	5	S & D overhead	10
	30		30

Salaries & Wages Control

Wage rate variance	15	WIP	250
Bank	425	Prod'n o/h	60
Deductions	50	Admin. o/h	100
		S & D	80
	490		490

Selling & Dist, Overhead Control

Salaries & Wages	80	Cost of sales	210
Expense creditors	120		
Over absorbed o/h	10		
	210		210

Sales

Returns	60	Debtors	2500
P & L	2440		
	2500		2500

Material Usage Variance

P & L	20	WIP	20

Labour Efficiency Variance

P & L	30	WIP	30

Production O'Head Expenditure Var.

Overheads	25	P & L	25

Discount Allowed

Debtors	35	P & L	35

Bad Debts

Debtors	25	P & L	25

Profit and Loss A/c for year

		£
Sales		2,440,000
Less cost of sales		2,210,000
		230,000
Add Favourable variances	£	
Material usage	20,000	
Wage rate	15,000	
Labour efficiency	30,000	
Overhead efficiency	40,000	105,000
		335,000
Less adverse variances		
Material price	35,000	
Overhead excpenditure	25,000	60,000
		275,000
Add Over absorbed overheads		5,000
		280,000
Less Net Discounts	10,000	
Bad Debts	25,000	35,000
= Net Profit		£245,000

Balance sheet

	£	£		£	£
Capital		1,000,000	Fixed Assets		
Reserves	200,000		Freehold buildings at cost		500,000
Unappropriated profit	245,000	445,000	Plant & mach. cost	350,000	
			less Depreciation	150,000	200,000
		1,445,000			700,000
Current liabilities			Current Assets		
Creditors	215,000		Stocks- mat'ls	225,000	
Deductions	50,000	265,000	WIP	55,000	
			Fin. gds.	40,000	
			Debtors	230,000	
			Bank	460,000	1,010,000
		1,710,000			1,710,000

A26.8

a. Can be taken from the text key points: standard costing can aid planning, control and motivation. Tends to make internal accounting and stock valuation simpler. main limitations; keeping standards up to date, tracing responsibility for variances.

b. A high rate of inflation does pass serious problems for standard costing systems. These include:
   – standards (& thus variances) soon became out of date due to price increases.
   – This volatility renders control more difficult and monitoring trends more of a problem.

   Of course standards can be adjusted frequently but this is expensive and cumbersome. A possible solution is to report internally controllable variances (eg, labour efficiency and material usage) in quantities, not values.

	Actual Revenues & costs		Standard Revenues & costs	Variances		
	£	£	£		£(F)	£(A)
Sales		259,000	245,000	PRICE	14,000	
Production costs:						
Direct Materials	65,570		64,000	PRICE	830	
				USAGE		2,400
Direct labour	107,100		96,000	RATE		5,100
				EFFICIENCY		6,000
Variable overheads	18,800			EXPENDITURE	2,600	
			51,200	VOLUME		6,000
Fixed overheads	39,000			EFFICIENCY		3,200
Royalties	8,000		6,400	EXPENDITURE		1,600
Production cost	238,470		217,600			
Closing stock (1/8)	27,200		27,200			
		211,270	190,400			
Operating profit		47,730	54,600			
Selling and distribution		12,000	14,000	EXPENDITURE	2,000	
		35,730	40,600		19,430	24,300
					Total	4,870 (A)

Chapter 27 Solutions

Exercises

A27.1

To: MANAGING DIRECTOR
From: COST ACCOUNTANT

Subject: UNIFORM COSTING SYSTEM

TERMS OF REFERENCE: To investigate and report upon the advantages to be obtained from becoming a member of the Uniform Costing System operated by the Trade Association.

There are several advantages to be gained from joining the scheme of which the major ones are as follows:

a. Access to detailed cost and operating characteristics of our competitors. This will enable us to compare costs and efficiencies and may show where improvements can be made.

b. Improvement to our tendering procedures.
   Having an information base from which we can obtain genuinely comparable cost data should enable us to improve our bidding particularly in competitive conditions.

c. The simplified uniform system will make it easier to introduce information technology.
   Having agreed systems and procedures will enable us to purchase ready made application software when inevitably we introduce information technology to deal with out cost accounting systems.

Although the above are major advantages and would probably lead to an organisation joining the scheme it should be remembered that if, there are some disadvantages including: the fee payable, changes to existing systems and valuation methods and the fact that competitors will have access to the organisation's costs and operational data albeit in an anonymous form.

Chapter 28 Solutions

Exercises

A28.1

Some of the overhead tasks which the computer could assist with are:

Accumulation of overheads expenditure by type of expenditure and location.

Apportionment over cost centres and departments of general overhead items eg, rates.

Statistical analysis of overhead expenditure for separation of fixed and variable elements, forecasting and decision analysis Budget preparation,

Budgetary control report production calculation and updating of O.A.R's overhead analysis for monthly operating statements.

A28.2

Six areas where 'what if' facility could be used.

> Exploration of different assumptions for budget preparation.
> Liquidity and cash budget statements.
> Product cost calculations with different material/labour and other costs.
> Testing effect on O.A.Rs of varying inflation rates/cost levels and so on.
> All forms of decision analysis utilising different assumptions/costs.
> Revenue and cost forecasting using different growth rates/inflation/costs.

Examination questions

A28.3

a. A notional cost is a hypothetical cost not actually incurred. Occasionally notional costs are used to render comparisons more valid or to illustrate 'true' costs.

   Examples include: a notional charge for interest may be included in a project statement even though no interest is paid (because internal funds are used) to make the project comparable with those that do carry an interest charge. When an asset is in use after being fully depreciated a charge is often still levied to produce more accurate job costs and to help comparability with other periods.

   Where there are separate cost and financial ledgers notional costs may be entered in the cost accounts without affecting the financial ones. This is not possible without complex Contra entries where there is an integrated system. This may thus be deemed to be a disadvantage, but the other benefits of integrated systems are likely to be outweigh this theoretical disadvantage.

b. It is very difficult to arrive at a cost of handling an account mainly because of the existence of high fixed costs and the common usage of facilities. Only by making numerous assumptions and the use of arbitrary conventions can any cost be established. In practice bank charges are based on what the market will stand rather than being cost based.

c. There are numerous advantages including:

   ❑ speed of communication, access and calculation
   ❑ better presentation
   ❑ flexibility eg, using 'what if' facilities on spreadsheets
   ❑ reducing real costs
   ❑ access to internal and external data-bases

   and so on.

A28.4

Can be taken from the text.

Index

ABB *347*
ABC *10, 148, 154*
Abnormal gain *190*
Abnormal process loss *190*
Absorption bases *72*
Absorption costing *77,251*
Absorption of overheads *10, 72*
Accounting rate of return *315*
Accounting systems *110*
Activity based accounting *13*
Activity based budgeting *13, 347*
Activity cost management *13, 347*
Activity level *230*
Added value *9*
Administration overhead absorption *76*
Advanced manufacturing technology *422*
AMT *421*
Assessment stage *224*
Attainable standards *365*
Attendance records *64*
Average cost method *194*
Average price *44*

Backflush accounting *110, 129*
Base stock *45*
Basic standards *365*
Batch costing *145, 148*
Behavioural aspects *337*
Bill of materials *30*
Bin card *33*
Block coding *19*
Bottlenecks *277*
Break even
   analysis *294*
   chart *296*
   point *295*
Budget
   centre *330*
   manual *343*
   officer *344*
   period *330*
Budgetary
   control *329*
   planning *329*
   slack *349*
Budgeting *224, 314*
Budgets *329*
Buffer stock *36*
Burden *14*
By product *210*
   costing *145, 210*

Capacity variances *383*
Capital investment appraisal *314*
Carrying costs *36*
Cash
   budgets *339*
      and computers *446*
   discount *48*
Centralised stores *28*
Check digit verification *19*
Classification *17*
   of fixed costs *235*
Closed notation *19*
Coding *9, 18*
Coefficient of determination *240*
Commitment accounting *343*
Communication *330, 339*
Computers *439*
Concave curve *232*
Continuous
   allotment *81*
   operation costing *145, 180*
   stocktaking *27*
Contract costing *145, 164*
Contribution *251*
Contribution to sales ratio *295*
Control *2, 223, 225*
Control accounts *110*
Control limits *414*
Control ratios *386*

Conversion cost *8*
Convex curve *232*
Corporate planning *223*
Cost *7*
   allocation *9*
   apportionment *9*
   attribution *9*
   behaviour *230*
   centre *9*
   control *67, 223*
   drivers *10, 72, 89*
   ledger control account *110*
   of capital *319*
   of work certified *165*
   pools *12, 72, 89*
   unit *7*
   unit absorption *72*
Cost accounting – definition *1*
   accounts (standard costing) *415*
   accounts *110*
Cost volume profit analysis *294*
Costing *9*
   and computers *439*
   methods *145*
CS ratio *295*
Current standards *365*
Curve fitting *232*
Curvilinear cost *232*
CVP analysis *294*

Data processing systems *441*
DCF (discounted cash flow) *317*
Decentralised stores *28*
Decision making *2, 210, 223, 266*
Decision packages *346*
Decision support systems *443*
Depreciation *84*
Differential costs *266, 273*
Differential piecework *57*
Diminishing balance depreciation *85*
Direct
   cost *7*
   costing *251*
   expenses *8*
   labour *7*
      hour absorption *72*
      variance *375, 379*
   materials *7*
      absorption *72*
      variances *377*
   wages *7, 67*
      absorption *72*
      variances *379*
Discounted cash flow (DCF) *317*
Distribution overhead absorption *76*
Double loop feedback *225*
DSS *443*

Economic ordering quantity *33, 37*
Economists break even chart *301*
End-user computing systems *443*
EOQ *33, 37*
Equivalent units *192*

Feedback *225*
FIFO (first in first out) *44, 194*
Financial accounting *3*
Financial ledger control account *110*
First in first out (FIFO) *44, 194*
Fixed budgets *334*
Fixed cost *234, 237*
Fixed overhead variances *383*
Flexible budgets *334*
Forecasting *230, 343*
Free stock *33, 36*
Function costing *180*

General jobbing account *157*
General ledger control account *117*
Goal congruence *338*
Goal definition *338*

Goods received note (GRN) *26*
GRN *26*
Group classification codes *19*
Group incentive schemes *57*

Hierarchical codes *19*
High day rate *55*
High/low method *237*
Human aspects *337, 369*

Ideal standards *365*
Idle time variance *380*
Incentive schemes *54,55*
Incremental decision packages *346*
Indirect
   costs *8*
   expenses *8*
   labour *8*
   materials *8*
   wages *67*
Information characteristics *227*
Information feedback *225*
Input material *193*
Integrated cost accounts *110*
Interest *88*
Interlocking cost accounts *110*
Internal rate of return (IRR) *318*
Inventory control *33, 35*
IRR *318*
Issue pricing *43*

JIT (Just-in-time) *4, 28, 422*
   production *29*
   purchasing *29*
Job
   card *64*
   cost card *152*
   costing *148*
   evaluation *67*
Joint classification *235*
   costs *210*
   product *210*
      (service industries) *214*
      costing *145, 210*
Just-in-time *see* JIT

Kanbans *29*
Key factors *266*

Labour remuneration *54*
   turnover *68*
   variances *379*
Last in First out (LIFO) *44*
Lead time *35*
Least squares *240*
LIFO *44*
Limiting factor *266, 330*
Linear approximation *233*
Linear cost *231*
Long term strategic planning *223*
Long term variable cost *89, 237*

Machine hour absorption *72*
Make or buy *272*
Management accounting *2*
Manufacturing response time *276*
Marginal cost *234, 251, 266*
   costing *77, 251, 266*
Marketing overhead absorption *76*
Master budget *329, 331*
Material
   classification *17*
   control *24*
   requisition *27*
   return note *27*
   variances *377, 386*
Materials requirement planning *30*
Maximum level, stocks *36*
Measured day work *55*
Memorandum account *117*
Merit rating *67*

Mixed cost 235
Mixture variance 387
Modulus II check digit 19
Motivation 330, 338
MRP 30
MRPII 30
Multi-product chart 299
Muliple regression analysis 243
Mutually-exclusive decision packages 346

Net asset cost 84
Net present value 317
Net realisable value 48
Non-linear cost 232
Non-programmed decisions 226
Normal equations 239
Normal process loss 190
Notional cost 88
Notional sales value basis 212
NPV 317

OAR 72
Objective classification 17
Objective stage 224
Objectives 338
Obsolescence 88
Oncost 14
Operating statement 110
Operation card 65
  costing 145, 180
Operational variances 423
Opportunity cost 273, 275
Ordering costs 35
Output costing 180
Over absorption 75
Overhead
  absorption 72
    rate 72
  recovery 10
  variances 381
Overheads 8, 72
Overtime 55

Parabola 232
Participation 338
Payback 316
Performance measurement 184, 423
Periodic stocktaking 27
Perpetual inventory system 28, 34
Personnel function 68
Physical unit basis 212
Piecework 56
Planning 2, 223
Planning variances 423
Plant register 87
Policy classification 235
Predetermined absorption rates 75
Price variance - materials 367
Pricing 2
Prime cost 8
  absorption 72
Principal budget factor 266, 330
Process
  costing 145, 189
  loss 189, 210

Procurement time 35
Product unit depreciation 86
Profit
  centre 330
  chart 298
  maximisation chart 301
  sharing 58
  volume ratio 302
Programmed decisions 226
Prorating costs 14
Public sector 180, 411
Purchasing 24
PV ratio 302

Quantity discounts 48

Ratios 386
Reciprocal servicing 81
Reducing balance depreciation 85
Regression analysis 240, 343
Relevance 227, 235
Reorder level 36
Reorder quantity 36
Repair reserve depreciation 87
Replacement
  cost 48
  price 45
Replenishment rate 37
Research overhead absorption 76
Revaluation depreciation 86
Revision of standards 368
Reward-penalty system 338
Risk analysis 320

Safety stock 36
Sales margin variances 404
Sales value basis 212
Sales variances 403
Scattergraph 238
Secondary apportionment 77
Selling overhead absorption 76
Semi-fixed cost 235
Semi-variable cost 235
Sensitivity analysis 320
Service cost centres 78
Service costing 180
Shift bonus 55
Short run 230, 266
Short-term variable cost 89, 237
Significance of variances 375, 413
Significant digit codes 20
Simultaneous equations method 81
Single loop feedback 25
Sinking fund 87
Software 444
Specific order costing 145
Specific price 45
Split off point 211
Spreadsheets 444
SSAP9 44, 165, 256
Standard
  cost 365
    card 368
  costing 365, 374, 403
  hour 367

marginal cost 368, 391, 406
marginal costing 406
price 45
process costing 409
Step costs 241
Stock
  audit 31
  out costs 35
  record card 33
  recording 33
  valuation 48, 254
Storage of materials 24, 26
Straight line depreciation 84
Subjective classification 17
Sum of the digits 86
Sunk costs 274
Systems 28

Taxation 88
Throughput accounting 266, 276
Throughput time 29
Time
  -based overhead absorption 74
  keeping bonus 55
  series analysis 343
  sheets 64
Total absorption costing 77
Total cost 8, 10
Total Quality Control (TQC) 29
Trade discounts 48
Transaction processing 441
Two bin system 38

Under absorption 75
Uniform costing 436
Unit
  costing 145
  price 45
Usage variance – materials 375

Value added tax (VAT) 48, 88
Value of work certified 165
Variable
  cost 231
  overhead variances 382
Variance 365, 374
  analysis 365
VAT 48, 88
Volume classification 235
Volume of activity 230
Volume variance 383

W-I-P (Work in progress) 17, 192
WACC 319
Wages
  determination 67
  procedure 66
Weighted average cost of capital 319
Work in progress (W-I-P) 17, 192

Yield variance 387

ZBB (Zero base budgeting) 345